Beyond the Balance of Power

This is a major new study of French foreign and security policy before, during and after the First World War. Peter Jackson examines the interplay between two contending conceptions of security: the first based on traditional practices of power politics and the second on internationalist doctrines that emerged in the late nineteenth century. He pays particular attention to the social and political context in which security policy was made and to the cultural dynamics of the policy-making process. The book reconsiders the evolution of French war aims and reinterprets the peace policy of the Clemenceau government in 1919. It also provides a new interpretation of the foreign policy of successive French governments in the early 1920s. Jackson shows that internationalist ideas were far more influential over this entire period than is commonly understood. The result is a thorough reassessment of France's security policy and a new perspective on international relations during this crucial period in European history.

Peter Jackson is Professor of Global Security in the History Department at the University of Glasgow.

Beyond the Balance of Power
*France and the Politics of National Security
in the Era of the First World War*

Peter Jackson

CAMBRIDGE
UNIVERSITY PRESS

University Printing House, Cambridge CB2 8BS, United Kingdom

Published in the United States of America by Cambridge University Press, New York

Cambridge University Press is part of the University of Cambridge.

It furthers the University's mission by disseminating knowledge in the pursuit of education, learning, and research at the highest international levels of excellence.

www.cambridge.org
Information on this title: www.cambridge.org/9781107039940

© Peter Jackson 2013

This publication is in copyright. Subject to statutory exception and to the provisions of relevant collective licensing agreements, no reproduction of any part may take place without the written permission of Cambridge University Press.

First published 2013

Printed in the United Kingdom by Clays, St Ives plc

A catalogue record for this publication is available from the British Library

ISBN 978-1-107-03994-0 Hardback

Cambridge University Press has no responsibility for the persistence or accuracy of URLs for external or third-party internet websites referred to in this publication, and does not guarantee that any content on such websites is, or will remain, accurate or appropriate.

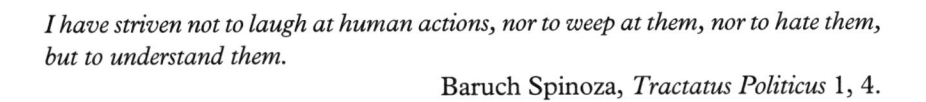

I have striven not to laugh at human actions, nor to weep at them, nor to hate them, but to understand them.

Baruch Spinoza, *Tractatus Politicus* 1, 4.

Contents

List of maps	page ix
Preface	xi
List of abbreviations	xvi
Introduction	1
Part I The sources of French security policy	15
1 The social dynamics of security policy making	19
2 Two approaches to security	47
Part II War and the politics of national security, 1914–1918	79
3 The primacy of the balance of power, 1914–1916	85
4 The coming of a new world order, 1917	133
5 National deliverance and post-war planning	163
Part III Peace and security, 1918–1919	197
6 The political contexts of peacemaking, 1918–1919	203
7 Towards a post-war security order: the eastern settlement, economic security and the League of Nations	235
8 The Rhineland settlement and the security of France	276
Part IV Imposing security	317
9 Post-war dilemmas: enforcement or engagement?	323
10 Briand and the emergence of a multilateral alternative, 1921	357

11	The politics of confrontation	391

Part V The Cartel des gauches and the 'internationalisation of security' — 427

12	A new approach: arbitration, security, disarmament	431
13	Locarno	469
	Conclusion	514
	Select bibliography	523
	Index	531

Maps

Map 1 The Rhineland in 1789. Adapted from M. Rowe, *From Reich to State*, Cambridge University Press, 2003, p. ix   *page* xviii

Map 2 Alsace-Lorraine and the Saar. Adapted from D. Stevenson, *French War Aims against Germany, 1914–1919*, Oxford University Press, 1982, p. 217   xix

Map 3 The Rhine basin in 1914. Adapted from D. Stevenson, *French War Aims against Germany, 1914–1919*, Oxford University Press, 1982, p. 221   xx

Map 4 Rhineland zones of occupation. Adapted from C. Fischer, *The Ruhr Crisis 1923–1924*, Oxford University Press, 2003, pp. x–xi   xxi

Preface

This book considers the impact of the First World War on the politics of national security in France. It argues that the sacrifice and suffering caused by the Great War created political space for internationalist doctrines of peace and security to play an important role in policy making. Two general approaches to the problem of security are identified. The first is defined as the *traditional* conception of security. It was based on long-standing practices of the balance of power and alliance politics. The second is described as the *internationalist* approach. It was understood chiefly in terms of peaceful cooperation between states under a regime of international law. This cooperation would be underpinned by international institutions designed above all to implement and enforce the rule of law in international society. While advocates of a purely internationalist conception of security remained for the most part marginalised from the decision-making process, the steady rise in support for this approach within both the public and parliamentary spheres constituted a factor that could not be ignored in the policy-making process. This fact has not received the attention it deserves from historians of this period. The traditional and internationalist approaches together provided the conceptual framework for debates about national security among political and policy elites.

These debates took place in an era of revolutionary change. In 1914 the international system entered a lengthy transition period that brought about the end of European dominance. Spring 1917 was a pivotal moment in this process. It witnessed the collapse of Imperial Russia, France's principal pre-war ally, into revolutionary chaos that would force it to leave the Great War. At the same time the United States, which was well on its way to becoming the world's most powerful state, entered the conflict as an 'Associated Power'. These developments had profound consequences for the post-war political order. They transformed the structural environment in which France's security policy was made in ways that have not been fully understood by historians of this period. Among the many legacies of the war were a new distribution of power and a new set of international norms. Both of these developments created new external and internal pressures to which French policy makers were forced to respond. Their chief consequence was to create favourable conditions for a more internationalist approach to security. This process did not come to full fruition until the advent of the centre-left Cartel des gauches political coalition inside France in May 1924. The Cartel government of Édouard Herriot responded with a multilateral security strategy based on the principles of interlocking mutual assistance, arbitration and close Franco-British cooperation. This strategy, in turn, laid the conceptual foundations for French policy leading to the Locarno Accords of 1925. It also opened the way for the more audacious efforts of Aristide Briand to achieve European peace based on Franco-German reconciliation and European federation in the late 1920s. Briandism did not emerge fully formed from the ether in 1925.

The book's focus on contending conceptions of security raises a number of interesting methodological challenges. As David Stevenson has observed, 'security' was an 'intangible' concept that could 'expand indefinitely' to mean everything from the restoration of Alsace-Lorraine to the destruction of Germany as a political entity.[1] The tension between various and often incompatible conceptions of security was never fully resolved. But it was central to the political and cultural context in which virtually all debates concerning foreign and defence policy took place. The book therefore pays careful attention throughout to internal discourses of national security and their role in shaping the policy context. Developments in the international sphere were equally important and receive equal attention. The strategies of other states, and in particular France's Great Power allies Britain and the United States, presented a different range of challenges and often constituted powerful restraints on France's freedom of action. Also important, however, was the transnational flow of ideas about peace and international legitimacy. The impact of new international norms is more difficult to assess but was also crucial in shaping the way policy makers understood and responded to the wider environment of international politics. The analysis that follows is therefore oriented systematically towards understanding the complex interaction of external and internal dynamics in the evolution of foreign and security policy. A central contention throughout is that the wider structures that conditioned policy decisions were constituted not only by the distribution of material power in the international system, but also by the emergence of new normative standards for state behaviour during the Great War.

It is with this latter point that I hope to make a small contribution to debates about the role of power and ideas among theorists of international relations. My chief aims, however, are first to reinterpret the course of French foreign and security policy during this period of upheaval and second to offer a case study for understanding the way policy-making elites adapt to seismic changes in their structural environment.

---

[1] D. Stevenson, *French War Aims against Germany, 1914–1919* (Oxford, 1982), 200–2.

Preface

The origins of this study stretch back to spring 2002 and to one of the many fruitful discussions that I have had over the years with Zara Steiner. Zara observed that French policy makers of the inter-war period seemed unusually concerned with embedding French policy in binding legal arrangements. She remarked that it would be interesting to explore the origins of this cultural reflex. Zara's remarks niggled away at me as I began a year's sabbatical leave to research a book on French security policy after 1919. It was clear to me that the juridical dimension of French policy practices was an expression of long-standing traditions within French political culture that could be traced back to the period before the revolution. But I also came to realise that certain of its characteristics could be traced to late nineteenth-century pacifist thought and in particular the movement for 'peace through law' that emerged along with the profession of international law during this period. I owe a significant debt for this realisation to the innovative and important work done on the French internationalist movement by a new generation of scholars that includes Norman Ingram, Carl Bouchard and especially Jean-Michel Guieu.

In the end I decided that it would be much more interesting to trace the evolution of French thinking about peace and security from the period before 1914 through to the aftermath of the First World War. The aim is to integrate the transnational history of internationalist thought into an archive-based study of the evolution of foreign and security policy. In order to explore the origins of various and often contending beliefs about security, I resolved to pay careful attention to the social and educational backgrounds of various policy elites as well as the cultural environment in which they worked. By the time I realised the scale of the project I had set for myself it was too late to turn back, and I found myself delving into such diverse literatures as the evolution of transnational civil society in the mid-nineteenth century, the social composition of the French officer corps, the military history of the Great War and the dynamics of veterans' politics after 1918. The result is a much longer book than I ever intended to write, but one that I enjoyed researching and writing much more than I ever thought possible.

This enjoyment owed much to the help and support of others. It is a pleasure to express official thanks for the invaluable financial assistance provided by the Arts and Humanities Research Council, the Staff Research and Learned Societies funds at Aberystwyth University, the Nuffield Foundation and the John Anderson Research Leadership scheme at the University of Strathclyde. I am also grateful for the opportunity to present my ideas at seminars at the Institut d'études politiques in Paris, the University of Nottingham, the Université de Paris IV, the University of Cambridge, Boston University, the Institute of Historical Research, the University of Glasgow, the University of Utah, the University of Western Australia, the Royal Military College of Canada, the University of Western Ontario and the Ohio State University. The project began while I was a research fellow at 'Sciences po' in 2002 and was finished while I was a visiting professor at the same institution in 2012–13. I am grateful to all of the above organisations. I am also happy to thank Michael Watson at Cambridge University Press for the faith he has shown in this book.

The assistance and support of friends and colleagues was also invaluable. Special thanks must go to Andrew Webster, who listened patiently to many hours of my ramblings as the idea for this book first took shape way back in 2002–3. And I am also very grateful to Mehmet Basutçu, Craig Ritchie and Alison Rodger for providing both a place to stay and excellent company during many research trips to Paris and London. I would also like to acknowledge the supportive research environment at the Department of International Politics in Aberystwyth (where I worked for more than twelve years). Lengthy books such as this one are increasingly rare in the era of the Research Assessment Exercise (now the Research Excellence Framework) in Britain. The fact that I was given the institutional support necessary to see the project through to conclusion is a credit to the research culture at 'Interpol' and in particular to the support of Andrew Linklater, Colin McInnis and Ian Clark. Ian deserves additional thanks for suggesting the title of the book. Other friends and colleagues at 'Aber' read portions of the manuscript and I would especially like to thank R. Gerald Hughes, Martin Alexander, Patrick Finney and Campbell Craig for their commentary on various drafts of the manuscript.

Beyond Aberystwyth I received extremely helpful insights and advice from Georges-Henri Soutou, John Ferris, Sally Marks, Hidemi Suganami, Nicolas Roussellier, William Keylor, Phillips O'Brien, Andrew Barros, Robert Young, Taylor Jackson, Robert Boyce, Claire Sanderson, Andrea Thomas, George Peden and Keith Neilson. My Ph.D. student Lora Gibson wrote an excellent thesis advancing an interpretation very much opposed to my own. It is a great pleasure to acknowledge the importance of her ideas in sharpening my own thinking. At the University of Strathclyde I was fortunate to work with a convivial and supportive group of friends and colleagues. I am particularly grateful to Allan MacInnes, Alison Cathcart, Rogelia Pastor-Castro and Richard Finlay for making my time there so enjoyable.

Three friends and colleagues read virtually every word of the manuscript and provided truly invaluable feedback. It is no stretch to say that the book could hardly have been written without the expert advice of Martin Thomas, Joe Maiolo and Talbot Imlay. I am also grateful to the two anonymous readers of the manuscript for Cambridge University Press, whose comments and suggestions strengthened the book. While the contribution of the aforementioned scholars was crucial, any errors of fact or interpretation in the pages that follow are my own.

My greatest debt, as ever, is to my family. My sister Mary-Jane has always been a source of inspiration and support for me. My children, Erika, Taylor, Eva and Cameron, have lived with this book for all or most of their lives. They have rarely seen the point to all of the time away, or the agonising over minor details. But without them the whole business would mean very little. My final and most important thanks go to Jackie, who provided love, support and the constant reassurance that one day I would finish this 'damn book'. She was right (as usual). And it is to her that this book is dedicated with a love that continues to grow after all these years.

Abbreviations

AFSDN	Association française de la Société des nations
AHR	*American Historical Review*
AN	Archives nationales
AS	Archives du Sénat
BDIC	Bibliothèque de documentation internationale et contemporaine
BL	British Library
BNF	Bibliothèque Nationale de France
CAEAN	*Commission des affaires étrangères de l'Assemblée nationale*
CAES	*Commission des affaires étrangères du Sénat*
CCAC	Churchill College Archives Cambridge
CDH	*Les Cahiers des droits de l'homme*
CEH	*Contemporary European History*
CISDN	Commission d'études interministérielles pour la Société des nations
CSDN	Conseil supérieur de la défense nationale
CSG	Conseil supérieur de guerre
CTP	Commission du Traité de paix (sub-commission of the *CAEAN*)
DAPC	Direction des affaires politiques et commerciales (foreign ministry)
DDF	*Documents diplomatiques français*
D&S	*Diplomacy & Statecraft*
EHR	*English Historical Review*
FHS	*French Historical Studies*
FRUS	*Papers Relating to the Foreign Relations of the United States*
GMCC	*Guerres mondiales et conflits contemporaines*
GQG	Grand quartier général
HJ	*Historical Journal*
HLRO	House of Lords Records Office
IHR	*International History Review*
IMCC	Inter-Allied Military Control Commission

List of abbreviations

IOL	India Office Library (British Library)
JCH	*Journal of Contemporary History*
JMH	*Journal of Modern History*
JO	*Journal officiel de la République française*
JSS	*Journal of Strategic Studies*
LDH	Ligue des droits de l'homme
MAE	Ministère des affaires étrangères
PAC	Permanent Advisory Commission on Military, Naval and Air Questions (League of Nations)
PPC	*Paris Peace Conference*
PPD	*La Paix par le droit*
PV-SDN	A. G. Lapradelle (ed.), *La Paix de Versailles*, vol. I; *La Conference de la Paix et la Société des Nations*
RDDM	*Revue des Deux Mondes*
RH	*Revue Historique*
RHA	*Revue historique des armées*
RHD	*Revue d'histoire diplomatique*
RI	*Relations internationales*
SDN	*Société des nations*
SFIO	Section française de l'Internationale ouvrière
SFSDN	Service français de la Société des nations (foreign ministry)
SGDN	Secrétariat général de la défense nationale
SHD-DAT	Service historique de la défense – Département de l'armée de terre
SLYU	Sterling Library, Yale University
TMC	Temporary Mixed Commission (League of Nations)
TNA-PRO	The National Archives – Public Records Office
VS	*Vingtième siècle*

xviii Map 1

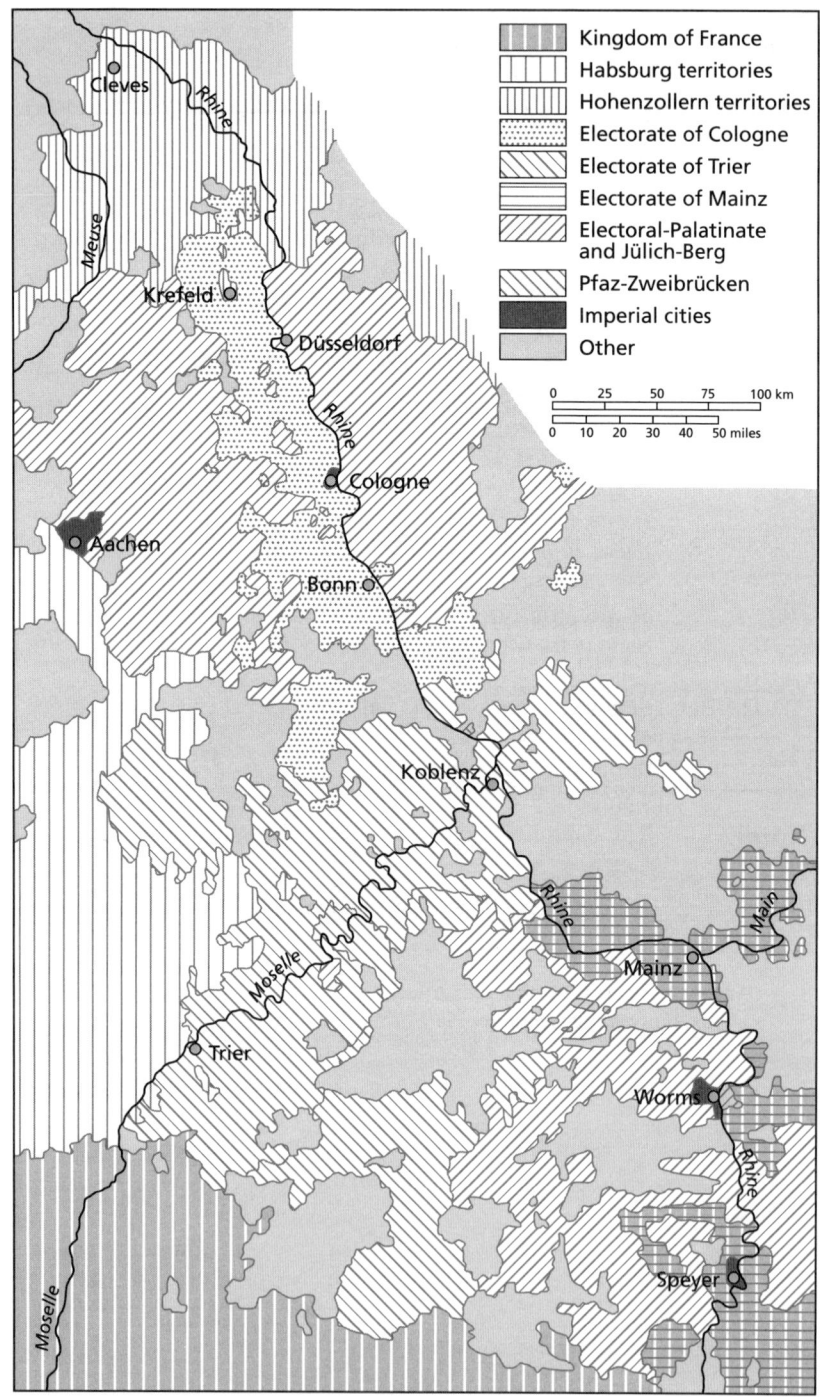

Map 1 The Rhineland in 1789. Adapted from M. Rowe, *From Reich to State*, Cambridge University Press, 2003, p. ix

Map 2   xix

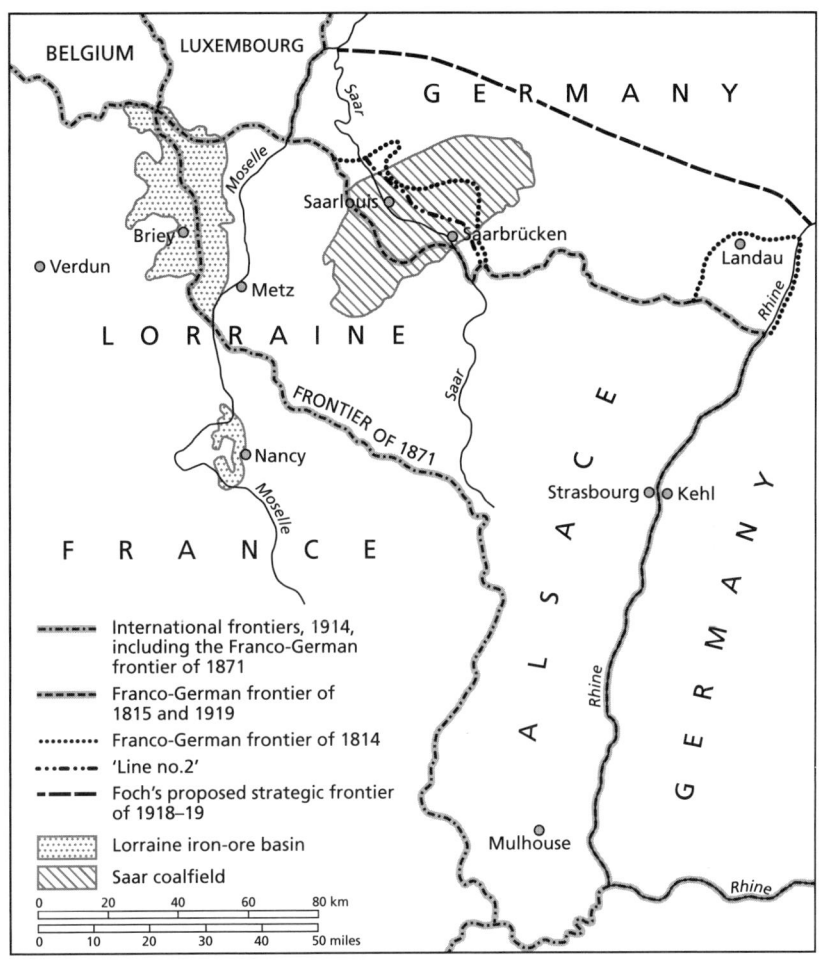

Map 2 Alsace-Lorraine and the Saar. Adapted from D. Stevenson, *French War Aims against Germany, 1914–1919*, Oxford University Press, 1982, p. 217

Map 3 The Rhine basin in 1914. Adapted from D. Stevenson, *French War Aims against Germany, 1914–1919*, Oxford University Press, 1982, p. 221

Map 4

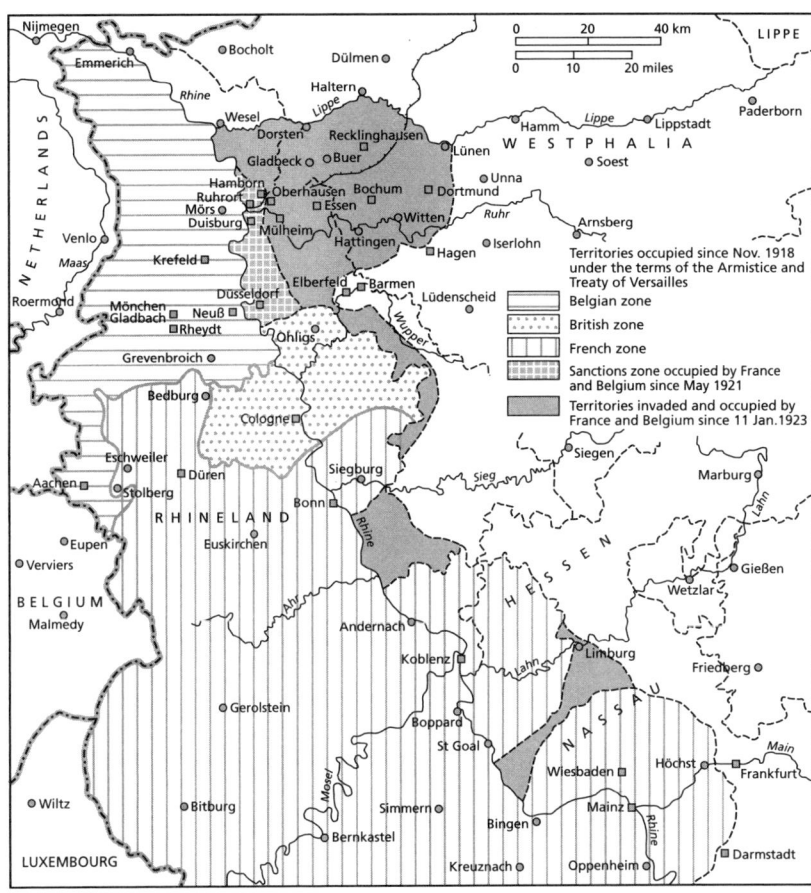

Map 4 Rhineland zones of occupation. Adapted from C. Fischer, *The Ruhr Crisis 1923–1924*, Oxford University Press, 2003, pp. x–xi

Introduction

The problems of peace, security and disarmament were long-term preoccupations for the internationalist movement in France. On 5 June 1911 a national congress of French peace societies convened to consider the conditions necessary for international disarmament. Discussion revolved around a report by Théodore Ruyssen, president of the Association de la paix par le droit. Ruyssen had concluded that

> Any lasting solution to the problem of disarmament must be subordinated to achieving durable security through the construction of a juridical international system capable of pushing aside or resolving disputes between nations.

Only compulsory international arbitration, Ruyssen argued, could provide the security necessary for nations to accept arms reductions.[1]

Thirteen years later French premier Édouard Herriot appeared before the Fifth Assembly of the League of Nations to give a celebrated speech on the problems of security and disarmament. Herriot here unveiled a new French policy for international security aimed at establishing a regime of compulsory arbitration that would provide the security necessary to allow for significant international disarmament. 'Arbitration, security, disarmament', Herriot proclaimed, 'are the three master pillars of the edifice of peace we must construct.'[2]

The prescriptions of Ruyssen in 1911 and Herriot in 1924 were part of an internationalist current in French thinking about peace and security that flowed through the First World War and into the inter-war period. Ruyssen's Association de la paix par le droit was the largest and most influential peace association in France. His juridically inspired analysis of the challenge facing international disarmament reflected the views of the overwhelming majority of his colleagues in the French peace movement. Herriot, meanwhile, was leader of a centre-left coalition government, the Cartel des gauches, that had come to power in May 1924 with a mandate to change the course of France's foreign

---

[1] P.-E. Decharme (ed.), *VIIème Congrès nationale des sociétés françaises de la paix: compte-rendu du congrès (4, 5, 6 et 7 juin 1911)* (Clermont-Ferrand, 1911), 196–7.

[2] Société des nations, *Journal officiel*, 1924, Herriot before the League Assembly, 5 September 1924.

policy. The triple-formula *arbitrage–sécurité–désarmament* outlined by Herriot to the League Assembly provided the conceptual foundations for new Cartel policy. It would shape French responses to the challenge of European security until the mid-1930s.[3] But Herriot's formula was essentially a rearticulation of the vision of international security outlined by Ruyssen in 1911 and pursued by French internationalists of all stripes before, during and after the First World War.

The impact of French internationalism has been ignored in the historiography of international relations in the era of the Great War. The foreign and security policies of France are nearly always characterised as 'realist' in inspiration and dominated by traditional practices such as the balance of power and military alliances. The prevailing view is that French policy was essentially a bid for strategic predominance over Germany. There is virtual consensus, moreover, that French policy elites were all but immune to the politics of internationalism.[4] The distinguished historian P. M. H. Bell, for example, argues that internationalist 'idealism' was an issue that 'came between the British and the French'. France, Bell asserts, was 'an old European country' whose policy elites 'thought primarily in terms of interests and power'. In Britain, conversely, internationalism 'touched a strong responsive chord'.[5]

As a concept, 'internationalism' defies easy definition.[6] It is generally associated with an outlook that attaches vital importance to the economic, social and cultural benefits of cooperation at the international level. A particularly

---

[3] France, Ministère des affaires étrangères (hereafter MAE), 1918–1940, *Série SDN*, 'Arbitrage, Sécurité, Désarmament', vols. 706–824.

[4] There is, by contrast, a large and growing literature on pacifism, non-state actors and support for Franco-German cooperation and the League of Nations. See esp. N. Ingram, *The Politics of Dissent: Pacifism in France, 1919–1939* (Oxford, 1991); J.-P. Biondi, *La Mêlée des pacifistes* (Paris, 2000); S. Lorrain, *Des Pacifistes français et allemands pionniers de l'entente franco-allemande* (Paris, 1999); C. Birebent, *Militants de la paix et de la SDN: les mouvements de soutien à la Société de nations en France et au Royaume-Uni, 1918–1925* (Paris, 2007); J.-M. Guieu, *Le Rameau et le glaive: les militants français pour la Société des Nations* (Paris, 2008); C. Bouchard, *Le Citoyen et l'ordre mondial (1914–1918): le rêve d'une paix durable au lendemain de la Grande Guerre* (Paris, 2008).

[5] P. M. H. Bell, *France and Britain, 1900–1940: Entente and Estrangement* (London, 1996), 116–17. The assumption that French policy was based on 'realist' power politics is so pervasive that listing the relevant literature would take up too much space. Among the most influential works specifically on French policy during the war and during the peace conference are G.-H. Soutou, *L'Or et le sang: les buts de guerre économiques de la Première Guerre mondiale* (Paris, 1989); D. Stevenson, *French War Aims Against Germany, 1914–1919* (Oxford, 1982); D. Stevenson, 'France and the German Question in the Era of the First World War' in S. Schuker (ed.), *Deutschland und Frankreich vom Konflikt zur Aussöhnung: Die Gestaltung der westeuropäischen Sicherheit 1914–1963* (Munich, 2000), 1–18; J.-B. Duroselle, *La Grande Guerre des Français* (Paris, 1994); P. Miquel, *La Paix de Versailles et l'opinion publique française* (Paris, 1972); J. Bariéty, *Les Relations franco-allemandes après la première guerre mondiale* (Paris, 1977).

[6] The following passage is indebted especially to P. Anderson, 'Internationalism: a breviary', *New Left Review*, 14 (March–April 2002), 5–6; but see also M. Geyer and J. Paulmann, *The Mechanics of Internationalism: Culture, Politics and Society from the 1840s to the First World War* (Oxford, 2001); P. Clavin, 'Conceptualising Internationalism between the World Wars' in

important form of internationalism, for the purposes of this study, was a doctrine that looked to the creation of institutions beyond the nation-state as the best means to promote economic progress and prevent war. Recent scholarship has underlined the importance of liberal and internationalist conceptions in the foreign policies of both Britain and the United States. Keith Neilson distilled the findings of a generation of work on British policy when he underlined the extent to which decision-making elites in London were 'caught between nineteenth century concepts of the balance of power, the experimentation that was collective security and old-fashioned alliance diplomacy'.[7] Work on the conceptual foundations of American policy during this period has advanced along similar lines. Historians have tackled issues ranging from Theodore Roosevelt's approach to world order to the ideological content of 'Wilsonianism' and the American movement to promote arbitration and the rule of law.[8] The prevailing picture of French foreign and security policy, conversely, has scarcely changed over the past thirty years. France's international posture continues to be represented in monochrome fashion as inspired exclusively by the power political assumptions of the pre-1914 era.[9]

D. Lacqua (ed.), *Internationalism Reconfigured: Transnational Ideas and Movements between the World Wars* (London, 2011) and G. Sluga, *Internationalism in the Age of Nationalism* (Philadelphia, 2013).

[7] K. Neilson, *Britain, Soviet Russia and the Collapse of the Versailles Order* (Cambridge, 2006), 318; see also, and among others, T. G. Otte, *The Foreign Office Mind: The Making of British Foreign Policy, 1865–1914* (Cambridge, 2011); J. Ferris, *The Evolution of British Strategic Policy, 1919–1925* (London, 1987); B. McKercher, 'Old Diplomacy and New: The Foreign Office and Foreign Policy, 1919–1939' in M. Dockrill and B. McKercher (eds.), *Diplomacy and World Power: Studies in British Foreign Policy, 1890–1950* (Cambridge, 1996), 79–114; B. McKercher, 'Austen Chamberlain and the Continental Balance of Power' in E. Goldstein and B. J. C. McKercher (eds.), *Power and Stability: British Foreign Policy, 1865–1965* (London, 2003), 207–36; E. Goldstein, 'The British Official Mind and the Lausanne Conference' in ibid., 185–206.

[8] See, again among many others, J. R. Holmes, *Theodore Roosevelt and World Order* (Washington, D.C., 2006); T. J. Knock, *To End all Wars: Woodrow Wilson and the Quest for a New World Order* (Princeton, 1992); L. Ambrosius, *Wilsonianism: Woodrow Wilson and his Legacy in American Foreign Relations* (London, 2002); E. Manela, *The Wilsonian Moment: Self-determination and the International Origins of Anti-colonial Nationalism* (Oxford, 2007); R. Kennedy, *The Will to Believe: Woodrow Wilson, World War I, and America's Strategy for Peace and Security* (Kent, Ohio, 2009); S. Wertheim, 'The league that wasn't: American designs for a legalist–sanctionist League of Nations and the intellectual origins of international organization, 1914–1920', *Diplomatic History*, 35, 5 (2011), 797–836; see also the many important insights into Anglo-American policy conceptions offered in P. Cohrs, *The Unfinished Peace after World War I* (Cambridge, 2006).

[9] Notable exceptions to this general rule are a number of important essays by G.-H. Soutou, such as 'L'Ordre européen de Versailles à Locarno' in G.-H. Soutou and C. Carlier (eds.), *1919: Comment faire la paix?* (Paris, 2001), 301–31 (although, as we shall see, Soutou has elsewhere characterised French policy in highly traditional terms); see also M. Trachtenberg, *Reparation in World Politics: France and European Economic Diplomacy, 1916–1923* (New York, 1980); N. Jordan, 'The reorientation of French diplomacy in the 1920s: the role of Jacques Seydoux', *EHR*, 117, 473 (2002), 867–88; and S. Jeannesson, 'Jacques Seydoux et la diplomatie économique dans la France de l'après-guerre', *RI*, 121 (2005), 9–24. None of the aforementioned scholars detects the influence of internationalist conceptions in French policy, however.

4   Introduction

The logical corollary of this historiographical consensus is the conclusion that the Great War made no impact on French policy elites other than to reinforce existing beliefs in power politics. France's leadership, according to standard interpretations, remained unswervingly committed to traditional practices based on the balance of power. Post-war security policy was aimed overwhelmingly at keeping Germany down. This strategy, it is argued, culminated in an attempt to compel Germany to accept the Versailles order by seizing control of the Ruhr industrial basin in February 1923. Only after this hardline approach failed did France's leadership change course and adopt a more conciliatory policy. This change, significantly, is nearly always interpreted as having been imposed on France by Britain and the United States. The failure of earlier coercive strategies, it is argued, left French decision makers with no choice but to accept Anglo-American political and financial intervention and to adapt French security policy accordingly. The settlements of London in 1924 and Locarno in 1925 are thus represented as a comprehensive defeat for French designs. The international politics of 'Briandism', meanwhile, are usually represented as an aberration that came out of nowhere and disappeared without a trace.[10]

This general interpretation of French security policy has endured without serious challenge since the early 1980s. It has remained largely unaffected by important and innovative research that has transformed our understanding of this entire period. Work on the cultural history of the Great War, for example, has made little or no impact on the historiography of French foreign and security policy.[11] Nor has the recent resurgence of interest in the international history of the 1920s resulted in any significant revision of the standard narrative. An ambitious reassessment of the post-war period by Patrick Cohrs, for example, represents French policy in essentially static terms as a 'bid to establish a continental hegemony *against* Germany'.[12] An important recent

---

[10] S. Schuker, *The End of French Predominance in Europe: The Financial Crisis of 1924 and the Adoption of the Dawes Plan* (Chapel Hill, 1977); see also S. Marks, *The Illusion of Peace: International Relations in Europe, 1918–1933*, 2nd edn (London, 2003); J. Bariéty, *Les Relations franco-allemandes après la première guerre mondiale* (Paris, 1977); C. Maier, *Recasting Bourgeois Europe: Stabilization in France, Germany and Italy in the Decade after World War I* (Princeton, 1975); W. McDougall, *France's Rhineland Diplomacy, 1914–1924: The Last Bid for a Balance of Power in Europe* (Princeton, 1978); D. Artaud, *La Question des dettes interalliées et la reconstruction de l'Europe 1917–1929*, 2 vols. (Paris, 1978); C. Wurm, *Die französische Sicherheitspolitik in der Phase der Umorientierung, 1924–1926* (Frankfurt, 1979); B. Kent, *The Spoils of War: The Politics, Economics and Diplomacy of Reparations, 1918–1932* (Oxford, 1989); J. Jacobson, 'Is there a new international history of the 1920s?', *AHR*, 88, 3 (1983), 617–45; J. Jacobson, 'Strategies of French foreign policy after World War I', *JMH*, 55 (1983), 78–9.
[11] It is also true that the cultural history of the First World War largely ignores the international political dimensions of that conflict: see A. Prost and J. Winter, *Penser la Grande Guerre: un essai d'historiographie* (Paris, 2004).
[12] Cohrs, *Unfinished Peace*, 604 (emphasis in original); when characterising the French 'form of statesmanship' Cohrs quotes Herbert Hoover's judgement that French policy had

Introduction 5

study of international relations in the post-war decade by Robert Boyce makes no mention of internationalism as an influence on France's security policy in the early and mid-1920s.[13]

This book offers an alternative interpretation. It will not argue that French policy makers were inspired throughout by an internationalist vision of peace and security. It will instead contend that internationalist ideas were more influential in the making of foreign and security policy than is generally assumed. Strategies for security were more varied and ambiguous than most historians have recognised. Amid the wide array of policy conceptions under consideration it is possible to identify two distinct currents of thought about the problem of security in Europe. The first, defined for the purposes of this study as the 'traditional' approach, favoured security through strategic preponderance and alliance politics. The alternative, a French variant of internationalist thought best described as 'juridical internationalism', advocated enmeshing Germany in a multilateral system based on the rule of law and backed up by provisions for the use of collective force.

The problem of German power was central to all French thinking about security in Europe. Germany had invaded France twice in living memory. Its larger population and more powerful industry placed France at a permanent disadvantage in the European strategic balance. Prescriptions for dealing with German power marked the clearest dividing line between traditional and internationalist conceptions of security. The traditional approach envisaged organising the European balance of power *against* Germany. The internationalist alternative envisaged *including* Germany in a system of inter-state cooperation under international law.

The traditional conception of security rested on two mutually dependent assumptions. The first was that military conflict was a permanent feature of politics among nations. The second was that international relations were driven chiefly by the pursuit of power. Proponents of the traditional approach assumed a permanent adversarial relationship with Germany. National safety, according to this understanding of security, rested inevitably on a superior combination of economic and military power and strong allies. The balance of power and alliance politics together constituted the core conventions of the traditional approach. Traditional prescriptions for the security of France therefore stipulated that Germany must be weakened, isolated and surrounded by a powerful combination of allies. This was the solution advocated consistently by the foreign ministry and army high command for most of this period.

---

maintained Europe's 'whole economic and political life ... in an atmosphere of war': ibid., 69; this is also the vision of France's security policy advanced by Sylvain Schirmann in *Quel ordre europeen? De Versailles à la chute du IIIème Reich* (Paris, 2006), 11–69.

[13] R. Boyce, *The Great Interwar Crisis and the Collapse of Globalization* (London, 2009), 77–141; see also S. Jeannesson, *Poincaré, la France et la Ruhr (1922-1924)* (Strasbourg, 1998); C. Fischer, *The Ruhr Crisis, 1923–1924* (Oxford, 2003); Z. Steiner, *The Lights that Failed: European International History, 1919–1933* (Oxford, 2005); S. Pedersen, 'Back to the League of Nations: review essay', *AHR*, 112, 4 (2007), 1091–117.

Traditional practices of security were embedded in the institutional cultures of these two crucial organs of state.

The internationalist vision of security, conversely, was rooted in a specifically French variant of peace activism that emerged in the late nineteenth and early twentieth centuries. Despite their common roots, this movement must be distinguished from the more liberal strains of pacifist internationalism in Britain or the United States. It was a product of the legalist political culture of the Third French Republic. As a result it was more muscular. French internationalists called for the establishment of a robust regime of binding international law supported by collective force. It was this general conception that inspired the proposals of both Ruyssen and Herriot. The prominence of force in their common vision reflected the link between the use of force and the principle of justice that is a defining feature of French politics. French internationalists had campaigned prominently for this conception of international order at the two Hague Peace Conferences of 1899 and 1907. Léon Bourgeois, a leading political figure of the Third Republic and head of the French delegation at both conferences, led a campaign to establish a system of compulsory international arbitration for the peaceful settlement of disputes between states. Arbitration and collective force became the twin pillars of the French 'juridical internationalist' movement. The emphasis on the use of force is particularly important because it provided a measure of common ground between internationalist and more traditional visions of security that would eventually open the way to combining the two approaches in the mid-1920s.

French internationalists had very little direct influence over policy making for most of the period considered in this book. The traditional approach provided the conceptual parameters for the formulation of security policy during the early and middle phases of the Great War. This policy was characterised by long-standing practices of balancing power and alliances supplemented by secret conventions and joint war planning. But the unprecedented scale and ferocity of that conflict, along with the huge sacrifices it demanded, eventually created political space for the internationalist alternative. By mid-1917 internationalist conceptions of 'peace through law' were increasingly prominent at the centre and on the left of the French political spectrum. This trend was reinforced by an omnipresent official discourse that represented the conflict as a struggle to establish the rule of law in international politics. The internationalist movement also benefited enormously from the public proclamations of American president Woodrow Wilson. The American president's call for transforming international politics generated widespread enthusiasm that stimulated support for a new approach to security. By the war's end France was committed to establishing a new international organisation to secure the peace. A high-profile inter-ministerial commission was created under the leadership of Bourgeois and charged with designing a blueprint for a 'society of nations'.

Introduction

The traditional approach to security nonetheless remained at the centre of official policy prescriptions into the post-war decade. This reflected the extent to which it was ingrained in the cultural reflexes of both security professionals and government ministers. Support for the internationalist agenda continued to grow after 1918, however. This process gained momentum after traditional attempts to transform the strategic balance, in particular the occupation of the Ruhr under Premier Raymond Poincaré, failed to deliver security. The advent of the Cartel des gauches in 1924 brought the internationalist approach to the centre of the French policy machine. The foreign and security policy that emerged thereafter was an amalgamation of the traditional power political reflexes of France's security professionals and the multilateral and legalist inclinations of the French internationalists. Within the Quai d'Orsay a growing number of officials – nearly all of whom were from the generation recruited into the foreign ministry after 1900 – were converted to the idea of enmeshing Germany in a multilateral security system underwritten by Britain and France. Such an approach was much closer to the internationalist conception of security than previous policies aimed at creating a vast anti-German coalition. This process culminated in the Locarno Accords of October 1925.

Another internationalist current that shaped policy debates focused on the promotion of greater economic cooperation. This current emerged as part of the steady growth of financial, industrial and commercial links between the European states in the decades before 1914. Research into this subject stresses the role of business leaders – primarily from the coal and steel-producing sectors in France, Germany and Belgium – in leading the way towards greater industrial integration in western Europe. French heavy industry was part of a regional system of industrial, financial and commercial cooperation that had proved very profitable before the war.[14] As we shall see, an inclination to restore cooperation with German heavy industry once peace returned persisted within France's industrial and policy elite right through the conflict. This tendency manifested itself in plans to devise a transatlantic system of post-war economic cooperation into which Germany would be integrated. But it also inspired projects for direct Franco-German financial and industrial cooperation that first surfaced during the Paris Peace Conference and gained momentum thereafter.

---

[14] See among others J.-F. Eck, S. Martens and S. Schirmann (eds.), *L'Économie, l'argent et les hommes: les relations franco-allemandes de 1871 à nos jours* (Paris, 2009); C. Strikwerda, 'The troubled origins of European economic integration: international iron and steel and labor migration in the era of World War I', *AHR*, 98, 4 (1993), 1106–29; Soutou, *L'Or et le sang*, 141–61; G.-H. Soutou, 'Le Coke dans les relations internationales en Europe de 1914 au plan Dawes', *Relations internationales*, 43 (1985), 249–67; R. Poidevin, *Les Relations économiques et financières entre la France et l'Allemagne de 1898 à 1914* (Paris, 1969); M. Lévy-Leboyer (ed.), *La Position internationale de la France: aspects économiques et financières XIXème–XXème siècles* (Paris, 1977), 347–61; J.-N. Jeanneney, *François de Wendel en république: l'argent et le pouvoir 1914–1940* (Paris, 1976).

A number of scholars have underlined the extent to which post-1919 French responses to the problems of reparation and economic reconstruction were based on the principles of multilateral cooperation and engagement with Germany.[15] But the link between this fundamentally internationalist policy orientation and French projects to construct a multilateral security regime in Europe has not been made. Indeed, in some cases the history of French thinking about security has been all but subsumed into the history of reparations and war debts. This fixation with 'the primacy of economics'[16] has even led to the judgement that French policy elites were inclined to 'define national security in economic terms'. The crucial reorientation in French policy in 1924, according to this view, demonstrated 'the dominance of reparations over security'.[17] The argument in this book, conversely, is that policy towards reparations and war debts must be understood within the larger context of debates about the security of France.

The challenge posed by economic security will therefore be considered through the analytical lens of contending 'traditional' and 'international' approaches to security. This provides an interesting new perspective on the role of economic considerations. It illuminates, in particular, the presence of both currents in thinking about economic security within the French policy elite. It also suggests, however, that economic considerations were not as dominant in national security policy as is often assumed. This was the case not only during the war but also in the 1920s. The issue of reparations was bound up intimately with the quest for political and territorial security.

Three aspects of this book distinguish it from other international histories of this period. The first is its chronological span – which rejects the traditional starting and ending points of 1914 and 1919. The year 1914, for example, is usually treated, along with 1789, as a great watershed of the modern era. Most studies either start or end with the outbreak of the First World War. The problem with this tendency is that it obscures the pre-1914 sources of wartime policy making. The same is true of 1919. Focus on the Versailles order and its discontents has meant that pre-war and wartime trends that carried over into the post-war period have too often been ignored. This book will trace the impact of traditional and internationalist impulses across these watersheds. The era of the First World War did not begin in 1914, and it did not end in 1919. We will therefore take up its story before 1914 and end after the Locarno

---

[15] See esp. Trachtenberg, *Reparation* and W. McDougall, 'Political economy versus national sovereignty: French structures for German economic integration after Versailles', *JMH*, 51, 1 (1979), 4–23.
[16] The title of the fourth chapter in Steiner, *Lights that Failed*, 182–250.
[17] Jordan, 'Reorientation of French Diplomacy', 877 and 879; Cohrs similarly characterises reparations as 'the core question of postwar politics': *Unfinished Peace*, 158. An important exception is Robert Boyce's *Great Inter-war Crisis*, which consistently analyses reparations policy as part of the wider question of national security.

Accords in 1925. The result is a more complete picture of the impact of the First World War on the practice of foreign and security policy.

A second important aim is to bring together three historiographical currents that have long existed in relative isolation. The dominant interpretation of French foreign and security policy is based on an untenable divorce between the history of French policy, on the one hand, and more recent work on transnational civil society, on the other. The past three decades have seen the emergence of a very significant body of research on both the international and the specifically French dimensions to transnational peace movements. But this research is virtually absent from the history of French foreign and security policy.[18] The same is true of recent work on the cultural history of the First World War. Over the past three decades several waves of path-breaking research have transformed our understanding of the First World War as a social, and especially a cultural, watershed in the history of modern Europe.[19] Yet this important work has made only limited impact on mainstream international history. One important strand in this literature emphasises the extent to which France's war effort was held together by a system of representations of the war as a crusade for civilisation, the rule of law and national survival. These representations operated at all levels of society, from political elites to schoolchildren. The great majority of the French population, according to this school of interpretation, internalised this construction of the war's meaning and considered the struggle both legitimate and necessary.[20] The argument that follows stresses the extent to which high policy was influenced by such representations. This process was important in establishing a central principle of French internationalism – the need to enforce the rule of law in international society – as one of France's major war aims.

A third distinctive aspect of this study is the systematic attention paid to the relationship between the cultural predispositions of policy actors and the wider structural context in which security policy was made. To tackle this problem in the specific case of French foreign and security policy, I have borrowed several concepts from the 'practice theory' of sociologist Pierre Bourdieu. I have used Bourdieu's conceptualisation of 'culture' as a historically derived set of predispositions that interact with the wider structural environment to form a basis for everyday practices. This process produces what Bourdieu termed a 'practical

---

[18] It is also fair to say that the activities of European (though not American) transnational civil society are too often studied without sufficient engagement with the history of international politics.

[19] For an excellent survey and analysis of much of this literature see Prost and Winter, *Penser la Grande Guerre*. The most impressive study of French security policy during and immediately after the Great War, David Stevenson's *French War Aims Against Germany*, was written when work on cultural history of the First World War was in its infancy.

[20] S. Audoin-Rouzeau and A. Becker, 'Violence et consentement: la "culture de guerre" du Premier Conflit mondial' in J.-P. Rioux and J.-F. Sirinelli (eds.), *Pour une histoire culturelle* (Paris, 1997), 251–71; L. Smith, 'The "Culture de guerre" and French historiography of the Great War of 1914–1918', *History Compass*, 5–6 (2007), 1967–79.

logic' that conditions the strategies generated by social actors. A central argument of this book is that a practical logic based on the traditional conception of security dominated the cultural reflexes of soldiers, diplomats and many political leaders during and immediately after the First World War. This logic came under pressure as early as 1917, however, as internationalist principles gained in popularity within the parliamentary and public spheres. It is possible to detect the influence of these ideas in the policy prescriptions of various key actors during the Paris Peace Conference. But the traditional approach did not lose its status as a practical logic until the advent of the Cartel in May 1924.[21]

If this study is successful in making a case for the importance of French internationalism, it will also contribute to the discipline of international relations theory. French thinking about war and peace during this period is utterly absent from standard accounts of the 'genealogy' of this discipline.[22] Even studies of 'idealism' between the two world wars ignore the active role played by French internationalists in efforts to derive a theoretical basis for peace in the 'real' world.[23] The result is a misrepresentation of the early phase of international relations theory, and in particular thinking about international organisation, as an exclusively Anglo-American enterprise.[24] In reality a small but vibrant community of academics, politicians and pundits elaborated a distinctly French perspective on the problem of international peace. Its leading figure was Léon Bourgeois but it also included such dynamic figures as Ruyssen, the international lawyer Georges Scelle and the sociologist Célestin Bouglé. The contributions of French international theorists have been ignored in standard narratives of the emergence of international politics as a distinct discipline after the First World War.[25] Excavating a distinctly French vision of

---

[21] The term 'security professionals' refers to the diplomats and senior military officials responsible for the framing of policy choices and the execution of policy decisions.

[22] See, for example, S. Smith, 'The Self-images of a Discipline: A Genealogy of International Relations Theory' in K. Booth and S. Smith (eds.), *International Relations Theory Today* (Cambridge, 1995), 1–37; B. Schmidt, *Political Discourses of Anarchy: A Disciplinary History of International Relations* (Albany, 1998).

[23] The classic example is E. H. Carr, *The Twenty Years' Crisis: An Introduction to the Study of International Relations*, 2nd edn (London, 2001). Carr's criticisms were aimed at British and American liberal internationalists; he ignored French contributions to this literature altogether. French 'thinkers' are also entirely absent in D. Long and P. Wilson (eds.), *Thinkers of the Twenty Years' Crisis: Inter-war Idealism Reassessed* (Oxford, 1995); recent examples of this trend are the anglocentric focus in D. Bell (ed.), *Victorian Visions of Global Order: Empire and International Relations in Nineteenth Century Political Thought* (Cambridge, 2007) and D. Gorman, *The Emergence of International Society in the 1920s* (Cambridge, 2012), esp. 175–212.

[24] See, for example, M. Mazower, *Governing the World: The History of an Idea* (London, 2012), 116–41.

[25] A lone partial exception is a study of thinking about world order by Andrew Williams. Williams acknowledges the importance attached to international law and arbitration by French statesmen; but he does not identify a distinctly French conception of 'world order', and follows the historical literature when he characterises the French programme for a League of Nations as 'a continuation of the wartime alliance': see A. Williams, *Failed*

Introduction

international peace does more than rectify a long-standing historiographical injustice, however. It enriches our understanding of the history of international political thought in two ways. First, it provides a fuller account of the diversity of thinking about international politics in the era of the Great War. Second, it illuminates the interpenetration of theory and practice during this early stage in the development of international relations theory as a distinctive field of enquiry and reflection in both Europe and North America.

The book's focus on the role of cultural factors in explaining policy decisions, meanwhile, has direct implications for one of the key debates within the discipline of international relations theory over the past thirty years: the theoretical divide between realism and constructivism.[26] 'Realist' international theory (and in particular 'structural' or 'neo-classical' realism) assumes that the anarchical character of the international system exerts pressure on states to pursue their own security at the expense of others. The distribution of military and economic power within the international system therefore determines the long-term course of world politics. The imperative to maximise security, combined with uncertainty concerning the intentions of other actors, makes competition and conflict permanent features of the international system.[27] Alliances, from a realist perspective, are self-help mechanisms used by states to improve their security. States will cooperate with one another when faced with an external threat to their vital interests that they cannot manage independently. Structural shifts in the balance of power are the main drivers of security policy in general, and alliance formation in particular.[28] Recently, 'neo-classical' international theorists have focused on 'unit-level' distortions of the policy process (primarily domestic politics) to understand why states 'misread' prevailing systemic pressures and adopt policies that do not reflect

---

Imagination? New World Orders of the Twentieth Century (Manchester, 1998), 19–78 and esp. 55–7; see also Williams' more recent 'Norman Angell and his French contemporaries, 1905–1914', *D&S*, 21, 4 (2010), 574–92.

[26] This is by no means the only important debate within 'IR theory'. Other influential theoretical perspectives include liberal institutionalism, post-structuralism/post-colonialism, neo-Marxism and the 'English School'. But the key divergence in the realist–constructivist debate is over the role of ideas in world politics. This obviously speaks directly to a central theme in this study.

[27] Classic statements of 'realist' theory include H. J. Morgenthau, *Politics Among Nations: The Struggle for Power and Peace*, 5th edn (New York, 1978); K. Waltz, *Theory of International Politics* (Toronto, 1979); R. Jervis, 'Co-operation under the security dilemma', *World Politics*, 30, 2 (1978), 167–214; R. Jervis, 'Realism, neoliberalism and co-operation: understanding the debate', *International Security*, 24, 1 (1999), 42–61; J. Mearsheimer, *The Tragedy of Great Power Politics* (New York, 2001); J. Vasquez and C. Elman, *Realism and the Balancing of Power: A New Debate* (Upper Saddle River, 2002); on the relationship between structural realism and history see E. May, R. Rosecrance and Z. Steiner (eds.), *History and Neo-Realism* (Cambridge, 2010).

[28] See esp. S. Walt, *The Origins of Alliances* (Ithaca, 1987); J. Levy and W. R. Thompson, 'Balancing on land and at sea: do states ally against the leading global power?', *International Security*, 35, 1 (2010), 7–43.

existing power balances.[29] In virtually all strains of realism, however, decisive importance is attributed to 'objective laws' that force states to compete for power under conditions of international anarchy.[30]

'Constructivist' international theory, conversely, denies the very existence of such 'objective laws'. Constructivists argue that the meaning of the balance of power is subjective and interpreted by policy actors within specific cultural contexts that vary over space and time. They place greater emphasis on identities and norms as sources of policy decisions. The objective distribution of power has no meaning independent of the subjective interpretations of policy makers. The 'laws' of international politics are therefore whatever decision-making elites imagine them to be.[31] Constructivism is often criticised, however, for failing to account for the role of power in shaping ideas and establishing the conditions for beliefs and norms to become influential.[32]

The case of French foreign and security policy in the era of the First World War illustrates strengths and limitations of both realism and constructivism. The immutable fact of German economic and demographic superiority was a fundamental constituent element of the international system. It posed a potentially mortal threat to France that could not be ignored. Yet 'systemic' pressures on French policy ran in more than one direction. The transformation of international norms brought about by the Great War presented a very different set of challenges to which French policy makers were forced to respond. This development placed both internal and external pressure on French policy to adapt to changed standards of state behaviour after 1918. The cultural backgrounds of French policy-making elites played a crucial role in shaping the way they responded to these pressures and adjusted to profound changes in both the domestic and international environments. A number of scholars have argued recently that the sociology of Pierre Bourdieu provides a framework for combining the realist focus on the effects of power with constructivist attention to the importance of beliefs and practices.[33] This study makes a

---

[29] See esp. S. Lobell, N. Ripsman and J. Talliaferro (eds.), *Neo-Classical Realism, the State and Foreign Policy* (Cambridge, 2009) and S. Lobell, N. Ripsman and J. Talliaferro (eds.), *The Challenge of Grand Strategy: The Great Powers and the Broken Balance between the World Wars* (Cambridge, 2012).

[30] This is the first of Morgenthau's 'six principles of political realism': *Politics Among Nations*, 4–5.

[31] A. Wendt, 'Anarchy is what states make of it: the social construction of power politics', *International Organization*, 46 (1992), 391–425; P. Katzenstein (ed.), *The Culture of National Security: Norms and Identity in World Politics* (New York, 1996); C. Reus-Smit, *The Moral Purpose of the State* (Princeton, 1999); T. Farrell, 'Constructivist security studies: portrait of a research programme', *Review of International Studies*, 4, 1 (2002), 49–72.

[32] W. Wohlforth, 'Reality check: revising theories of international relations in response to the end of the Cold War', *World Politics*, 50, 4 (1998), 659–80; J. Snyder, 'Anarchy and culture', *International Organisation*, 56, 1 (2002), 7–45; M. Barnett and R. Duvall, *Power in Global Governance* (Cambridge, 2005).

[33] M. C. Williams, *Culture and Security: Symbolic Power and the Transformation of the International Security Order* (London, 2007); F. Mérand and V. Pouliot, 'Le Monde de Pierre Bourdieu: éléments pour une théorie sociale des relations internationales', *Canadian Journal of Political*

modest contribution to this project by highlighting how the interplay between the subjective understandings of French policy elites and structures of power set the parameters for all strategies of national security.

The book is organised chronologically and into five parts. Part I outlines the social and cultural context in which foreign and security policy was made. It also examines the origins and development of both the traditional and the internationalist conceptions of security. Part II traces the interplay between traditional and internationalist approaches during the First World War. While the traditional current remained indisputably dominant within the policy elite, the terrible losses France suffered, when combined with representations of the war as a crusade for justice and democracy, underpinned growing consensus in the public sphere that the international system must be reformed to prevent another such conflict. Part III reassesses the peace programme of the Clemenceau government at the Paris Peace Conference. It argues that French policy at the conference was based, to a much greater extent than is generally understood, on a commitment to the principles of democracy and self-determination. Plans for the creation of a North Atlantic strategic and economic condominium lay at the heart of the Clemenceau government's programme. Part III also illuminates the importance of the internationalist vision of peace through law to France's proposal for a league of nations in 1919. This proposal foundered in the face of Anglo-American opposition and indifference on the part of Clemenceau. But this conception of the league would be resurrected in the mid-1920s to provide one of the pillars of French security policy.

Part IV is devoted to examining policy responses to the changed normative context of the post-1918 era. It traces the domestic and international tensions created by pursuit of an essentially traditional conception of security early in this period. It shows how the changed international context led even the traditionalists such as Alexandre Millerand to contemplate multilateral solutions to the problem of economic security. A willingness to embrace such alternative solutions was even more pronounced under Millerand's successor Aristide Briand in late 1921. The advent of Raymond Poincaré as head of government in early 1922 reversed this trend. The result was a series of efforts to force Germany to comply with the treaty that culminated in a highly traditional attempt to overthrow the Versailles order and establish French predominance. But Poincaré's security policy, like that of Millerand, encountered both international and domestic opposition that was central to the electoral victory of the Cartel des gauches in 1924. The fifth and final section of the book focuses on the response of a series of Cartel governments to the problem of

Science, 41, 3 (2008), 603–25; P. Jackson, 'Pierre Bourdieu' in N. Vaughan Williams and J. Edkins (eds.), *Critical Theorists and International Relations* (London, 2009), 89–101; V. Pouliot, *International Security in Practice: The Politics of NATO–Russia Diplomacy* (New York, 2010); E. Adler and V. Pouliot, *International Practices* (Cambridge, 2011); R. Adler-Nissen (ed.), *Bourdieu in International Relations* (London, 2012).

security in the mid-1920s. It reinterprets the foreign and security policy of the Herriot government, demonstrating the extent to which it placed the League of Nations at the heart of its strategy for security. This process culminated in the Geneva Protocol of September 1924. The demise of the Protocol led to negotiations leading to the Locarno Accords for security in western Europe the following autumn. This section of the book underlines the difficult choices that French policy makers faced in their effort to construct a viable Europe-wide security regime based on principles of compulsory arbitration and mutual assistance but underwritten by a continental commitment from Great Britain.

The structure of individual chapters reflects the diverse aspects of France's European security policy. Most chapters are organised into a series of themes, all of which run through the book: security in western Europe; policy towards Russia and eastern Europe; economic security; and, after 1917, the challenge of post-war international organisation. Most also provide systematic discussions of the structural context that conditioned policy choices. Categorising the different elements of security policy in this way inevitably imposes artificial distinctions between strands of policy that were interdependent. This is a price worth paying, however, in order to explore specific themes thoroughly over time. This manner of structuring chapters breaks down altogether, interestingly, in Part V when the Cartel government attempted to unite the various strands in an ambitious policy for Europe-wide security based on a reformed League of Nations.

There are inevitable gaps in the analysis that follows. The focus of the book is France's foreign and security policy in Europe. The security of France's empire was a pressing strategic issue through most of this period, but falls outside the parameters of this study. The same is true of internal security in general and anti-communism in particular. Attempting to incorporate these issues would have taken much time and effort, and resulted in an even longer book. Fortunately, there is a growing body of first-rate scholarship on both imperial and domestic security during this period by historians whose expertise in these areas far outstrips my own.[34] I have therefore chosen to concentrate on French policy for security in Europe. The focus throughout is on alternative conceptions of an international order that would remove the risk of another German bid for continental domination. The central argument is that internationalist ideas about peace and security played a much more important role in the evolution of French policy than is generally understood. By the mid-1920s French policy makers were thinking beyond the balance of power.

---

[34] On empire and security see esp. M. Thomas, *Empires of Intelligence? Security Services and Colonial Disorder in North Africa and the Middle East, 1914–40* (Berkeley, 2007); M. Thomas, *Violence and Colonial Order: Police, Workers, and Protest in the European Colonial Empires, 1918–40* (Cambridge, 2012); on internal security see O. Forcade, *La République secrète: histoire des services spéciaux français de 1918 à 1939* (Paris, 2008); G. Vidal, *La Grande Illusion? Le Parti communiste français et la défense nationale* (Lyon, 2006).

Part I

The sources of French security policy

The past two decades have witnessed the 'pervasive rise of culture' in the practice of international history. 'Culturalist' approaches have broadened and deepened our understanding of the nature of international politics and the sources of policy making. A central feature of the 'cultural turn' is a focus on the social imagination of policy actors.[1] This book contributes to this literature with an analysis of the role of contending conceptions of national security in the making of foreign and defence policy.

Any attempt at a systematic analysis of the role of ideas in policy making must address the difficult questions 'where do ideas come from?' and 'how do they affect policy making?'. At the heart of both questions is the problem of culture – or, more precisely, the cultural context within which policy is made. Ideas about peace and security emerge within specific social and historical contexts. They cannot be understood properly without taking these contexts into account. This, in turn, requires detailed consideration of the social backgrounds, education, training and everyday practices of those political, diplomatic and military elites involved in making foreign and security policy. It was through these 'background' factors that policy elites acquired a durable set of cultural predispositions that conditioned their responses to the international challenges of this period. The role of these predispositions must then be understood in relation to the institutional culture of the various organs of state in which most policy actors were embedded. Just as important were the wider domestic and international contexts in which policy was made. Factors such as parliamentary or public opinion, the balance of military and economic power or the policies of other actors in the international system all placed structural

---

[1] For useful discussions see P. Finney, 'Introduction: what is international history?' and A. Rotter, 'Culture', both in P. Finney (ed.), *Palgrave Advances in International History* (London, 2006), 2 and 17 and 267–99 respectively; J. C. E. Gienow-Hecht and F. Schumacher (eds.), *Culture and International History* (Oxford, 2004); A. Iriye, 'Culture and International History' in M. Hogan and T. Paterson, *Explaining the History of American Foreign Relations*, 2nd edn (Cambridge, 2004), 241–56; S. Brewer, '"As Far as we Can": Culture and US Foreign Relations' in R. Schulzinger (ed.), *A Companion to American Foreign Relations* (Oxford, 2003), 15–30; and D. Reynolds, 'International history, the cultural turn and the diplomatic twitch', *Cultural and Social History*, 3 (2006), 75–91.

constraints on policy choices. Any study of the role of ideas and beliefs must consider their interrelationship with these outside structures.

Many international historians tackle these problems almost by instinct. Much of the best international history is written without any engagement with social or political theory. My own approach to the role of cultural reflexes in policy decisions owes an intellectual debt that must be acknowledged to sociologist Pierre Bourdieu's 'theory of practice'.[2] Bourdieu's theoretical framework provides a useful conceptualisation of culture as a set of predispositions that are internalised by social actors over time. These predispositions, which Bourdieu refers to as the actor's 'habitus', are acquired by a process of formal and informal learning as well as the cumulative impact of daily practices. The habitus is therefore the product of the social agent's social background, education and training but also of the position that they occupy within a given field of social relations. The habitus provides actors with an ingrained orientation to the external world that generates expectations and understandings about how the world works and how things should be done. These constitute a 'practical logic' which shapes the actor's engagement with the social world. Crucially, the habitus is in a continual state of evolution as it responds and adapts to the changes in the external environment. It is durable but in no way static, and is thus capable of producing a multitude of different strategies and practices, depending on the external structures to which it is responding.[3]

An important characteristic of the concepts of habitus and practical logic is that they can be applied to collective actors as well as individuals. Institutions with a reasonable degree of social cohesion will often develop their own corporate identity and a common practical logic to function more effectively as social actors.[4] The chapters that follow will identify the operation of various practical logics as they evolve in response to the changing circumstances of war, peacemaking and international stabilisation. This approach provides a useful template for asking why French policy makers responded *in the way that they did* to profound transformations in both the internal and external environment. Careful attention is paid throughout to the interaction between the cultural disposition of various policy elites and wider structural factors that set limits on policy choices. But this is not a Bourdieusian study of French policy. Bourdieu's general conceptualisation of 'culture', along with the more specific concept of a 'practical logic', are part of the deeper infrastructure of the book.

---

[2] For more detailed discussion see P. Jackson, 'Pierre Bourdieu, the "cultural turn" and the practice of international history', *Review of International Studies*, 34, 1 (2008), 155–81; P. Jackson, 'Pierre Bourdieu' in N. Vaughan Williams and J. Edkins (eds.), *Critical Theorists and International Relations* (London, 2009), 89–101.
[3] P. Bourdieu, *Le Sens pratique* (Paris, 1980); D. Swartz, *Culture and Power: The Sociology of Pierre Bourdieu* (Chicago, 1997); V. Pouliot, 'The logic of practicality', *International Organization*, 62, 2 (2008), 257–88.
[4] See esp. P. Bourdieu, *La Noblesse d'état: grandes écoles et esprit de corps* (Paris, 1989), 11–26, 44–7.

Yet the intellectual debt to Bourdieu is significant, even if the evidence and arguments are not expressed in Bourdieusian language.

The following two chapters consider the institutional and ideological sources of French policy. The first examines the social background, education and everyday practices of political, diplomatic and military elites. It seeks to map out the cultural and institutional settings within which ideas about national security evolved and identify the dynamics of the wider field of security policy making during and after the Great War. The second will introduce the two general conceptions of peace and security that structured both official and public sphere discourse on international relations. It will consider the origins and evolution of both the traditional and internationalist approaches as well as the extent to which each was embedded in prevailing cultural practices of national security on the eve of the First World War.

1 The social dynamics of security policy making

The human sinews of national security policy making in France are the subject of this chapter. Political elites, foreign ministry officials and senior military figures comprised the three dominant constituencies in the making of foreign and security policy under the Third Republic. Each occupied a distinct position within the field of policy making. Although there were internal divisions over individual policy issues within all three constituencies, each was characterised by a distinct set of practices and predispositions that shaped their institutional responses to questions of national security. This chapter will examine the social backgrounds, education, formal training and everyday practices of France's politicians, diplomats and soldiers. It will then outline the organisational structure of national security policy making. In its treatment of 'policy elites' as distinct social groupings whose background, beliefs and comportment shaped their responses to policy challenges, the discussion that follows owes a considerable intellectual debt to pioneering studies by D. C. Watt and Zara Steiner.[1] It combines the methodologies developed by Watt and Steiner with Bourdieu's concept of 'culture' to provide an overall picture of the social and cultural context within which foreign and defence policy evolved.

I

Perhaps the central theme in the early political history of the Third Republic was the effort of elected officials to assert their control over the machinery of state. By the eve of the First World War this process was virtually complete in the realm of national security. Parliament had secured unchallenged authority over the making of foreign and defence policy. French parliamentarians, interestingly, were an ideologically disparate group drawn from a relatively narrow cross-section of society. Among those senators and deputies who came of age in the late nineteenth and early twentieth centuries, barely 7 per cent were of

---

[1] D. C. Watt, *Personalities and Policies: Studies in the Formulation of British Foreign Policy in the Twentieth Century* (Notre Dame, 1965); Z. Steiner, *The Foreign Office and Foreign Policy, 1898–1914* (Cambridge, 1969); see also K. Neilson, *Britain and the Last Tsar: British Policy and Russia, 1894–1917* (Oxford, 1995), 11–37.

working-class origin. And only 10 per cent were from the ranks of the *grands notables* that had dominated French politics before 1870. The remaining 83 per cent were from the bourgeoisie.[2] This bourgeois domination was even more pronounced when it came to ministerial posts. Ninety-two per cent of government ministers in France between 1900 and 1930 came from the ranks of the bourgeoisie – and virtually all those who held senior posts were products of French higher education.[3] Governments were made up of familiar combinations of politicians from the centre-right, centre and centre-left.[4]

Another factor contributing to the striking social cohesion of the 'ruling elite' was the operation, at the entry level of the party and parliamentary hierarchy, of what Christophe Charle and Gilles Le Béguec have identified as a system of 'self-selecting networks' and 'pathways'. The function of this system was to thrust some candidates forward and to filter out others. The governing elite was in this way able to reproduce itself.[5] The Paris Bar was by far the most prolific network for the production of political elites. The legal profession had occupied a central position in French political culture at least since the constitution of the Estates-General in early 1789. Two-thirds of the deputies elected to represent the Third Estate in that year possessed legal qualifications.[6] Lawyers and the law have played a pivotal role in shaping the political history of France ever since. The first two decades of the twentieth century marked the zenith of the legal profession in French political life. Thirty per cent of the deputies elected to the French Chamber in spring 1914 were lawyers. And the proportion of *avocats* within the governing elite was much greater. Two-thirds of

---

[2] On the social and professional background of French parlementarians see M. Dogan, 'La Stabilité du personnel parlementaire sous la Troisième République', *Revue française de science politique*, 2 (1953), 319–48; M. Dogan, 'Les Filières de la carrière politique en France', *Revue française de science politique*, 7 (1967), 468–92; M. Offerlé (ed.), *La Profession politique XIXème–XXème siècles* (Paris, 1999); and J.-M. Mayeur, J.-P. Chaline and A. Corbin (eds.), *Les Parlementaires de la Troisième République* (Paris, 2003), of which the chapters by Christophe Charle, Éric Anceau and Gilles Le Béguec were especially useful.

[3] C. Charle, 'Les Parlementaires: avant-garde ou arrière-garde d'une société en mouvement?', in Mayeur, Chaline and Corbin (eds.), *Parlementaires de la Troisième République*, 49, 47, 63. See also É. Philippeau, 'La fin des notables revisitée' in Offerlé (ed.), *La Profession politique*, 69–92 and J. Bécarud, 'Noblesse et représentation parlementaire: les députés nobles de 1871 à 1968', *Revue française de science politique*, 23, 5 (1973), 972–93. On the importance of higher education see É. Anceau, 'Les Écoles du Parlement: les types de formation des parlementaires' in Mayeur, Chaline and Corbin (eds.), *Parlementaires de la Troisième République*, 167–95.

[4] Standard sources on French politics during this era remain J.-M. Mayeur, *La vie politique sous la Troisième République* (Paris, 1984), 195–294 and S. Berstein, *Histoire du Parti Radical*, vol. I: *À la recherche de l'âge d'or* (Paris, 1980). See also, among many others, P. Lévêque, *Histoire des forces politiques en France*, vol. II: *1880–1940* (Paris, 1994), esp. 31–94.

[5] Charle, 'Les Parlementaires', 61–3 and G. Le Béguec, 'Les Réseaux' in Mayeur, Chaline and Corbin (eds.), *Parlementaires de la Troisième République*, 241–62. Le Béguec's massively detailed *thèse d'état* is indispensable on the character of these networks: 'L'Entrée au Palais Bourbon: les filières privilégiées d'accès à la fonction parlementaire: 1919–1939', 5 vols., Université de Paris X (Nanterre), 1989.

[6] D. Bell, *Lawyers and Citizens: The Making of a Political Elite in Old Regime France* (Oxford, 1994), 146.

cabinet ministers during the period under consideration in this book were drawn from the ranks of the legal profession.[7] Any list of the political luminaries of this period is dominated by lawyers. Raymond Poincaré, Alexandre Millerand, Louis Barthou, René Viviani, Marcel Sembat and Aristide Briand were all members of the Bar. The same was true of many of the rising stars of the next generation, including Marius Moutet, Joseph Paul-Boncour, Paul Reynaud, Vincent Auriol, Anatole de Monzie, Pierre Cot and Pierre Laval. All were to play key roles in security policy making during the inter-war years. The influence of the juridical profession was most pronounced in foreign affairs. Six of seven foreign ministers during the 1920s were lawyers. Only Édouard Herriot, who briefly combined the offices of premier and foreign minister in 1924–5 and for three days in 1926, was not a member of the Bar.[8]

There are two central reasons for the dominance of the juridical profession during this period. The first is the character of French politics. Under the constitution of the Third Republic the balance of political power rested decisively with the legislature over the executive authority of the president or cabinet. It was no coincidence that the period 1900–30 was the golden age of deliberative democracy in France. Success in politics, more than at any time before or since, required both 'eloquence' and skill in set-piece parliamentary debates. These were also attributes required in the courtroom.[9] Just as important was the role of the Paris Bar in establishing structures specifically aimed at facilitating political careers for its members. The most important of these was the Conférence des avocats du barreau de Paris, an annual competition for newly qualified lawyers. Each year twelve 'secretaries' of the Conférence were appointed based on their performance in competitions emphasising oratory and debating skills. The *cadre* of former *secrétaires* constituted a powerful network of political influence that, under the Third Republic, produced 3 presidents, 12 premiers, 5 presidents of the chamber of deputies, 41 ministers and 139 parliamentarians.

This network was particularly influential in the recruitment of aspiring politicians to positions within the entourages of ministers. Poincaré and Millerand, for example, were former secretaries of the Conférence des avocats who went on to become both premier and president in the decade 1914–24. Both were notorious for recruiting their private secretaries from the ranks of the Conférence. This political reflex extended to the appointment of ministerial colleagues when constituting governments. Eight of thirteen ministers and

---

[7] Figures from G. Le Béguec, *La République des avocats* (Paris, 2003), 24–5 and 38–9; see also Y.-H. Gaudemont, *Les Juristes et la vie politique sous la IIIème République* (Paris, 1970).
[8] Le Béguec, *République des avocats*, 115–21; R. Young, *French Foreign Policy 1918–1945*, 2nd edn (Wilmington, 1993), 303–4.
[9] N. Roussellier, *Le Parlement de l'éloquence: la souveraineté de la délibération au lendemain de la Grande Guerre* (Paris, 1997), 3–12 and 44–5; J. Starobinski, 'La Chaire, la tribune, le barreau' in P. Nora (ed.), *Les Lieux de mémoire*, 3 vols. (Paris, 1997), II, 2009–62.

three of six under-secretaries of state in the government formed by Poincaré in 1922 were members of the Bar.[10] This practice of self-selection and benefaction was by no means unique to Poincaré. It was an essential feature of the political culture of the Third Republic. The dominance of the legal profession in the French political elite was significant in the evolution of security policy after 1918. It contributed to the emergence of a juridical cultural reflex that shaped the course of French strategy and diplomacy well into the 1930s.

Another defining feature of French politics, which was a product of the practices of patronage and self-selection described above, was the enduring influence of a relatively limited number of parliamentarians who appeared and reappeared in different ministerial combinations. This meant that, despite the almost legendary ministerial instability of the Third Republic, there was a remarkable continuity in terms of those who governed. The result was a system in which most senior parliamentarians, whatever their ideological position, were on familiar terms with one another. The late nineteenth and early twentieth centuries were truly the era of the *république des camarades*.[11] There were certainly important ideological fissures within this elite. But there were also powerful shared beliefs about the proper role of France in European and world politics. Among the most widely held such beliefs were a reflex assumption of France's cultural greatness, its duty to uphold the rule of law and its unique mission to educate and even to 'civilise' the rest of humanity. These convictions were prominent in political discourse from the nationalist right to the mainstream of the socialist movement.[12]

The only significant challenge to these core beliefs came from the revolutionary politics of extreme-left Socialists, trade unionists and anarchists. These movements professed not to recognise France as a distinct political community. They preached instead the doctrine of international class struggle. The emergence of increasingly well-organised socialist parties in the latter half of the nineteenth century had transformed the European political landscape. And yet, despite the growing authority of trade unions, and the political success of the unified Section française de l'Internationale ouvrière (SFIO) after its formation in 1905, this ideology remained far from the levers of political power in France. There were, moreover, limits to the ideology of class struggle as a counterpoint to national allegiance in France. Absolute opposition to war in 1914 was confined to a doctrinaire minority within the workers' movement. The vast majority of the left, including the trade union and SFIO leadership, opted for patriotism over international class loyalty and were co-opted into the

[10] Le Béguec, *République des avocats*, 51–5 and 18–19.
[11] R. de Jouvenel, *La République des camarades* (Paris, 1914).
[12] These constructions can be traced back at least to the eighteenth century. See D. A. Bell, *The Cult of the Nation in France, 1680–1800* (Cambridge, Mass., 2001), esp. 91–8 and 143–9; on constructions of national identity see also P. Birnbaum, *La France imaginée* (Paris, 1998); T. Conley and S. Ungar (eds.), *Identity Papers: Contested Nationhood in Twentieth Century France* (London, 1996).

Union sacrée. It was this decision, significantly, that brought socialist ministers for the first time into government.[13]

The late nineteenth and early twentieth centuries were the 'golden age' of the French Radical Party. A decisive effect of the Dreyfus Affair had been to galvanise support for the republican regime in France from the moderate right to the socialist left. The foundation of the Radical and Radical Socialist Parties in 1901 was part of this larger movement of 'republican defence' against the forces of conservative nationalism. French Radicals were fixed firmly in the centre of the French political spectrum, between the Socialists to their left and the 'moderate' republicans on their right. The Radical Socialist Party (which emerged as the dominant political organ of French Radicalism) straddled the right–left divide in French politics. Its centrist political orientation – from left to right and back – allowed the party to tip the electoral scales in nearly every election through 1940. This permitted the Radicals, the first 'modern' French political party, to assume the role of the 'party of government' for much of the first half of the twentieth century. Radical politicians participated in virtually every government from 1906 through to the end of the 1920s. After 1902 a succession of Radical-dominated governments undertook the 'republicanisation' of the French army and the separation of Church and State in the decade before 1914.[14]

A common historiographical judgement is that international affairs were not a decisive issue in the domestic politics of the Third Republic. Most historians point to the fact that governments were rarely overthrown over questions of foreign policy or national defence. Even the official history of the foreign ministry observes that foreign policy was 'rarely the cause of ministerial crises, or even lively parliamentary debates'.[15] There are good reasons to doubt this judgement for the entire period from 1871 through 1940. But it is patently wrong for the era of the First World War. French politics were dominated by national security issues before, during and after the Great War. The single most important issue in French politics in 1912–14, for example, was the question of the Three Year Military Service Law. The proposed law was to extend the term of service for French conscripts from two to three years. It aimed to increase the size of France's army from 545,000 to 690,000 by the spring of 1914 and to 730,000 by 1916. This armaments programme was conceived as a response to

---

[13] A. Bergounioux and G. Grumberg, *L'Ambition et le remords: les socialistes et le pouvoir (1905–2005)* (Paris, 2005), 17–79; J.-P. Brunet, *Histoire du socialisme de 1871 à nos jours* (Paris, 1989); G. Lefranc, *Le Mouvement socialiste sous la IIIème République* (Paris, 1963); J. Kergoate, *Histoire du Parti Socialiste* (Paris, 1997).

[14] Berstein, *Recherche de l'âge d'or*, 41–86; Mayeur, *Vie politique*, 226–81; Lévêque, *Forces politiques*, 54–90.

[15] J. Baillou (and collaborators), *Les Affaires étrangères et le corps diplomatique français*, 2 vols. (Paris, 1984), II, 42–3; see also J. E. Howard, *Parliament and Foreign Policy in France* (London, 1948), 164–5; R. J. Young, 'The Foreign Ministry and Foreign Policy' in *French Foreign Policy, 1918–1945: A Guide to Research and Research Materials* (Wilmington, 1991), 27–8.

legislation under preparation in the German Reichstag that intended to increase the size of Germany's army dramatically.[16] The 'Three Year Law' occasioned a fevered national debate before it was passed by parliament in the summer of 1913. It was championed by the nationalist right as essential to national security. It was opposed by most of the left as a dangerous step down the road towards militarism and war.[17] Radicals were deeply divided over the issue. The vast majority remained suspicious of the military establishment, unenthusiastic about France's alliance with absolutist Russia and were uneasy about the increase in the power of the army that would result. But a significant proportion were also convinced that the law was necessary, at least as a temporary measure, for the security of France. This attitude was decisive, and left-wing opposition to the law failed.[18]

The politics of national security inevitably dominated political discourse during the First World War. As we shall see, however, it continued as an important element in the public sphere well into the post-war period. The government of Aristide Briand was overthrown by opposition to its foreign policy in early 1922. Thereafter foreign policy issues, principally the need to enforce the Treaty of Versailles, were a central theme in the public posture of Briand's successor, Raymond Poincaré. And foreign policy was a pivotal issue in the elections that brought an end to Poincaré's government in May 1924. The crucial importance of foreign affairs is illustrated not least in the decision of successive premiers Georges Leygues, Alexandre Millerand, Briand, Poincaré and Édouard Herriot to combine the foreign minister's portfolio with that of head of government during this period. Political elites could not ignore the profound impact of the war and its legacy on both public perceptions and parliamentary dynamics.

II

The ministry of foreign affairs was the second influential constituency in the making of national security policy. The institutional history of the 'Quai d'Orsay' was steeped in the long tradition of French power in Europe. The portraits of Richelieu, Colbert and Vergennes that lined the corridors of the ministry served as a constant reminder of the glorious legacy of French predominance.[19] This legacy combined with the social backgrounds, education

---

[16] D. Stevenson, *Armaments and the Coming of War: Europe, 1904–1914* (Oxford, 1996), 301–18.
[17] The best study of this question remains G. Krumreich, *Armaments and Politics in France on the Eve of the First World War: The Introduction of Three-Year Conscription, 1913–1914* (Leamington Spa, 1984). But see also J.-J. Becker and S. Audoin-Rouzeau, *La France, la nation et la guerre: 1850–1920* (Paris, 1995), 237–64.
[18] Berstein, *Recherche de l'âge d'or*, 66. On the Radicals and the Three Year Law see also Krumreich, *Armaments and Politics*, 70–117 and 103–17.
[19] A. Outrey, 'Histoire et principes de l'administration française des affaires étrangères', published in three parts in the *Revue française de science politique*, 3 (1953), 298–318, 491–510 and 714–38. See also Baillou et al., *Affaires étrangères*; Young, 'Foreign Policy', 9–44; and M. Vaïsse, 'L'Adaptation du Quai d'Orsay aux nouvelles conditions diplomatiques (1919–1939)', *Revue d'histoire moderne et contemporaine*, 32 (1985), 145–62.

and training of French diplomatic personnel to produce a remarkably durable set of policy predispositions that shaped the practice of foreign policy within the Quai d'Orsay during the early decades of the twentieth century.

From its origins in the fifteenth century through to the late nineteenth century the foreign ministry had been the near-exclusive preserve of France's aristocratic families. As late as the 1870s more than 74 per cent of its personnel were of noble extraction.[20] As the Third Republic became progressively more 'republican', however, it embarked on a programme to 'republicanise' and 'democratise' the Quai d'Orsay. Reforms introduced by foreign minister Charles de Freycinet in 1880 and 1882 aimed at eliminating the most reactionary elements within the diplomatic corps.[21] All potential candidates were carefully vetted by the Sûreté nationale to ensure that they held political views that were neither too far to the right nor too far to the left. Careful note was made of the results of these enquiries in the dossiers that were compiled for each candidate before their entry into the diplomatic service.[22] At the same time, the imposition of more rigorous and standardised entrance examinations (*concours*) introduced greater professionalism among ministry personnel.[23] The cumulative effect of these measures was a notable decline in the proportion of aristocrats from nearly three-quarters to barely one-fifth by 1914 and a dramatic increase in the number of diplomats who had rallied to the republic.[24]

The Quai d'Orsay remained a strikingly cohesive bastion of elitism within the machinery of the French state despite these efforts to open up the diplomatic profession. One reason for this was that the aristocracy was not purged altogether. Those members of the nobility who did not express open hostility to the republican regime kept their positions. There was a functional logic to retaining aristocrats in the diplomatic corps. Envoys from the nobility were typically better received in the predominantly monarchical courts of European

---

[20] I. Dasque, 'La Diplomatie française au lendemain de la grande guerre: bastion d'une aristocratie au service de l'État?', *VS*, 99, 3 (2008), 34–5; I. Dasque, 'À la recherche de Monsieur de Norpois: les diplomates sous la Troisième République, 1871–1914', thèse de doctorat, Université de Paris IV (Sorbonne), 2007.

[21] MAE, Papiers d'agents – Archives privées (hereafter PA-AP) 77, *Papiers Charles de Freycinet*, vol. 1, 'Oeuvres administratives de M. de Freycinet au Ministère des Affaires Étrangères en 1880 et 1882'; see also C. de Freycinet, *Souvenirs*, vol. II: *1878–1893* (Paris, 1913), chapter 6, 'Le Grand ministère'.

[22] See the personal dossiers of foreign ministry officials from this period which are available for consultation in MAE, *Dossiers de personnel*, 2ème série.

[23] Successive ministerial decrees from the 1880s onward aimed at standardising the entrance examination. The most far-reaching of these were part of the ministerial reforms of 1907. See especially Baillou et al., *Affaires étrangères*, II, 110–51; P. G. Lauren, *Diplomats and Bureaucrats: The First Institutional Responses to Twentieth Century Diplomacy in France and Germany* (Stanford, 1976), 44–72; M. B. Hayne, *The French Foreign Office and the Origins of the First World War, 1898–1914* (Oxford, 1993), 9–28; M. B. Hayne, 'Change and continuity in the structure and practices of the Quai d'Orsay, 1871–1914', *Australian Journal of Politics and History*, 37 (2008), 61–76.

[24] Dasque, 'Diplomatie française', 34–9 and 'À la recherche', 270–9.

Great Powers in the pre-1914 era.[25] Nor were candidates from anti-republican backgrounds necessarily excluded. It was essential that candidates expressed support for the republican regime when applying, but the politics of diplomatic personnel were not monitored once they passed the initial vetting stage of the recruitment process. The Comte Charles de Beaupoil de Saint-Aulaire, for example, entered the foreign ministry a committed republican but finished his career as an inveterate critic of republican foreign policy. This trajectory was not unusual during this period.[26]

Equally important in the ongoing elitism of the Quai d'Orsay, however, were the selection procedures of the ministry itself. While in principle the diplomatic profession remained open to talent, in practice the social, economic and cultural capital necessary to make it through the selection process restricted entry to the sons of aristocrats or of France's wealthiest families. A substantial independent income was essential. Before being considered for the final round of the admissions competition, candidates were required to work as unpaid *stagiaires* for at least twelve months.[27] Moreover, in order to qualify to sit the entrance examination, applicants needed to hold either a university degree or a diploma from one of the institutes established to train French military and administrative elites. The École libre des sciences politiques, founded in 1872 to train patriotic civil servants, was particularly successful in preparing candidates for the foreign ministry's entrance competition. In the era of the First World War more than 80 per cent of new recruits to the foreign ministry were graduates of 'Sciences po'. By 1935 this figure had risen to more than 90 per cent. The annual fee for this programme, however, automatically excluded all but the wealthy elite. Ninety-two per cent of students enrolled in this programme were from the upper reaches of the bourgeoisie.[28] The overall effect of

---

[25] V. Steller, 'The Power of Protocol: On the Mechanisms of Symbolic Action in Diplomacy in Franco-German Relations, 1871–1914' in M. Mösslang and T. Riotte (eds.), *The Diplomat's World: A Cultural History of Diplomacy* (Oxford, 2008), 197–205; I. Dasque, 'À la recherche de Monsieur de Norpois: prosopographie des ambassadeurs et ministres plénipotentiaires sous la Troisième République', *Revue d'histoire diplomatique*, 114, 4 (2000), 261–88.

[26] MAE, *Dossiers de personnel*, 2ème série, vol. 118: Auguste Félix Charles de Beaupoil de Saint-Aulaire; see also Comte de Saint-Aulaire, *Confession d'un vieux diplomate* (Paris, 1953) and Comte de Saint-Aulaire, *Je suis diplomate* (Paris, 1954).

[27] This probationary period was reduced to two-and-a-half months in 1907: Baillou et al., *Affaires étrangères*, II, 115–16 and 417–19.

[28] J. Keiger, 'Patriotism, Politics and Policy in the Foreign Ministry, 1880–1914' in R. Tombs (ed.), *Nationhood and Nationalism in France* (London, 1991), 260; according to M. B. Hayne, between 1899 and 1936 249 of 284 new recruits were from the École libre: *The French Foreign Office*, 27–8. A more commonly cited figure is 153 of 192 between 1905 and 1927 – this originates from W. R. Sharp, 'Public Personnel Management in France' in *The French Civil Service: Bureaucracy in Transition* (New York, 1931), 112; the figure for 1935 is from E. N. Suleiman, *Politics, Power and Bureaucracy in France: The Administrative Elite* (Princeton, 1974), 48; see also S. Jeannesson, 'La Formation des diplomates français et leur approche des relations internationales à la fin du XIXème siècle', *Revue d'histoire diplomatiques*, 122, 4 (2008), 364–9. On the École libre see also T. Osborne, *A Grande École for the Grands Corps: The Recruitment and Training of the French Administrative Elite in the Nineteenth Century* (New York, 1983), 69–75.

the ministry's entrance requirements was to reserve diplomatic careers almost exclusively for the academically gifted sons of the aristocracy and *haute bourgeoisie*. In 1901, for example, 77 per cent of the diplomatic corps possessed inheritances of 100,000 francs or more.[29] Aristocratic privilege was thus displaced by a new form of elitism that was no less exclusionary.

Another factor that contributed to the social cohesiveness of foreign ministry officials was that, despite efforts to 'democratise' the ministry that continued through to the eve of the First World War, the practice of self-selection was scarcely curtailed.[30] While the examination (the *concours*) served to weed out the less academic applicants, the ultimate decision to admit or reject candidates rested with a *jury* comprised of current and former diplomats (later expanded to include outside experts who were nonetheless selected by the ministry). Key categories in the selection criteria, moreover, were the candidate's 'family position', 'private conduct' and 'general culture'. Among the chief characteristics sought in the latter category were urbanity, self-control, tact, discretion and conversational skill.[31] Also highly valued was an ability to write with both verve and nuance. This important category was part of the long tradition of the writer-diplomat that stretched back to the earliest years of the ministry and continues to this day.[32] Because possession of such attributes was impossible to measure with precision, the process of selection remained highly subjective.

The nature of the ministry's entrance requirements and vetting procedures, when combined with the ongoing practice of self-selection, ensured that diplomats retained the traditions, comportment and idiom that set them apart from the rest of French officialdom. All of this only reinforced a belief in the distinctiveness of 'the career' that is evident in virtually every memoir account written by foreign ministry personnel of this period. The Comte de Saint-Aulaire, a long-serving and distinguished veteran of this era, emphasised the importance of the 'force of co-optation' that 'made "the career" a selective club whose members were bound by the same sense of solidarity as a religious brotherhood' into which 'any intrusion was as sacrilege'.[33]

---

[29] C. Charle, *Les Élites de la République, 1880–1900*, 2nd edn (Paris, 2006), 97; P. Jackson, 'Tradition and adaptation: the social universe of the French foreign ministry in the era of the First World War', *French History*, 24, 2 (2010), 164–8.

[30] 'On Démocratise au Quai d'Orsay', *Le Matin*, 19 Apr. 1909. See also the dossier entitled 'Suppression des titres de noblesse dans l'Annuaire Diplomatique de 1909' in MAE, PA-AP 12, *Papiers Maurice Horric de Beaucaire*, vol. 10.

[31] These categories and considerations are evident in the personnel dossiers cited above. See also the interesting discussions in J. Cambon, *Le Diplomate* (Paris, 1926), 63–4 and C. Charle (ed.), *Les Hauts fonctionnaires en France au XIXe siècle* (Paris, 1980), 155–8. For a vivid memoir account of the process see Saint-Aulaire, *Confession*, 7–19.

[32] P. Sellal, 'L'Écrivain diplomate entre littérature et politique'; L. Bély, 'L'Écrivain diplomate des temps modernes: entre nécessité politique et pratique culturelle'; and L. Badel, 'Le Verbe et le corps: anthropologie du diplomate écrivain', all in L. Badel, G. Ferragu, S. Jeannesson and R. Meltz (eds.), *Écrivains et diplomates: l'invention d'une tradition, XIXème–XXIème siècles* (Paris, 2012), 17–20, 31–42 and 398–408 respectively.

[33] Saint-Aulaire, *Confession*, 34–5.

This sense of distinctiveness was reinforced by the long tradition of family dynasties that continued through the First World War and beyond. Nearly 40 per cent of ministry personnel were connected by birth or marriage to another family within the Quai d'Orsay. By the early 1920s the names of bourgeois diplomatic dynasties such as Herbette, Cambon, Henry, Conty and Seydoux were firmly established in the *Annuaire diplomatique* alongside aristocratic names such as d'Ormesson, Saint-Aulaire, de Laboulaye, de Margerie, and de Vitrolles.[34] The result was a remarkably cohesive elite that viewed itself as the nation's repository of expertise on international politics. The sense of entitlement with which Quai d'Orsay officials approached diplomacy, and the ill-disguised disdain with which they often viewed civilian and military collaborators, reflected the social and intellectual elitism underpinning practices of recruitment and selection within this institution.

It is impossible to understand the internal dynamics of the foreign ministry without taking into account the endemic practice of patronage. Raoul Girardet rightly judged that 'the principle of patronage' was one of the fundamental operational codes of the Quai d'Orsay.[35] Networks of patronage were a fundamental source of social capital and were wired into every level of career advancement, from the admission of candidates to promotion to the rank of *ambassadeur de France*. Family relations were one of the most pervasive and important forms of patronage. More important still – particularly for promotion to the upper reaches of *la carrière* – was the support of senior ministry officials and friends in parliament. A brilliant career required both internal and external forms of patronage. Practices of recruitment and career progress were intimately bound up with the inveterate *clientèlisme* of the Third Republic.

The long and distinguished careers of the four 'greats' of the pre-1914 period – the brothers Paul and Jules Cambon, Jules Jusserand and Camille Barrère – provide an admirable illustration of the importance of patronage. All four deployed complex networks of sustained political support to further their careers. The Cambons had entered the diplomatic service after stellar careers as prefects and colonial administrators. Both enjoyed the backing of such luminary political figures as Adolphe Thiers, Jules Ferry, Léon Gambetta and Théophile Delcassé.[36] Barrère, ambassador to Italy from 1897 to 1924, was yet another protégé of Gambetta. Jusserand, who headed the embassy in Washington from 1903 through 1924, enjoyed the backing of Barthélemy

---

[34] On family dynasties within the foreign ministry see, among others, F. Le Moal, 'Diplomates et diplomatie en France entre 1900 et 1914', *Revue d'histoire diplomatique*, 114, 4 (2000), 289–330; Dasque, 'À la recherche'; Dasque, 'Diplomatie française'.
[35] R. Girardet, 'L'Influence de la tradition sur la politique étrangère de la France' in J.-B. Duroselle (ed.), *La Politique étrangère et ses fondements* (Paris, 1954), 147–9.
[36] L. Villate, *La République des diplomates: Paul et Jules Cambon, 1843–1935* (Paris, 2002), 16–23, 147–80, 199–200.

Saint-Hilaire, de Freycinet and later Delcassé.[37] Maurice Paléologue, political director at the Quai d'Orsay in 1912 and ambassador to Russia in 1914, had been a classmate of Raymond Poincaré at the Lycée Louis-le-Grand. Paléologue's successor as political director, Pierre de Margerie, was sponsored by the Cambon brothers as well as Poincaré and Delcassé.[38]

The formal intellectual training received by diplomatic officials was just as important in shaping institutional reflexes. Teaching at the École libre was predominantly historical and the tone was forthrightly nationalist. The larger aim was to apply the principles of nineteenth-century positivism to train a new generation of officials who would renovate and modernise state and society in France.[39] The intellectual preparation received by aspiring diplomats also reflected the centrality of law and legalism in French political culture. The vast majority of successful candidates for the diplomatic service, including those who had obtained a diploma from the École libre, had studied in one of the nation's law faculties and were *licencié en droit*.[40] The specific character of this legal training was important. French jurisprudence was rooted in the positive law tradition, with its emphasis on the role of written laws in bestowing rights and duties on both individuals and groups. The teaching of international law in France was thus more concerned with its codification and practice than with the sources of international justice. For diplomats, the 'law of nations' was in essence the history of international treaties.[41]

The foreign ministry entrance examination reflected the importance attached to international law. It was an ordeal that included up to seventeen hours of written examinations, interrogation in either German or English and then a further four hours of oral examinations. The subjects examined were political economy, constitutional law, international law, physical and political geography and diplomatic history. By the turn of the century the *jury* responsible for selecting candidates typically included either the ministry's chief legal

---

[37] Baillou et al., *Affaires étrangères*, II, 57–60; R. J. Young, *An American by Degrees: The Extraordinary Lives of French Ambassador Jules Jusserand* (Montreal, 2009), 10–27.
[38] MAE, PA-AP 113, *Papiers Pierre de Margerie*, vols. 9–10; B. Auffray, *Pierre de Margerie et la vie diplomatique de son temps, 1861–1942* (Paris, 1976), 63–111, 143–60 and 226–333; Jackson, 'Tradition and adaptation', 169–71.
[39] Keiger, 'Patriotism, Politics and Policy', 260–2; Osborne, *A Grande École for the Grands Corps*, 53–68, 91–9; G. Thuillier, *L'ENA avant L'ENA* (Paris, 1983).
[40] According to Stanislas Jeannesson, before 1914 91 per cent of French diplomats were *licencié en droit*: 'Formation', 364, 377; of the thirty-seven personnel dossiers consulted for this study, which focused on ministry officials admitted between 1885 and 1910, twenty-seven possessed some form of legal qualification. The dossiers are held in MAE, *Dossiers de personnel*, 2ème Série. This 'licence' did not qualify its holder to practise law. It was instead an indication that the candidate had received instruction in the social sciences. In a practice that reveals a great deal about the juridical character of the French approach to politics during this period, subjects such as political economy, comparative government and public finance, along with what would now be described as international relations, were all taught in faculties of law: see R. Valeur, *L'Enseignement du droit en France et aux États-Unis* (Paris, 1928).
[41] M. Koskenniemi, *Gentle Civilizer of Nations: The Rise and Fall of International Law, 1870–1960* (Cambridge, 2001), 269–72.

counsel or a representative from the law faculty of the University of Paris.[42] Positivist legal training, with its emphasis on the letter rather than the spirit of the law, was increasingly prominent in the institutional culture of the foreign ministry. It conditioned both the way diplomats approached problems and the way they framed responses.

The growing importance of this juridical reflex was expressed by the creation of an office of legal experts responsible for advising the ministry on an ever wider range of issues. The post of legal counsellor (*jurisconsulte*) was first created in 1722 but not established as a permanent fixture in the ministry's bureaucracy until the late nineteenth century.[43] In the early 1880s the growing prominence of international law in trade and political relations between states led to the establishment of a Direction du contentieux politique et commerciale and a Sous-direction de droit public. The increased importance placed on ensuring that foreign policy rested on a solid legal grounding led to the creation of the office of the *jurisconsulte* under the direction of Louis Renault in 1891. In 1907 this office was upgraded to become the Section juridique. The following year a Commission du droit international was created, comprising twelve senior officials and presided over, again, by Renault.[44]

By the First World War, therefore, international law was firmly established as a central element in the bureaucratic machinery of the Quai d'Orsay. All important policy initiatives passed through the Section juridique, which was responsible for advising all branches of the ministry. By the mid-1920s the influence of Renault's successor, Henri Fromageot, was widely considered to be 'second only to that of the secretary general'.[45] In practice this meant that careful attention was always paid to crafting a solid legal justification for French policy. It did not mean that professional diplomats understood international law, in itself, as a source of security for France. International public law was instead understood as an expression of the interests of specific states. As it was written in treaties, so too could it be altered should the interests of those involved change as part of the evolution of the balance of power.

If the gradual institutionalisation of legal counsel was a response to changes in the scope and pace of international politics, this was true to an even greater extent of the ambitious structural reforms of 1907. The Quai d'Orsay was in need of renovation. Its structures and procedures had changed hardly at all since the days of Talleyrand. Officials worked by candlelight, usually without the use of typewriters or telephones. The typical working day began in the late

---

[42] MAE, PA-AP 12, *Papiers de Beaucaire*, vol. 10, 'Conditions d'admission dans les carrières diplomatique et consulaire', 20 Nov. 1894 and 'Conditions d'admission', 24 Apr. 1900 (these are two presidential decrees, the latter modifying the former); Baillou et al., *Affaires étrangères*, II, 150–7. The system was modified slightly in 1906–7 when candidates were required to possess a working knowledge of a third language; see Jeannesson, 'Formation', 378.
[43] J. Baillou and P. Pelletier, *Les Affaires étrangères* (Paris, 1962), 129–30.
[44] Baillou et al., *Affaires étrangères*, II, 104–7.   [45] Quoted in Young, 'Foreign Policy', 19.

morning and finished in the afternoon with long breaks for lunch and five o'clock tea. More problematic still was the institutional segregation of political and commercial affairs that had remained in place since the Napoleonic era. The *direction politique* was responsible for political relations with other states conducted through France's embassies and legations abroad. The *direction commerciale* managed trade and industrial relations using the network of French consuls. The *direction politique* was unquestionably the senior department and was staffed by members of the diplomatic corps. The consular service, meanwhile, was less prestigious, less well paid and in the main comprised officials who had done less well in the *concours*. There was little interaction between the two departments and almost no policy coordination. This was at a time when an explosion in international trade and a revolution in communications technology had transformed the role of economic factors in international relations and dramatically increased the volume of information required to conduct policy. New conditions demanded a much greater diversity of expertise to use information effectively and make decisions more quickly.[46]

The reorganisation of the ministry was begun by Théophile Delcassé, the industrious minister of foreign affairs from 1898 through 1904 whose ambitious policy initiatives expanded the scope and intensity of France's global policy.[47] And yet, if the reforms of 1907 institutionalised the more professional approach introduced by Delcassé, they bear the unmistakable imprint of their chief architect: Philippe Berthelot.[48] The son of Marcellin Berthelot – the founder of organic chemistry and a lifetime senator – Philippe was a product of the late nineteenth-century French republican aristocracy. He remained a committed republican throughout his long career as a diplomat. This career in many ways mirrored the many contradictions in his personality. Berthelot's family background determined the conditions of his entry into the Quai d'Orsay, but was also the reason he twice failed to gain entry into the diplomatic service via the standard entry procedure. Despite passing the *concours* with distinction in 1889 and again in 1890, and being classed *admissible* on both

---

[46] Jackson, 'Tradition and adaptation', 176–8; Le Moal, 'Diplomates et diplomatie', 304–6; Vaïsse, 'L'Adaptation du Quai d'Orsay', 148–54; see also D. P. Nickles, *Under the Wire: How the Telegraph Changed Diplomacy* (Cambridge, Mass., 2003).

[47] C. Andrew, *Théophile Delcassé and the Making of the Entente Cordiale* (London, 1968); J.-C. Allain, 'L'Affirmation internationale à l'épreuve des crises, 1898–1914' in *Histoire de la diplomatie française*, vol. II: *De 1815 à nos jours* (Paris, 2005), 214–83; J. Delauney (ed.), *Aux vents des puissances* (Paris, 2009).

[48] This discussion is drawn from A. Bréal, *Philippe Berthelot* (Paris, 1937); J.-L. Barré, *Philippe Berthelot: l'éminence grise, 1866–1934* (Paris, 1998); P. Claudel, *Accompagnements* (Paris, 1949), 182–209; *Bulletin de la Société Paul Claudel*, 28 (1967) (a special issue devoted to Berthelot); J. Chastenet, *Quatre fois vingt ans, 1893–1973* (Paris, 1974), 116–24; R. Challener, 'The French Foreign Office in the Era of Philippe Berthelot' in G. Craig and F. Gilbert (eds.), *The Diplomats, 1919–1939* (Oxford, 1953), 49–85.

occasions, he was not selected for the intake in either year.[49] Berthelot eventually joined the ministry during his father's short tenure as foreign minister in the government of Léon Bourgeois in 1895. Crucially, this made him an *intru* (the contemptuous term often used by career diplomats for those who owed their status to political influence).[50] But Berthelot possessed a formidable intellect, an exceptional memory and a tremendous capacity for hard work. To these qualities were added an unshakeable resolve to impose himself and his views on the formulation and execution of foreign policy.[51] These attributes, along with powerful support from the key figures from the centre-left in parliament, facilitated his swift rise up the career ladder within the ministry. This ascent culminated in his appointment as director of political and commercial affairs in 1919 and then secretary general in 1920. Berthelot's close relationship with Aristide Briand formed the basis of one of the most enduring and successful careers in the history of French diplomacy.

Despite his obvious gifts and his unstinting dedication to France's interests, Berthelot attracted considerable resentment. This was in part owing to his status as an *intru*. His overt republicanism was also held suspect by several of his more conservative colleagues. The fact that he was an intimate of Léon Blum, a rising star within the Socialist Party who lived in the same apartment block on the Boulevard du Montparnasse, was not a mark in his favour within this milieu. But Berthelot's behaviour also contributed to the divided sentiments of his colleagues. He was not good at concealing either his considerable ambition or his disdain for convention. Jules Laroche, one of his protégés, remarked that Berthelot seemed to regard himself as 'above customary practices, if not the law itself'.[52] With the exception of a two-year mission to China, Berthelot's career was forged exclusively in Paris. This was in contravention of the norm that officials would gain experience in a series of foreign postings before being elevated to the senior echelons of the ministry. Berthelot was also an *habitué* of Paris literary salons. His vast social network included, at one time or another, such diverse characters as Maurice Barrès, Marcel Proust, Toulouse-Lautrec, Oscar Wilde, Collette and Jean Cocteau. As his influence within the ministry grew, he became patron to a generation of writer-diplomats that included Paul Claudel, Jean Giraudoux, Paul Morand, Jean Mistler and Alexis Léger. One of Berthelot's nicknames was 'le directeur ami des lettrés'.[53]

---

[49] MAE, *Dossiers de personnel*, 2ème Série, vol. 157, Philippe Berthelot, 'Concours d'admission', 15 Jan. 1890; see also Barré, *Berthelot*, 24–61.

[50] See esp. Saint-Aulaire, *Confession*, 33.

[51] See, for example, the glowing assessment of Berthelot in MAE, *Dossiers de personnel*, 2ème Série, vol. 157, Philippe Berthelot, 'Notes de chefs de poste', Cabinet du Ministre, 1901.

[52] Jules Laroche, *Au Quai d'Orsay avec Briand et Poincaré (1913–1926)* (Paris, 1957), 32.

[53] Claudel, *Accompagnements*, 53–7; Barré, *Berthelot*, 12; R. Meltz, 'Âge d'or ou naissance d'une tradition? Les Écrivains diplomates français dans l'entre-deux-guerres' in Badel et al. (eds.), *Écrivains et diplomates*, 70–95.

Berthelot's combination of talent, ambition and disregard for convention earned him the enmity of a number of influential politicians and press commentators. Raymond Poincaré, for example, could tolerate neither Berthelot's disdain for rules and procedure nor his mastery of the policy machine. British statesmen and diplomats considered him anti-British, while German observers accused him of Germanophobia. Both assessments were wide of the mark. Berthelot was a consistent proponent of the Franco-British entente and was a relatively early convert to a policy of cautious rapprochement with Germany. Paul Morand observed wryly in April 1917 that

The press of the far left ... attacks Berthelot as a reactionary, as an agent of the Church and as the master of censorship ... This is comical given that here in the Department we see Berthelot defend the perspective of the [Russian] revolutionaries and the most progressive ideas ... in fact his independent cast of mind and his modest cynicism make him suspicious to everyone. And no one can pardon his disdain for accolades.[54]

Berthelot's first priority throughout his long career remained the interests of France. He was arguably the single most influential French diplomat of the twentieth century.

Berthelot's career was emblematic of the transformations in international politics more widely between 1895 and 1932. It began at the close of the era of the amateur diplomat and flourished in an era of greater specialisation and larger, more influential bureaucracy. This period witnessed, with the rise of summit diplomacy and the growing influence of multilateral institutions, a greatly enhanced role for the press and public opinion as well as a decline in the independence and influence of ambassadors. It was also marked by the emergence of the Franco-British entente as a cornerstone of European politics, the destruction of the four great autocratic empires of central and eastern Europe and the advent of the United States as a bona fide world power.

Named the *rapporteur* of the Commission des réformes administratives in 1906, Berthelot was pivotal in adapting the structure and practices of the Quai d'Orsay to these new conditions. The appointment reflected his growing importance within the ministry. But it was due also to his status as an *intru*. The centre-left government of Georges Clemenceau viewed the ministry as a bastion of aristocratic privilege. Its reform was therefore entrusted to a relative outsider with impeccable republican credentials. Clemenceau's foreign minister, Stephen Pichon, was a diplomat and also an *intru*. The overriding aim of the reform programme Berthelot devised was to adapt the ministry 'to new conditions and to the requirements of modern diplomacy'.[55] Among these requirements were the need to introduce greater specialisation and to bring an

---

[54] Paul Morand, *Journal d'un attaché d'ambassade, 1916–1917* (Paris, 1963), 213.
[55] France, *Journal officiel de la République française* (hereafter *JO*), 1907, 'Rapport de la Commission des réformes administratives du Ministère des Affaires étrangères', 3 May 1907. On the 1907 reforms see also Lauren, *Diplomats and Bureaucrats*, 80–94; Hayne, *French Foreign Office*, 144–71; and Young, 'Foreign Policy', 8–13.

end to the antiquated separation of political and commercial affairs. A new Direction des affaires politiques et commerciales (DAPC) was created and divided geographically into four *sous-directions*. At Berthelot's insistence, a *conseiller commercial et financier* was assigned to each of these *sous-directions*. The DAPC was placed under the authority of the political director and quickly became the nerve centre of the foreign policy machine.[56] The authority of the political director was enhanced – a particularly important innovation in an era where the portfolio of foreign minister changed hands at the bewildering rate of once every seventeen months during the period 1871 to 1914.[57]

To manage relations with the growing number of non-state actors in world politics, a new Département des affaires administratives et des unions internationales was created. An awareness of the growing influence of 'opinion' (both at home and abroad) led to the creation of a propaganda organ, the Bureau des communications. The activities of this office were amplified in 1909 by the creation of a Service des écoles et des oeuvres françaises à l'étranger that was charged with promoting French language and culture around the world. During the war the Bureau des communications was transformed, once again at Berthelot's initiative, into a much larger Maison de la presse, which evolved in 1920 into the Service de presse et d'information. This process of modernisation was accelerated with the introduction of greater numbers of typewriters, duplicating machines, telephones and even automobiles.[58]

The increasing importance of international law, and especially arbitration, was reflected in a ministerial decree enlarging the office of the *jurisconsulte* and creating the post of deputy legal counsel. A separate section responsible for arbitration treaties and future peace conferences was created within the DAPC. Léon Bourgeois was given an office within this unit. Both Bourgeois and his secretary, Joseph Maximilien Jarousse de Sillac, envisaged it as a bridge both to the world court and to an eventual 'society of nations'.[59] Its function in Berthelot's reforms, however, was to make effective representation to international tribunals and thereby provide French policy with legitimacy within both domestic and international public opinion. It was thus an expression of the linkage between international law, public opinion and political legitimacy that

---

[56] Baillou et al., *Affaires étrangères*, II, 47–56; Vaïsse, 'L'Adaptation du Quai d'Orsay', 145–62; Lauren, *Diplomats and Bureaucrats*, 91–104; Hayne, 'Change and Continuity', 71–4; Outrey, 'Histoire et principles', 714–21; and Allain, 'Affirmation internationale', 247–51.

[57] When the seven-year tenure of Delcassé is left aside, this average shrinks to less than eight months: Baillou et al., *Affaires étrangères*, II, 41.

[58] J.-C. Montant, 'L'Organisation centrale des services d'information et de propagande du Quai d'Orsay pendant la Grande Guerre' in J.-J. Becker and S. Audoin-Rouzeau (eds.), *Les Sociétés européennes et la guerre de 1914–1918* (Nanterre, 1990), 133–5; R. J. Young, *Marketing Marianne: French Propaganda in America, 1900–1914* (London, 2004), 14–16.

[59] J.-M. Guieu, 'Les Apôtres français de "l'esprit de Genève": les militants pour la Société des nations dans la première moitié du XXe siècle', thèse de doctorat, Université de Paris I (Sorbonne), 2004, 44–7.

emerged in international society during this period and was given expression in the popular enthusiasm surrounding the two Hague Peace Conferences.[60]

These measures, along with the wider international trends to which they were a response, transformed working conditions and brought a definitive end to the leisurely and almost familial atmosphere of the Quai d'Orsay at the turn of the century. Officials were required to work longer hours to cope with the 'avalanche du papier' that crossed their desks. Diplomatic correspondence nearly doubled between 1895 and 1914 and increased at an even faster rate thereafter.[61] The passing of the institution of five o'clock tea marked the end of an era within the foreign ministry and the advent of a trend towards ever-greater levels of professionalisation and bureaucratisation that would continue through the remainder of the twentieth century.[62]

Perhaps the most important consequence of the 1907 reforms was the appearance of a generation of officials with more specialised training. The concept of distinct generations, always important in structuring social and political understanding in France,[63] is particularly vital in the case of the Quai d'Orsay in the era of the First World War. Recruiting a new cohort of foreign policy professionals was Berthelot's chief priority. 'Everything is a question of people,' he confided to Paul Claudel while in the midst of drafting the reforms. 'Whom should we appoint? That is the most important and perhaps even the only question.'[64] Berthelot's aim was not only to bring greater levels of legal and commercial expertise into the ministry, however; he was also determined to entrench his own influence. And circumstances favoured Berthelot's ambitions to establish a strong power base within the ministry. His appointment first as head of the foreign minister's personal *cabinet* under Pichon and, later, Aristide Briand, and then as political director and secretary general, enabled him to further the careers of his protégés (and thus his personal influence over policy). Between 1900 and 1920 the personnel in the central administration in Paris doubled. By 1914 86 per cent of the 152 foreign ministry officials trained at the École libre were under forty-four years of age.[65] Berthelot was the unquestioned leader and chief patron of this new generation. He was at the centre of an emerging generational cleavage within the diplomatic corps between those diplomats who had come to maturity by the turn of the century and those who were products of the new atmosphere within the ministry after 1907.

---

[60] See esp. I. Clark, *International Legitimacy and World Society* (Oxford, 2007); G. Sluga, *Internationalism in the Age of Nationalism* (Philadelphia, 2013), 21–8.
[61] Vaïsse, 'L'Adaptation du Quai d'Orsay', 158; Hayne, 'Change and Continuity', 71–5.
[62] On the transformation in conditions within the Quai d'Orsay see Young, 'Foreign Policy', 9–10; Lauren, *Diplomats and Bureaucrats*, 94–104; and esp. Jules Laroche's reminiscences in *Au Quai d'Orsay*, 11–12.
[63] P. Nora, 'La Génération' in Nora (ed.), *Lieux de mémoire*, II, 2975–3015.
[64] MAE, PA-AP 010, *Papiers Philippe Berthelot*, vol. 4, Berthelot to Claudel, 4 Aug. 1907.
[65] Keiger, 'Patriotism, Politics and Policy', 261.

The 'Berthelot reforms' have come in for heavy criticism, principally because they increased the size and influence of the ministry's central administration at the expense of diplomats posted abroad. The inevitable result was tension between senior ambassadors and their more junior counterparts working in the ministry in Paris. Jules Cambon, ambassador in Berlin, complained to his brother Paul in London about the 'young wolves' who had 'carved out for themselves personal domains within the Ministry'. He denounced the 'impudence of these presumptuous and ambitious youngsters' and advocated a return to pre-1907 structures and procedures.[66] This critique has been endorsed by at least one distinguished historian.[67] There is room for disagreement, however. It is true that Berthelot's reforms increased the numbers and influence of ministry officials and brought to the fore a new breed of 'technocratic mandarin'. They also reconfigured the factionalism that had long existed within the ministry. But it is equally true that they were a response to profound and irreversible changes in the international environment. The 1907 restructuring must also be understood as part of the wider trend towards larger bureaucracies and greater specialisation that characterised the evolution of the modern industrial state in the twentieth century. They anticipated similar measures that would be taken in Britain, Germany and elsewhere. The era of the semi-independent ambassador making policy 'on the ground' was passing away and that of summit diplomacy between heads of state relying on the counsel of specialist advisers was about to arrive.[68] The clock could not be turned back on this process.

III

France's military elite comprised the third influential collective actor in security policy making. Although the French navy boasted a long and proud tradition, the army had long been the dominant service within the military establishment. Defeat in 1870–1 had underlined the army's role as chief guardian of national security, and the Great War only reinforced its dominance over the making of strategic policy. Funding for naval construction ceased almost altogether from 1915 as the French war effort focused on the land campaign and relied ever more on British naval power. France's soldiers were credited with delivering victory in 1918; senior army commanders were fêted as national saviours.

---

[66] J. F. V. Keiger, *France and the Origins of the First World War* (London, 1983), 29, 183; see also Saint-Aulaire, *Je suis diplomate*, 103–8.
[67] Keiger, 'Patriotism, Politics and Policy', 258–9.
[68] K. Hamilton and R. Langhorne, *The Practice of Diplomacy: Its Evolution, Theory and Administration*, 2nd edn (New York, 2011), 141–84; G. Craig, 'The Professional Diplomat and his Problems, 1919–1939', in *War, Politics and Diplomacy: Selected Essays* (London, 1966), 155–69.

The conservative social and religious backgrounds of the majority of senior officers shaped the politics of the army leadership during this period. These politics, when combined with the intellectual formation and professional experience of the vast majority of French officers at this time, resulted in a deeply pessimistic perspective on international politics. While the social composition of the army officer corps as a whole was relatively diverse, the upper reaches of the military hierarchy were the preserve of conservative elites drawn from a surprisingly narrow cross-section of society. Since the revolutionary period the French army had aimed to draw roughly two-thirds of its officers from the ranks of non-commissioned officers. The remaining one-third was reserved for graduates of France's elite military academies, the École spéciale militaire de Saint-Cyr and the École polytechnique (which also produced France's engineering elite).[69] Officers from the ranks, meanwhile, passed through the academies of Saint-Maixent (for the infantry), Saumur (for the cavalry) and Versailles (for artillery officers and engineers). Thereafter, although in principle advancement was determined on merit, formal and informal practices for promotion favoured graduates of the elite military schools and in particular well-educated sons of aristocratic and wealthy bourgeois families. The first five criteria according to which young officers were rated upon graduation were 'character', 'education', 'intelligence', 'conduct' and 'bearing'. These categories then provided a basic structure for the performance reports written by their superiors for the rest of their careers.[70] William Serman has observed that 'in this game, "young men of means" performed brilliantly. They comported themselves with grace and confidence, they understood what to do and what not to do, and they rose rapidly up the army hierarchy.'[71]

Statistics for promotion bear this out. One in two officers of aristocratic or 'high' bourgeois origins rose to the rank of general. Prospects were not as good for officers from less privileged backgrounds. Only one in ten officers from the middle and lower bourgeoisie reached the rank of general, while only one in thirty of those from the working class reached this rank.[72] Efforts made to 'republicanise' promotion procedures from the early 1880s had only limited effect because they were aimed at eliminating open opposition to the Republic

---

[69] W. Serman, *Les Officiers français dans la nation, 1848–1914* (Paris, 1982); R. Girardet, *La Société militaire de 1815 à nos jours*, 2nd edn (Paris, 1998); C. Croubrois (ed.), *Histoire de l'officier français des origines à nos jours* (Saint-Jean d'Angély, 1987); J.-C. Jauffret, *Parlement, gouvernement, et commandement: l'armée de métier sous la Troisième République*, 2 vols. (Vincennes, 1987); O. Forcade, 'Les Officiers de l'état, 1900–1940' in M.-O. Baruch (ed.), *Serviteurs de l'état: histoire de l'administration française, 1870–1945* (Paris, 2000), 261–77.

[70] Quoted from the personnel dossier of General Édouard Réquin which can be consulted in Service historique de la défense–Département de l'armée de terre (hereafter SHD-DAT), Dossiers et états de service (personnel dossiers), 13Yd, dossier 953.

[71] See Serman, *Officiers français*, 228. See also A. Bach, *L'Armée de Dreyfus: une histoire politique de l'armée française de Charles X à 'l'Affaire'* (Paris, 2004), 21–43 and 512–16.

[72] Serman, *Officiers français*, 17–18.

rather than altering the social composition of the officer corps.[73] Indeed, the proportion of officers from the privileged classes increased in the final decades of the nineteenth century as the military profession became increasingly popular among conservative and Catholic families seeking a 'last institutional bastion against the politics of the republic'.[74]

At the apex of the army hierarchy were the general staff and the Conseil supérieure de guerre (CSG). The general staff was the engine room of the army. It was responsible for planning and implementation of everything from recruitment and promotion to intelligence, military operations and logistics. Entry into this citadel was determined chiefly by academic excellence. The first hurdle in this process was the fiercely competitive *concours* for entry into the École supérieure de guerre – the training school for general staff officers. In 1908, for example, eighty officers were admitted to the École from a pool of more than a thousand applicants. Upon graduation after two years of intensive study, officers were ranked from first to last according to their academic performance. Those graduating in the top 10 per cent of their class were identified as high flyers and typically assigned to the army general staff or the military *cabinet* at the war ministry. Officers who excelled at staff work were usually appointed as instructors at one of the military academies or the École supérieure de guerre. These various stages were interspersed by command assignments. The pinnacle of a career in the army was appointment to the CSG, the organ responsible for the formulation of nearly all aspects of French military policy. The CSG was staffed by the army's senior generals. Its vice-president was also the commander-in-chief designate.[75]

The system of self-selection and co-optation that determined promotion within the French army was criticised from the right for the excessive importance it attributed to academic performance and from the left for the advantage it accorded to well-educated candidates from privileged backgrounds. This criticism made little impact on practices, and the higher echelons of the army remained dominated by academically gifted graduates of Saint-Cyr and the École polytechnique.[76] In 1920 the personnel bureau of the army general staff

---

[73] This mirrored wider trends in recruitment and promotion within the French civil service as a whole. Christophe Charle has found that only 10.7 per cent of senior civil servants in France were not drawn from the aristocracy or the upper bourgeoisie: 'Le Recrutement des hauts fonctionnaires en 1901', *Annales*, 35, 2 (1980), 380–409.

[74] Forcade, 'Les Officiers et l'état', 271; see also Jauffret, *Parlement, gouvernement, commandement*, 402–3 and P.-M. de la Gorce, *The French Army: A Military–Political History* (London, 1963), 21–9.

[75] Jauffret, *Parlement, gouvernement, commandement*, 388–456. By 1914 many of the CSG's prerogatives in the making of high policy had been circumscribed. Its official role was to recommend policy to the government through the minister of war who, in principle, presided over its meetings.

[76] Bach, *Armée de Dreyfus*, 511–17; Girardet, *Société militaire*, 141–46; and Jauffret, *Parlement, gouvernement, commandement*, 401–13; see also the memoirs of army chief of staff General Marie-Eugène Debeney, *La Guerre et les hommes: réflexions d'après-guerre* (Paris, 1937), 9–12.

went so far as to advocate the institutionalisation of this state of affairs by creating an 'elite' officer corps drawn exclusively from the two *grandes écoles*.[77] Officers of modest means who managed to obtain appointment to the general staff or the CSG had invariably internalised modes of comportment that had long prevailed within the general staff and were a legacy of an era when the military was dominated by the nobility. All of this meant that, despite measures implemented to 'republicanise' recruitment and promotion procedures, the army leadership remained a relatively homogeneous group of conservative elites.[78] This state of affairs was reflected in prevailing attitudes towards both domestic and international politics.

A durable alliance emerged in the late nineteenth century between the politics of the military establishment and the conservative nationalism of the French right.[79] In the early 1870s conservative legislators responsible for the creation of the post-1871 army were haunted not only by defeat at the hands of Prussia but also the bloody experience of the Paris Commune. Policy towards the army reflected, on the one hand, popular conceptions of its role as the vehicle for national *redressement* and, on the other, pervasive fears of revolution. As the Catholic and conservative legislator Albert de Mun observed, 'The more the country becomes democratic, the more the army must remain undemocratic in order to preserve its capacity for sustaining social order.'[80] Once republican politicians gained firm control of the legislature in the late 1870s, however, the dynamics of civil–military relations changed dramatically. The Dreyfus Affair threatened to open a permanent breach between the republic and its army. A succession of Radical-dominated governments asserted parliamentary authority by intervening in the promotion process. The army's role in the making of national policy was limited constitutionally to providing 'technical' advice on issues of national defence. The political and religious views of conservative officers were monitored, and became criteria in decisions over career advancement within the war ministry. While this policy succeeded in affirming civilian authority over the military, it did not alter the conservative character of the army leadership.[81] Enforcing silence among officers proved easier than changing their ideological convictions. These convictions, crucially, received continual reinforcement through the rituals of military society,

---

[77] SHD-DAT, Série 1918–1940, 1N 23–6, 'Note sur l'encadrement de l'armée', 11 May 1920.
[78] Girardet, *Société militaire*, 118–62.
[79] M. Bernard, 'Les Militaires dans les partis conservateurs sous la Troisième République: un engagement naturel?' in O. Forcade, E. Duhamel and P. Vial (eds.), *Militaires en république, 1870–1962: les officiers, le pouvoir et la vie publique en France* (Paris, 1999), 395–404.
[80] Albert de Mun cited in G. Krumreich, 'The Military and Society in France and Germany between 1870 and 1914' in K. J. Müller (ed.), *The Military in Politics and Society in France and Germany* (Oxford, 1995), 29.
[81] D. B. Ralston, *The Army of the Republic: The Place of the Military in the Political Evolution of France, 1870–1914* (Cambridge, 1967); J.-F. Bédarida, 'L'Armée et la République', *RH*, 22 (1964), 119–64.

which were organised around the principles of authority and respect for tradition that remained the bedrock of social practices within the military.[82]

While a majority of army officers may well have disapproved of the Third Republic – there is no doubt that a majority disapproved of its religious politics – the temptation to overthrow the regime in a military *coup d'état* was entirely foreign to the French military tradition. The cult of discipline and of service to the state remained at the very centre of the belief system of the officer corps.[83] Strict limitations had long been placed on soldiers' political rights. These restrictions assumed ever greater importance after the experience of Boulangism in the late 1880s. The need to 'keep quiet' (*se taire*) on issues of domestic politics was 'elevated to the status of a military ethic' during the Third Republic.[84] The vast majority of active officers of all ranks refrained from openly expressing their political views. The result was what one distinguished product of this system described as 'a virtual absence of political culture' which left military elites 'impregnated with the summary political views inherited from our families'.[85]

All of this contributed to what André Beaufre described as the 'political illiteracy' of French officers.[86] A disdain for politics imbued military leaders with a narrow perspective on international affairs. It produced military responses to the problem of security that were, on the whole, technical rather than political and inflexible rather than adaptable. This did not, however, prevent senior active and retired officers from periodically communicating their views on strategic issues and defence policy to the wider public. Most did so indirectly via friendly journalists and elected representatives in the chamber or senate. But a minority opted to write articles in both the general and specialised press (after first obtaining approval for their contributions from the ministry of war).[87]

The influence of the high command peaked in the aftermath of the First World War. Victory carried the prestige of the military to levels unprecedented since the Napoleonic era. When Marshals Ferdinand Foch and Philippe Pétain expressed views on national policy, they were able to invoke not only the credibility that accrued to them as a result of victory, but also the sacrifices of the two million soldiers killed or permanently disabled on the battlefields of the Great War.[88] This provided military leaders with unrivalled symbolic capital and a dominant voice in the debates over national security that unfolded in the aftermath of the war.

[82] Serman, *Officiers français*, 227. [83] Girardet, *Société militaire*, 185–91.
[84] See Forcade, 'Les Officiers de l'état', 266. For this reason the French army was also known as the *grande muette* (the great silence). On the conservative and Catholic politics of the majority of the officer corps see also Serman, *Officiers français*, 65–123.
[85] A. Beaufre, *Mémoires: 1920–1940–1945* (Paris, 1965), 35. [86] Ibid., 34–8.
[87] For a discussion see O. Forcade, 'Les Murmures de la "Grande Muette" sous la Troisième République', in Forcade, Duhamel and Vial (eds.), *Militaires en république*, 507–19.
[88] J. Nobécourt, *Une Histoire politique de l'armée*, vol. I: *De Pétain à Pétain* (Paris, 1967), 13–58.

This kind of prestige, however, is nearly always a diminishing asset. It was undermined, moreover, by the system of recruitment, education, training and promotion employed by the French military, which left its leadership ill-equipped to adjust to the new international environment of the post-war era after 1918. The influence of the military in the realm of national security declined steadily in the early 1920s.

IV

It is now time to turn to the machinery of foreign and security policy making. During the first decade of the twentieth century a succession of governments created a range of bureaucratic structures intended to bring political, diplomatic and military elites together to discuss strategic policy. Chief among these was the Conseil supérieure de la défense nationale (CSDN). The aim was greater coordination between foreign policy, armaments policy and military planning in a system firmly under the ultimate control of parliament.

One of the few constitutional legacies of the *Ancien Régime* to modern France is the formal authority of the executive in the execution of foreign policy. In the constitution of 1875, the president of the Republic (the head of state elected by the chamber and senate every seven years) was nominally responsible for all aspects of foreign policy. The president signed all international treaties, made formal declarations of war and was the authority to which foreign representatives were accredited. In addition to this role in the domain of foreign policy, the president was also formally responsible for convening meetings of the *conseil des ministres* (the cabinet) and for calling on individual parliamentarians to form a government. These formal powers were limited in practice. All presidential acts required a countersignature by a government minister to become law. When a majority of parliamentarians opposed the policy of a given government, they could (and often did) overthrow it in a vote of confidence. The president would then be forced to choose another head of government. In addition, all peace treaties, any agreement engaging state finances and all declarations of war were to be ratified by both chambers. The result was that most presidents exercised their authority indirectly by deploying the substantial symbolic capital attached to their office when urging a particular line of policy.[89]

A determined president could, however, play a decisive role in foreign policy if government ministers lacked the willpower to resist pressure from the Élysée Palace. Poincaré, for example, exercised considerable influence during much

---

[89] Nicolas Rousselier refers to the 'gilded prison' inhabited by presidents under the Third Republic, especially after 1879: *Parlement de l'éloquence*, 16; see also J.-L. Clément, 'Pouvoir exécutif et pouvoir législatif en France de 1879 à 1914' in J. Garrigues (ed.), *Assemblées et parlements dans le monde* (Paris, 2011), 914–26; Howard, *Parliament and Foreign Policy*, 28–37; W. R. Sharp, *The Government of the French Republic* (New York, 1938), 77–81.

of his tenure as president from 1912 to 1919. Alexandre Millerand enjoyed similar authority between 1920 and 1924. Both saw their influence undermined in the face of resolute opposition, however. Poincaré was marginalised during Georges Clemenceau's premiership, while Millerand was forced to resign as president after an unsuccessful attempt to intervene directly in the parliamentary elections of 1924.[90]

Parliamentary authority over foreign policy was usually exercised indirectly through standing commissions of deputies and senators in a system that had evolved gradually from the late 1890s onward. The six crucial organs for foreign and defence policy were the army, foreign affairs and finance commissions of both the chamber and senate.[91] Ministers and permanent officials appeared regularly before these commissions to explain or defend key aspects of foreign or defence policy. Commission membership reflected proportional representation within the two houses. In practice this meant that the senate commissions were more conservative than those of the chamber. It also meant that debates within the latter commission were animated by a wider array of political perspectives because socialist and, later, communist deputies played a much more prominent role. The proceedings of the chamber foreign affairs commission, in particular, provide a rich perspective on contending conceptions of peace and security among parliamentarians at this juncture.[92]

Commission members were elected by their parliamentary peers, usually on the basis of interest and experience. The foreign affairs commissions always included former ministers with vast experience in international relations. The chairmen and *rapporteurs* of each commission were figures of considerable authority and influence. The chairman set the tone of debates and was responsible for calling the relevant minister for an *audition* before their commission. The *rapporteur*, meanwhile, presented the commission's views to parliament. This was a particularly important function during debates over budgets or the ratification of treaties. The budget of the foreign ministry, for example, was determined in negotiations between the ministry's Service du personnel et de la comptabilité and the *contrôleur des dépenses engagées* from the finance ministry. It was then presented for discussion before foreign affairs and finance commissions of both the chamber and senate. The *rapporteurs* from each commission would then report to parliament. Debates over military reforms, treaties and

---

[90] Mayeur, *Vie politique*, 242–50; J.-J. Becker and S. Berstein, *Victoire et frustrations, 1914–1929* (Paris, 1990), 246–8.
[91] R. K. Gooch, *The French Parliamentary Committee System* (London, 1969); Howard, *Parliament and Foreign Policy*, 96–112; Young, 'Foreign Policy', 26–9; M. Schumann, 'La Commission des affaires étrangères et le contrôle de la politique extérieure en régime parlementaire' in *Les Affaires étrangères* (Paris, 1959), 21–55; A. Duménil, 'La Commission sénatoriale de l'armée' in Forcade, Duhamel and Vial (eds.), *Militaires en République*, 313–24; P. Géroudet, *Le Parlement et l'armée: la commission de l'armée de la Chambre des députés* (Paris, 1990); Rousselier, *Parlement de l'éloquence*, 76–82.
[92] The only drawback was that *auditions* by ministers and senior officials were sometimes more circumspect for fear that their words would be leaked to the press (as they sometimes were).

general policy orientations within the commissions were also occasions for bringing parliamentary views to bear on the government. This system rarely resulted in reversals of policy. It did, however, provide a forum for free-ranging debate concerning fundamental issues of national security policy. This was not least because, with the important exception of socialist and later communist deputies, the phenomenon of party discipline was not yet entrenched in the French political and parliamentary culture.[93]

It was chiefly through the machinery of the parliamentary commissions, significantly, that the ministry of finance exercised much of its influence over foreign and defence policy. While the power and prestige of institutions such as the Inspection des finances and the Cours des comptes had increased steadily over the nineteenth century, there was no tradition of direct finance ministry intervention in national security policy. Indeed, the inter-ministerial machinery of government was only just taking shape, and finance ministry officials played no role in the formulation of strategy and diplomacy. There was no French equivalent, for example, of the redoubtable Warren Fisher, the permanent secretary of the British treasury who intervened in all aspects of high policy.[94]

Direct control over foreign and defence policy was exercised by the *conseil des ministres* through the ministers of finance, foreign affairs, war and (for naval policy) the *marine*. Ministers had final authority over all operations pertaining to their department, including budgetary issues, internal promotion and, of course, the overall direction of policy. Senior military or diplomatic officials, on the other hand, were formally restricted to the role of technical advisers. The powers of cabinet ministers thus verged on the arbitrary. The ministers of war and foreign affairs could, and did, intervene in personnel decisions of all kinds within their departments. Added to this was the prerogative of the premier and foreign minister to withhold even the most important international engagements from public scrutiny by invoking the principle of national security. The military convention attached to the Franco-Russian alliance in 1895 and the Grey–Cambon Letters of 1912 are examples of agreements kept secret during this period.[95]

There was no forum for the coordination of the national security policy, however, until the CSDN was created in 1906. The aim of this measure, which had close parallels with the formation of the Committee of Imperial Defence in Britain, was to establish 'a higher organ of co-ordination' to ensure that political, financial, diplomatic and military considerations were integrated in

---

[93] Roussellier, *Parlement d'éloquence*, 77–8; Howard, *Parliament and Foreign Policy*, 80–112; Gooch, *French Parliamentary Committee System*, 34–76; Young, 'Foreign Policy', 26–8.
[94] E. O'Halpin, *Head of the Civil Service: A Study of Sir Warren Fisher* (London, 1989); on the background and role of ministry of finance officials see Charle, *Hauts fonctionnaires*, 183–214.
[95] F. Schuman, *War and Diplomacy in the French Republic: An Inquiry into Political Motivations and the Control of Foreign Policy* (New York, 1931), 321–4; Young, 'Foreign Policy', 28–9.

the formulation of national security policy.[96] In practice the CSDN provided a forum for political, diplomatic and military decision makers to gather together to consider strategic policy. Planning for such a council had been under way since 1897. The war ministry at this time emphasised the need for collaborative study of 'all questions relating to the exploitation, for the defence of the nation, of the entire array of forces that constitute its power'.[97] Full membership of the CSDN was limited initially to the ministers of foreign affairs, finance, war, the *marine* and the colonies. In yet another expression of political control over the machinery of state, the chiefs of the army and naval general staffs, along with the ranking military official within the colonial ministry, attended in an advisory capacity only. They were denied a vote in the council's deliberations. Chairmanship of CSDN meetings was restricted to either the premier or the president of the Republic. To facilitate the effective functioning of the council, the Comité d'études, comprising the director of the DAPC at the foreign ministry as well as the army and naval chiefs of staff, was created. It was charged with preparing preliminary study papers to inform discussion and debate within the council. The CSDN was also served by a secretariat staffed with military officers.[98]

Several minor alterations were made to the structure of the CSDN before 1914. The minister of the interior became a full member in 1911. Changes to the army and naval command structures brought the commanders-in-chief designate of both services (General Joffre and Admiral Boué de Lapeyrère) on to the council in consultative roles. The Comité d'études was replaced first by a smaller Section d'études and then by a larger Commission d'études.[99] The aftermath of the Great War saw more dramatic restructuring. A large Secrétariat général (SGDN) was created and placed under the command of a senior army officer. The Commission d'études, meanwhile, was enlarged and divided into four sections. These sections, which were served by the ever-expanding SGDN, were charged with preparing studies of virtually all aspects of national security policy from arms limitation to planning the military, economic and social organisation of the nation in wartime.[100]

---

[96] SHD-DAT, 2N 3–1, 'Évolution des attributions du Conseil supérieur de la Défense nationale', 4 Feb. 1929; see also F. Guelton, 'Les Hautes instances de la Défense nationale sous la Troisième République' in Forcade, Duhamel and Vial (eds.), *Militaires en République*, 53–64.
[97] SHD-DAT, 2N 1–1, 'Rapport au président de la République', 27 Jan. 1897.
[98] SHD-DAT, 2N 3–1, 'Évolution des attributions du Conseil supérieur de la Défense nationale', 4 Feb. 1929.
[99] Guelton, 'Hautes instances', 54–5.
[100] SHD-DAT, 2N 3–1, 'Évolution des attributions du Conseil supérieure de la Défense nationale', 4 Feb. 1929; 'Procédure de collaboration entre le Conseil supérieur de la Défense nationale, la Commission d'études et le Secrétariat général permanent', 6 Mar. 1922; 'Notes sur l'organisation et la mission du Conseil supérieur de la Défense nationale', 18 Sept. 1924; SHD-DAT, 2N 3–2, 'Listes des membres de la Commission d'études', 5 Feb. 1924; see also T. Imlay, 'Preparing for total war: industrial and economic preparations for war in France between the two World Wars', *War in History*, 15, 1 (2008), 43–71.

The CSDN met a total of eleven times from its inception to the outbreak of war in 1914. These sessions focused almost exclusively on land and naval armaments policy and the evolution of mobilisation plans. Even after it was enlarged after 1919, however, the CSDN rarely discussed foreign policy in any depth. The strategic dimensions of France's alliance policy were sometimes addressed. But the bases of external policy were never up for discussion. The Quai d'Orsay was successful in maintaining its control of the formulation and execution of France's external policy.[101]

The above survey illuminates important differences in the background, training and practices of political, diplomatic and military elites during this period. All three constituencies were drawn overwhelmingly from a relatively privileged stratum of French society. Senior members of each had risen to occupy influential positions within the hierarchy of the French state. But the military profession was distinguished by a very different set of core practices from those of the politician or diplomat. An essential skill for both the politician and (especially) the diplomat is the ability to negotiate, to find common ground in order to achieve objectives without conflict. The influence of politicians and diplomats decreases once shooting starts. The core function of military officials, conversely, is to execute political violence in pursuit of national aims. The application of military force is the elemental activity around which nearly all military training and ritual revolves. Negotiating skill and political acumen were much less highly valued in the hierarchy of military attributes. A second important distinction was the juridical background of most politicians and diplomats. Military elites did not receive the same level of legal training and were little disposed to see the rule of law as a source of security.

All of this meant that political leaders and foreign ministry officials were better equipped in a cultural sense to adapt to the changed normative environment after 1918. The progressive militarisation of European international politics before 1914 had placed military expertise at a premium in the field of foreign policy.[102] Military influence over national policy peaked during the First World War as the strategic exigencies of the military campaign dominated all other political considerations. But military officials found themselves at a disadvantage after the war, in an era where military violence was increasingly discredited as a legitimate tool of foreign policy. This point may seem obvious, but it is rarely acknowledged in the literature on French security policy after the

---

[101] The *procès-verbaux* for nearly all meetings of the CSDN from 1907 through 1935 are available for consultation in SHD-DAT 2N 4; the supporting documentation for these meetings are available in cartons 2N 5–2N 7.
[102] D. Stevenson, 'Militarization and diplomacy in Europe before 1914', *International Security*, 22, 1 (1997), 125–61.

First World War. The changed normative context proved a boon, on the other hand, for foreign ministry officials. The skill-set of the diplomat was much better suited to the tenor of European politics in the post-war decade. The result was a reassertion of foreign ministry dominance in the field of foreign and security policy at the expense of France's military elite.

2 Two approaches to security

The decade prior to the outbreak of war in 1914 was characterised by a dramatic rise in international tensions. This brought foreign and defence policy to the forefront of the public consciousness in France. The result was an extraordinary expansion in both official and public-sphere discourse on the subject of national security.[1] Amid the array of policy conceptions advocated during this period it is possible to identify two reasonably distinct currents of thought about the problem of security in Europe. The first, which for the purposes of this study will be termed the 'traditional' approach, favoured security through strategic preponderance and alliance politics. It was based on an essentially pessimistic understanding of international relations as a perpetual struggle for greater power. The second, which is defined as the 'internationalist' conception, favoured security through cooperation between states under the rule of international law. The internationalist alternative was based on the more optimistic assumption that greater interdependence and cooperation, along with the creation of a robust regime of international law, could provide lasting security for France and other members of civilised world society.

This chapter will examine both the traditional and internationalist approaches as historically specific regimes of knowledge that produced contending visions of peace and national security.[2] It will examine the conceptual underpinnings of both approaches as well as areas of actual or potential overlap between them. It will also consider their relative influence over the policy-making process. The primary conclusion drawn is that only the traditional approach could claim the status of a 'practice' among French policy elites on the eve of the First World War.

---

[1] G. Krumreich, *Armaments and Politics in France on the Eve of the First World War* (Leamington Spa, 1984), esp. 13–20 and 231–41. On the varying levels of public interest in foreign affairs see J.-J. Becker and S. Audoin-Rouzeau, *La France, la nation et la guerre* (Paris, 1995), 38–9 and 264–5; and the still useful E. M. Carroll, *French Public Opinion and Foreign Affairs, 1871–1914* (London, 1931).

[2] The concept of historically specific assumptions about security is borrowed from M. Foucault, 'Truth and Juridical Forms' (trans. R. Hurley) in J. D. Faubion (ed.), *Michel Foucault: Essential Works, 1954–1984*, vol. III: *Power*, 11–19.

47

I

At the heart of the traditional approach to security was the conviction that world politics were driven by the pursuit of power. From this core belief flowed two operating assumptions. The first was that the chief interest and responsibility of the state is to achieve security by increasing its power wherever the costs for doing so did not outweigh the benefits that accrued. The second was that all power is relational in that it can only be measured against the power of other states. This meant that a significant increase in the aggregate power of one state always has the potential to threaten others.

These core assumptions made the balance of power a central element in all traditional conceptions of international politics. The organising principle of the balance of power is that, in the event of one state becoming over-powerful, others will combine their efforts in order to counter-balance any bid to dominate the international system.[3] Pursuit of a balance of power operated through a series of conventions, or practices, that were understood by the policy elites of all of the Great Powers before 1914. The most important of these were: compensations; alliances; joint military planning; the principle that power relationships determine interests; and, finally, the conviction that territory is a source of power.[4]

The notion of compensations was based on the practice of balancing strategic advantages obtained by one actor with commensurate advantages granted to others. This principle imbued traditional understandings of international relations with a 'zero-sum' character: the assumption tended to be that strategic gains by one actor were necessarily to the disadvantage of others. Hence the need for compensation. Alliances were mechanisms of self-help used by states to increase their influence and security. Powers pooled security resources and coordinated strategic plans when confronted with an external threat to their vital interests that could not be managed independently. Joint military plans (or staff conversations) were a means of outlining the precise strategic commitments of alliance partners. In a world of power politics, however, such

---

[3] Important studies of the balance of power as a belief system in international history include M. Wright (ed.), *The Theory and Practice of the Balance of Power, 1486–1914* (London, 1975); special issue of the *Review of International Studies*, 15, 2 (1989); H. M. Scott, *The Birth of a Great Power System, 1740–1815* (London, 2005); J. Haslam, *No Virtue like Necessity: A History of Realist Thought in International Relations since Machiavelli* (New Haven, 2002); and especially P. W. Schroeder, *The Transformation of European Politics 1763–1848* (Oxford, 1994). On balance-of-power theory see, among many others, H. J. Morgenthau, *Politics among Nations: The Struggle for Power and Peace* (New York, 1948); K. Waltz, *Theory of International Politics* (New York, 1979); S. Walt, *The Origins of Alliances* (Ithaca, 1987); M. Sheehan, *The Balance of Power: History and Theory* (London, 1996); J. Mearsheimer, *The Tragedy of Great Power Politics* (New York, 2001); R. Little, *The Balance of Power in International Relations* (Cambridge, 2008); J. Levy, 'Hegemonic threats and Great Power balancing in Europe, 1495–2000', *Security Studies*, 14, 1 (2005), 1–30.

[4] Two of these categories (compensation and alliances) are borrowed from Schroeder, *Transformation*, 5–9; see also Haslam, *Realist Thought*, 89–127.

arrangements were unlikely to endure once the common threat receded or was removed. This was also the logic underpinning the principle that interests were determined by power relationships. Because they were rooted in material conditions of power, interests were considered the only reliable guide to state behaviour. Belief in territory as a source of power, finally, was a pivotal organising principle in all balance-of-power calculations during this period. It also underpinned another important element in the traditional approach to security: the ideology of 'natural frontiers'. Paul Schroeder has argued persuasively that, for most of the period between 1763 and 1815, balance-of-power practices 'governed conduct in the sense that statesmen accepted them as the way politics had to work'.[5] The same was true in the case of most French policy elites during and immediately after the First World War.

Belief that France's security rested on a favourable *équilibre européen* can be traced back at least as far as the late fifteenth century. Some of the earliest systematic reflections on the concept of the balance of power in any language were those of the French statesman and man of letters Philippe de Commynes dating from the fifteenth century.[6] Half a century later Henri de Rohan produced one of the earliest arguments for the systematic calibration of power and interests in the practice of statecraft.[7] François de Salignac de la Mothe Fénelon, archbishop of Cambrai in the era of Louis XIV, published a widely read tract on 'The Necessity of Forming Alliances both Offensive and Defensive against a Foreign Power which manifestly aspires to Universal Monarchy'.[8] Even Voltaire urged European statesmen to pursue 'the wide policy of maintaining among themselves as far as possible an equal balance of power'.[9]

Raoul Girardet has argued that the balance of power was one of the oldest, most pervasive and most powerfully entrenched traditions within the French foreign ministry.[10] There is much evidence to support this argument. For centuries France's reflex reaction to the rise of any powerful state in central Europe was to ally with powers to that power's north and east. Little importance was attached to the religious or political character of these allies. The first example of this strategy of an 'eastern counterweight' was the alliance between King François I and the Ottoman Empire against the Habsburgs in 1536. Both Henri IV and the Cardinal de Richelieu adopted a strategy of counterbalance to deal with Habsburg power.[11]

---

[5] Schroeder, *Transformation*, 6.
[6] P. de Commynes, *Mémoires*, ed. J. Blanchard, 2 vols. (Paris, 2004); see also Haslam, *Realist Thought*, 91–2.
[7] H. de Rohan, *Traité de l'intérêt des princes et états de la Chrétienté*, cited in C. Dupuis, *Le Principe d'équilibre et le concert européen de la paix de Westphalie à l'acte d'Algésiras* (Paris, 1909), 19–20.
[8] Reproduced in Wright (ed.), *Theory and Practice*, 39–45.
[9] Quoted in F. H. Hinsley, *Power and the Pursuit of Peace: Theory and Practice in the History of Relations between States* (Cambridge, 1963), 163.
[10] R. Girardet, 'L'Influence de la tradition sur la politique étrangère de la France' in J.-B. Duroselle (ed.), *La Politique étrangère et ses fondements* (Paris, 1954), 153–6.
[11] Dupuis, *Principe d'équilibre*, 17–19.

Significantly, the most distinguished history of Richelieu's statecraft at this time was a six-volume study written by Gabriel Hanotaux, a career diplomat who was also foreign minister from 1894 to 1898.[12] For Hanotaux and his contemporaries, the modern version of this counterbalancing strategy was the Franco-Russian alliance. At the heart of this alliance was a detailed military convention directed specifically against Germany and Austria-Hungary. An exchange of letters between the French and Russian foreign ministers on 9 August 1899 reaffirmed the objective of the alliance as 'the maintenance of general peace and the balance of European power'.[13] The conclusion of the Russian alliance, significantly, was a defining moment for a generation of French diplomats. It ended France's isolation in the Great Power system and opened the way for a more active period in French diplomacy that culminated in the Entente Cordiale with Britain in 1904. After war broke out in 1914, President Raymond Poincaré described the alliance with Russia as 'the salvation of France'.[14]

Another balance-of-power reflex of long standing was the tradition of support for smaller European states, whose existence prevented a concentration of power in the hands of one of France's rivals. Provided their existence was guaranteed by the majority of the Great Powers, these 'intermediary states' provided strategic buffers between larger rivals. The strategy, pursued by Richelieu as a means of preventing Austrian domination of the smaller German states, was endorsed by Montesquieu in *The Spirit of Laws* as a cost-effective means of promoting stability in Europe while at the same time reinforcing the security of France's northern and eastern frontiers.[15] The Comte de Vergennes, foreign minister under Louis XVI, agreed. 'It would be better', observed Vergennes in 1777, 'that France remains the most powerful monarchy in a Europe divided up into smaller states than to compete, in perpetual rivalry, for the domination of a Europe reduced to several great sovereignties.'[16] This conception had underpinned French support for states such as

---

[12] G. Hanotaux, *Histoire du Cardinal Richelieu*, 2 vols. (Paris, 1888); Hanotaux's tenure at the foreign ministry was interrupted for three months in 1896.

[13] France, Ministère des affaires étrangères, *Documents Diplomatiques: l'alliance franco-russe* (Paris, 1918), Delcassé (France) to Count Muraviev (Russia), 28 Jul.–9 Aug. 1899, doc. no. 94: 130; on the impact of the alliance see G. F. Kennan, *The Fateful Alliance: France, Russia and the Coming of the First World War* (Manchester, 1984) and A. Sorel, 'Deux précurseurs de l'alliance russe' in *Lectures historiques* (Paris, 1913), posthumous, 197–214.

[14] R. Poincaré, *Au Service de la France: neuf années de souvenirs*, 9 vols. (Paris, 1926–74), vol. V: *L'invasion (1914)* (Paris, 1928), 154; see also the analysis of Poincaré's emphasis on the Franco-Russian alliance in S. Schmidt, *Frankreichs Aussenpolitik in der Julikrise 1914: Ein Beitrag zur Geschichte des Ausbruchsdes Ersten Weltkrieges* (Munich, 2009), esp. 72–104.

[15] C. de Montesquieu, *De l'Esprit des lois* (Paris, 1999), vol. II, book IX, chapters 9 and 10; see also F. Hildesheimer, 'Guerre et paix selon de Richelieu' in L. Bély (ed.), *L'Europe des traités de Westphalie: esprit de la diplomatie et diplomatie de l'esprit* (Paris, 2000), 31–54.

[16] Quoted in A. Sorel, *L'Europe et la révolution française*, vol. I: *De l'Origine des traditions nationales dans la politique extérieure avant la Révolution française* (Paris, 1882), 46.

Poland and Bavaria in the eighteenth century. It was abandoned during the Revolutionary and Napoleonic Wars. By 1914 most of Europe's intermediary states had been largely swallowed up. The focus of Great Power tensions was the fate of several small powers in the Balkans and, ultimately, Belgium.[17] The strategy of support for smaller states as counterweights and strategic buffers would be resurrected in France's peace programme after 1918.

Over the past 250 years both the theory and practice of balancing power have been criticised as a flawed approach to achieving international stability. Some critics have argued that the competitive dynamic underpinning the concept renders any system resting on a balance of power at best precarious.[18] Others have stressed that all perceptions of balance are necessarily subjective. As early as 1730 the French ambassador in Vienna observed that the notion of a balance of power was 'a thing of pure opinion, which each interprets according to their views and their particular interests'.[19] What is a favourable balance for one state is very often entirely unacceptable to another. Professor Schroeder has argued persuasively that seeking durable peace through a balance of power is futile because there can never be consensus as to what constitutes the right balance.[20]

This latter criticism is borne out in the records left behind by the French policy machine for the era of the First World War. Although French officials referred repeatedly to the need for an *équilibre européen*, what they nearly always *meant* by this was a situation of French strategic preponderance at Germany's expense. The concept of *équilibre* was therefore shorthand not for a stable balance of power but instead for a favourable *imbalance* of power. Notwithstanding this paradox, calculations of power remained central to the traditional approach to security that dominated policy making for most of this era.

The core assumptions of the traditional power-politics approach to security were reinforced by the explosion in colonial expansion in the final decades of the nineteenth century. Thanks to the technological breakthroughs of the mid-1800s, European power politics could be projected across the entire globe at much greater speed, and with much greater public involvement, than ever before. The result, as James Joll has argued, was to reinforce collective

---

[17] On the role of intermediary powers see P. Schroeder, 'The lost intermediaries: the impact of 1870 on the European System', *IHR*, 6, 1 (1984), 1–27. Schroeder argues that support for intermediaries is better decribed as a policy of equilibrium than balance. The problem with this thesis is that it was also a tactic for ensuring France's power position relative to that of its rivals.
[18] This is the central argument in Schroeder, *Transformation*; see also P. Schroeder, 'Did the Vienna Settlement rest on a balance of power?', *AHR*, 97, 3 (1992), 683–706 and the discussion in Haslam, *Realist Thought*, 89–127; for contemporaneous criticisms see Dupuis, *Principe d'équilibre*, *passim*.
[19] Cited in Sorel, *Traditions nationales*, 34.
[20] Schroeder, *Transformation*, 10; M. S. Anderson, 'Eighteenth Century Theories of the Balance of Power' in R. Hatton and M. S. Anderson (eds.), *Studies in Diplomatic History* (London, 1970), 183–98.

understandings of international politics as driven by competition rather than cooperation. The 'new imperialism' was driven by a 'zero-sum' conception of world politics that became entrenched as never before in the belief systems and practices of European policy elites.[21]

II

An influential ideological current within the traditional approach that merits special attention was the discourse of France's 'natural frontiers'.[22] The idea that France's rightful frontiers were bounded by 'the natural limits of Gaul' – from the Atlantic to the Alps and the Pyrenees to the Rhine – went back centuries. France's alleged natural frontier on the Rhine had been the chief preoccupation of this discourse since the rise of Habsburg power.[23] Richelieu considered a presence on the Rhine as a vital element to his forward policy towards the German states.[24] The doctrine was embraced by Montesquieu and Jean-Jacques Rousseau and developed into a full-blown ideological programme for expansion by the national convention in 1792–3.[25] The convention's celebrated *arrêté* of 24 October 1792 declared that France would fight 'until the enemies of the Republic have been pushed back across the Rhine'. The Rhine was represented in this case as the physical guarantee of the security of the Republic and the 'frontier of liberty'.[26]

Military success in the autumn of 1792 left the new Republic in control of much of the Left Bank of the Rhine (as well as Savoy, Nice and Belgium). To justify the regime's decision to annex the Left Bank (taken in 1795), the doctrine of France's natural and ancient limits was married to the ideology of political self-determination. From this propaganda exercise a durable myth emerged that the overwhelming majority of Rhinelanders embraced their new

---

[21] J. Joll, *The Origins of the First World War* (London, 1992), 56–91; see also M. Reynolds, *Shattering Empires: The Clash and Collapse of the Ottoman and Russian Empires, 1908–1918* (Cambridge, 2011), 7–8.

[22] Important recent scholarship includes P. Sahlins, 'Natural frontiers revisited: France's boundaries since the seventeenth century', *AHR*, 95, 5 (1990), 1423–51; D. Nordman, *Frontières de France: de l'espace au territoire, XVI–XIX siècles* (Paris, 1999); D. Nordman, 'Des limites d'état aux frontières nationales' in P. Nora (ed.), *Lieux de mémoire*, 3 vols. (Paris, 1997), I, 1125–46.

[23] Though the much-cited aphorism of Jean le Bon, 'When Paris drinks from the Rhine, all Gaul will be fulfilled', dates from 1568: quoted in D. Nordman, 'Le Rhin est-il une frontière?', *L'Histoire*, 201 (1996), 30–1.

[24] H. Weber, 'Richelieu et le Rhin', *RH*, 239 (1968), 265–80. The doctrine was more than mere propaganda, however; it was also a tool of state building aimed at projecting the image of a coherent and unified national space: see Sahlins, 'Natural frontiers', 1433–5; Nordman, 'Aux frontières nationales'.

[25] Sahlins, 'Natural frontiers', 1431–6.

[26] A. Sorel, *L'Europe et la revolution française*, vol. III: *La Guerre aux rois, 1792–1793* (Paris, 1885), 152–3.

status as citizens with great enthusiasm.[27] The Left Bank's status as a staging ground for invasions across the Franco-German frontier was thus overlaid with ideologically charged discourses of revolution, liberty and natural frontiers.[28] The result was a potent vision of France's political destiny that was central to nearly all traditional conceptions of France's security.

Albert Sorel famously argued that the doctrine of natural frontiers was inherited by the revolutionary regime from its monarchist predecessor. The national convention followed the 'classic idea of the Rhine' that was 'the grand dream of Louis XIV and all kings of France'.[29] While Sorel did not always allow for the changing character of this doctrine over time, there is no doubt that the discourse of natural limits was embraced by the entire spectrum of the French policy elite during the revolutionary and Napoleonic periods. Nor did it disappear as a foreign policy aim after 1815. Napoléon III tried unsuccessfully to bargain French neutrality in the Austro-Prussian war in exchange for control over the Left Bank of the Rhine.[30]

The idea of a natural frontier on the Rhine was overshadowed in the public sphere after 1871 with the loss of Alsace-Lorraine and the resulting discourse of the 'lost provinces'. But it remained a potent undercurrent that resurfaced during the war to shape traditionally inspired conceptions of post-war security among both policy elites and political commentators. The 'Gallic' character of the Rhenish population was asserted, along with the myth of Rhineland solidarity with revolutionary France. The Rhine was once again represented as the 'frontier of liberty'.[31] Similar discursive strategies were deployed in support of French claims to the coal-rich Saarland.[32] Gabriel Hanotaux confidently predicted that, once Prussian power was broken, 'the territories between France and Germany will regain their freedom and will choose spontaneously, as they did in 1792, to move under the protection of French liberties'.[33] The holy grail of the Rhine frontier endured even after France's defeat and occupation during the Second World War. In a conversation with Soviet leader Joseph Stalin in

---

[27] This legend is dismantled persuasively by T. C. W. Blanning, *The French Revolution in Germany: Occupation and Resistance in the Rhineland, 1792–1802* (Cambridge, 1983) and M. Rowe, *From Reich to State: The Rhineland in the Revolutionary Age* (Cambridge, 2003).
[28] See esp. Sahlins, 'Natural frontiers', 1445–9.   [29] Sorel, *Guerre aux rois*, 151.
[30] L. Theis, 'Entre Besoin de repos et désir de gloire (1815–1870)' in *Histoire de la diplomatie française*, vol. II: *De 1815 à nos jours* (Paris, 2005), 119–24; V. Martin, 'Une Diplomatie révolutionnaire? Les Agents diplomatiques francais en Italie (1774–1804)', thèse de doctorat, Université de Paris I (Sorbonne), 2001.
[31] MAE, PA-AP 166, *Papiers André Tardieu*, vol. 417, 'Note sur le statut politique des pays de la rive gauche du Rhin', 20 Jan. 1919; 'Note sur le rôle international du Rhine comme "Frontière de la Liberté"', 20 Jan. 1919.
[32] SHD-DAT, *Fonds Georges Clemenceau*, 6N 73–4, 'Note sommaire sur la frontière de 1814 et le Bassin de la Sarre'; see also MAE, PA-AP 166, *Papiers Tardieu*, vol. 415, 'Titres de la France à la frontière de 1814', n.d. but Jan. 1919.
[33] MAE, *Série A*, vol. 60, 'De la future frontière', 11 Nov. 1918.

late 1944, Charles de Gaulle invoked the 'geographic and historic frontier of France' that was 'constituted by the Rhine'.[34]

III

The ideology of natural frontiers, like the tradition of power politics more generally, was rooted in an approach to international relations that looked backward to an era of French predominance. The status of this approach as a 'practical logic' owed much to the intellectual preparation received by aspiring soldiers and statesmen. Institutions such as the École libre des sciences politiques, together with the prestigious military *écoles*, played a crucial role not only in the intellectual formation of politicians, diplomats and soldiers, but also in the reproduction of traditional understandings of international politics.

Established in the aftermath of the national defeat of 1871, the central mission of the École libre was to train a new generation of patriotic civil servants better equipped to avert another such catastrophe. Teaching staff were, in the main, conservative liberals, and nearly always included several practising diplomats. Impatience with abstract principles and a commitment to the historical method were hallmarks of the intellectual environment at the École.[35] The stated aim of the preparatory course for the foreign ministry entrance examination offered at the École was to provide graduates with a 'specialist doctrine' for the practice of international politics.[36] This approach was later criticised by Bertrand de Jouvenel, a famous graduate of the École, for producing 'minds that were specialised not only in their knowledge, but almost in their souls'.[37] The most influential instructor on the preparatory course was unquestionably Albert Sorel. A member of the foreign ministry since 1866, Sorel is widely considered the founder of diplomatic history in France. He had served in Léon Gambetta's government of national defence in 1870–1 and then as private secretary to various foreign ministers in the mid-1870s. It was the teaching post at the École libre, however, that provided Sorel with a platform for the dissemination of his ideas to the political and policy elite of the new Republic. He was best known for his multi-volume diplomatic history of the French Revolution. His thesis that the foreign policies of nations

---

[34] P.-J. Rémy, *Trésors et secrets du Quai d'Orsay: une histoire inédite de la diplomatie française* (Paris, 2001), 'Compte-rendu de l'entretien du général de Gaulle avec le maréchal Staline', 2 Dec. 1944: 859–60.

[35] T. Osborne, *A Grande École for the Grands Corps: The Recruitment and Training of the French Administrative Elite in the Nineteenth Century* (New York, 1983), 53–99; J. Keiger, 'Patriotism, Politics and Policy in the Foreign Ministry, 1880–1914' in R. Tombs (ed.), *Nationhood and Nationalism in France* (London, 1991), 260–2; G. Thuillier, *L'ENA avant L'ENA* (Paris, 1983), 122–59; on the politics of the French system of *grandes écoles* see P. Bourdieu, *La Noblesse d'état: grandes écoles et esprit de corps* (Paris, 1989).

[36] P. Jackson, 'Tradition and adaptation: the social universe of the French foreign ministry in the era of the First World War', *French History*, 24, 2 (2010), 172–4.

[37] B. de Jouvenel, *Après la défaite* (Paris, 1941), 50.

were determined by 'national traditions' was particularly influential for several generations of aspiring diplomats.[38] 'For over thirty years', notes one historian of this period, 'Sorel shaped generations of diplomats and political leaders who would occupy embassies and exercise power right up to the outbreak of the Second World War.'[39]

Sorel provided his students with a sophisticated but deeply pessimistic picture of international relations. The history of France's international policy, he argued, was essentially an expression of two powerfully entrenched traditions. The first was to 'forge a homogenous nation and an effective state'. The second was to 'ensure by sound frontiers the independence of the nation and the power of the state'.[40] Since the Capetian dynasty France had expanded steadily in pursuit of its supposed 'natural limits'. For Sorel, this quest was determined not only by France's geography but also by the 'mysterious ties' that bound the nation together and provided its dynamism.[41] Yet this metaphysical conception of the sources of French policy was tempered by a strong element of political realism. Sorel was no apologist for expansionist policies in the name of natural frontiers. He argued instead that the quest for 'natural limits' had more often than not provided a pretext for expansionist programmes. He pointed out that rivers, which were most frequently invoked as natural frontiers, were 'in fact means of communication and [constitute] a link between peoples'. To make a river a frontier was therefore 'to violate nature by separating arbitrarily that which history has united'.[42] Sorel was similarly critical of the way the 'myth of Gaul' had long been used to justify an expansionist policy that was often inimical to France's interests:

France has sacrificed rivers of blood to conquer the limits accorded to it by the doctrine of natural frontiers; it has attained these limits only to lose them sooner or

---

[38] Isabelle Dasque refers to him as the 'véritable figure de proue' at Sciences po during this period: 'A la recherche de Monsieur de Norpois: les diplomates sous la Troisième République, 1871–1914', thèse de doctorat, Université de Paris IV (Sorbonne), 2007, 271; see also J. Bariéty, 'Albert Sorel, L'Europe et la Révolution française, 1885–1904' in J. Bariéty (ed.), *1889: centenaire de la Révolution française* (Berne, 1992), 129–44.

[39] D. Decherf, *Bainville: l'intelligence de l'histoire* (Paris, 2000), 94; John Keiger agrees that Sorel 'profoundly influenced a whole generation of French foreign office officials between 1872 and 1906': 'Patriotism, Politics and Policy', 261–3; see also S. Jeannesson, 'La Formation des diplomates français et leur approche des relations internationales à la fin du XIXème siècle', *RHD*, 122, 4 (2008), 370–3; I. Dasque, 'Écriture et usages de l'histoire chez les diplomates de la Troisième République' in L. Badel, G. Ferragu, S. Jeannesson and R. Meltz (eds.), *Écrivains et diplomates: l'invention d'une tradition, XIXème–XXIème siècles* (Paris, 2012), 166–80.

[40] Sorel, *Traditions nationales*, 6–7.

[41] Ibid., 7–8; see also A. Sorel, *L'Europe et la Révolution française*, vol. IV: *Les Limites naturelles, 1794–1795* (Paris, 1892), esp. 469–70.

[42] A. Sorel and T. Funck-Brentano, *Précis du Droit des gens* (Paris, 1887), 18–19; this critique was taken up in the 1930s by the distinguished historian Gaston Zeller in 'Histoire d'une idée fausse', *Revue de Synthèse*, 56, 2 (1936), 115–32; see also Sahlins, 'Natural frontiers'.

later after more bloody disasters, and yet the most prosperous periods of its history were those where it did not possess them.[43]

Sorel had time neither for the positivist vision of the march of progress nor for the romantic conviction that France was destined to dominate Europe once again from a place on the Rhine.

At the centre of Sorel's political catechism was instead the measured calculation of national interests. 'States', he asserted, 'have no other judge than themselves and no other laws than their interests.' But he added that the system of inter-state relations provided its own moderating dynamic. The state of anarchy was regulated by the competing interests of nations:

> The source of the excesses of this system also provides its moderating force. To the paradoxes of the doctrine of reason of state there is an antidote: common sense. To the dangerous excesses of national ambitions there is an ineluctable impediment: the interests of other states.

At the centre of Sorel's vision of international politics was the 'law' that 'all political actions generate consequences'. States that sought to dominate their neighbours would 'infringe upon the interests of other states in the system' and 'inevitably call up a coalition of rivals to oppose them'. 'It is this', he observed, 'that we call the balance of forces or the European balance of power.' Although he was inclined to use the language of the 'balance of interests' rather than the balance of power, the organising principle was the same.[44]

If Sorel considered the balance of power a 'fact', he placed only limited faith in its capacity to provide peace and stability. He stressed that episodes of effective equilibrium were rare. Nor could they endure. 'The same causes that produce [a balance] tend to destroy it,' he argued. 'In order to subsist, a balance of power requires stasis, which is impossible ... the balance of power is thus neither a principle of order nor a guarantee of justice.' The only reliable guide to national policy was therefore the astute analysis of the state's interests in an international environment characterised by more or less permanent instability. The balance of power was not an end in itself, but a condition that could sometimes serve the interests of France. Sorel's chief criticism of the foreign policy of France's revolutionary leaders was that they pursued the 'grand dream' of a frontier on the Rhine and in so doing 'disregarded their interests and ignored the balance of forces in Europe'.[45]

It was this complex and fundamentally pessimistic conception of the nature of international politics that Sorel conveyed to generations of future diplomats.

---

[43] Sorel and Funck-Brentano, *Précis du Droit des gens*, 20; see also Sorel, *Traditions nationales*, 48–51.

[44] Quotes from Sorel, *Traditions nationales*, 31, 33–4 and Sorel and Funck-Brentano, *Précis du Droit des gens*, 16, 18–19; see also Jeannesson, 'Formation', 372–3.

[45] Quotes from Sorel, *Guerre aux rois*, 151–2; see also Sorel, *Limites naturelles*, 64–71, 143–53, 174–86, 291–3, 353–60, 449–51, 456–69.

The only durable feature of the international system was the role of power and interests. It followed, therefore, that Sorel was no starry-eyed advocate of *revanche* in the decades following the defeat of 1871. He stood instead for a robust conception of France's place among the Great Powers, which, he argued, depended on astute diplomacy and judicious manipulation of the balance of power.[46]

Louis Renault was another influential teacher at the École libre. It is difficult to overstate Renault's influence in the evolution of international law as both an academic discipline and a practice of statecraft. Not only did he hold France's first chair in international law at the Sorbonne, he was also chief legal counsel at the Quai d'Orsay. For nearly fifty years Renault was 'the personification of the French conception of international law'.[47] His vision of the driving forces in international relations, interestingly, was close to that of Sorel. Although he served as deputy head of the French delegation at both Hague Peace Conferences, Renault advocated a carefully circumscribed understanding of the role of international law in international politics. In his hugely influential *Introduction à l'étude du droit international* he defined international law as essentially the written expression of the shared interests of states. Renault also considered international law as *sui generis* and thus fundamentally different in nature from domestic law. The latter, he argued, was a law of *subordination* in which individuals recognised limitations on their personal sovereignty. The former, conversely, was a law of *coordination* in which individual actors recognised no limitation on their sovereignty.[48] This made Renault sceptical of the campaign to achieve peace through the creation of a powerful regime of international law. 'Peace can only be assured', he observed, 'if peaceful nations are stronger than warlike nations.'[49] These were lessons that future statesmen on the preparatory course at the École libre took to heart.

Sorel and Renault also played important roles in the selection process for new entrants into the foreign ministry. They helped devise the entrance examination each year and sat regularly on the *jury* that selected new entrants. Their areas of expertise were consistently the most important components of the *concours*.[50] Sorel considered that his teachings would 'furnish future diplomats with a number of notions that are indispensable [for the practice of foreign

---

[46] Bariéty, 'Albert Sorel'.
[47] M. Koskenniemi, *The Gentle Civilizer of Nations: The Rise and Fall of International Law, 1870–1960* (Cambridge, 2001), 274–5.
[48] Renault defined international law as 'l'ensemble des règles destinées à concilier la liberté et les intérêts de chacun avec ceux des autres': *Introduction à l'étude du droit international* (Paris, 1879), 6.
[49] Quoted in Saint-Aulaire, *Confession*, 10, 11 respectively; on the distinction between subordination and coordination see H. Lauterpacht, *The Function of Law in the International Community* (Oxford, 1933), 183–94 and H. Suganami, 'Reflections on the domestic analogy', *Review of International Studies* (1986), 146–7.
[50] Baillou et al., *Affaires étrangères et le corps diplomatique français*, 2 vols. (Paris, 1984), II, 64 and 154–6. For a fascinating glimpse into the examination and selection procedure from the

policy]'.[51] The Comte de Saint-Aulaire, a career diplomat and future ambassador in London, recalled that the 'rays of wisdom' provided by Sorel and Renault constituted a 'collection of fundamental truths' and 'a source of illumination' that had guided him throughout his career.[52] Jacques Seydoux, a crucial figure in the foreign ministry during the 1920s, similarly stressed the intellectual debt that he owed to 'the eminent historian and philosopher Albert Sorel'.[53] Sorel's influence was also formative in the intellectual development of Jacques Bainville, perhaps the most influential historian and commentator on foreign policy during this period.[54] Bainville, along with the vast majority of French diplomats of this era, placed calculations of power and interest at the centre of his vision of ideal policy making. The following summation of the 'permanent bases' of French foreign policy by Jules Cambon, composed in 1926, could well have been written by Albert Sorel forty years earlier:

> Foreign policy is not an affair of sentiment. Its fundamental objective is to accommodate incidental facts with the permanent laws that shape the destiny of nations. These laws exist; they do not owe their existence to the diplomats or lawmakers. The interests of peoples do not vary; it is the nature of their geographic situation and their specific character that determine them ... Just as the interests of peoples do not change, the foreign policy of a nation, whatever revolutions that occur in the character of its domestic government, must follow these traditions.[55]

This highly traditional approach to foreign policy would characterise the foreign ministry's response to the security challenges of the First World War and after.

Traditional assumptions were just as central to military understandings of international politics. Within the French military elite war and the use of force tended to be represented as fundamental to the practice of statecraft. This belief was inevitably linked to the position military officials occupied within the machinery of the state. The use of armed force was (and remains) central to the identity of the military professional.[56] It is impossible to understand cultural reflexes within the military without taking account of this basic fact. Belief in the necessity of political violence was translated into a more specific approach

---

perspective of one of the members of the *jury* see dossiers for the *concours* for 1895, 1896, 1897 and 1898 in MAE, PA-AP 12, *Papiers de Beaucaire*, vol. 10; see also Jeannesson, 'Formation', 366–70.

[51] A. Sorel, 'L'Enseignement de l'histoire diplomatique', *Nouveaux essais d'histoire et de critique* (Paris, 1898), 85.

[52] Saint-Aulaire, *Confession*, 10.

[53] MAE, PA-AP 261, *Papiers Jacques Seydoux*, vol. 12, Seydoux to Sydney Waterlow (foreign office expert on reparations), 20 Dec. 1921; Jeannesson disagrees, however: see his 'Formation', 374.

[54] Decherf, *Bainville*, 93–6 and C. Dickès, *Jacques Bainville: les lois de la politique étrangère* (Paris, 2008), esp. 59–65.

[55] J. Cambon, *Le Diplomate* (Paris, 1926), 17.

[56] C. Moskos, *Soldiers and Sociology* (London, 1989); T. Lindemann and M. L. Martin, 'The Military and the Use of Force: Corporate Interest and War' in G. Caforio (ed.), *Sociology of the Military*, 2nd edn (New York, 2006), 99–109.

to world politics by the intellectual training and professional experience of French officers. While the intellectual level of teaching at the elite military academies – at Saint-Cyr, the École polytechnique and, for high-flying officers, the École supérieure de guerre – was high, the range of subjects studied was limited. At Saint-Cyr officer candidates were introduced to moral philosophy, but the focus of the curriculum was military issues rather narrowly conceived. Subjects such as law and political economy were eschewed in favour of military history and geography, diplomatic history and the rudiments of strategy and tactical doctrine. At the École polytechnique, where most artillery officers were trained, the focus was on the science of war. These subjects came together at the École supérieure, where tactical and strategic doctrine were studied intensively by officers tipped for senior-level staff work and higher command. Political economy was added to the curriculum only after the First World War brought an increased appreciation of the importance of economics in modern war. With the notable exception of the laws of war, juridical science was almost entirely neglected in the *formation* of French officers.[57] This reflected, but also contributed to, the silent contempt in which the majority of the army officers held lawyers and politicians – particularly after the Dreyfus Affair drove a painful wedge between army and society at the turn of the century.[58]

The result was a very traditional set of assumptions about international security. A survey of writings on foreign and defence policy by both active and retired soldiers before 1914 underlines the deeply pessimistic conception of international relations that prevailed among military elites at this juncture.[59] Military alliances and the use of force were represented as 'part of the ineluctable pattern of the modern world'.[60] Alternative approaches to security and international politics, meanwhile, were viewed with a mixture of contempt and anxiety. 'In the state of human imperfection', one general officer remarked in 1911, 'it is manifest that war has its role in the economy of societies and that it responds to a moral law as wind and tempest are necessary to the perfection of order in the equilibrium of material life.'[61] Even more moderate military commentators on international relations manifested a profound scepticism towards the concept of peace through international cooperation. While it was acknowledged that these efforts might one day bring about peace, this day was a

---

[57] J. Delmas, 'Le Développement de l'enseignement militaire supérieur en France, 1876–1975' in R. Hudemann and G.-H. Soutou (eds.), *Elites en France et en Allemagne aux XIXème et XXème siècles: structures et relations* (Munich, 1994), 235–48. On the increased importance of economics in assessments of the strategic balance see P. Jackson, *France and the Nazi Menace: Intelligence and Policy-Making, 1933–1939* (Oxford, 2000), 82–5.

[58] For an excellent discussion see P.-M. de la Gorce, *The French Army: A Military–Political History* (London, 1963), 32–61.

[59] J. Cairns, 'International politics and the military mind: the case of the French Republic, 1911–1914', *JMH*, 25, 3 (1953), 273–85.

[60] Ibid., 276. [61] General Cherfils, '"L'Armée nouvelle" et l'armée', quoted in ibid., 283.

long way off: 'what is certain ... is that neither we nor our children nor our grandchildren will see such an era of concord and prosperity'.[62]

Professional experience only reinforced existing assumptions about the role of war in international politics. As Olivier Forcade has shown, depictions of the military in art and literature at this time focused overwhelmingly on campaigns and battles. Representations of army life similarly tended to 'telescope' time into brief moments of combat at the expense of the more mundane aspects of life in the barracks or on the parade ground.[63] French army officers devoted the whole of their professional lives to studying and preparing the most effective deployment of armed force. It is scarcely surprising, therefore, that the primacy of war in international politics was seldom questioned.

In sum, the traditional approach, with its emphasis on power, interests and the role of force, constituted what Bourdieu would have termed a 'practical logic' for both diplomats and military professionals. This logic was the product of long-standing tradition as well as formal and informal learned experience. And it was reinforced by everyday practices within both the foreign ministry and the military services. Traditional understandings did not predetermine policy decisions in a crude sense. They instead inclined policy elites to gravitate towards traditional solutions to France's security dilemma.[64] They provided a set of predispositions that would prove very durable when challenged by alternative approaches to national security based on more optimistic premises of cooperation among nations and the rule of international law.

IV

The second half of the nineteenth century was a period of dramatic technological change and interesting transnational intellectual ferment. Technological revolutions in communications, transport, industry and commerce brought about profound structural changes in international society. The cumulative impact of steam power, railways and telegraphic communications was to shrink the globe, facilitate the 'new imperialism' and transform the scope and character of international relations. Information could for the first time be transmitted across vast distances in something close to real time, accelerating the pace of international politics and transforming the management of global empires.[65]

---

[62] Lt. Col. Gondré in a speech to the Société polytechnique militaire, 24 Jan. 1913, quoted in ibid., 283.

[63] O. Forcade, 'Le Temps militaire à l'époque contemporaine: pratiques et représentations', *Bibliothèque de l'École des Chartes*, 157, 2 (1999), 479–91.

[64] P. Bourdieu, *The Logic of Practice*, trans. R. Nice (Palo Alto, 1990), 27–9; an interesting and insightful study of the 'practical logic' of NATO officials is V. Pouliot, *International Security in Practice: The Politics of NATO–Russia Diplomacy* (New York, 2010).

[65] The classic study of this process is D. Landes, *The Unbound Prometheus: Technological Change and Industrial Development in Europe from 1750 to the Present*, 2nd edn (Cambridge, Mass., 2003); see also K. H. O'Rourke and J. G. Williamson, *Globalization and History* (Cambridge,

Technological change also stimulated the growth of internationalism. The movement of people and ideas increased dramatically as part of the 'expansion of international society'.[66] The late 1850s onward witnessed the creation of increasing numbers of international institutions. Most were established to manage the tremendous increase of global trade. Among the most important were the International Telegraphic Union (1865), the Universal Postal Union (1874), the International Union for Weights and Measurements (1875), the International Union of Customs and Tariffs (1890) and the International Office for Public Hygiene (1907). By the turn of the century a growing number aimed at promoting transnational technological and cultural exchange and other forms of intellectual cooperation.[67] Before 1850 the number of international bodies of this kind could be counted on one hand. By the 1890s, however, ten such organisations were being established each year. One result of these trends was the emergence of what one historian has termed 'new forms of international sociability' that reflected 'a world shrinking under the influence of commercial and cultural interdependence'.[68]

The notion of growing interdependence was central to internationalist doctrines predicting increased peaceful cooperation among nation-states. Late nineteenth-century theorists of interdependence, working in the intellectual tradition of Jeremy Bentham, John Stuart Mill and Richard Cobden, argued that the dramatic increase in global intercourse would lead to growing awareness of the common interest among states. War would become unprofitable and therefore increasingly unlikely.[69] This theory of interdependence provided

Mass., 2001); D. R. Headrick, *When Information Came of Age: Technologies of Knowledge, 1700–1850* (Oxford, 2000); D. R. Headrick, *The Tentacles of Progress: Technology Transfer in the Age of Imperialism, 1850–1940* (Oxford, 1988).

[66] H. Bull and A. Watson, *The Expansion of International Society* (Oxford, 1984).

[67] On these developments see, among others, M. Mazower, *Governing the World: The History of an Idea* (London, 2012), 13–116; M. Geyer and J. Paulmann (eds.), *The Mechanics of Internationalism: Culture, Politics and Society from the 1840s to the First World War* (Oxford, 2001); J. Boli and G. M. Thomas, *Constructing World Culture: International Nongovernmental Organizations since 1875* (Palo Alto, 1999); A. Iriye, *Global Community: The Role of International Organizations in the Making of the Contemporary World* (Berkeley, 2002), 9–22; D. Held, A. McGrew, D. Goldblatt and J. Perraton, *Global Transformation: Politics, Economics and Culture* (Stanford, 1999), esp. 39–81 and 154–7; and G. Sluga, *Internationalism in the Age of Nationalism* (Philadelphia, 2013); also still useful is F. S. L. Lyons, *Internationalism in Europe* (Leiden, 1963); an interesting, if idiosyncratic, contemporary perspective is W. F. Crafts, *A Primer of Internationalism: With Special Reference to University Debates* (Washington, D.C., 1908).

[68] Sluga, *Internationalism*, 11–19; see also D. Laqua, 'Transnational Endeavours and the "Totality of Knowledge"' in G. Brockington (ed.), *Internationalism in Britain and Europe at the Fin-de-siècle* (Oxford, 2009), 247–71 and Mazower, *Governing the World*, 31–66 and 94–115.

[69] V. Grossi, *Le Pacifisme européen, 1889–1914* (Brussels, 1994), 139–67; Hinsley, *Power and the Pursuit of Peace*, 141–3; P. Laity, *The British Peace Movement, 1870–1914* (Oxford, 2001), 114–214; and C. Bouchard, *Le Citoyen et l'ordre mondial: le rêve d'une paix durable au lendemain de la Grande Guerre* (Paris, 2008), 46–8; on antecedents to the nineteenth-century European peace movement see J.-P. Bois, *La Paix: histoire politique et militaire, 1435–1878* (Paris, 2012).

a stimulus to older national and transnational movements to eradicate war that had emerged in the aftermath of the Napoleonic Wars. The result was the evolution of what one scholar has described as a 'robust global civil society' of peace activism.[70] By 1900 there were at least 425 peace organisations worldwide, many of which collaborated in the organisation of large annual 'Universal Peace Congresses'.[71]

The idea of using arbitration as a means of settling disputes between states had been central to doctrines of international peace on both sides of the Atlantic since the early 1860s. While the concept of arbitration can be traced back at least to Grotius, its emergence in the mid-nineteenth century coincided with the rise of international law as both a profession and an academic discipline. There was considerable ideological and sociological overlap between international law and peace activism. Both movements were drawn almost exclusively from the ranks of the well-educated bourgeoisie. The normative assumptions of both reflected the prevailing intellectual climate, and in particular positivist convictions concerning the inevitability of progress and the perfectibility of mankind.[72]

The movement to establish international legal institutions in general, and arbitration regimes in particular, assumed that the codification of international law would impose reciprocal duties and obligations on states which would, in turn, act as constraints on the use of violence as a tool of policy. The objective of 'peace through law' was understood as a gradual process requiring the perfection of existing structures and the creation of new institutions. Binding international arbitration agreements and the creation of a world court would provide a framework for the peaceful settlement of political disputes among 'civilised peoples'. By the turn of the century a host of private associations as well as inter-parliamentary unions had been created in the United States, Britain and France to promote the cause of international arbitration. This movement coincided with the rising importance of arbitration in relations between states. Between 1872 and 1914 at least 194 treaties containing

---

[70] Quote from J. Keane, *Global Civil Society?* (Cambridge, 2003), 44; see also W. Mulligan, *The Origins of the First World War* (Cambridge, 2010), 133–76.
[71] W. H. van der Linden, *The International Peace Movement, 1815–1874* (Amsterdam, 1987), 239; P. Brock, *Freedom from War: Nonsectarian Pacifism, 1814–1914* (Toronto, 1991); S. Cooper, *Patriotic Pacifism: Waging War on War in Europe, 1815–1914* (New York, 1991); M. Ceadel, *Thinking about Peace and War* (Oxford, 1987); M. Ceadel, *Semi-Detached Idealists: The British Peace Movement and International Relations, 1854–1945* (Oxford, 2000); D. S. Patterson, *Toward a Warless World: The Travail of the American Peace Movement, 1887–1914* (Bloomington, 1976); R. Chickering, *Imperial Germany and a World without War: The Peace Movement in German Society, 1892–1914* (Princeton, 1975); J. Bariéty and A. Fleury (eds.), *Mouvements et initiatives de paix dans la politique internationale* (Berne, 1987).
[72] Hinsley, *Power and the Pursuit of Peace*, 20–3, 164–5; Koskenniemi, *Gentle Civilizer of Nations*, 22–85; Mazower, *Governing the World*, 65–93; A. Fitzmaurice, 'Liberalism and empire in nineteenth century international law', *AHR*, 117, 1 (2012), 122–40.

Two approaches to security 63

arbitration provisions were signed, and these provisions were employed successfully to settle ninety separate international disputes.[73]

The influence of juridical conceptions of international peace peaked at the Hague Peace Conferences of 1899 and 1907. Efforts to create a binding international legal regime that would, in turn, provide an atmosphere conducive to arms reductions became central themes at both conferences. Legal experts and civil society activists were particularly active in lobbying for new international machinery for the peaceful settlement of disputes between states at the Second Hague Conference. These efforts met with limited success. Although a Permanent International Court of Arbitration was created in 1899, efforts to establish a system of compulsory arbitration for the settlement of international disputes failed at both conferences. Considerable progress was made, nonetheless, in the codification of international public law in general, and in particular the laws of war. Many scholars have also argued that the Hague conferences marked an important moment in the development of international society. Ian Clark has rightly described them as an early example of the intrusion of an 'international public conscience' into the practice of international relations.[74]

Though their role is often overlooked, French internationalists were involved in the transnational movement for peace through the rule of law from its beginnings. Parliamentarian Frédéric Passy, an early and voluble advocate of international arbitration with long-standing ties to the British peace movement, was the driving force behind the organisation of the first 'Universal Peace Congress' in Paris in 1889.[75] Out of this meeting, which was the first of twenty-one such congresses held before 1914, emerged the Inter-Parliamentary Union for Arbitration. This organisation was an international gathering of elected officials whose aim was to coordinate efforts to introduce legislation for arbitration treaties and a permanent international court.[76]

---

[73] Figures from M. Howard, *War and the Liberal Conscience* (Oxford, 1989), 53; on the movement for arbitration generally see Hinsley, *Power and the Pursuit of Peace*, 126–33; Bouchard, *Citoyen*, 48–50.

[74] I. Clark, *International Legitimacy and World Society* (Oxford, 2007), 18; S. Rosenne (ed.), *The Hague Peace Conferences of 1899 and 1907 and International Arbitration: Reports and Documents* (The Hague, 2001); Cooper, *Patriotic Pacifism*, 91–115; S. Cooper, 'International Organization and Human Rights Ideals of the European Peace Movement, 1889–1914' in Bariéty and Fleury (eds.), *Mouvements et initiatives de paix*, 37–58; J. B. Scott (ed.), *The Hague Conventions and Declarations of 1899 and 1907: Accompanied by Tables of Signatures, Ratifications and Adhesions of the Various Powers and Texts of Reservations*, 2nd edn (New York, 1915); Sluga, *Internationalism*, 24–8.

[75] M. Clinton, 'Coming to terms with "pacifism": the French case, 1901–1918', *Peace & Change*, 26, 1 (2001), 1–30; M. Clinton, 'Frédéric Passy (1821–1912): a patriotic pacifist', *Journal of Historical Biography*, 2 (2007), 33–62.

[76] Y. Zarjevski, *La Tribune des peuples: histoire de l'Union interparlementaire 1889–1989* (Lausanne, 1989), 41–89; N. Ingram, 'Pacifisme ancien style, ou le pacifisme de l'association de la paix par le droit', *Matériaux pour l'histoire de notre temps*, 30 (March, 1993), 2–5; Cooper, *Patriotic Pacifism*, 93–8 and Ceadel, *Semi-Detached Idealists*, 136–8.

France sent as many as 500 delegates to each of the Universal Peace Congresses before 1914. In 1901 Passy became the first recipient of the Nobel Peace Prize. The Groupe parlementaire français de l'arbitrage international, the French arm of the Inter-Parliamentary Union, counted a membership of 168 of 300 senators and 344 of 584 deputies. There were also close ties with the United States in a transatlantic network of arbitration enthusiasts. The two most influential French associations for the promotion of peace through arbitration, the Comité de conciliation internationale and the Association de la paix par le droit, were both subsidised by the Carnegie Foundation.[77]

Juridical solutions to international disputes held a predictable appeal to the positivist ideology and legalist cultural reflexes of French internationalists in the era of the *république des avocats*. French international lawyers were prominent in the transnational community of international legal expertise centred around the Institut de droit international. From the mid-1890s the Paris-based *Revue générale de droit international* was the most influential journal in this field.[78] Passy expressed the conviction of a generation of French 'juridical internationalists' when he observed:

Arbitration is on its way to becoming the custom of the world, either in the form of permanent and general treaties ... or as limited specific treaties for particular cases ... We say that it is the true sign of the superior civilization which has developed toward the end of the nineteenth century.[79]

Théodore Ruyssen, another leading figure in this movement, insisted that the 'primordial condition' of international peace was 'the substitution of a juridical order for the anarchy that currently prevails among nations'.[80]

The most important civil society organisation for peace was the Association de la paix par le droit. The Association had been founded in 1887 by Ruyssen and Paul d'Estournelles de Constant. By the 1890s it had its own journal, *La Paix par le droit*, and boasted a membership of 1,200 in 1902 and nearly 4,000 by 1912.[81] It was at the centre of what one historian has described as 'a new

---

[77] J.-M. Guieu, 'Les Apôtres français de "l'esprit de Genève": les militants pour la Société des nations dans la première moitié du XXe siècle', thèse de doctorat, Université de Paris I (Sorbonne), 2004, 48–64; C. Bouchard, 'Projets citoyens pour une paix durable, en France, en Grande Bretagne et aux États-Unis (1914–1924)', thèse de doctorat, Paris III and Université de Montréal, 2004, 115–22.

[78] Koskenniemi, *Gentle Civilizer of Nations*, 274–9.

[79] Quoted in S. Cooper, 'Pacifism in France, 1889–1914: international peace as a human right', *FHS*, 17, 2 (1991), 362.

[80] Decharme (ed.), *VIIème Congrès nationale des sociétés françaises de la paix*, 161; also quoted in J.-M. Gueiu, *Le Rameau et le glaive: les militants français pour la Société des nations* (Paris, 2008), 22; see also T. Ruyssen, *La Philosophie de la paix* (Paris, 1904), 32–5 and T. Ruyssen, *Les Sources doctrinales de l'internationalisme*, 3 vols. (Paris, 1954–61).

[81] Guieu, 'Les Apôtres', 25–6; R. Fabre, 'Un Exemple du pacifisme juridique: Théodore Ruyssen et le mouvement de la paix par le droit', *VS*, 39 (1993), 38–54; M. Clinton, 'Revanche ou relèvement? The French peace movement confronts Alsace and Lorraine, 1871–1918', *Canadian Journal of History*, 40, 3 (2005), 425–48.

religion of peace through law' which would eventually constitute the backbone of the French League of Nations movement before, during and after the First World War.[82] French delegates were among the most voluble in calling for an international arbitration regime at the two Hague Peace Conferences. French parliamentarian Léon Bourgeois presided over the Arbitration Commission at both conferences. Louis Renault received the Nobel Peace Prize in 1907 for his role in drafting and presenting the Final Act for both conferences.[83] Renault was one of six French recipients of the Nobel Prize during this period: Passy (1901), d'Estournelles de Constant (1909), Bourgeois (1920), Aristide Briand (1926) and Ferdinand Buisson (1927) were similarly honoured.[84]

For nearly three decades Bourgeois was the most influential voice of French juridical internationalism. As Serge Berstein has observed, Bourgeois was the 'archetype' French Radical politician of this period.[85] He was from a lower-middle-class background, was a trained lawyer (with a doctorate in law), had begun his career as a lawyer and prefect, and was a long-standing member of the most influential of France's Freemason lodges, the Grand Orient. After defeating General Boulanger in the parliamentary elections of 1888, Bourgeois went on to become one of the dominant political figures in France. During his long political career he was leader of the first Radical-dominated government in 1896, held major ministerial posts in a series of centre and centre-left governments before and during the war, and served as president of both the chamber of deputies and the senate. As head of the French delegations to both Hague Conferences, Bourgeois also acquired an international reputation as a leading proponent of arbitration and a tireless promoter of the idea of a 'society of nations'. It was his championing of this latter idea that led to his appointment as the head of the inter-ministerial commission created in 1917 to design a French blueprint for a post-war international organisation of states. After serving as French delegate to the League of Nations Commission at the Paris Peace Conference, Bourgeois became the first president of the League Council in 1920 (the same year he received the Nobel Peace Prize).[86]

Bourgeois' approach to international peace and security was rooted in the social philosophy of *solidarisme*, the unofficial doctrine of the Radical Party during this period. Bourgeois was a central figure in the elaboration of this influential social theory. Conceived in response to the socialist challenge to late nineteenth-century liberal politics, the doctrine of *solidarité* assumed that the

---

[82] Guieu, *Rameau et glaive*, 13.
[83] L. Renault (ed.), *Les Deux conférences de la paix de 1899 et 1907: recueil des textes arrêtés par ces conférences et de différents documents complémentaires* (Paris, Rousseau, 1908).
[84] G. Lundestad, 'The Nobel Peace Prize' in A. W. Levinovitz and N. Ringertz (eds.), *The Nobel Prize: The First 100 Years* (London, 2001), 163–97.
[85] Quoted in Guieu, 'Les Apôtres', 56.
[86] M. Sorlot, *Léon Bourgeois: un moraliste en politique* (Paris, 2005); M.-A. Zeyer, 'Léon Bourgeois, père spirituel de la Société des nations: solidarité internationale et service de la France (1899–1919)', doctoral thesis, École des Chartes, 2006; M. Vaïsse and A. Niess, *Léon Bourgeois: du solidarism à la Société des nations* (Langres, 2007).

individual is born with a 'social debt' to the society in which they live. Bourgeois explained that 'the individual, living in society and unable to live without society, is at all times a debtor towards society'. The 'social debt' formed 'the basis of one's duties and is the price of one's liberty'. It was expressed and given a tangible structure through the elaboration of public and private law, which codified the 'mutual obligations' owed by individuals to one another. For Bourgeois, observing the rule of law was 'obedience to one's social duty' and 'to acknowledge one's debt to society'.[87]

In the *solidariste* vision ties of 'social solidarity' linked individuals to their wider communities. Moral and material progress did not happen naturally. It was instead a result of social organisation based on the principle of interdependence. *Solidarisme* posited an associative conception of political community that was inspired by Émile Durkheim's theory of collective consciousness and emphasis on social roles as determinants of individual behaviour.[88] The true interests of individuals were determined by their social role and their obligation to society. Laws, like individual interests, were functions of social and economic imperatives.[89] In a departure from the revolutionary tradition, *solidariste* thought attached greater importance to obligations than to rights. Law codified and legitimated the individual's responsibilities. It also provided a framework for punishing those who did not honour their 'social debt'. The rule of law, backed up by the force of the state, provided a framework for the 'mutualisation' of individual security in society.[90] The aim of the lawmaker, in Bourgeois' own words, was to 'transform, little by little, purely moral engagements into precise contractual obligations with the necessary sanctions'.[91] *Solidarité* was immensely influential, particularly on the centre-left of the political spectrum, where the notion that 'every man his neighbours' debtor' was deployed in answer to Proudhon's claim that 'all property is theft'. *Solidarisme* provided the Radical movement with an intellectual framework for its social policies. 'To the Declaration of the Rights of Man', Bourgeois observed, 'we must now add a declaration of his social debts.'[92]

Radical doctrine on international affairs was essentially an application of the concepts of *solidarité* to world politics. Léon Bourgeois was by far the dominant

---

[87] L. Bourgeois, *Solidarité* (Paris, 1896), 101–2 and 131–2; see also C. Bouglé, *Le Solidarisme* (Paris, 1907), 69–78, 152–5.
[88] Bouglé, *Solidarisme*, 110–14 and 290–1; see esp. É. Durkheim, *De la Division du travail social* (Paris, 1893).
[89] Koskenniemi, *Gentle Civilizer of Nations*, 269–70.
[90] L. Bourgeois, 'L'Idée de la solidarité et ses conséquences sociales' in *Essai d'une philosophie de la solidarité* (Paris, 1907), 48–50.
[91] Bourgeois quoted in V. d'Eitchal, 'Solidarité sociale et solidarisme', *Revue politique et parlementaire* (1903), 116.
[92] J. E. S. Hayward, 'The official social philosophy of the Third Republic: Léon Bourgeois and Solidarism', *International Review of Social History*, 6 (1961), 19–48; see also S. Elwitt, *The Third Republic Defended: Bourgeois Reformers in France, 1880–1914* (Baton Rouge, 1986), 181–214.

voice on this subject. His vision of international relations was based on the idea that the 'civilised' nations of the world constituted a 'society' bound together by responsibilities to one another. In his conception 'civilised states' functioned as 'moral persons' with a 'duty' to reflect upon the consequences of their actions. Only states that had reached a sufficient stage of civilisation (which was never defined but was presumably to be judged using France as a benchmark) were 'capable' of considering 'justice and law' as a 'higher good in the interests of all to safeguard'.[93] The successful reorganisation of world politics therefore depended upon each state recognising and honouring its 'social debt' to civilised international society. It was at Bourgeois' insistence that the phrase 'society of civilised nations' had been introduced into the arbitration convention adopted by the First Hague Conference.[94]

Thereafter, in his frequent speeches advocating arbitration and a league of nations, Bourgeois returned repeatedly to the concept of the 'social debt' states owed to one another by dint of their status as 'civilised' polities. This debt, he emphasised, must be prescribed and enforced by international law. Summing up the results of the First Hague Conference in 1904, Bourgeois stressed the 'crucial importance of the new conception expressed in the conventions of the peace conference ... states must recognise the ties of mutual solidarity that unite their individual interests ... It is this principle of solidarity that is the basis of the Convention for the Pacific settlement of international conflicts.'[95]

In arguing that each state possessed a 'responsibility' to the other members of the civilised world, Bourgeois was transposing *solidariste* notions into the international sphere. Predictably, a central theme in his attempt to derive a new approach to peace was the mutual obligations of states towards one another. 'As soon as the threat of war appears between two states,' he argued in 1907, 'the other states that make up international society must not remain impassive ... they must instead act together as neighbours in solidarity who are responsible for safeguarding the peace.'[96] In the aftermath of the Hague Conferences, Bourgeois called for the formation of 'a society of law among nations'.[97] He envisaged the Permanent Court of Arbitration at the Hague as the foundation from which the machinery of collective action would emerge in a 'process of creative evolution' that he described as the 'juridical organisation of international life'.[98] For Bourgeois – and for two generations of French juridical internationalists – the rule of law served as the organising principle of international society and the foundation of peace among nations.

---

[93] L. Bourgeois, *Pour la Société des nations* (Paris, 1910), 233–4; Bourgeois' ideas are discussed briefly in H. Suganami, *The Domestic Analogy and World Order Proposals* (Cambridge, 1989), 90.
[94] Guieu, 'Les Apôtres', 55–61.
[95] Bourgeois, 'Ni scepticisme, ni impatience' in *Pour la Société des nations*, 121–2.
[96] Bourgeois, 'L'État du droit entre nations' in *Pour la Société des nations*, 131–2.
[97] Bourgeois, 'Les Conditions de la paix' in *Pour la Société des nations*, 23–4.
[98] Bourgeois, 'La Société des nations' in *Pour la Société des nations*, 228 and 192 respectively.

The transposition of the principles of *solidarisme* to the international sphere is a good example of the 'domestic analogy' that was a common feature in proposals for world order in the era of the First World War.[99] The juridical internationalist doctrine was a specifically French contribution to this movement in thinking about war and peace. Yet it has been ignored almost altogether in virtually all standard narratives of the evolution of international theory. One important reason for this neglect is that E. H. Carr's *The Twenty Years' Crisis*, one of the foundation texts in the 'new science' of international theory, targeted British and American liberal conceptions of world politics and ignored almost all other thinking on the subject. Carr's example has been followed by the great majority of international theorists ever since.[100]

There were important differences that set French thinking about international order apart from the liberal strand of internationalism that prevailed in Britain and the United States. The French approach was more legalist and more muscular. It combined a focus on the construction of an international legal order with a refusal to divorce the rule of law from the use of force. An 'integral pacifism', which rejected war under all circumstances, did not emerge as a significant movement in France until the late 1920s.[101] Nor was disarmament, the other great issue taken up by the international peace movement, considered a crucial source of peace by most French internationalists. It remained, in Passy's words, a 'distant aim'.[102] Bourgeois was more categorical. 'Disarmament', he asserted, in a formulation that would be taken up by French policy makers in the 1920s, 'is a consequence rather than a cause of security.'[103] Armed force was instead considered a necessary corollary to the rule of law.

The link between law and force has a long tradition in the history of French political thought. It can be traced back at least as far as Blaise Pascal's seventeenth *pensée* 'Justice without force is impotent, force without justice is tyranny'.[104] Pascal's formulation has been deployed ever since to justify a strong state as the best guarantor of security. Maximilien Robespierre paraphrased Pascal in his infamous justification of terror in 1793: 'the springs of popular government in revolution are at once *virtue and terror*: virtue, without which terror is fatal; terror, without which virtue is powerless'. Maurice Barrès did the same in his plea for national unity in 1914: 'Where there is no force, there can be no law; when force is present, the rule of law shines forth.' Three years later premier Alexandre Ribot invoked Pascal to argue for the creation of a powerful

---

[99] For a thorough and rigorous analysis of this issue see above all Suganami, *Domestic Analogy*.
[100] E. H. Carr, *Twenty Years' Crisis: An Introduction to the Study of International Relations*, 2nd edn (London, 2001); see also B. Schmidt, *Political Discourses of Anarchy: A Disciplinary History of International Relations* (Albany, 1998).
[101] On this phenomenon see N. Ingram, *The Politics of Dissent: Pacifism in France, 1919–1939* (Oxford, 1991).
[102] Quoted in Cooper, 'Pacifism in France', 372.
[103] 'L'Empire du droit', in Bourgeois, *Pour la Société des nations*, 175–6.
[104] Blaise Pascal, 'Pensées 298–99' in *Pensées*, ed. P. Sellier (Paris, 1976), 137–8.

league of nations: 'What is the rule of law without force', Ribot demanded, 'if not the humiliation of justice oppressed by violence?' Premier Georges Clemenceau made similar use of Pascal to argue for dealing firmly with Germany in 1919.[105] For centuries a significant current in French political culture has envisioned both force and justice as the indispensable pillars of all political order.

This is borne out in an important comparative study of French, British and American conceptions of international organisation by Carl Bouchard, which shows that French internationalists were almost twice as likely to favour the use of military sanctions as were their counterparts in Britain. Nearly 92 per cent of French internationalists favoured recourse to military force, as compared to 59 per cent in Britain and only 44 per cent in the United States.[106] French internationalists were also more willing to accept encroachments on national sovereignty in exchange for international security. Nearly 70 per cent of French proposals for international order envisaged surrendering a measure of sovereignty, as compared to only 36 per cent of those from Britain and 53 per cent from the United States.[107]

Armed force was therefore an integral element in even the most liberal French visions of a just international order. The greater willingness on the part of French internationalists both to approve the use of force and to accept limitations on national sovereignty illustrates the difficulties with the general categories of 'pacifism' or 'liberal internationalism' that structure the literature on this subject. Pre-1914 French internationalism was without doubt less pacifist and less liberal than American and especially British variants. Maurice Vaïsse has used the term 'Jacobin pacifism' to distinguish French thinking from other variants of peace activism.[108] While this expression captures the greater prominence of force in French conceptions, it ignores the legalist foundations of French conceptions of international order. Pierre Cot, a prominent politician and internationalist of the inter-war period, underlined this point when comparing French, British and American approaches to the problem of peace:

The country of Descartes and Voltaire prefers technical solutions to spiritual hymns ... The Anglo-Saxon, we hear, traverses the globe with his bible. The Frenchman carries his legal code. We should not be ashamed of this natural and

---

[105] M. Robespierre, 'On the Moral and Political Principles of Domestic Policy' in *Oeuvres completes*, vol. X (Paris, 1967), 357; M. Barrès, *La Grande pitié des Églises de France* (Paris, 1914), 360; Ribot cited in *JO*, 1917, *Débats parlementaires*, 1917, 2 Aug. 1917; Clemenceau in P. Mantoux (ed.), *Les Délibérations du Conseil des quatre (24 mars–28 juin 1919)*, 2 vols. (Paris, 1955), I, 43: 27 Mar. 1919.
[106] Bouchard, 'Projets citoyens pour une paix durable', 129 and 138–41.
[107] Ibid., 133–4; see also the published version in Bouchard, *Citoyen*, 114 and 121 respectively.
[108] M. Vaïsse, 'Pour une histoire comparée des pacifismes européens' in M. Vaïsse (ed.), *Le Pacifisme en Europe des années vingt aux années cinquante* (Brussels, 1993), 441.

national tendency. We have a conception of peace that is more juridical than mystical.[109]

One does not have to accept Cot's rather crude stereotypes to acknowledge that it captures the legalist spirit of French internationalism during this period.

The *solidariste*-inspired theory of peace did, however, share a common weakness with Anglo-American 'domestic analogies': it did not take sufficient account of the interrelated problems of sovereignty and anarchy in the international system. The doctrine advocated by Bourgeois and his colleagues was based on the implicit assumption that the issue of sovereignty was essentially the same in both the domestic and international spheres. This was a misjudgement that ignored Renault's distinction between the power of domestic versus international legal regimes. In the domestic context the state functions as a higher sovereign authority with powers to limit the sovereignty of individual members of society. No such authority exists at the international sphere. Sovereignty is instead an attribute of states themselves. Hence the condition of anarchy. A higher international authority can never exist unless states agree to substantial limitations on their sovereign rights. This is something most are unwilling to do. Historically, in fact, the larger and more powerful the state, the greater is its reluctance to give up any of its sovereignty or sacrifice its own vital interests to the rule of international law.[110]

The issue of state sovereignty therefore constituted an intractable problem at the heart of French internationalist conceptions. This was compounded by another fundamental contradiction. While virtually all juridical internationalists rejected the idea of a 'super-state', their insistence on the need for a powerful world court and a robust system of sanctions assumed the existence of just such a higher authority. This contradiction, as we shall see, undermined the case made by French internationalists and hamstrung their efforts to shape the structure and functioning of the League of Nations in 1919 and after.

V

Another current of internationalism in pre-1914 France was more concerned with the pursuit of profits than the promotion of peace. Patterns of economic development in nineteenth-century Europe were increasingly based on international cooperation. On the eve of the First World War the west-European economy reached a level of integration that was not achieved again until the late 1960s. Franco-German cooperation was especially pronounced, interestingly, in the sectors of coal, iron and steel, which were crucial to the French and

---

[109] Pierre Cot, 'La Conception française de la lutte contre la guerre', *PPD*, Apr.–May 1929, 164, quoted in Guieu, 'Les Apôtres', 16.
[110] On the problems of sovereignty for the domestic analogy see Suganami, *Domestic Analogy*; on anarchy and sovereignty see H. Bull, 'Society and Anarchy in International Relations' in H. Butterfield and M. Wight (eds.), *Diplomatic Investigations* (London, 1966), 35–48.

German defence industries. This trend was facilitated by the more or less free movement of semi-skilled labour across Europe that was possible during this period.[111]

The essential complementarity of the French and German coal and steel sectors was a pivotal factor in the growing interdependence of heavy industry in western Europe. France lacked coal and Germany lacked iron ore. From the late nineteenth century France was forced to import at least one-third of its coal. Its 'energy deficit' was particularly acute when it came to coke. Since the 1880s coke, the material obtained from bituminous coal by destructive distillation, was the key energy source used in the smelting process for steel production. Although France lacked coal suitable for making coke, it did possess several of the richest iron-ore fields in Europe. Germany, conversely, possessed abundant resources of coal and coking coal but was forced to import much of its iron ore (though this deficit was reduced after it annexed the iron-ore deposits of Lorraine in 1871). Out of this situation emerged a mutually beneficial set of arrangements whereby France provided Germany with more than a third of its iron-ore imports and Germany provided nearly 80 per cent of French coke imports.[112]

But these figures on their own fail to capture either the level of cooperation between French and German heavy industry or the fundamentally international character of business activity in this sector. German and Belgian investment in France provides a striking illustration of these aspects of economic integration. Before the Great War, foreign nationals enjoyed virtually full rights of incorporation throughout western Europe.[113] By 1914 German and Belgian industrial concerns had exercised this right to control of a significant proportion of French iron ore. Among the German firms involved were the Ruhr industrial giants Thyssen, Krupp and Deutsche-Luxembourg (controlled by the steel magnate Hugo Stinnes). Also active were the Aciéries réunies de Burbach, Eich et Dudelange founded in 1911 with capital from Belgium, Germany, France and Luxembourg to form Europe's first large multinational steel-producing concern. Thyssen, in fact, used French capital to build a large

---

[111] C. Strikwerda, 'The troubled origins of European economic integration: international iron and steel and labor migration in the era of World War I', *AHR*, 98, 4 (Oct. 1993), 1106–29; see also the response by Paul Schroeder: 'Economic integration and the European international system', *AHR*, 98, 4 (1993), 1130–7.

[112] N. J. G. Pounds and W. N. Parker, *Coal and Steel in Western Europe: The Influence of Resources and Techniques on Production* (Bloomington, 1957); F. Crouzet, 'Le Charbon anglais en France au XIXème siècle' in L. Trénard (ed.), *Charbon et sciences humaines* (Paris, 1966); G.-H. Soutou, 'Le Coke dans les relations internationals en Europe de 1914 au plan Dawes', *RI*, 43 (1985), 249–67.

[113] B. Barth, 'Les Ententes financières franco-allemandes et l'expansion économique avant 1914' and E. Langlinay, 'Apprendre de l'Allemagne? Les Scientifiques et industriels de la chimie et l'Allemagne entre 1871 et 1914', both in J.-F. Eck, S. Martens and S. Schirmann (eds.), *L'Économie, l'argent et les hommes: les relations franco-allemandes de 1871 à nos jours* (Paris, 2009), 15–38 and 113–30 respectively.

steel plant in Caen in Normandy. By 1913 German and Belgian capital controlled nearly 15 per cent of the French iron and steel industry. French firms, in turn, invested on a more modest scale in the German coal industry, raising much of the capital for this investment on the German money market. The overall result was the internationalisation of western Europe's coal and steel industries.[114]

The cross-border flow of investment created large and complex networks of mutual interest. Of the seventeen directors of the most powerful French iron cartel, the Comptoir métallurgique de Longwy, eight represented either German or Belgian firms. Thyssen was similarly represented on the Comité des forges, the powerful and politically active association of French iron and steel producers. The iron and steel concern owned by the de Wendel family in French Lorraine, meanwhile, possessed mines and factories on both sides of the Franco-German border.[115] These links were supplemented by the activities of interest groups such as the Comité commercial franco-allemande in France or the Deutsche–Französischer Wirtschaftsverein in Germany. These and similar networks were active right up to 1914 in promoting cooperation both in their respective national parliaments and within French and German chambers of commerce.[116] On the eve of war, lobbying in political circles called for a tramway that would connect France, Germany, Belgium and Luxembourg and a new railway linking energy mines and industrial plants in France and Germany. There were also attempts to devise a coordinated response by governments and industrialists to trade union pressure for improved working conditions.[117]

Increased levels of industrial cooperation in the private sector were paralleled by an impressive expansion in international commerce. The trend, again, continued right up to the outbreak of war. Tariffs were much lower before 1914 than at any point up to the creation of the European Common Market. Trade

[114] Strikwerda, 'Troubled origins', 1113–19; R. Poidevin, 'Placements et investissements français en Allemagne, 1898–1914' in M. Lévy-Leboyer (ed.), *La Position internationale de la France: aspects économiques et financiers XIXème–XXème siècles* (Paris, 1977), 347–61; J.-M. Moine, *Les Barons du fer: les maîtres de forges en Lorraine du milieu du 19ème siècle aux années trente* (Nancy, 1989), 56–81; D. Woronoff, *Histoire de l'industrie en France: du XVIe siècle à nos jours* (Paris, 1994), 361–6; A. Broder, 'Entreprises françaises à l'étranger, entreprises étrangers en France avant 1914' in P. Milza and R. Poidevin (eds.), *La Puissance française à la belle époque* (Brussels, 1992), 109–23.
[115] D. Fraboulet, 'L'Union des industries métallurgiques et minières: organisation, stratégies et pratiques du patronat métallurgique (1901–1940)', *VS*, 114, 2 (2012), 119–27; D. Fraboulet, *Quand les patrons s'organisent: stratégies et pratiques de l'Union des industries métallurgiques et minières 1901–1950* (Villeneuve-d'Ascq, 2007), esp. 23–41; Strikwerda, 'Troubled origins', 1116–18; J.-N. Jeanneney, *François de Wendel en république: l'argent et le pouvoir 1914–1940* (Paris, 1976), 17–38.
[116] L. Coquet, *Politique commerciale et coloniale franco-allemande* (Paris, 1907); Lucien Coquet was the founder of the Comité commercial franco-allemande. For a balanced corrective see R. Poidevin, 'Le Nationalisme économique et financier dans les relations franco-allemandes avant 1914', *Revue d'Allemagne*, 28, 1 (1996), 63–70.
[117] Strikwerda, 'Troubled origins', 1110–11 and 1120–4.

between France and Germany was at an all-time high when the July Crisis broke out. Between 1904 and 1913, for example, the proportion of German iron-ore imports provided by France grew from 5 to nearly 35 per cent.[118] Before 1914 the European economy was becoming steadily more integrated in terms of investment, industrial cooperation, the movement of labour and commerce. What is more, iron and steel production, the sector most closely associated with the armaments industries, was leading the way in the trend towards interpenetration and interdependence.

The wider conclusions to be drawn from these trends are not straightforward. The growth of economic interdependence proceeded at the same time as an intense upsurge of nationalism. Criticism of the role of German industry in France's mining and iron and steel sectors was a consistent theme in French nationalist rhetoric that intensified as tensions mounted.[119] French investment in Germany, meanwhile, must be placed in context. It was dwarfed by the huge public and private investment in Tsarist Russia during the same period. Loans to Russia, moreover, were sponsored by a succession of French governments and reflected France's strategic interest in a strong eastern counterweight to Germany.[120] Similarly, private-sector lobbying for better rail links between the industrial regions of France and Germany took place against the backdrop of the huge resources devoted by both countries to the construction of ever-larger networks of strategic railways.[121]

The driving force of the economic integration that took place before 1914 was profit. Peace, crucially, was not understood as the only means to profit. The judgement that 'many business leaders saw peaceful ties between states as the best means to economic growth' is not supported by detailed evidence.[122] Indeed, it flies in the face of much of the evidence in Georges-Henri Soutou's magisterial study of the economic aims of the great powers during the First World War. This research leaves no doubt that the great majority of industrialists considered themselves patriots and cooperated with the nationalist programmes pursued by their respective governments. This precluded open opposition to decisions for war or resistance to national war efforts. It did not, however, rule out support for the resumption of industrial cooperation after the war. As we shall see, both government officials and senior figures within French heavy industry hesitated between this option and a strategy

---

[118] R. Poidevin, *Les Relations économiques et financières entre la France et l'Allemagne de 1898 à 1914* (Paris, 1969), esp. 752–79, 833–85; W. Ashworth, 'Industrialization and the economic integration of nineteenth century Europe', *European Studies Review*, 4 (1974), 291–314; I. Berend, *An Economic History of Twentieth Century Europe* (Cambridge, 2006), 10–41; Woronoff, *Histoire de l'industrie*, 358–61.
[119] Poidevin, *Relations économiques et financières*, 844–92.
[120] R. Girault, *Emprunts russes et investissements français en Russie, 1887–1914* (Paris, 1973).
[121] A. Mitchell, *The Great Train Race: Railways and the Franco-German Rivalry, 1815–1914* (Oxford, 2006), 175–269.
[122] Strikwerda, 'Troubled origins', 1107 and 1129.

aimed at seizing control of Europe's coal and steel industry for France.[123] This tension within the policy elite gave economic security an ambiguous character that would endure through the Great War and into the 1920s.

VI

The internationalist reflexes of many French industrialists were therefore of a very different character from those of Léon Bourgeois and other juridical internationalists. Yet it was the latter variant that would eventually emerge as a genuine alternative to traditional power politics. Advocates of 'peace through law' were concentrated at the centre and centre-left of French politics. They included the moderates of the centre and centre-right such as d'Estournelles de Constant, Joseph Barthélemy and Paul Painlevé as well as leading Socialists such as Jean Jaurès. But the heart of the movement beat within the Radical Party. A striking number of French internationalists were Radicals. Among the most prominent were Bourgeois, Ferdinand Buisson, Célestin Bouglé, Charles Beauquier, Lucien Le Foyer, Pierre Cot and Henry de Jouvenel.[124]

There were also multiple overlaps between internationalist and other civil society networks. Many of the most active internationalists were also Freemasons. The Paris Cosmos and Grand Orient lodges were particularly active in support of the juridical internationalist movement. The same was true of the Ligue des droits de l'homme (LDH), an influential civil society association founded in the heat of the Dreyfus Affair in 1898. Membership of the LDH was drawn from the moderate centre to the socialist left of the political spectrum. Many juridical internationalists had played prominent roles in its foundation. Both Ferdinand Buisson, its president from 1914 to 1926, and his successor, Victor Basch, were active juridical internationalists.[125] The LDH affiliated itself officially with the International Peace Bureau in 1906 and played a prominent role thereafter in the campaign for compulsory international arbitration.[126]

Basch was also part of another web of contacts linking reformist socialists to the juridical internationalist movement. International arbitration was increasingly prominent in official SFIO doctrine in the pre-war decade. Under the leadership of Jean Jaurès the Socialists criticised the traditional policy of alliance

---

[123] G.-H. Soutou, *L'Or et le sang: les buts de guerre économiques de la Première Guerre mondiale* (Paris, 1989), see esp. 141–70.
[124] S. Berstein, *Histoire du Parti Radical*, vol. I: *À la recherche de l'âge d'or* (Paris, 1980), 31–6.
[125] This paragraph is drawn principally from Gueiu, 'Les Apôtres', 23–64; Gueiu, *Rameau et glaive*, 18–51; C. Birebent, *Militants de la paix et de la SDN: les mouvements de soutien à la Société de nations en France et au Royaume-Uni, 1918–1925* (Paris, 2007), 23–67; W. D. Irvine, *Between Justice and Politics: The Ligue des droits de l'homme, 1898–1945* (Stanford, 2007), 132–47.
[126] E. Naquet, 'Entre justice et la patrie: la Ligue des droits de l'homme et la Grande Guerre', *Mouvement social*, 183 (1988), 94–6; Gueiu, 'Les Apôtres', 53–6; and Irvine, *Between Justice and Politics*, 132–3 and 135–6.

blocs and championed the cause of arbitration. Jaurès argued for the 'regular convocation of international conferences with a view to establishing mechanisms for the development of international legislation'.[127] It was the idea of a society or league of nations that captured the imaginations of internationalist-minded socialists most powerfully, however. The cause dominated Socialist international policy prescriptions during the First World War. Among the most active in this campaign were a younger generation of socialist leaders (many of whom were graduates of the École normale supérieure) that included Edgard Milhaud, Albert Thomas and Léon Blum. Milhaud and Thomas were tireless advocates of League-based internationalism and would work together in Geneva for much of the 1920s. Blum, meanwhile, was an eloquent supporter of the League – which he described as the 'juridical expression of the civilised world' – through to the outbreak of the Second World War.[128]

It would be wrong, however, to represent juridical internationalism as anything but marginal to the making of national security policy before 1914. Even within the Radical Party the focus was above all on domestic issues of 'republican defence'. Radical politics were preoccupied with threats posed to the Republic (and to the interests of the *classes moyennes*) by the reactionary right and the revolutionary left. Schemes for the juridical reorganisation of international politics elicited little more than a 'polite silence' from the majority of Radicals.[129] It would take the trauma of the Great War to put an end to this relative indifference.[130] The wartime experience would create the necessary political space for the internationalist movement to grow in influence.

It was also the case that the juridical and socialist variants of internationalism were in the long run incompatible. Even the more moderate members of the SFIO envisaged the eventual destruction of the existing international political order and the rise of post-national cooperation among the working classes. Liberal juridical internationalists, conversely, aimed to preserve the existing order. The SFIO officially sponsored plans to convert the French army into a

---

[127] L. Barcelo, 'Aux Origines de la Cour permanente d'arbitrage: la première conférence de La Haye (1899)', *GMCC*, 189 (1998); S. Milner, *The Dilemmas of Internationalism: French Syndicalism and the International Labour Movement, 1900–1914* (Oxford, 1991); P. Buffotot, *Le Socialisme français et la guerre: du soldat-citoyen à l'armée professionnelle, 1871–1998* (Paris, 1999), 50–76.

[128] Quote from L. Blum, 'Le Bilan', *Le Populaire*, 16 août 1921. On this network, many of whose members were also influenced by Lucien Herr, the head librarian at the École normale, see also J.-F. Sirinelli, *Génération Intellectuelle: Khâgneux et Normaliens dans l'entre-deux-guerres* (Paris, 1994), 308–94 and esp. C. Prochasson, *Les Intellectuels le socialisme et la guerre, 1900–1938* (Paris, 1993), 122–9.

[129] Berstein, *Recherche de l'âge d'or*, 64.

[130] Cf. Guieu, 'Les Apôtres', iii. On the issue of public attitudes towards internationalism and the League of Nations see also M.-R. Mouton, *La Société des nations et les intérêts de la France (1920–1924)* (Berne, 1995), 18–23; C. Manigand, *Les Français au service de la Société des nations* (Berne, 2003); and J. L. Hogge II, 'Arbitrage, Sécurité, Désarmement: French Security and the League of Nations, 1920–1925', Ph.D. dissertation, New York University, 1994.

national militia. The left wings of both the socialist and trade union movements were sympathetic to the virulent anti-patriotism and anti-militarism advocated by figures such as Gustave Hervé. Jaurès, significantly, did not rule out an international general strike as a means to prevent war.[131] These attitudes and policy positions were denounced by bourgeois juridical internationalists. While most remained suspicious of militarism and favoured gradual reductions in levels of armaments, the overwhelming majority were thoroughly middle class, deeply patriotic and opposed to the SFIO's radical plans for military reform and a 'new army' at a time when war with Germany seemed increasingly imminent.[132]

The internationalist cause was all but submerged by the rise in international tensions that brought France to the brink of war with Germany during the Agadir Crisis in late 1911. One important result of these tensions was a surge of national and patriotic feeling across France. The result was the emergence of what Rod Kedward has termed 'normative nationalism' within the political mainstream.[133] These trends had a profound effect on both domestic and foreign policy. Historians disagree over the social and political dynamics of the 'national revival' in France. What is not in doubt, however, is that international events had intruded on the public consciousness to a greater extent than at any time since the 'war scares' of the previous century.[134] The popular nationalism of the pre-war years had little in common with the anti-republicanism that dominated nationalist politics on the extreme right. A new generation of intellectuals called for a rehabilitation of the military, as well as the martial virtues of honour and sacrifice. Support for this cause reverberated not only on the right but also at the centre and centre-left of French politics. A major consequence was much greater consensus concerning the need for stability at home and firmness in international affairs.[135]

A series of centre and centre-right governments cultivated this public mood assiduously in the years before the outbreak of war. Regular military parades, which had been banned since the 1890s, were reinstated and proved very popular. Most conservative nationalists looked on with approval as a more

---

[131] A. Kriegel and J.-J. Becker, *1914: la guerre et le mouvement ouvrier français* (Paris, 1964), esp. 16–77; M. Dreyfus, *Histoire de la CGT* (Paris, 1995), 37–75; Krumreich, *Armaments and Politics*, 58–70, 83–102; D. E. Sumler, 'Opponents of War Preparation in France, 1913–1914' in S. Wank (ed.), *Doves and Diplomats: Foreign Offices and Peace Movements in Europe and America in the Twentieth Century* (Westport, 1978), 109–26; M. B. Loughlin, 'Gustave Hervé's transition from socialism to National Socialism: continuity and ambivalence', *JCH*, 38, 4 (2003), 515–38.

[132] See Guieu, 'Les Apôtres', 40–2; Krumreich, *Armaments and Politics*, 70–6 and 103–80; and M. E. Nolan, *The Inverted Mirror: Mythologizing the Enemy in France and Germany, 1898–1914* (Oxford, 2005), esp. 87–104.

[133] R. Kedward, *La vie en bleu: France and the French since 1900* (London, 2005), 48–56.

[134] On this issue see, in particular, J.-J. Becker, 'La Genèse de la Union sacrée' and M. Baumont, 'Psychose de guerre en 1914', both in M. Boivin (ed.), *1914, les psychoses de guerre?* (Rouen, 1985).

[135] See in particular R. Girardet, *La Société militaire de 1815 à nos jours*, 2nd edn (Paris, 1998), 176–85 and Becker and Audoin-Rouzeau, *La France, la nation et la guerre*, 254–9.

assertive strain of national feeling spread across the political spectrum. Maurice Barrès, the most eminent theoretician of traditional nationalism in France, observed with satisfaction that former socialist politicians such as Aristide Briand and Alexandre Millerand had become converts to the nationalist cause. 'What does it matter', he asked, 'that the nationalist party is losing ground when at the same moment we are witnessing the nationalising of the opposing parties?'[136] The First World War marked the high point of national feeling in France while at the same time establishing the conditions for the internationalist approach to grow in influence and popularity.

Before 1914, however, national security policy was dominated by the time-honoured traditions of military strength and the balance of power. No political leader in France was more committed to the traditional approach to security than Raymond Poincaré.[137] A lawyer of international repute, Poincaré was also one of the longest-serving politicians of his or any other generation (he was a member of parliament from 1887 through to his death in 1934). A committed republican of the centre-right, he was also a fervent patriot, born in Lorraine before the Franco-Prussian War. As a political leader, Poincaré combined a fine intellect and an extraordinary capacity for hard work with conservative instincts and a profound respect for procedure and the letter of the law. His overriding aim upon assuming the premiership in January 1912 was to unite France behind a policy of strength and resolve in international affairs. His ministerial declaration called for unity in defence of the 'superior interest of national security'. These interests, he asserted, were best served by cultivating France's alliances and strengthening the armed services.[138] As John Keiger has observed, 'Poincaré, with characteristic juridical precision, wanted the balance of power observed to the letter – a total separation of the two [alliance] blocs and a strict refusal to allow any penetration of the alliance system.' For Poincaré the traditional principles of the balance of power and alliance politics constituted the 'lasting and indestructible interests of French foreign policy'.[139]

Poincaré became president of the Republic in February 1913. This ensured that all those summoned by him to lead governments shared his traditional convictions. He took the broadest possible interpretation of his constitutional prerogatives as president and intervened actively in all aspects of policy making. A succession of wartime premiers found it difficult to resist his influence. This situation endured until Georges Clemenceau formed a government in the midst of a national crisis in November 1917. Clemenceau had the confidence and willpower to keep the president at arm's length from the levers of policy.

[136] *L'Echo de Paris*, 13 Jul. 1913.
[137] Excellent biographies include J. F. V. Keiger, *Raymond Poincaré* (Cambridge, 1996) and F. Roth, *Raymond Poincaré, un homme d'état républicain* (Paris, 2006); see also D. Amson, *Poincaré: l'acharné de la politique* (Paris, 1997). P. Marcus, *Raymond Poincaré, l'architecte d'une carrière d'état* (Paris, 2006) is more critical.
[138] Keiger, *Poincaré*, 130–1 and Krumreich, *Armaments and Politics*, 31–3.
[139] Quote in J. F. V. Keiger, *France and the Origins of the First World War* (London, 1983), 56.

Through the first three-and-a-half years of the conflict, however, there was no more influential voice in the making of foreign and security policy than that of Poincaré.[140]

Two general approaches to the problem of national security shaped attitudes and understandings in France on the eve of the First World War. The traditional and internationalist conceptions of security were based on very different assumptions about the nature of international relations and the prospects for lasting peace. The traditional approach was rooted in long-standing practices of power politics embedded within the policy-making elite. Its proponents tended to look back for inspiration to an era of French predominance and to well-established conventions such as the balance of power and alliance politics as the bases of international order. At the core of the traditional approach was the belief that lasting security could only be achieved through strategic preponderance. This general conception of security was dominant within the policy elite during the First World War and after.

The internationalist approach to peace and security emerged as part of the nineteenth-century transnational movement to eradicate war. Internationalists looked to the growth of international institutions to provide a framework for the peaceful resolution of international disputes. The French variant of this movement was characterised by its juridical character and its emphasis on the role of collective force. It aimed to replace the balance of power with the rule of law and assumed that the practice of compulsory arbitration, when embedded in a robust regime of international law and backed up by powerful sanctions, would provide the basis for peace among nations. Before 1914 this movement exerted little or no influence on national security policy.

It is important to emphasise, finally, that there was considerable potential for overlap between the traditional and internationalist approaches. It was not only in the realm of economic security that traditionalist and internationalist impulses could coexist. Both conceptions, crucially, attributed decisive importance to the role of force in any international order. Adherents to both approaches also shared similar notions of France's international role as a champion of justice and civilisation. It was therefore possible for traditional and internationalist impulses to coexist even in the minds of individual policy makers. The result, in the mid-1920s, was the rise of a hybrid policy that sought to construct international peace through a system of interlocking mutual assistance pacts based on the principles of compulsory arbitration and a British strategic commitment. The aim of this system was to enmesh German power in a Europe-wide web of political and legal obligations that would contain its aggressive impulses. Power and interest were thus combined with the rule of law in a policy that culminated in the Locarno Accords.

[140] See vols. VI through X of Poincaré's war-time memoirs: *Au service de la France*; an invaluable source that must nonetheless be used with great care.

Part II

War and the politics of national security, 1914–1918

For fifty-two months between August 1914 and November 1918 French society was engaged in an unprecedented struggle for national survival. The Great War transformed nearly every aspect of French politics and wrought a similar revolution in the character of international relations. French planning for post-war security was inevitably shaped by this experience. In important respects, however, the conceptual foundations of this planning remained rooted in the beliefs and practices of the pre-1914 period. The following three chapters trace the evolution of security policy from the outbreak of war through to the armistice in 1918. Despite the seismic changes brought about by the First World War, neither the traditional nor the internationalist conceptions of security were altered fundamentally. Proponents of both approaches found justification for their convictions in the events of 1914 and after.

The transformations in the structural environment were nonetheless immense. They combined to alter both popular and official discourse on the subject of post-war security. For most of the first three years of the conflict, public discussion of war aims and peace conditions was restricted by the politics of the Union sacrée and the effects of government censorship. This state of affairs was transformed by the crises of 1917 and the breakdown of the Union sacrée. The febrile political atmosphere inside France was heightened by the fall of the Tsarist regime in February 1917 and the Bolshevik victory the following October. These events inspired the revolutionary left in France but left conservative nationalists with a sense of foreboding. The political rhetoric of revolution would become a permanent feature of the French political landscape between the wars. Paradoxically, an important effect of this turn of events was a weakening of the French Socialist Party. By the war's end French socialism entered a period of internecine warfare that would undermine its influence as a factor in the making of national security policy.

The manner in which the war was represented to the French public played a pivotal but little-recognised role in attitudes towards peace and security. Official discourses aimed at bolstering public support for a 'total' war effort constructed the meaning of the war around a complex of oppositions between France and Germany. Historians have argued persuasively that these meanings were at the heart of a 'war culture' that emerged in France after 1914, without which the sacrifices made both at the front and behind the lines would have been impossible.[1] This 'culture' has been defined as 'a body of representations of the conflict crystallised into a veritable system, giving the war its fundamental meaning'.[2] Within this system, crucially, the war was nearly always depicted as a crusade for 'civilisation' aimed at establishing peace through the rule of law. France was cast as the cradle of civilisation and the defender of international justice. A German victory, conversely, would mean the triumph of brute force.[3]

This discourse was omnipresent in public-sphere constructions of the war's meaning. Albert Sarraut, the Radical minister of education, provided the following vision of the war's purpose for dissemination to French schoolchildren:

It is once again against the human beast whose evolution has been retarded, against the Hun of old, who has changed his armour without changing his conscience, yes, it is against the Vandal, unchanged after more than fifteen centuries of human progress that, like a gleaming knight from days gone by, Latin France draws its sword. It is once again the violent clash of civilisation against barbarism, the struggle between light and the shadows ... German hatred for France is the hatred of the beast that crawls for the bird that takes flight, the hatred of the reptile for the star. [Germany] hates the French soul, the most pure reflection of the universal conscience ... France is the glory of the human patrimony and the second home of all men who think ... France's genius, unchanged through the ages and despite the diversity of its history, is eternally in the service of the same inspirations of generosity that have led it to bring to the oppressed multitudes the language of the Declaration of the Rights of Man ... France must always be the magnificent evangelist of a new rule of law.[4]

The French and German national characters were thus defined by a series of oppositions: civilisation versus barbarism, humanity versus inhumanity, the

---

[1] The discussion that follows is based primarily on 'Représenter la guerre, 1914–1918': a special issue of *GMCC*, 171 (1993); J.-J. Becker and S. Audoin-Rouzeau, *La France, la nation, la guerre, 1850–1920* (Paris, 1995), 237–337; S. Audoin-Rouzeau and A. Becker, *14–18: retrouver la guerre* (Paris, 2000), 129–230; J.-J. Becker, *La France en guerre, 1914–1918: la grande mutation* (Brussels, 1999); A. Becker, *Les Oubliés de la Grande Guerre: humanitaire et culture de guerre, 1914–1918* (Paris, 2003); S. Audoin-Rouzeau and A. Becker, 'Violence et consentement: la "culture de guerre" du Premier Conflit mondial' in J.-P. Rioux and J.-F. Sirinelli (eds.), *Pour une histoire culturelle* (Paris, 1997); L. Smith, 'The "Culture de guerre" and French historiography of the Great War of 1914–1918', *History Compass*, 5–6 (2007), 1967–79. This school of interpretation has been challenged in F. Rousseau, *La Guerre censurée: une histoire des combattants européens de 14–18* (Paris, 1999). See also the discussion in A. Prost and J. Winter, *Penser la Grande Guerre: un essai d'historiographie* (Paris, 2004), 140–3; H. Strachan, *The First World War*, vol. I: *To Arms* (Oxford, 2001), 1114–39; and F. Cochet, *Survivre au front 1914–1918: les poilus entre contrainte et consentement* (Paris, 2005).
[2] Audoin-Rouzeau and Becker, *14–18*, 145.
[3] S. Tison, *Comment sortir de la guerre? Deuil, mémoire et traumatisme (1870–1940)* (Rennes, 2011), 241–73.
[4] Albert Sarraut, *Bulletin administratif du ministère de l'instruction publique*, 3 Oct. 1914, no. 2144, cited in Becker and Audoin-Rouzeau, *La France, la nation, la guerre*, 297–8.

rule of law versus the rule of force. The effect of these binary categories was to reinforce constructions of the conflict as an elemental struggle for national survival.

These representations were present from the very outset of the war. They were given eloquent expression by the writer Charles Péguy, a militant campaigner for social justice and a Dreyfusard who converted to Catholicism in 1910. Péguy's patriotic reflections brought together many of the diverse strands of French political and cultural life. In August 1914, before leaving for the front where he would be killed in one of the early actions of the Battle of the Marne, he wrote that 'in the modern world, the French people remain the eminent, and perhaps even the only, true representatives of the race of freedom ... the Germans are the eminent, and perhaps even the only, representatives of the race of domination'. 'Never', Péguy insisted, 'will Germany be able to understand France. It is a question of race. She will never understand liberty and grace. She will only ever understand empire and domination.'[5]

All of the key themes in prevailing constructions of both the identity of France and the significance of the war are distilled in the above two passages by Sarraut and Péguy. There are references to France's unique role as the repository of reason, the sponsor of freedom and the universal conscience of humanity. France was not only the home of the rights of man but also the 'evangelist of the new rule of law'. These discursive strategies were part of a long-standing tradition of linking the interests of France with those of humanity. Security for France therefore meant the preservation of civilisation. The war brought about a far more expansive dissemination and generalisation of these oppositions and associations. But the role of these representations in shaping attitudes and understandings has not been integrated into the literature on French foreign and security policy. The conviction that France stood against Germany in defence of civilisation and justice was central not only to understandings of the war's purpose, but also to conceptions of what might constitute a 'just' post-war order. One of the most common linkages was that between French war aims and the rule of law.

Official discourse on the meaning of the war was saturated with references to justice and the rule of law. This was true in the first public proclamations on war aims, which were made on 22 December 1914 after parliament and government returned from a brief exile in Bordeaux. Before the combined ranks of the senate and chamber of deputies, premier René Viviani declared that France's overriding war aim was to 'reconstruct a regenerated Europe upon the principles of justice'.[6] Paul Deschanel, the president of the chamber, added that France 'will not relent until we have fulfilled our duty to the central

---

[5] Charles Péguy, 'Note conjointe sur M. Descartes et la philosophie cartésienne' in *Charles Péguy: oeuvres en prose complètes, 1909–1914* (Paris, 1992), III, 1344 and 1346.
[6] Assemblée Nationale, *JO*, Chambre des députés, *Débats parlementaires*, 1914 (hereafter *JO*, Chambre, *Débats*), 22 Dec. 1914.

thought of our race: the rule of law must win out over the rule of force'.[7] Aristide Briand, upon succeeding Viviani as premier in October 1915, depicted France as 'the champion of justice' and pledged that it would continue the struggle 'until victory restores the rule of law'.[8] Alexandre Ribot, who became premier in March 1917, pledged to pursue the 'definitive triumph of the rule of law'.[9] His successor, Paul Painlevé, duly assured parliament that France's central objectives were 'those of the rule of law itself'.[10] The same trope was present in Georges Clemenceau's first parliamentary address as wartime premier when he assured the nation that the 'unifying thought' of his government would be 'war without limit' to achieve 'the apotheosis of the rule of law'.[11]

Establishing the 'rule of law', as we have seen, held very different meanings to different political constituencies. For French internationalists it would serve as the basis of a transformed international order. For more traditionally inclined policy elites, conversely, it signified entrenching a more favourable strategic balance in a new body of international treaties. Hence even apparently similar prescriptions for security could hold very different meanings.

The same is true of the frequently expressed aim to 'destroy Prussian militarism'. This resolution, with its modern-day connotations of 'regime change', was first articulated publicly by Viviani when he asserted that an end to Prussian militarism was an essential prerequisite for European reconstruction.[12] It was an objective upon which opinion across the political spectrum could agree. For socialist leaders such as Marcel Sembat and Albert Thomas the responsibility of the militarist Prussian ruling class for causing the war was beyond doubt.[13] Poincaré, for his part, described the aim of 'smashing Prussian militarism' as 'the only peace the Republic can accept' as a 'guarantee of European security'.[14] Théophile Delcassé, restored to the foreign ministry in August 1914, referred in official correspondence to the 'unshakeable resolution of the Allies not to lay down arms until Germany is reduced to impotence and it is incapable of further harm'.[15] Briand endorsed this aim as premier when he wrote in May 1916 that 'the conclusive defeat of Germany's militarism and ambition to dominate is a matter of life and death for France, and the sole guarantee of the future liberty of the world'.[16]

---

[7] J.-B. Duroselle, *La Grande Guerre des Français* (Paris, 1994), 133.
[8] *JO*, Chambre, *Débats*, 1915, session of 3 Nov. 1915; see also S. Unger, *Briand: le ferme conciliateur* (Paris, 2005), 307.
[9] *JO*, Chambre, *Débats*, 1917, 21 Mar. 1917.
[10] *JO*, Chambre, *Débats*, 1917, 18 Sept. 1917.
[11] *JO*, Chambre, *Débats*, 1917, 20 Nov. 1917.
[12] *JO*, Chambre, *Débats*, 1914, 22 Dec. 1914.
[13] See esp. P. Buffotot, *Le Socialisme français et la guerre: du soldat-citoyen à l'armée professionnelle, 1871–1998* (Paris, 1999), 18–37 and J.-L. Robert, *Les Ouvrières, la Patrie et la Révolution: Paris, 1914–1919* (Paris, 1995), 21–30, 60–1 and 82–5.
[14] Poincaré, *Au Service de la France*, vol. VII: *Guerre de siege (1915)* (Paris, 1931), 10.
[15] MAE, PA-AP 211, *Papiers Théophile Delcassé*, vol. 25, Delcassé to Paul Cambon (London) and Maurice Paléologue (Petrograd), 6 Dec. 1914.
[16] MAE, PA-AP 93, *Papiers Jean Jules Jusserand*, vol. 31, Briand to Jusserand, 27 May 1916.

Yet underneath this apparent consensus over the need to 'break' Prussian militarism was an ambiguity that helps illuminate the divergent character of security prescriptions among the French elite. For adherents to the traditional approach to security, breaking Prussian militarism meant breaking German power. The threat to France's security, according to this analysis, lay with German industrial and demographic superiority. Germany must therefore be weakened for France to have greater security. Inherent in this conviction was the assumption that Germany would pose a threat to European peace whatever its political make-up. A very different set of assumptions underpinned internationalist diagnoses of the security problem. For both liberal and socialist internationalists, breaking Prussian militarism meant changing the political culture of the Reich. The problem lay with German political practices, which needed to be democratised. Once this was achieved Germany could be reintegrated into the European political community without posing a threat to the security of France.

The main reason that political elites confined themselves to generalities in public expressions of war aims and peace conditions was the desire to prevent these ambiguities surfacing to become issues of public discord. In this they were largely successful through mid-1917. As the Union sacrée came under strain, however, contending conceptions of security and international order occasioned bitter debate in secret sessions of parliament. This process was repeated in late 1918 and again the following summer as disagreements over the best route to national recovery and the foundations of a durable peace structured public discourse over the peace settlement.

A final set of representations that coalesced and became increasingly prominent after the spring of 1917 depicted the war as a crusade for 'democracy'. The combination of the Russian Revolution and American entry made it much easier to represent the war as a struggle between western democracy and eastern autocracy. Traditional republican constructions of France as the home of democracy and human rights were duly deployed in opposition to stock images of German absolutism. In the public sphere in France and elsewhere, war came to be depicted as a struggle between belief systems in which defeat would mean political and cultural annihilation. This dimension to the conflict was first articulated in public statements of Allied resolve to bring an end to Prussian militarism. But it was given further definition as democratisation gradually became a central war aim of the Allied and Associated Powers over the course of 1917–18.[17] This opened the way for the discourse of self-determination to play an ever more influential role in shaping conceptions of the post-war order.

---

[17] On this issue see D. Stevenson, *Cataclysm: The First World War as Political Tragedy* (New York, 2004), 103–22, 216–39, 260–1, 318–20 and esp. 379–406; see also H. E. Goemans, *War and Punishment: The Causes of War Termination and the First World War* (Princeton, 2000).

These developments in the way the war was represented and understood had limited direct impact on the process of security policy making. Traditionalist assumptions continued to inspire the policy conceptions of the vast majority of security professionals. Yet it is also possible to detect the influence of internationalist alternatives, particularly in the realms of economic security and programmes for post-war international order. French security policy towards these issues was more ambiguous and less utterly committed to traditional practices than has generally been assumed.

Crucially, representations of the conflict as a war to establish the rule of law only added to the long-term credibility of the internationalist cause. For policy elites, this sort of language may have been intended chiefly as a means of bolstering national resolve and demanding ever greater sacrifices from society. But it left important hostages to fortune for future policy because it was understood by all parties as carrying with it an implicit political commitment for greater social justice and reforms to the international system that could not be ignored once the guns fell silent.

The conflict was to shape both popular and elite attitudes in ways that policy makers could not anticipate. If the outbreak of war appeared to confirm the wisdom and legitimacy of alliance politics and the balance of power, the scale and ferocity of the conflict revitalised and provided a much wider and more receptive audience for internationalist calls for a new basis for international politics. The public utterances of United States president Woodrow Wilson functioned as a magnetic pole for the internationalist movement.[18] After France's political leadership committed publicly to cooperate in the establishment of an international organisation to preserve peace in January 1917, internationalists were fired with missionary zeal to contribute to this project. The role of the Great War in creating the conditions necessary for internationalism to flourish is the central paradox running through the entire period 1914–25.

---

[18] See especially E. Manela, *The Wilsonian Moment: Self-determination and the International Origins of Anti-colonial Nationalism* (Oxford, 2007), 3–53.

3 The primacy of the balance of power, 1914–1916

The period from the outbreak of the First World War through to the spring of 1917 witnessed the emergence of a coherent programme for post-war security in western Europe. This programme was animated in nearly all respects by the traditional approach to security outlined in the previous chapter. This was because foreign and security policy during the first three years of the war was controlled by political leaders and security professionals who remained committed to the tried and tested practices of power politics.

The traditional approach enjoyed wide support inside the government, in parliament and in French society. The pivotal ministries of war and foreign affairs remained in the hands of strongly patriotic politicians committed to the principles of the balance of power and alliance politics. The traditional orientation of policy did not rule out regular expressions of support for internationalist causes, including transatlantic calls for a league or society of nations to prevent future wars. But such expressions did not reflect genuine support for transforming the bases of international relations.[1] Such a transformation would have been inimical to the core views of the great majority of the political elites and security professionals responsible for the framing of France's national security programme.

French internationalists, conversely, were forced into retreat during the early stages of the war as popular opinion rallied overwhelmingly to the war effort. The outbreak of the war was a grievous setback for the juridical internationalist cause. Many modified or even renounced their internationalist stance in order to assert their credentials as patriots. The great majority of socialist internationalists supported the war in line with both SFIO and Confédération générale du travail (CGT) policy of temporary cooperation with the bourgeois parties in defence of the nation against German imperialism. Dissidents were inhibited by censorship and by the politics of the Union sacrée.

Two aspects of the conflict augured well for the future of the internationalist conception, however. The first was the sheer scale of the conflict and its horrific

---

[1] A point also made in S. Blair, 'La France et le pacte de la Société des nations: le rôle du gouvernement français dans l'élaboration du pacte de la Société des nations, 1914–1919', thèse de doctorat, Université de Paris I (Sorbonne), 1991, 21–2.

human and material costs. As the conflict expanded and losses mounted, a crucial cumulative effect of the war was to add legitimacy to calls for transforming international relations. The second was the fact that, virtually from the opening of hostilities, the French war effort was represented as a struggle for justice and the rule of law against an opponent who represented barbarism and the rule of force. This official discourse provided legitimacy to the internationalist cause and generated longer-term support for its vision of an international society based on a 'law of nations'. From summer 1914 through to spring 1917, however, these developments remained in their early stages. French policy remained centred firmly on a traditional approach to security.

I

'France', declared President Poincaré in a celebrated message to parliament on 4 August 1914, 'has just been the object of premeditated aggression in insolent defiance of the law of nations . . . She will be defended heroically by all her sons, and in the face of the enemy nothing will break this sacred union.'[2] The Union sacrée was fundamental to the political context in which security policy was made during the first three years of the war. While there remains considerable debate about the precise character of the 'sacred union' proclaimed by Poincaré, there can be no doubt that the omnipresent discourse of national unity played a fundamental role in conditioning the way the war was both represented and understood among French policy elites.

Poincaré's message was greeted with unanimous enthusiasm in both houses of parliament. The president noted the following day that the sentiments and convictions of the Union sacrée had 'spread over the country as if by enchantment'.[3] The ideal expressed by this concept, evoked repeatedly in the press and in public declarations by political leaders in the ensuing months, was one of political, economic and spiritual unity before a mortal threat to the French nation. And it included virtually all of the major threads of the identity of France: republican, nationalist, socialist and Catholic. Individual and group interests were to be set aside for the duration of the conflict. 'There are no political distinctions now,' declared Louis Barthou, a former premier and key figure on the nationalist centre-right, 'no separate confessions and no class struggles. There is only France.'[4]

This was obviously a discursive construction formulated for political purposes. It cannot capture the complexity of French responses to the German invasion. Historians nonetheless agree that, in the weeks and months that followed, an 'incontestable current of harmony and national reconciliation' flowed through

[2] Poincaré, *Au service de la France*, vol. IV: *L'Union sacrée (1914)* (Paris, 1927), 547–8.
[3] Ibid., vol. V: *L'Invasion (1914)* (Paris, 1928), 2.
[4] Anonymous, *Ceux qui nous mènent* (Paris, 1922), 6. See also R. Kedward, *La Vie en bleu: France and the French since 1900* (London, 2005), 69–73.

French society.[5] This current provided powerful testimony to the strength of national feeling at all levels of French society. But the reality of the Union sacrée was less theatrical and, at the same time, more substantial in its medium and long-term effects. It can be understood on two levels. The first is that of the public performance of French elites. The second is the more substantive reactions of the French political movements and the population at large.[6]

The performative aspects of the Union sacrée were declarations and gestures made in public by French elites that were both genuine expressions of unity and resolve and attempts to shape public sentiment. Perhaps the most dramatic and effective of these was the funeral of Socialist leader Jean Jaurès on the morning of 4 August. Jaurès had been assassinated by a nationalist fanatic on 31 July. His funeral became an elaborate ritual of national unity attended not only by all of the key figures of the socialist and trade unions movement, but also by Poincaré, prime minister Viviani, the presidents of both the senate and chamber of deputies as well as representatives of the largest nationalist associations, including Maurice Barrès of the Ligue des patriotes. Léon Jouhaux, secretary general of the CGT, made an impassioned speech invoking the Jacobin legacy of the French left and the need to 'throw back the invader' in order to 'save the patrimony of civilisation'. Jouhaux subsequently received harsh criticism for this speech from others on the left. On 4 August 1914, however, his words were greeted with enthusiasm and interpreted as public affirmation of trade union support for the national war effort.[7]

Subsequent symbolic acts further solidified the image of national union. In the chamber of deputies Edouard Vaillant, eminent Socialist and veteran of the Paris Commune, clasped hands with Albert de Mun, leader of the Catholic right and a former officer in the army that crushed the Commune.[8] The newspaper *Le Temps* introduced a regular column entitled *L'Union sacrée*, and the chamber declared a state of siege, voted credits for the war effort, introduced censorship and increased the volume of notes printed by the Bank of France.[9]

Set-piece theatrics and symbolic politics were in many ways superficial and transitory manifestations of the national response to the outbreak of war.[10] The

---

[5] J.-J. Becker and S. Berstein, *Victoire et frustrations, 1914–1929* (Paris, 1990), 27.
[6] This conceptualisation is borrowed from J.-J. Becker and S. Audoin-Rouzeau, *La France, la nation et la guerre: 1850–1920* (Paris, 1995), 271–83. See also J.-J. Becker's 'Union sacrée et idéologie bourgeoise', *RH*, 264 (1980), 65–74.
[7] B. Georges and D. Tinant (with M.-A. Renauld), *Léon Jouhaux: cinquante ans de syndicalisme*, vol. I: *Des origines à 1921* (Paris, 1962), 468 and 46; see also M. Dreyfus, *Histoire de la CGT* (Paris, 1995), 80–7 and J.-J. Becker, *1914: comment les Français sont entrés dans la guerre* (Paris, 1977), 400–5; S. Audoin-Rouzeau and S. Becker, *14–18: retrouver la guerre* (Paris, 2000), 134–5.
[8] L. Smith, S. Audoin-Rouzeau and A. Becker, *France and the Great War, 1914–1918* (Cambridge, 2003), 27.
[9] J.-B. Duroselle, *La Grande Guerre des Français* (Paris, 1994), 49–51.
[10] See esp. the analysis of Maurice Agulhon in *La République*, vol. I: *(1880–1932)* (Paris, 1999), 249–61 and Becker, *1914*, 425–84.

substance of the Union sacrée, which was to underpin more than three years of unparalleled sacrifice, was embedded in the lone point of true national consensus in 1914: the need to defend French soil from unjustified aggression. German policy, and in particular the strange imperatives of the Schlieffen plan, contributed greatly to cementing this consensus. The relatively passive French position at the height of the crisis, which included a decision to hold all troop concentrations ten kilometres back from the German frontier, stood in sharp contrast with Germany's aggressive strategic posture. 'For the sake of public opinion,' the cabinet decided, 'let the Germans put themselves in the wrong.'[11] As a result, when war came, Germany was cast in the role of the aggressor and violator of international law.

This made it much easier for the mainstream political left, which had been caught off-guard by the swift deterioration of the international situation in late July, to rally to the war effort. 'Whatever our adversaries might say,' Jaurès observed in the Socialist paper *L'Humanité* during the July Crisis, 'there is no contradiction between making the maximum effort to ensure peace and, if this war breaks out despite our efforts, making the maximum effort to preserve the independence and integrity of the nation.'[12] The implication was clear: Socialist participation in a war in defence of French soil would be legitimate.[13] On the same day the Comité confédéral of the CGT voted against mounting a general strike at the outbreak of war. Four days later, as German troops concentrated on the eastern frontiers of Belgium and France, Edouard Vaillant, now the senior figure in the SFIO, declared that 'in the face of this aggression, French Socialists will fulfil all of their duties, for the *Patrie*, for the Republic and for the International'. Other prominent voices on the left were more direct. 'National defence above all,' proclaimed Gustave Hervé, a one-time militant anti-patriot who in 1914 changed the title of his newspaper from *La Guerre sociale* to *La Victoire*.[14] There were isolated cases of opposition to the Union sacrée and calls for a general strike from a small number of anarchists and radical trade unionists. But this resistance was the exception. It was also,

---

[11] Notes taken by Abel Ferry, the French under-secretary of state for foreign affairs, at the 30 July 1914 meeting of the cabinet, cited in J. F. V. Keiger, *Raymond Poincaré* (Cambridge, 1996), 175. On the government's strategy for managing the crisis see the contending interpretations in J. Keiger, 'France' in K. Wilson (ed.), *Decisions for War* (London, 1995), 121–50; R. A. Doughty, *Pyrrhic Victory: French Strategy and Operations in the Great War* (Cambridge, Mass., 2005), 51–4; and S. Schmidt, *Frankreichs Aussenpolitik in der Julikrise 1914: Ein Beitrag zur Geschichte des Ausbruchsdes Ersten Weltkrieges* (Munich, 2009), 55–104, 289–354.

[12] Jaurès in *L'Humanité*, 18 Jul. 1914, quoted in A. Kriegel, 'Jaurès en juillet 1914', *Mouvement social*, 49 (1964), 69.

[13] Becker, *1914*, 224–6; see also A. Kriegel and J.-J. Becker, *1914: la guerre et le mouvement ouvrier français* (Paris, 1964), 218–77 and Duroselle, *Grande Guerre*, 52–3.

[14] Quotes from J.-J. Becker, *L'Année 1914* (Paris, 2004), 22 and G. Heuré, 'Gustave Hervé, le tournant d'avant guerre', *Mil neuf cent: revue d'histoire intellectuelle* 19, 1 (2001), 87; see also M. B. Loughlin, 'Gustave Hervé's transition from socialism to National Socialism: continuity and ambivalence', *JCH*, 38, 4 (2003), 524–32.

out of necessity, both muted and secret. As Jean-Jacques Becker observed, 'there can be little doubt that, far from the reaction that had been anticipated, the circumstances surrounding the outbreak of war provoked a disintegration of the anti-patriotic and anti-war movements'.[15]

At the other end of the political spectrum the Catholic Church, which had fought a bitter rearguard action with the Republic for more than a generation, also rallied to the Union sacrée, as did the influential monarchist voice of the Action française. 'The only thing that matters', observed Charles Maurras, 'is victory; we will not win with internal dissension.'[16] This spirit of reconciliation and commitment to national defence was reciprocated by the government. On 1 August 1914 interior minister Louis Malvy decided, with the approval of the rest of the cabinet, not to arrest those whose names appeared on the *Carnet B*, a list of alleged revolutionaries who, it was anticipated, were planning to sabotage mobilisation.[17] In fact, mobilisation proceeded much more smoothly than expected. The army staff had expected more than 10 per cent of French conscripts to ignore the call to the colours; the actual number who failed to report was less than 1.5 per cent.[18] Public reaction to the mobilisation decree was complex. In Paris and other large cities, where the nationalist associations were strongest, there were numerous demonstrations of enthusiastic support. Outside these urban centres it was more often greeted with consternation followed by a determined resignation that would endure through the entire war.[19] The sinews of French resolve were knit together by the imperative need to defend France from the German invader.

But beneath the façade of 'sacred union' there remained fissures that threatened to overturn the edifice of national unity and undermine the war effort. France was a deeply divided society before 1914. Political and social tensions, the roots of which stretched back to the revolutionary era, were not forgotten with the outbreak of war. They were instead put on hold in widespread expectation of a short campaign. As the conflict continued, they re-emerged to shape public discourse over such crucial issues as war aims and peace strategies. While there was consensus over the need to defend France, the diverse constituencies making up the Union sacrée were in reality fighting for very different objectives. In general, the left of the political spectrum tended to understand the war as a defence of social democracy against a militarist Prussian autocracy. 'If France is attacked,' asked Socialist leader Jean Longuet, the grandson of

---

[15] Becker and Audoin-Rouzeau, *La France, la nation et la guerre*, 274 and 272; see also P. Buffotot, *Le Socialisme français et la guerre: du soldat-citoyen à l'armée professionnelle, 1871–1998* (Paris, 1999), 73–87 and N. Roussellier, 'Le "Gouvernement de guerre" et les socialistes' in R. Ducoulombier (ed.), *Les Socialistes dans l'Europe en guerre: réseaux, parcours, experiences, 1914–1918* (Paris, 2010), 33–44.
[16] S. Berstein and M. Winock, *La République recommencée* (Paris, 2004), 16–20.
[17] J.-J. Becker, *Le Carnet B: les pouvoirs publics et l'antimilitarisme avant la guerre de 1914* (Paris, 1973).
[18] P. Boulanger, *La France devant la conscription, 1914–1922* (Paris, 2001), 170–5.
[19] Becker, *1914*, esp. 573–90.

Karl Marx, on 3 August 1914, 'how could we Socialists not be the first to defend the France of the Revolution and of Democracy, the France of the Encyclopaedia, of Pressensé and of Jaurès?'[20] This justification for defending France was combined, on a more abstract level, with the conviction that the war demonstrated the need to transform international relations. Péguy expressed this conviction on the day the war broke out: 'We soldiers of the Republic leave for the front to fight for general disarmament and an end to all wars.'[21] Socialist support for the war effort was not an endorsement of the traditional alliance politics upon which French foreign policy was based. It was instead a reconciliation of national defence with the politics of internationalism.

On the right, conversely, the war tended to be understood in terms of a struggle to preserve traditional aspects of French life that included family, the soil of France, the army and the Catholic Church. The coming of war was more often interpreted as proof that the pacifist theorising of the internationalist movement was dangerous nonsense. 'For militants on the right,' Jean-Baptiste Duroselle observed, '... the France of Joan of Arc ranged itself quite naturally not only against the German Hun, but also the "chimeras" of "internationalism".'[22] In this conception, the war was not a crusade for democracy but instead a long-foreseen clash between France and her traditional enemy. Although its scale and virulence transformed it into an existential fight to the death, it remained a struggle between the French and German nations. This conservative construction of the nature and meaning of the war translated into traditional analyses of France's security requirements in the post-war era.

In practice the politics of the Union sacrée favoured a conservative vision of society in which social tensions and public agitation for greater social justice were set aside for the greater good of the nation in its moment of supreme danger. As Serge Berstein has argued, as the war evolved into a costly stalemate, the discourse of 'sacred union' increasingly came to represent 'the system of values and reference points of the right'.[23] This was certainly the case when it came to security policy. On 4 August 1914 a tight regime of censorship was established by the Viviani government which prohibited all public discussion of peace conditions. Censorship was intended to preserve consensus at home while projecting an image of unity and social cohesion abroad.[24] But an important practical effect of the politics of unity in general,

---

[20] *L'Humanité*, 3 Aug. 1914. The allusion is to Francis de Pressensé, a former editor of *Le Temps*, Dreyfusard and convert to socialism, who also died in 1914.
[21] A. Ducasse, J. Meyer and G. Perreux, *Vie et mort des Français, 1914–1918* (Paris, 1962), 26–7; on the left and the Union sacrée see also Becker, *1914*, 425–36 and Becker and Audoin-Rouzeau, *La France, la nation et la guerre*, 276–8.
[22] Duroselle, *Grande Guerre*, 57; see also Becker, *1914*, 439–76.
[23] Berstein cited in Becker and Audoin-Rouzeau, *La France, la nation et la guerre*, 280; see also Becker, 'Union sacrée et idéologie bourgeoise'.
[24] O. Forcade, 'La Censure et l'opinion publique française face à l'Allemagne en 1914–1918', unpublished paper delivered to the conference Burgfriede und Union sacrée at the University

and censorship in particular, was to ensure that the balance-of-power approach to security favoured by the government remained unchallenged both in the public sphere and in parliamentary debate. Only after severe cracks began to appear in the Union sacrée in mid-1917 was the government's security policy subjected to sustained challenge – and even then this challenge was mounted only in secret sessions of parliament.

If the rhetoric of the Union sacrée was most pervasive among parliamentarians, it was among this group that it was most tenuous in practice.[25] Premier Viviani responded to the exigencies of war on 4 August 1914 with a slight modification of his cabinet, the chief result of which was to augment the number of the Radicals in government. As the military situation worsened in the ensuing weeks Viviani came under increased pressure to form a new cabinet that reflected the Union sacrée. He yielded grudgingly to this pressure on 26 August. The resulting 'government of national unity' included stalwarts from the political centre such as Alexandre Millerand (as minister of war), Théophile Delcassé (foreign affairs), Alexandre Ribot (finance) and Aristide Briand (justice) but also, for the first time, Socialists Jules Guesde (minister without portfolio) and Marcel Sembat (public works).[26] Predictably, Guesde and Sembat were kept away from the making of security policy. The key ministries of war, finance and foreign affairs went to politicians with strong nationalist credentials who had backed the Three Year Law. The committed internationalism of both Socialist ministers thus played no role in key government debates over war aims and peace conditions.

Political opposition to the government was muted in both the chamber and the senate during the first half of the war. A parliamentary recess was declared as German troops approached Paris and the government moved temporarily to Bordeaux. When the two assemblies reconvened in the capital the following December, it was to reaffirm the politics of national union and to give unanimous approval to the government's proposed budget for 1915. For many months thereafter, patriotic self-censorship all but precluded open attacks on government policy in parliament. Opposition manifested itself chiefly in intrigue in the corridors of the two assemblies, directed most often against war minister Millerand (whose unyielding support for commander-in-chief Joffre was deeply unpopular with many parliamentarians) and Delcassé (who was widely considered a spent force at the Quai d'Orsay). The most significant pressure on the government was exercised through the parliamentary commissions. It was through the work of these commissions, which met and

---

of Stuttgart, 17 June 2007; see also O. Forcade, 'La Censure politique en France pendant la Grande Guerre', thèse de doctorat, Université de Paris X (Nanterre), 3 vols., 1999, vol. I, esp. 94–109; F. Bock, *Parlementarisme de guerre* (Paris, 2002), 78–80 and 121–2.

[25] J.-M. Mayeur, *La Vie politique sous la Troisième République* (Paris, 1984), 234–7.

[26] Bock, *Parlementarisme de guerre*, 75–8; Duroselle, *Grande Guerre*, 50–9 and 129–37; G. (and E.) Bonnefous, *Histoire politique de la Troisième République*, vol. II: *La Grande Guerre* (Paris, 1957), 11–72.

deliberated in secret, that parliament gradually asserted its authority in the prosecution of the war. The key organs in this process were the army and finance commissions, and the central issues at stake were armaments and munitions production and civil–military relations. The foreign affairs commissions were less influential. And government planning for security after the war proceeded largely independently of direct parliamentary influence.[27] The overriding need to preserve the Union sacrée meant that political leadership avoided substantive discussion of war aims in the public sphere.[28]

It was foreign affairs, however, that occasioned the first of four wartime ministerial crises and brought down the Viviani government. The pretext was the entry of Bulgaria into the war on the side of the Central Powers on 22 September 1915. The real cause of the crisis was growing evidence of incapacity on the part of the foreign minister and the nervous exhaustion of the prime minister. Briand, Poincaré and even Viviani became convinced that Delcassé was no longer capable of managing the foreign ministry. He sometimes appeared disoriented in cabinet meetings, would lose his train of thought in the midst of policy discussions and, after his son was captured by the Germans, was prone to outbursts of uncontrolled sobbing.[29] Delcassé resigned on 13 October. Viviani, meanwhile, was fatigued, weakened by illness and under constant siege from the critics of Millerand and Joffre in the press, in parliament and even within his cabinet. He resigned on 29 October on the understanding that Poincaré would replace him with Briand.[30]

Briand lasted longer than any other wartime premier, becoming head of government on 29 October 1915 and staying on until 17 March 1917. He took the foreign minister's portfolio along with the premiership and appointed a succession of army generals (Joseph Gallieni, Pierre Roques and Louis-Hubert Lyautey) as war ministers. Briand's first cabinet included five 'ministers of state', senior political figures intended to embody the Union sacrée, ranging from Guesde and the arch anti-clerical Émile Combes to the Catholic monarchist Denys Cochin. His tenure as premier included the national agony of Verdun, the earliest signs of a wavering of public resolve in the autumn of 1916 and the first secret sessions of parliament convened to debate the prosecution of the war. Briand was most effective in his role as foreign minister (in which capacity he depended heavily on the energy and abilities of his *chef de cabinet* Philippe Berthelot). It was under Briand that a full-blown post-war security programme was first hammered out within the Quai d'Orsay and approved by cabinet in January 1917. Pressure from parliament forced Briand to change his cabinet in December 1916. Guesde and Sembat left the

[27] Bock, *Parlementarisme de guerre*, 121–50.
[28] D. Stevenson, *The First World War and International Politics* (Oxford, 1988), 113.
[29] Poincaré, *L'Invasion*, 261–4; Duroselle, *Grande Guerre*, 133 and 139; and Keiger, *Poincaré*, 219–20.
[30] Duroselle, *Grande Guerre*, 132–41; Mayeur, *Vie politique*, 239–41.

government, leaving reformist Albert Thomas (minister of armaments) as the only Socialist in the cabinet. The system of ministers of state was abandoned and Briand experimented with the creation of a restricted war cabinet that included the ministers of war, foreign affairs, the *marine*, finance and armaments. The French model was less successful than its British counterpart, however, because it did not have power of decision and could only make policy recommendations to the full cabinet.[31]

Briand's second government eventually collapsed in mid-March 1917 amid the storms created by setbacks in the Near East, open conflict between war minister Lyautey and parliament and, most importantly, the fall of the Tsar and the advent of a provisional government in Russia. The fall of Briand ushered in a period of political crisis for France that lasted through to the end of 1917. These months also witnessed the transformation of the international landscape, first by the entry of the United States into the war and then by the Bolshevik revolution in Russia. The international context intruded increasingly on calculations in Paris as the war dragged on and France's status as a world power ebbed away in the bloodletting on the western front.

Through to the spring of 1917 all planning for post-war security was predicated on the assumption of victory. And the nature of the war dictated that this victory must be total. The duration and intensity of the conflict undermined prospects for a negotiated peace. These prospects were never great to begin with because the political objectives of the belligerents remained fundamentally incompatible. The major factor in this equation was German military success in the west in the opening phase of the war.[32] By late autumn 1914 Germany was in possession of nearly all of Belgium as well as a large swathe of France's industrial heartland concentrated in the ten provinces closest to its north-eastern frontier. This gave the Reich a commanding position in the event of peace negotiations. It also forced a succession of French governments to submit to a long and costly war in which absolute victory was the only acceptable outcome. The result was sacrifice on a hitherto unimagined scale at Verdun, on the Somme and along the Chemin des Dames.[33]

One of the important early conclusions drawn from the military situation was a confirmation of the importance for France of the alliance with Russia. In mid-August 1914 the Imperial Russian army committed seventy-four divisions to an ambitious dual offensive against Germany and Austria-Hungary. These

---

[31] This paragraph is drawn from Mayeur, *Vie politique*, 239–43; Bock, *Parlementarisme de guerre*, 177–210 and 243–65; Duroselle, *Grande Guerre*, 147–90; and G. Suarez, *Briand: sa vie, son oeuvre, avec son journal et de nombreux documents inédits*, 6 vols. (Paris, 1938–52), vol. III: *Le Pilote dans la tourmente, 1914–1916* (Paris, 1939).

[32] Excellent discussions of the course and consequences of the war on the western front are H. Strachan, *The First World War*, vol. I: *To Arms* (Oxford, 2001), 208–80 and D. Stevenson, *Cataclysm: The First World War as Political Tragedy* (New York, 2004), 37–50 and 75–85.

[33] On this issue see esp. Doughty, *Pyrrhic Victory*.

operations achieved important initial successes, compelling the German high command to shift two army corps to the eastern front. This provided much-needed relief for the French in the west at a crucial stage in the war of movement. By the end of 1914, despite defeat at Tannenberg, Russian forces had overrun large swathes of Habsburg territory and were tying down more than one-third of Germany's armed forces in the eastern theatre.[34] If victory on the Marne was publicly attributed to the valour of France's army, it was clear that operations on the eastern front were important to the Entente's prospects for victory. Russia was crucial to the strategic conception developed by French leaders in late 1914. The aim was to force the Central Powers to disperse their resources in a multifront war to prevent Germany from massing overwhelming force against France. This would provide the Entente with time to muster its superior war potential in preparation for decisive operations. Commander-in-chief Joffre envisaged a series of Franco-British attacks in the west that would preoccupy the German army so that the Russians could 'finish the business' with a decisive offensive in the east. He held to this strategy well into 1916.[35] 'The military and political importance of our Russian ally can never again be called into question,' observed Delcassé in a February 1915 note to Paul Cambon in London.[36] Poincaré, as we have seen, described the Russian alliance as the 'salvation' of the French war effort.[37]

Yet another consequence of the military campaign was an intensification of the ideological character of the conflict. In its advance through Belgium and northern France, the German army murdered more than 6,400 civilians and destroyed thousands of public and private buildings in retribution for largely imagined partisan operations. Many more civilians were used as human shields. These operations, in conjunction with the use of Zeppelin airships to bomb civilian targets, were vividly portrayed in Allied propaganda and served to reinforce existing representations of the war as a defence of civilisation from the evils of Prussian militarism. Parliamentary commissions appointed to investigate and document these atrocities published dozens of reports replete with the testimony of hundreds of witnesses. The image of the German soldier that emerged to dominate the French imagination for the duration of the war was that of a murderous brute. This representation should not be dismissed as mere propaganda and thus of little real importance to policy making. It was accepted widely and functioned as automatic frame of reference for both popular and elite opinion. It played a central role in shaping both official and public responses to the German question well into the post-war period.[38]

---

[34] N. Stone, *The Eastern Front, 1914–1917*, 2nd edn (London, 1998), 44–143; Strachan, *To Arms*, 316–35, 347–73; and Stevenson, *Cataclysm*, 51–66, 75–8.
[35] Doughty, *Pyrrhic Victory*, 107–12 (quote p. 112) and 251–3.
[36] MAE, *Série Guerre (1914–1918)*, vol. 86, Delcassé to Cambon, 7 Feb. 1915.
[37] Poincaré, *L'Invasion*, 154.
[38] J. Horne and A. Kramer, *German Atrocities, 1914: A History of Denial* (New Haven, 2001); Audoin-Rouzeau and Becker, *14–18*, 142–8.

A final important effect of the nature and course of the conflict was its stark affirmation of the elemental importance of demography, access to raw materials and industrial and financial power to success on the battlefield and thus to the post-war strategic balance. The insatiable demands of modern industrial war only heightened existing anxieties concerning the Franco-German balance of power and reinforced calls for a post-war order that would alleviate Germany's industrial and demographic superiority over France. 'The first lesson we must draw from our experience in this war', asserted a general staff study in 1916, 'is that the Germany of 1871 is an industrial and military monstrosity alongside which France cannot continue to exist.' France's 'first objective' must be 'to put an end to this baleful project by liberating the industrial regions of the Rhine placed under the Prussian yoke in 1815'. This would allow for an 'effective balance' which alone could ensure a stable and lasting peace in Europe.[39]

II

The foreign policies of other major powers constituted important structural factors with which French policy elites had to contend in all post-war planning. This familiar challenge was made all the more difficult by the revolutionary character of the world war. By mid-1916 the financial and industrial costs of the conflict had placed France in a position of almost abject economic dependence, not only on its British ally but also on the neutral United States. This state of affairs would have far-reaching consequences for the development of post-war security conceptions.

A central issue in the development of French policy was the impossibility of achieving a mutually satisfactory settlement with Germany. For most of the war, even the most moderate formulation of official German aims envisioned crippling France through annexations and the imposition of a heavy indemnity.[40] The fundamental objective was the permanent destruction of France's Great Power status and an end to its ability to threaten Germany's western frontier. The chief targets for annexation were the iron-ore deposits and heavy concentrations of steel mills in the Briey–Longwy basin. Belgium would become a German satellite, losing its economic independence along with control over foreign policy. There were also plans for a permanent German military presence in Flanders as well as a network of bases in the Mediterranean

---

[39] SHD-DAT, 4N 92-1, *État-major du Maréchal Foch*, 'Traité de paix: considérations préliminaires', n.d. but certainly Aug.–Sept. 1916. This handwritten document was included in a dossier on the Rhineland compiled by Foch's staff in Nov. 1918.

[40] The discussion that follows is drawn from F. Fischer, *Germany's Aims in the First World War* (London, 1967); L. L. Farrar, *The Short War Illusion: German Policy, Strategy and Domestic Affairs* (Santa Barbara, 1973); and Stevenson, *International Politics*, 89–106. See also Stevenson, *Cataclysm*, 129–36 and G.-H. Soutou, *L'Or et le sang: les buts de guerre économiques de la Première Guerre mondiale* (Paris, 1989), chapters 1–3, 11, 14–16.

and the Atlantic. In economic terms German planning envisaged the construction of a *Mitteleuropa* that would consolidate the Reich's commercial domination over central Europe and impose a favourable trading regime on France and the low countries.[41] Projects for territorial annexation, in particular, enjoyed massive support within German civil society and were prominent in public discourse concerning war aims in the Reich. In early December 1915 all of the non-Socialist parties in the Reichstag issued a declaration stipulating that 'Germany's military, economic, financial and political interests must be permanently guaranteed to their full extent and by all means, including the necessary territorial acquisitions'. This level of public support for ambitious war aims convinced German policy elites that a compromise settlement would endanger the Reich's internal stability.[42]

All of this virtually precluded substantive negotiations. There was little hope for an end to the fighting short of decisive victory for one side. German aims were more flexible in eastern Europe, where it was hoped that Russia could be persuaded to conclude a separate peace with the offer of concessions over the fate of Poland and the Baltic states. The Central Powers made a disingenuous public offer to negotiate on 12 December 1916. This 'Peace Note' was greeted with hostility by the Allies. The growing authority of the military in Germany over the course of the war only compounded this situation. Under the influence of Hindenburg and Ludendorff, German war aims became more ambitious and less flexible. There was some benefit in this development from the French perspective. In late 1916 and early 1917 the Oberste Heeresleitung (high command) rode roughshod over Chancellor Bethmann Hollweg and forced through a decision to wage unrestricted submarine warfare.[43] This decision was crucial in facilitating the entry of the United States into the war and, ultimately, victory for the Entente.

The war aims of the other Central Powers had less impact on the evolution of France's European security policy. Austro-Hungarian ambitions were focused on the Balkans and on Poland. In January 1916 the joint cabinet of the Habsburg Empire agreed on a programme that included annexing at least half of Serbia (and if possible more) as well as the coastline of Montenegro. Designs for Poland centred on uniting the Russian and Austrian regions of that partitioned state into one semi-autonomous kingdom under Habsburg sovereignty.[44] Both sets of aims were directed against Russian power. Neither

[41] See esp. Soutou, *L'Or et le sang*, 15–107, 569–708.
[42] Stevenson, *International Politics*, 101, quoting Fischer, *Germany's Aims*, 177; all belligerents devoted extensive resources to monitoring the war aims of their enemies.
[43] H. Herwig, 'Total Rhetoric, Limited War: Germany's U-Boat Campaign' in R. Chickering and S. Förster (eds.), *Great War, Total War: Combat and Mobilisation on the Western Front, 1914–1918* (Cambridge, 2000), 192–7.
[44] R. W. Kapp, 'Divided loyalties: the German Reich and Austria-Hungary in Austro-German discussions of war aims', *Central European History*, 17, 3 (1984), 120–39; Stevenson, *International Politics*, 95–100.

conflicted with vital French interests. This explains why French policy makers were tempted by the possibility of a separate peace settlement with Austria-Hungary during the war. The need to maintain the alliance with Russia was the chief obstacle to this strategy. The policy objectives of Bulgaria and the Ottoman Empire impinged even less on French security in Europe. Bulgaria aimed chiefly at regaining the territory lost to Romania, Greece and especially Serbia in the Second Balkan War.[45] Although the war aims of Ottoman Turkey were of central importance to French imperial power, they affected policy in Europe only indirectly. Before the war's outbreak there had been general consensus among the Great Powers that the continued existence of the Ottoman Empire was preferable to any alternative scenario. Almost as soon as the Turks entered the war, however, the Entente states began planning to divide up Ottoman territory.[46] The effect on French planning for security in Europe was limited.

Of France's allies, Russia played the most prominent role in shaping postwar security planning during the early stages of the war. The Tsarist government defined its objectives soon after the fighting began and took the lead in initiating discussion of war aims among the Entente states. It initiated the 5 September 'Pact of London' in which Russia, France and Britain committed themselves not to seek a separate peace and to consult and agree on peace conditions before undertaking any negotiations with the enemy. Russia remained loyal to this commitment despite being the chief target of German and Austrian efforts to divide the Entente. Even more than the German leadership, the Tsarist government feared that a compromise peace would threaten its legitimacy and perhaps even its longer-term viability.[47]

The political aims and negotiating tactics of the Tsarist regime were essentially those of the eighteenth century. Insisting that 'when the time comes the conditions of peace must be *dictated* to Germany and Austria-Hungary', the Russian government put together a shopping list of territorial annexations that exceeded even that of Germany.[48] Its chief objectives lay in Poland and the Dardanelles Straits. On 25 September Russian foreign minister Sergei Sazonov presented a programme of war aims to the French and British. Sazonov's 'Thirteen Points' envisaged rolling back the western frontiers of the German and Habsburg empires by detaching Galicia from Austria-Hungary and Posen, southern Silesia and territory in eastern Prussia around the Niemen river delta from Germany. The German Reich, in the initial Russian conception, would

---

[45] Stevenson, *International Politics*, 58–61.
[46] C. Andrew and A. S. Kanya-Forstner, *France Overseas: The Great War and the Climax of French Imperial Expansion* (London, 1981), 64–77 and 87–97; M. Kent (ed.), *The Great Powers and the End of the Ottoman Empire* (London, 1984), esp. 52–75, 141–205.
[47] See generally C. J. Smith, *The Russian Struggle for Power: A Study of Russian Foreign Policy during the First World War* (New York, 1956); A. Dallin (ed.), *Russian Diplomacy and Eastern Europe, 1914–1917* (New York, 1963).
[48] MAE, *Série A Paix*, vol. 54, Paléologue to Delcassé, 15 Nov. 1914.

remain united but would lose substantial territory in the east and the west. Austria-Hungary would lose its Polish, Ukrainian and South Slav subjects. Both states would be forced to pay heavy indemnities.[49] Petrograd had also issued a proclamation calling for the Polish people to be 'united under the sceptre of the Russian Emperor'. The new Polish entity would receive the territories lost to Germany and Austria-Hungary and was promised 'self-government' (although in practice the Tsarist government intended to maintain control of its foreign policy, public finance and armed forces).[50]

Russian demands for Ottoman territory were equally ambitious. Turkey's entry into the war presented an opportunity to assert Russia's strategic interests in the region. For centuries Russian elites had nurtured aspirations to gain control of both Constantinople and the Dardanelles. The former was a religious centre for the Orthodox faith while the latter was a vital year-round artery for Russian commerce that could open the way for the projection of Russian power into the Mediterranean basin.[51] A series of demands made by the Tsar, Sazonov and other Russian ministers in late 1914 and early 1915 eventually included the annexation of Constantinople, the European coastline of the Dardanelles, the coastline of the Bosphorus Sea in Asia Minor and part of Armenia.[52] The Tsarist government maintained and even expanded its war aims despite a series of military catastrophes that cast serious doubt on its ability to stay in the war.

Russia's ambitious set of demands, when combined with the familiar antipathy for Tsarist autocracy on the centre-left and left of French politics, posed a potential problem for the Viviani government. The demand for Constantinople and the Straits violated principles of national self-determination that had acquired ever-greater legitimacy in nineteenth-century Europe. It also threatened long-standing French political and commercial interests in the region. Russian plans for Poland were another source of tension given the long tradition of sympathy for Polish independence among French elites. Support for this cause was amplified by the activities of a well-organised and voluble network of émigré Polish nationalists. Among those members of the French political elite who openly expressed support for the cause of Poland were

---

[49] W. A. Lenzi, 'Who composed Sazonov's "Thirteen Points"? A re-examination of Russia's war aims of 1914', *AHR*, 88, 2 (1983), 347–57; see also Stevenson, *Cataclysm*, 111–12.
[50] R. Bobroff, 'Devolution in wartime: Sergei D. Sazonov and the future of Poland, 1910–1916', *IHR*, 22, 3 (2000), 511–19.
[51] R. Bobroff, *Roads to Glory: Late Imperial Russia and the Turkish Straits* (London, 2006), 116–48; A. Bodger, 'Russia and the End of the Ottoman Empire' in Kent (ed.), *Great Powers and the End of the Ottoman Empire*, 76–110.
[52] MAE, *Série A*, vol. 54, Paléologue to Delcassé, 15, 16 and 22 Nov. 1914 and 6 Feb. 1915; MAE, PA-AP 133, *Papiers Maurice Paléologue*, vol. 2, Paléologue to Delcassé, 4, 5 Mar. 1915 and Paléologue to Poincaré, 16 Apr. 1915. See also M. A. Reynolds, *Shattering Empires: The Clash and Collapse of the Ottoman and Russian Empires, 1908–1918* (Cambridge, 2011), 107–65; Bodger, 'Russia', 96–101; and Stevenson, *Cataclysm*, 112–13.

Léon Bourgeois, Georges Clemenceau, André Tardieu, Gabriel Hanotaux, Stephen Pichon and Marcel Sembat.[53]

The Tsarist government insisted, however, that Poland was a matter of Russian internal policy. It warned that French interference over this issue could jeopardise the alliance. This did not prevent Socialist deputies from raising the question openly in the chamber. But it did impose an uncomfortable reticence on the French government. Socialist minister for munitions, Albert Thomas, commented ruefully on 'this Polish question which has troubled Franco-Russian relations for so long' during a mission to Petrograd in April 1916. He regretted that the 'violent hostility' manifested by the Russians at the mere mention of Poland meant that 'it is necessary to be extremely prudent even in the affirmation of one's own principles'. The result was an unpleasant need to choose between sympathy for Poland and the requirements of the French war effort. 'It will be very difficult', Thomas concluded, 'to conciliate our traditional policy with the vital interests of our country.'[54] Polish aspirations, support for which Thomas interestingly characterised as France's 'traditional policy', were subordinated to the exigencies of the military alliance with Russia.

There were also substantial financial costs to maintaining the alliance. The pre-war flow of French credits to Russia continued and even accelerated during the war. But the nature of this lending changed from private investment before the war to government loans during the conflict. By the end of the war the Russian debt to France stood at 3.53 billion francs.[55] Moreover, because the war industries of both Britain and France were taken up almost entirely by the urgent requirements of their own war efforts, Russia was forced to place orders for armaments and munitions in the United States. This posed a problem because Petrograd had limited access to the American money market. This was resolved by using British and French credit. During the period of American neutrality more than 70 per cent of British and French borrowing from the United States went towards financing Russian purchases. France contracted a debt of over $460 million in Russia's name.[56]

---

[53] P. Wandycz, *France and her Eastern Allies, 1919–1925: French–Czechoslovak–Polish Relations from the Paris Peace Conference to Locarno* (Minneapolis, 1962), 7–8.

[54] France, Archives nationales (hereafter AN), 94 AP 174, *Archives Albert Thomas*, dr. 1, undated handwritten note composed upon Thomas' return from Russia in 1916. Thomas also noted that the dilemma facing French policy was 'all the greater because the Poles expect, even demand, a great deal from us'. See also D. Stevenson, *French War Aims against Germany, 1914–1919* (Oxford, 1982), 26–32 and K. Hovi, *Cordon Sanitaire or Barrière de l'Est? The Emergence of the New French European Alliance Policy, 1917–1919* (Turku, 1975), 34–6 and 42–4.

[55] L.-C. Petit, *Histoire des finances extérieures de la France pendant la guerre (1914–1919)* (Paris, 1929), 163–6; Martin Horn puts the figure at 3.225 billion francs in *Britain, France and the Financing of the First World War* (Montreal, 2002), 183.

[56] See the detailed summary in Strachan, *To Arms*, 956–7.

Russia's participation in the war therefore came at considerable political and financial cost for France. But its value as a military ally was undeniable. Russia mobilised between 14 and 15.5 million troops during the war, and by 1916 had suffered nearly 5.5 million casualties.[57] The alliance was of considerable political value as well. The Tsarist government expressed a willingness to underwrite whatever settlement the French deemed desirable in western Europe. This, in addition to the dozens of German divisions tied down on the eastern front, explains the crucial importance attached by successive French governments to keeping Russia in the war.[58]

The strategic importance of Britain, its empire and dominions to France increased steadily over the course of the conflict. The British Expeditionary Force had played a crucial role in halting German attempts to turn the Allied right flank in autumn 1914. Thereafter, the number of British troops committed to the continent grew steadily: to 907,000 in late 1915; to 1,379,000 in October 1916; to a peak of 1,801,000 in October 1917. Britain's contribution was particularly important as the size of the French army in the field diminished from a maximum of 2,234,000 in 1916 to 1,888,000 in 1917.[59] Just as important was the contribution of British sea power. The Royal Navy assumed near-total responsibility for containing the German 'high seas fleet', for protecting Allied commerce and for imposing an increasingly effective naval blockade on the Central Powers. France was dependent on British merchant shipping for nearly half of the imports it required to maintain its war industry and feed its population. In addition, German occupation of its major coalfields made France vitally dependent on steady deliveries of British coal.[60] Finally, Britain's role as the banker of the Entente was vital to the French war effort. The Allies were more effective than their adversaries at coordinating their financial resources and externalising their debt primarily because of Britain's position as the world's leading creditor. France's modest pre-war trade surplus with Britain quickly evaporated and, by 1915, became a deficit of nearly 3 billion francs. By late 1916 the French government had borrowed 7.8 billion francs from Britain and was utterly dependent on British treasury support for its purchases in the United States. At the same time Britain was financing the Russian war effort to the tune of £24 million per month.[61] All of this made the alliance with Britain indispensable to France's survival.

---

[57] A. Wildman, *The End of the Imperial Russian Army*, vol. I: *The Old Army and the Soldiers' Revolt (March–April 1917)* (Princeton, 1980), 82–96.
[58] See, among others, Duroselle, *Grande Guerre*, 223–8.
[59] All figures cited from Stevenson, *Cataclysm*, 160–6.
[60] K. Neilson, 'Reinforcements and Supplies from Overseas: The British Strategic Sealift in the First World War' in G. Kennedy (ed.), *The Merchant Marine in International Affairs, 1850–1950* (London, 2000), 31–58; E. Greenhalgh, *Victory through Coalition: Britain and France during the First World War* (Cambridge, 2005), 114–19; W. Philpott, *Anglo-French Relations and Strategy, 1914–18* (London, 1996), 18–94; Stevenson, *Cataclysm*, 200.
[61] Horn, *Financing*, 117–41; Duroselle, *Grande Guerre*, 164; Strachan, *To Arms*, 962–71.

A continuation of the Franco-British wartime entente was therefore central to every plan for post-war security conceived by French elites during and after the Great War. But neither Herbert Asquith's government nor its successor under David Lloyd George fashioned a detailed programme of war aims. In general terms British policy makers were less focused on Europe and less committed to transforming the continental balance of power than were their Russian and French counterparts. There was consensus in London that German naval power must be destroyed so that it could no longer pose a threat to Britain's dominions, its colonies and its commerce. But there was little enthusiasm among either policy elites or the British public for far-reaching territorial readjustments in Europe.[62]

The political objectives of France's other European allies – Italy, Belgium, Romania, Serbia and Montenegro – were not as important to calculations in Paris. Italy entered the war after it had been promised Allied support for an imposing list of territorial demands whose cumulative aim was to establish Italian dominance over both sides of the Adriatic Sea and bolster its status as a great power.[63] Nearly all of its claims were approved by the Allies in the secret Treaty of London of April 1915. This agreement, which envisaged Italian annexation of 250,000 ethnic German speakers in the north and 700,000 Slavs in the south, was yet another throwback to an earlier era of Great Power exchanges of territory and peoples.[64] While Italy did manage to tie down a credible number of mainly Austro-Hungarian divisions, it was also a heavy drain on Allied finances.[65]

Belgium was more important. The liberation of that country was a fundamental French war aim from the outset. Its position as a natural corridor for invasion made this an issue of major strategic importance. The Belgian government spent most of the war in exile in Normandy and was in a position of chronic dependence on France and Britain. A significant current of thought within both the army staff and foreign ministry envisaged bringing Belgium firmly within the political and economic orbit of France. Belgium's own policy objectives – which included annexation of the Duchy of Luxembourg – had only limited impact on long-term thinking about post-war security in Paris.

---

[62] D. French, *British Strategy and War Aims, 1914–1916* (London, 1986); V. Rothwell, *British War Aims and Peace Diplomacy, 1914–1918* (Oxford, 1971); Stevenson, *International Politics*, 106–13.

[63] J. Whittam, 'War Aims and Strategy: The Italian Government and High Command' in B. Hunt and A. Preston (eds.), *War Aims and Strategic Policy in the Great War, 1914–1918* (London, 1977), 82–104.

[64] On this point see esp. Stevenson, *International Politics*, 51–2; also R. J. B. Bosworth, *Italy and the Approach of the First World War* (London, 1983), 121–41; for the text of the 1915 Treaty of London see HMSO, Command Paper (Cmd.) 671, Miscellaneous No. 7, 2–7 (London, 1920).

[65] Strachan, *To Arms*, 961–2; P. Milza, 'Les Relations financières franco-italiennes pendant le premier conflit mondial' in P. Guillen (ed.), *La France et l'Italie pendant la première guerre mondiale* (Grenoble, 1976), 306–15.

The same was true to an even greater extent when it came to Romania, Serbia and Montenegro. All three were considered desirable allies during the war, and their relations with France remained close throughout the period covered in this study. Yet, particularly after Romania's swift military collapse in the autumn of 1916, the future of all three states depended on the fortunes of the Entente. Their ability to influence French planning was strictly limited.

The neutral country with the greatest potential to influence French policy was unquestionably the United States. As the war evolved into a test of economic power and societal resolve, American finance, raw materials, foodstuffs and steel production became increasingly vital to the French war effort.[66] American neutrality benefited the Allies as they were better able both to finance their purchases in the USA and to transport them to Europe. Between 1914 and 1916 US trade with the Entente quadrupled in value while that with the Central Powers fell to approximately 1 per cent of its pre-war levels.[67] By the end of the war France was in a relationship of economic dependence on American power that approached, though never equalled, its dependence on Britain. Purchases in the USA threatened to bankrupt the French treasury, rising from 795 million francs in 1914, to 6.16 billion in 1916 and 9.77 billion in 1917.[68] The result was a severe balance of payments crisis and a trade deficit that ballooned from 1.6 billion francs in 1914 to 21.5 billion in 1917.[69] To finance these purchases the French borrowed heavily both in London and New York. The annual value of American loans to France increased from 510,000 francs in 1914 to 7.5 billion in 1917.[70] In early 1917 Allied finances reached breaking point as Britain's ability to secure loans using its gold reserves and dollar holdings was nearly exhausted. When Germany declared unrestricted submarine warfare in late February, the end of the Entente's purchasing power in the USA was only weeks away.[71]

The German decision thus saved France and its allies from grave difficulties. There would have been no sudden collapse in the Allied war effort. Nor, however, would there have been a First World War equivalent of the American Lend-Lease programme of 1940–1. By late 1916 relations between the USA and the Entente were showing increased strain. President Woodrow Wilson's repeated attempts to mediate a compromise settlement were resented in policy-making circles in Paris. The same was true of his call for a new world order. At the heart of Wilson's world-view was a faith in democratisation and national self-determination, a commitment to freedom of the seas and to the construction of an international organisation designed to prevent future wars.

[66] Y. H. Nouailhat, *France et les États-Unis: août 1914–avril 1917* (Paris, 1979), 85–123.
[67] Stevenson, *International Politics*, 67.
[68] Petit, *Finances extérieures*, 693 and 695; Horn, *Financing*, 86 and 117–65.
[69] Duroselle, *Grande Guerre*, 163; Petit, *Finances extérieures*, 28, 33–45.
[70] Duroselle, *Grande Guerre*, 164; Nouailhat, *France et les États-Unis*, 266–95.
[71] Strachan, *To Arms*, 975 and, more generally, Horn, *Financing*, 142–65.

His international vision was structured around a fundamental opposition between democracy and the rule of law, on the one hand, and militarism and the dominance of force, on the other.[72]

Over the course of the war, the US president became convinced that it was America's special mission to intervene in the conflict to establish a new moral and political basis for international relations. The creation of a 'League of Nations' was an openly declared objective of American policy from May 1916. Wilson's chief advisers, Treasury Secretary William McAdoo, Secretary of State Robert Lansing and his personal emissary Colonel Edward House, were all broadly sympathetic to the Allied cause. All agreed with his conviction that the USA had a responsibility to act as an 'influence for good'.[73] This sense of mission was bound up with the more self-serving assumption that the amplification of American power, along with its extension further into the international sphere, was an inevitable precondition for progress towards a better international order.

In January 1917 Wilson called publicly for 'peace without victory' and argued that the traditional balance of power must be replaced by a 'community of power' based on democracy and a league of nations.[74] This was antithetical to the policy objectives of *all* of the belligerents. It implied that the ambitions of the European Great Powers must be contained by a new moral and political framework in which balance of power would be eradicated as a legitimate practice of statecraft. American policy in this way challenged the conceptual foundations of traditional European power politics.[75] In setting out his vision in ever-greater detail from mid-1916 onwards, Wilson established himself as a contending pole of attraction for all French advocates of an alternative to the balance of power – from juridical internationalists to reform-minded Socialists.

In sum, French security policy was formulated in an international environment in which the core aims of its chief adversary, Germany, threatened France's very existence as a significant European power. The policy objectives of its Russian ally, meanwhile, envisaged vast annexations that, if realised, would dismantle German power and provide the bases for security, and

---

[72] This interpretation of 'Wilsonianism' draws substantially on T. J. Knock, *To End all Wars: Woodrow Wilson and the Quest for a New World Order* (Princeton, 1992); R. Kennedy, *The Will to Believe: Woodrow Wilson, World War I, and America's Strategy for Peace and Security* (Kent, Ohio, 2009), 43–127; L. Ambrosius, *Wilsonianism: Woodrow Wilson and his Legacy in American Foreign Relations* (London, 2002), esp. 21–64; and J. Milton Cooper (ed.), *Reconsidering Woodrow Wilson: Progressivism, Internationalism, War and Peace* (Washington, D.C., 2008).
[73] E. R. May, *The World War and American Isolation, 1914–1917* (Cambridge, Mass., 1959), 153; see also R. W. Tucker, *Woodrow Wilson and the Great War: Reconsidering America's Neutrality, 1914–1917* (Charlottesville, 2007), 54, 104–6.
[74] 'Peace Without Victory Address', in A. S. Link et al. (eds.), *The Papers of Woodrow Wilson*, 69 vols. (Princeton, 1966–94), XL, 533–9; Knock, *To End All Wars*, 111–13; and Kennedy, *Will to Believe*, 71–80 and 96–103.
[75] D. Stevenson, 'French war aims and the American challenge, 1914–1918', *HJ*, 22, 4 (1979), 877–94.

perhaps even hegemony, for France in Europe for many decades. Significantly, however, Russian war aims were dramatically out of step with the norm of democratic self-determination. British policy, although aiming at annexations outside Europe, was non-committal when it came to the question of transforming the balance of power through territorial revisions in western Europe. The policy of the Wilson administration in the USA, meanwhile, aimed at overthrowing existing practices of statecraft and introducing a new international order based on the ideals of democratic peace. This posed a major challenge to the traditional security practices of the French policy elite. Crucially, however, it was inspired by many of the same principles and assumptions of both socialist and juridical internationalism in France.

III

Traditional prescriptions for security, and in particular a transformation of the European strategic balance in France's favour, were at the heart of a series of ambitious and uncompromising prescriptions for France's security developed within the military. One of the earliest and most interesting of these was undertaken in late 1914 by two members of commander-in-chief Joffre's staff: Major Maurice Gamelin and Captain André Tardieu. Both would rise to the highest echelons of the French military and political hierarchies. Gamelin was a rising star in the general staff and Tardieu was already a prominent deputy and celebrated publicist.[76] The study they prepared together argued that a frontier on the Rhine was the most effective security guarantee for France. If this proved impossible, it recommended the construction of a *strategic glacis* that was to include most of the Saarland, Luxembourg and western Belgium in a defensive network aimed at containing Germany. A subsequent study, also prepared by Tardieu, advocated that France's military frontier be established on the Rhine with bridgeheads on the German side of the river.[77]

These preliminary reflections by Gamelin and Tardieu anticipated two further prescriptions for the post-war settlement prepared by the *deuxième* (intelligence) *bureau* of the Grand quartier général (GQG) in August and October 1916. The origin of both studies was a request from Poincaré to Joffre for an analysis of the military terms for an armistice with the Central Powers. This request came at a relatively favourable juncture of the war. The German offensive against Verdun had been halted, Franco-British coordination had improved in anticipation of another attack on the Somme and Romania was poised to enter the conflict on the side of the Entente. In a manifestation of its sense of its own authority within the policy establishment,

---

[76] A. Tardieu, *Avec Foch: août-novembre 1914* (Paris, 1939), 174–208.
[77] R.-A. Pichot-Duclos, *Réflexions sur ma vie militaire: au GQG de Joffre* (Grenoble, 1948), 360–1; see also R. Prete, 'French military war aims, 1914–1916', *HJ*, 28, 4 (1985), 890–1.

Joffre's staff went beyond its remit to produce two studies entitled 'Peace Conditions'.[78] Both expressed traditional currents of thought about the requirements of French security that would animate French policy into the mid-1920s. Both, moreover, were approved personally by Joffre and are reproduced in summary fashion in his memoirs.[79]

The August document envisaged restoring France as the strongest power in Europe. It called for the return of Alsace-Lorraine as well as the whole of the Saar coalfield in a re-establishment of the French frontier of 1790. Germany would also be deprived of the Left Bank of the Rhine – which would be occupied for thirty years while the German government paid off an indemnity. The provinces of this region could then choose either to maintain their independence or unite to form two states. In either case they would be 'politically separate' from the rest of Germany. France would dictate the size and character of their parliamentary assemblies and have the right of approval for their heads of state 'in perpetuity'. The area would further be tied to France by a permanent customs union. Luxembourg could choose to unite either with France or with Belgium. This strategy for the Rhineland, which resurrected the centuries-old quest for 'natural frontiers' in the east, offered the twin advantages of depriving Germany of a significant portion of its industrial strength while at the same time closing off this region as an avenue for invasion. Belgium, meanwhile, would end its neutrality and enter a full-blown military alliance and customs union with France in an arrangement characterised as 'intimate co-penetration'. Finally, Germany would be forced to pay a 'war indemnity' of 6 billion francs within a year, followed by 1.8 billion francs (estimated to be two-thirds of the annual German military budget for 1913–14) per year for thirty years without the possibility of early payment (which would shorten the period of military occupation).[80]

The second study, submitted the following October, advocated an even more ambitious programme centred around dismembering the Reich.[81] It began with the observation that France could never be secure as long as Germany was dominated by a large and populous Prussia. It aimed, therefore, to 're-establish the balance of power' by breaking the Reich up into nine separate states. Prussia's population would be reduced from 40 million to 11.5 million. It would also be deprived of the concentrations of heavy industry in Silesia and the Ruhr. The authors of the study further recommended that the Austro-Hungarian Empire be dismantled into its constituent nationalities, with significant territory going to pre-existing states allied to France such as

---

[78] The originals are in SHD-DAT, carton 14N 35-3, 'Armistice général' and 'Conditions de paix', both undated but certainly mid- to late Aug. 1916, and 'Conditions de paix – le statut de l'Allemagne', Oct. 1916. See also Stevenson, *French War Aims*, 42–4 and G.-H. Soutou, 'La France et les marches de l'est, 1914–1919', *RH*, 528 (1978), 355–6.
[79] J.-J. C. Joffre, *Mémoires du Maréchal Joffre, 1910–1917*, vol. II (Paris, 1932), 371–80.
[80] SHD-DAT, 14N 35-3, 'Conditions de paix', Aug. 1916.
[81] SHD-DAT, 14N 35, 'Conditions de paix – le statut de l'Allemagne', Oct. 1916.

Romania, Serbia, Italy and, inevitably, Russia. The question of an independent Polish state was also addressed. This was considered preferable to an extension of Russian domination over Poles from former German and Austria–Hungarian territory. It was acknowledged that such an outcome was unlikely, however, and the best that could be hoped for was probably that the Tsarist government would grant a measure of autonomy to a new Polish state within the Russian empire.[82]

At the heart of the military vision of post-war security were two key convictions. The first was the assumption of permanent Franco-German enmity. The second was the unshakeable belief that the only sure way to deal with this problem was to destroy German power. Both convictions rested on familiar constructions of both European history and the French and German national characters. 'History', it was asserted in the August document, had shown that the 'security of France ceased' the day that the small states on the Left Bank of the Rhine had lost their independence to an 'avid and hostile' Prussia. The discourse of France's 'natural and historic frontier' was then invoked to justify bringing this region back into the French orbit. This was combined with an expression of confidence in the 'attractive qualities' of France that made it likely that the peoples of the Left Bank of the Rhine would opt for eventual union:

> Let a generation pass. The settlement of the indemnity will assure us an occupation of 31 years. The customs union will bring about economic union. Time and our attractive qualities will do the rest and bring about moral union. As common historical memories reawaken, under the influence of economic need, of constant contact, but above all the example of French behaviour, the peoples [of the Rhineland] will ask to be reattached to us.[83]

The document cited Maurice Barrès in asserting the 'Latin' character of the Rhinelanders. To this was added 'a certain Catholic consciousness' that made attaching the Left Bank to France all the more attractive to French soldiers.[84]

These very particular constructions of history and national character were crafted to serve the overriding aim of overthrowing the existing balance of power in Europe. Annexation of the Saar coal basin would increase France's economic power at the expense of Germany. Similar logic underpinned the creation of the new Rhenish states as well as small independent states out of the remnants of the Hohenzollern and Habsburg Empires in east–central Europe. As the authors of the October note stressed, France's allies in eastern Europe would be major beneficiaries of these measures and thus share a common interest in upholding the status quo created by such a settlement.[85]

---

[82] Ibid.
[83] SHD-DAT, 14N 35, section entitled 'Observations justificatives' in 'Conditions de paix', Aug. 1916.
[84] Ibid.; see also W. McDougall, *France's Rhineland Diplomacy, 1914–1924: The Last Bid for a Balance of Power in Europe* (Princeton, 1978), 118.
[85] SHD-DAT, 14N 35, 'Conditions de paix – le statut de l'Allemagne', Oct. 1916.

Military professionals charged with considering the issue of post-war security had predictably little time for internationalist conceptions. It is nonetheless interesting to note that both general staff studies sought wider legitimacy for their prescriptions by couching them in the discourse of self-determination. This was particularly the case in the August document, which claimed 'fidelity with the principles of the French Revolution according to which peoples have the right to govern themselves'. In a rhetorical strategy aimed at pre-empting critics of traditional power politics both in France and elsewhere, the strategic benefit of transforming the balance of power was elided with the normative objective of 'liberty' for 'subjugated peoples'. Even the French army staff felt the need to pay lip service to the discourses of international legitimacy that were gaining momentum at the time. The same argument could be made concerning another discursive strategy that would reappear again and again in French official memoranda in the years to come: that of representing France as the 'guardian' of 'western' and 'European' security and the Rhineland as the 'frontier of liberty'.[86] The true inspiration of military prescriptions, however, were traditional calculations of the balance of power and national self-interest.

IV

Policy recommendations within the foreign ministry were based on a similar approach to national and international security. Alliance politics and the future strategic balance were at the centre of nearly all formulations of France's international position produced by French diplomats. Rivalry and resentment among the three senior officials at the ministry – Jules Cambon, Pierre de Margerie and Philippe Berthelot – at times led to bitter disagreements about specific issues. All three, however, held basically similar operating assumptions about the nature of international relations. They believed in the primacy of the balance of power and were strident advocates of strengthening the strategic position of France and its allies at the expense of Germany.

Berthelot advocated annexing a significant portion of the Rhineland along with the Grand Duchy of Luxembourg. His conception of post-war security at this stage is distilled in his assessment of Luxembourg's importance to European politics:

The rare combination of iron and coal [in Luxembourg] makes it a region of global strategic importance ... It is essential that France controls the entire basin ... [this] ... would put us in a position to surpass even the United States in this regard and would deprive Germany of one of its most important means of waging war ... One would have to have no understanding of the capital importance of economic and industrial factors for the future position of France to abandon Luxembourg to Belgium.[87]

[86] SHD-DAT, 14N 35, 'Conditions de paix', Aug. 1916.
[87] MAE, *Série A*, vol. 281, undated 'Note', from late Dec. 1916 or early Jan. 1917.

Berthelot did not need to add that Luxembourg was a major European railway hub and thus of significant military importance for the defence of France and Belgium. This was reflected in his further insistence that France must secure political dominance over the Low Countries once the war ended. This would mean an end to Belgium's status as a neutral. 'If the history of the present war has demonstrated anything,' Berthelot argued, 'it is that Belgium can no longer live as an independent neutral: this conception is too dangerous for France ... [Belgium] must be brought into our financial, military and customs orbit.'[88] Berthelot, like nearly all of his colleagues in the diplomatic corps, was a committed practitioner of traditional power politics. The Belgian ambassador in Paris recognised this when he observed that Berthelot and Briand had taken up the policy of Louis XIV and aimed at the dismemberment of Germany and domination of the Rhineland.[89]

The prescriptions of other senior Quai d'Orsay officials were founded on essentially the same principles.[90] Paul Cambon was the eloquent and persuasive advocate-in-chief of a Paris–London axis to French policy. But his influence extended beyond Franco-British relations. Working closely with Barrère, he played a key role in the secret negotiations leading to the Treaty of London.[91] Cambon was impatient with internationalism of all varieties. He referred to Woodrow Wilson with contempt as 'that professor', criticising the American president's 'dogmatism' and 'sanctimonious airs'.[92]

From Petrograd, ambassador Paléologue insisted that the post-war peace settlement must instead be 'dictated' by victors to the vanquished.[93] The future strategic balance was at the centre of his preoccupations. The ultimate aim, he argued, must be the end of German power in Europe. 'The German Empire', he observed to Tsar Nicholas II of Russia, 'is directed manifestly against France ... the territorial sacrifices that we are resolved to impose must have as an inevitable consequence the destruction of the Reich.' Significantly, Paléologue was not interested in the democratisation of Germany. He instead agreed with the Tsar that Prussia should be returned to its seventeenth-century

---

[88] Both passages quoted in Soutou, 'Marches de l'est', 343 n39; see also D. Stevenson, 'Belgium, Luxemburg and the Defence of Western Europe, 1914–1920', *IHR*, 4, 4 (1982), 504–23.
[89] McDougall, *Rhineland Diplomacy*, 21.
[90] P. Jackson, 'Tradition and adaptation: the social universe of the French foreign ministry in the era of the First World War', *French History*, 24, 2 (2010), 164–96.
[91] MAE, PA-AP 141, *Papiers Stephen Pichon*, vol. 4, 'Accords avec l'Italie', P. Cambon to Delcassé, 26 Apr. 1915; see also L. Villate, *La République des diplomates: Paul et Jules Cambon, 1843–1935* (Paris, 2002), 322–3.
[92] Paul Cambon to Henri Cambon, 21 Dec. 1916 in P. Cambon, *Correspondance, 1870–1924*, vol. III: *(1912–1924) Les Guerres balkaniques. La Grande Guerre. L'Organisation de la paix* (Paris, 1946), 135.
[93] MAE, *Série A*, vol. 54, Paléologue to Delcassé, 22 Nov. 1914.

status as a 'simple kingdom'. Such an outcome, he judged, would be a 'great source of security for France'.[94]

There was general agreement that the Reich must be deprived of the industry and raw materials in the Rhineland. 'The unavoidable logic of European politics', de Margerie observed in February 1916, 'leaves us no choice but to amputate this region, which is such an important source of German economic and military power.' Such a policy, he insisted, was 'dictated by our responsibility to assure the future security of our race'.[95] Jules Cambon, supported by Poincaré, opposed Berthelot's assertion that France must annex Luxembourg. He warned that alienating the Belgians by denying their claims to Luxembourg would be short-sighted. Jules agreed with his brother that cooperation with Belgium was essential to constitute a crucial 'ring' that would bind the Franco-British alliance after the war.[96] There was almost certainly an element of personal animosity to the dispute between Cambon and Berthelot, which came to a head in late 1916 when the former was charged with drafting a programme of war aims and peace conditions. In this document Cambon advocated allowing the population of Luxembourg to decide between union with France or Belgium through a plebiscite. Berthelot opposed this and succeeded in excising all references to the future of Luxembourg from the final text sent to London.[97]

The dispute with Berthelot left both Cambon brothers angry.[98] But it did not arise from fundamentally opposed security conceptions. Both Berthelot and Cambon agreed that France must dominate the Grand Duchy along with the rest of the Left Bank of the Rhine as part of the peace settlement. Cambon attributed greater importance to cooperation with Britain than did Berthelot at this juncture. The latter stressed the need to control land and resources. Both analyses, however, were rooted in traditional conceptions of the nature of international relations.

A commitment to the balance of power and alliance politics also shaped foreign ministry responses to persistent American efforts to mediate an end to the conflict. These initiatives were always unwelcome in Paris. In early 1915, for example, Delcassé responded to such an initiative by Wilson's emissary, Colonel House, by insisting that there could be no peace until Germany had

---

[94] Ibid. and M. Paléologue, *Le crépuscule des Tsars: journal (1914–1917)* (Paris, 2007), 123–5.
[95] MAE, *Série A*, vol. 291, 'Note' (by de Margerie), 1 Sept. 1916. See also Soutou, 'Marches de l'est', 352 and Stevenson, *French War Aims*, 31.
[96] MAE, *Série A*, vol. 281, 'Note en réponse' (Jules Cambon), 22 Jan. 1917 and 'Question du Luxembourg', 30 Jun. 1917, which summarises the debate.
[97] There are several versions of Cambon's draft 'Projet', including one with Berthelot's annotations, in MAE, *Série A*, vol. 55 and MAE, PA-AP 141, *Papiers Pichon*, vol. 4. The final version is in MAE, *Série A*, vol. 58, 'Conditions de paix', Briand to (Paul) Cambon, 12 Jan. 1917 and in PA-AP 141, *Papiers Pichon*, vol. 4; see also Soutou, *L'Or et le sang*, 279–83; Villate, *République des diplomates*, 331–4.
[98] Villate, *République des diplomates*, 338–40 and 398 n60.

been 'broken'.[99] House returned to Paris in early February 1916, this time raising the prospect of US intervention under the condition that France adhere to a new international order based on a liberal condominium of the three Atlantic powers. The implicit corollary was that France would renounce the Russian alliance.[100] This was unpalatable to policy makers who were unwilling to relinquish not only the independence France enjoyed as a result of the relationship with Russia but also the implicit approval given by the Tsar to French ambitions in the Rhineland. Paul Cambon dismissed the House mission as an 'electoral ploy'.[101] Jules Jusserand, the French ambassador in Washington, agreed. Within the ministry, both Jules Cambon and Berthelot were also opposed. 'Neutral states', the latter observed, 'dream always of playing a decisive role in the conclusion of the peace. It is the result of a combination of self-interest, pride and a secret sense of discomfort at having selfishly remained aloof from a struggle where so much is at stake.'[102]

Resentment and mistrust of Wilson's tactics among career diplomats in Paris only intensified in May 1916 with his declaration that 'the peace of the world must depend upon a new and more wholesome diplomacy' and advocacy of a 'universal association of nations'.[103] The president's public 'peace note' in December of that year, which called on all belligerents to state their requirements for peace, was greeted with hostility by permanent officials in Paris. De Margerie speculated that the American initiative had been 'concerted with Germany'. He articulated the consensus view within the ministry when he asserted that 'when the day comes that we consent to treat [with Germany], it can only be by imposing our conditions, because in doing so we will keep out enemies at our mercy and force them despite themselves to keep to their engagements'.[104] Although Berthelot did not share de Margerie's interpretation of American motives, he was just as adamant that France must negotiate

---

[99] E. M. House, *The Intimate Papers of Colonel House*, ed. C. Seymour, 4 vols. (New York, 1926), I, 201; see also Nouailhat, *France et les États Unis*, 144–6.

[100] MAE, *Série Guerre*, vol. 498, 'Conversation du Colonel House avec Jules Cambon', 2 Feb. 1916 and 'Deuxième entrevue du Colonel House' (with Briand), 7 Feb. 1916; see also Stevenson, *French War Aims*, 14–15.

[101] Cambon, *Correspondance*, III, 99: Paul Cambon to Henri Cambon, 13 Feb. 1916; see also MAE, *Série Guerre*, vol. 499, P. Cambon private letter to Briand, 22 Feb. 1916.

[102] MAE, PA-AP 93, *Papiers Jusserand*, vol. 31, Briand [Berthelot] to Jusserand, 28 May 1916; see also MAE, *Série Guerre*, vol. 498, Briand [Berthelot] to Cambon and Jusserand, 9 Feb. 1916; for Jusserand's views: MAE, *Série Guerre*, vol. 499, Jusserand to Briand, 15 Feb. and 31 Mar. 1916; Villate, *République des diplomates*, 333; J. L. Barré, *Philippe Berthelot: l'éminence grise, 1866–1934* (Paris, 1998), 309–11 and Nouailhat, *France et les États Unis*, 319–28.

[103] Knock, *To End All Wars*, 77.

[104] MAE, PA-AP 43, *Papiers Jules Cambon*, vol. 19, 'Paix', de Margerie note, 20 Dec. 1916; MAE, *Série A*, vol. 33, 'Propositions de paix: note allemande du 12 décembre 1916', de Margerie note, 19 Dec. 1916; 'Notes pour le Ministre', de Margerie notes, 15 and 16 Dec. 1916; 'Proposition d'ouverture de négociations de paix: Project de réponse', Cambon note annotated by Berthelot, 17 Dec. 1916 and 'Ouvertures de paix', 19 Dec. 1916; Paul Cambon to Henri Cambon, 21 Dec. 1916, Cambon, *Correspondance*, III, 135; see also Soutou, 'Marches de l'est', 362 and Stevenson, 'American challenge', 881–3.

only when in a position to impose a victor's peace on Germany. He therefore took charge of drafting the French response to Wilson's note, which aimed above all at bringing an end to the exchange.[105]

The traditional perspective at the heart of these responses was shared throughout the diplomatic community. Jean Doulcet, first secretary at the French embassy in Moscow, argued for breaking up Germany, the 'resurrection' of an independent Hanover and the establishment of a string of small neutralised states along France's eastern marches.[106] From within the ministry Henri de Manneville agreed that a return to the situation before 1871 was unrealistic. He argued instead for the 'amputation' of Alsace-Lorraine and Poland from Germany and for the seizure of the Saar coalfields. But de Manneville reckoned that these measures would be insufficient in themselves to provide security. 'We will be forced to place [Germany] in irons for the foreseeable future.' He judged that this could only be achieved by imposing a large indemnity on the Reich along with 'very severe commercial stipulations'. The result would be 'an effective economic yoke' that would prevent a further German bid for economic and political dominance by 'placing her economically in a situation of dependence [in relation to] the victors. *Vae victis*.'[107] This strategy for future security was endorsed by Léon Geoffray, the French ambassador in Madrid. Geoffray argued that, while the frontier of 1814 (which included the coalfields of the Saar) was a 'strategic imperative', in order for France to have 'enduring security' it was 'indispensable' to impose 'financial and economic measures that will prevent Germany from pursuing a policy of military and naval expansion'.[108]

The call for overturning the economic balance of power between France and Germany would be taken up elsewhere within France's policy machinery. The main point to be made here is that, as a strategy for future security, it reflected the traditionalist reflexes of French professional diplomats. Even Paul Claudel, often considered one of the more moderate and far-sighted of French diplomats of this era, was convinced that the 'rectification' of the imbalance in German and French economic power was an 'essential condition' of peace and security in Europe. France, Claudel argued, must become 'master of as much territory in the Rhineland as is deemed necessary' but also establish control over the coal production of the Ruhr industrial basin.[109] This articulation of France's security requirements was a product of the institutional

---

[105] Nouailhat, *France et les États Unis*, 394–6; Stevenson, *French War Aims*, 46–7.
[106] MAE, PA-AP 240, *Papiers Jean Doulcet*, vol. 21, personal letter from Doulcet to Henri de Manneville, 19 Aug. 1914.
[107] *Vae victis* is Latin for 'Woe to the vanquished'. MAE, PA-AP 240, *Papiers Doulcet*, vol. 21, two personal letters from de Manneville to Doulcet, 22 Nov. 1914 and 23 May 1915. This exchange is also cited in Soutou, *L'Or et le sang*, 163–4.
[108] MAE, PA-AP 240, *Papiers Doulcet*, vol. 21, personal letter from Geoffray to Doulcet, 9 Jun. 1915.
[109] MAE, *Série A*, vol. 290, 'Note sur les conditions de la paix économique avec l'Allemagne', 31 Jul. 1916; see also Soutou, *L'Or et le sang*, 172–3.

commitment to the balance of power within the French foreign ministry in the era of the First World War.

V

The traditional prescriptions of foreign ministry mandarins were echoed in planning for post-war economic security. Under the energetic leadership of Étienne Clémentel the commerce ministry assumed an influential role in strategic planning. Before analysing the official programme for economic security elaborated in 1916–17, however, it is worth considering the views articulated during this period by influential experts outside the government and policy machine. Among the more important of these were views of the Bureau d'études économiques and the Comité des forges. The former was set up in July 1915 under Senator Jean Morel and was composed of both parliamentarians and permanent officials. Its influence was considerable in 1915–16, when it functioned as a 'laboratory of ideas' concerning both the prosecution of economic warfare and prescriptions for economic security in the post-war period. The Bureau d'études économiques also functioned as a mechanism for coordinating the positions adopted by the government and the parliamentary commissions. Although the Bureau never formulated a coherent programme, its individual prescriptions consistently assumed a state of economic warfare with Germany even after the military conflict ended. The Bureau was therefore much closer to the traditional than the internationalist approach to security. Its influence waned, however, as post-war economic planning came to be dominated by the commerce ministry.[110]

The most important non-governmental association in debates about the post-war economic order was the Comité des forges. The influence of this powerful combine only increased with the unprecedented demands placed on the iron and steel industry by modern warfare. Both political leaders and state agencies consulted frequently with the Comité in an effort to achieve maximum cooperation with private industrialists in the war effort. To ensure that the interests of the metallurgy industry were represented in government post-war planning, a 'peace treaty commission' was established within the Comité in 1915 under the direction of its secretary general, Robert Pinot. This commission was charged with studying the implications of possible territorial readjustments for the iron and steel industry. Officially, the views of the commission were communicated to political elites in forums such as meetings of the Bureau d'études économiques and the 'Commission on French Economic Expansion' of the senate. But unofficial links were just as important. Some members of the commission, including François de Wendel, were also deputies. Briand

---

[110] Soutou, *L'Or et le sang*, 147–69 and Stevenson, *French War Aims*, 24–5.

consulted privately with Pinot on several occasions. The interests of the iron and steel masters, in sum, were well represented at the heart of government.[111]

A major preoccupation of the Comité des forges was the industrial implications of the recovery of Alsace-Lorraine. The return of the rich iron-ore deposits in Lorraine, along with its extensive steel-producing plant, presented major potential difficulties for French heavy industry. The return of Lorraine would double France's steel-producing capacity. While this was obviously attractive to French government officials focused on the industrial balance of power, it would also destroy the industrial and commercial arrangements upon which the French iron and steel industry had come to depend. Lorraine, crucially, lacked substantial coal deposits of its own. Its return would therefore only aggravate France's existing energy deficit and in particular its lack of the coking coal required for producing steel. The addition of the steel factories of Lorraine was expected to raise the coke requirements of French industry from 4 to nearly 7 million tons per year. Nor could annexation of the Saar coalfields alleviate this problem. The coal of this region yielded only limited amounts of lower-quality coke that was consumed entirely by local foundries. As a result, French iron and steel producers would be forced to buy even more coke from Germany after the war.[112]

Another, equally vexing, problem was one of markets. The iron and especially the steel produced in the region was at present integrated into the German market. Should these commercial links be cut by the return of Lorraine, the French metallurgical industry would be thrown into a crisis of overproduction. And acquisition of the Saar coalfields would only worsen the situation, as a market would also have to be found for the 1.3 million tons of iron and steel produced in the Saarland. The peace treaty commission consequently approved the return of Alsace-Lorraine more out of patriotism than self-interest. The same was true of its attitude towards demands for the Saar coalfields. The 13 million tons of coal produced annually in this region would be an obvious benefit to the French economy as a whole, but it was not in the interests of the iron and steel industry.

The peace commission of the Comité des forges also considered the future status of the Left Bank of the Rhine. There were concerns that absorbing this region into France's industrial and commercial orbit would raise similar problems in terms of internal competition. In the end, and only after considerable deliberation and a round of consultations with government officials, the commission added its voice to calls for altering the political status of the Left Bank.

---

[111] Soutou, *L'Or et le sang*, 169–70, 182–9 and 284–95; J.-N. Jeanneney, *François de Wendel en république: Argent et pouvoir 1914–1940* (Paris, 1976), 25–39; Stevenson, *French War Aims*, 23–5 and 38–40; and Suarez, *Briand*, III, 403–12. See also Robert Pinot's account of the war-time activities of the Comité: *Le Comité des forges au service de la nation, août 1914–novembre 1918* (Paris, 1919).

[112] Soutou, *L'Or et le sang*, 181–2 and Jeanneney, *L'Argent et le pouvoir*, 36–8 for this paragraph and the next.

There were certainly key figures within the metallurgical industry who advocated using force to bring about a radical transformation of the Franco-German industrial and commercial balance. The most prominent was Camille Cavallier, the *patron* of the powerful steel-producing concern Pont-à-Mousson. Cavallier proposed seizing control of the coal-producing region of Westphalia.[113] For the majority of those on the Comité peace commission, however, memories of the mutually beneficial relationships that had grown up between the French and German metallurgical industries during the pre-war decade remained crucial. The fundamental complementarity of French iron ore and German coal and markets remained a central consideration in all debates within the peace commission.

The appeal of the pre-war arrangements, and of the economic liberalism they embodied, was reflected in the initial policy proposals put forward by Pinot in late 1915 and early 1916. Before the Bureau d'études économiques on 10 December 1915, Pinot presented a picture of the post-war economic order based on ongoing Franco-German cooperation: 'We must preserve the necessary economic relations between France and Germany. This [will ensure] that we will continue to obtain coke from Westphalia and Westphalia will continue to receive iron ore from us in exchange.' He added that these commercial links could not be severed because they constituted 'one of the most serious guarantees of a durable peace'.[114] A report summarising the views of the Comité des forges was prepared early the following May. This document, approved by the Comité peace commission, insisted that 'It is essential that French industry is able to depend upon the German market as it did before the war. [Any future] peace treaty must therefore contain a clause assuring France of German coke at favourable prices.'[115] This vision of French security, with its emphasis on post-war economic collaboration with Germany, was in complete opposition to the more traditional projects based on annexations that were under construction within the army staff and foreign ministry.

The result was standoff behind the scenes between the Comité des forges and the Briand government. This was an encounter that, in the charged atmosphere of 1916, the Comité was bound to lose. A copy of the Comité peace commission report of early May found its way to Berthelot on 10 May and was circulated throughout the policy establishment.[116] Accounts of debates within the commission had also leaked to several journalists. The result was a vibrant press campaign denouncing French iron and steel magnates for

---

[113] Soutou, *L'Or et le sang*, 181 and 184–5.
[114] MAE, *Série A*, vol. 257, 'Déposition faite par M. Robert Pinot, secrétaire général du Comité des forges, devant le Bureau d'études économiques du Ministère des affaires étrangères', 3 and 10 Dec. 1915 and 'La Métallurgie française et le future Traité de paix', 10 Dec. 1915.
[115] Cited in Soutou, *L'Or et le sang*, 284.
[116] MAE, *Série A*, vol. 257, Pierre Comert (London) to Berthelot, 10 May 1916; see also Soutou, *L'Or et le sang*, 283–4.

their lack of patriotism.[117] It was at this stage that Briand appears to have intervened directly to place pressure on Pinot to obtain proposals more in line with the thinking of French officialdom. In late June 1916 the Comité officially declared that 'any extension of our territory or our economic domain beyond Alsace-Lorraine and the Saar could only simplify the resolution of the problems created for our industry by the recovery or the annexation of these provinces by providing new markets, greater combustible resources and the transport facilities of the Rhine'.[118] France's iron and steel magnates thus fell into line with the majority of public-sphere discourse on the question of security. Crucially, however, most appear to have done so only reluctantly and under pressure from both the government and the patriotic press. The pre-1914 reflex towards collaboration with German heavy industry continued to shape preferences concerning post-war order among the leaders of French heavy industry. This reflex was suppressed in 1916. But it would re-emerge to play a significant role in policy making after the peace conference.

It is possible to identify similar ambiguities in the economic and commercial policy developed by the commerce ministry. The evolution of this policy owed much to the energy and convictions of commerce minister Clémentel, who joined the newly constituted Briand government in October 1915. A lawyer by training, Clémentel was a figure of growing importance on the left of the Radical Party and a political ally of Bourgeois.[119] He had exhibited little interest in international relations before the war. There are nonetheless interesting parallels between his approach to international economic issues and juridical internationalist conceptions of international relations. A consistent theme in Clémentel's vision of the wartime and post-war international economy was the importance of inter-state collaboration based not only on shared interests but also on common political and cultural values.

As was the case with internationalist visions of a juridical political order, the economic programme developed under Clémentel was derived from 'essentially theoretical notions regarding ideal economic structure'.[120] Clémentel was an early advocate of the 'planning' approach to economic policy that would become dominant in France after 1945. He was also a determined proponent of seeing the war through to victory whatever the cost (*jusqu'au boutisme* in the grammar of the French political elite at the time) and of limiting German power after the war. The economic strategies he advocated as minister of commerce combined the collaborative and multilateral currents of the internationalist approach with the more widespread conviction that Germany

---

[117] Jeanneney, *L'Argent et le pouvoir*, 35 and 71–2. Pinot's memoir was written in response to this campaign: see *Comité des forges*, 2–7.
[118] Pinot, *Comité des forges*, 233–4; see also Stevenson, *French War Aims*, 38–9; Soutou, *L'Or et le sang*, 285–6; and Suarez, *Briand*, III, 412–13.
[119] M. Sorlot, *Léon Bourgeois: un moraliste en politique* (Paris, 2005), 182 n47, 249 and 259.
[120] M. Trachtenberg, '"A New Economic Order": Etienne Clémentel and French economic diplomacy during the First World War', *FHS*, 10, 2 (1977), 318.

must be deprived of the means to wage economic or military war in the future.

This ambiguity has led to disagreement over the precise nature of the programme elaborated by Clémentel and his team. Georges-Henri Soutou has argued that the overriding objective of this programme was to transform the economic balance of power in France's favour. Soutou emphasises the anti-German character of Clémentel's policy conception and, in particular, its default assumption that France and Germany would continue to wage an 'economic war' long after military operations were brought to an end. Marc Trachtenberg, conversely, stresses the multilateral and cooperative character of the strategies proposed by the ministry of commerce under Clémentel.[121] While Soutou's interpretation is most persuasive for the wartime period, he does not acknowledge the ambiguous character of much ministry of commerce planning. This ambiguity arose from tensions between the programme's anti-German character, on the one hand, and its forthrightly multilateral conception of economic security, on the other.

The central pillar of the commerce ministry's strategy was the creation of an Allied 'economic bloc' capable of combating German projects for a *Mitteleuropa* customs union dominated by Berlin and Vienna.[122] Two officials, in particular, played important roles in the elaboration of this strategy: Fernand Pila at the foreign ministry and Henri Hauser at the ministry of commerce. Pila was the foreign ministry's representative on the Bureau d'études économiques and the central figure in economic planning within the Quai d'Orsay during the war.[123] Hauser was a professor of history and geography at the University of Dijon who by late 1915 had written numerous pamphlets and articles on the historical, political and especially economic aspects of the war. The most widely read of these was a short book entitled *Les Méthodes allemandes d'expansion économique* which emphasised the aggressive character of Germany's pre-war commercial policy.[124]

Hauser's chief concern was German efforts to dominate European commerce by dumping cheap manufactures on neighbouring markets. This strategy, he argued, aimed to create a vast commercial bloc in the heart of Europe. If it was successful, he warned, France would lose its economic independence in

---

[121] Soutou, *L'Or et le sang*, esp. 234–70, 279–305 and 549–67; Trachtenberg, '"New Economic Order"'; M. Trachtenberg, *Reparation in World Politics: France and European Economic Diplomacy, 1916–1923* (New York, 1980), 1–25.
[122] Two essential documents are MAE, *Série Guerre*, vol. 1216, 'Projet d'entente économique entre alliés: note de M. Pila', 14 Apr. 1916 and AN, *Série* F12 (commerce ministry), vol. 7988, 'Avant la conférence économique. La situation en novembre 1915', n.d. but almost certainly drafted in May–Jun. 1917. See also Clémentel's own account: *La France et la politique économique interalliée* (Paris, 1931), 68–70.
[123] Soutou, *L'Or et le sang*, 159–62 and Stevenson, *French War Aims*, 10–11.
[124] H. Hauser, *Les Méthodes allemandes d'expansion économique* (Paris, 1915); S.-A. Marin and G.-H Soutou (eds.), *Henri Hauser (1866–1946): humaniste, historien, républicain* (Paris, 2006), esp. 147–84.

The primacy of the balance of power, 1914–1916   117

the shadow of a *Mitteleuropa*-dominated economic order.[125] Hauser did not join the commerce ministry officially until May 1917. But his influence on French policy can be identified much earlier. His conviction that Germany must be denied Most Favoured Nation status in the post-war commercial regime was a cornerstone of planning from mid-1916 onwards.[126]

The first stage in the evolution of a coherent French programme was a 20 December 1915 note from Clémentel to Briand which stressed the heavy sacrifices made by France to the Allied cause. France, Clémentel asserted, was 'economically and geographically at the centre of the Allied war effort'. The note deployed the familiar language of national victimhood, noting that for forty-five years France had been 'the designated victim of German commercial tactics'. It was therefore vital that the French government take the lead in coordinating the economic power of the Entente. Clémentel proposed that an inter-Allied economic conference be organised to facilitate 'the establishment... of a community of views aimed at obtaining, for each member of the Entente, all possible commercial and industrial advantages for the present and in the future'.[127]

Clémentel's suggestion, which complemented the priority given by the Briand government to improving inter-Allied diplomatic and military unity, was embraced by the Quai d'Orsay. An outline of the programme was circulated to the embassies in London, Rome and Petrograd on 21 December. This was superseded three weeks later by a more ambitious project that extended planning into the post-war era and envisaged 'the constitution of an economic bloc' capable of 'responding to the grouping of Central Powers'.[128] Professor Soutou has rightly attributed the 'hardening' of the French project to an intervention by Berthelot. The addition of post-war issues to the conference agenda, and in particular the reference to common customs regimes, was in tune with Berthelot's conception of a post-war political and economic order that strengthened France at Germany's expense.[129]

The French programme rested on an interpretation of German economic behaviour that was every bit as bleak as assessments of German political intentions within the army staff and foreign ministry. An analysis prepared by the ministry of commerce in February 1917 cited the following declaration by

---

[125] Hauser, *Méthodes allemandes*, 6–22; H. Hauser, *L'Allemagne économique, l'industrie allemande considérée comme facteur de guerre* (Paris, 1915).
[126] MAE, *Guerre, 1914–1918*, vol. 1216, 'Projet d'entente économique entre alliés', Pila overview, 14 Apr. 1916; AN, F12 7985, 'La Clause de la nation la plus favorisée dans les conventions commerciales à venir', Pila note, 30 Septembre 1916; AN, F12 7988, 'Conférence des Alliés dans l'ordre économique: mesures transitoires', n.d. and 'Avant la conférence économique', May–Jun. 1917. See also Soutou, *L'Or et le sang*, 148, 152–3 and 160.
[127] Clémentel, quoted in MAE, *Série Guerre*, vol. 1216, 'Projet d'entente économique entre alliés', Pila overview, 14 Apr. 1916.
[128] Ibid.   [129] Soutou, *L'Or et le sang*, 240–1.

the German defence ministry as representative of the core convictions of all German political and industrial elites:

> War is eternal. In the situation in which we find ourselves it is essential that we internalise this truth ... War, like birth and death, is a natural function ... All improvement in the human condition is based on struggle. That which we call peace is nothing more than a less extreme state of war. A complete absence of combat is found only in a world of illusions.[130]

This image of German society as permanently oriented towards organising for war underpinned the expectation of a German commercial offensive after the war. This expectation could only have been reinforced by the increased prominence of *Mitteleuropa* in German political discourse in late 1915 and by intelligence detailing German plans to establish a 'general staff for economic war' which would exist in peacetime. The anticipated offensive would be all the more formidable given that Germany's industrial production had been enhanced significantly during the war while many of the key industrial areas of France had suffered systematic destruction under German occupation.[131] Policy elites were haunted by the spectre of a powerful German economy securing control over vital markets in the post-war era.

This anxiety was a central feature of planning for post-war economic security. There were three underlying objectives to this planning. First, to ensure that France would have access to crucial raw materials. Second, to establish a system of mutual commercial preference among the allies and friendly neutral states 'for as long a time as possible after hostilities'. Third, to reduce 'to the greatest extent possible' Allied commercial dependence on the Central Powers.[132] Two sets of measures were envisaged to achieve these objectives. The first were war-winning strategies aimed at pooling the resources of the Entente states and tightening the economic blockade of Germany. The second were post-war 'transitional measures' intended to provide significant economic advantages to France and its Allies in relation to Germany in peacetime. The stated aim was to establish the conditions necessary for the full recovery of the French and Belgian economies. The 'transitional' provisions included continued pooling of those raw materials necessary for reconstruction. This, crucially, would ensure France full access to the natural resources of the British Empire while at the same time denying such access to ex-enemy states. The coordination of Allied transport would also be continued during the

---

[130] AN, F12 7988, 'Allemagne', 22 Feb. 1917.
[131] AN, F12 7988, 'Préparation d'après guerre', 31 Jan. 1917 and Clémentel, *Politique économique*, 68–70. On the prominence of *Mitteleuropa* at this juncture see H. C. Meyer, *Mitteleuropa in German Thought and Action, 1815–1945* (The Hague, 1955), 232–79; Soutou, *L'Or et le sang*, 92–7 and 240–1.
[132] All quotations from MAE, *Série Guerre*, vol. 1216, 'Projet d'une entente économique', Pila note, 14 Apr. 1916; but see also MAE, PA-AP 141, *Papiers Pichon*, vol. 4, 'Note sur les conditions de la paix', 6 Nov. 1916 and AN, F12 7985, 'La Clause de la nation la plus favorisée', Pila note, 30 Sept. 1916.

'transitional period' to facilitate reconstruction. Tariff policies would be harmonised to prevent German dumping. Finally, a series of 'coercive measures in the economic realm' would be imposed on former enemy states until reconstruction was complete and reparations had been paid.

This transitional regime was envisaged for a period of between five and twenty years.[133] It was to be supplemented, however, by a series of 'permanent measures' aimed at 'preventing the Central Powers from' pursuing a policy of economic domination'. This would be achieved by a system of commercial and financial accords based on the principle of 'mutual assistance [*entre'aide*]'. These accords would serve as a 'departure point towards a general economic entente' that 'must be based around a Franco-British condominium'.[134] The underlying objective was the construction of a peacetime economic bloc strong enough to confront future German bids for continental economic hegemony.

The commerce ministry's programme, finalised in mid-April, was approved by the cabinet and presented to France's allies at the Economic Conference held in Paris on 14–17 June 1916. Briand opened the conference with an impassioned warning of the danger presented by German efforts to subject the states of Europe to a form of 'economic slavery' and the need to 'organise a defence against the common danger through the reordering of our alliance'. French negotiators succeeded in obtaining agreement on the essentials of their programme. The Allied states declared their 'solidarity' in the task of reconstruction, agreed to conserve key raw materials primarily for themselves, to take concerted action against post-war dumping by pursuing economic independence from the Central Powers in general, and in particular by denying Germany Most Favoured Nation status for an undetermined period.[135]

Although the official declarations issuing from the Paris conference greatly alarmed the Central Powers, the Allies did not agree on detailed plans to implement the French programme. The British were reluctant to commit to an indefinite period of economic punishment for the Central Powers that would hurt their own commerce. Russia and Italy, meanwhile, feared losing Germany as an export market for their agricultural produce. In the USA, moreover, the prospect of a formidable Allied trading bloc was viewed with deep hostility.[136] The structural dynamics of the world economy stood in the way of the economic solutions envisaged for French security at this juncture.

There are nonetheless important affinities between these solutions and the traditional approach to security. As Soutou has observed, the over-arching aim of the French proposals was to 'reinforce France's economic power and to

---

[133] MAE, *Série Guerre*, vol. 1216, 'Projet d'une entente économique générale et la prochaine conférence économique de Paris', Pila note, 14 Apr. 1916 and AN, F12 7988, 'Conférence des Alliés dans l'ordre économique: mesures transitoires', n.d.
[134] MAE, *Série Guerre*, vol. 1216, 'Projet d'une entente économique', 14 Apr. 1916.
[135] AN, F12 7988, 'La Conférence économique de Paris: les négociations', n.d.
[136] Soutou, *L'Or et le sang*, 261–305 and 353–63; Stevenson, *French War Aims*, 34–5.

improve its security by strengthening its ties with its allies and by weakening Germany'.[137] This is clear from Pila's observation that a key aim of French post-war commercial policy must be to 'degermanise' the economies of friendly and neutral states. The traditional conception similarly runs through Henri Hauser's analysis of France's economic security requirements in September 1916. Hauser began, significantly, by dismissing liberal theories of economic interdependence:

> It was generally assumed that the complexity of international political and commercial relations would prevent another war between the European powers ... But it has been necessary to face up to bitter evidence ... Competition for political and economic power between rival European states must be accepted as a permanent reality.[138]

Hauser's analysis of international commerce followed from this conclusion. Long experience, he warned, had illustrated 'the immense appetites for economic and territorial conquests' that animated German policy. There could be no doubt that 'behind its military operations Germany is preparing a [programme of] economic aggression that is every bit as fearful'. An Allied military victory would therefore be insufficient if it left Germany with 'the means to re-establish in a short period of time its economic power'. Hauser's analysis was based on the assumption of permanent economic warfare between France and Germany: 'Once military action is terminated, it will be indispensable to establish the conditions within which to continue the war effectively in the commercial and industrial sectors with the aim of assuring that our victory does not become an economic defeat.'[139] Pila, for his part, predicted 'the probable persistence after the war, in the economic domain, of more or less exclusive groupings of states'.[140]

There is, in other words, a great deal of evidence to support Soutou's contention that French economic policy should be understood as a power political programme aimed at securing a dominant position in Europe. Yet it is hard to avoid the conclusion that he pushes this argument too far. Soutou's interpretation does not take sufficient account either of the specific context in which French policy was made or of the ambiguities inherent in its conception. Two points are worth emphasising. The first is that the French programme was devised in the midst of a desperate struggle for national survival. The outcome of this struggle was by no means clear in the winter and spring of 1916 as the battle for Verdun hung in the balance. Whatever the rhetoric deployed to rally the national war effort, comprehensive victory over Germany was a remote prospect at this juncture of the war. This meant that French commercial strategy, unlike programmes for political or military security, was not based

---

[137] Soutou, *L'Or et le sang*, 257–8.
[138] AN, F12 7988, 'Avant la conférence économique', May–Jun. 1917.   [139] Ibid.
[140] AN, F12 7985, 'La Clause de la nation la plus favorisée', 30 Sept. 1916.

on the assumption of total victory. It was assumed instead that a powerful German-dominated economic bloc would continue to exist in central and eastern Europe after the war.

As Pila put it, the 'primordial requirement' of French policy was to 'respond to the powerful economic grouping of our enemies that we must anticipate facing after the war'. 'We must prepare ourselves', he warned, 'against the probable and formidable return of the economic offensive mounted by our adversaries [before the war].'[141] The anti-German character of the French programme must therefore be set in its proper context. Soutou's analysis emphasises 'the depth of French economic hostility towards Germany'.[142] But this sentiment was hardly remarkable given that France and Germany were fighting a war of unprecedented dimensions that demanded hitherto unimaginable human and material sacrifices from their populations.

A second important consideration is that, despite the expectation that the post-war system would be dominated by rival economic blocs, a multilateral current persisted in French planning. This reflected the continued influence of economic liberalism among both policy makers and business elites. The economic strategy formulated in 1916 was designed to confront Germany with an ever-widening web of commercial, financial and industrial relationships that would include both the victorious powers and neutral states. Crucially, nearly all of the 'permanent' conditions envisaged were defensive in character. What is more, they aimed overwhelmingly at containing, rather than destroying, German economic power. Pila described the French proposals as a 'common policy of economic defence'. He advocated that an inter-Allied customs regime be established 'for as long as possible'. He did not envisage permanent commercial discrimination against Germany. On the contrary, he warned several times against using the language of permanent economic warfare. He predicted that such rhetoric would only stiffen the resolve of German economic elites to fight to the end while at the same time generating suspicions among Allied and neutral states that the Allies sought economic domination.[143]

Even more significantly, Pila argued that 'we cannot reasonably hope to exclude Germany from the world economy'. He stressed that German industry and the German market were too important for the functioning of the European economy to be marginalised in a future economic regime. Any attempt to do so would 'lead to insoluble difficulties' in the post-war era and make true economic recovery impossible. A far more prudent strategy, he

---

[141] Quoted in ibid. and AN, F12 7985, 'Du danger des cris de guerre économique', 22 Feb. 1916 respectively.
[142] Soutou, *L'Or et le sang*, 269. Soutou admits evidence of 'tactical and even at times strategic divergences' in the French programme but argues that its central characteristic was 'firmness'.
[143] MAE, *Série Guerre*, vol. 1216, 'Projet d'une entente économique', 14 Apr. 1916; see also Pila's observations before the Bureau d'études économiques in AN, F12 7985, 'Bureau d'études économiques: procès-verbal du séance du 17 mars 1916'.

argued, would be to 'ensure that German economic expansion no longer takes place directly at our expense ... We must curb and contain [German expansion]; we must not dream that we can put an end to it.'[144] Even Hauser agreed with this line of argument, acknowledging that 'there can be no question of maintaining the German and Austro-Hungarian people in a permanent state of economic misery'. What was crucial was instead to deny both countries the opportunity to mount future economic offensives based on unfair commercial practices.[145] Before the Bureau d'études économiques in March 1916, Pila speculated that, once Germany had been forced to end its unfair commercial practices, it would likely be in France's economic interest to renew commercial ties with the Reich 'much sooner than is generally admitted'.[146]

The multilateral dimensions to French planning for economic security would become more prominent as prospects for a German-dominated *Mitteleuropa* receded. But it is important to recognise that they were present from the outset. The roots of this current in French thinking lay in the mutually profitable pre-1914 commercial and industrial relationship between France and Germany as well as the ideology of economic liberalism that underpinned this relationship.

VI

The policy prescriptions for post-war security advocated by the army staff, the foreign ministry and the ministry of commerce were not formulated in a vacuum. Policy planning was influenced by the wartime domestic context in general and public sphere civil society discussion of the security problem in particular. Much of this discussion, significantly, was dominated by the traditional themes of alliance politics and the balance of power. Historical constructions of France's identity and interests were used to justify claims for territorial annexations that went well beyond the recapture of Alsace-Lorraine. In this discourse, the interests of France were depicted as virtually coterminous with those of Europe and humanity as a whole. Alongside evocations of history and the future of European civilisation, however, were more prosaic considerations of a military and economic character.

Official censorship played an important role in shaping public sphere discussion of post-war security. An ambitious regime of censorship was imposed

---

[144] All quotations from AN, F12 7985, 'Du Danger des cris de guerre économique', 22 Feb. 1916 (prepared for the Bureau d'études économiques but also circulated widely within the commerce and foreign ministries).
[145] AN, F12 7988, 'Avant la conférence économique', May–Jun. 1917.
[146] AN, F12 7985, 'Bureau d'études économiques: séance du 17 mars 1916'. Pila went even further to hold out the possibility of a coalition of German financial, commercial and industrial elites that might act to bring about an end to the war before Germany's economic wealth was destroyed altogether: see F12 7985, 'Du Danger des cris de guerre économique', 22 Feb. 1916 and MAE, *Série Guerre*, vol. 1216, 'Projet d'une entente économique', 14 Apr. 1916.

by the Viviani government at the outset of the war and maintained by its successors. This regime functioned through sets of instructions (*consignes*) issued to both the national and regional press by the premier's office and other interested ministries in collaboration with President Poincaré's staff. Between 1914 and 1919 over 1,100 such *consignes* were issued. These could be either temporary or permanent, of a general or a particular character. The overriding aim was to suppress public discourse in favour of a compromise peace. Instructions issued on 1 February and 28 April 1915, for example, forbade the publication of any articles discussing the character of a future peace settlement. Specific exception to this rule was made only for those authors who called in general terms for the 'triumph of Justice and Law'.[147]

Censorship was useful not just for controlling public discourse on the meaning and the aims of the war, but also as a means of forming opinion. It was to this end, significantly, that the censors approved the publication of a series of articles by Maurice Barrès in February, March and April 1915, all of which insisted that German sovereignty over the Rhineland must be brought to an end. The objective was to build consensus for a traditional vision of France's security. To make this claim, Barrès used the familiar ideology of natural frontiers. He stressed the alleged racial and cultural affinities between the Rhenish population and the 'Latin civilisation' of France. These ties, combined with long-standing resentment of Prussian domination in the region, constituted the foundations for an independent and neutral Rhineland that would be brought firmly within the French orbit. Barrès also postulated that the Rhinelanders might eventually even choose annexation by France. Albert Sorel would no doubt have smiled to see France's most influential conservative nationalist deploy the arguments of the National Convention of 1792 to justify a presence on the Rhine.[148]

Barrès' arguments reflected the convictions not only of historians of the right such as Jacques Bainville and Edouard Driault, but also moderate republican Ernest Lavisse and Radical Alphonse Aulard. And his interpretation of France's post-war security interests reflected the views of a significant public movement that emerged in favour of a 'Rhenish peace'. The parties of the right virtually all believed that France should have a military frontier on the Rhine. Louis Marin of the Fédération républicain lobbied discreetly for annexation of the Left Bank, as did minister of agriculture Jules Méline.[149] But the traditional prescription for security extended well into the centre and centre-left of the

---

[147] Quoted in P. Renouvin, 'Les Buts de guerre du gouvernement français, 1914–1918', *RH*, 516 (1966), 7; see also Forcade, 'La Censure politique', I, 88, 104–18.

[148] Most of the articles by Barrès appeared in *L'Echo de Paris* and are reproduced in his *Chronique de la Grande Guerre*, vol. III: *(1 janvier–11 mars 1915)* (Paris, 1921) and vol. IV: *(12 mars–31 mai 1915)* (Paris, 1915).

[149] P. Schöttler, 'The Rhine as an object of historical controversy: towards history of frontier mentalities', *History Workshop Journal*, 39, 1 (1995), 1–9; Stevenson, *French War Aims*, 19–20.

political spectrum. It animated the 'war aims bloc' that emerged in parliament in early 1915, which included mainly nationalist politicians from the right but also a significant number of Radicals. This movement was given expression in civil society through the Ligue des patriotes of Barrès, the royalist Action française, and, in more moderate terms, by the Comité de la rive gauche du Rhin, whose membership stretched from Barrès on the right through to Édouard Herriot, a rising star within the Radical Party, on the centre-left. These associations were intended as an answer to the patriotic leagues in Germany. But they were smaller, less well organised and less influential.[150]

When censorship was relaxed in late summer 1916, the majority of press discussion was in favour of detaching the Left Bank. Several commentators went even further to demand the political destruction of the Reich. Former foreign minister Gabriel Hanotaux argued in the influential *Revue des deux mondes* that federal ties between the largest German states must be dissolved. Charles Maurras used stronger language in urging that the German Empire be 'drawn and quartered'. This prescription, with its implicit emphasis on destroying the balance of power established in 1871, was a common theme in both the moderate and nationalist press from *La Victoire*, *Le Matin* and *Le Figaro* to the *Journal des débats* and the radical outlet *L'Oeuvre*.[151] A traditional solution to French security enjoyed wide favour in French civil society and in the public sphere.

The same was true, if to a slightly lesser degree, of discussion of the post-war order within the Comité d'études. The Comité d'études was a semi-official study group established during the war that was attached to the premier's office. First proposed by Poincaré, it was tasked with preparing studies on key issues that were expected to shape the future peace settlement. Charles Benoist, a centre-right deputy and political editor of the *Revue des deux mondes*, was charged with selecting its membership. Benoist, convinced that 'true policy must have its basis in geography and history', drew almost exclusively on these disciplines in his selection of predominantly conservative academics.[152] Ernest Lavisse, professor of modern history at the University of Paris and director of the École normale supérieure, was named its president. The studies produced by the Comité, which met weekly through early 1919 at the Sorbonne's Institute of Geography, were forwarded to the offices of both

---

[150] Renouvin, 'Buts de guerre', 3–14; McDougall, *Rhineland Diplomacy*, 16–17.

[151] See the detailed discussion in Renouvin, 'Buts de guerre', 10–12; on the political contours of the French press see P. Miquel, *La Paix de Versailles et l'opinion publique française* (Paris, 1972), 19–25.

[152] C. Benoist, *Souvenirs de Charles Benoist (1902–1933)*, vol. III: *Vie parlementaire, vie diplomatique* (Paris, 1934), 324–7; see also D. Kitsikis, *Le Rôle des experts à la conférence de la paix de 1919: gestation d'une technocratie en politique internationale* (Ottawa, 1972); J. Bariéty, 'Le "Comité d'études" du Quai d'Orsay et la frontière rhénane' in C. Fink and C. Baechler (eds.), *L'Établissement des frontières en Europe après les deux guerres mondiales* (Berne, 1996), 251–62; and O. Lowczyk, *La Fabrique de la paix: du comité d'études à la conférence de la paix, l'élaboration par la France des traités de la première guerre mondiale* (Paris, 2010).

Poincaré (who read them) and Briand (who did not). It would be misleading, however, to represent this commission as a key actor in the policy process. The formulation of security policy took place elsewhere, within the general staff, the ministry of commerce and the foreign ministry. The Comité d'études is more important for what its output can tell us about the wider context of informed opinion within which policy was formulated.[153]

Several of the reports prepared for Comité meetings provided well-documented support for the idea of an independent Left Bank. A central theme was the 'historical persistence' of a 'French sentiment' among the Rhenish population. Historian Christian Pfister insisted that the people of the Rhineland had 'given themselves to France with enthusiasm' during the Revolutionary Wars.[154] Philippe Sagniac, another historian, judged that, although France had been 'driven' from the Rhineland in 1814, 'morally it has remained in this region' because the local population looked to France 'with gratitude for having ended their political fragmentation, their feudalism and their lethargy by attaching [the Rhinelanders], to their happiness, to the most powerful and modern state in Europe'.[155] If this narrative of Rhineland politics during the Revolutionary Wars has since been dismantled by historians, this should not obscure the fact that it was widely accepted within the French public sphere.[156]

The discourse of natural frontiers was also invoked in a report entitled 'The North and North-Eastern Military Frontier' by General Émile Bourgeois, head of the geographical section of the army general staff. 'The only frontier capable of assuring a durable peace for France', Bourgeois concluded, 'is the frontier of the Rhine.' He argued that this could best be accomplished by establishing an independent Rhenish polity on the Left Bank with a permanent French military presence.[157] Even Lavisse, whose views regarding the peace settlement were less uncompromising than those of the majority of his colleagues, favoured an independent Rhineland 'protected by France' that would, if necessary, be placed under French military occupation.[158]

---

[153] Lowczyk, *Fabrique de la paix*, 469–75; Kitsikis, *Le Rôle des experts*, 12–29; Schöttler, 'The Rhine', 3–5; on Lavisse see P. Nora, 'Lavisse: instituteur national' and 'L'"Histoire de France" de Lavisse' in P. Nora (ed.), *Lieux de mémoire*, 3 vols. (Paris, 1997), I, 239–75 and 851–902 respectively.

[154] C. Pfister, 'Le Sort des pays rhénans depuis les invasions barbares jusqu'à la Révolution', in Bibliothèque nationale de France (hereafter BNF), *Travaux du Comité d'études*, vol. I: *L'Alsace-Lorraine et la frontière du nord-est* (Paris, 1919), 372.

[155] P. Sagniac, 'L'Esprit publique dans les pays rhénans de 1789 à 1814' in *Travaux du Comité d'études, L'Alsace-Lorraine et la frontière du nord-est*, 391–2.

[156] See esp. T. C. W. Blanning, *The French Revolution in Germany: Occupation and Resistance in the Rhineland, 1792–1802* (Cambridge, 1983); M. Rowe, *From Reich to State: The Rhineland in the Revolutionary Age* (Cambridge, 2003).

[157] G. Bourgeois, 'La Frontière militaire du Nord et du Nord-Est' in *L'Alsace-Lorraine et la frontière du nord-est*, 319–24; see also Lowczyk, *Fabrique de la paix*, 129–77.

[158] Soutou, *L'Or et le sang*, 176.

If the traditional approach was predominant in the security prescriptions of elite opinion, there remained important counter-currents within French civil society that would grow in importance over the course of the war. These alternative prescriptions for national security would prove crucial to the evolution of policy making in the longer term. The coming of war was a terrible blow for most French internationalists. Many had struggled to the bitter end to build links across the Rhine and to exert pressure on policy makers to seek Franco-German rapprochement. What was more, Germany's disregard for international law appeared to undermine the credibility of the juridical internationalist position. Advocates of 'peace through law' were criticised for their 'dangerous idealism', which, according to one prominent commentator on international relations, threatened to 'soften the hearts of the population and weaken the nation's resolve'. 'We must acknowledge publicly', declared the committed internationalist Antoine Pillet, 'that all doctrines of perpetual peace are vain and perilous; we must combat them because we are not strong enough to prevent war.'[159]

Nearly all French internationalists responded to the outbreak of fighting with emphatic declarations of patriotism and support for the war effort. German actions, both during the final days of peace and in the early stages of the war, made it easy for most to adopt this position.[160] Indeed, the official discursive strategy of representing the war as a crusade for justice and the rule of law would prove a long-term boon to the internationalist cause. Jean-Michel Guieu has rightly stressed the 'omnipresence' of references to law in official, semi-official and unofficial justifications of the French cause. Justice was the first clearly enunciated war aim by Poincaré in the summer of 1914. As we have seen, a commitment to the rule of law was reaffirmed by every government thereafter. The French people were represented as '*soldats du droit*' in a phrase deployed frequently in official propaganda. The emphasis on law and justice proved crucial in allowing the internationalist movement to interpret the war as a struggle between civilised law-abiding nation-states and those 'outside of the law'.[161] Ferdinand Buisson, president of the LDH, described the conflict as 'not a duel between two nations but between two spirits'. He contrasted the 'German spirit', which had made force a 'divinity', with the 'French spirit', which rested on 'national and international justice, on the eternal laws of the human conscience'.[162]

[159] Antoine Pillet cited in C. Bouchard, 'Projets citoyens pour une paix durable, en France, en Grande Bretagne et aux États-Unis (1914–1924)', thèse de doctorat, Paris III and Université de Montréal, 2004, 64.
[160] S. Cooper, 'The Reinvention of the "Just War" among European Pacifists before the First World War' in H. L. Dyck (ed.), *The Pacifist Impulse in Historical Perspective* (Toronto, 1996), 303–19.
[161] T. Ruyssen, 'La Force et le droit', *Revue de métaphysique et de morale*, 6 (1914), 850.
[162] J.-M. Guieu, 'Les Apôtres français de "l'esprit de Genève": les militants pour la Société des nations dans la première moitié du XXe siècle', thèse de doctorat, Université de Paris I (Sorbonne), 2004, 75–6.

Just as importantly, as the war widened and losses mounted, the internationalist cause was steadily strengthened. The resolution '*plus jamais ça*' emerged alongside calls for waging the war '*jusqu'au bout*'. The sacrifices the war demanded of French society eventually provided the most powerful argument for a new approach to politics among nations. This created the political space for juridical internationalists to state their case with increasing confidence. In 1915 Edgard Milhaud published a long essay denouncing balance-of-power politics entitled 'From the law of force to the force of law'.[163] In June of that year the Association de la paix par le droit outlined a 'minimum programme' for the construction of a post-war international order. This programme had three objectives: self-determination; the 'completion of the juridical project undertaken at the Hague peace conferences'; and the constitution of a 'society of peaceful nations committed to compulsory arbitration'.[164] The Masonic Congress of France, meanwhile, appointed a study group to examine the bases of a future international organisation that convened under the direction of Léon Bourgeois in July 1916.[165]

The LDH articulated its own peace programme that was also based on the principles of law and international organisation. Victor Basch insisted in April 1915 that the war must end with 'the establishment of the rule of law, among states as among individuals, and the creation of a Society of Nations animated by the principles of international justice'.[166] In an influential volume entitled *La Guerre de 1914 et le droit*, published several weeks later, Basch further developed this argument but added that the advent of democracy in Germany was a crucial precondition for European peace.[167] The following December the LDH overwhelmingly rejected a motion calling for a compromise peace. But it also approved a programme calling for compulsory international arbitration and opposing any peace conditions based on breaking up nations or annexing territories in violation of the principle of national self-determination. 'Durable peace', it resolved, 'is only possible through the establishment of a society of nations.'[168]

---

[163] E. Milhaud, *Du Droit de la force à la force du droit* (Geneva, 1915).
[164] T. Ruyssen, 'Notre programme minimum', *PPD*, 10–25 Oct. 1915, 466–7 and 'Le Problème de la paix durable', *PPD*, 10–25 Jun. 1915, 382–3; Guieu, 'Les Apôtres', 92–3.
[165] Referred to in MAE, Société des nations [hereafter SDN], vol. 1, 'Séance d'ouverture', 28 Sept. 1917.
[166] V. Basch, 'La Ligue des droits de l'homme et la guerre', *Bulletin officiel de la Ligue des droits de l'homme* (Apr. 1915), cited in Guieu, 'Les Apôtres', 90.
[167] V. Basch, *La Guerre de 1914 et le droit* (Paris, 1915), 93–5. See also the discussion in W. D. Irvine, *Between Justice and Politics: The Ligue des droits de l'homme, 1898–1945* (Stanford, 2007), 133–5.
[168] M.-R. Mouton, 'L'Idée d'organisation internationale en France et en Italie pendant la premiere guerre mondiale' in Guillen (ed.), *France pendant la premiere guerre mondiale*, 104–5; Renouvin, 'Buts de guerre', 10.

Juridical internationalist prescriptions for post-war order and security posed a direct challenge to the more traditional solutions favoured by government officials. A number of articles in *La Paix par le droit* were banned by government censors and the correspondence of Théodore Ruyssen was placed under official surveillance.[169] Deliberations within the Comité national d'études politiques et sociales – a 'broad-church' grouping consisting mainly of politicians and trade unionists chaired by Léon Bourgeois – provide further evidence of tensions between internationalist conceptions and mainstream opinion. During the spring and summer of 1916 the Comité debated two resolutions, one in favour of compulsory arbitration and the other opposed not only to any annexations but also to a lengthy post-war occupation of the Rhineland. This alarmed some of the more conservative members of the Comité. Several, including the industrialist François de Wendel, advised Briand and Poincaré of the tenor of the debate. The premier and the president were also alarmed – not least because Bourgeois was a minister of state in Briand's government. Both therefore met privately with Bourgeois. After this meeting Bourgeois continued to oppose annexations but accepted the need for an occupation as a means to ensure future reparations payments. He also agreed to adjourn discussion of these issues within the Comité.[170] The episode provides a good example of the way the informal networks of the *république des camarades* could be used to stifle unwelcome discussion of post-war security conditions.

The Briand government was much less successful in controlling discussion of post-war issues on the far left.[171] The silent minority within the CGT and the SFIO that had opposed the war in 1914 gained the confidence to articulate its opposition over the course of 1915. At an inter-Allied conference of Socialists held in London in February of that year, SFIO representatives Marcel Sembat, Jean Longuet and Pierre Renaudel adhered to a vague internationalist declaration condemning the Tsarist regime. This caused predictable embarrassment for the Viviani government and outrage within the Quai d'Orsay. At the SFIO national council the following July, a minority element within the party led by Longuet abstained from voting for a motion against a compromise peace. Longuet would become the leading voice of the *minoritaire* movement within the SFIO that would eventually oppose the war openly. Trade unionist opponents of the war, meanwhile, were less cautious than Socialist parliamentarians. The union of metalworkers led the way in creating a 'committee of

---

[169] Mouton, 'L'Idée d'organisation internationale', 111–12.
[170] Poincaré, *Au Service de la France*, vol. VIII: *Verdun (1916)* (Paris, 1931), 13 Aug. 1916: 314; ibid., vol. IX: *L'Année trouble*, 7 Oct. 1916: 4; see also Jeanneney, *L'Argent et le pouvoir*, 35–6 (which includes de Wendel's scathing assessment of a report on international arbitration prepared by Milhaud); Sorlot, *Bourgeois*, 262; and Suarez, *Briand*, III, 412–13.
[171] The following discussion is drawn principally from A. Kriegel, *Aux Origines du communisme français, 1914–1920*, 2 vols. (Paris, 1964), I, 100–25; L. Robert, *Les Ouvrières, la Patrie et la Révolution, Paris, 1914–1919* (Paris, 1995), 36–100; and Duroselle, *Grande Guerre*, 142–4.

international action' and passing a motion calling for 'peace without annexations or indemnities'.[172]

The internationalist instincts of French Socialists also revived during this period. There was considerable support among the rank and file of both the SFIO and the CGT for establishing contact with socialists in enemy countries. This led to the participation of two French Socialists in the Zimmerwald peace conference in Switzerland in September 1915, where the war was condemned as an imperialist struggle and a motion was passed calling for a compromise peace. Among the thirty-eight participants at this conference were two German delegates as well as Russian exiles Vladimir Lenin and Léon Trotsky. The Zimmerwald proposals did not win the approval of a significant portion of working-class opinion. A vast majority within both the SFIO and even the CGT was hostile to the *Zimmerwaldiens* and remained committed to the pro-government position of the Socialist leaders Guesde, Sembat, Thomas and Vaillant. Yet an alternative to this position had been established in the form of revolutionary workers' pacifism.[173]

This alternative would become increasingly attractive on the far left as the fighting stretched into its third year with no end in sight. In January 1916 the CGT established a 'Committee for the Resumption of International Relations', the backbone of which came from pacifist-inclined members of the metalworkers' and teachers' unions. At the same time the number of *minoritaires* within the SFIO in favour of a negotiated peace grew steadily. At the party's national council of 7 August 1916 their number had increased to 1,081, as against 1,850 *majoritaires*.[174] The Socialist leadership was less divided over the question of an independent Left Bank state. Opinion was unanimous on two key points. The first was opposition to any annexations. The second was that the political fate of the Left Bank should be determined by the Rhinelanders themselves in a plebiscite.[175]

Virtually the entire Socialist programme for post-war security was thus incompatible with traditional approaches based on the need for a strategic barrier as well as calculations of the post-war balance of power. In the chamber on 3 November 1915 Renaudel, who represented the majority of the SFIO that supported the Allied war effort, pressed Briand to expressly disavow a policy of conquest and annexations. Briand refused.[176]

There remained significant overlap between juridical and socialist internationalism. Both movements opposed annexation, advocating instead

---

[172] Dreyfus, *Histoire de la CGT*, 84–93; N. Ingram, 'Le Pacifisme de guerre: refus de l'Union sacrée et de la synthèse républicain?' in R. Cazals, E. Picard and D. Rolland (eds.), *La Grande Guerre: pratiques et expériences* (Toulouse, 2005), 77–86.
[173] Kriegel, *Origines du communisme*, I, 124–5.   [174] Duroselle, *Grande Guerre*, 143.
[175] There was even support within the SFIO for a plebiscite to determine the future of Alsace-Lorraine.
[176] Bonnefous, *Grande Guerre*, 97–9; Renouvin, 'Buts de guerre', 11–12; Stevenson, *French War Aims*, 19–20.

self-determination and the rule of law. Both, moreover, also supported the idea of an international organisation that would draft and impose the rule of law. But the fundamental divergence between the two movements remained. Juridical internationalists' commitment to national sovereignty continued to be at variance with the class-based ideology of mainstream socialists. The gulf between the two internationalisms would only increase as a growing number of socialists embraced revolutionary pacifism as an alternative to patriotism and support for the war effort. This process remained in its early stages in 1916. It would be accelerated by news from Russia over the course of 1917 and culminate in the destruction of socialist unity.

Both currents of internationalism gained credibility and momentum from Woodrow Wilson's widely disseminated criticisms of traditional diplomatic practices as causes of the war. The same was true of his 27 May 1916 commitment to a league of nations. This initiative received enthusiastic support from both *majoritaires* and *minoritaires* within the Socialist Party and became one of the chief themes of Socialist agitation in the chamber. The LDH signalled its unanimous approval for the idea during its congress in November 1916. This was all part of what one scholar has described as a 'veritable Wilsonian mystique' among French internationalists of all stripes.[177] With the partial exception of Léon Bourgeois, however, juridical and socialist internationalists were not part of the machinery of policy making.

VII

Alliance politics, territorial annexations and calculations of the future balance of power remained central elements in the making of high policy through spring 1917. Foreign minister Delcassé initially favoured breaking up the Reich into nine independent or semi-independent states, with Prussia losing its predominant position.[178] He subsequently agreed to an even more draconian programme suggested by the Tsarist government aimed at ending German power in Europe. The Russians proposed eighteenth-century-style reciprocal annexations of German, Austro-Hungarian and Ottoman territory. The idea was that Russia would annex large swathes of German- and Austro-Hungarian-controlled Poland. It would also gain control of Constantinople and the Dardanelles Straits. France, in return, would regain the lost provinces of Alsace-Lorraine and, along with Belgium, would annex the entire Left Bank

---

[177] Guieu, 'Les Apôtres', 95; see also S. Lorrain, *Des Pacifists français et allemands pionniers de l'entente franco-allemande* (Paris, 1999); Bouchard, 'Projets citoyens pour une paix durable', 63–80; and Blair, 'La France et le pacte', 22–32.

[178] Delcassé outlined this vision of the post-war settlement to Russian ambassador Alexander Isvolski in September 1914; see the latter's report of 30 Sept. 1914 in F. Stieve (ed.), *Isvolski and the World War: Based on the Documents Recently Published by the German Foreign Office* (Freeport, 1978); Stevenson, *French War Aims*, 26–8, 43; McDougall, *Rhineland Diplomacy*, 17–18.

The primacy of the balance of power, 1914–1916   131

of the Rhine and also receive sections of the Palatinate. 'Take the Left Bank of the Rhine, take Mainz, take Koblenz, go even further if you deem it necessary,' Tsar Nicholas II urged French ambassador Paléologue in March 1915.[179]

It is difficult to imagine a purer expression of the power-politics approach to international relations than that of the Russian programme. There was, significantly, general approval within the French policy elite for the principles upon which the Russian proposal was based, if not the specific terms on offer. Paléologue warned of the danger that Russia might leave the war. He urged his government to accept the tsar's proposal. Delcassé was amenable, and responded that he was in 'general accord' with the 'bases' of the Russian scheme.[180] In early 1915 he invited his counterpart Sazonov to a conference to establish a post-war settlement, the 'essential bases' of which would be reciprocal annexations. Delcassé's chief aim was to obtain French control of the Left Bank of the Rhine.[181]

Opposition to Delcassé's strategy in official circles, interestingly, was focused not on the traditional principles underpinning his approach but instead on the sense that France was giving up too much and that the result would be an over-powerful Russia that could threaten French interests in the Mediterranean. De Margerie made this argument in a widely circulated memorandum of early April 1915.[182] Poincaré, always determined to exercise his presidential prerogatives in the domain of foreign policy, intervened in the debate along the same lines. If France agreed to Russia's demands, he argued, 'the European balance will be changed completely ... such an increase in [Russian] power would be acceptable only if we receive equivalent advantages'. Poincaré was thus no less devoted to the power-balancing approach to international relations than were Delcassé and his advisers at the foreign ministry. 'We can support Russia's desires', he concluded, 'only in proportion to the satisfactions that we receive in return.'[183] In the end, the desire to bolster French power by extending it into the Rhineland combined with the fear that Russia might leave the war to overcome long-standing anxieties over Russia's ambition to control the Dardanelles. In March 1915 the French government reluctantly agreed to back Russian claims in the 'Straits Agreement'.[184]

---

[179] MAE, *Série A*, vol. 223, Paléologue (Petrograd) to Delcassé (Paris), 4 Mar. 1914; also in MAE, PA-AP 133, *Papiers Paléologue*, vol. 2; see also Soutou, 'Marches de l'est', 345–54.
[180] MAE, *Série A*, vol. 54, Delcassé to Paléologue, 15 Nov. 1914; see also Delcassé's telegram to Paléologue of 10 Oct. 1914 in the same dossier.
[181] Quoted in Stevenson, *French War Aims*, 27.
[182] MAE, PA-AP 211, *Papiers Delcassé*, vol. 25, 'Note pour le ministre' by de Margerie, 9 Mar. 1915.
[183] MAE, PA-AP 133, *Papiers Paléologue*, vol. 2, Poincaré to Paléologue, 9 Mar. 1915 (also in PA-AP 43, *Papiers Jules Cambon*, vol. 18); these passages were excised from the version of the exchange published in Poincaré's memoirs, *Au Service de la France*, vol. VI: *Les Tranchées (1915)* (Paris, 1930), 92–5; see also Soutou, 'Marches de l'est', 349–51.
[184] Stevenson, *Cataclysm*, 112–13.

An ambition to overturn the European balance of power was central to both public discourse and official policy. French planning for post-war security policy as it emerged in 1916 aimed at bolstering France's industrial position by securing control over the coalfields of the Saar basin and, crucially, access to the metallurgical coking coal (vital for steel production) produced in the Ruhr industrial region. It also sought to dominate the Left Bank of the Rhine. The end result would be to establish an effective barrier to a future German invasion and to weaken the sinews of German economic power while at the same time greatly enhancing the productive capacities of France's steel industry. Security would be obtained through unchallengeable strategic preponderance. France's 'historic' frontiers were constructed so as to coincide with this programme. The traditional approach to security constituted a 'practical logic' that went virtually unchallenged within the policy-making elite during the first half of the Great War.

The internationalist approach to security, conversely, remained largely marginalised. The politics of the Union sacrée, reinforced by official censorship, inhibited the articulation of an alternative conception for post-war security based on political transformation, multilateral cooperation and international law. At the same time, however, internationalist currents endured. The continuing preference among many of France's most powerful iron and steel magnates for industrial cooperation with Germany after the war provides a good illustration of this basic fact. So too do the ambiguities in post-war economic planning within the Quai d'Orsay and ministry of commerce. Just as important for the internationalist cause was the unprecedented ferocity of the war, which generated calls for a new approach to international relations both inside and outside France. Yet another boon to internationalists was the omnipresence of tropes such as 'law' and 'justice' in official representations of the conflict. This discourse, which was intended to secure legitimacy for the French war effort both at home and abroad, culminated in the Briand government's commitment to the creation of a 'society of nations' in its response to president Wilson's 'peace note' in January 1917. All of this provided the internationalist cause with the political space to make its case with increasing confidence. These trends only accelerated as the bonds of the Union sacrée came apart in mid-1917 and the government's security policy came under open challenge in parliament.

4 The coming of a new world order, 1917

In late May 1917 Paul Morand, a junior official at the foreign ministry, reflected on the seismic changes in both the domestic and international contexts in which France was waging war: 'I have been re-reading our initial war aims, the instructions given to Paul Cambon by Briand. How we are far from all that (the Left Bank, the Saar basin Constantinople, etc.).'[1] The first six months of 1917 had brought about a profound transformation in the political character of the war. Revolution in Russia in February (and then again in October), combined with the decision of the United States to enter the war on the side of the Allies in April, laid the foundations of a new world order that would endure in its essentials through to the end of the twentieth century.

To these international developments were added an unmistakable wavering in the French nation's resolve to see the conflict through to victory. The grinding frustration and unending losses that characterised the middle phases of the war had a profound effect on both popular and elite understandings of its purpose. One historian has judged that the losses sustained at Verdun, on the Somme and elsewhere had raised the question as to 'whether the war could yet be won, and whether winning had any longer much meaning'.[2] The costly and futile offensive on the Chemin des Dames in spring 1917 provided the catalyst for a wave of mutinies and an alarming series of strikes on the home front. The result was steadily increasing support for a compromise peace among politicians of the left and centre-left. By October of that year the Union sacrée lay in ruins, Russia had left the war and the prospect of final victory seemed more remote than at any time since the disastrous opening phases of the war.

These developments posed powerful challenges to the traditional conception of security. With the collapse of Tsarist Russia, France lost the ally most willing to support its plans to overturn the European strategic balance with a forward policy in the Rhineland. French decision makers instead came under intense pressure to alter their policies in response to proposals emanating from Petrograd and, especially, from Washington. At the same time, domestic advocates of both socialist and juridical internationalism were emboldened to

---

[1] Morand, *Journal d'un attaché*, 26 May 1917, 248.
[2] D. Stevenson, *Cataclysm: The First World War as Political Tragedy* (New York, 2004), 143.

133

articulate alternative visions of a future international order that revolved around the creation of a league or society of nations. Despite these internal and external challenges, official policy planning remained wedded to a traditional approach to security. Seismic changes in the national and international spheres manifested themselves only gradually in the policy process. The result would be ever greater ambiguity in the aims and objectives of post-war planning as the changing fortunes of war confronted France with one of the darkest moments in its history.

I

In early 1917 the balance of power and traditional assumptions about the nature of international relations were as dominant as ever in official policy conceptions. This is clear from a series of high-level discussions of war aims and peace conditions that culminated in the 'Cambon Letter' of 12 January 1917. The impetus for these consultations was concern that Russia might negotiate a separate peace with the Central Powers. Anxiety over Russian intentions had been growing since the previous summer. It gave rise to a general sense that France must formulate its security requirements in preparation for inter-Allied discussions aimed at keeping its ally in the war.

An important initial stage in this process was a four-hour luncheon at the Élysée Palace on 7 October 1916.[3] In attendance were Poincaré, Briand, the presidents of the chamber and senate, Paul Deschanel and Antonin Dubost respectively, and the two influential ministers of state in Briand's cabinet, Léon Bourgeois and Charles de Freycinet. The chief issue discussed was France's policy towards the Left Bank of the Rhine. Socialist ministers Albert Thomas and Marcel Sembat were not invited. This meeting was typical of the informal way in which important decisions were often taken in unofficial consultations among the key parliamentary power-brokers of the Third Republic.[4] Deschanel and Dubost both argued that the only way to achieve security was to weaken German power and to bolster that of France by annexing the Left Bank of the Rhine. De Freycinet, a fixture of centrist politics since the 1870s, proposed that France make it clear to its allies that it was 'indispensable' to consider the question of the Left Bank as 'a matter of French policy'. Poincaré endorsed this manner of proceeding. Only Bourgeois was unequivocally opposed to annexing the Left Bank. He argued instead for a 'lengthy occupation' of this region as a 'guarantee' of German compliance to Allied peace terms and to the 'organisation of international law'. But he was outnumbered. It was agreed that soundings should be taken in London along

---

[3] Poincaré, *Au Service de la France*, vol. IX: *L'Année trouble, 1917* (Paris, 1932), 3–4 and 79; G. Suarez, *Briand: sa vie, son oeuvre, avec son journal et de nombreux documents inédits*, 6 vols. (Paris, 1938–52), vol. III: *Le Pilote dans la tourmente, 1914–1916* (Paris, 1939), 411–14; see also D. Stevenson, *French War Aims against Germany, 1914–1919* (Oxford, 1982), 41–2.

[4] G.-H. Soutou, 'La France et les marches de l'est, 1914–1919', *RH*, 528 (1978), 356.

the lines suggested by de Freycinet and Poincaré. An envoy would then be sent to Russia to advise the Tsarist government of Franco-British views concerning the future of Germany and Austria-Hungary.[5] The balance of power clearly trumped juridical internationalism at this meeting.

The aim of establishing a special French interest in the Left Bank was a central theme in the Cambon Letter. This document was intended to guide discussions with the British about Allied war aims.[6] Although it was drafted in the first instance by Jules Cambon, it drew together the views of senior foreign ministry officials, the prescriptions of the army general staff and the majority view at the 7 October meeting at the Élysée Palace. A first draft of the document was completed in late November. It was then revised substantially, most notably by Berthelot, before eventually coming before the cabinet for discussion and approval in early January 1917.[7] As the product of a relatively lengthy process of inter-ministerial reflection and consultation, the Cambon Letter has rightly been characterised as 'the most authoritative statement of French objectives' to appear during the course of the war.[8] Despite the careful scrutiny it has received, however, little attention has been paid to the fundamental assumptions that underpin this document, the terms in which it represented the security problem and the language that it deployed.

As an expression of France's security requirements the Cambon Letter was in many ways a virtual distillation of the traditional approach to security. A passage in the second paragraph of the document provides an illuminating summary of the power-political principles at the heart of the French programme:

Each power has its own aspirations; it is essential to know these in order to somehow balance the satisfactions that can be accorded with the sacrifices that can be demanded of each. It is for this reason that the negotiations that will open in London with Italy on the subject of Asia Minor must not be considered in isolation, without taking into account the considerable advantages that the government of Rome has secured in the Adriatic or in the Alps.[9]

Great Power horse-trading would remain the order of the day.

---

[5] See Poincaré, *L'Année trouble*, 4. In his analysis Soutou asserts that this meeting demonstrates that even Bourgeois favoured the neutralisation of the Rhineland. This is not borne out by Poincaré's notes on the meeting in question.
[6] The original is in MAE, *Série A*, vol. 58, 'Conditions de paix', Briand to (Paul) Cambon, 12 Jan. 1917.
[7] See for example Jules Cambon's 'Projet' of Nov.–Dec. 1916, with detailed annotations by Berthelot, in MAE, *Série A*, vol. 55 and MAE, PA-AP 141, *Papiers Pichon*, vol. 4.
[8] D. Stevenson, 'France and the German Question in the Era of the First World War' in S. Schuker (ed.), *Deutschland und Frankreich Vom Konflikt zur Aussöhnung: Die Gestaltung der westeuropäischen Sicherheit 1914–1963* (Munich, 2000), 9; see also Stevenson, *French War Aims*, 36–51; W. McDougall, *France's Rhineland Diplomacy, 1914–1924: The Last Bid for a Balance of Power in Europe* (Princeton, 1978), 16–23; Soutou, 'Marches de l'est'; and P. Renouvin, 'Les Buts de guerre du gouvernement français, 1914–1918', *RH*, 516, (1966).
[9] MAE, *Série A*, vol. 55, 'Conditions de paix', Briand to (Paul) Cambon, 12 Jan. 1917; also in *Série A*, vol. 58 and in MAE, PA-AP 141, *Papiers Pichon*, vol. 4.

At the same time, however, the document is replete with universalist claims concerning both the motives and the objectives of French policy. It makes reference to Germany's responsibility for starting the war and reminds Paul Cambon to stress the common ideological sources of French and British policy. As democracies, both states shared the 'same ideal of liberty'. There are many passages where universalist claims sit alongside traditionalist objectives aimed at providing France with strategic advantage. While insisting that France pursued 'no particular advantage' in the outcome of the war, the note also asserts the French right to 'positive satisfaction' in Europe. The tensions between universalism and self-interest are even more pronounced in the following passage:

> Honour, loyalty to engagements, the defence of weaker peoples and the maintenance of our independence and that of Europe will inspire us during the final settlement as it has throughout the war and will distance us from any thought of conquest. At the same time, we have a duty to look out for the interests of France, which include certain territorial guarantees and the reparation of our rights violated in 1871, and which rest on respect for the law of nations.[10]

French demands for a revolution in the balance of power were thus couched in the discourse of international legitimacy. One of the most interesting aspects of the Cambon Letter is the fact that its authors seem to have been unaware of, and indeed were perhaps unable to recognise, the contradictions between the language used and the claims being advanced.

After an allusion to 'the generous sentiments of our democracy', the note deployed history and popular memory to lay out a programme of territorial changes aimed at transforming Europe. It called for a return of Alsace-Lorraine 'not mutilated as they were by the treaty of 1815 [at the Congress of Vienna] but restored to their status before 1790'. This would include virtually all of the Saar basin, 'the possession of which is essential to our industry'. Restitution of the lost provinces, it was emphasised, 'must not enter into the balance sheet' as 'an advantage' or 'a net gain' for France. Moving on to address 'positive satisfactions' for France, the document stressed the need to neutralise the Left Bank. It underlined popular support in France for reincorporating the Left Bank. Regaining this 'lost heritage of the French Revolution' was described as 'one of the oldest traditions of our national policy'. Acknowledging that annexation of this region might be misinterpreted as conquest, it proposed that the Left Bank be neutralised following a temporary occupation. The letter further stipulated that France must have 'a preponderant voice' in the precise constitution of this state.[11]

Turning to central Europe, the note advocated the creation of a strong Poland at Germany's expense. This would provide a military counterweight on the Reich's eastern marches. The question of a financial indemnity was also

---

[10] Ibid. [11] Ibid.

raised, but not examined in any systematic way. The final paragraph of the note alluded to President Wilson's proposal to create an international organisation to prevent future conflicts. The Cambon Letter approved of this idea but clearly envisioned any institution that emerged from it as an organisation in which Allied powers 'might unite more intimately by treaties of alliance' and create 'an association of force that would command respect on its own'. In conclusion it stressed that the French proposal was 'an expression of a policy of reason and moderation' which sought 'only to re-establish in Europe the balance between the powers that is the surest means of maintaining the peace'.[12]

From beginning to end the Cambon Letter advocated a traditional solution to France's post-war security requirements. Although it used the familiar tactic of eliding these requirements with the interests of Europe and the rest of the world, its fundamental aim was to transform the strategic balance by territorial revision in both east and west at the expense of the Reich. At the same time, however, the rhetorical strategies employed in the letter should not be dismissed as window-dressing. The tactic of stressing France's democratic credentials as a means to establish legitimacy for its security requirements was new, and reveals a sensitivity to the changing normative environment in which France was operating. Democracy was increasingly a source of legitimacy in Great Power politics. French policy was thus expressed in a language designed to take advantage of this important development – which would only accelerate in the months to come as the USA entered the war and Tsarist Russia collapsed. Nor should the sincerity of claims to represent the interests of Europe and the world be dismissed altogether. The vast majority of French officials certainly believed that the war effort was more than a struggle to defend the national interests of France. If this fundamental truth was assumed to be self-evident, it did no harm to remind France's allies of both the nature and scale of its sacrifice in negotiations over the shape of the post-war order.

The changes made to earlier versions of the Cambon Letter are instructive in this regard.[13] In addition to Berthelot's removal of references to the fate of Luxembourg (mentioned in the previous chapter) a number of other significant changes were made. In the original, for example, Jules Cambon had made a distinction between 'the direct demands of France' and 'the French programme for the future organisation of Europe'.[14] This distinction was dropped in the final version. There were fewer details about French plans for the frontiers and political orientation of an independent Rhineland. In particular, references to a customs union between this region and France were removed.

[12] Ibid.
[13] The following two paragraphs compare the various versions of Jules Cambon's 'Projet' drafted in November and December 1916 (one of which is extensively annotated by Berthelot) with the final version: all versions can be consulted in MAE, *Série A*, vol. 55.
[14] MAE, *Série A*, vol. 55, 'Projet' J. Cambon note, 12 Dec. 1916.

Also excised was a lengthy section on the dismemberment of the Austro-Hungarian Empire and the crucial role its successor states would play in the construction of a future eastern 'rampart against Germanism'.

The cumulative effect of these changes was to moderate the scope of the French programme for conversations in London and, just as importantly, to present it as a proposal for 'the security of Europe' as opposed to a list of French desiderata. The changes did not reflect a moderation of French ambitions. Berthelot, who assumed chief responsibility for editing the document, was if anything even more hardline than Cambon. The alterations reflect instead Berthelot's sensitivity to the predispositions of British policy makers. He rightly judged that far-reaching plans for a Rhenish vassal state and the constitution of an anti-German political order in east–central Europe would only alarm the new Lloyd George government. Paul Cambon in London agreed. He judged that the British would consider even this more restrained formulation of French aims excessive. Consequently, he did not even discuss the Letter with British foreign secretary Arthur Balfour until 2 July 1917 (nearly six months after its dispatch).[15] The Cambon Letter would be overtaken by the tumultuous events of the first half of 1917.

II

The collapse of Tsarist Russia in February, followed by the gradual erosion of all political authority in that country in the months that followed, deprived France of its ally of longest standing. The entry of the United States into the war the following April was just as important, not least because it threw up a powerful obstacle to French aspirations for the post-war order. Military setbacks on the western front in April and May, moreover, contributed mightily to a crisis of morale within the army, and within French society more generally. To these problems were added increasingly militant labour unrest that culminated in a wave of strikes in May and June. These latter factors were part of a broader wavering of the national commitment to prosecuting the war that ranged from doubts that the war was winnable (mainly on the right) to growing support for a negotiated peace (mainly on the centre-left) to revolutionary pacifism (among a minority on the left).[16] Taken together these developments weakened France's war effort and increased its dependence on Britain and the United States. Neither the British nor the Americans, significantly, were sympathetic to the traditional conception of post-war security that prevailed in official circles in Paris.

---

[15] L. Villate, *La République des diplomates: Paul et Jules Cambon, 1843–1935* (Paris, 2002), 333–4; Stevenson, *French War Aims*, 48–51.
[16] L. Robert, *Les Ouvriers, la Patrie et la Révolution, Paris, 1914–1919* (Paris, 1995), 116–55, 177–94 and 203–362.

Important changes altered the political situation of France's chief enemy. After the German army failed to break France's will at Verdun, Generals Paul von Hindenburg and Erich Ludendorff succeeded in imposing their radical vision of both the prosecution of the war and the character of the post-war order. The result was the 'Kreuznach Programme', drafted and approved in April 1917. This document called for German control for 'at least a century' of Luxembourg, Liège, the entire Flanders coastline and France's Briey-Longwy iron-ore fields. Russian Poland would come under German domination and the Baltic states of Courland and Lithuania would be annexed. The overriding aim was to ensure that Germany was best-placed to achieve victory in future European wars.[17]

There was resistance to this programme for continental domination from both parliament and the political elite in Germany. Chancellor Bethmann was convinced that Germany must make some concessions in its bargaining position, and signed the Kreuznach Programme under protest.[18] He was forced to resign as chancellor shortly thereafter. His successor, Georg Michaelis, also worked to introduce greater flexibility in Germany's bargaining position. He was supported by the centre-left and left in the Reichstag. There were, however, strict limits on the willingness of even moderate elements in Germany to make significant compromises.[19] The democratic opposition in Germany posed no genuine threat to the war effort. Its chief contribution to the settlement of the war was instead to constitute a possible democratic alternative to the regime when the military situation took a turn for the worse in late 1918.[20] French decision makers were provided with an essentially accurate picture of German intentions at this juncture by the Deuxième bureau and by the sources at the disposal of the Quai d'Orsay.[21] This intelligence only reinforced existing interpretations of the conflict as an elemental struggle for national survival, and had no material effect on post-war planning in Paris.

The situation in Austria-Hungary was worse. The war had radicalised the politics of the Polish, Czech and South Slav minorities living under Habsburg rule. This process accelerated as the war dragged on and strains on the empire mounted. The decline of the Habsburg army, along with the general deterioration of the economy and living conditions, created the conditions under which minority leaders were able to demand autonomy, and even full

---

[17] F. Fischer, *Germany's Aims in the First World War* (London, 1967), 345–53; Stevenson, *Cataclysm*, 282–3.
[18] K. H. Jarausch, *The Enigmatic Chancellor: Bethmann Hollweg and the Hubris of Imperial Germany* (New Haven, 1973), 411–522.
[19] T. Oppelland, *Reichstag und Aussenpolitik im Ersten Weltkrieg: Die deutschen Parteien und die Politik der USA* (Düsseldorf, 1995), 172–88.
[20] R. Chickering, *Imperial Germany and the Great War, 1914–1918* (Cambridge, 1998), 160–72.
[21] G.-H. Soutou, 'Un Exemple d'influence: le renseignement français et le problème des nationalités, le cas de l'Office central des nationalités' in P. Lacoste (ed.), *Le Renseignement à la française* (Paris, 1998), 131–47.

independence.[22] Concerns for the future of the empire led the Vienna government to explore the option of a compromise peace through secret contacts with the French government in April 1917, and then again the following autumn. These exploratory efforts led nowhere mainly because the Dual Monarchy was unwilling to consider a separate peace that would leave Germany isolated.[23]

Events in Russia posed formidable challenges to French policy. The convulsive process that brought about the withdrawal of Russia from the war was already under way even as a high-ranking delegation of French officials under the direction of colonial minister Gaston Doumergue arrived in Petrograd to discuss the post-war settlement in early February 1917.[24] The Russian war effort was in serious difficulty, hamstrung by the decline in the combat effectiveness of the army, an acutely devalued currency and a workforce on the verge of insurrection.[25] On 8 March Petrograd was paralysed by a generalised strike and a massive demonstration. The capital's military garrison refused to put down the protesters with force. When the chief of the garrison reported that he had lost control of the city, the army leadership declined to stand by the regime. On 15 March Tsar Nicholas II abdicated. Russia was declared a republic and a provisional government was established.

Two contending centres of authority emerged. The first was the provisional government, led by parliamentary politicians committed to constitutional change. The second was the Petrograd Soviet of workers' and soldiers' deputies, led by socialist revolutionaries. The provisional government and the army general staff both hoped to channel the energies of the revolution into an invigorated war effort. When this proved impossible, they aimed instead at establishing the political bases for a negotiated peace. The Petrograd Soviet, conversely, increasingly favoured withdrawal from the conflict and a separate peace. It was also the more powerful of the two power centres. The Soviet's 'Army Order No. 1' asserted its authority over the army and also its right to countermand orders given by the provisional government. This contributed mightily to the erosion of discipline within the Imperial Army.

Despite its fraught political position, the provisional government initially assured the Allies that it would honour the secret agreements negotiated by the

---

[22] Z. A. B. Zeman, *The Break-up of the Habsburg Empire, 1914–1918: A Study in National and Social Revolution* (London, 1961), 318–31; A. Sked, *The Decline and Fall of the Hapsburg Empire, 1815–1918*, 2nd edn (London, 2001), 296–334.

[23] H. Herwig, *The First World War: Germany and Austria-Hungary, 1914–1918* (London, 1996), 294–387.

[24] The following paragraphs are drawn principally from O. Figes, *A People's Tragedy: The Russian Revolution, 1891–1924* (London, 1997), 291–551; T. Hasegawa, *The February Revolution: Petrograd, 1917* (London, 1981); and M. A. Reynolds, *Shattering Empires: The Clash and Collapse of the Ottoman and Russian Empires, 1908–1918* (Cambridge, 2011), 140–266.

[25] D. R. Jones, 'Imperial Russia's Forces at War' in A. Millett and W. Murray (eds.), *Military Effectiveness*, vol. I: *The First World War* (Boston, 1988), 252–79; B. D. Taylor, *Politics and the Russian Army: Civil–Military Relations, 1689–2000* (Cambridge, 2003), 64–137.

The coming of a new world order, 1917   141

Tsarist regime. It also reiterated Russia's claim to Constantinople and the Dardanelles. The Petrograd Soviet responded by issuing the 'Petrograd Formula' calling on the peoples of the world to rally to a peace settlement based on self-determination without either annexations or indemnities. Foreign minister Pavel Miliukov was forced to resign and the provisional government was restructured. The new cabinet abandoned all territorial claims and on 13 June 1917 proposed an inter-Allied conference to revise war aims. In mid-July, after receiving evasive replies from the Entente to its proposals, the Russian leadership changed tack and proposed a meeting in Stockholm of representatives from the socialist parties of *all* belligerents.[26] It was this proposal that provoked the political crisis in France, the ultimate result of which was the end of the Union sacrée.

When the provisional government pressed ahead with a major offensive against the Central Powers, the Russian army began to disintegrate. By September 1917 the eastern front had effectively ceased to exist.[27] Military collapse in turn created the conditions under which the Bolsheviks, the movement most committed to ending the war almost at any cost, were able to seize power in early November 1917. The central foreign policy objective of the Bolsheviks was to transform the capitalist war between states into a revolutionary conflict between classes. Immediately after the November revolution the new regime immediately issued a 'Peace Decree' denouncing secret diplomacy and proposing 'immediate negotiations' for a 'just and democratic' settlement without annexations or indemnities. It also published all of the secret treaties negotiated by the Entente. The secret Allied arrangements for the Straits, eastern Europe and the Rhineland thus entered the public domain immediately after the Bolsheviks took power.[28]

The revolutionaries failed in their aim to provoke a Europe-wide class war, however. The Bolsheviks were forced to seek an armistice with the Central Powers. The agreement that was eventually signed at Brest-Litovsk on 3 March 1918 forced Russia to relinquish its authority in Poland and the Ukraine. It was also deprived of nearly one-third of its population, much of its heavy industry and coal production and most of its best agricultural land.[29] Russia had not only left the war, it had been removed as a factor in the European balance of power for the foreseeable future. The revolution wrought a profound transformation of the political and strategic contexts in which French security policy was made.

The second momentous change was America's entry into the war as an 'Associated Power' on 6 April 1917. The Wilson administration imposed no conditions for joining the conflict, and loudly proclaimed that it harboured no

---

[26] R. Wade, *The Russian Search for Peace, February–October 1917* (Stanford, 1969), 51–73.
[27] Figes, *People's Tragedy*, 330–1; A. Wildman, *The End of the Imperial Russian Army*, vol. I: *The Old Army and the Soldiers' Revolt (March–April 1917)* (Princeton, 1980), 176–92.
[28] Stevenson, *Cataclysm*, 313–22.
[29] R. K. Debo, *Revolution and Survival: The Foreign Policy of Soviet Russia, 1917–1918* (Liverpool, 1979), 14–24 and 72–88.

territorial ambitions. This allowed the president to retain his self-appointed role as an honest broker who spoke for the 'principles of mankind'. He fully intended to use this status to dominate the peace proceedings once the fighting was over. The chief American objectives were the democratisation of Germany and a transformation of international politics.[30] Neither of these aims, significantly, was in line with the priorities of the traditional approach to international security.

Wilson and his chief advisers were convinced that the ambitions of both the Allies and the Central Powers must be restrained in the interests of a lasting peace. In the president's rather hazy vision of the post-war order, this restraint would be institutionalised by the League of Nations. In his 'Peace Without Victory' speech Wilson had stressed the importance of a post-war 'League for Peace'. He insisted that the USA would participate in such an institution only if it was inclusive and not merely a de facto alliance of victorious states.[31] Pronouncements such as these were intended to encourage opponents of traditional Great Power politics within Allied states as well as the Central Powers. This strategy met with considerable success in France. From early 1917 French internationalists of all stripes were ever more confident in asserting their vision of the post-war order. From within the Quai d'Orsay Paul Morand remarked that 'Wilson's message has had an important impact on the French socialist milieu. Numerous letters of congratulation. We tell ourselves that this message has greatly embarrassed the Germans, but it is just as much an embarrassment for the Allies.'[32]

Nor could France count on Britain to support its traditional designs to transform the balance of power in Europe. As British policy towards the post-war period took shape, a reformed and moderately powerful Germany at the heart of Europe was considered both inevitable and desirable. Support for liberal internationalist doctrines was more widespread in Britain than in France, and much stronger among policy elites. There were proposals to cripple German economic power. And the British government did participate in various schemes to construct imperial and allied economic blocs after the war. But Germany had been Britain's second-largest export market before 1914. The British treasury, which wielded far more influence over policy than did the ministry of finance in France, doubted whether such schemes were either practicable or in Britain's long-term interests.[33]

---

[30] T. J. Knock, *To End all Wars: Woodrow Wilson and the Quest for a New World Order* (Princeton, 1992), 105–93; E. Manela, *The Wilsonian Moment: Self-determination and the International Origins of Anti-colonial Nationalism* (Oxford, 2007), esp. 3–53.

[31] 'Peace Without Victory Address', in Link et al. (eds.), *The Papers of Woodrow Wilson*, XL, 5363–8.

[32] Morand, *Journal d'un attaché*, 148; see also C. Bouchard, *Le Citoyen et l'ordre mondial (1914–1918): le rêve d'une paix durable au lendemain de la Grande Guerre* (Paris, 2008), 84–94.

[33] See esp. V. Rothwell, *British War Aims and Peace Diplomacy, 1914–1918* (Oxford, 1971), 265–71; R. Bunselmeyer, *The Costs of the War: British Economic War Aims and the Origins of Reparation* (Hamden, Conn., 1975), 21–72.

The coming of a new world order, 1917   143

There was therefore little prospect of British support for a policy of annexations aimed at destroying German power. Foreign secretary Arthur Balfour characterised the Cambon Letter as a 'rather wild project' when it was divulged to him. He urged his colleagues to oppose the French programme. British thinking inclined instead towards a relatively swift reintegration of a reformed Germany into the international system. Nor was the Lloyd George government immune to power-political calculations. There was widespread acknowledgement, for example, that a strong Germany would serve as an effective geostrategic counterweight to future designs for continental hegemony on the part of either France or Russia. In the autumn of 1917 Lloyd George refused even to make a clear statement of support for French claims to Alsace-Lorraine.[34]

These transformations of the international context happened just as France entered its most difficult period of the war. The core elements of the moral crisis that would shake the war effort in 1917 were in place in late 1916. But it was the bloody failure of the Chemin des Dames offensive, in which great hopes for a breakthrough had been invested, that led to widespread disillusionment within both the army and the civilian population. The French army suffered 271,000 casualties in two attacks along the Aisne in April 1917. In the two months following these operations nearly two-thirds of the army was affected by a wave of mutinies. Most of the incidents involved soldiers refusing to re-enter the front line, and especially to attack. But there were also extensive protests against the war and, significantly, demands for peace without annexations or indemnities. Revolutionary rhetoric was prevalent in some units, and there were even threats to march on Paris.[35] The government responded by sacking General Robert Nivelle, the commander of the French armies on the western front responsible for planning and executing the offensive. General Philippe Pétain was appointed as his replacement while General Ferdinand Foch was named chief of army staff. Pétain and Foch would dominate French military planning for the next decade.[36]

The breakdown in discipline and morale was all the more serious because it coincided with a looming manpower crisis. The army staff was forced to disband six divisions in November 1917. It anticipated that another nine divisions would be inoperable by the following spring, a number that was expected to rise to twenty-five by the end of 1918. The French war effort, in other words, had peaked and was in decline by mid-1917.[37] This was reflected

---

[34] D. French, *The Strategy of the Lloyd George Coalition, 1916–1918* (Oxford, 1995), 13–39 and 204–5; Rothwell, *British War Aims*, 64–5; Stevenson, *French War Aims*, 83–4.

[35] G. Pédroncini, *Les Mutineries de 1917* (Paris, 1967); L. V. Smith, *Between Mutiny and Obedience: The Case of the French Fifth Infantry Division during World War I* (Princeton, 1994); R. A. Doughty, *Pyrrhic Victory: French Strategy and Operations in the Great War* (Cambridge, Mass., 2005), 361–5.

[36] Doughty, *Pyrrhic Victory*, 356–69; G. Pédroncini, *Pétain: le soldat, 1914–1940* (Paris, 1998), 107–23.

[37] See the excellent discussion in Doughty, *Pyrrhic Victory*, 416–17.

in the scaled-back objectives of French military planning at this stage of the war. On 19 May Pétain issued 'Army Directive No. 1' which asserted that a breakthrough was impossible under the existing 'equilibrium of forces'. It stated that the French army would concentrate on limited operations to conserve manpower until the arrival of American troops altered the balance and made a war-winning strategic offensive possible. With an eye on peace negotiations, Pétain's staff judged that the main French effort at this time should be directed towards Alsace.[38] But the larger reality was that France was increasingly dependent on the military efforts of its coalition partners.[39]

The pronounced deterioration in the military situation was central to the national crisis of 1917. Between June and September postal censors reported an increase in pessimism among the French population as well as growing support for a compromise peace. The interior ministry prepared a lengthy study in late June which judged that morale was 'bad' in eight departments and 'mediocre' in twenty-nine more. It described public confidence as 'fairly good' in thirty departments and 'good' in only three.[40] The strikes of May–June 1917 provided further evidence of wavering national resolve. Strike action began on May Day and by the end of the month more than 160,000 workers were on strike in Paris alone.[41] The taboo against striking during wartime was thus overcome. At the same time, however, strikers' demands focused on wages and working conditions. The French defence industries, moreover, remained little affected. This was not the case the following spring. Industrial action in May 1918 was more widespread and better coordinated. And this time industrial action affected many armaments and munitions factories. Even more significantly, they were often aimed at forcing the government to make peace. These strikes were thus a much greater threat to the war effort than those of the previous year. Yet the importance of worker unrest should not be exaggerated. The 1918 strikes tended to be short-lived; most lasted no more than ten days. They took place within the context of marked improvement in national morale and greater commitment to the war effort. The line between workers' desire for peace and revolutionary defeatism was very rarely breached even by the most extreme elements in the strike movement. As Jean-Jacques Becker has observed, 'the immense majority of workers, no less than the rest of the nation, continued to believe that it was not in their interest to lose the war'.[42]

---

[38] Pédroncini, *Pétain*, 114–55; and esp. Doughty, *Pyrrhic Victory*, 392–3 on the strategy of an offensive into Alsace.
[39] W. Philpott, *Anglo-French Relations and Strategy, 1914–18* (London, 1996), 144–9.
[40] J.-J. Becker, *The Great War and the French People* (Oxford, 1985), 225–30.
[41] Robert, *Les Ouvriers*, 137–50.
[42] J.-J. Becker and S. Audoin-Rouzeau, *La France, la nation et la guerre: 1850–1920* (Paris, 1995), 334; see also Becker, *Great War*, 251–301; for a different view, Robert, *Les Ouvriers*, 205–49.

The coming of a new world order, 1917 145

This did not mean that the workers' movement opposed a negotiated peace. Indeed, one of the central causes of the political crisis of 1917 was growing opposition to the idea of 'war to the end' on the centre-left and left of the political spectrum. The strength of the *minoritaire* opposition to the war increased steadily within the SFIO. It threatened to become generalised when the nature of the secret arrangements with Imperial Russia became apparent in May. A minority of Radicals concentrated around the president of the party, Joseph Caillaux, were also open to the idea of negotiations. Nearly all agreed, however, that any settlement that did not return Alsace-Lorraine to France was unacceptable.[43] The social and military challenges confronting the French war effort contributed to a long-running political crisis that brought down four successive governments and culminated in the end of the Union sacrée the following autumn.

Briand survived several votes of confidence over his ministry's prosecution of the war before finally resigning on 20 March 1917. He was replaced as premier and foreign minister by Alexandre Ribot. Eloquent and urbane, Ribot was a vastly experienced parliamentarian whose first term as premier in 1892–5 had witnessed the creation of the Franco-Russian alliance. Although to the right of Briand in domestic politics, he had a reputation for open-mindedness and commanded respect from all sides of the chamber.[44] Poincaré considered Ribot one of the last hopes for continued national unity behind the war effort. Though committed to pursuing the war to victory, Ribot was sceptical of plans to destroy German power on the continent. He was also more sympathetic to the juridical internationalist cause than any of his predecessors. He would preside over the demise of both the alliance with Russia and the Union sacrée.

Ribot became head of government on the eve of the Nivelle offensives. He was forced to deal with mutiny in the army, the May strikes and the gradual erosion of Socialist commitment to a government of national unity. His ministry survived a fraught series of parliamentary debates over France's war aims and security requirements that were held in secret in early June. Repeated pleas for national unity allowed him to maintain his government through to the following autumn.[45] Ribot was forced to cede the premiership to Paul Painlevé in September, however, when his decision to dismiss interior minister Malvy from his cabinet drew the ire of the Socialists and left-leaning Radicals in parliament.[46] He was replaced as premier by war minister Paul Painlevé, a

[43] These included Louis Malvy (the interior minister), Léon Accambray and rising star Anatole de Monzie; see J.-C. Allain, *Joseph Caillaux*, vol. II: *L'Oracle, 1914–1944* (Paris, 1981), 132–47; S. Berstein, *Histoire du Parti Radical*, vol. I: *À la recherche de l'âge d'or* (Paris, 1980), 93–7.
[44] M. Schmidt, *Alexandre Ribot: Odyssey of a Liberal in the Third Republic* (The Hague, 1974); A. Ribot, *Journal d'Alexandre Ribot et correspondances inédits* (Paris, 1936); A. Ribot, *Lettres à un ami: souvenirs de ma vie politique* (Paris, 1924).
[45] See esp. G. (and E.) Bonnefous, *Histoire politique de la Troisième République*, vol. II: *La Grande Guerre* (Paris, 1957), 241–67.
[46] Malvy was accused of being lenient towards defeatists and even of having links with German agents in France; see J.-B. Duroselle, *La Grande Guerre des Français* (Paris, 1994), 298–300.

world-famous mathematician and Independent Republican who had good relations with deputies across the centre-left and left of the chamber.

This last, rather desperate, attempt to keep the Union sacrée together failed from the beginning. The SFIO refused to participate in the new government when Painlevé retained Ribot as foreign minister.[47] For two difficult months Painlevé attempted to retain his parliamentary support amid a series of controversies, the most serious of which were secret contacts between German officials and Briand. Another stormy secret session over this issue once again exposed the extent to which parliamentary support for the war was wavering. Painlevé's ministry fell on 13 November 1917, the only wartime ministry to be overturned by parliamentary vote, amid yet another crisis (created this time by the Bolshevik takeover in Petrograd).[48] France had reached the most desperate point of its war effort when Poincaré called on Georges Clemenceau to form a government.

III

The dominance of the traditional approach to security reached its zenith in an agreement with Tsarist Russia in February 1917. The chief French negotiator, Gaston Doumergue, was a relatively moderate stalwart of the centre of the Radical Party. Although Russia was on the eve of the February Revolution, the Tsarist government's appetite for expansion had abated little. The Doumergue mission to Petrograd negotiated an agreement that was more reminiscent of eighteenth-century power politics than an era of self-determination and democratisation.

The terms of the agreement reached between Doumergue and Tsar Nicholas II on 3 February 1917 were more extensive and specific than the general aims outlined in the Cambon Letter (a copy of which Doumergue was given before he left Paris). Doumergue reported with satisfaction that Tsar Nicholas had reaffirmed his 'ardent desire' that France should 'come out of the war as strong as possible' and thus his willingness to 'underwrite in advance whatever we wish to do regarding the Left Bank of the Rhine'. In exchange for approval of Russian demands to extend the western frontiers of a Russian-dominated Poland at Germany's expense, France would obtain 'at the very least' the return of Alsace-Lorraine with the frontier of 1790 and 'the entire coal district of the Saar Valley'. As for the Left Bank of the Rhine, the agreement stipulated that 'those areas of this region not annexed by France' would be organised into neutral states to be placed under French occupation until 'the

---

[47] J.-J. Becker and S. Berstein, *Victoire et frustrations, 1914–1929* (Paris, 1990), 117–20; though there were exceptions to the SFIO party line: see Y. Billard, 'Des impénitents de l'Union sacrée: les Quarante de la France libre' in R. Ducoulombier (ed.), *Les socialistes dans l'Europe en guerre: réseaux, parcours, experiences, 1914–1918* (Paris, 2010), 73–83.
[48] L. Smith, S. Audoin-Rouzeau and A. Becker, *France and the Great War, 1914–1918* (Cambridge, 2003), 140–3; Bonnefous, *Grande Guerre*, 147–263.

complete execution of all peace conditions' was achieved. The expectation was clearly that France would annex at least part of the Left Bank. This went well beyond the programme outlined in the Cambon Letter. Doumergue and the Tsar further agreed on the need to isolate Prussia from the rest of Germany and to speculate on the chances of Imperial Germany coming apart in the event of an Allied victory.[49]

Ambassador Paléologue had since the previous autumn urged his government to transform the verbal assurances of the Tsar into a written document. The terms of the agreement between Doumergue and the Tsar were therefore spelled out in an exchange of letters between Paléologue and the Russian foreign minister Nikolai Pokrovsky on 14 February 1917. Crucially, in return for acquiescence to French territorial aims in western Europe, the Russian government demanded a free hand to settle its western frontiers with the Central Powers.[50] The agreement had bleak implications for an independent Poland and was corrosive to Franco-Polish relations after it was published by the Bolsheviks. Significantly, the precise terms of the Paléologue–Pokrovsky exchange were not divulged to the cabinet. Briand, after some hesitation, eventually approved the agreement as achieving the 'necessary enfeeblement of Germany' that would 'guarantee' the 'security and economic development of [France and Russia]'.[51]

The terms of this agreement would prove highly embarrassing to the French government when they were conveyed to various SFIO deputies visiting Russia the following May. Briand, who had doubts about the wisdom of Doumergue's mission, would nonetheless defend it vigorously in the chamber.[52] But all of this should not obscure the key point that traditional solutions to security remained dominant among even relatively moderate elements within the French policy-making elite at this time. Indeed, most of the misgivings among key policy makers stemmed not from its power-political character, but rather from worries that France had bargained away too much. The Briand government was at the same time considering an equally traditional scheme of using some of the same territories offered to Russia as enticements to

---

[49] MAE, *Série A*, vol. 223, Doumergue telegram to Briand, 5 Feb. 1917; Secretary of State for Foreign Affairs, Cmd. 2169, *Papers Respecting Negotiations for an Anglo-French Pact* (London, 1924), 7: 'Note from the Russian Foreign Ministry to the French Ambassador at Petrograd', 1 Feb. 1917.
[50] This exchange is in MAE, *Série A*, vol. 223, dated 14 Feb. 1917; see also ibid., Berthelot (for Briand) to Paléologue, 9 Feb. 1917; the negotiations are explained most clearly in Stevenson, *French War Aims*, 53–6.
[51] MAE, *Série A*, vol. 223, Briand telegram to Paléologue, 16 Feb. 1916. In a secret session of the chamber on 4 June, Socialists criticised the exchange of letters as 'the personal policy of Berthelot': *JO*, Chambre, *Débats*, 1925, 'Comité secret du 1er juin 1917', quotation from the session on 4 Jun. 1917.
[52] Poincaré, *L'Année trouble*, 64–5; Suarez, *Briand*, vol. IV: *Le Pilote dans la tourmente, 1916–1918* (Paris, 1940), 134–6; S. Unger, *Briand: le ferme conciliateur* (Paris, 2005), 351–2.

lure Austria-Hungary into a separate peace. This possibility was raised by Jules Cambon in secret talks with the Belgian princes Sixte and Xavier de Bourbon-Parme during the first half of 1917. Both were staff officers related by marriage to Karl I, who succeeded Franz Josef as emperor of Austria-Hungary in late 1916. Although these conversations came to nothing, they illustrate the extent to which French war aims and peace planning remained in flux at this time.[53]

The subsequent turmoil in Russia posed a challenge to French planning. The 'Petrograd Formula' and the provisional government's call for an international peace conference were profoundly antithetical to the traditional foundations of French war aims. Policy elites were faced with difficult choices but also new opportunities. The fall of the Tsar revitalised representations of the war as democracy against autocracy and liberty against despotism. It also opened the way for innovative planning for the post-war territorial settlement, particularly in eastern Europe.

News of the overthrow of the Tsar was greeted with enthusiasm by much of the French political establishment. On the left events tended to be interpreted through the historical prism of the French Revolution and of Valmy. Albert Thomas, who had spent more time in Russia than any other member of the government, was optimistic that a 'new patriotic spirit' would emerge out of the upheaval to reinvigorate the Russian war effort.[54] A socialist delegation led by deputies Marcel Cachin and Marius Moutet travelled to Russia in April–May 1917. They returned convinced of the determination of the new regime to continue the war and optimistic about its prospects for success.[55] 'The worthless tyrant has been overthrown,' enthused Georges Clemenceau in his newspaper, *L'Homme enchaîné*. 'Forward Russia,' he proclaimed four days later, hailing 'the exquisite beauty of this revolutionary drama'.[56]

The right tended to be much more pessimistic. From Petrograd, Paléologue concluded from the outset that anarchy was inevitable and worried about the effect of the revolution in France. He advised his government that it could no longer count on the Russian alliance.[57] Poincaré, though less alarmist, also feared that Russia would withdraw from the war. This anxiety was shared by the majority of permanent officials within both the Quai d'Orsay and the military establishment.[58] On 27 July 1917 army chief of staff Foch prepared a memorandum on the consequences of events in Russia. Foch reckoned that the

---

[53] G. Pédroncini, *Les Négociations secretes pendant la Grande Guerre* (Paris, 1969), 58–67; Villate, *République des diplomates*, 338–9; W. Bihl, 'La Mission de médiation des princes Sixte et Xavier de Bourbon-Parme en faveur de la paix', *GMCC*, 170 (1993), 31–75.
[54] Ribot, *Journal*, 94–5; Duroselle, *Grande Guerre*, 225–56.
[55] Bonnefous, *Grande Guerre*, 241–5.
[56] Clemenceau in *L'Homme enchaîné*, 17 and 21 Aug. 1917, cited in J.-B. Duroselle, *Clemenceau* (Paris, 1988), 614.
[57] Paléologue, *Crépuscule des Tsars*, 415–34.
[58] A. Hogenhuis-Seliverstoff, *Les Relations franco-soviétiques 1917–1924* (Paris, 1981), 17–23.

Entente must anticipate a Russian collapse.[59] With the advent of the Bolsheviks, French policy moved towards a strategy of intervention aimed at resurrecting some semblance of an eastern front and denying Germany control of Russia's raw materials.[60]

The alternative peace conditions articulated by the Petrograd Soviet had a profound effect. Doubts about both the wisdom and morality of pressing forward in pursuit of a 'victorious peace' became stronger and more widespread within the SFIO and CGT. Moutet and Cachin returned from Moscow in late May 1917 with information concerning Franco-Russian territorial bartering. This news strengthened the *minoritaire* argument that the SFIO was supporting a traditional imperialist conflict. By this time the *minoritaires* were actually close to gaining a majority within the party executive. A delegation of SFIO officials visited Ribot to demand a parliamentary discussion of war aims and passports for party officials to attend the international peace conference in Stockholm.[61] Ribot and his cabinet refused to grant passports to SFIO delegates but accepted a secret session of parliament to debate the issue.[62] This session, which began on Friday 1 June and ran over to the following Monday, witnessed the most sustained parliamentary discussion of war aims and peace conditions of the entire war.

At stake in the secret debates was the continued political cooperation of the SFIO that most politicians considered essential to the successful prosecution of the war. 'This is the most important debate of the entire war,' observed Pierre Renaudel, the leading advocate of the Union sacrée on the SFIO executive. 'Our entire cooperation is yours for a war of justice and national defence,' he declared to the chamber. 'But the day when this war becomes one of imperialism, we will say to you "do not count on us".'[63] This opened the way for a debate over France's security requirements that has rightly occupied a prominent place in the historiography. For Pierre Renouvin and Jean-Baptiste Duroselle, this debate provides evidence that the Ribot government had moderated its objectives after the setbacks of early 1917.[64] For David Stevenson, and still more for Georges-Henri Soutou, the ambiguity of the final resolution that closed the debate indicates that far-reaching territorial adjustments remained a central aim of the governing political elite.[65]

---

[59] F. Foch, *Mémoires pour server l'histoire de la guerre de 1914–1918*, 2 vols. (Paris, 2007), II, xxx–xxxi.
[60] K. Hovi, *Cordon Sanitaire or Barrière de l'Est? The Emergence of the New French European Alliance Policy, 1917–1919* (Turku, 1975), 51–112; Hogenhuis-Seliverstoff, *Relations franco-soviétiques*, 32–105.
[61] A. Kriegel, *Aux Origines du communisme français, 1914–1920*, 2 vols. (Paris, 1964), I, 152–79. For the international dimensions of this issue see J.-J. Becker, *1917 en Europe: l'année impossible* (Brussels, 1997), 134–9.
[62] Ribot, *Journal*, 138–41.
[63] *JO*, Chambre, *Débats*, 1925, 'Comité secret du 1er juin 1917', quote from 2 Jun. 1917.
[64] Renouvin, 'Buts de guerre', 22–4 and 35–6; Duroselle, *Grande Guerre*, 296–8.
[65] Soutou, 'Marches de l'est', 368–70; Stevenson, *French War Aims*, 6–72.

Viewed from a different perspective, however, the chamber's secret session reveals the strength of internationalism not only among deputies of the left but also those on the centre-left and even the centre of the chamber. This reflected the growing influence of internationalist doctrine in the public sphere. As the prominent juridical internationalist Antoine Pillet observed, one of the chief effects of the war was that it had 'transported into the political arena pacifist ideas that had long been confined to the domain of pure speculation'.[66] While more traditional conceptions based on security through territorial adjustment remained strong, growing support for a post-war order based on democracy and the rule of international law extended even to premier Ribot. Aristide Briand, who would one day become a hero of the internationalist peace movement, was cast in the role of chief defender of secret diplomacy and traditional power politics. Debate opened in earnest when Cachin challenged Briand to admit that as head of government he had approved a plan to trade Constantinople for the Left Bank of the Rhine. 'Yes!' was Briand's response.

Briand, who privately regretted the exchange of letters with the Tsarist government, now found himself in the uncomfortable position of having to explain and defend this policy.[67] He deployed the now-familiar rhetorical strategy of eliding France's ambitions to dominate the Rhineland with its claim to Alsace-Lorraine. The return of the lost provinces, he argued, could not be considered either a conquest or an annexation. 'Legally', he observed, 'we have the right to say that they have never left [France].' The issue of Alsace-Lorraine, Briand asserted, was 'inseparable from that of our eastern frontiers'. It was essential, therefore, that France secure the right, during post-war negotiations, to 'interpret the terms "Alsace-Lorraine" ... in the largest sense possible, whether from the political and ethnic points of view or from that of iron and steel'. Nor could a demand for reparation of the damages done to France during the war be characterised as an indemnity along the lines of that imposed on France by Imperial Germany in 1871. In order to secure these vital 'interests', Briand added, his government had been forced to 'obtain certain letters, certain promises and certain guarantees'.[68]

Ribot assumed very much the same position. He denied utterly the charge that French policy aimed at conquests or annexations of any kind. Both Briand and Ribot also insisted that French policy was entirely in line with the principle of self-determination. To make this case Briand rather disingenuously invoked

---

[66] A. Pillet, *De L'idée d'une Société des nations* (Paris, 1919), 18–19.
[67] The February 1917 exchange was approved by the Quai d'Orsay in Briand's absence and was probably the policy of Poincaré and Berthelot. Poincaré argued it was necessary to remove the 'obscurity' that characterised Russia's commitments to France. Berthelot, for his part, almost certainly drafted the instructions sent to Petrograd: see Poincaré, *L'Année trouble*, 63–4 and Unger, *Briand*, 351–2 and 362–4.
[68] *JO, Chambre, Débats*, 1925, 'Comité secret du 1er juin 1917', quote from 2 Jun. 1917.

his government's support for a reunified Poland.[69] The Socialist deputies were not placated. 'Tell us about the Left Bank of the Rhine!' shouted Jean Longuet to cheers from his party colleagues.[70] Pierre Renaudel then intervened to make a series of trenchant critiques of government policy. He began by hammering away at the contradiction between official statements of French war aims and secret planning within the corridors of government. 'France', he declared,

... from the first day of the war has affirmed that it is fighting to defend itself and restore the rule of law ... When M. Viviani spoke on this issue in December [1914] or in March 1915, or when premier Briand took the floor to speak of the question of returning Alsace-Lorraine to France, we were assured that France aimed at 'nothing else' ... Never since has one word been uttered either in parliament or in public on this question ... We hold to all of the public declarations of successive governments. They have said 'War for the rule of Law' ... But what was the Doumergue mission?[71]

The profound contradiction between official representations of the war as a crusade for civilisation and the rule of law, on the one hand, and secret planning aimed at territorial adjustments to overturn the European balance of power, on the other, had finally surfaced in open debate. The result was a major political crisis.

Cachin intervened to argue for abandoning 'these old forms of diplomacy' which had created such problems for the government and the war effort. Renaudel agreed and denounced any attempt to obtain security through annexation of territory. Against this model of security he articulated an alternative vision based on international organisation and the rule of law. 'How', he demanded, 'can the goals of President Wilson be made to conform with the war aims of the Allies?'[72] He then argued that 'France does not have the right to stand aside while the peace of the world remains unachieved; but a just peace can never be a territorial peace. A just peace can only mean a society of nations.'[73] Renaudel reminded Briand and Ribot that both had made a

---

[69] Ibid.; for a more sympathetic assessment of Briand's position see Suarez, *Briand*, IV, 216–23 and Unger, *Briand*, 363–5.
[70] *JO*, Chambre, *Débats*, 1925, 'Comité secret du 1er juin 1917', quote from 2 Jun. 1917.
[71] Ibid., quote from 4 Jun. 1917.
[72] Ibid., quote from 2 Jun. 1917. Georges-Henri Soutou has argued that Renaudel 'did not rule out a Rhenish policy'. This is open to question; the Socialist deputy did say on 4 June that he was 'not sure' that France 'should not seek measures of national organisation' on the Left Bank. But he immediately contradicted himself by insisting that such measures 'should not touch, in any way, the territorial property of Germany'. He then insisted that any temporary occupation of Germany must be charged to an 'international force' rather than France alone. In sum, Renaudel's strange observation ran against virtually everything else he said over the course of the secret session – and, indeed, the entire war. See Soutou, 'Marches de l'est' and *JO*, Chambre, *Débats*, 1925, 'Comité secret du 1er juin 1917', quote from 4 Jun. 1917.
[73] *JO*, Chambre, *Débats*, 1925, 'Comité secret du 1er juin 1917', quote from 2 Jun. 1917. On the issue of SFIO support for the idea of a society or league of nations see P. Buffotot, *Le Socialisme français et la guerre: du soldat-citoyen à l'armée professionnelle, 1871–1998* (Paris, 1999), 81–3 and J.-M. Guieu, *Le Rameau et le glaive: les militants français pour la Société des nations* (Paris, 2008), 46–7.

public commitment to peace through 'a worldwide juridical organisation with international powers of sanction'. Such a commitment, he proclaimed, 'would constitute a kind of antidote to guarantees through annexation'. Cachin joined Renaudel in urging the Ribot government to 'take a very clear public position' and 'renounce deliberately in form and in substance ... this formula for the Left Bank of the Rhine'. Otherwise, he warned, the support of the SFIO was in doubt.[74]

Briand responded that such 'transactions' were the everyday currency of international politics. French war aims, he asserted, were modest indeed when compared to those formulated in Germany. He added that any French foreign minister had a duty to pursue 'the particular interests of France'. This required obtaining 'certain guarantees and certain precautions' that served as essential 'currency of negotiations' in dealings between states. Turning to the rows of Socialists to his left, Briand asserted: 'You would do well to help your Russian friends to understand things that they will need to grasp in the future, because they will themselves be obliged to practise them if they desire to be a government.'[75]

Briand then proceeded to outline 'two methods for assuring peace'. The first was 'guarantees obtained through an international organisation with sanctions'. This approach, he asserted, could not deliver the necessary security. 'Even at the end of this war, even allowing for the evolution of the human mind and the progress of self-determination that has appeared so strikingly over the course of the war, such an organisation could not deliver the necessary guarantees, especially from the point of view of sanctions.' Hence the need, Briand argued, for a second approach that envisaged the creation of a 'neutralised buffer state' between France and Germany. This requirement, he explained, lay behind the allusions to the Left Bank of the Rhine in both the Cambon Letter and the Paléologue–Pokrovsky exchange. The aim of his government had been to ensure that France possessed a 'free hand' when it came to peace negotiations.[76]

Briand's critics dismissed his policy as 'imperialism under the cover of strategic necessity'. And this criticism did not come exclusively from SFIO deputies. Republican Socialist Victor Augagneur, an ally of Joseph Caillaux, also called for an alternative approach. 'These diplomatic methods,' he asserted, 'caught up as they are in old traditions, may be excellent under a monarchy, but they are deplorable for a democratic country.' He urged the government to moderate its war aims. Jean Hennessy, the centre-left deputy and heir to the family cognac dynasty, similarly argued that a society of nations would constitute a more effective guarantee of peace than strategic annexations. Briand responded by dismissing internationalist doctrine as 'mere

---

[74] *JO*, Chambre, *Débats*, 1925, 'Comité secret du 1er juin 1917', quotes from 4 Jun. 1917.
[75] Ibid., quote from 2 Jun. 1917.
[76] Ibid., quote from 4 Jun. 1917; see also Bonnefous, *Grande Guerre*, 241–61.

words'. French security, he insisted, must rest on more than 'vague philosophical formulas'. What was needed were 'guarantees' and 'securities'.[77] This was a very long way from the post-war Briand of Geneva and the politics of European federation.

Ribot, meanwhile, was in the difficult position of having to explain and justify a security policy bequeathed to him by his predecessor. Of the five wartime heads of government, Ribot was easily the most sympathetic to the internationalist cause. His investiture speech to the chamber in March had included a clear commitment to a post-war 'society of nations' and stated his preference for 'moral' guarantees of peace as opposed to 'conquests'.[78] Ribot had returned to these themes in a public address on 22 May, where he observed that the best hope for a peaceful European order was political transformation in Germany and the creation of a society of nations.[79] In private, he described the Doumergue agreement as 'all bad'. He also expressed doubts about schemes to change the status of the Left Bank of the Rhine.[80]

Ribot's reservations concerning traditional solutions to security were evident in the secret session debates. He returned several times to the theme of democratic change and a 'society of nations' as fundamental conditions for lasting peace. He argued that France must insist on reparations and the return of the Alsace-Lorraine of 1790 (rather than 1814 or 1871). But he distanced himself from the annexationist character of the Doumergue agreement. 'Had the agreement been deliberated in cabinet,' Ribot assured his fellow deputies, 'I would, for my part, have expressed reservations.' The agreement was of 'a rigidity that did not at all express the intentions of the government'. He added, moreover, that he did not consider the agreement binding and would be happy to release the Russian government from its obligations.[81]

Ribot then turned to his own vision of future security. 'It has been suggested', he observed, 'that we could neutralise the territories on the Left Bank rather than annex them. They would then serve as a buffer between Germany and France and permit us to live in relative security.' Such an arrangement, he argued, could not guarantee lasting peace:

It is not enough that we retake our former frontiers if we are forced to live side by side with a formidable empire which at any moment could move against us and destroy us. We can imagine all manner of guarantees. I have already stated at this tribune that, for my part, the most effective [guarantee] would not be the appropriation or

---

[77] *JO*, Chambre, *Débats*, 1925, 'Comité secret du 1er juin 1917', quote from 2 Jun. 1917.
[78] *JO*, Chambre, *Débats*, 1917, Ribot's ministerial declaration, 21 Mar. 1917.
[79] *JO*, Chambre, *Débats*, 1917, 22 May 1917; Scott Blair concludes, strangely, that Ribot's commitment is questionable because he failed to proclaim a society of nations as the *only* guarantee of security (as opposed to the best): S. Blair, 'La France et le pacte de la Société des nations: le rôle du gouvernement français dans l'élaboration du pacte de la Société des nations, 1914–1919', thèse de doctorat, Université de Paris I (Sorbonne), 1991, 101–4.
[80] Cited in Stevenson, *French War Aims*, 65.
[81] *JO*, Chambre, *Débats*, 1925, 'Comité secret du 1er juin 1917', quote from 2 Jun. 1917.

neutralisation of territories, but instead to ensure that, in the future, we will not have, as a perpetual menace on our immediate frontier, an armed and well-organised autocracy that can at any moment force us to accept the horrible sacrifices that we have made for the past three years. This does not depend on us; this depends on the German people.[82]

Democracy in Germany was a more reliable source of security than territorial adjustments.

The same was true, Ribot went on to argue, of a future international organisation. 'We will not do what von Moltke and Bismarck did,' he insisted. 'We will not make a German peace, we will make a French peace founded on the rights of peoples, a democratic peace founded on law and on justice.' Contradicting Briand, he insisted that France could put its signature alongside that of 'the noble president Wilson' because 'we have the same ideal, the same orientation, the same conception of the public order of the future'. For Ribot a 'society of nations' must be at the centre of the post-war order:

What is necessary is that all nations, and by this I mean democratic nations, those who have reached the stage where they are master of their destiny, form together that which is called on the other side [of the Atlantic] a league of nations, to ensure the compliance, if need be by force, of those peoples who have not reached this stage and who refuse to join the league, with the laws of civilisation, the modern law of peoples that it will be our duty to define... This is the way of the future, the way in which wars will cease to afflict humanity.[83]

Ribot's vision was of a league of democracies maintaining the peace. Germany, given the logic of his earlier declarations, would participate in this enterprise once its people progressed from autocracy to a democratic form of government. Ribot returned to these themes in an address to the chamber the following September:

We have made terrible sacrifices, but we will not have made them in vain if we can aid in the establishment of a new rule of law that will not be based on violence, on the balance of power, but instead on justice and a society of nations.

The most effective guarantee of such a peace, Ribot reiterated, was one coming from the will of the German people itself rather than its autocratic rulers.[84] There is a striking harmony between this conception of peace and the core tenets of the internationalist cause.

After Ribot's intervention a series of *ordres du jour* were proposed in an effort to find common ground among deputies that could be presented to the French public as evidence of continued solidarity. The majority were sponsored by figures on the centre and right, and articulated a traditional conception of

---

[82] Ibid.; see also Stevenson, *French War Aims*, 76–8.
[83] *JO*, Chambre, *Débats*, 1925, 'Comité secret du 1er juin 1917', quote from 4 Jun. 1917; see also the analysis in Blair, 'La France et le pacte', 92–116.
[84] *JO*, Chambre, *Débats*, 1917, session of 19 Sept. 1917.

security. The formulation sponsored by Charles Benoist, for example, anticipated 'victory' that would 'ensure' France's 'historic rights, its political and economic interests ... and its future development'.[85] Nearly half, however, were of an internationalist character and sponsored by Socialist or Radical deputies. During a break of nearly three hours a compromise formula was hammered out which was accepted by government and the chamber. The resolution, sponsored by Radical deputy Charles Dumont, reiterated the claim to Alsace-Lorraine and reparations. It then articulated a compromise between internationalist and more traditional conceptions of post-war security:

> Far removed from any thought of conquest or subjugation of foreign populations, [the French parliament] counts on the effort of the armies of the Republic and the Allied armies to provide, once Prussian militarism has been destroyed, durable guarantees of peace and independence for peoples, great and small, within an organisation, to be prepared immediately, of the society of nations.[86]

The 'Dumont Resolution' passed by a majority of 467 to 52. Thirty-nine Socialists, including Renaudel, voted with the government; forty-seven voted against.[87]

In the senate, where the Socialist Party did not have a strong power base, another resolution was passed unanimously, and with much less debate, on 6 June 1917. The need for 'guarantees' was expressed more forthrightly in the senate's formulation of France's security requirements. Significantly, however, Ribot tried to include an approving reference to a society of nations in this resolution. He was thwarted, however, by the opposition of Georges Clemenceau.[88]

The evidence from the secret debates provides an illuminating perspective on the security conceptions of political elites during one of the bleakest moments of the war. Three aspects of these deliberations are of particular importance. The first is the prominence of Woodrow Wilson as a symbol of a new approach to international relations. Wilson was evoked no less than fifteen times during the secret session, always as a source of legitimacy in criticisms of traditional power politics. Second, the debates brought out into the open the contradiction between public discourse and secret planning. Critics were able to use official representations of the conflict's meaning and purpose to condemn plans for post-war security based on the balance of power. Third, and most significantly, the tone and substance of the secret parliamentary discussions reveal the increasing strength of internationalist conceptions of peace and

---

[85] Also highlighted in Soutou, 'Marches de l'est', 371.
[86] *JO*, Chambre, *Débats*, 1925, 'Comité secret du 1er juin 1917', from 4 Jun. 1917.
[87] *JO*, Sénat, *Débats*, 1968, 'Comité secret du 6 juin 1917'; Bonnefous, *Grande Guerre*, 265–7.
[88] Bonnefous, *Grande Guerre*, 267–8; Ribot, *Lettres à un ami*, 246–7; and Blair, 'La France et le pacte', 97–103.

security, which extended even to the head of government. These aspects of the secret sessions have not received the attention they deserve.

Woodrow Wilson's much-publicised calls for a league of nations reverberated powerfully among French internationalists. Their effect was so pronounced, however, because Wilson was preaching to the converted and providing stimulus to projects for international organisation that pre-dated the war. Wilsonian reverberations are discernible even within the predominantly conservative Comité d'études. At the closing session of the Comité's first series of meetings, for example, the distinguished historian Charles Seignobos mounted a spirited defence of internationalist principles. France, he asserted, would need to choose between 'traditional' and 'juridical' approaches to post-war security.

> Given the present state of humanity, when armed peace and the balance of power have proven their inability to prevent war, it is only international law, founded on the respect of treaties and the reciprocal limitation of state sovereignties, [that] can put an end to the sickness of insecurity that causes war.[89]

The chair of the Comité, Ernest Lavisse, endorsed this point of view, observing that 'the old diplomatic methods produced a state of almost perpetual war. Only the new method, that of law armed with sanctions, provides hope for security in the future.'[90]

If support for an international organisation was on the rise among liberals on the centre and centre-left, it remained concentrated most potently within the Socialist Party. As early as July 1915 the SFIO party council had called for 'respect for the political and economic independence of nations ... the limitation of armaments, the democratic control of all engagements undertaken by governments, the constitution of an international force of sanction'.[91] Socialist agitation for a society of nations did not abate after the secret parliamentary debates, despite the government's commitment to such a society in the Dumont Resolution. When tensions mounted between SFIO deputies and the Ribot government in July 1917, armaments minister Albert Thomas recommended a diplomatic gesture of support for Wilson as a means of calming Socialist nerves.[92]

The Ribot government's decision to appoint an inter-ministerial commission to devise a programme for a society of nations should therefore be understood as a response to internal as well as external pressures. This has not been

---

[89] BNF, *Travaux du Comité d'études*, vol. I: 'Séance de clôture', 447–8; see also A. Prost, 'Charles Seignobos revisité', *VS*, 43 (1994), 100–18.
[90] BNF, *Travaux du Comité d'études*, *L'Alsace-Lorraine et la frontier du nord-est*, 'Séance de clôture', 449; Lavisse, significantly, had supervised Seignobos' *thèse d'état*.
[91] Cited in M.-R. Mouton, 'L'Idée d'organisation international en France et en Italie pendant la premiere guerre mondiale' in P. Guillen (ed.), *France pendant la premiere guerre mondiale* (Grenoble, 1976), 101–2.
[92] Poincaré, *L'Année trouble*, 203, cited in Stevenson, *French War Aims*, 246 n70.

acknowledged in the historiography. The premier's support for a league or society of nations has instead been characterised as disingenuous. The Dumont Resolution has similarly been interpreted as a vague compromise that allowed the government to maintain its commitment to a traditional programme. David Stevenson characterises its pledge to support the League project as 'a rhetorical sleight of hand'. Georges-Henri Soutou similarly represents the allusion to the League as a 'wink and a nod' rather than a substantive commitment.[93]

This view does not stand up to careful scrutiny. Ribot, as we have seen, expressed his sympathy for the league of nations project in his ministerial declaration, in subsequent public addresses and in the secret sessions of both the chamber and senate in early June. The wording of the Dumont Resolution, it is worth noting, stipulated that 'guarantees' were to be obtained 'within an organisation' of 'the society of nations' ('dans une organisation... de la société des nations'). Read in this way, the resolution appears not just as an anodyne compromise, but instead as a surprisingly firm commitment to a future international organisation. Even if, for many deputies, this wording was a public gesture to preserve political unity, the fact that they felt compelled to pay lip service to an alternative vision of post-war order is evidence of the growing influence of juridical internationalism both in parliament and in the public sphere. Ribot reaffirmed his commitment to an international organisation in speeches to the chamber on 2 August and 19 September.[94] But this evidence of the increased prominence of internationalist conceptions in both the public and parliamentary spheres in 1917 has been ignored in the existing literature. As a result, an important dimension to the political dynamics of the period has been written out of the international history of the First World War.

IV

Neither the deterioration of France's military situation nor the growing support for internationalism among political elites had much impact on those responsible for the formulation and implementation of policy. Traditional prescriptions for security remained as firmly embedded as ever within the policy machine in 1917–18. They extended from the Élysée Palace to the Quai d'Orsay and the army general staff. In a note to Ribot on 20 March 1917, Poincaré took issue with Ribot's expressed intention to rule out territorial annexations when outlining French war aims in his ministerial declarations. He warned that such a declaration would 'shock all those in the chamber and in

---

[93] Stevenson, *French War Aims*, 70–1 and 65; Soutou, 'Marches de l'est', 368–72.
[94] *JO*, Chambre, *Débats*, 1917, 2 Aug. and 19 Sept. 1917. Even David Stevenson acknowledges that Ribot was 'the only French wartime statesman to suggest that German democratisation was a possible alternative rather than a supplement to more concrete guarantees': *French War Aims*, 70–1 and 65.

the country who are convinced that more or less extensive territorial guarantees are desirable for the security of France'. This conviction, Poincaré advised, was held by the majority of the public as well as the presidents of both the chamber and the senate. It had also, he added, guided Doumergue during negotiations in Petrograd.[95] Poincaré remained an advocate of security through a transformation in the balance of power.

The traditional vision was the organising principle of a memorandum by the operations department (the *troisième bureau*) of the army staff in July 1917.[96] When this document was drafted, revolution in Russia and bloody failure on the western front had reversed the fortunes of war. Nor had the enormous strategic potential of the United States yet been translated into significant military power in Europe. The author of this study not surprisingly acknowledged that 'the conditions of the future peace treaty' depended on 'factors that remain impossible to evaluate'. Three categories of 'conditions' were identified. The first was the military situation at the moment hostilities ceased. The second was 'the intentions of certain of our allies', several of whom 'might fear a resurgence of French imperialism in the event of extensive territorial gains'. The third was the internal political situation in France and, in particular, the 'influence of the socialist party'. Socialist calls for a peace without annexations or indemnities were characterised as a threat to 'the vital conditions of our national survival'.[97] All three factors would condition the nature of the peace that could be negotiated.

The *troisième bureau* study then outlined the acceptable conditions for the future security of France. The positions of the British and American governments were represented as favouring a formula of 'restitutions and reparations' in which France would receive Alsace-Lorraine and limited compensation for wartime damages. These were considered 'manifestly insufficient' to prevent another war that would 'threaten the very existence of France'. What was needed instead were territorial annexations and an independent Left Bank. The optimal solution was an annexation of the Saar coalfields and the creation of a Rhenish 'protectorate' occupied permanently by French troops. A second formula attributed to the Rhineland the status of a 'buffer state' occupied by an inter-Allied force. A third scenario was considered in which the Rhineland remained in German hands with French territorial gains limited to the return of Alsace-Lorraine and the annexation of the Saarland. The latter was an 'absolute minimum' condition for peace. In this case, however, the judgement was that France 'must begin preparing for the next war with Germany'.

In all cases, the study concluded, Belgium must end its neutrality and enter into a military and economic alliance with France. 'It would be useless for us to

---

[95] Poincaré, *L'Année trouble*, 78–80; see also Soutou, 'Marches de l'est', 368.
[96] SHD-DAT, 12N 35, 'Note sur les conditions du futur traité de paix (frontières belges et françaises)', 12 Jul. 1917.
[97] Ibid.

establish a solid barrier to our east and north-east if the enemy can once again outflank our defences by invading Belgium.' The study concluded with the familiar injunction of the universal character of French national interests: 'The weaker the French security barrier, the greater the chances of war ... the realisation of French interests in the coming treaty constitutes the essential factor in the European balance. Our interests, along with those of Europe and the entire world, demand that France must be as strong and as well-protected as possible.'[98] Interestingly, although the military situation had deteriorated significantly at the time this document was prepared, the core assumptions of the army leadership had not changed. The general staff memo of July 1917 could serve as a classic statement of the traditional approach to French security.

Another study of post-war security, prepared almost simultaneously by Major Herscher, deputy head of Painlevé's military staff within the war ministry, mooted an alternative but equally traditional programme for future security.[99] Herscher's analysis was influenced by the serious consideration being given in Paris to a separate peace with Austria-Hungary at this time. It took for granted that Great Power rivalry and calculations of the military balance would continue to determine the course of international relations after the war. Herscher judged that the threat of revolution made a negotiated peace in the interests of all belligerents. He further observed that 'economically, the peoples of Europe are being driven to ruin to the profit of Japan and North America'. The 'evident bases' for a 'French peace' must be a 'respect for nationalities' and a 'balance of power in Europe'.

Yet Herscher said nothing about nationalities. He concentrated instead on the balance of power. Contrary to all other prescriptions emanating from the general staff, however, Herscher submitted that the destruction of German power, and in particular the German fleet, was not in France's interests. Such a solution, he argued, would leave Britain supreme and 'submit our colonial and economic life to her pleasure'. It was therefore necessary that Germany 'continue to play a role in the balance of forces' on the condition that crucial 'precautions' were taken to ensure it could no longer threaten France.

Herscher dismissed the commerce ministry's projects to 'contain Germany in economic webs' as 'chimerical'.[100] He similarly discounted the idea that democratic regime change would alleviate the German problem, warning that imposing a republic on Germany 'would be the surest means of making it unpopular'. He concluded instead that France must 'follow the old tradition and establish a powerful counterweight to Germany in the European balance'. The only viable option for such a counterweight was the Habsburg empire. An

---

[98] Ibid.
[99] AN, 313 AP 129, *Archives Paul Painlevé*, 'Étude sur les conditions d'une paix française', 12 Jul. 1917.
[100] Ibid.

alliance between France and a reformed Austria-Hungary, bolstered by a close relationship with a reunified and semi-independent Poland ruled by a Habsburg-appointed prince, would be sufficient to keep Germany 'permanently on its knees'.[101] Although it offered a different solution to the problem of future security – which was not surprising given that prospects for a decisive victory seemed remote at the time – Herscher's analysis was every bit as much a product of the traditional conception as other studies emanating from the military establishment during the conflict.

Major Herscher's power-political vision reflected support for the idea of a compromise peace with Austria-Hungary that existed within the war ministry and army staff in mid-1917. This was a response to the new strategic context created by the collapse of Tsarist Russia. War minister Painlevé's advisers, in consultation with the army Deuxième bureau and with General Foch, sought to recreate the balance of power by substituting Austria-Hungary for Russia as the chief eastern counterweight to Germany.[102] In early August Painlevé authorised secret contacts between an officer of the Deuxième bureau and a representative of the Habsburg court. The aim was to induce Vienna to agree to a separate peace, the return of the lost provinces and the neutralisation of the Left Bank of the Rhine. The intelligence officer charged with this mission went beyond his remit to raise the possibility of Habsburg sovereignty over Poland, Silesia and even Bavaria. Neither the foreign ministry nor Ribot, significantly, had approved these terms, which took the traditional principle of bartering for territory and peoples to the extreme. Austria-Hungary was unwilling to contemplate a compromise peace in any case.[103] The episode, which was reprised briefly in late February 1918, is interesting chiefly for what it reveals about the highly traditional character of post-war security conceptions within the army staff and war ministry.

Traditional policy reflexes were also manifest, in rather different and attenuated form, in a 'Preliminary note on the reorganisation of Germany' prepared by the Quai d'Orsay in late October 1917.[104] This study outlined two 'directing ideas'. The first called for the permanent demilitarisation of the Left Bank of the Rhine and tight restrictions on German railways. The second envisioned a post-war federal Germany divided into three categories of states:

---

[101] Ibid.; for other analyses of this document see Stevenson, *French War Aims*, 73–4; G.-H. Soutou, *L'Or et le sang: les buts de guerre économiques de la Première Guerre mondiale* (Paris, 1989), 449–50; and A. Adamthwaite, *Grandeur and Misery: France's Bid for Power in Europe, 1914–1940* (London, 1995), 37.

[102] Pédroncini, *Négociations*, 73–5; G.-H. Soutou, 'Paul Painlevé et la possibilité d'une paix négociée en 1917', *Cahiers du CEHD*, 22 (2004), 27–43; and D. Stevenson, *The First World War and International Politics* (Oxford, 1988), 164–9, 196–7.

[103] M. Bourlet, 'Le Deuxième bureau et la diplomatie secrète: les négociations Armand-Revertera de 1917', *GMCC*, 221 (2006), 33–49; Pédroncini, *Négociations*, 67–75.

[104] Nanterre, Bibliothèque de documentation internationale et contemporaine (hereafter BDIC), *Archives Louis-Lucien Klotz*, dr. 18, 'Note préliminaire sur la réorganisation de l'Allemagne', 27 Oct. 1917 (also in MAE, *Série A*, vol. 60).

the Prussian-dominated Protestant states; a 'Catholic bloc' including Bavaria and Württemberg; and, finally, the Rhineland and German Austria. In this resurrection of Napoleon's strategic conception, the *Zollverein* binding the German empire economically would be dissolved and the latter two categories of states, in particular Austria and the Rhineland, would be granted preferential treatment in commercial relations with the Allies. The aim was to erode their political relationship with Prussia. 'These arrangements', the author of this study noted, 'do not violate the right of peoples to determine their government.' They therefore complemented the decisive precondition of any such arrangement: post-war political and economic coordination between France, Britain and the United States. This coordination, it was envisaged, would make possible a 'permanent regime of international control' to oversee the comprehensive demilitarisation of the Rhineland.[105]

Two things stand out in this interesting snapshot of foreign ministry thinking about the post-war order. First, although it was based, as its title suggests, on a traditional conception of the future security of France, the study also reflects the growing importance of Wilsonianism (the principle of self-determination) in internal planning at the foreign ministry. The strategic importance of the United States intruded on all levels of French policy formulation. Second, and in stark contrast to thinking within the war ministry, the note assumed the dissolution of the Austro-Hungarian Empire. Here again the changing political and military context opened up new opportunities even as others were closed down. American entry into the war combined with the gradual withdrawal of Imperial Russia to accelerate the rise of democratisation and self-determination to a central position in French security planning. These trends posed a profound challenge to the balance of power as an animating doctrine of this planning. And they did not bode well for the multinational Habsburg Empire. Planning for a new order in eastern Europe would accelerate over the ensuing twelve months as French security policy continued to adjust to the political transformations of 1917–18.

In parliament the temptation of a compromise peace remained well into the autumn of 1917. That summer the high-ranking German foreign ministry official Baron Oskar von der Lancken sponsored a plan to meet with Briand to discuss terms. The Germans did not intend to offer any substantial concessions to France, but instead hoped that peace offers would have a divisive effect on the Allies. Briand, with the approval of newly appointed premier Painlevé, was willing to attend. The project foundered amid opposition from both Ribot (still foreign minister), Poincaré and the majority of the cabinet.[106] When rumours of these contacts appeared in the press, however, they provoked

---

[105] BDIC, *Archives Klotz*, dr. 18, 'Note préliminaire sur la réorganisation de l'Allemagne', 27 Oct. 1917.
[106] Soutou, 'Paix négociée', 35–42; Ribot, *Journal*, 212–15; and Poincaré, *L'Année trouble*, 298–9.

another stormy secret session of parliament dominated by the divisive issue of a compromise peace. Poincaré judged that one-third of the deputies in the chamber desired peace.[107]

Growing support for internationalism in both parliament and the public sphere was a product of the domestic and international transformations that characterised the middle period of the war. Revolution in Russia and American participation altered the ideological character of the conflict. This presented internationalists with new opportunities to challenge the traditional bases of official planning. Particularly interesting was the way the official discourse of a war for the rule of law was used against the government by critics of the Franco-Russian agreements over the Straits and the Rhineland. Representing the meaning of the war in internationalist language had left hostages to fortune that were used against official policy in June 1917.

Viewed from the perspective of contending conceptions of security, the continued status of the traditional approach as a practical logic among policy makers is striking. The operating assumptions of most policy elites were scarcely affected by the profound changes in the structural environment in which policy was made. Thinking about the traditional conception as a 'practical logic' helps explain the durability of power politics in post-war planning. Traditional predispositions were so ingrained in the individual and collective habitus of security professionals that it was all but impossible for them to conceive of a post-war order that was not based on strategic preponderance. This is why internationalist prescriptions were virtually absent from the various programmes for security generated by the policy machine through 1917 and beyond.

The increasingly bleak strategic situation resulting from the Bolshevik takeover did bring about a major political change in France. After Painlevé's ministry was overthrown by a vote in the chamber on 13 November, Poincaré was left with a difficult decision regarding his replacement. The choice seemed to nearly all observers to be between Caillaux, who favoured a compromise peace that would leave German power intact, or Georges Clemenceau, who advocated 'war to the end'. For Poincaré this was no choice at all. The president opted for Clemenceau, who shared his determination to impose a victor's peace on the enemy but was cut from a very different political cloth than any of his predecessors.[108] This decision would have important consequences for the direction of national security policy.

[107] *JO*, Chambre, *Débats*, 1933, 'Comité secret du mardi 16 October 1917'; rumour of secret contacts was first published by Clemenceau in *L'Homme enchaîné* on 15 October 1917; Poincaré, *L'Année trouble*, 365.
[108] J. F. V. Keiger, 'Poincaré, Clemenceau and Total Victory' in R. Chickering and S. Förster (eds.), *Great War, Total War: Combat and Mobilisation on the Western Front, 1914–1918* (Cambridge, 2000), 247–63.

5 National deliverance and post-war planning

On New Year's Day 1918 the French cabinet received an army general staff assessment of the 'general situation' which began with the observation that 'the year 1917 ends with the disappointment of the hopes that we quite understandably entertained in late 1916'. This was a spectacular understatement. Russia was in revolutionary turmoil, Allied offensives had failed to break through in the west, and intelligence indicated that German morale had improved dramatically. The Central Powers, the assessment predicted, would eventually move between sixty-five and seventy divisions from the eastern front. Powerful offensives were expected on the western front and in northern Italy. 'The political configuration of Europe has been transformed,' it concluded, 'and the fate of the Allied war effort depends on our ability to withstand a German offensive in the west which will come in the spring.'[1]

Over the next eleven months the changing fortunes of war would deliver France from the brink of ruin to victory and national salvation. The dramatic turnaround forced the issue of post-war security to the forefront of government preoccupations. By November 1918 the foundations of a programme for post-war security were taking shape. The traditional approach to international politics provided most of the cement holding policy conceptions together. But important counter-currents were present in the planning process. These would carry through to the armistice and beyond. Among the most important such currents were a blueprint for a future league of nations inspired by the juridical internationalist vision and a programme for a new international economic order based on the principle of wide-ranging multilateral cooperation.

I

Georges Clemenceau was a veteran republican of the generations of 1848 and 1870.[2] His political career had begun in the aftermath of the French defeat by Prussia. He participated first-hand in the tragedies of the siege of Paris and the

---

[1] SHD-DAT, 3N 7, 'Situation générale à la date du 30 décembre 1917'.
[2] The portrait of Clemenceau that follows is drawn mainly from D. Watson, *Georges Clemenceau: A Political Biography* (London, 1974); J.-B. Duroselle, *Clemenceau* (Paris, 1988); R. K. Hanks,

Commune as mayor of Montmartre. He also voted against the peace settlement of 1871 that surrendered Alsace and Lorraine to Germany. These experiences left a profound mark on 'the Tiger', who would remain a leading political figure even after his retirement in 1920. In the early years of the Third Republic he was a prominent voice on the radical left and a staunch defender of civil liberties and secular values. Clemenceau's political outlook was characterised by a profound commitment to democratic freedoms and an abiding belief that German power posed an existential threat to France. These core convictions made him an ardent defender of republican ideals, a ferocious critic of the Tsarist regime in Russia and a committed advocate of *entente* with Great Britain. Clemenceau's worldview is nonetheless remarkable for its contradictions. His pessimistic pronouncements regarding the human condition were famous. Yet his passion for democracy was a genuine expression of the nineteenth-century positivist tradition, with all of its optimistic assumptions concerning mankind's potential for self-improvement. He combined ardent patriotism and profound belief in the genius of France with a thoroughly cosmopolitan outlook informed by a lifelong passion for travel and wide knowledge of the world beyond France. He spent a year in the USA as a young man, married an American woman (briefly, as it turned out), spoke fluent English and developed an extensive network of friends and political contacts across the Channel. Clemenceau, in other words, possessed a highly unusual set of skills and experiences for a bourgeois politician of the Third Republic.

Clemenceau had spent the early years of the Third Republic on the far left but had drifted steadily towards the centre with the emergence of the Socialist Party. He had played a pivotal role in the Dreyfus Affair by publishing Émile Zola's famous denunciation of the wrongful conviction of the army captain. Opposed to colonisation on ideological grounds, he was also convinced that imperial adventures weakened France's capacity to concentrate its resources against Germany.[3] His first tenure as premier from 1906 to 1909 had witnessed the forceful repression of a series of large-scale strikes. While this move was highly divisive and gained for Clemenceau the enduring enmity of French Socialists, it also demonstrated his belief in forceful leadership and his willingness to take difficult decisions. In terms of foreign policy, significantly, his first government attributed fundamental importance to nurturing the Entente Cordiale. This was a policy priority to which Clemenceau would adhere with even greater conviction throughout his epochal second term as premier from November 1917 through January 1920.

The appointment of the seventy-seven-year-old 'Tiger' was a move that Poincaré had resisted up to November 1917. The president had been a frequent target of Clemenceau's relentless attacks on the overall management of

'Culture versus Diplomacy: Clemenceau, Anglo-American Relations and the First World War', Ph.D. thesis, University of Toronto, 2002; and the excellent sketch in D. Stevenson, *With our Backs to the Wall: Victory and Defeat in 1918* (London, 2011), 494–7.

[3] Watson, *Clemenceau*, 73–8 and 90–1; Duroselle, *Clemenceau*, 205–10 and 217–27.

the war from his position as president of the powerful senate army and foreign affairs commissions as well as in the pages of his newspaper, *L'Homme enchaîné*.[4] Clemenceau took control of the government at the lowest point in the war for France. In Russia the Bolsheviks had agreed to an armistice and appeared ready to sign terms that would greatly strengthen the Central Powers.[5] Their publication of the secret Allied agreements was another major blow. Official claims that the conflict was a selfless crusade for international justice were undermined by details of the Allies' traditional horse-trading of territories and peoples. France's army, meanwhile, was in a state of convalescence after the military disasters of the previous spring. And the threat of labour unrest continued to cast a shadow over the entire war effort.[6]

Clemenceau's response was to impose his authority on the prosecution of the war. The new premier accepted the end of the Union sacrée, which removed the need to adjust policy to keep the SFIO on side. Clemenceau's premiership saw a transformation in the practice of government that rolled back the authority of parliament. He put an end to the debilitating practice of secret parliamentary sessions and assumed powers of decree in economic policy. The new government also mounted a vigorous campaign of arrest and prosecution of 'defeatists', 'anti-patriots' and 'traitors'. The premier proclaimed: 'No more pacifist campaigns, no more German intrigues ... war, nothing but war ... the country will know that it is defended.'[7] Political heavyweights such as Ribot, Millerand and Briand were excluded from ministerial posts to ensure that Clemenceau would dominate his government. He took the war minister's portfolio for himself and appointed a range of less-forceful politicians to various cabinet posts. Stephen Pichon, Clemenceau's long-time protégé and loyal collaborator, returned to the foreign ministry. Pichon was not a strong character, and rarely took a decision of any kind without consulting the premier. Cabinet met rarely under Clemenceau and deliberated vital strategic issues even less frequently. Poincaré was in this way kept at arm's length from policy decisions, and lost much of his former influence. The important exception to this general rule of ministerial effacement was Clémentel, who remained at the ministry of commerce and managed to retain a measure of influence and

---

[4] J. V. F. Keiger, *Raymond Poincaré* (Cambridge, 1996), 228–36; F. Bock, *Parlementarisme de guerre* (Paris, 2002), 288–96; and Duroselle, *Clemenceau*, 586–629.
[5] SHD-DAT, 3N 7, 'Situation générale à la date du 30 decembre 1917'.
[6] R. A. Doughty, *Pyrrhic Victory: French Strategy and Operations in the Great War* (Cambridge, Mass., 2005), 405–6; J.-B. Duroselle, *La Grande Guerre des Français* (Paris, 1994), 192–231; J.-J. Becker, *1917 en Europe: l'année impossible* (Brussels, 1997), 163–71.
[7] *JO*, Chambre, *Débats*, 20 Nov. 1917; also in SHD-DAT, *Fonds Clemenceau*, 6N 79-1. Joseph Caillaux, who had uncertain relations with a number of German and Hungarian agents, was arrested and imprisoned; see Duroselle, *Grande Guerre*, 317–18; J.-J. Becker, 'Le Procès Caillaux: une justice politique?' in M.-O. Baruch, V. Duclert and A. Bancaud (eds.), *Justice, politique et République* (Brussels, 2002), 211–18; Watson, *Clemenceau*, 275–92; R. K. Hanks, '"Generalissimo" or "Skunk"? The impact of Georges Clemenceau's leadership on the western alliance in 1918', *French History*, 24, 2 (2010), 197–217.

independence in an area where Clemenceau had little expertise and few clearly established ideas.[8]

Clemenceau otherwise dominated policy making for the duration of the war through the peace negotiations of 1919. He disliked detail, avoided making hard-and-fast commitments that would hamper his freedom of manoeuvre and resisted all pressure to specify his war aims. 'I believe first that when one is engaged in an action, it is best to speak as little as possible... when you demand to know my war aims, I can only respond that my aim is to win.' All public talk of plans for the Rhineland was subject to official censorship.[9]

Clemenceau's accession threatened the foreign ministry with marginalisation. The premier was famously mistrustful of professional diplomats. He preferred to take important decisions in consultation with a small circle of trusted collaborators. Very often this group did not include the foreign minister, let alone senior diplomats. The post of secretary general created by Briand was suppressed under Clemenceau. Jules Cambon was moved to a newly created post of chief counsellor on Franco-American affairs (where he was eclipsed by Clemenceau favourite André Tardieu at war's end). Quai officials thus lost most of the access to the upper reaches of decision making that they had enjoyed under Briand and Ribot.[10] Yet Pichon's lack of forcefulness also created opportunities for foreign ministry mandarins when it came to issues where the premier had no fixed ideas. A number of leading officials took advantage of this situation to exercise decisive influence over the evolution of French policy towards central and eastern Europe. Berthelot, who had worked closely with Pichon during Clemenceau's first ministry, established a position of 'undisputed primacy' within the ministry in 1918–19.[11]

The international environment presented important challenges for post-war planning under Clemenceau. Woodrow Wilson was determined to impose his own conception of international order on 'Old Europe'. This had been apparent at least since August 1917, when the American president sent a private note to the British and the French urging them to abandon plans for territorial 'aggrandisement' and 'exclusive economic arrangements'.[12] British attitudes towards post-war order were also cause for concern. Foreign secretary Arthur Balfour opposed French projects for an independent 'buffer state' on the Left

---

[8] See esp. Duroselle, *Clemenceau*, 638–70 and Bock, *Parlementarisme de guerre*, 275–309.
[9] Clemenceau cited from *JO*, Chambre, *Débats*, 20 Nov. 1917; on censorship under Clemenceau see O. Forcade, 'La Censure politique en France pendant la Grande Guerre', thèse de doctorat, Université de Paris X (Nanterre), 3 vols., 1998.
[10] L. Villate, *La République des diplomates: Paul et Jules Cambon, 1843–1935* (Paris, 2002), 340–9; J.-L. Barré, *Philippe Berthelot: l'éminence grise, 1866–1934* (Paris, 1998), 322–37; B. Auffray, *Pierre de Margerie et la vie diplomatique de son temps, 1861–1942* (Paris, 1976), 118–78.
[11] D. Stevenson, *French War Aims against Germany, 1914–1919* (Oxford, 1982), 96–7; P. Jackson, 'Tradition and adaptation: the social universe of the French foreign ministry in the era of the First World War', *French History*, 24, 2 (2010), 189–90.
[12] See Stevenson, *French War Aims*, 77–8.

Bank of the Rhine before the House of Commons in December 1917.[13] Lloyd George, for his part, came out against the destruction of German power in a speech on war aims delivered at Caxton Hall on 5 January 1918. 'Germany has occupied a great position in the world,' he observed. 'It is not our wish or intention to question or destroy that position for the future.' There were clear indications from the Lloyd George government that Britain would focus on imperial interests and distance itself from Europe after the war.[14]

The clearest exposition of a post-war programme by any belligerent, however, was Woodrow Wilson's 'Fourteen Points' address made three days later. Like Lloyd George's Caxton Hall speech, Wilson's Fourteen Points were an attempt to rally wavering liberals and socialists in the charged atmosphere created by the Bolshevik revolution. But just as important to Wilson was the need to bind the Allies to his vision of the post-war order. 'The programme of the world's peace', Wilson declared, 'is our programme ... the only possible programme.'[15] The president's Fourteen Points presented a direct and formidable challenge to traditional approaches to security. They emphasised the need for 'open diplomacy', freedom of the seas, free trade and reduction of armaments 'to the lowest point consistent with domestic safety'. Another passage, which demanded 'the removal, as far as possible, of all economic barriers and the establishment of an equality of trade conditions', posed a direct challenge to French plans for post-war economic security. Wilson also called for a series of detailed territorial adjustments, including German withdrawal behind its 1914 frontiers, the restoration of an independent Belgium, a newly constituted Poland and the rectification of 'the wrong done to France by Prussia in 1871 in the matter of Alsace-Lorraine'.

Wilson stopped short of demanding an end to autocratic rule. But he did use the language of democratisation when discussing the future of territories dominated by the Hohenzollern, Habsburg and Ottoman Empires. His final point returned to the need for a 'general association of nations'. Such an association, he asserted, would guarantee the independence and territorial integrity of 'great and small states alike' by establishing the rule of law as the arbiter of international relations.[16] The American president did not use the term 'self-determination' in the Fourteen Points. He introduced the concept when adding 'Four Principles' to his list of requirements in a speech before Congress on 11 February 1918. The peace, he insisted, must accord 'utmost

---

[13] Cmd. 2169, *Negotiations for an Anglo-French Pact*, 4–5: 'Extracts from a Debate in the House of Commons on December 19, 1917'. Balfour was responding to a parliamentary question concerning publication of details of the Doumergue negotiations by the Bolsheviks.
[14] Reprinted in D. Lloyd George, *War Memoirs of David Lloyd George*, 2 vols. (London, 1938), II, 1510–17: quotation from 1511.
[15] 'President Wilson's Fourteen Points', doc. 3 in R. S. Baker (ed.), *Woodrow Wilson and World Settlement*, 3 vols. (London, 1923), III, 42–5.
[16] Ibid., 44–5.

satisfaction' to 'well-defined national aspirations'.[17] Like nearly all of Wilson's statements on the post-war order, this formulation left considerable room for interpretation.

American diplomacy aimed at convincing both the Allied and Central Powers to accept the Fourteen Points as the basis for peace. Wilson continued to see his country's role as that of mediator.[18] When the military fortunes of the Central Powers declined in the summer of 1918, the American president declared publicly that the 'western powers' had 'no jealousy of German greatness' and did not wish to 'block in any way her legitimate influence or power'.[19] This position could hardly have been further from French planning for a transformation in the balance of power. 'The Americans', lamented Berthelot, 'are necessary undesirables.' France had no choice but to seek the their assistance. 'Europe', he predicted, 'will pay dearly.'[20]

II

The power vacuum created in the east by the collapse of Russia posed both an imminent and longer-term threat to French security. In the short term it allowed the Central Powers to transfer large numbers of troops and equipment to the western and southern European theatres. In the longer term it was feared that, even if Germany lost the war, its economic penetration and exploitation of eastern Europe and European Russia would alter the strategic balance decisively in its favour. The Bolsheviks were perceived as enabling this process. From the outset, therefore, the Bolshevik and German challenges were commingled in official perceptions. The foreign ministry and the intelligence services were aware of German assistance to the Bolsheviks. The Bolsheviks, along with their supporters in Europe, were consistently referred to as '*les agents allemands*' by French officials. The Deuxième bureau produced a study of the alleged German-Jewish origin of many Bolshevik leaders and also warned of the danger that Germany would gain control of Russian industry and raw materials.[21]

The strategic implications of German domination of Russia were a source of profound anxiety. In early 1918 Berthelot drafted a note on the problem for all French embassies that began with the observation:

---

[17] J. B. Scott (ed.), *Official Statements of War Aims and Peace Proposals, December 1916–November 1918* (Washington, 1921), 269–70.
[18] T. J. Knock, 'Wilsonian Concepts and International Realities at the End of the War' in M. Boemke, G. Feldman and E. Glaser (eds.), *The Treaty of Versailles: A Reassessment after 75 Years* (Cambridge, 1998), 117.
[19] See K. Schwabe, 'Germany's Peace Aims: Domestic and International Constraints' in Boemke et al. (eds.), *The Treaty of Versailles*, 40.
[20] See Morand, *Journal d'un attaché*, 180.
[21] MAE, *Série Guerre*, vol. 658, 'Membres du Soviet de Petrograd où agents des Soviets suspectés d'être soudoyés par l'Allemagne', 7 Nov. 1917; ibid., vol. 669; SHD-DAT, 3N 7, 'Situation générale de l'ennemi à la date du 30 janvier 1918'.

The Russian revolution poses a problem not only for the war but even more for the future of the world after the peace. If Russian unity is not reconstituted, or if Russia becomes a colony under German control ... the war, even if victorious, will be lost. Hence the need to reconstitute a federal Russian state entirely free of German domination.[22]

Out of this analysis emerged the logic for intervention in Russia.[23] The spectre of German–Bolshevik collusion would continue to haunt French policy makers though to the end of the 1920s.

Disorder in Russia added ever-greater urgency to existing schemes to reconstruct a balance of power in central Europe after the war. Policy elites were divided over the best means of achieving this. The war ministry continued to favour strengthening the Habsburg monarchy as a means of balancing German power in the east. 'Rather than permit the constitution of a powerful "Mitteleuropa" under the hegemony of the Prussian military,' asked the army Deuxième bureau (which had acquired a taste for policy recommendation during Painlevé's tenure at the war ministry), 'would it not be preferable to create a German Catholic confederation in the south to oppose the Protestant bloc in the north?'[24] This general conception had also underpinned Jules Cambon's secret discussions with Vienna via Sixte de Bourbon-Parme.

A contending current within the Quai d'Orsay argued for the reconstitution of a strong and independent Poland. Political director de Margerie was the foremost advocate of this project, which he formulated in classic balance of power terms:

There is here no question of sentiment, but [instead] a territorial issue in which the entire future European balance is at stake. Settlement in the sense desired by the Poles is of the greatest interest to all of the Allies because it is the only means to prevent Germany and Austria-Hungary, even if they are defeated, from achieving their fatal aim of a powerful 'Central Europe' for the domination of eastern Europe.[25]

De Margerie's chief concern was that Polish territories would be subsumed in projects for *Mitteleuropa*. His solution, to create a strong Poland that could help counterbalance German power, became increasingly central to French postwar plans after secret talks with the Habsburgs failed, the USA entered the war and Russia collapsed into revolutionary disorder.

---

[22] MAE, *Série Guerre*, vol. 669, Pichon (Berthelot) circular, 13 Feb. 1918; see also ibid., vol. 667, 'Les Évènements de la Russie et les Alliés', 19 Dec. 1917.
[23] On this issue see A. Hogenhuis-Seliverstoff, *Les Relations franco-soviétiques 1917–1924* (Paris, 1981), 19–86; K. Hovi, *Cordon Sanitaire or Barrière de l'Est? The Emergence of the New French European Alliance Policy, 1917–1919* (Turku, 1975), 92–103; and M. Carley, *Revolution and Intervention: The French Government and the Russian Civil War, 1917–1919* (Montreal, 1983), 6–29.
[24] SHD-DAT, 14N 23-3, 'La Situation militaire, politique et économique de l'Autriche-Hongrie', 7 Mar. 1917.
[25] MAE, *Série Guerre*, vol. 719, 'Répliques russes à l'action austro-allemande', 16 Nov. 1916.

Arguments in favour of an entirely independent Poland were part of a larger reorientation in French planning in anticipation of the break-up of the Tsarist and Habsburg empires. The thrust of planning shifted from acquiescence to Russia's expansion (in exchange for its support of French ambitions on the Rhine) to a new policy of support for east European nationalities. The aim was to create a new political order that would provide France with allies in the east to help counterbalance German power. This strategy, significantly, complemented the discourses of democratisation and self-determination that were increasingly prominent on both sides of the Atlantic.

It was de Margerie who first articulated the strategy of an 'eastern barrier' to counterbalance Germany and resist its eastward expansion after the war. In late November 1917 he argued that the collapse of Russia made it imperative that the Allies address 'their duties and their interests' with regard to Poland.[26] Combining cultural essentialism with strategic calculation, de Margerie described Poland as a 'centre of western culture' between the 'Germanic' and 'Slav' cultural blocs. A reconstituted Poland 'with the aid of an enlarged Romania' would form 'the best barrage against German and Austro-Hungarian expansion towards the east'. He further argued that Russia was liable to remain 'weakened, unreliable and possibly even split up'. Poland would therefore play the vital role of 'the vanguard of the west against Germany for the future development of Russia'.[27] History, cultural affinity and strategic considerations were packaged together in this essentially traditional project for a Polish counterweight to German power.

De Margerie outlined his vision to the Belgian minister in Paris, the Baron de Gaiffier, early the following January. Czechoslovakia and the Ukraine, significantly, were at this time included as potential elements in what he described as an 'eastern barrier' to contain German power. He added that the project had the support of the army staff, Pichon and Clemenceau.[28] This was evident when the Clemenceau government pressed for a clear statement of support for an independent Poland with access to the sea during an inter-Allied conference in late November 1917. Although the idea was rejected as premature by France's allies, Pichon went ahead with a unilateral declaration of support for an independent Poland in a speech to the chamber on 17 December.[29]

---

[26] MAE, *Série Guerre*, vol. 728, 'La Question de la Pologne', de Margerie note, 26 Nov. 1917; see also Hovi, *Cordon Sanitaire*, 72–3.

[27] MAE, *Série Guerre*, vol. 728, 'La Question de la Pologne', de Margerie note, 26 Nov. 1917. There was also a powerful military logic in waging a propaganda war against the Central Powers' efforts to recruit hundreds of thousands of Poles into their armed forces with vague promises of autonomy after the war: see G. Rothenberg, *The Army of Francis Joseph*, paperback edn (West Lafayette, 1998), 210–15.

[28] Cited in Hovi, *Cordon Sanitaire*, 75.

[29] The British and American governments followed suit in public declarations of their war aims in early January 1918: see P. Wandycz, *France and her Eastern Allies, 1919–1925: French–Czechoslovak–Polish Relations from the Paris Peace Conference to Locarno* (Minneapolis, 1962), 8–17.

The signature of the Treaty of Brest-Litovsk, which granted Germany a dominant political and economic position in central Europe and European Russia, intensified the importance attributed to the national movements of this region in French planning.[30] A study prepared by the DAPC concluded that a fully reconstituted Poland with access to the sea 'must function as one of the essential elements in the future European balance'. It added, however, that such a strategy would be most effective if Poland formed part of a wider network of eastern states that included 'Romania to the south and, it is to be hoped, by the Czech people similarly restored to its independence'. Such a system of states would 'constitute the indispensable barrier' between Germany on the one hand and Russia and the Baltic region on the other.[31] The overriding aim was incontestably to oppose German political and economic domination in the east rather than to prevent the spread of Bolshevism to the west.

As France's eastern policy evolved in early 1918, the discourse of self-determination was again put at the service of balance-of-power calculations. De Margerie drafted a note which made repeated reference to the 'rights of Poland' and the principle of 'respect for nationalities'. He argued that the Treaty of Brest-Litovsk was a clear violation of the 'right of peoples to determine their own political fate'.[32] This thesis formed the basis for a circular signed by Pichon and sent to the embassies of France's four Great Power allies. This document underlined France's 'duty' to support Poland's claim to independence. French diplomats were instructed to press the governments to which they were posted to agree to a common declaration that an independent Poland with access to the sea was 'a fundamental element in the organisation of a Europe based on the principle of nationalities ... and self-determination'. Only such a regime, it was argued, could 'guarantee a just and durable peace'.[33] French foreign ministry officials were calibrating their language to respond to the growing normative importance of self-determination in the international sphere.

The same discursive framing of the *barrière à l'est* strategy was deployed over the question of Czech and Slovak independence. These national movements could not draw on the same level of historical sympathy for their cause within France as that enjoyed by the Poles. But the Czechoslovak National Council, under the able and energetic leadership of Tomas Masaryk, Edvard Beneš and Milan Stefànik, proved effective at lobbying French officials. Berthelot, who admired the poetry of Stefànik, was perhaps the most influential patron of the Czechoslovak national cause in Paris and facilitated its access to key decision

---

[30] Jules Cambon observed that Brest-Litovsk 'would cure France forever of an alliance with Russia': Laroche, *Quai d'Orsay*, 46.
[31] MAE, *Série Guerre*, vol. 732, 'Note pour le Ministre: état de la question polonaise', 4 Mar. 1918.
[32] MAE, *Série Guerre*, vol. 732, 'Déclaration sur la Pologne', 5 Mar. 1918.
[33] MAE, *Série Guerre*, vol. 732, 'Déclaration sur la Pologne', Pichon to embassies in London, Rome, Washington and Tokyo, 7 Mar. 1918.

makers. Clemenceau met with Beneš on 22 May 1918 to assure him that France would work towards an Allied declaration of support for Czechoslovak independence.[34] On 29 June Pichon recognised the Czechoslovak National Council as the 'supreme organ representing all interests of the nation and as a foundation of the future Czecho-Slovak government'. Official French support was given to the campaign for an independent state based on the frontiers of the historical kingdom of Bohemia (thus including the German population in the Sudetenland). Pichon concluded by expressing the hope that the new state would constitute, 'in close union with Poland and a Yugoslav state, an insurmountable barrier to German aggression'.[35]

The Clemenceau government was ahead of its allies in support for the national movements within the Habsburg Empire. Its aim was a political order capable of containing German power and economic influence after the war. Historians have interpreted this policy exclusively as an expression of the traditional approach to security.[36] There is scope for a more nuanced interpretation, however. A purely traditional approach would have aimed at maintaining the Habsburg monarchy as the most effective counterweight to Germany east of the Rhine. This, significantly, had been the preferred strategy of the war ministry and army staff as well as a number of senior diplomats (most notably Paléologue). Yet it was abandoned by early 1918 in favour of a new conception based on 'successor states'. This is not to say that this new approach was not traditional in its fundamental orientation. It surely was. The point is instead that it provides an interesting example of the way French foreign policy elites adapted their traditional power-political principles to the new context thrown up by the war. This trend would continue into the next decade.[37]

III

Ambiguities in French thinking about post-war order are more apparent in planning for post-war economic security. Policy elites in this domain were forced to adjust their strategies to changes in the structural environment in general, and to the growing importance of American power in particular.

[34] Hovi, *Cordon Sanitaire*, 109–12; Wandycz, *Eastern Allies*, 9–15; Barré, *Berthelot*, 314–15; and B.-M. Unterberger, *The United States, Revolutionary Russia and the Rise of Czechoslovakia*, 2nd edn (College Station, 2000), 32–104. G.-H. Soutou has emphasised the role of the chamber in exerting pressure on Clemenceau to recognise Czechoslovak national aspirations: 'Jean Pélissier et L'Office central des nationalités, 1911–1918: renseignement et influence', *RI*, 78 (1994), 177–94. The Czechoslovak cause was further strengthened by the exploits of the Czech Legion in revolutionary Russia: see D. Stevenson, *Cataclysm: The First World War as Political Tragedy* (New York, 2004), 353–4.
[35] Cited in E. Beneš, *Souvenirs de guerre et de revolution (1914–1918): la lutte pour l'indépendance des peuples*, 2 vols. (Paris, 1929), II, 230–2; see also Wandycz, *Eastern Allies*, 14–15 and Stevenson, *French War Aims*, 107–8.
[36] See esp. Hovi, *Cordon Sanitaire*; and Carley, *Revolution and Intervention*.
[37] Jackson, 'Tradition and adaptation', 186–94.

One element of consistency in all planning was an alarmist assessment of the threat that German commercial policy would pose to France after the war. The nightmare vision of post-war German economic domination was exacerbated by the fact that France had run up an enormous foreign debt to finance the war. Germany had not. Added to this was the fact that the Reich's industrial infrastructure had suffered negligible damage. The industrial heartland in northern France, meanwhile, had been devastated. Clémentel's description of peacetime German commercial policy as 'the economic methods of brutal German militarism' was typical of the way the problem was represented in official memoranda.[38]

The Treaty of Brest-Litovsk only confirmed this bleak assessment. Brest-Litovsk, one foreign ministry assessment concluded, was 'essentially a specific application of the general methods of economic pangermanism', the principal aim of which was

to form around the military and customs bloc of central Europe a belt of secondary states, allegedly autonomous or independent but in reality existing as vassals to the German empire from an economic point of view. This is a modern transposition of the ancient religious idea of a Germanic Holy Roman Empire. The German state thus extends its domination beyond its territorial limits ... the power exercised over the inhabitants of this region is not through legal possession of territory but instead economic domination through banking and commerce.

Economic imperialism of this sort, the foreign ministry memo added, left the way open for 'the annexationist ambitions of military pangermanism'.[39] A commerce ministry study of the 'economic conditions of a German peace' began by observing that 'it is a banality to say that the war was begun for economic reasons, by the desire of Germany to assure its industry and commerce of unlimited expansion'. German war and peace aims could be reduced to 'one single and unifying goal: world economic domination'.[40] Germany would continue to constitute a serious threat to French economic security after the war. Henri Hauser summed up this view when he warned that France must prepare for 'the economic war that will follow inevitably from the present military conflict'.[41]

To counter this threat, the attention of policy elites focused on including the vast resources of the USA in existing strategies for post-war raw-material sharing and the construction of a more favourable international commercial regime. The aim remained to place Germany at a permanent economic

---

[38] AN, F12 7819, untitled and undated document prepared for an appearance before the senate by Clémentel in early 1918.
[39] AN, F12 7819, 'Brest-Litovsk: le traité entre l'Ukraine et la Quadruplice', memorandum by the DAPC of the foreign ministry, Feb. 1918.
[40] AN, F12 7985, 'Tableau des conditions économiques de la paix allemande', Sept. 1918; see also ibid., 'Le Plan économique de l'Allemagne et ses alliés', 29 Jul. 1918.
[41] AN, F12 7988, 'L'Approvisionnement de l'Allemagne en matières premières après la guerre', n.d. but almost certainly summer 1917.

disadvantage and to ensure France post-war access to the grain, coal and other crucial raw materials that it lacked. But this thinking ran against an influential current of opinion in favour of commercial protectionism after the war. Calls to revise France's commercial arrangements both in parliament and in the public sphere intensified as nationalist feeling surged after 1914. As early as April 1916 the Bureau d'études économiques recommended that all commercial treaties with enemy states be annulled after the war. It expanded its recommendations to include the denunciation of existing agreements with neutral states and an end to the practice of granting Most Favoured Nation status to other states.[42] This was anathema to Clémentel, however. The commerce minister approved the principle of discrimination against Germany but opposed the rising tide of generalised protectionism that characterised parliamentary and popular opinion.[43]

The issue of post-war commercial arrangements was taken up by Fernand Pila in a long study prepared in September 1917. Pila began by alluding to the fact that the return of Alsace-Lorraine would mean a significant expansion of French iron and steel manufacturing at the expense of that of Germany. This, in turn, made it essential that France secure new markets. The solution, Pila argued, must be to establish a network of intimate bilateral commercial arrangements with key trading partners such as Britain and its empire, the USA, Italy and Belgium. Trade with Germany would continue, but it would be much reduced and the Most Favoured Nation regime, considered a mechanism for German dumping, would be abolished.[44]

On 23 April 1918 Clemenceau's cabinet approved the decision to abolish all existing commercial accords but to maintain agreements with its allies on a rolling three-monthly basis.[45] As Professor Soutou has pointed out, in place of the 'liberal cosmopolitanism' at the heart of commercial policy before the war, French planners aimed to substitute a network of bilateral trade agreements varying in character according to the partner in question.[46] Pila described this strategy as expressing 'a new understanding of our interests, and in particular concern for our economic defence'.[47] This meant, at least when it came to tariff policy, that internationalism was in retreat in the face of a growing anti-German economic nationalism.

Planning for post-war control of raw materials was more ambiguous and less firmly rooted in traditional conceptions of power and interest. Policy

---

[42] AN, F12 8105, minutes and 'avis' of the 7 Apr. 1916 meeting of the Bureau d'études économiques; see also G.-H. Soutou, *L'Or et le sang: les buts de guerre économiques de la Première Guerre mondiale* (Paris, 1989), 298–302. The analysis that follows relies heavily on Soutou.
[43] Soutou, *L'Or et le sang*, 300–2 and 552–7.
[44] MAE, *Série A*, vol. 353, 'Régime de l'après guerre', 11 Sept. 1917.
[45] AN, F12 7985, 'La Dénonciation des traités de commerce', Apr. 1918.
[46] Soutou, *L'Or et le sang*, 550–2.
[47] MAE, *Série A*, vol. 276, Pila to de Fleuriau, 12 May 1918.

concerning this issue built upon the declared intention of the Allied states to pool raw materials both during and immediately after the war that was expressed at the Allied Economic Conference in Paris the previous June. The effective functioning of the Allied Wheat Executive, established in December 1916, provided a good example of the benefits of such pooling. Commerce ministry plans envisaged extending the system deployed for wheat to a wide range of other important raw materials. The aim, Clémentel explained to Ribot, was to achieve the effective coordination of industrial policy in Britain, France and the USA. Coordination on this scale, he predicted, would 'assure that Allied industries will be in a dominant position in relation to Germany after the war'.[48] The fact that this strategy, along with plans for an inter-Allied post-war tariff regime, was in contradiction with the second of Wilson's Fourteen Points (calling for a return to free-trade after the war) does not seem to have been understood. Here, as in other areas, the vagueness of Wilson's language (calling for the elimination of trade barriers 'as far as possible') provided ample scope for misinterpretation.

Clémentel played down the aim of crippling German trade and industry in discussions with the British Board of Trade and Treasury. Interestingly, he emphasised instead the role that economic sanctions could play in maintaining the post-war political order. Control over access to raw materials, he argued, would provide 'civilised peoples' with a 'powerful diplomatic instrument ... much more effective than force of arms' with which to enforce peace and international arbitration.[49] The tension at the heart of the project for pooling raw materials – between the traditional aim of weakening German power and the internationalist aspiration to construct a multilateral system of economic cooperation after the war – became more pronounced as the Clemenceau government sought to persuade its chief allies to take part. Clémentel and his colleagues remained relatively sanguine that US policy makers could be convinced of the wisdom of a transatlantic economic order based on collaboration.[50]

Pila tried to reconcile the tension in French plans in a series of memoranda on the question of raw materials in late 1917. He distinguished between 'national' and 'collective' measures to be taken in pursuit of economic security. Noting that Wilson's attitude towards the French scheme was uncertain, he recommended that efforts to induce the USA to take part should focus on the scheme's potential to complement, or even form part of, a future league of nations in establishing 'peace, order and prosperity in the world'.[51] The

---

[48] MAE, *Série Guerre*, vol. 1276, Clémentel memo for Ribot, 5 Aug. 1917.
[49] MAE, *Série Guerre*, vol. 1276, 'Rapport sur la conférence de Londres, 16–27 août 1917'; see also M. Trachtenberg, *Reparation in World Politics: France and European Economic Diplomacy, 1916–1923* (New York, 1980), 2–11 and 352 n49.
[50] Soutou, *L'Or et le sang*, 511–29.
[51] AN, F12 7988, 'Question d'un contrôle international des matières premieres', Pila note, 2 Dec. 1917.

normative legitimacy of the league was deployed in an effort to promote French plans for economic security. This framing was not merely window dressing, however. Pila's vision of the post-war economic order continued to be based on the assumption that Germany would eventually be admitted into the projected system for sharing raw materials on the condition that it provided 'serious guarantees' that it would not resume its aggressive commercial practices.[52]

The potential contradictions between the traditional and internationalist aspects of the raw-materials project created other telling ambiguities in Pila's analysis. On the one hand, he stressed the importance of the 'economic arm' as a means of threatening Germany should it refuse to agree to territorial adjustments during peace negotiations; on the other, he predicted that German participation in a post-war raw-materials regime could constitute the basis of general economic cooperation with France.[53] The same ambiguities emerge in a resolution produced by the Bureau d'études after it debated the Clémentel proposal for sharing raw materials on 30 November 1917. The Bureau approved the nascent programme as an *'arme de combat'* for defeating Germany and a 'guarantee of the highest value for peace negotiations'. But it also described the plan as 'one of the bases of the new European and international order that must be established after the war'. This order, it added, 'will need to embrace Germany in order to take advantage of the export market it provides for our industrial production'.[54]

Similar tensions are manifest in a personal letter from Clémentel to the US president on 6 October 1917. Clémentel's aim was to persuade Wilson to agree to another Allied economic conference that would put into place a system of raw-material coordination based on the model of the Wheat Executive. Pila and de Margerie advised Clémentel to 'seduce' Wilson with the argument that such coordination would reinforce the functioning of a post-war international organisation. Clémentel therefore began with the assertion that Allied control of raw materials was 'the most powerful means of maintaining the peace after the defeat of German militarism and the most effective sanction for ensuring respect for the decisions of the League of Nations'. An international organisation for the control of raw materials, he argued, could open the way to a new and more humane international order in which economic sanctions would take the place of armed force.[55]

---

[52] See esp. AN, F12 7988, 'Question d'un contrôle international des matières premieres', 2 Dec. 1917.

[53] Ibid.; see also Soutou, *L'Or et le sang*, 494–5.

[54] AN, F12 7988, Communiqué of the resolution of the Bureau d'études économiques, 30 Nov. 1917 (appended to the procès-verbal of the séance of this date); 'Avis du Bureau d'études économiques', 4 Dec. 1917; see also G.-H. Soutou, 'Henri Hauser et la première guerre mondiale' in S.-A. Marin and G.-H. Soutou (eds.), *Henri Hauser (1866–1946): humaniste, historien, républicain* (Paris, 2006), 159.

[55] AN, F12 7819, 'Lettre de M. Clémentel au président Wilson', 6 Oct. 1917; see also Trachtenberg, *Reparation*, 13–14 and 352; Soutou, *L'Or et le sang*, 490–500; and Stevenson, *French War Aims*, 84–6.

Clémentel's letter is most notable, however, for its conceptual muddle. The control of raw materials, it insisted, constituted 'the most formidable arm at the disposal of the Allies' in their effort to 'end the war victoriously' by 'paralysing the industry of our enemies'. Clémentel assured Wilson, however, that 'it would not be good to continue to wage war after the war'. At the same time, he laid great emphasis on the utility of raw-material controls in peacetime, when populations were less willing to accept the privations forced on them by economic sanctions. The threat of such sanctions, he observed, would be 'particularly terrible to an industrious people like the Germans' and would thus increase the likelihood that they would rise against the 'military caste' that controlled the Reich.[56] At no point in this missive did Clémentel distinguish between the way his proposed system would function in peacetime as opposed to wartime. Although he admitted the impossibility of continuing the economic war after the fighting ceased, he was in effect arguing that measures intended to bring the war to a victorious close were also the best means to guarantee peace in the post-war period. A peaceful order would in essence be an order organised to threaten Germany most effectively.

At the heart of the contradictions in Clémentel's letter were two goals that sat uneasily alongside one another: the desire to keep Germany weak after the war while at the same time creating a 'new economic order' based on multilateral cooperation. When Clémentel unveiled his conception of post-war economic security to the French senate in February 1918, he framed it as a 'guarantee' against the return of 'the industrial and commercial forms of pangermanism'. The control and coordination of Allied raw materials, he advised, 'is not just a matter of mutual support and assistance in the reconstruction of our ruins, it is also the most formidable arm directed at an adversary who remains deaf to the repeated calls of the rule of law and humanity'.[57]

All of this was to underline the traditional characteristics of a project aimed at weakening and containing German power. Yet Clémentel also insisted that 'the organisation that we desire to see established ... will be closed to our enemies only if they themselves close the doors and refuse to subscribe to the peaceful methods of economic intercourse that inspire the Entente, to the conditions of a just and humane peace'. Priority in raw-material allocations would be given, during the period of reconstruction, to states that had suffered the most destruction during the war. Clémentel explained that this was a temporary measure, however. Significantly, when one senator characterised his programme (approvingly) as a means to 'perpetuate the industrial ruin

---

[56] AN, F12 7819, 'Lettre de M. Clémentel au président Wilson', 6 Oct. 1917; also 'Contrôle interalliés des matières premières', Clémentel to Tardieu (Washington), 16 Apr. 1918 and 'Télégramme du M. Clémentel à M. Paul Cambon', 19 Apr. 1918.

[57] AN, F12 7819, undated and untitled manuscript that served as the basis of Clémentel's discourse before the senate on 7 February 1918; see also Trachtenberg, *Reparation*, 14–15; Soutou, *L'Or et le sang*, 558–9; and D. Stevenson, 'The First World War and European integration', *IHR*, 34, 4 (2012), 852–8.

[and] prevent the recovery of our principal enemy', Clémentel demurred. 'There can be no question of creating a sort of aggressive and exclusive league,' he responded. 'This would only perpetuate conflict.'[58]

Clémentel, it is worth remembering, was speaking before a French audience when he made these remarks.[59] The multilateral and constructive aspects of his programme were not merely for foreign consumption. They were integral elements of the wider conceptual framework within which economic security policy was made. They were also part of a longer-term continuity in official French thinking about the political dimensions of economic cooperation. An increasingly influential voice in international economic planning during the conflict was Jean Monnet, who is now known as one of the chief architects of European integration after the Second World War. The most thorough biography of Monnet rightly identifies a 'family resemblance' between the Clémentel Plan and post-1945 projects for European reconstruction.[60] The tension between the traditional and internationalist impulses of French economic planning policy gave it an ambiguous character that would endure through the following year to shape preparations for the peace conference.

IV

Another dimension of post-war planning centred on the design and functioning of a future international organisation. This issue assumed increasing importance as calls for the creation of a league or society of nations intensified. In the aftermath of the secret parliamentary sessions of June 1917 Ribot appointed an inter-ministerial commission under the chairmanship of Léon Bourgeois. The Commission d'études interministérielles pour la Société des nations (CISDN) was charged with drafting a blueprint for the new international body. Historians have characterised the programme that resulted as a traditionally inspired attempt to perpetuate the wartime anti-German coalition in peacetime. This view is entrenched not only in the literature on French policy, but also in the wider historiography of twentieth-century international relations.[61] A close look at the evidence provides a different perspective, however.

---

[58] AN, F12 7819, undated and untitled manuscript that served as the basis of Clémentel's discourse before the senate on 7 February 1918; see also *JO*, Sénat, 1918, *Débats parlementaires*, 7 Feb. 1918.

[59] Although the Quai d'Orsay monitored press reaction in Germany carefully: MAE, *Série Guerre*, vol. 1217, 'Les Déclarations de M. Clémentel sur la guerre économique (7 février 1918) et la presse allemande', Feb. 1918.

[60] F. Duchêne, *Jean Monnet: First Statesman of Interdependence* (New York, 1984), 40; see also Stevenson, 'European integration', 855–8.

[61] Duroselle, *Grande guerre*, 310–12; Stevenson, *French War Aims*, 65–6, 78, 109–10; S. Blair, 'La France et le pacte de la Société des nations: le rôle du gouvernement français dans l'élaboration du pacte de la Société des nations, 1914–1919', thèse de doctorat, Université de Paris I (Sorbonne), 1991, 170–87; M.-R. Mouton, *La Société des nations et les intérêts de la*

The programme devised by the CISDN was inspired in the main by pre-1914 juridical internationalist concepts. It envisaged a league of democratic states organised to preserve peace by establishing and upholding the rule of international law. The central components of this organisation were an international council, a permanent court of arbitration, a robust system of legal, political, economic and military sanctions and a powerful international force with a permanent command structure. Crucially, the organising principle of the French conception was the rule of law rather than the political interests of member states.

Planning for the *commission interministérielle* began within the Quai d'Orsay in the immediate aftermath of the secret sessions of parliament. On 8 June 1917 Bourgeois' office within the foreign ministry circulated a memo summoning a variety of permanent officials, politicians and academics to take part in studying ways in which 'nations might associate with one another in the common aim of mutual guarantee'.[62] Members of the CISDN were selected by Bourgeois and Jules Cambon. The inevitable result was a commission dominated by legal experts and foreign ministry officials.[63] Of the twenty-one eventual CISDN members, only five were not drawn from these two constituencies. Eight were serving or former diplomats, and eight more were from the legal profession (four of whom were also *jurisconsultes* at the Quai d'Orsay). Most influential among the diplomats were Cambon, Gabriel Hanotaux, Jean Gout and Fernand Pila. Key legal experts were Louis Renault, Henri Fromageot, André Weiss and Paul Matter.[64] The dominant voice on the commission, however, was undoubtedly that of Bourgeois.

From before its first meeting it was apparent that the CISDN was divided into two broad camps. One point of view – which included Cambon, de Margerie, Renault and Fromageot – was generally sceptical of projects for security through international law. They argued consistently for an

---

France (1920–1924) (Berne, 1995), 12–13; A. Sharp, *The Versailles Settlement: Peacemaking in Paris, 1919* (London, 1991), 47; A. Williams, *Failed Imagination? New World Orders of the Twentieth Century* (Manchester, 1998), 54–7.

[62] MAE, *SDN*, vol. 7, 'Un problème de guerre urgent: la Société des nations formée par les Alliés', 8 Jun. 1917; see also MAE, PA-AP 029, *Papiers Léon Bourgeois*, vol. 17, 'Note pour M. le rapporteur du budget des affaires étrangères sur la Commission de la Société des nations', 25 Jan. 1918.

[63] See, for example, MAE, PA-AP 029, *Papiers Bourgeois*, vol. 17, Cambon to Bourgeois, 20 Jul. 1917.

[64] Hanotaux was an eminent historian and former foreign minister; two more diplomats, Jarousse de Sillac and Comte Bertrand Clauzel (a future head of the SFSDN), served as secretaries. There were two academics, Ernest Lavisse and Paul Appell; neither intervened much in debates. There were also three military officials: Vice-admiral Lucien Lacaze (who spoke very rarely), army captain René Petit (who drafted a report on military sanctions) and General Pierre Vidalon (who never spoke at all). See MAE, *SDN*, vol. 1, 'Commission de la Société des nations: membres', n.d., as well as the material in vols. 1–9 and MAE, *Série A*, vol. 62; see also the discussion in Blair, 'La France et le pacte', 119–33 and S. Blair, 'Les Origines en France de la SDN: la commission interministérielle d'études pour la Société des nations, 1917–1919', *RI*, 75, 3 (1993), 277–92.

organisation that would facilitate the continued functioning of France's wartime alliances. Cambon had expressed this scepticism the previous February: 'for the moment', he had advised Bourgeois' secretary, Jarousse de Sillac, 'the most effective means of maintaining the peace is to form a close alliance or a sort of confederation between the powers of western Europe and the American states'.[65] Renault and Fromageot were equally doubtful that states would surrender their sovereignty in return for the promise of collective security. Hanotaux, interestingly, combined a genuine commitment to a powerful international organisation with the iron conviction that Germany must be broken up into its constituent parts. De Margerie was more unequivocal, insisting that 'everything involved with [The Hague] peace conferences – arbitration, mediation, international enquiries – is now discredited'. The experience of the war, he argued, had only reinforced traditional practices of alliances and military conventions. 'It will be in another direction that we move,' de Margerie predicted. 'The system that will be created after the war will be an organisation of war.'[66]

A contending perspective was advanced consistently by Weiss, Gout, Pila, Matter and Bourgeois. Weiss, another professor of international law, was a protégé of Bourgeois who had written extensively on the question of collective sanctions as well as German violations of international law.[67] Gout, who would become the first head of the Quai d'Orsay's Service française de la Société des nations after the war, argued throughout for a multilateral approach to security that would eventually include enemy states. Pila and Matter advocated the utility of collective action, and especially economic sanctions, in the post-war security order. But the leading proponent of internationalist themes was Léon Bourgeois. The shorthand for the CISDN among political and policy elites was the 'Bourgeois commission'. Bourgeois would place his personal stamp on both its deliberations and the final report it produced.

Bourgeois had outlined his vision of international organisation before the civil society study group the Comité national d'études politiques et sociales on 13 November 1916. Criticising traditional policies based on the balance of power as benefiting 'the most numerous and the most brutal', he argued that the chief task of a future 'society of civilised nations' would be to 'uphold the rule of law in international life'. Only a powerful international legal regime could 'provide us with a new and superior guarantee of security'. Bourgeois combined this juridical conception of international order with a profound suspicion of Germany. He acknowledged that his vision of peace and security was possible only if the autocratic regime in Berlin was defeated and

---

[65] MAE, PA-AP 029, *Papiers Bourgeois*, vol. 17, de Sillac memorandum of a conversation with Jules Cambon, 8 Feb. 1917.
[66] MAE, PA-AP 029, *Papiers Bourgeois*, vol. 17, de Sillac memorandum of a conversation with de Margerie, 14 Feb. 1917.
[67] C. Manigand, *Les Français au service de la Société des nations* (Berne, 2003), 14–15; Blair, 'La France et le pacte', 127–8.

overthrown. He also admitted that, in defeat, even a democratic German government would be vengeful and prone to violence. He therefore favoured placing the Rhineland under international occupation 'as a guarantee of our reparations and compliance with our demands relative to an organisation of international law'.[68]

In early 1917 Bourgeois further developed his thoughts to argue that it was 'essential first to defeat Germany, disarm it, then bind it in an international organisation without ceasing to be suspicious and watchful'.[69] This complex attitude towards Germany was typical of nearly all French internationalists. It was assumed that Germany must be punished for its violations of the law of peoples and made to pay for the damage it had inflicted. It did not follow from this, however, that it should be placed permanently outside the community of nations. The aim was instead to enmesh the Reich in a post-war regime of international law that would constrain its revisionist impulses and encourage its development as a responsible member of international society.[70]

Bourgeois opened the first session of the CISDN on 28 September 1917 by invoking Pascal's association of force and justice. He declared that the two imperatives of the commission were to 'form an association of law among nations' and to 'give expression to the common coercive forces charged with maintaining the peace'.[71] The priorities of international justice and international force dominated discussion and debate. Bourgeois described the final proposal that issued from this process on 8 June 1918 as 'a contractual and permanent organisation' of juridical relations between states'.[72] The link between the rule of law and the use of force was at the heart of the French conception. The need for an executive body to take decisions and govern the activities of the envisaged society, conversely, did not figure initially among the priorities set for the commission by Bourgeois. In fact it was the last major issue to be addressed by the CISDN.

The rule of law was the pivot around which all discussions within the commission revolved. Bourgeois insisted on the 'realism' underpinning projects for an 'international regime of law'. Rejecting the charge that this vision was for 'dreamers', he insisted that 'we are realists, alas, all too well-informed by the bloody experience that has afflicted humanity in this war'. Peace was the overriding objective for all projects for post-war order. 'And only law can establish this peace,' Bourgeois observed. André Weiss endorsed this

---

[68] L. Bourgeois, 'Politique des alliances où politique de la Société des nations?', excerpt from the minutes of the 13 Nov. 1916 meeting of the Comité national d'études politiques et sociales, published in his *Le Pacte de 1919 et la Société des nations* (Paris, 1919), 12–21.
[69] MAE, PA-AP 029, *Papiers Bourgeois*, 'Note' by Jarousse de Sillac summarising a conversation with Bourgeois, 14 Feb. 1917.
[70] Bourgeois, 'Politique des alliances où politique de la Société des nations?' in *Pacte de 1919*, 12–19.
[71] MAE, *SDN*, vol. 1, 'Séance d'ouverture', 28 Sept. 1917.
[72] MAE, *Série A*, vol. 62, 'Textes adopté par la Commission: exposé des principes sur lesquels peut être constituée la Société des nations', 8 Jun. 1918.

conception: 'Law is the guarantor of security at the international level as well as the national ... membership in international society confers legal obligations.'[73] Gout concurred, insisting that 'the new association of nations must rest on the ideal of law rather than the power of armed force'.[74]

There was therefore general consensus within the CISDN that the central function of a future society of nations must be to 'define the mutual legal obligations that states must assume towards one another'. It would therefore need to 'codify and proclaim the law between nations as a result of international jurisprudence and conventions'. The words 'organised international law', interestingly, were used virtually interchangeably with 'society of nations' by all members of the commission. Membership in a future international organisation, it was further agreed, would require both observance of international laws and participation in their enforcement. In a phrase that speaks volumes about the juridical foundations of his conception of the league, Bourgeois argued that the international tribunal at The Hague must constitute the 'brain and central nervous system' of the international organisation.[75] In a note intended for Woodrow Wilson, he summarised the commission's programme as 'the design of a regime of durable peace through the organisation of international law'.[76]

These allusions to the importance of the 'rule of law' or the 'reign of law' by internationalists on the commission were more than just rhetorical flourishes. At stake was the character of the international organisation that would emerge after the war. A society of nations based on the rule of law was understood by juridical internationalists as very much in opposition to a post-war organisation based on transitory mutual interests. This is clear from an exchange between Bourgeois and Henri Bergson, the world-famous French moral philosopher, at a meeting of the Comité d'études politiques et sociales the previous November.[77] Here Bergson asserted that any attempt to construct a 'society' of nations was premature given the 'primitive state' of the 'mental evolution' of France's enemies. He argued instead for the constitution of a 'permanent federation' of France's wartime allies as the best means of imposing peace on Germany. Bourgeois disagreed. Such a system, he argued, 'would have as its only basis the common interests of the Allies', which 'will last only as long as these interests coincide'. Germany would exploit differences between former allies

---

[73] MAE, PA-AP 029, *Papiers Bourgeois*, vol. 17, Bourgeois' handwritten notes for the first meeting of the CISDN, 27 Sept. 1917; MAE, *SDN*, vol. 1, 'Séance d'ouverture', 28 Sept. 1917.
[74] MAE, *SDN*, vol. 1, second meeting of the CISDN, 21 Nov. 1917.
[75] MAE, *SDN*, vol. 1, 'Note du Président', Bourgeois memorandum to the commission, 15 Dec. 1917; see also the minutes from the second meeting of the CISDN, 21 Nov. 1917 as well as the preliminary 'Exposé des principes' produced by Bourgeois on 16 Jan. 1918.
[76] MAE, *SDN*, vol. 7, Pichon to Jusserand (drafted by Bourgeois). There are several drafts of this note in both this volume and in *SDN*, vol. 3.
[77] MAE, PA-AP 029, *Papiers Bourgeois*, vol. 16, 'Comité nationale d'études politiques: séance du lundi 20 novembre 1916'.

to isolate France and defy the terms of any peace treaty. 'What then constitutes a more solid foundation for peace?' Bourgeois asked. 'I know of only one: the law.'[78]

Bergson's argument was taken up within the CISDN, in different ways, by Henri Fromageot and Jules Cambon. Fromageot argued that it was precisely the sovereign right of states to defend what they considered to be their 'vital interests', a right consecrated in international law, that made the effective functioning of an international legal regime all but impossible. He predicted that states would never accept compulsory arbitration over issues where they deemed their vital interests to be at stake. He therefore argued for a more exclusive 'society' limited to 'those states with common interests'.[79]

Jules Cambon criticised the internationalist commitment to the rule of law from a different perspective. Noting the widespread tendency to attack 'the policy of the balance of power' he expressed the hope that:

We do not allow ourselves, seduced by the vision of a new world organisation, to abandon that which appears to me to be the essential base of the institutions of liberty, upon which rests the defence of the weak and small against the abuses of the strong. We must face the realities of the world as it is ... the balance of power will not disappear as a result of our deliberations. It will continue to determine the behaviour of nations after the war as it did before.

As a result, Cambon warned, 'it will be necessary to constitute forces capable of resisting the expansionist instincts of the German people and this can only mean to arrive, one way or another, at the old policy of the balance of power'. The lessons of history, Cambon argued, did not augur well for messianic internationalism.[80]

Bourgeois responded to these challenges by revisiting, almost word for word, his argument to Bergson of several months earlier. 'To build the peace on the maintenance of a federation of Allies', he repeated, 'would be to build it on sand.' Only a legal regime could ensure that the shifting currents of national interest did not undermine international peace and security. 'I do not consider the prolongation of the alliance as sufficient,' he observed. 'This may well be a necessary transition, but not in itself a sufficient condition for future security. We need a juridical organisation.'[81] Gout supported Bourgeois, warning that an exclusive organisation of former Allies would constitute a modern version of the post-1815 Holy Alliance, leading inevitably to the return of opposing coalitions and, ultimately, war. 'Our new union of nations must therefore

---

[78] Ibid.
[79] Fromageot interventions in the first and second sessions of the CISDN: MAE, *SDN*, vol. 1, 28 Sept. and 21 Nov. 1917.
[80] MAE, *SDN*, vol. 2, CISDN tenth session, 13 Feb. 1918.
[81] Ibid.; see also similar discussion on 21 Nov. 1917 in vol. 1. Scott Blair erroneously judges Bourgeois as aiming at a league that would be a de facto military alliance in 'La France et le pacte', 170 and 182.

rest not on force but instead on laws.' Hanotaux intervened to observe that 'the old policy of power balancing has failed. It unleashed the war.'[82]

These disagreements revolved around the concrete question of Germany's role in the post-war international system. There was no place for the Reich in the society of nations advocated by Fromageot and Cambon. Their argument was to organise a league *against* Germany. Such a view was utterly incompatible with the internationalist conception of a society that must one day include Germany.

Democratic institutions would be the fundamental prerequisite for membership in this society. Hanotaux, for example, judged that 'the condition for the [successful] realisation of this project is the destruction of the Hohenzollern dynasty'. Bourgeois concurred:

The Allies, who represent the free peoples of the world, must confer together to establish the bases of a society which, by its juridical character, would be open to all, but can admit only those peoples who conform to the necessary condition of being represented by free institutions.

Only states with representative institutions could be trusted to support the cause of international peace. 'Germany', Bourgeois observed, 'has far to go in its evolution towards freedom, peace and democracy.' At the same time, he insisted, the Reich could not be excluded from international society indefinitely. If, once defeated, it adopted a democratic government, disarmed and paid its share of the costs of reconstruction, it must be admitted.[83] The distinction between this conviction and the interest-based conception of Fromageot and Cambon was fundamental.

There was much less disagreement when it came to elaborating a regime of sanctions backed up by an international armed force to impose them on recalcitrant states. Ribot's only observations upon opening the first session of the commission had been to exhort its members to 'devise the sanctions that provide practical value [to an international organisation]'. The long tradition of associating the use of force with the rule of law had only been intensified by the experience of invasion and occupation. Support for equipping the league with robust powers of sanction stretched across the political spectrum. The socialist position outlined by Albert Thomas to the chamber was that 'sanctions are the essential guarantee of any future Society of Nations'. Their enforcement must rest on 'a union of the forces of its members'.[84] Bourgeois agreed. 'Sanctions are an absolute necessity. This is the glaring truth that emerges from the present war.'[85]

---

[82] MAE, *SDN*, vol. 2, CISDN tenth session, 13 Feb. 1918; vol. 1, second session, 21 Nov. 1917.

[83] Quotations from MAE, *SDN*, vol. 1, CISDN second session, 21 Nov. 1917; vol. 2, CISDN tenth session, 13 Feb. 1918; MAE, PA-AP 029, *Papiers Bourgeois*, vol. 17, 'SDN. Exposé des principes', 16 Jan. 1918.

[84] *JO*, Chambre, 1917, *Débats*, 20 Nov. 1917.

[85] MAE, *SDN*, vol. 1, 'Séance d'ouverture', 28 Sept. 1917; significantly, Bourgeois was quoting from a speech made by Ribot to the chamber on 2 Aug. 1917.

Weiss prepared a detailed thirty-nine-page study of diplomatic, juridical and economic sanctions for the CISDN meeting of 30 January 1918.[86] It was at this point that Pila joined the commission to make a compelling case for utility of the 'economic arm' in future efforts to enforce international law.[87] The Allied blockade, he argued, illustrated the potential power of economic sanctions to isolate a given state and compel it to change its behaviour. A similar measure, particularly in peacetime, would require the coordination of the commercial policies of the major economic powers. A league of nations of the kind envisaged by the CISDN, Pila observed, held out the possibility of achieving such coordination. He added that the British blockade minister Robert Cecil was thinking along very similar lines. It was agreed that an international economic organ should be created within the society of nations and charged with planning 'measures of economic harmonisation' among member states. Harmonisation of this kind, CISDN members agreed, would be necessary in order to 'mutualise' the commercial costs of embargo to individual states. With these arguments, Pila succeeded in importing the essentials of the Clémentel Plan into the CISDN programme for international sanctions. From being almost an afterthought in the initial report prepared by Weiss, economic measures moved to the centre of the sanctions regime adopted by the CISDN.[88]

The most detailed provisions for collective action, however, were those for military sanctions. The report on this subject, which was prepared by army general staff officer Captain René Petit, described 'recourse to arms' as the 'supreme means' by which the envisaged society of nations would enforce its decisions.[89] Petit's report therefore called for the creation of a powerful international force comprising contingents from all member states. It further envisaged the creation of a permanent general staff for this force, whose task would be to determine the nature of each national contingent. This staff would even have the right to intervene to standardise levels of training and armaments. The system envisaged by Petit and approved by the CISDN was highly intrusive and implied significant infringements on the sovereignty of member states. Officers from the international staff would inspect the armed forces of each member state 'at least twice per year'. The anticipated functions of the international force would range from occupying disputed territory and patrolling rivers and sea lanes to mounting full-scale military operations against recalcitrant states. In contrast to the detailed discussion of the land forces, the role of naval units, much more pivotal in the imposition of economic sanctions, was left unspecified.

---

[86] MAE, *SDN*, vol. 1, 'Rapport de M. Weiss sur les sanctions diplomatiques, juridiques et économiques', 30 Jan. 1918; see also a preliminary report by Weiss entitled 'La Société des nations: sanctions diplomatiques, juridiques et économiques' and dated 15 Dec. 1917.
[87] MAE, *SDN*, vol. 2, seventh session of the CISDN, 31 Jan. 1918.   [88] Ibid.
[89] MAE, *SDN*, vol. 2, 'La Société des nations: sanctions militaires. Rapport présente par M. le capitaine Petit', 11 Feb. 1918.

French thinking when it came to sanctions was dominated by previsions of future conflict with Germany.[90]

One of the most remarkable, yet least understood, aspects of the French plan for an international force was its implications for national armed services. Petit drafted his report on the assumption that the creation of an international force would lead inevitably to the imposition of strict limitations on the sizes of the armies and navies of all member states. He anticipated a system whereby states would submit their military budgets for the approval of the society or league of nations.[91] This generated heated discussion within the commission. Gout pointed out that, without generalised arms limitations, there was little point to the constitution of an international force. Bourgeois agreed, observing that 'the question is whether or not we will have arms limitations in the future. If we do not, there will be no society of nations.' This point of view was opposed with great vigour by Hanotaux, in particular, who argued that it was pointless to discuss arms limitations in the future while France was waging an unprecedented war for survival in the present. The issue was dropped and not taken up again in a substantive way until after the armistice.[92] But it was clear that the issue of arms limitation would cause difficulties in the future.

The final issue debated by the CISDN was the composition and role of an 'international council'. Such a structure, significantly, did not figure in the initial conception outlined by Bourgeois in September 1917. For Bourgeois the core functions of a future international organisation would be the codification and application of the law of nations. It was Gout who first pointed out the need for an 'engine' to drive the league's processes of mediation, arbitration and collective security. Bourgeois responded, revealingly, that these functions could be performed by the international bureau of the Hague tribunal. Gout observed that the Hague machinery was a 'receiver' when what was needed was a 'transmitting organ'. Despite unanimous antipathy for anything that suggested a 'super-state', Bourgeois and the rest of the commission were convinced by this argument. Gout was charged with preparing a study of this issue.[93]

Gout was assisted by Jules Basdevant, professor of international law and an acclaimed expert on Grotius, who would become chief legal counsel at the Quai d'Orsay during the 1920s. Together they prepared a series of reports that sparked lively and lengthy debates over the composition, functions and powers

---

[90] Both Cambon and Lacaze criticised the complete neglect of naval power by Petit; see MAE, SDN, vol. 2, CISDN seventh session, 31 Jan. 1918 and 'La Société des nations: sanctions militaires. Rapport présente par M. le capitaine Petit', 11 Feb. 1918.
[91] See esp. Petit's contribution to commission discussions on 11 Feb. in 'La Société des nations: sanctions militaires. Rapport présente par M. le capitaine Petit', 11 Feb. 1918.
[92] MAE, SDN, vol. 2, ninth and eleventh sessions of the CISDN, 11 and 20 Feb. 1918.
[93] MAE, SDN, vol. 1, 'Séance d'ouverture', 28 Sept. 1917; for Basdevant's expertise see his contribution to Les Fondateurs du droit international: leur oeuvres, leur doctrines (Paris, 1904).

of an international council.[94] The text of these debates illuminates once again the deep fissure within the CISDN between those in favour of an international organisation to prolong France's wartime alliances and those who advocated a juridical vision in which members would agree to surrender a measure of sovereignty in exchange for collective security. Disagreement centred on the relationship between the council and the Permanent Court of Arbitration at The Hague. Cambon and Fromageot pointed out that many disputes between states were of a political rather than a juridical character and were not suitable for settlement before the Hague tribunal. Bourgeois and Weiss, conversely, insisted that the vast majority of such disputes could be resolved by arbitration if priority was given to developing an ever-more comprehensive and precise corpus of international law. This profound divergence over the nature of international politics was obscured in a compromise document drafted by Gout that left the precise functioning of the council purposefully vague and open-ended.[95]

The final programme adopted by the CISDN on 8 June 1918 marked a victory for the juridical internationalist position. It outlined a robust regime of diplomatic, juridical and economic sanctions. It called for the creation of an international economic organisation to be responsible for the implementation of embargoes and blockades. It also included a detailed discussion of military sanctions with details on the creation of an international force and permanent general staff. At the heart of the CISDN programme, however, was the aim to establish a legal basis for international politics. The final proposal was imbued from start to finish with a juridical internationalist vision of world order. It proclaimed at the outset that the 'unifying goal of the Society of Nations' was to 'maintain peace through the substitution of law for force in the settlement of international conflicts'.[96] Nor, crucially, would Germany be excluded permanently. The CISDN called for a 'society of democratic peoples' with a

---

[94] For the reports: MAE, *Série A*, vol. 62, 'Rapport préliminaire rédigé par M. Basdevant sur l'organe politique de la SDN', 27 Mar. 1918; 'Composition du Conseil international et de la Délégation permanente' (Gout), 29 Apr. 1918; 'Exposé des motifs de la rēsolution relative au rôle et au fonctionnement du Conseil international' (Basdevant), 3 Jun. 1918; for the commission's debates, MAE, *SDN*, vol. 3, twelfth and thirteenth CISDN sessions, 27 and 28 Mar. 1918; vol. 4, fourteenth and fifteenth CISDN sessions, 10 and 17 Apr. 1918.

[95] A committee was to be established within the council to determine whether disputes were of a juridical or a political nature; the former were to be referred to The Hague and the latter would be dealt with through mediation by the council. But the composition of this committee was not addressed, neither was the criteria to be applied to make this determination. See MAE, *Série A*, vol. 62, 'Exposé des motifs de la résolution relative au rôle et au fonctionnement du Conseil international' (Basdevant), 3 Jun. 1918 and 'Exposé des motifs de la résolution relative à la composition du Conseil international et de la Délégation permanente' (Gout), 4 Jun. 1918.

[96] MAE, *SDN*, vol. 10, 'Textes adoptés par la Commission interministérielle française de la Société des nations: exposé des principes sur lesquels peut être constituée la Société des nations', 8 Jun. 1918; also in MAE, *Série A*, vol. 62 and in published form in A. G. de Lapradelle (ed.), *La Paix de Versailles*, 12 vols. (Paris, 1929–36), vol. I: *La Conference de paix et la Société des nations* (hereafter *PV-SDN*), 120–7.

'universalist orientation'. Any state with representative institutions that demonstrated a willingness to 'observe certain rules for the maintenance of peace through respect for international law' would be admitted. Germany, in other words, would be allowed to join once it had transformed its political institutions and demonstrated good faith. Provided the Allies were victorious and Prussian militarism overthrown, a democratic Germany would eventually take its place in post-war international organisation.[97]

The French conception was therefore much more than merely a club of victorious states. Its purpose was to establish a legal basis for international politics as well as the machinery to enforce the law of nations. The Allied nations would draft this law. Indeed, it could not be otherwise in the light of French constructions of the meaning of the conflict as a struggle to impose the rule of law on Prussian tyranny. Crucially, however, the legal regime that resulted was always intended to be applied to *all* states (or at least all states with a common European heritage). It was not conceived to disadvantage Germany permanently. The CISDN programme was an expression of the juridical internationalist vision of peace and security.

Bourgeois and his fellow internationalists had prevailed. Interestingly, however, they do not seem to have recognised a fundamental contradiction at the heart of their conception of the league. There was unanimous opposition to the idea of a super-state that would compromise the national sovereignty of its member states. Yet the plan for an international force implied substantial interference in the defence policies of member states. The same was true, to an even greater extent, of the aim to ensure the *automatic* participation of member states in the imposition of diplomatic, economic and even military sanctions. The tension between the imperatives for robust collective security, on the one hand, and state sovereignty, on the other, would prove decisive when the powers gathered to design the League in Paris in early 1919. Nor has this dilemma been resolved in the structure and functioning of the Security Council of the United Nations nearly one hundred years later.

How to explain this blind spot in the French internationalist conception? One factor, surely, was the influence of the theory of *solidarité*. According to *solidariste* doctrine, a 'society of nations' could only be an association of states with common cultural values, all of which accepted the need for mutual obligations (defined by law) to preserve peace and security. Germany posed the obvious immediate challenge to such a society. This would remain the case until it joined the ranks of democratic and 'civilised' powers in the indeterminate future. In this heavily juridical vision, observance and enforcement of the rule of international law necessarily implied restrictions on the sovereignty of member states. Bourgeois skated over the tricky implications of this reality by deploying the solidarist theory of mutualisation:

---

[97] *PV-SDN*, 120–7.

In conceding to this international organ the powers necessary for the maintenance of peace, nations abdicate nothing of their true sovereignty. When a citizen exercises his liberty in assuming an engagement that he deems to be in his interests, how is he giving up his liberty? ... Sovereignty is nothing more than liberty, something that is absolute. But the liberty of every individual is limited by the liberty of others; the sovereignty of a state is limited by the equal sovereignty of other states, small or large. And the contract they enter into, as long as they are equally free in doing so, alienates nothing of their liberty but is instead an arrangement of mutual consent.[98]

Bourgeois' ultimate aim was to achieve peace by replacing international anarchy with the rule of law. He assumed that state leaders would see the reason of his argument and accept the limitations on their freedom of action necessary to achieve this.

There was little chance that such arguments would fly even within the French policy elite. Clemenceau was not seduced by the idea of security through international organisation. He made no reference to the project during his investiture speech. He addressed the issue only when pressed to do so by Socialist deputies. 'You believe that the formula of the Society of Nations can resolve everything,' he responded. 'I share your idealism. But I am also aware of the reality of things.' The security provided by such a society would rest ultimately on the good faith of its members and as such was insufficient given 'the present state of humanity'.[99] In private Clemenceau mocked Bourgeois and his approach to security. When his government received a copy of the CISDN programme, it forwarded it to London and Washington without comment.[100]

V

Clemenceau, to be fair, had other pressing concerns. Russia was out of the war, Italy had suffered a crushing defeat at Caporetto and a powerful German offensive was anticipated on the western front. The German attacks, when they began in March, achieved startling initial successes that placed acute pressure on the Franco-British alliance. The result was a military and political crisis that led to the creation of a unified command structure and the nomination of Ferdinand Foch as supreme commander of the Allied armies.[101]

But the 'last throw' of the Central Powers failed to achieve its objective of a massive breakthrough. By late July the long-anticipated influx of US troops had tilted the military balance irrevocably in favour of the Allied and Associated

[98] MAE, *SDN*, vol. 7, 'Discours prononcé à l'Assemblée générale constitutive du 10 novembre 1918 par M. Léon Bourgeois'.
[99] *JO*, Chambre, *Débats*, 1917, 20 Nov. 1917.
[100] Poincaré, *Au service de la France*, vol. X: *Victoire et armistice* (Paris, 1933), 25 Jun. 1918: 245; MAE, *SDN*, vol. 7, 'Note au sujet de "Société des nations"', Pichon to Jusserand, 20 Jun. 1918.
[101] Excellent sources on French policy during this crisis are G. Pédroncini, *Pétain: le soldat, 1914–1940* (Paris, 1998), 214–40; Doughty, *Pyrrhic Victory*, 418–59; Hanks, 'Clemenceau's leadership', 204–17; on the wider course of the war see above all Stevenson, *Backs to the Wall*.

Powers. Germany's armies were unable to halt Allied counter-attacks that came all along the western front. The army Deuxième bureau reported that Austria-Hungary was on the verge of collapse and that even the German government was contemplating peace negotiations.[102] This assessment may have been premature, but it proved accurate. On 5 October 1918 the newly appointed moderate chancellor Prince Max of Baden wrote to Woodrow Wilson to ask for armistice negotiations on the bases of the Fourteen Points. The German note set in train a month-long series of exchanges that culminated in the armistice of 11 November.[103]

The swiftness with which the course of the war turned was unexpected. It forced French policy makers to begin concrete preparations for a post-war settlement that would be negotiated under very different conditions from those that had prevailed for the majority of the conflict. The collapse of Russia, the ally most supportive of France's ambitions to transform the European balance of power with a forward policy in the Rhineland, was a crucial factor in the new geo-political landscape. The other was the United States, whose president was determined to replace the balance of power with a new framework for international relations.

Woodrow Wilson's love of points and principles did not clear up uncertainty over American policy. The president failed even to respond to Clémentel's letter of the previous October outlining plans for sharing raw materials. This uncertainty persisted despite the efforts of André Tardieu – France's talented and energetic high commissioner to the United States – to obtain clarification concerning American intentions. As fighting drew to a close French planning faced a wide array of imponderables.

In the event, the armistice signed on 11 November 1918 brought to a close more than a month of debate among security professionals in Paris. This debate centred initially on the wisdom of agreeing to a ceasefire before shifting to focus on the necessary conditions under which France could agree to an armistice. An influential current of opinion favoured rejecting German armistice demands in favour of carrying the war into Germany. General Pétain demanded authorisation to launch the long-planned assault into western Germany. The principal objective of this offensive, tellingly, was the Saar coalfield. Ambassadors Jusserand in Washington and Paul Cambon in London both advocated such an offensive as the best means to drive home the meaning of defeat to the German people. Paul Deschanel, still president of the chamber, agreed. Poincaré was the foremost proponent of this view, however. He wrote to Clemenceau to urge him to avoid 'the trap' of an armistice which would 'hamstring' France's troops and 'give us no strength in negotiations'.

---

[102] SHD-DAT, 14N 23-3, 'La Question de la paix en Allemagne et en Autriche-Hongrie', 21 Jul. 1918.
[103] See the printed documents annexed in P. Renouvin, *L'Armistice de Rethondes: 11 novembre 1918* (Paris, 1968), 376–422.

Clemenceau responded with a threat to resign that forced Poincaré to step back from decision making. The premier's control of policy was further strengthened.[104]

There were strong counter-arguments to an offensive if the necessary 'diplomatic and military guarantees' could be obtained in an armistice.[105] The most important were certainly humanitarian. Neither Clemenceau nor commander-in-chief Foch was willing to continue to expend lives in costly military operations if France could obtain its political objectives in armistice terms. There was also genuine concern that revolution would engulf Germany and spread to other areas of Europe if the forces of order in that country were smashed altogether. Finally there was an argument for ending the conflict before US military power on the continent eroded France's negotiating position at the peace table.[106]

A central figure in this process was Foch, the commander-in-chief of Allied armies since the previous spring. Born in 1851 to a conservative, religious and highly patriotic family, Foch was 'brought up to worship French predominance'.[107] The defeat of 1871 was one of the great formative events in his life, prompting his decision to take up a military career. Educated by Jesuits before entering the École polytechnique, Foch was a brilliant student. He made his name as an officer of extraordinary intellect, energy and charisma. Before 1914 he served as commander of the École supérieure de guerre and was widely considered one of France's foremost philosophers of war. A Clausewitzian, Foch understood war as a struggle between peoples in which military action must be determined by an understanding of political objectives. His Jesuit education, however, had imbued him with the conviction that ends should not be subordinated to means. 'The essential thing is to know what one wants to do' was one of his favourite observations on the nature of strategy. This lent his strategic thought a dynamic and aggressive character that would also shape his conception of the post-war order.[108]

Foch had played an important role in the war from its beginning. Named commander of the northern army group in early 1915, he directed the French

---

[104] Renouvin, *Armistice de Rethondes*, 255–67; J.-J. Becker, *La France en guerre, 1914–1918: la grande mutation* (Brussels, 1999), 127–8; G. Wormser, *Le Septennat de Poincaré* (Paris, 1977), 141–77; Duroselle, *Grande Guerre*, 406–13; and Keiger, *Poincaré*, 247–9.

[105] Pierre Renouvin and David Stevenson note that even the SFIO opposed an armistice that did not deliver such guarantees: see P. Renouvin, 'Die öffentliche Meinung in Frankreich während des Krieges, 1914–1918', *Vierteljahrshefte für Zeitgeschichte*, 18 (1970), 269–71; Stevenson, *French War Aims*, 117.

[106] Renouvin, *Armistice de Rethondes*, 262–5; Soutou, *L'Or et le sang*, 556–9; Watson, *Clemenceau*, 307–8; Stevenson, *Backs to the Wall*, 509–45.

[107] J.-C. Notin, *Foch* (Paris, 2008), 18; the following paragraphs draw heavily on this study as well as R. Recouly, *Le Mémorial de Foch: mes entretiens avec le maréchal* (Paris, 1929).

[108] Notin, *Foch*, 17–18; A. Martel, *Relire Foch au XXIème siècle: stratégies et doctrines* (Paris, 2008), 23–69; P. Jackson, 'Foch et la politique de sécurité française, 1919–1924' in F. Cochet and R. Porte (eds.), *Ferdinand Foch (1851–1929): apprenez à penser* (Paris, 2010), 333–47.

attack on the Somme the following summer. The failure of this offensive led to his reassignment as chief of army staff, where he excelled. His energy and resolve during the darkest moments of the German spring offensives led to his promotion as Allied commander-in-chief, a position he would continue to hold into the 1920s. By war's end Foch was one of the most distinguished and popular soldiers in French history. His command during the decisive campaigns of 1918 came to personify France's victory every bit as much as Clemenceau's defiance and determination. And the loss of his eldest son in the fighting of early 1914 meant that he also embodied France's sacrifices. Foch would use this immense symbolic authority to intervene repeatedly in an effort to shape the peace settlement according to his own vision of security, at the centre of which was a permanent French presence on the Rhine.

The general outlines of Foch's post-war vision are discernible in a draft memorandum on peace conditions he prepared as Allied victory became increasingly certain in August 1918. He began by observing that to settle for the return of Alsace-Lorraine and the imposition of an indemnity would be to 'see the struggle begin again in twenty years'. What was needed was a settlement that would establish 'a long-lasting European balance'. This, in turn, meant 'ending German sovereignty west of the Rhine'.[109] This conception of post-war order underpinned a subsequent note Foch prepared for Clemenceau on 8 October 1918. Allied representatives were at this point gathered in Paris to discuss the German request for a ceasefire. Foch advised the premier that any armistice must go beyond the liberation of occupied territory to include control of strategic bridgeheads on the Rhine, the withdrawal of all German military units at least thirty kilometres east of that river, and, equally crucially, Allied military occupation of the Left Bank. The latter measures, Foch explained, were a way to 'take in hand guarantees for the reparations ... that are to be demanded during peace negotiations'.[110] In carefully circumscribed language, Foch was advocating seizing control of German territory on the Left Bank of the Rhine.

The marshal went further in another missive of 16 October which addressed the future status of the Left Bank of the Rhine directly:

What will be the future of this territory? Will our occupation be permanent? Will we annex all or part of this country? Or will we rather pursue the creation of neutral states, autonomous, independent, forming a buffer? ... Because it is certain that the armistice must place in our hands the sureties that will guarantee that in peace negotiations we obtain those conditions that we wish to impose on the enemy, and it is clear that only the advantages embedded in the armistice are certain to remain

---

[109] SHD-DAT, Fonds Privés (DITEEX), *Papiers du maréchal Ferdinand Foch*, 1K 129, carton 2, 'Note', n.d. but certainly Aug. 1918.
[110] SHD-DAT, 14N 35-1, 'Note sur les conditions d'un armistice avec l'Allemagne', 8 Oct. 1918.

National deliverance and post-war planning 193

assured [in subsequent negotiations]; the only definitive territorial sacrifices will be those conceded by the enemy when the armistice is concluded.[111]

For Foch, a permanent presence on the Left Bank held the key to France's future security. Occupation of this territory was therefore vital to ensure that French policy makers would have the final say over this crucial issue. This foray into the realm of foreign policy making led Pichon to complain to Clemenceau that the marshal had far exceeded his remit to provide technical counsel.[112] Clemenceau agreed, forwarding Pichon's complaint to Foch and reminding him that his role was that of 'military counsellor'. He had no business speculating on the political status of any foreign territory.[113] The exchange was a harbinger of things to come.

If Foch was censured for trying to make policy, his analysis was not rejected. Both Pichon and Clemenceau agreed that the armistice conditions would be crucial for the peace negotiations to come. Berthelot, now the leading voice within the Quai d'Orsay, initiated a round of consultation within the policy establishment with the observation that international law placed no limits on what could be demanded in armistice talks.[114] Allied military officials on the Supreme War Council at Versailles responded by advocating the seizure of 'material guarantees' in the form of fortified areas along Germany's western frontier and in the North Sea. These guarantees were 'to ensure that Germany respects its promises'.[115] Finance minister Louis-Lucien Klotz also intervened to demand clear stipulation that any financial measures imposed on Germany in the armistice must be 'subject to all demands and claims that might subsequently be made on the part of the Allies'.[116] This important proviso was intended to secure future claims for full reparation of damages.

Marshal Joffre's counsel was sought through the offices of Berthelot (who was in close contact with nearly all senior military commanders). Joffre endorsed Foch's idea for an occupation. He also forwarded a peace plan of his own. It is difficult to imagine a plan more out of touch with the political realities of the period than this programme, which proposed breaking up the

---

[111] Foch to Clemenceau, 18 Oct. 1918, reproduced in Foch, *Mémoires pour servir*, II, 229–31; see also SHD-DAT, *Fonds Clemenceau*, Foch to Clemenceau (recounting a conversation with British field marshal Douglas Haig), 18 Oct. 1918; for further analysis see Jackson, 'Foch et la politique de sécurité française', 336–7 and esp. Stevenson, *French War Aims*, 122.
[112] SHD-DAT, *Fonds Clemenceau*, 6N 70–1, 'Au Sujet d'une lettre du Maréchal Foch', Pichon to Clemenceau, 21 Oct. 1918 (though the tone, cadence and logic of this note suggest that Berthelot was the author).
[113] SHD-DAT, *Fonds Clemenceau*, 6N 70–1, 'Au Maréchal Foch', 23 Oct. 1918.
[114] MAE, *Série A*, vol. 279, 'Armistices', 22 Oct. 1918.
[115] MAE, PA-AP 141, *Papiers Pichon*, vol. 6, 'Avis collectif: étude des conditions d'un armistice avec l'Allemagne et l'Autriche-Hongrie', 8 Oct. 1918; also MAE, *Série A*, vol. 279, 'Conditions d'armistice', 28 Oct. 1918: subsection entitled 'Conditions des représentants militaires et navals permanents du Conseil supérieur de guerre de Versailles'.
[116] SHD-DAT, *Fonds Clemenceau*, 6N 73–1, 'De la Part de M. Klotz après accord avec M. Pichon: en cas d'armistice avec les Puissances Centrales', 19 Oct. 1918.

German empire into a loose confederation of states with no army or navy. The leader of the resulting polity would be a 'prince chosen among the ruling families of the different states' who would serve for a five-year period.[117]

A range of studies produced by the foreign ministry were more realistic but no less rooted in a power-political conception of the current situation and the peace settlement that would follow. Typical of these was a set of proposals drafted by Robert de Caix, the influential conservative-nationalist editor of the *Journal des débats* on secondment to the Quai d'Orsay in 1918. De Caix formulated an ambitious list of demands intended to clear the way for an extensive territorial reordering of Europe at Germany's expense. He argued that France should press for independence of the Bavarian Palatinate, the Left Bank, Schleswig-Holstein, German Poland, Austria and even the Ruhr industrial basin.[118] He also drew attention to the dangerous situation in eastern Europe resulting from the turmoil in Russia. His recommendation was that Germany be forced to facilitate the transfer of Polish and Czechoslovak troops to their national homelands as quickly as possible to contain the 'Bolshevik danger'. He added that 'a small French contingent' should be sent to both regions 'to remind our future clients to whom they owe their liberation'. De Caix concluded by warning that 'we cannot count on the goodwill of our allies once peace negotiations begin'. France's vision for the transformation of Europe must therefore be entrenched in the armistice.[119] For de Caix this vision centred on breaking German power and installing France as the arbiter of an exhausted Europe.

These various prescriptions for armistice terms were outlined and analysed in a crucial study prepared by Berthelot for Pichon on 28 October. In this document Berthelot endorsed Foch's demand for bridgeheads, the occupation of the Left Bank and the demilitarisation of a thirty-kilometre strip along the right bank. Berthelot went further, however, to advocate the inter-Allied occupation of Essen in the Ruhr basin as well as control of Germany's rail system and all German ports. He also recommended that the Central Powers should be forced to renounce the Treaty of Brest-Litovsk and evacuate not only all Russian territory, but also Polish, Czech, Slovak and Serb lands in order to facilitate the state-building process in these new countries. 'Acceptance of president Wilson's conditions', Berthelot observed, 'changes every aspect of the position [in eastern Europe].' He also underlined the importance of the reservation requested by Klotz, but added that reparations in kind were preferable to any gold indemnity that France might obtain.[120] Nearly all of these

[117] SHD-DAT, 14N 35-2, 'Dossier remis par M. Berthelot au Maréchal le 14 octobre'; 'Conditions possibles d'un armistice', 13 Oct. 1918; 'Projet de Traité', 17 Oct. 1918.
[118] MAE, *Série A*, vol. 279, '[Note] sur l'armistice en ce qui concerne l'Allemagne', n.d. but certainly 22-24 Oct. 1918.
[119] MAE, *Série A*, vol. 279, 'Note sur les demandes d'armistice', 24 Oct. 1918.
[120] MAE, PA-AP 141, *Papiers Pichon*, vol. 6, 'Conditions d'armistice', 28 Oct. 1918; also in MAE, *Série A*, vol. 279.

National deliverance and post-war planning 195

recommendations were reproduced in a memorandum forwarded to Clemenceau in Pichon's name three days later. This document went even further, however, to advocate Allied occupation of the entire industrial region of Westphalia.[121]

Nearly all of the armistice conditions mooted by policy elites in Paris ran counter to the spirit of the Fourteen Points. Pichon, echoing the views of Berthelot and other senior officials within the Quai d'Orsay, warned that Wilson's programme was too vague and presented opportunities for Germany to subvert the peace during negotiations. Clemenceau, who had received a virtual blank cheque from cabinet to negotiate armistice terms, concurred. He was dismissive of Wilson's sermonising and resented the president's tactic of negotiating without prior consultation with the Allies. But he eventually gave way and accepted the Fourteen Points after difficult inter-Allied discussions on 29–30 October 1918. The lone reservation upon which he insisted (along with Lloyd George) was a statement indicating that the Allies could claim reparation for damage to their civilian populations and property. This reflected Clemenceau's well-founded judgement that reparations would be a central preoccupation with French public opinion once the fighting ceased.[122]

On 8 November 1918 Marshal Foch communicated Allied armistice conditions to the German delegation at Rethondes. That evening Clemenceau and his military *chef de cabinet*, General Jean Mordacq, celebrated revenge for the defeat of 1871 and fulfilment of 'the supreme object of our existence'.[123] Clemenceau had largely succeeded in securing Allied agreement on the military conditions laid out by Foch. These did not go as far as the occupation of Westphalia advocated by the Quai d'Orsay. But they did include occupation of the whole of the Left Bank, the bridgeheads at Mainz, Koblenz and Cologne as well as the creation of a forty-kilometre-wide demilitarised zone on the east bank of the Rhine. This placed France in a favourable position to address the crucial issues left unresolved by the Fourteen Points: the frontiers of Alsace-Lorraine and the new eastern European states; the political status of the Rhineland; and Germany's obligation to help pay for Allied reconstruction.[124]

And yet it is worth pausing for a moment to consider the ambiguities in French policy. Clemenceau had accepted Wilson's Fourteen Points as the

[121] SHD-DAT, *Fonds Clemenceau*, 6N 73–1, 'Notes pour les clauses militaires de l'armistice allemand', 1 Nov. 1918.
[122] The French records of the meetings of the Supreme War Council of 29 Oct.–4 Nov. 1918 to debate armistice terms are in SHD-DAT, 6N 64–1 and 64–2; Poincaré, *Victoire et armistice*, 29 Oct.: 396; see also the analysis in Stevenson, *Backs to the Wall*, 521–9.
[123] G. Mordacq, *Le Ministère Clemenceau: journal d'un témoin*, 3 vols. (Paris, 1931), II, 345, cited in Stevenson, *French War Aims*, 129.
[124] Renouvin, *Armistice de Rethondes*, 214–20; Stevenson, *French War Aims*, 126–9; Stevenson, *Backs to the Wall*, 509–44.

bases for both the armistice and subsequent peace negotiations. The French government had publicly endorsed the principle of the League of Nations and produced a relatively detailed plan for its creation. These facts reflected not only the importance of American and British power in French strategic planning, but also the political affinities between France and its chief democratic allies. At the same time, the Clemenceau government had secured coalition agreement on Foch's 'military conditions' which were, in reality, political conditions designed to put France in the strongest possible position to shape a favourable balance of power in the post-war order to be constructed.[125] The familiar tradition of the balance of power sat uneasily alongside internationalist agendas aimed at a fundamental transformation of world politics. Both currents would shape French policy in the peace negotiations to come.

[125] This argument is advanced most powerfully in Stevenson, *French War Aims*, 125–32.

Part III
Peace and security, 1918–1919

On 16 November 1918, with the ink newly dry on the armistice, premier Clemenceau met with a gathering of senior foreign ministry officials to discuss peace conditions and negotiating strategies. There was general agreement that there were two central objectives to be obtained for the future security of France. The first was a transformation of the European strategic balance through peace conditions that would weaken German power while at the same time strengthening that of France. The second was a continuation of the wartime coalition to secure the political and military support of both Britain and the USA in the post-war era. It was by no means clear that these two aims could be reconciled. 'One cannot always satisfy Jacques without displeasing Jean,' Clemenceau observed.[1] Compromises would have to be made.

At the heart of plans to overturn the European power balance were familiar projects to detach the Rhineland from Germany and create a buffer state which would be drawn into France's political orbit. This bid for a 'Rhenish peace', advanced formally by the Clemenceau government in late February 1919, has cast a long shadow over the historiography of French security policy. The French peace programme is nearly always represented as a traditional bid to achieve security through military preponderance. This interpretation is part of a wider narrative of the peace conference as a struggle between the power politics of 'old Europe' and the idealism of Woodrow Wilson. The earliest and one of the most extreme articulations of this view was John Maynard Keynes' *Economic Consequences of the Peace*. In what remains probably the most influential book ever written about the peace conference, Keynes characterised Clemenceau as a French Bismarck and the chief advocate of a 'Carthaginian peace'.[2] This judgement has been endorsed by historians ever since. Clemenceau's approach to international politics, according to one

---

[1] Cited in K. Hovi, *Cordon Sanitaire or Barrière de l'Est? The Emergence of the New French European Alliance Policy, 1917–1919* (Turku, 1975), 139–40.
[2] John Maynard Keynes, *The Economic Consequences of the Peace* (London, 1919), 32 and 35 respectively: 'His theory of politics was Bismarck's. He had one illusion – France; and one disillusion – mankind.' Recent iterations of this thesis are P. Cohrs, *The Unfinished Peace after World War I* (Cambridge, 2006), 30–67 (esp. 48–51) and H. Kissinger, *Diplomacy* (New York, 1994), 20–2, 44–54; more nuanced are M. MacMillan, *Paris 1919* (New York, 2001), 29–32

eminent scholar of the peace conference, 'was based first and foremost on *Realpolitik* and an avowed belief in the balance of power'.[3]

There is much evidence to support this interpretation. Although a number of historians have tried to argue that French policy was inspired chiefly by the threat of revolution, even a cursory look at the relevant archival material leaves no doubt that French planning and policy was dominated by the German problem. The conviction that limiting German power was crucial to France's future security was a core element in this planning. Projects to create strong 'successor states' on the Reich's eastern marches, limitations on its armed forces, punitive economic measures and plans to detach and neutralise the Rhineland were all traditional solutions based on power-political calculations. The traditional dimension to French peace policy is a central theme in the memoirs of both Clemenceau and his chief adviser, André Tardieu. Both emphasised that the Versailles Treaty weakened Germany considerably and, if enforced properly, would have made another German bid for power impossible.[4]

Yet a favourable Franco-German balance was not the only motivation guiding French policy. The three chapters that follow will argue that the French peace programme was more open-ended and innovative than is generally recognised. Internationalism did not provide the guiding principles for the Clemenceau government's policy. But internationalist themes, from an international organisation based on the rule of law backed up by powerful sanctions to a multilateral economic system that would include Germany, were part of the French programme. Even more significant was the importance attached to democratic transformation in Germany and to the principle of self-determination. These dimensions to French policy have not received the attention they deserve in the existing literature.

The stock image of Clemenceau, that of an incorrigibly cynical statesman who saw no future apart from a permanent effort to keep Germany down, is overdrawn and misleading.[5] There can be no denying his profound suspicion of Germany. The premier was convinced that many years must pass before the Allies could put faith in Germany's democratic transformation. But emphasis

and 157–203; Z Steiner, *The Lights that Failed: European International History, 1919–1933* (Oxford, 2005), 21–4 and 69–70; and R. Boyce, *The Great Inter-War Crisis and the Collapse of Globalization* (London, 2009), 23–74.

[3] A. Lentin, 'A Comment' in M. Boemke, G. Feldman and E. Glaser (eds.), *The Treaty of Versailles: A Reassessment after 75 Years* (Cambridge, 1998), 229; see also A. Sharp, *The Versailles Settlement: Peacemaking in Paris, 1919* (London, 1991), 188–94; P. M. H. Bell, *France and Britain, 1900–1940: Entente and estrangement* (London, 1996), 110–19, 157–203. For penetrating assessments of the historiographical issues at stake see W. R. Keylor, 'Versailles and International Diplomacy' and D. Stevenson, 'French War Aims and Peace Planning', both in Boemke et al. (eds.), *Treaty of Versailles*, 469–505 and 87–109.

[4] Georges Clemenceau, *Grandeurs et misères d'une victoire* (Paris, 1930); André Tardieu, *La Paix* (Paris, 1921).

[5] It is difficult to find studies of either French policy, or the peace conference more generally, that do not attribute critical importance to the premier's pessimism, cynicism or 'realism'. Partial exceptions, interestingly, are Clemenceau's biographers David Watson and Jean-Baptiste Duroselle.

on his pessimism ignores other aspects of his political catechism that also shaped his approach to peace making. The Tiger had a long record as a radical defender of democratic liberties in both parliament and the press. His commitment to the principles of self-determination and democracy was genuine. It determined his position when it came to the most fundamental issues shaping the peace settlement. Alongside the aims of territorial adjustment and a weakening of German power was a thoroughly transatlantic conception of a democratic post-war order that allowed for the possibility of political and economic cooperation with a reformed and democratic Germany. The flexible and fundamentally multilateral character of this 'larger strategic design' overlapped with prevailing internationalist visions of peace and security in ways that have not been acknowledged in the existing literature.[6] French policy was certainly more ambiguous than Clemenceau was later willing to admit. Along with his chief lieutenant, André Tardieu, he would spend much of the 1920s denouncing the failure of successive governments to impose the letter of the Versailles Treaty.[7] But this post-war posturing has done much to obscure the complex character of his government's peace programme.

At the war's end Clemenceau had secured an unusually powerful position from which to speak for France in peace making. Fêted as *père-la-victoire*, the premier enjoyed unprecedented levels of popular support for a politician of the Third Republic. His popularity, which only increased after he survived an assassination attempt the following February, was rivalled only by that of Marshal Foch. It translated into immense political authority and placed him in a virtually unassailable position in relation to parliament. Clemenceau used this authority to claim absolute control of peace negotiations. Virtually all of the crucial decisions during the peace conference were taken by the premier in consultation with his narrow circle of advisers. Leading parliamentarians were rarely informed about the course of negotiations and never consulted. Even Clemenceau's cabinet was marginalised and played no part in deliberations over momentous issues such as France's frontier with Germany, the fate of eastern Europe or reparations.[8]

Yet the premier and his team could not make peace in any way they liked. From the outset, Clemenceau sensed that absolute security in the traditional sense was unattainable. 'We may not have the peace that you and I should wish for,' he observed to Poincaré even before the fighting had ceased.[9] In

---

[6] Exceptions include S. Schuker, 'The Rhineland Question: West European Security at the Paris Peace Conference of 1919' and G.-H. Soutou, 'The French Peacemakers and their Homefront', both in Boemke et al. (eds.), *The Treaty of Versailles*, 275–312 and 167–88 respectively; as well as D. Stevenson, 'France and the German Question in the Era of the First World War' in S. Schuker (ed.), *Deutschland und Frankreich Vom Konflikt zur Aussöhnung: Die Gestaltung der westeuropäischen Sicherheit 1914–1963* (Munich, 2000), 1–18.
[7] See esp. J.-B. Duroselle, *Clemenceau* (Paris, 1988), 896–952 and M. Trachtenberg, *Reparation in World Politics: France and European Economic Diplomacy, 1916–1923* (New York, 1980), 102.
[8] D. R. Watson, *Georges Clemenceau: France* (London, 2008), 331–43; Duroselle, *Clemenceau*, 720–31.
[9] Poincaré, *Au Service de la France*, vol. X: *Victoire et armistice*, 6 Sept. 1918: 336.

November 1918 the pre-war order had been destroyed. France's population emerged traumatised from a conflict that had pushed it to the very limit of national endurance. The terrible human and material costs of the war, along with the expectations for social and political transformation that came with victory, placed powerful constraints on French policy. Popular expectations, crucially, often ran counter to the policy aims of France's allies.

British and American policy presented a formidable challenge to French peacemakers. Wilson had repeatedly framed the war as a struggle to install a new international system based on morality and cooperation rather than power politics: 'The question upon which the whole future peace and policy of the world depends,' the US president had insisted,

... is this: Is the present war a struggle for a just and secure peace, or only for a new balance of power? ... There must be, not a balance of power, but a community of power; not organized rivalries, but an organized common peace.[10]

The early optimism of French mandarins that France's chief allies could be brought round to support the central objectives of French security policy was unfounded. Though they disagreed on specific issues, both British and American leaders were united in rejecting all projects for breaking up Germany or placing any part of German soil under permanent occupation. All of these complications were compounded by important changes in the normative context within which foreign and security policy was made. In 1919 the global tide of popular enthusiasm for transforming world politics – and more specifically for replacing the balance of power with international cooperation and collective security – could not be ignored.

There were nonetheless powerful counter-currents to this trend that were also a product of the wartime experience. By 1918 a consensus existed within French opinion that Germany bore overwhelming responsibility for the war and must be punished. There was also wide agreement that the very nature of the German national character posed a permanent threat to peace.[11] This marked an important change from pre-war understandings, particularly on the centre-left. On the eve of war, internationalist-minded observers had retained the view that, however distasteful the Kaiser's regime might be, the fundamental threats to peace were systemic. For doctrinaire socialists the problem was international capitalism. For juridical internationalists the problem was a lack of the rule of law in international society. In 1918, however, nearly all residual conceptions of a 'good' Germany had been submerged by four-and-a-half years of human sacrifice, material destruction and official war propaganda. The assumption that Germany was malign, that it had caused the war and that it must be forced to pay for reconstruction went virtually

---

[10] Link et al. (eds.), *The Papers of Woodrow Wilson*, vol. XL, Wilson Speech, 22 Jan. 1917, 535–6.
[11] This paragraph is drawn principally from P. Miquel, *La Paix de Versailles et l'opinion publique française* (Paris, 1972), 236–48.

unchallenged across the political spectrum. More importantly for post-war conceptions of peace and security, the notion that the German national character could be reformed was greeted with scepticism, particularly within mainstream opinion. 'If the spirit of the world has changed,' observed *Le Temps*, the centrist newspaper with close ties to the Quai d'Orsay, 'that of Germany is untouched and remains dominated by pride, megalomania and a lust for conquest.'[12] Only on the left, among more class-conscious socialists and trade unionists, was this deeply pessimistic interpretation of the German national character rejected in favour of a more hopeful vision of a reformed social democratic Germany that would play a responsible role in European political progress.

These ambiguities and complexities were an important part of the structural context in which security policy took shape. But this policy was also shaped to an important extent by the instincts and ideological convictions of the premier. These are impossible to categorise neatly; they had been acquired over the course of a political career that stretched back to the Franco-Prussian War and the Paris Commune.

Clemenceau, the patriot of the generation of 1871, aimed at a peace based on a favourable balance of power and territorial guarantees against future German aggression. The old radical of the generation of 1848, conversely, believed in democratisation and self-determination. He therefore attached greatest priority to cooperation with the great Atlantic democracies. The ambiguity that resulted, which reflected wider divergences over national security within the French public sphere, was a central characteristic of peace planning. The problem is that historians have underlined the importance of 1871 in shaping Clemenceau's peace programme but ignored that of 1848.[13]

It was precisely because of its open-ended and Atlanticist character that Clemenceau's final peace programme came in for virulent criticism from advocates of a more traditional approach. Foch was only the foremost of a large and influential number of soldiers, diplomats and deputies who argued that the centre of gravity for France's security policy must be the Rhine.

The three chapters that follow will not provide a blow-by-blow narrative of the months between the armistice and the ratification of the various treaties that made up the Paris settlement. They will instead focus on the conceptual architecture of French security policy as it evolved from autumn 1918 through summer 1919. If the dominant consideration in this policy was the problem of German power, the policy process was complicated by a host of domestic and international constraints. Together these challenges conditioned all French efforts to shape a new international order.

---

[12] *Le Temps*, 11 Feb. 1919.
[13] These ambiguities are also acknowledged in D. Watson, *Georges Clemenceau: A Political Biography* (London, 1974), 331–76; Duroselle, *Clemenceau*, 720–7; and Soutou, 'French Peacemakers', 169–72.

6 The political contexts of peacemaking, 1918–1919

'You can be sure', Aristide Briand had predicted to parliament in 1917, 'that after this war, after so many funerals and so much sacrifice, in France a cry will rise up for a peace that can never be troubled again.'[1] Popular expectations for peace and security would be enormous. The Paris Peace Conference of 1919 marked the first time that a fundamental reordering of the international system was undertaken by democratic leaders of modern nation-states. Planning for peace and post-war order took place in a highly fraught atmosphere. The French public was traumatised by the war, but also delirious with expectation that peace would deliver security, prosperity and social transformation. The sheer scale and daunting complexity of the task facing the peacemakers was without precedent. This chapter will survey the domestic and international contexts within which plans for the peace settlement took shape.

The majority of both elite and popular opinion in France anticipated a peace based on traditional power politics that would return France to a dominant position in the European strategic balance. This was also the reflex aim of the majority of French security professionals, whose background, training and experience conditioned them to aim for a post-war order that would transform the balance of power in France's favour. Ranged against these expectations were the policy priorities of France's key coalition partners. Although Britain and the USA pursued different and often divergent strategies at the peace conference, neither aimed to replace Germany with France as a potential continental hegemon.

The end of the war brought about far-reaching changes in international norms concerning the proper behaviour of states. The significance of this normative transformation is impossible to deny, even if it is very hard to measure. It is evident not least in growing enthusiasm for a new international order embodied in a league or society of nations. While internationalists remained a minority in the French public sphere, the movement was voluble and increasingly well organised. And it embraced the indistinct discourse of Woodrow Wilson before the peace conference with much greater enthusiasm

---

[1] *JO*, Chambre, *Débats*, 1925, 'Comité secret du 1er juin 1917', quotation from the session on 4 Jun. 1917.

than it would the details of his programme of the League when they were made public the following February. The sheer diversity of opinion regarding the best bases for a just and durable peace left no hope for a peace settlement that would leave all constituencies even relatively satisfied.

I

During the secret sessions of early June 1917, premier Ribot had assured parliament that:

Conditions of peace will be fixed by the national sovereignty, and you, sirs, constitute this national sovereignty in your role as representatives of the country. The government will do nothing without you, without your counsel, without your authority. This much I can promise you.[2]

This principle of parliamentary supremacy was ignored by Clemenceau. During the course of negotiations neither the senate nor the chamber were consulted on specific issues related to the peace settlement. The same was true, to only a slightly lesser extent, of the cabinet. The premier's strategy was to keep a free hand in negotiations and to seek cabinet and parliamentary approval only once the core elements of the peace were agreed. Senators and deputies were then presented with what amounted to a fait accompli that they could reject only at the risk of a major political crisis.[3]

Decision making during the peace conference was concentrated within a small circle of key advisers that included Clémentel, Louis Loucheur, General Mordacq and André Tardieu. Pichon and Louis Klotz were sometimes present at key meetings, but neither had decisive influence over any aspect of the government's programme. Clemenceau continued to treat Pichon as a junior aide, often neglecting to keep him abreast of the state of negotiations over such crucial issues as France's frontiers with Germany. Klotz was manifestly out of his depth as finance minister, and did not play a central role in the elaboration of reparations policy.[4] The chief voices in the domain of commercial, industrial and financial policy were those of Clémentel and Loucheur. Clémentel was particularly important in late 1918 and early 1919. But his influence waned considerably after his grand scheme for transatlantic coordination was rejected by the Wilson

---

[2] Ibid.
[3] F. Bock, *Parlementarisme de guerre* (Paris, 2002), 305–9; J.-B. Duroselle, *Clemenceau* (Paris, 1988), 725–6 and 736–42.
[4] J.-J. Becker, *Clemenceau, chef de guerre* (Paris, 2012), 75–6, 143–57; R. Poincaré, *Au service de la France*, vol. XI: *À la recherche de la paix (1919)*, ed. J. Bariéty and P. Miquel (Paris, 1974), 436; Laroche, *Quai d'Orsay*, 58–69; D. Watson, *Georges Clemenceau: A Political Biography* (London, 1974), 331–63; D. Stevenson, *French War Aims against Germany, 1914–1919* (Oxford, 1982), 162; and Duroselle, *Clemenceau*, 761–2.

administration. By mid-February 1919 he had been supplanted by Loucheur as the dominant voice in all aspects of economic policy.[5]

Born in 1871, Loucheur was a graduate of the École polytechnique and had been a rising figure among French industrialists before 1914. During the war he had worked closely with Albert Thomas in managing the reorganisation of France's munitions industry. He was named under-secretary for war production in December 1916 and replaced Thomas as minister of armaments in September 1917. Having earned Clemenceau's confidence, he remained at the head of this department when it was converted into the ministry for industrial reconstruction in November 1918. Loucheur was an early prototype of the technocratic elite that would emerge to play an increasingly influential role in French politics through to the late 1950s. For him the war had driven home the dangers of untrammelled industrial and commercial competition. By 1919 he had become a firm advocate of cooperation between the state and private enterprise. This inclination towards collaboration would shape Loucheur's attitude towards Franco-German relations in the post-war decade.[6]

The most influential member of Clemenceau's inner circle was André Tardieu.[7] Born into a conservative bourgeois family in Paris, Tardieu was a brilliant student whose achievements included ranking first in the entry examinations of the École normale, the foreign ministry and the ministry of the interior.[8] His remarkable career is as notable for its inconsistency as for its undeniable achievement, for its spectacular failures as well as its stunning successes. Tardieu left the École normale after only a few weeks. He left the foreign ministry – which he dismissed as 'an upper-class caravan ... which offers amateurs a comfortable front seat at the human comedy' – after less than a year to serve as personal secretary to premier Pierre Waldeck-Rousseau in 1899. Thereafter he took up journalism, becoming diplomatic editor of *Le Temps* in 1905 at the age of twenty-nine. While at *Le Temps* Tardieu developed such an impressive array of contacts that German chancellor Bernhard von Bülow described him as the 'seventh great power of Europe'.[9] Elected to the chamber in 1914, he volunteered for the army at the outbreak of war. His wartime service included a posting to Foch's general staff (where he wrote an important memo

---

[5] See esp. M. Trachtenberg, *Reparation in World Politics: France and European Economic Diplomacy, 1916–1923* (New York, 1980), 31–40 and G.-H. Soutou, 'The French Peacemakers and their Homefront' in M. Boemke, G. Feldman and E. Glaser (eds.), *The Treaty of Versailles: A Reassessment after 75 Years* (Cambridge, 1998), 169–70.

[6] S. Carls, *Louis Loucheur and the Shaping of Modern France, 1916–1931* (Baton Rouge, 1993); see also L. Loucheur, *La Reconstruction de l'Europe et le problème des réparations* (Paris, 1922).

[7] The following two paragraphs are drawn principally from L. Aubert, I. Martin, M. Missoffe, F. Piétri, A. Pose and G. Puaux, *André Tardieu* (Paris, 1957) and F. Monnet, *Refaire la République: André Tardieu, une dérive réactionnaire, 1876–1945* (Paris, 1993).

[8] Tardieu's examiners for the foreign ministry *concours* praised his 'formidable intellectual faculties', the 'exceptional clarity' of his ideas and the 'extraordinary logical power' of his expositions: MAE, PA-AP 12, *Papiers de Beaucaire*, vol. 10, dr. 2, 'Dossier de concours 1898'.

[9] Monnet, *Refaire la République*, 50–1.

on war aims cited above) and at the front, where he was wounded. Returning to parliament as one of its first veteran deputies, Tardieu joined the chamber army commission (then under Clemenceau's presidency) before being named by Ribot as French high commissioner to the United States in April 1917. He returned in November 1918 to join Clemenceau's team and play a leading role in peace planning. Tardieu's signal contribution to the evolution of French policy would be his consistent emphasis on the growing importance of US power in world politics and the need for France to make a close strategic relationship with Washington a pillar of its planning for post-war security.

Clemenceau named himself, Tardieu, Pichon, Klotz and Jules Cambon as France's official delegates to the peace conference. These choices reflected the premier's determination to dominate policy making in those areas he considered vital for France's security: France's strategic relationship with the USA and Britain; the territorial settlement in western Europe; and the financial and commercial aspects of the settlement. He stubbornly resisted pressure to involve other elected officials in negotiations. Pressed by Poincaré to consider naming at least one or two elected officials as delegates, Clemenceau replied that he preferred his own choices to 'political men'.[10] This inevitably generated resentment among political heavyweights such as Briand, Barthou and, not least, Poincaré himself. As president, Poincaré felt entitled to a voice in deliberations and became exceptionally bitter when this was refused. His resentment became obsessive, and led to his involvement in various schemes to undermine Clemenceau. The premier, however, maintained firm control over decision making despite the presence of powerful critics in parliament, the Élysée Palace, the press and the army high command.[11]

Clemenceau's approach to policy making facilitated the elaboration of a coherent peace programme. Negotiations over core issues proceeded in close coordination with one another because they remained in the hands of his small circle of confidants. But there was a cost. The marginalisation of powerful political figures eroded the legitimacy of the peace settlement among parliamentarians, many of whom would subsequently be charged with upholding it. The same is true of the tactic of presenting the peace treaty to parliament in the form of an ultimatum to be accepted or rejected.[12] Clemenceau's decision-making style also presents particular challenges for the historian. The premier avoided committing his precise ideas to paper, and most key decisions were taken in closed discussions with his inner circle, usually in the evening at his apartment on the rue Franklin. Policy coherence was achieved at the expense of transparency and parliamentary legitimacy.

[10] Poincaré, *Recherche de la paix*, 9 Jan. 1919: 49.
[11] J. F. V. Keiger, *Raymond Poincaré* (Cambridge, 1996), 252–65 is excellent on this, as are Duroselle, *Clemenceau*, 536–41 and Watson, *Clemenceau: A Political Biography*, 215–34.
[12] A point made by E. Beau de Loménie in *Le Débat de ratification du Traité de Versailles à la chambre des députés et dans la press en 1919* (Paris, 1919), 197–8.

II

The First World War wrought far-reaching changes to the normative environment of international politics. David Stevenson has pointed to 'a deeper transformation of western attitudes towards armed conflict' that was 'one of the war's enduring legacies'.[13] Expectations for the behaviour of 'civilised' states were altered in a fundamental sense by four years of industrial-scale slaughter. The response of the victors, as Ian Clark has argued, was to try to introduce a 'new normative architecture' that would establish the framework for 'a genuine international society'. The central conditions for membership in this society were the 'adoption of democratic principles' and 'adherence to the rule of law'.[14] The impact of these changes on the evolution of French policy has not received the consideration it merits.

To understand the impact of the new normative context it is essential to define what we mean by 'norms' and to consider how they affect policy. A norm, for our purposes, is best defined as a collective expectation for the proper behaviour of actors in a given political realm.[15] The political realm in this case is the sphere where states interacted with one another in the shadow of the greatest conflict in history. Norms emerge out of inter-subjective understandings. They can range from semi-conscious practices to formalised laws and institutional procedures. International relations theorists point out that norms can be regulative, constitutive, or both at the same time. An influential norm for the period 1880–1945, for example, was that Great Powers possessed capital ships. This expectation regulated state behaviour in important ways, inducing powers such as Germany, Japan and Italy to construct large battleships. But it was also constitutive, reinforcing the self-image of these states as international Great Powers.[16] Norms are most influential when they are internalised by actors to become something close to what James Joll defined as 'unspoken assumptions' or what Bourdieu described as 'background knowledge'.[17] But such instances are relatively rare and did not obtain in the case of the new international norms after 1918.

---

[13] D. Stevenson, *Cataclysm: The First World War as Political Tragedy* (New York, 2004), 143 and 244.
[14] I. Clark, *Legitimacy in International Society* (Oxford, 2005), 110–12, quotes from 112.
[15] M. Finnemore and K. Sikkink, 'International norm dynamics and political change', *International Organization*, 52, 4 (1998), 887–917; R. Jeppert, A. Wendt and P. Katzenstein, 'Norms, Identity and Culture in National Security' and P. Kowert and J. Legro, 'Norms, Identity and their Limits: A Theoretical Reprise', both in P. Katzenstein (ed.), *The Culture of National Security: Norms and Identity in World Politics* (New York, 1996), 33–75 and 451–97 respectively.
[16] This example is taken from P. Katzenstein, 'Alternative Perspectives on National Security' in Katzenstein (ed.), *Culture of National Security*, 5–6.
[17] J. Joll, '1914: the unspoken assumptions', inaugural lecture, London School of Economics and Political Science, 25 April 1968; P. Bourdieu, *The Logic of Practice*, trans. R. Nice (Palo Alto, 1990), 84–7.

Two further points about norms merit special mention. First, they are always to some extent arbitrary. Germany, after all, was a Great Power after 1880 whether or not it possessed capital ships. The power of norms therefore depends on the extent to which they are accepted by all actors in a given political realm. If they are rejected without significant cost by one or more actors, their power to shape politics is diminished, if not undermined altogether.[18] Second, although norms are inter-subjective understandings, they are by no means static phenomena to which policy makers respond passively. They are instead dynamic, and their meanings are nearly always being negotiated and re-negotiated by actors seeking to improve their position relative to others.[19] Policy makers are active agents in the process of interpreting norms and determining their implications for international politics.

Two norms were particularly influential in shaping the international political realm of 1918–19. The first and most powerful was 'self-determination'. This principle, never defined with precision by Wilson or any other major political figure, was intended primarily to signify the right to democratic representation. Wilson famously proclaimed that a central aim of the war, and a guiding principle of the peace, must be to make the world 'safe for democracy'.[20] Jan Smuts proclaimed 'No annexations and the self-determination of nations' in his hugely influential pamphlet on the League of Nations.[21] French officials typically referred to self-determination as 'the right of peoples to determine their own political destiny' and represented it as firmly within the revolutionary tradition.

As one recent study of self-determination has shown, however, public advocacy for this concept took on a life of its own that was quite independent of the intentions of its proponents.[22] Accepting self-determination as one of the core principles of the peace thus had far-reaching implications for peacemaking. Local populations would no longer be treated as spoils of war in Great Power horse-trading to establish a favourable balance of power. This opened up the Pandora's Box of ethnicity and national identity. The politics of self-determination played an important role not only in shaping the peace settlement, but also in undermining post-war attempts to achieve political

---

[18] Finnemore and Sikkink, 'International norm dynamics', 891–7; Kowert and Legor, 'Norms, Identity and their Limits', 463–84.
[19] Katzenstein, 'Alternative Perspectives', 24; Finnemore and Sikkink, 'International norm dynamics', 888–904.
[20] W. R. Keylor, 'Versailles and International Diplomacy' in Boemke et al. (eds.), *The Treaty of Versailles*, 474–6; see also, more generally, C. Bouchard, *Le Citoyen et l'ordre mondiale (1914–1918): le rêve d'une paix durable au lendemain de la Grande Guerre* (Paris, 2008), 112–14; J. Milton Cooper, *Breaking the Heart of the World: Woodrow Wilson and the Fight for the League of Nations* (Cambridge, 2001), esp. 9–56. See also J. Winter, *Dreams of Peace and Freedom: Utopian Moments in the Twentieth Century* (New Haven, 2006), 48–74.
[21] J. Smuts, *The League of Nations: A Practical Suggestion* (London, 1918), 12.
[22] E. Manela, *The Wilsonian Moment: Self-determination and the International Origins of Anticolonial Nationalism* (Oxford, 2007), 10.

stability in Europe and maintain the sinews of imperial control in Asia and Africa.[23]

A second increasingly influential norm in 1918–19 was the aspiration to transform international politics by replacing power politics and the use of force with an institution to facilitate cooperation and impose the rule of law. Although this 'transformative' norm pervaded the public utterances of virtually all political elites both during and after the war, it was even less well defined than self-determination. It underpinned widespread support for a league of nations among both elite and popular opinion. Yet details concerning the form the league should take, or how such a profound remaking of the international sphere might be achieved, were thin on the ground as fighting ceased.

Wilson's 'Fourteen Points' and 'Five Principles' constituted probably the most ambitious attempt to lay out a new normative international order. His public calls for political transformation reached an unprecedented global audience.[24] The principle of democracy-promotion achieved normative status when Wilson stipulated regime change as a prerequisite for armistice negotiations with Germany. Clemenceau himself observed that the United States had 'opened a new ethical era in relations between peoples'.[25] And yet, for all of their undeniable influence, Wilson's public declarations are as notable for their vagueness as they are for the new world order that they purported to herald. German leaders, for example, seized on the Fourteen Points, and in particular the principle of self-determination, as a guarantee that Germany's European frontiers would remain more or less intact. For French policy makers, conversely, self-determination provided a potential justification for breaking up the Reich. There was, in other words, wide scope for interpreting the meaning and implications of these norms as the peace conference opened.

An international order based on the rule of law had been a constant theme in official constructions of the war's meaning inside France since 1914. The link between this principle and the movement for an international organisation had been endorsed publicly by the Ribot government when it established the study

---

[23] Ibid., 6–62; A. Sharp, *The Versailles Settlement: Peacemaking in Paris, 1919* (London, 1991), 130–84; C. Fink, 'The Minorities Question at the Paris Peace Conference' in Boemke et al. (eds.), *Treaty of Versailles*, 249–74; C. Fink, *Defending the Rights of Others: The Great Powers and International Minority Protection* (Cambridge, 2004), 133–70; J. Mayall, *Nationalism and International Society* (Cambridge, 1990), 39–45; and E. Weitz, 'From the Vienna to the Paris system: international politics and the entangled histories of human rights, forced deportations and civilising missions', *AHR*, 113, 5 (2008), 1313–43.

[24] On this issue see above all Manela, *Wilsonian Moment*. The legacy of 'Wilsonianism' has been highly contested in American politics ever since; apart from the importance of international engagement, its precepts are open to dramatically different interpretations: see J. A. Thompson, 'Wilsonianism: the dynamics of a conflict concept', *International Affairs*, 86, 1 (2010), 27–47 and L. Ambrosius, 'Wilson and the Culture of Wilsonianism' in his *Wilsonianism: Woodrow Wilson and his Legacy in American Foreign Relations* (London, 2002), 21–9.

[25] Sterling Library, Yale University (SLYU), MS 466, *Papers of Col. Edward Mandell House*, Series II (Diary), vol. 6: 26 Dec. 1918.

commission for a 'society of nations' under Bourgeois the previous autumn. The aim to promote democracy, meanwhile, had always been implicit in the much-invoked objective of destroying 'Prussian militarism'. Its prominence was amplified after the fall of the Tsar and US entry into the war opened the way for representations of the conflict as a democratic crusade. France, with its revolutionary heritage and republican politics, was considered a natural defender of self-determination even by the conservative elements within the Quai d'Orsay and the army staff. Yet, as we shall see, efforts by foreign ministry officials to harness the principle of self-determination to the traditional aim of constructing strategically viable frontiers bear witness to the extent to which this norm was open to divergent interpretations.

France had made a series of public commitments to these principles in its responses to Wilson's various peace initiatives, most notably its statement on war aims of 10 January 1917 and its acceptance of the Fourteen Points the following year. The frequency with which these themes appear in internal memoranda testifies to their impact on French planning. Gabriel Hanotaux, in a widely circulated memorandum prepared the day of the armistice, stressed the 'irresistible force' of the 'new international spirit'. 'The right of peoples to determine their political status', he argued, 'must be united with the principle of the rule of law to become the foundations of a sound world order for the future.'[26] Jules Laroche, a rising star within the foreign ministry, acknowledged that 'France cannot do what Germany did in 1871' and that the post-war settlement must 'take into account the principle of self-determination'.[27] Tardieu agreed, judging that 'France must remain scrupulously loyal to the principles for which its armies waged war'. Foremost among these, he added, were the rule of law and the democratic rights of oppressed peoples.[28] Berthelot, for his part, predicted that a principal challenge for peacemaking would be to 'conciliate the guarantees necessary for our security with the right of peoples to determine their own political destiny'.[29]

As planning for the peace conference began in earnest, there was optimism among security professionals that Wilsonian principles could be interpreted to complement more traditional conceptions. 'The general inspiration of all the speeches of president Wilson is our own,' Clemenceau's staff at the war ministry concluded. 'We seek, like him, only to increase existing guarantees of a durable peace both in terms of the obligations to be imposed on Germany

[26] MAE, *Série A*, vol. 60, 'De la future frontière', 11 Nov. 1918; also in MAE, PA-AP 166, *Papiers Tardieu*, vol. 417 and BDIC, *Archives Klotz*, dr. 18.
[27] MAE, *Série A*, vol. 289, 'Les Frontières de l'Alsace-Lorraine et le statut de la rive gauche du Rhin', 1 Nov. 1918.
[28] MAE, PA-AP 166, *Papiers Tardieu*, vol. 415, 'Note présentée à M. Clemenceau par M. Tardieu au sujet du Bassin de la Sarre', Jan. 1919; vol. 417, untitled note about the British position and French interests, 10 Feb. 1919.
[29] MAE, *Série A*, vol. 60, 'Préliminaires de paix avec l'Allemagne', n.d. but certainly early Nov. 1918.

and the engagements that we will undertake among ourselves for the benefit of all civilised peoples.'[30] Tardieu, along with most foreign ministry officials, reckoned that the new 'international spirit' could complement efforts to alter the strategic balance.[31] 'It is essential to first define the forms that these principles might assume', Tardieu observed, 'so that they can be applied to reinforce our overall programme.'[32] One commerce ministry official underlined the importance of maintaining a 'Wilsonian façade' when formulating France's demands.[33] Louis Aubert, the young historian who served as Tardieu's secretary, liaised with the American delegation and helped draft many of the memoranda produced by the French delegation at the peace conference, gave expression to this strategy when he emphasised the need to 'orient our argumentation in the American sense wherever possible' so as to 'secure the support of president Wilson for our fundamental aims'.[34] Georges-Henri Soutou has described this as an exercise in *'captatio benevolentiae'*, a strategy of 'using language apparently compatible with Wilsonianism to advance aims of a very different inspiration'.[35] This is true. But it is worth adding that adopting such a strategy was in effect acknowledging both the legitimacy of the new norms and the limitations of more traditional language. The consequences of this normative engagement were impossible to foresee as the peace conference opened.

There were words of caution concerning the merits of this strategy. Henri Bergson had met with the American president during a series of lectures on democracy in 1917. He warned that French negotiators should 'avoid giving the impression that we are merely paying lip service to [Wilson's] principles in order to secure his confidence'. It would be better, Bergson advised, 'to accept these principles in general but, when applying them, to state frankly and *with*

---

[30] SHD-DAT, *Fonds Clemenceau*, 6N 73–1, 'Dossier du président', Nov. 1918.
[31] See, for example, MAE, *Série A*, vol. 289, 'Les Frontières de l'Alsace-Lorraine et le statut de la rive gauche du Rhin' (Laroche), 1 Nov. 1918; 'Note sur la future frontière entre l'Alsace-Lorraine et l'Allemagne' (Berthelot), 10 Nov. 1918; MAE, PA-AP 166, *Papiers Tardieu*, vol. 296, 'Examen des conditions de la paix', 15 Nov. 1918; BDIC, *Archives Klotz*, dr. 18, 'Préliminaires de paix avec l'Allemagne', n.d.
[32] MAE, PA-AP 166, *Papiers Tardieu*, vol. 415, 'Réponse à une objection sur le parallélisme des revendications françaises et italiennes', n.d. but certainly Jan.–Feb. 1919.
[33] AN, F12 8106, 'Note pour M. le ministre', undated and untitled marginal commentary by an unknown commerce ministry official in a dossier entitled 'Clauses générales'.
[34] MAE, PA-AP 166, *Papiers Tardieu*, vol. 415, 'Note sur le dossier relatif au bassin de la Sarre', 12 Dec. 1918. Aubert would remain an influential member of the French policy elite through to the eve of the Second World War. He helped elaborate disarmament policy as a member of the French delegation to Geneva and remained influential in Radical Party circles – intervening decisively in policy debates as late as 1938–9. See M. Vaïsse, *Sécurité d'abord: politique française en matière de désarmement, 1930–1934* (Paris, 1981), esp. 50 and 131–2; J.-B. Duroselle, *La Décadence: politique etrangere de la France, 1932–1939* (Paris, 1979), 370–2; and D. Hucker, *Public Opinion and the End of Appeasement in Britain and France* (London, 2010), 74–5.
[35] G.-H. Soutou, *L'Or et le sang: les buts de guerre économiques de la Première Guerre mondiale* (Paris, 1989), 769–70.

firmness that which appears necessary to us for the security of France and the maintenance of peace'.[36]

Those French military elites who recognised that the international atmosphere had changed also tended to be more pessimistic about its implications for French policy. In a thoughtful analysis of the security challenges facing France, General Marie Émile Fayolle, commander of the two French armies on the Rhine, observed that the 'new theories of peace' that had 'seduced too many well-meaning spirits' could not be ignored. He judged that:

> If France was on its own on the Rhine, it could no doubt say 'I am here by historic right and by the right of victory; by law and for the sake of justice I am here and I will remain here' ... But it is all too evident today that between France and her natural frontier stands the Wilson programme which Germany is already brandishing against us; France will suffer from the principle of nationalities, of self determination etc. It is therefore probable – otherwise the peace would already have been signed – that *theories* will dominate *realities* and that the question of the Rhine will not be settled with a clarity that would assure the peace of the world for a long time to come, by teaching Germany the only lesson that she is capable of understanding.[37]

For Fayolle, as for the vast majority of the military establishment, the new international environment posed a grave threat to French security.

Marshal Foch concurred with Fayolle. There were three central pillars to Foch's geo-strategic conception.[38] The first was a highly pessimistic vision of international politics as a struggle for domination. The chief lesson of history, for Foch, was that 'war is a permanent feature of the condition of mankind'.[39] His second core conviction, a preference for material advantages over political combinations, flowed from the first. Alliances, for Foch, were ultimately expressions of temporary shared interests. They could never take the place of solid natural frontiers and a strong national army. 'We can only build with what we have in our own hands,' he insisted. France must therefore not 'abandon tangible guarantees that are in our hands in exchange for [Allied] promises for the future that are easier to make than to keep'.[40] This was all the more important in the light of the third core element in Foch's world view: the assumption that German power posed a permanent and existential threat to France. A different political constitution, argued the marshal, would not change the fact that a desire for conquest and domination had been ingrained

---

[36] AN, F12 8106, 'Conversation avec M. Bergson', 23 Dec. 1918 (emphasis in original).
[37] MAE, PA-AP 166, *Papiers Tardieu*, vol. 417, 'Note relative à la paix', 14 Feb. 1919 (emphasis in original).
[38] P. Jackson, 'Foch et la politique de sécurité française, 1919–1924' in F. Cochet and R. Porte (eds.), *Ferdinand Foch (1851–1929): apprenez à penser* (Paris, 2010), 334–9.
[39] Quoted in M. Motte, 'Foch théoricien: faut-il brûler *Des principes de la guerre?*' in Cochet and Porte (eds.), *Foch*, 55.
[40] Quotes from Jackson, 'Foch et la politique de sécurité française', 337 and J.-C. Notin, *Foch* (Paris, 2008), 454 respectively.

in Germany's political culture from its beginnings. 'Germany', Foch warned, 'will remain for a long time to come ... a fearsome menace to civilisation.'[41]

Foch's views were important because in 1919 his stature was greater than that of any French soldier since Napoleon.[42] In the aftermath of victory he was hailed as a national saviour. On the nationalist right, in particular, enthusiasm for the marshal assumed 'the form of a veritable cult'.[43] He also enjoyed enormous prestige abroad. The Lloyd George government made him a British field marshal and the Poles accorded him the same honour. At home he was elected to a seat among the 'immortals' in the Académie française. This combination of public honours and popular adulation provided Foch with vast reserves of what Bourdieu defined as 'symbolic capital': an accumulation of prestige and authority that allows one to impose categories of meaning in a given realm.[44] The fact that Foch possessed enormous symbolic capital in 1919 was at least as important for his efforts to dominate security policy as was the logical power of his arguments. He understood this and resolved to use his capital to resist to the end the 'new theories of peace' to which Fayolle referred and to champion the call for a permanent position on the Rhine. In 1919 Foch was France's most prominent advocate of a traditional conception of security.

III

As Clemenceau and his advisers understood more clearly than many of their compatriots, the victory of 1918 had been a coalition victory; the peace would therefore be a coalition peace. The policies of France's wartime partners were crucial in shaping the context in which the government's peace programme evolved. Also important was the situation with its former enemies.

The collapse of the German, Hapsburg and Russian empires occasioned a free-for-all in which nearly every continental actor, including the newly proclaimed but not yet fully formed states of Poland, Czechoslovakia and Yugoslavia, compiled a list of territorial desiderata to be pressed home at the peace conference. Belgian political leaders developed territorial claims that challenged French projects for Luxembourg.[45] Italy demanded not only fulfilment of the terms of the highly traditional 1915 Treaty of London, but also the cession of French territory along the Franco-Italian border and territory along the Adriatic coast that threatened the strategic interests of the newly

---

[41] SHD-DAT, *Fonds Clemenceau*, 6N 73–2, Foch 'Note' to Clemenceau, 27 Nov. 1918.
[42] See, for example, discussion in F. Gaquère, *Vie popular du maréchal Foch* (Arras, 1954) or Recouly, *Mémorial de Foch*; see also Notin, *Foch*, 439–49; F. Cochet, 'Foch, de l'hagiographie à l'histoire' in Cochet and Porte (eds.), *Foch*, 19–44.
[43] R. Porte, 'Avant-propos' in Cochet and Porte (eds.), *Foch*, 17.
[44] P. Bourdieu, 'The Forms of Capital' in J. Richardson (ed.), *Handbook of Theory and Research for the Sociology of Education* (New York, 1986), 241–58.
[45] S. Marks, *Innocent Abroad: Belgium at the Paris Peace Conference* (Chapel Hill, N.C., 1981); D. Stevenson, 'Belgium, Luxemburg and the defence of Western Europe, 1914–1920', *IHR*, 4, 4 (1982), 515–21.

proclaimed South Slav kingdom of Serbs, Croats and Slovenes (which would become Yugoslavia).[46] Romania, meanwhile, lodged an ambitious set of claims against neighbouring Central Powers and supported them with military operations in defiance of the express wishes of the Allied Supreme Council.[47]

For the security of France, however, the most important eastern territorial questions concerned the borders of Czechoslovakia and Poland. The newly established Czechoslovak state was in physical possession of most of the territory it demanded, and its interests were well represented in Paris. Thomas Masaryk and Edvard Beneš portrayed the new state as a bastion of Western civilisation and democracy in a region threatened by revolutionary chaos. These were arguments that played well with the Great Powers.[48] Polish ambitions, conversely, were crippled by internal divisions between the pro-French Polish National Committee and a provisional government led by Jozef Piłsudski, the left-wing leader of Polish military forces on the ground in east-central Europe. Both factions were united in demanding the restoration of Poland's historical boundaries (which would include millions of Germans and Ukrainians). Defensible frontiers for either Poland or Czechoslovakia would mean substantial violations of the principle of self-determination.[49] And any decisions taken regarding the political order in this region were threatened by the political convulsions in Russia.

Russia was the greatest enigma in world politics in 1919, and would remain so for the entire inter-war period. The surpassing brutality of the civil war in that country reverberated through Europe in the form of rumour and unconfirmed official reporting. Allied intervention in that conflict was ill conceived, badly coordinated and succeeded only in convincing the Bolsheviks that they were encircled by predatory capitalist powers that desired their destruction.[50] The Soviet leadership concluded that survival depended on the spread of the workers' revolution to industrialised Europe.[51] When a continent-wide

---

[46] Stevenson, *French War Aims*, 144, 260; see also H. J. Burgwyn, *The Legend of the Mutilated Victory: Italy, the Great War and the Paris Peace Conference* (Westport, Conn., 1993), esp. 223–92.

[47] M. MacMillan, *Paris, 1919* (New York, 2001), 109–35; Z. Steiner, *The Lights that Failed: European International History, 1919–1933* (Oxford, 2005), 96–9.

[48] Beneš further promised minority rights for the millions of Germans, Hungarians, Ruthenes and Poles to be included within the borders of the new state: D. Perman, *The Shaping of the Czechoslovak State: A Diplomatic History of the Boundaries of Czechoslovakia* (Leiden, 1962), 8–118 and 156–223.

[49] K. Lundgreen-Nielsen, *The Polish Problem at the Paris Peace Conference*, trans. A. Borch-Johansen (Odense, 1979); the essays in P. Latawski (ed.), *The Reconstruction of Poland, 1914–1923* (London, 1992); and the excellent synthesis by Piotr Wandycz, 'The Polish Question' in Boemke et al. (eds.), *Treaty of Versailles*, 313–35.

[50] On French policy and intervention see A. Hogenhuis-Seliverstoff, *Les relations franco-soviétiques 1917–1924* (Paris, 1981), 35–163 and M. J. Carley, *Revolution and Intervention: The French Government and the Russian Civil War* (Montreal, 1983).

[51] A. Di Biagio, *Le origini dell'isolazionismo sovietico: l'unione sovietica et l'Europa dal 1918 al 1928* (Milan, 1990), 15–26; R. K. Debo, *Revolution and Survival: The Foreign Policy of Soviet Russia*,

uprising failed to materialise, the new regime responded with a dual foreign policy that aimed at securing stable diplomatic and commercial relations with the major powers while at the same time promoting revolutionary subversion in Europe and its empires. Pursuit of conventional international policy was the responsibility of the Commissariat of Foreign Affairs (Narkomindel). Propaganda and subversion was the responsibility of the Communist International (Comintern), which was created in 1919 to operate through communist parties in Western democracies.[52] The First World War and the Russian Revolution ushered in an era of profound ideological ferment such as the international system had not witnessed since the 1790s.

It was Britain and the United States, however, that posed the most immediate and formidable challenges to French policy. Both states had contributed decisively to the defeat of Germany. Both were determined to impose their own vision of post-war order at the peace conference. British prime minister David Lloyd George was a formidable negotiator at the height of his powers. Imaginative and non-doctrinaire, he could be charming and persuasive. And he was indefatigable in pursuit of his bargaining objectives. But Lloyd George was not a great statesman. His knowledge of the non-British world was alarmingly limited, and he was inclined to attach greatest priority to his domestic political position. Most importantly, from the perspective of French security, Lloyd George failed to appreciate the temporary character of France's military preponderance at the war's end. This led him to suspect French designs and to seek a moderate settlement on all issues that did not concern Britain directly.[53]

British policy was characterised by a hardline position over reparations and the destruction of German imperial and naval power but an essentially moderate stance when it came to territorial issues. The fact was that most of Britain's key strategic objectives had been satisfied by the armistice. By early 1919 the High Seas Fleet was in British hands and its U-boat squadrons were disabled. Outside Europe, Palestine and Mesopotamia were under British occupation along with most of Germany's African colonies. The Lloyd George government's chief aim thereafter was a settlement that established

---

1917–1918 (Liverpool, 1979), 350–2; T. Uldricks, *Diplomacy and Ideology: The Origins of Soviet Foreign Relations, 1917–1930* (London, 1979), 12–76; G. Gorodetsky (ed.), *Soviet Foreign Policy, 1917–1991: A Retrospective* (London, 1994).

[52] P. Broué, *Histoire de l'Internationale Communiste, 1919–1943* (Paris, 1997); M. Narinsky and J. Rojhan (eds.), *Centre and Periphery: The History of the Comintern in Light of New Documents* (Amsterdam, 1996); T. Rees and A. Thorpe, *International Communism and the Communist International, 1919–1943* (Manchester, 1998); and K. McDermott and J. Agnew, *The Comintern: A History of International Communism from Lenin to Stalin* (Basingstoke, 1996).

[53] For sympathetic treatments of Lloyd George at the peace conference see MacMillan, *Paris 1919*, 36–45 and esp. M. G. Fry, *And Fortune Fled: David Lloyd George: The First Democratic Statesman, 1916–1922* (New York, 2011); for more critical perspectives see A. Lentin, *Guilt at Versailles: Lloyd George and the Pre-history of Appeasement* (London, 1984); A. Lentin, 'Several types of ambiguity: Lloyd George at the Paris Peace Conference', *D&S*, 6, 1 (1995), 223–51; S. Marks, 'David Lloyd George: An Infernally Clever Chap' in S. Casey and J. Wright (eds.), *Mental Maps in the Era of the Two World Wars* (London, 2008), 21–35.

the best possible conditions for Britain's economic resurgence. Such a treaty would punish Germany and force it to make reparation for at least part of Britain's war costs. But it would also ensure the Reich's economic recovery so that it could once again provide a lucrative trading partner for Britain.[54] Lloyd George was the first of a series of inter-war British statesmen to base their nation's strategic policy on a fundamental misreading of the long-term balance of power in Europe.

Woodrow Wilson arrived in Europe in December 1918 with surprisingly few fixed ideas on the character of the peace settlement.[55] At the centre of his conception of international security remained a new order structured by representative government, economic liberalism and, above all, the League of Nations. For the president, the chief function of the League would be the moral regeneration of world politics. This would be achieved by ensuring that 'force of arms' was replaced by 'the force of world opinion' as the ultimate arbiter in international relations.[56] Any imperfections in the peace settlement, he believed, could be rectified in time by the power of public opinion operating through the machinery of the League. The president therefore insisted on creating the League before dealing with other aspects of the settlement. The League Covenant, once finalised, constituted the opening articles of each of the peace treaties with the Central Powers.

Wilson expected that the leaders of 'old Europe' would try to subvert his bid for a new international order. 'Too much success or security on the part of the Allies', he observed, 'will make a genuine peace settlement exceedingly difficult, if not impossible.'[57] The president was willing to use economic leverage to put pressure on Allied leaders to bend to his conception of a just and durable peace. He was in a position to do so. US loans to France and Britain would total nearly $9.5 billion by mid-1919. And further American financial support would be required for post-war reconstruction. There was no chance,

---

[54] E. Goldstein, *Winning the Peace: British Diplomatic Strategy, Peace Planning and the Paris Peace Conference, 1916–1920* (Oxford, 1991), esp. 104–62; D. Newton, *British Policy and the Weimar Republic, 1918–1919* (Oxford, 1997); R. Bunselmeyer, *The Costs of the War, 1914–1918: British Economic War Aims and the Origins of Reparation* (Hamden, Conn., 1975), 61–104; M. Dockrill and D. Goold, *Peace Without Promise: Britain and the Peace Conferences, 1919–1923* (London, 1981), 17–29.

[55] T. J. Knock, *To End All Wars: Woodrow Wilson and the Quest for a New World Order* (Princeton, 1992), 182–209.

[56] Quoted in Wilson's address to the second plenary session of the peace conference on 25 Jan. 1919 in *PV-SDN*, 8; on Wilson and the League to Enforce Peace see esp. S. Wertheim, 'The league that wasn't: American designs for a legalist–sanctionist League of Nations and the intellectual origins of international organization, 1914–1920', *Diplomatic History*, 35, 5 (2011); on Wilson's overall conception see Ambrosius, *Wilsonianism*, 51–64; Knock, *To End All Wars*, 44, 126–7, 149–53, 207; and R. Kennedy, *The Will to Believe: Woodrow Wilson, World War I, and America's Strategy for Peace and Security* (Kent, Ohio, 2009), 182–202.

[57] Link et al. (eds.), *The Papers of Woodrow Wilson*, vol. LI, Wilson to House, 28 Oct. 1918: 473; S. Schuker, 'The Rhineland Question: West European Security at the Paris Peace Conference of 1919' in Boemke et al. (eds.), *Treaty of Versailles*, 278.

moreover, that the USA would agree to participate in the transatlantic economic condominium proposed by the French. The Americans also opposed compelling Germany to pay huge sums in reparation. The economic reconstruction of France and the rest of Europe, US officials judged, should be financed by private lending from the USA rather than reparation from Germany.[58] The American president was closer to the French point of view, however, in his conviction that Germany had caused the war and in his sceptical attitude towards the democratic credentials of the new German government created at Weimar in January 1919.[59]

The overriding aim of German policy was to preserve the Reich's status as a Great Power. The abdication of the Kaiser and the constitution of a German republic at Weimar were widely considered sufficient measures to secure Germany's re-entry into the Great Power club with full participation in postwar peace negotiations leading to a moderate 'peace of understanding'.[60] Even those among the German policy elite who were more realistic about the prospects for achieving such a settlement were resolved to use the Fourteen Points as the basis for a revisionist foreign policy after peace was negotiated.[61]

A small German-speaking Austrian republic was created in mid-October. Its overriding ambition was to preserve as much German-speaking territory as possible in the peace settlement. Its failure to achieve this stoked popular support for *Anschluss* (union) with Germany.[62] Hungary, meanwhile, descended into anarchy. A putatively liberal democratic regime established in late 1918 faced territorial claims from virtually all the successor states and eventually gave way to revolution and a self-proclaimed Soviet republic led by Béla Kun in spring 1919. Austria and Hungary would emerge from the peace

[58] Soutou, *L'Or et le sang*, 807–40; Trachtenberg, *Reparation*, 29–97; S. Schuker, 'Origins of American Stabilisation Policy in Europe: The Financial Dimension, 1918–1924' in H.-J. Schröder (ed.), *Confrontation and Co-operation: Germany and the United States in the Era of World War* (Providence, R.I., 1994), 377–408; S. Schuker, 'Europe's Banker: The American Banking Community and European Reconstruction, 1918–1922' in M. Petricioli (ed.), *A Missed Opportunity? 1922 and the Reconstruction of Europe* (Berne, 1995), 47–59; E. Glaser, 'The Making of the Economic Peace' in Boemke et al. (eds.), *Treaty of Versailles*, 371–99; Steiner, *Lights that Failed*, 36–40.

[59] T. Knock, 'Wilsonian Concepts and International Realities at the End of the War' in Boemke et al. (eds.), *Treaty of Versailles*, 111–29; K. Schwabe, *Woodrow Wilson, Revolutionary Germany and Peacemaking, 1918–1919: Missionary Diplomacy and the Realities of Power* (Chapel Hill, 1985), 50–71, 161–84 and 210–52; Ambrosius, 'Wilson, Clemenceau and the German Problem at the Paris Peace Conference' in *Wilsonianism*, 65–73.

[60] K. Schwabe, 'Die Amerikanische und die deutsche Geheimdiplomatie und das Problem eines Verständigungsfriedens im Jahre 1918', *Vierteljahrshefte für Zeitgeschichte*, 19, 1 (1971), 1–32; P. Krüger, *Versailles: deutsche Aussenpolitik zwischen Revisionismus und Friedenssicherung* (Munich, 1986), 32–61.

[61] K. Schwabe, 'Germany's Peace Aims: Domestic and International Constraints' in Boemke et al. (eds.), *Treaty of Versailles*, 40; P. Krüger, 'German Disappointment and Anti-Western Resentment, 1918–1919' in Schröder (ed.), *Confrontation and Co-operation*, 323–36.

[62] A. D. Low, *The Anschluss Movement, 1918–1919, and the Paris Peace Conference* (Philadelphia, 1974).

conference heavily truncated, with millions of their co-nationals living under the rule of rival powers in central and southern Europe.[63]

IV

Planning for peace and security took place in a highly fraught domestic environment. The shadow of the war loomed over every aspect of government policy. France's human losses were staggering. Total deaths were officially estimated at over 1.35 million, but widely reported to be nearly 2 million. Over 55 per cent of French males over the age of nineteen were war veterans. And 28 per cent of all French combatants had died on the battlefield. A staggering 10 per cent of the *entire* French peasant class had perished in the fighting.[64] The generation born between 1887 and 1895 suffered most terribly, losing 40 per cent of its male population. During the opening phase of the war the average death toll reached 2,000 per day and never fell below 400 for the duration of the conflict. Nearly one-third of the *total* population born in the year 1894 died in the fighting. And these figures do not include the number of wounded. Roughly half of all surviving veterans of the front had been wounded. These were the highest proportional losses of any Great Power combatant.

The conflict had also given rise to a new phenomenon in French society: a constituency of more than 2 million 'war victims' that included more than 1 million permanently incapacitated war veterans, over 650,000 war widows and over 1.1 million orphans or offspring of war invalids. The national birth rate, meanwhile, virtually collapsed over the course of the conflict. Overall the French population was reduced by nearly 3 million lives as a result of the Great War. In 1921 the total population for metropolitan France, including the newly recovered provinces of Alsace and Lorraine, stood at 39.2 million, more than 500,000 less than the figure for 1914. Despite successive waves of immigration during the 1920s (mainly from eastern Europe), France did not reach its 1914 population level again until 1950. These losses were particularly alarming for a nation accustomed to understanding national power in terms of dynamic population growth.[65]

---

[63] One eminent Hungarian scholar refers to the 'unparalleled mutilation' of Hungary in 1919–20: see M. Ádám, *The Versailles System and Central Europe* (London, 2004), 29–54, esp. 32.

[64] The figures cited in this paragraph are drawn from O. Faron, 'Une Catastrophe démographique majeure', *Collections de l'Histoire*, 21 (2003), 86–9; O. Faron, *Les Enfants du deuil: orphelins et pupilles de la nation de la première guerre mondiale, 1914–1941* (Paris, 2001), 4–6; L. Smith, S. Audoin-Rouzeau and A. Becker, *France and the Great War, 1914–1918* (Cambridge, 2003), 68–71; J.-J. Becker and S. Berstein, *Victoire et frustrations, 1914–1929* (Paris, 1990), 155–75; F. Monier, *Les Années 20* (Paris, 1999), 12–16.

[65] J. Dupâquier (ed.), *Histoire de la population française*, vol. IV: *1914 à nos jours* (Paris, 1988), 34–61; on immigration and the politics of *dénatalité* see G. Noriel, *Le Creuset français: histoire de l'immigration, XIXe–XXe siècles* (Paris, 1988), 13–69 and R. Tomlinson, 'The disappearance of France: French politics and the birth rate, 1896–1940', *HJ*, 28, 2 (1985), 405–16.

The political contexts of peacemaking, 1918–1919   219

To the shocking human costs of the war were added the physical devastation of the ten *départements* that together constituted France's industrial heartland. During its retreat from this region the German army did everything it could to ensure that this area would be crippled for years to come. Industrial plant was blown up, mines were flooded, and half a million homes were destroyed along with 11,000 public buildings, most roads and 5,000 kilometres of railway. In addition to this purposeful and systematic destruction, more than 2.5 million hectares of tillable fields were unusable, marred by craters, barbed wire, unexploded shells, networks of trenches and other detritus of industrial war.[66] Industrial production had fallen to 57 per cent of its 1913 level and did not reach its pre-war level again until late 1924.[67] Albert Lebrun, the minister for blockade and liberated regions, estimated that a return to pre-war standards of economic life in these areas was impossible for at least four years. The systematic destruction inflicted by the Germans, he observed, was part of longer-term preparations for post-war economic domination.[68]

Vast resources would be required to accomplish the task of physical reconstruction from a country that had been forced heavily into debt to finance its war effort. In terms of 'strict war expenses' the cost of the war was estimated at 140 billion in 1913 gold francs. To put this sum in perspective, the average annual expenditure for the years before 1914 had been less than 5 billion francs. In 1919 the French government was spending more than 7 billion gold francs per year merely to service its public debt. Internal and external debts were on a scale that would have been unimaginable before the war. France's international debt approached 35 billion gold francs – virtually all of which was owed to Britain and the United States. Between 1913 and 1919 the internal public debt rose from 33.6 billion to 204.7 billion gold francs. Of this total, less than 75 billion was long-term debt (mainly fixed-income government bonds). The remainder was a floating debt that was vulnerable to demands for short-term payment. This made the confidence of creditors a crucial factor in managing the economy. Lack of confidence could induce panic and a wave of demands for short-term payment.[69]

The fundamentals of French finance were hardly conducive to confidence building, however. The 6 billion worth of currency in circulation in 1914 had risen to more than 30 billion by 1918, while the gold holdings of the Bank of France remained essentially the same. The result was runaway inflation costing the franc nearly 80 per cent of its value.[70] This bleak financial situation was

---

[66] Becker and Berstein, *Victoire et frustrations*, 150–1.   [67] Monier, *Années 20*, 28–9.
[68] SHD-DAT, *Fonds Clemenceau*, 6N 73–1, 'Clauses à insérer dans les conditions de l'armistice', 1 Nov. 1918; see also *Série A*, vol. 59, 'Ministère du Blocus: études et textes susceptibles d'être utilisés en vue de la préparation du traité de la paix', Dec. 1918.
[69] K. Mouré, *The Gold Standard Illusion: France, the Bank of France, and the International Gold Standard, 1914–1939* (Oxford, 2002), 41–3; A. Sauvy, *Histoire économique de la France*, 4 vols. (Paris, 1967), I, 19–38; Becker and Berstein, *Victoire et frustrations*, 223–5.
[70] Mouré, *Gold Standard Illusion*, 35.

further darkened by the evaporation of French holdings in Russia after the Bolshevik regime repudiated Tsarist debts. On top of all of this was the need to factor in pensions for the many millions of incapacitated veterans as well as the widows and children of France's war dead. The consensus view, unsurprisingly, was that Germany must be forced to pay for the damage it had inflicted.[71]

Jean-Jacques Becker has argued persuasively that victory in 1918 marked the 'zenith of national feeling' in France's long history.[72] Yet with victory came expectations that peace would deliver not only security but also social transformation. The First World War was a 'forcing house of social change' in which calls for a redistribution of national wealth and a more equitable social order accompanied hopes for lasting peace.[73] Yet the economic transition from war to peacetime was particularly difficult. The process of demobilisation placed huge strains on the labour market at a time when the nation's finances teetered on the verge of bankruptcy. France was vitally dependent on the continued flow of short-term loans from across the Atlantic in order to avoid bankruptcy. This was a major challenge for French negotiators. 'When the war is over', Wilson had predicted in July 1917, 'we can force [Britain and France] to our way of thinking because by that time they will, among other things, be financially in our hands.'[74]

At the same time, the cost of living continued to rise despite expectations that economic life would improve as a result of victory.[75] Membership of the CGT increased by 600 per cent from 100,000 in 1916 to 600,000 in 1918, and May–June 1919 saw a fresh wave of strikes sweep across France. All of this occurred against the backdrop of the Russian Revolution and criticisms of Allied policy towards the Soviet government.[76] The wartime experience had fired similar aspirations among the several hundred thousand women who had joined the workforce after 1914. The resulting tensions would help define French politics well into the post-war years.[77]

The volatility of public sentiment is evident in the swift collapse of Woodrow Wilson's popularity as his priorities for the peace, and in particular his vision of

---

[71] See P. Miquel, *La Paix de Versailles et l'opinion publique française* (Paris, 1972), 424–33.
[72] J.-J. Becker, *La France en guerre, 1914–1918: la grande mutation* (Brussels, 1999), 107.
[73] R. Kedward, *La Vie en bleu: France and the French since 1900* (London, 2005), 93; see also T. Stovall, *Paris and the Spirit of 1919: Consumer Struggles, Transnationalism and Revolution* (Cambridge, 2012).
[74] Quoted in A. Mayer, *Political Origins of the New Diplomacy, 1917–1918* (New Haven, 1958), 332; figures from Steiner, *Lights that Failed*, 38.
[75] J.-C. Asselain, *Histoire économique de la France*, vol. II (Paris, 1984), 3–29; Sauvy, *Histoire économique*, I, 19–38; Miquel, *Opinion publique*, 9–32 and 419–22; C. Maier, *Recasting Bourgeois Europe: Stabilization in France, Germany and Italy in the Decade after World War I* (Princeton, 1975), 29–33, 43–6, 76–85.
[76] M. Dreyfus, *Histoire de la CGT* (Paris, 1995), 94–5.
[77] L. Robert, *Les Ouvriers, la Patrie et la Révolution, Paris, 1914–1919* (Paris, 1995), 319–413; Becker and Berstein, *Victoire et frustrations*, 181–6; S. Couré, *La Grande lueur à l'Est: les Français et l'Union soviétique 1917–1939* (Paris, 1999); Kedward, *Vie en bleu*, 62–98; and S. Reynolds, *France between the Wars: Gender and Politics* (London, 1996), 20–9, 132–49.

the League of Nations, became clear in early February. Not only was the centre-right mainstream alienated, but also internationalists of all stripes who had hoped for a muscular international organisation to enforce the rule of law.[78] French opinion was truly united on only two issues: the return of Alsace-Lorraine and the need for vast reparation payments from Germany.

From the nationalist right came eloquent demands for an independent Rhineland and an eastern counterweight. Among the most influential voices in this campaign were those of Maurice Barrès and the monarchist historian and political commentator Jacques Bainville. For Bainville, writing in the *Action française*, the essential objective was to alter the Franco-German strategic balance. A Rhenish state tied to France would serve this aim in the west. Bainville lamented the end of the Russian and Habsburg Empires and advocated replacing the Russian alliance with a network of client states in eastern Europe to counterbalance German power.[79] The policy advocated by Barrès and his Ligue française was more ambiguous and in many ways more interesting: an autonomous and permanently demilitarised Rhineland would serve not only as a 'necessary buffer' between France and Germany but eventually as a cultural bridge between the two countries.[80] A series of resolutions passed by the Comité de la rive gauche du Rhin combined these two policy visions in a programme demanding France's 1814 frontier, an Allied military protectorate on the Left Bank and the occupation of the Ruhr basin until Germany had paid off an indemnity.[81]

The issue of the Rhineland was almost absent, conversely, from discourses of peace and security on the left. Both the SFIO and the CGT insisted that self-determination, democratic reform in Germany and a society of nations must constitute the central elements of France's peace programme.[82] As Professor Soutou has rightly observed, the guiding principle for French socialists was that it was both necessary and possible to achieve better relations with a democratic Germany in the long run.[83] After German elections of 19 January 1919 resulted in victory for a moderate socialist coalition, the SFIO demanded that representatives from the 'Weimar' government be invited to join in

---

[78] Miquel, *Opinion publique*, 37–213; Soutou, 'French Peacemakers', 181–2.
[79] Miquel, *Opinion publique*, 244–6 and 304–16; J. Bainville, *Les Conséquences politiques de la paix* (Paris, 1996), esp. 25–58; J. Bainville, *L'Allemagne*, 2 vols. (Paris, 1939), II, 1–49; C. Dickès, *Jacques Bainville: les lois de la politique étrangère* (Paris, 2008), 47–182.
[80] M. Barrès, *La Politique rhénane: discours parlementaires* (Paris, 1922), *passim*; M. Barrès, *Les Grands problèmes du Rhin* (Paris, 1930), esp. 27–39, 83–6, 134–9 and 229–71.
[81] Other influential commentators such as Pertinax (André Géraud), writing in *L'Echo de Paris*, argued for similar solutions: see Stevenson, *French War Aims*, 149–56 and Miquel, *Opinion publique*, 314–32.
[82] See, for example, the Socialist contributions to the great foreign policy debate in the chamber on 29 Dec. 1918: *JO, Chambre, Débats*, 1918, second séance, 29 Dec. 1918; see also Miquel, *Opinion publique*, 47–144 and G. B. Noble, *Policies and Opinions in Paris, 1919: Wilsonian Diplomacy, the Versailles Peace and Public Opinion* (New York, 1935), 98–104.
[83] Quoted in Soutou, 'French Peacemakers', 186.

negotiations. This did not rule out imposing substantial reparations on Germany, something a majority of the left supported.[84] It suggested instead a desire to coexist with a chastened and politically reformed Germany. But the SFIO had limited influence in the national debate over the peace settlement because Clemenceau did not depend on Socialists for parliamentary support. Just as significantly, from mid-January 1919 the party entered a period of internal crisis over the divisive questions of Bolshevism and world-wide revolution.[85]

For French liberal or juridical internationalists, still concentrated on the centre-left, the chief preoccupation remained the creation of a society of nations. The problem was that internationalists such as Ferdinand Buisson, Yvon Delbos, Alfred Dominique and Lucien Le Foyer struggled to secure unequivocal support for their project even within the Radical Party. Although the Radical Party Congress had adopted the creation of a society of nations as one of its official aims in October 1917, Buisson and his colleagues remained a smallish minority within the party.[86] Proponents of a traditional approach to security prevailed within the Radical executive committee. The most notable of these, Henry Franklin-Bouillon, favoured a highly traditional security policy. And this vision of the post-war settlement was approved by a substantial majority within the party's executive committee.[87] Centre and centre-left opinion tended in general to support a broadly harsh treaty that would weaken Germany and provide territorial and economic security for France.

Nor was there effective lobbying for the League from within French civil society at the war's end. The process of amalgamating and galvanising such support, which lagged well behind similar movements in Britain and the USA, began to gather momentum only with the constitution of the Association française de la Société des nations (AFSDN) in late 1918. The general membership of the AFSDN brought together a diverse array of public figures, from the Archbishop of Paris to the leadership of the CGT. Its driving force, however, was a small group of committed internationalists that included Ferdinand Buisson, Albert Thomas, Jules Prudhommeaux, Georges Scelle and Léon Bourgeois.[88] Under their direction, the AFSDN sponsored an 'Inter-Allied

---

[84] Miquel, *Opinion publique*, 419–32.
[85] Ibid., 127–45, 190–207, 324–7, 425–31; G. Candar, 'Les Socialistes contre Clemenceau, tout contre' in R. Ducoulombier (ed.), *Les Socialistes dans l'Europe en guerre: réseaux, parcours, experiences, 1914–1918* (Paris, 2010), 205–17; M. Rebérioux, 'Le Socialisme et la première guerre mondiale' in J. Droz (ed.), *Histoire générale du socialisme*, vol. II (Paris, 1974), 632–4; Becker and Berstein, *Victoire et frustrations*, 140–1; Kriegel, *Origines du communisme*, 358–420.
[86] J.-M. Guieu, *Le Rameau et le glaive: les militants français pour la Société des nations* (Paris, 2008), 39–40; S. Berstein, *Histoire du Parti Radical*, vol. I: *À la recherche de l'âge d'or* (Paris, 1980), 91–2.
[87] 'Séance plénière du Comité exécutif: 24 Nov. 1918', *Bulletin du Parti républicain radical et radical-socialiste*, 14 Dec. 1918.
[88] F. Buisson, A. Thomas and J. Prudhommeaux, *Appel en vue de la fondation d'une Association française pour la Société des nations* (Paris, 1918); Guieu, *Rameau et glaive*, 47–9.

Conference' of civil society associations for a league of nations held in Paris from 26 through 31 January 1919. Bourgeois, who chaired the conference, described its mission as 'the preparation of texts of a juridical order' to be forwarded to the secretariat of the peace conference.[89] Bourgeois, who was also the association's first president, aimed to use the AFSDN to pressure the Clemenceau government into incorporating the internationalist agenda as a central element in its peace programme.[90]

This was never likely to succeed. Not only was Clemenceau sceptical of the idea of an international organisation, there was also long-standing antipathy between the two men that was only exacerbated by the relatively close relations that prevailed between Bourgeois and Poincaré.[91] The AFSDN would evolve during the inter-war period into a mass movement in support of the peace, disarmament and the League of Nations. It was less successful, however, in its initial function as a lobby group. A mission statement was drafted that approved the principle of self-determination and resolved to establish close cooperation with civil society movements in other states. It called on Allied governments to constitute an international organisation of democratic states charged with 'assuring a durable peace by substituting the existing rule of force with a regime of organised law'.[92] This legalist conception was incorporated into a 'programme of action' submitted to the premier on 18 December 1919. Clemenceau pledged to do all he could to realise this 'noble vision for the future of humanity'.[93] Thereafter he ignored the AFSDN completely. And yet, even if internationalist enthusiasm could be disregarded in the short term, it would continue to grow and would make its mark on policy during the post-war decade.

Internationalist alternatives were marginalised almost completely in surveys of opinion and the press collated for the government by the foreign ministry. In December 1918, for example, the Maison de la presse prepared a synthesis of public sphere conceptions of peace and security that is most interesting for the insight it provides into thinking within the Quai d'Orsay. The study cited the 'dismemberment of Germany' as the 'one idea that dominates all projects elaborated for the peace'. Public discussion of self-determination, meanwhile, was represented as providing normative justification for overthrowing the

---

[89] 'Une Manifestation des comites alliés', *L'Éclair*, 27 Jan. 1919; 'Un Projet de status de la Société des nations: texte présenté par les associations des pays alliés', *L'Avenir*, 2 Feb. 1919.
[90] S. Blair, 'France et le pacte de la Société des nations: le rôle du gouvernement français dans l'élaboration du pacte de la Société des nations, 1914–1919', thèse de doctorat, Université de Paris I (Sorbonne), 1991, 275–7.
[91] Bourgeois was a regular visitor to the Élysée Palace throughout the war and particularly after the armistice: M. Sorlot, *Léon Bourgeois: un moraliste en politique* (Paris, 2005), 274–82.
[92] 'Notre association', *Bulletin de l'Association française pour la Société des nations*, 2 Jan. 1919; see also Guieu, *Rameau et glaive*, 47.
[93] MAE, *SDN*, vol. 7, 'La Société des nations: un texte à soumettre au gouvernement' and 'Pour le traité de paix: Monsieur Clemenceau préconise la Société des nations', 18 Dec. 1918; see also Blair, 'La France et le pacte', 440–2.

224 Peace and security, 1918–1919

existing geo-political order. The authors of the survey predicted that popular enthusiasm for the 'principle of the rights of nationalities' would translate into support not only for the dissolution of the Habsburg and Ottoman Empires but also for the creation of an autonomous polity on the Left Bank of the Rhine.[94] This line of argument would surface repeatedly in official memoranda over the months to come. Clemenceau is likely to have seen through such partisan representations of civil society views. Not only did he receive regular bulletins on the state of opinion from both the intelligence services and the police, his vast experience as a political journalist, not to mention his formidable influence over large swathes of the daily press, provided him with an independent perspective on the ebbs and flows of public opinion.[95]

V

It was the Quai d'Orsay that made the first bid to take control of peace planning. By the time the armistice was signed Philippe Berthelot, Jules Laroche and Gabriel Hanotaux had all drafted lengthy study papers on the nature of the future peace settlement. Shortly afterwards, both Paul Cambon and Berthelot produced detailed proposals for the organisation of the peace conference. All of these memoranda advocated traditional conceptions of the future European order.[96]

Interestingly, it was the older generation of foreign ministry officials who expressed the deepest unease at the prospect of American influence shaping the peace settlement. Hanotaux acknowledged the importance of American power, but also insisted that 'European questions are European and they must be addressed by accord between European powers'. The United States, he insisted, lacked 'sufficient understanding' of 'certain problems that have not concerned it in the past'.[97] Paul Cambon, for his part, judged Wilson 'incapable of understanding the complexity of European problems' and described his 'abstractions' as 'a grave threat to France'. Cambon's prescription for dealing with this problem was prior agreement with Britain. This, he

---

[94] MAE, *Série A*, vol. 221, 'Les Conditions générales de la paix', 15 Dec. 1918; see also the bibliography compiled by the Comité d'études in the same volume.

[95] For intelligence and policy reporting see SHD-DAT, *Fonds Clemenceau*, 6N 146–52; see also police reports in AN, F7 cartons 12,970–13,023; on the Clemenciste press see see the invaluable *classement* provided by Miquel in *Opinon publique*, 22–34.

[96] MAE, *Série A*, vol. 289, 'La Frontière de l'Alsace-Lorraine et le statut de la rive gauche du Rhin', 1 Nov. 1918; 'Note sur la future frontière entre l'Alsace-Lorraine et l'Allemagne: raisons stratégiques, économiques et politiques', 10 Nov. 1918; vol. 60, 'De la Future frontière' and 'Du Sort de l'Allemagne unifiée', both dated 11 Nov. 1918; see also MAE, PA-AP 166, *Papiers Tardieu*, vol. 417, 'Deux notes de M. Hanotaux', n.d.; MAE, PA-AP 141, *Papiers Pichon*, vol. 6, 'Examen des conditions de paix' (Paul Cambon), 22 Nov. 1918; MAE, PA-AP 42, *Papiers Paul Cambon*, vol. 14, 'Note sur le congrès de la paix' (drafted by DAPC under Berthelot), n.d. but certainly 20–25 Nov. 1918 (also in MAE, PA-AP 166, *Papiers Tardieu*, vol. 296); MAE, PA-AP 141, *Papiers Pichon*, vol. 6, 'État de paix' (Berthelot), n.d. but late Nov. 1918.

[97] MAE, *Série A*, vol. 60, 'De la Future frontière', 11 Nov. 1918.

advised, would present Wilson with a united front over territorial issues when negotiations began.[98] When putting this idea to the British foreign secretary Arthur Balfour, however, Cambon went overboard with warnings of a future global struggle pitting Britain and France against an alliance of Germany and the USA. Balfour found Cambon's analysis 'little short of insanity'. The French ambassador's apocalyptic vision of the future only strengthened existing predispositions in London towards cooperation with Washington.[99]

Berthelot also favoured a preliminary understanding with the Lloyd George government. In mid-November he took the lead in drafting a detailed plan for the organisation, aims and agenda of the peace conference.[100] Berthelot laid out not only a programme for the conference, but also a framework for a new political and territorial order in Europe. This document, along with subsequent drafts, provides eloquent testimony to the continued dominance of the traditional approach to security within the foreign ministry. Berthelot considered that the 1815 Congress of Vienna provided the best template for the upcoming peace conference. The Vienna settlement, he noted approvingly, was 'inspired by past principles of political balance'. The two great flaws in that settlement were, first, its failure to account for the rise of national feeling and, second, its extension of Prussian power to the Rhine. He judged that both must be corrected in the settlement to come.[101]

Berthelot therefore proposed an organisational and procedural framework in which the key elements of the peace settlement would be hammered out by the victorious great powers (France, Britain, Italy and the USA), with input from 'little states' and 'emerging states' only on issues that affected them directly. Russia, significantly, would not be invited. Its interests would be considered by an inter-Allied committee.[102] The first priority would be what Berthelot termed the 'settlement of the war proper'. The 'core issues' of this settlement

---

[98] Institut de France, *Correspondance Stephen Pichon*, MS 4396, *pièce* 150, Paul Cambon to Pichon, 15 Nov. 1918; MAE, PA-AP 141, *Papiers Pichon*, vol. 6, 'Examen des conditions de paix', 22 Nov. 1918; see also P. Cambon, *Correspondance, 1870–1924, vol. III: (1912–1924) Les Guerres balkaniques. La Grande Guerre. L'Organisation de la paix* (Paris, 1946), Cambon to Clemenceau, 14 Nov. 1918: 282–3; and BDIC, *Archives Klotz*, dr. 18, 'Préliminaires de paix avec l'Allemagne', n.d.

[99] House of Lords Records Office (HLRO), *David Lloyd George Papers*, LG F/3/3/35, Balfour to Lloyd George, 29 Nov. 1918; see also MAE, PA-AP 42, *Papiers Paul Cambon*, vol. 14, 'Procès-verbal d'une conversation Lloyd George–Cambon [17 Nov. 1918]', 22 Nov. 1918 (de Fleuriau memo).

[100] MAE, PA-AP 166, *Papiers Tardieu*, vol. 296, 'Note sur le congrès de la paix', n.d. but certainly 15–18 Nov. 1918; SHD-DAT, 6N 72, 26 Nov. 1918; MAE, PA-AP 141, *Papiers Pichon*, vol. 6, Pichon to London, Rome and Washington, 27 Nov. 1918; ibid., vol. 6, 'Documentation française du Congrès', 6 Dec. 1918. Berthelot had also helped Paul Cambon and his *chargé d'affaires* in London, Aimé de Fleuriau, draft their preliminary programme: MAE, PA-AP 166, *Papiers Tardieu*, vol. 296, 'Examen des conditions de la paix', 15 Nov. 1918.

[101] MAE, PA-AP 166, *Papiers Tardieu*, vol. 296, 'Note sur le congrès de la paix'.

[102] MAE, PA-AP 141, *Papiers Pichon*, vol. 6, 'Documentation française du Congrès', 6 Dec. 1918 and MAE, PA-AP 166, *Papiers Tardieu*, vol. 296, 'Note sur le congrès de la paix'.

were: 'the future regime of Germany'; the frontiers of eastern Europe; the calculation of 'indemnities and compensations'; and, finally, 'the elaboration of military guarantees on land and at sea' which would include 'territorial occupations'.[103] Only after agreement had been reached on these 'core issues', Berthelot advised, could the peacemakers move on to 'the organisation of a society of nations'. He stressed the distinction between the two stages. The first entailed the political and territorial reordering of Europe while the second was essentially an experiment with a new legal order. 'Any consideration of the second question implies, in effect, the solution of the first,' he asserted. 'We must not confuse the settlement of concrete questions with the application of stipulations of general public law.'[104] This sharp distinction between the territorial settlement and the League project illuminates the traditional assumptions underpinning Berthelot's approach to peacemaking. The League, for Berthelot, could not be an integral element either of the peace settlement itself or the security system that would emerge afterwards.

In addition to these procedural recommendations, Berthelot proposed a normative framework based on four 'directing principles'. The first, significantly, was 'the right of all peoples to democratic representation and self-determination'. The second was the 'inviolability' of all metropolitan and colonial territory possessed by the Allies on 1 August 1914. The third was the 'solemn repudiation of all human rights violations'. The fourth, and most controversial, was 'the renunciation of all prior treaties and agreements'. Berthelot asserted that not only should the various agreements with Tsarist Russia be repudiated, but also the promises made to Italy in the Treaty of London and, crucially, adoption of the Fourteen Points as the basis of all peace negotiations. Wilson's 'fourteen propositions', Berthelot observed, 'are no more than principles of public law and cannot furnish a concrete base for the work of the conference'. They were much better suited, he argued, to serve as guidelines for the establishment of the League of Nations.[105]

In sum, Berthelot urged that France must assert itself to determine the character of the peace settlement. He advocated what was in essence a traditional exercise in Great Power politics that would remake the strategic balance to France's advantage at Germany's expense. By taking the initiative in proclaiming the importance of self-determination he aimed to define the meaning and application of this principle in the negotiations to come. His project posed a direct challenge to American conceptions of post-war order. It also threatened hopes of drawing on US political, military and financial support after the war.

---

[103] MAE, PA-AP 166, *Papiers Tardieu*, vol. 296, 'Note sur le congrès de la paix'.
[104] MAE, PA-AP 141, *Papiers Pichon*, vol. 6, Pichon (Berthelot) to London, Rome and Washington, 27 Nov. 1918.
[105] Ibid.

The dangerous consequences of alienating the USA were driven home by Tardieu upon his return from New York. Tardieu's tenure as high commissioner had only strengthened his conviction that American power would play a dominant role in world politics. He had long argued that France must cultivate a strong political relationship with the USA.[106] He took up this theme in a note to the premier on 26 November, stressing 'the significance for France of America's entry into world affairs', which had taken place 'two generations sooner than would otherwise have been the case'. Tardieu argued that this presented French policy with a chance to 'bring the United States around to the idea of an alliance under the cover of the League of Nations'. This opportunity would be undermined by an open rejection of American policy initiatives. 'It would be disastrous', Tardieu warned, 'if the President and the [American] people drew the conclusion from their experience at Paris ... that Washington and Monroe were right after all, and that the United States is better off leaving Europe to its own affairs.'[107] This was a judgement that Clemenceau, with his long-standing personal and professional links to the USA, was predisposed to accept.

Clemenceau was nonetheless tempted by the idea of a prior understanding with the British. He had been shocked by American unilateralism and threats to make a separate peace during armistice negotiations, and travelled to London with Foch in early December to explore prospects for establishing such an understanding. But the visit was not a success. Lloyd George, Balfour and other British policy makers were either non-committal or openly opposed to such a strategy. By late December Clemenceau's ideas concerning post-war order revolved once again around a close strategic relationship with both America and Britain.[108]

The premier's long-standing hostility towards professional diplomats, meanwhile, was only intensified by Berthelot's attempt to assert foreign ministry control over policy making. Dismissing Quai d'Orsay personnel as 'technicians', he took measures to ensure that decision making over core issues was concentrated within his narrow circle of advisers. Berthelot was passed over

---

[106] A. Tardieu, *Notes sur les États-Unis* (Paris, 1908). Tardieu's correspondence with the premier's staff from New York is in SHD-DAT, *Fonds Clemenceau*, cartons 6N 136 and 137. Tardieu's admiration for American political processes helped shape his call for reform of the French state in the early 1930s: see Monnet, *Refaire la République*, esp. 78–101 and N. Roussellier, 'André Tardieu où la crise du constitutionnalisme libéral', *VS*, 21 (1989), 57–70.

[107] SHD-DAT, *Fonds Clemenceau*, 6N 137-3, 'L'Opinion française et le président Wilson: note pour le président du conseil', 26 Nov. 1926; see also Stevenson, *French War Aims*, 146–7.

[108] Mordacq, *Ministère Clemenceau*, III, 11, 12 and 13 Nov. 1918: 6–7; SHD-DAT, *Fonds Clemenceau*, 6N 72, 'Minutes of a Conference at 10 Downing Street', 2 Dec. 1918; ibid., 6N 73-2, 'Conversation entre M. Lloyd George et le maréchal Foch', 1 Dec. 1918; Stevenson, *French War Aims*, 144–6; Dockrill and Goold, *Peace Without Promise*, 22–4; on the 'Atlanticist' predispositions of British policy elites see M. G. Fry, *Illusions of Security: North Atlantic Diplomacy, 1918–1922* (Toronto, 1972), 7–25.

when the premier named Paul Dutasta, a family friend and long-time protégé, as secretary general to the conference. The foreign ministry was sidelined from decision making over the crucial questions of reparations and west European security as well as discussion and debate within the Council of Four.[109]

Most senior diplomats were outraged at this state of affairs and criticised the government's peace programme for both its method and its strategic conception. Paul Cambon described French policy as 'disorganised and lamentable'. France, he judged, was about to enter 'a period of the most acute difficulties, and all as a result of the same cause, a neglect of diplomacy'.[110] He might have added a neglect of tradition. 'Everything', he complained, 'has become part of the marmalade upon which, at the bidding of president Wilson, we construct a new edifice with no foundations other than useless abstractions.'[111] Barrère, meanwhile, travelled to Paris after the armistice to advise Clemenceau that frontier questions must be 'the foundations of the peace'. He was incensed when the premier appeared to have little time for his 'professional ideas'. The government, he complained, had entered negotiations 'in dispersed fashion, without order, method or a clear government doctrine concerning issues upon which our national future depends'.[112] Maurice Paléologue similarly dismissed the premier as 'a catastrophe' and predicted that France would suffer the consequences of his ill-informed and irresponsible approach to peacemaking.[113]

Berthelot, whose proposed conference programme was jettisoned, also complained about the marginalisation of the Quai d'Orsay. 'M. Pichon himself is only given fragmentary information on the state of negotiations,' he lamented. 'All questions are referred to the Council of Four – without documentation or critical analysis – and decided after usually very brief discussion before M. Hankey is charged with preparing the minutes in English (which are not communicated to us).' The ministry was thus placed in 'a position where it is impossible for us to do much useful work'.[114] But Berthelot's response differed from that of the generation of senior ambassadors. Under his direction ministry officials worked assiduously to assert the ministry's expertise in negotiations.

---

[109] See Berthelot's description of procedures in MAE, PA-AP 008, *Papiers Camille Barrère*, vol. 1, Berthelot to Barrère, 14 Jun. 1919; see also Jules Cambon's reflections in 'La Paix (Notes inédites – 1919)', *Revue de Paris*, 1 Nov. 1937 (Nov./Dec. 1937), 5–38 (compiled by Geneviève Tabouis); Laroche, *Au Quai d'Orsay*, 58–69; Watson, *Clemenceau: A Political Biography*, 331–63; and Duroselle, *Clemenceau*, 671–82.

[110] Citations from Cambon, *Correspondance*, III, 299–300 and 362, Paul to Henri Cambon, 28 Jan. and 19 Oct. 1919; see also L. Villate, *La République des diplomates: Paul et Jules Cambon, 1843–1935* (Paris, 2002), 347–54 and P. Jackson, 'Tradition and adaptation: the social universe of the French foreign ministry in the era of the First World War', *French History*, 24, 2 (2010), 182–4.

[111] Cambon, *Correspondance*, III, 345, Paul to Jules Cambon, 11 Jul. 1919.

[112] MAE, PA-AP 008, *Papiers Barrère*, vol. 6, 'Note de M. Barrère', 15 May 1919.

[113] Poincaré, *Recherche de la paix*, 287: 27 Mar. 1919.

[114] MAE, PA-AP 008, *Papiers Barrère*, vol. 1, Berthelot to Barrère, 14 Jun. 1919.

They were successful in this enterprise particularly over the question of eastern Europe. Berthelot succeeded even in overcoming the distrust of the premier. By the following May British and American officials considered him 'the moving spirit' within the Quai d'Orsay and judged his influence to be second only to that of Tardieu among Clemenceau's advisers. When Lloyd George enquired as to his precise role, Berthelot laughed and responded *'tout et rien'*.[115]

Tardieu remained the most influential voice within the premier's inner circle, however. In early December he was charged with synthesising the views of key ministries into a single programme. With the help of Aubert, he drew together the core strands of French security policy into an impressively coherent whole based on the twin pillars of an 'Atlantic community' of democracies and the neutralisation of the Left Bank of the Rhine.[116] The work of the Comité d'études was fed into the planning process either through the foreign ministry or via informal contacts between Benoist, Lavisse and Tardieu's staff.[117] Business and civil society groups, meanwhile, had little direct impact on the preparation of this programme.

In the aftermath of the armistice the Quai d'Orsay was deluged with policy advice from hundreds of civil society associations. Virtually all of these were filed away without comment by overburdened ministry officials. Influential figures from business or the press could sometimes gain an audience with Berthelot or one of his colleagues, but there is little evidence that this sort of private lobbying made any impact on the elaboration of policy making. The most powerful business association, the Comité des forges, remained badly divided over the issue of industrial cooperation with Germany and made no systematic effort to influence the economic settlement (though it afterwards complained loudly that it was not sufficiently consulted). All of this meant that France's peace programme was developed without significant input or interference from parliamentary, business or civil society interest groups.[118]

The enhanced importance of the USA in this strategic conception was evident in the proposed conference programme drafted by Tardieu in early January 1919.[119] This plan identified the 'central task' of the conference as 'to prepare, by the settlement of the war, a new organisation for international relations'. Its list of 'directing principles' began with open diplomacy and included freedom of the seas, self-determination and the establishment of an

---

[115] Quotes from Jackson, 'Tradition and adaptation', 183 and 184; see also J.-L. Barré, *Philippe Berthelot: l'éminence grise, 1866–1934* (Paris, 1998), 333–41.
[116] Quote from L. Aubert, 'Haut commissaire et homme d'état' in Aubert et al., *Andre Tardieu*, 65–7; see also Tardieu, *La Paix*, 93–110 and Stevenson, *French War Aims*, 147–9.
[117] Comité d'études material fed directly into the planning process can be found in MAE, *Série A*, vols. 220–2 and SHD-DAT, *Fonds Clemenceau*, 6N 294.
[118] There are nearly two hundred volumes of material received from business and civil society groups during this period in *Série A*; see also Miquel, *Opinion publique*, esp. 288–97; Stevenson, *French War Aims*, 149–52; Soutou, *L'Or et le sang*, 765–806.
[119] MAE, PA-AP 166, *Papiers Tardieu*, vol. 412, 'Congrès de la paix: plan général', 5 Jan. 1919.

international arbitration regime linked to a 'society of nations'. But Tardieu also made explicit reference to key French security aims such as post-war international economic collaboration, reparations and a regime of 'guarantees and sanctions'. This, significantly, would mean 'territorial rectifications' as well as 'the military neutralisation of certain zones'. Tardieu further underlined the need for 'new economic bases for international relations' to provide guarantees against German commercial imperialism.[120] In sum, although Tardieu's conference programme incorporated a number of internationalist themes, at its centre was an essentially traditional understanding of peace and security based on territorial adjustment and the balance of power.

This was the principal reason it was rejected. The American delegation observed that 'the nature and power of the League will necessarily affect many, if not all, other questions'.[121] It followed that the structure and functioning of the League must be agreed before territorial and economic questions could be addressed. At the first meeting of Great Power delegates on 12 January 1919 Wilson, supported by Lloyd George, insisted that the first task of the conference must be to create the League of Nations. Clemenceau, unwilling to place France in the invidious position of opposing the creation of the League, assented to this order of business.[122]

Nothing was put in place of Tardieu's proposed programme, however. The conference organisation remained ad hoc virtually throughout. While the official decision-making body of the conference was its huge plenary sessions, all important negotiations took place first in the Council of Ten or 'Supreme Council' (comprising two delegates each from France, Britain, Italy, Japan and the USA). Most of the detailed work, on issues such as the League of Nations, economic arrangements, reparations, the territorial settlement in eastern Europe and the colonial settlement, was undertaken by eight expert commissions appointed by the Council of Ten. During the most intense and important phase of the conference, from mid-March onward, high-level discussion and decision making was concentrated in the 'Council of Four' (Wilson, Clemenceau, Lloyd George and Italian premier Orlando) which met in Wilson's rooms at the Hotel Crillon. The inevitable result was delay. Peace terms were not agreed and offered to the German delegation until 7 May 1919. The Treaty of Versailles, by far the most important of the various treaties resulting from the peace conference, was not signed until 28 June 1919.[123]

---

[120] Ibid.; the plan is reproduced in Tardieu, *La Paix*, 97–101.
[121] United States Department of State, *Papers Relating to the Foreign Relations of the United States* (hereafter *FRUS*): *The Paris Peace Conference, 1919* (hereafter *PPC*), 13 vols. (Washington, 1942–7), I, 'Observations on Plan des premières conversations entre les ministres Alliés à partir du 13 janvier, 1919', 12 Jan. 1919, 399.
[122] *FRUS: PPC*, III, Council of Ten, 12 Jan. 1919, 492 and 535–6; Blair, 'La France et le pacte', 326–32.
[123] Sharp, *Versailles Settlement*, 37–40 and 180–4; MacMillan, *Paris 1919*, 53–62; and Keiger, *Poincaré*, 249.

VI

All of the core elements in the peace programme devised by Tardieu and his staff were developed in close consultation with the premier. Clemenceau's reluctance to commit his thoughts to paper during this period makes it difficult to pinpoint precisely when he formulated his strategy for peace negotiations. But he provided a glimpse into his thinking during a major foreign policy debate in the chamber of deputies on 29 December 1918. 'There is an old system', the premier remarked when called upon to offer his thoughts on the post-war order, 'which nowadays appears doomed but to which I am nevertheless unafraid to say that I remain in part faithful. In this system states are responsible for their own defence: They strive for solid and well defended frontiers, armaments and something called a balance of powers.'

The tradition of the balance of power, Clemenceau argued, had evolved to meet a recurrent challenge: 'The truth is that since time immemorial peoples have engaged in constant struggles with one another for the satisfaction of their appetites and their selfish interests. I did not write this history any more than any of you. It exists.' He expressed scepticism about 'international guarantees which remain to be defined and which will be perhaps more difficult to establish in reality than in speeches and writings'. He then praised President Wilson's '*candeur*' (which in French can imply naivety) before assuring the chamber that there were significant divergences between the American and French perspectives on the peace. 'America', he observed, 'is a long way away from Germany.'[124]

These observations give undeniable weight to the 'French Bismarck' interpretation of Clemenceau's approach to peace and security. It is important, however, to set the evidence in its proper context. Clemenceau's chief aim in this debate was to secure parliamentary backing for complete freedom of action in the negotiations to come. He was opposed in this by a significant number of deputies who desired to assert parliamentary control over policy. Clemenceau's most voluble and influential opponent in this debate was Franklin-Bouillon, who was not only a leading figure on the right of the Radical Party, but also a close ally of Briand and president of the chamber's powerful foreign affairs commission. Franklin-Bouillon called for the annexation of the Saar coalfield and argued that the 'moral guarantee' offered by a league of nations must be supplemented by the 'material guarantee' of a permanent military presence on the Rhine.[125]

It was to this nationalist prescription for security that Clemenceau was forced to respond in order to ensure himself of parliamentary support. And it is within this context that his approving references to 'traditional methods' and the

---

[124] *JO*, Chambre, *Débats*, 1918, second *séance*, 29 Dec. 1918; Pierre Renaudel described the reference to Wilson's '*candeur*' as 'abominable'.
[125] Ibid.

balance of power should be understood. The truth is that Clemenceau had never been a proponent either of traditional geo-politics or of a frontier on the Rhine. In fact, it is impossible to find a single reference to France's 'natural frontiers' in the vast corpus of his political writings dating back to the late 1860s. His first government, significantly, had accorded far more importance to the Entente with Britain than to the more traditional alliance with Russia.[126]

With these facts in mind it is interesting to note that during the foreign policy debate of 29 December Clemenceau also insisted on the need for a new approach to peace and international security. He stressed the need to 'alter the sentiments that prevailed before the war' and to 'construct a new edifice'. Such an effort was not possible, he argued, 'using only the traditional procedures of the old architecture'. He declared that the peacemakers must 'introduce a new spirit in international relations'. He also recognised the 'superior authority' that statesmen could call upon when pursuing the aim of cooperation and reconciliation.[127] There was an idealistic dimension to the premier's discussion of peacemaking. When Albert Thomas asserted that France's allies had greater faith in the realisation of a better future for international politics, Clemenceau's response was 'I am not so sure of that.'[128] Clemenceau's reflections on the nature of international security before the chamber in late December 1918 were more ambiguous than historians have tended to acknowledge.

This ambiguity was intended in part to preserve the government's freedom of manoeuvre: 'There are demands that I intend to make,' he informed the chamber, 'but I am not willing to share them with you at the moment. Why? Because some of them I can and perhaps must sacrifice to a larger interest.' There were abundant clues as to the nature of the 'larger interest' and to the inner core of the premier's vision of the post-war order. Both his own statements and those of foreign minister Pichon were replete with references to the importance of Allied unity in the post-war period. Although he was otherwise vague in his intervention, Pichon made no less than fourteen references to the importance of Allied solidarity and inter-Allied cooperation. 'Accord with our Allies', he insisted, 'brought us victory and it is this accord that will also deliver peace and justice to the world in the years to come.' Allied unity was the central theme of Clemenceau's intervention. He referred again and again to the crucial importance of prolonging the wartime coalition in peacetime. 'If we do not arrive at an accord with our Allies, our victory will have been in vain and the nightmares that we have just experienced will sooner or later return.'[129]

This Atlanticist orientation in Clemenceau's policy vision has not always been acknowledged in a historical literature that has tended to fixate on the Rhine. Yet the premier assured the chamber that the peacetime unity of the wartime Allies would be his 'directing thought' during peace negotiations. 'To

---

[126] Duroselle, *Clemenceau*, 526 on natural frontiers and 524–41 generally.
[127] *JO*, Chambre, *Débats*, 1918, second *séance*, 29 Dec. 1918. [128] Ibid. [129] Ibid.

this unity', he pledged, 'I will make every sacrifice.'[130] He would prove true to his word.

At the end of the First World War nationalist enthusiasm in France reached perhaps its highest levels since the revolutionary and Napoleonic eras. At the same time, however, France was more dependent on its allies in 1919 than at any point in its peacetime history. The gulf between domestic expectations of a peace of reparation and security guarantees, on the one hand, and the policy priorities of France's Great Power allies, on the other, did not augur well for a peace settlement that would satisfy either elite or popular opinion. The dilemma this posed to policy making was not immediately apparent in the febrile afterglow of victory. But external constraints on France's freedom of action would force its leaders to adjust their core security requirements in a process that much of the political and policy elite would find difficult to accept.

One of the most important but least understood aspects of both the domestic and international contexts of policy making was the emergence of new normative standards for state behaviour as a result of the conflict. Popular enthusiasm for a new approach to international politics posed a major challenge to the traditional predispositions of political elites and security professionals. The tendency in the existing literature to dismiss their engagement with self-determination and international organisation as mere window dressing has prevented scholars from posing two important questions. First, why did France's policy elite feel compelled to engage with these norms at all? Efforts to try to co-opt them into a more traditional policy are in themselves evidence of their power and agency. They could not simply be ignored.[131] Second, what were the consequences of this engagement? Incorporating the language of self-determination and the League would take French policy in unforeseen and often unintended directions in the medium and longer term. Accepting the principle of self-determination, for example, would also mean accepting the unity of Germany if arguments for independence were not embraced by the inhabitants of the Rhineland.

Of more immediate importance for peace planning, however, was support for a democratic settlement. The war, it is worth remembering, had been represented as a struggle between democratic freedoms and autocratic tyranny. A commitment to democratic freedoms underpinned hopes for eventual peaceful coexistence between France and a reformed and democratic Germany. In the aftermath of the First World War these hopes remained tentative and circumscribed even among committed internationalists. Yet they provided an

---

[130] Ibid.
[131] Mark Mazower has made a similar point in connection with Great Power engagement with the UN: 'even if it were true [that the UN was intended to be an instrument of great power politics], it would still remain important to see why certain powers at a certain point in history came to define their security needs in ways necessitating membership in a world body' (M. Mazower, *No Enchanted Palace: The End of Empire and the Ideological Origins of the United Nations* (Princeton, 2009), 10).

alternative vision of the long-term political future of Europe to which even premier Clemenceau could subscribe. The two chapters that follow will focus on the interplay between these alternative currents and the traditional impulses that continued to dominate the formulation of policy. The result, I hope, will be a more nuanced history of French policy that captures many of the ambiguities that have been lost in a literature that has focused overwhelmingly on French 'realism' at the peace conference.

7   Towards a post-war security order: the eastern settlement, economic security and the League of Nations

The foundations of a new political and economic order in Europe were laid down during three months of difficult negotiations beginning in mid-January and lasting through mid-April 1919. The traditional approach to security predominated in French policy towards eastern Europe and colonial issues. Traditional calculations were also influential in shaping the government's strategy for economic security. And yet alternative currents were also present in the security programme pursued by French officials. The government's proposal for a new commercial order aimed at enmeshing Germany in a system that would constrain its aggressive tendencies. There was also a significant impulse towards future Franco-German industrial cooperation within the policy elite. These aspects of the French peace programme cannot be reconciled with the traditional approach. Finally, while the government did not attach great importance to the League of Nations, the French delegates on the League of Nations Commission, Léon Bourgeois and Ferdinand Larnaude, fought hard for the juridical internationalist model of an international order based on the rule of law and collective force. There were, in other words, different and often contending currents in French security policy at the peace conference.

I

No aspect of French policy at the peace conference was more heavily influenced by the traditional approach than that towards the territorial settlement in eastern Europe. This was not least because it was the issue over which the Quai d'Orsay was given effective control. The eastern settlement demanded detailed regional knowledge, but was not a priority for Clemenceau. The foreign ministry, driven by Berthelot's undiminished energy and desire to dominate policy, was therefore able to assert its expertise and ensure that balance-of-power considerations remained at the centre of France's eastern policy.

All aspects of this policy were fraught with uncertainty owing to the frightful chaos that had engulfed Russia. If policy elites despaired at the state of their former ally, they were also remarkably reluctant to write off all hope of reviving the Russian counterweight to German power. France was the last of the Great

Powers to give up on the idea that Allied intervention could reverse the military and political tide and overthrow the Bolshevik regime. A central pillar of this commitment was the conviction that the Soviets remained the allies of German imperialism. And the operating assumption of foreign ministry officials was that Germany would 'continue to pursue a strategy of conquest and absorption to its east' in the post-war era.[1] Assessments emanating from both the foreign and defence ministries were replete with references to a 'Russo-German bloc' or a 'Germano-Bolshevik' alliance.[2] The constant flow of intelligence concerning Bolshevik efforts to stimulate revolution in western Europe only reinforced the existing desire among policy professionals to 'liberate Russia from both the German yoke and Bolshevik anarchy'.[3]

Just as important as fear of German-inspired Bolshevik subversion, however, were traditional conceptions of the European strategic balance. Underpinning nearly all policy prescriptions for eastern Europe in 1918–19 was the assumption that Russia would sooner or later resurface from revolutionary mayhem to resume its role as a European Great Power. Berthelot judged that Russia was undergoing an inevitable 'period of dissolution' prior to 'reforming itself and resuming its role as a great power'.[4] A subsequent foreign ministry note warned that France 'must reckon with the fact that Russia will re-emerge as a great power and will then ask of us what we have done for her, or against her'.[5] The army general staff was the most strident advocate of a large-scale intervention by 'free nations' to 'destroy Bolshevism, restore order and calm in Russia' so that it could 'take its place once again as an important factor in the European balance of forces'.[6] Clemenceau endorsed the judgement that such an outcome

---

[1] MAE, Série Z (Europe 1918–1940), Pologne, vol. 68, 'Le Territoire de la Pologne', DAPC analysis, 1 Mar. 1919.

[2] See, for example, MAE, Série Z, URSS, vol. 208, 'Plan d'ensemble d'action des Alliés en Russie', Pichon to Clemenceau, 1 Oct. 1918; Clemenceau to Pichon, 11 Oct. 1918; vol. 210, 'Une Méthode d'action en Russie', 4 Dec. 1918; PA-AP 141, Papiers Pichon, vol. 5, 'Le Problème russe et l'intervention japonaise', n.d.; SHD-DAT, Fonds Clemenceau, 6N 73, 'Coopération germano-russe', 8 Dec. 1918 and 'Note sur le plan d'action militaire de l'Entente', 2 Nov. 1918; 6N 81, 'Allemagne et le propagande bolcheviste dans les pays de l'Entente', 30 Apr. 1919. There was an anti-Semitic dimension to this analysis. Louis Barthou, for example, advised the senate foreign affairs commission that the Bolshevik movement was controlled by 'a cabal of Jews of German origin': France, Archives du sénat (hereafter AS), Commission des affaires étrangères du Sénat (hereafter CAES), vol. 1891, 69S 264, Barthou audition, séance of 12 Nov. 1917.

[3] MAE, Série Z, URSS, vol. 208, Clemenceau to Pichon, 11 Oct. 1918; on incoming intelligence see the voluminous material in SHD-DAT, Fonds Clemenceau, 6N 81 and MAE, Série Z, Allemagne, vol. 320, as well as summaries in MAE, PA-AP 141, Papiers Pichon, vol. 7.

[4] MAE, PA-AP 141, Papiers Pichon, vol. 5, 'Le Problème russe et l'intervention japonaise', marked '1er note de Berthelot', n.d. but certainly late Oct. 1918.

[5] MAE, Série Z, URSS, vol. 210, 'Une Méthode d'action en Russie', 4 Dec. 1918.

[6] MAE, Série Z, URSS, vol. 208, 'Note sur l'orientation de l'action des Alliés en Russie', 17 Oct. 1918; the author of this note, Lt. Col. Alphonse Georges, was chief of the operations bureau of the army general staff and a protégé of Foch.

was 'the only way to re-establish the European balance of power and to secure the benefits of a peace so laboriously acquired'.[7]

France's Great Power allies were increasingly unwilling to participate in such a venture. And, although Foch advocated large-scale intervention well into 1919, by January both the premier and the foreign ministry were resigned to a limited effort to contain Bolshevism and prevent Soviet–German collusion.[8] As early as 16 November 1918 Berthelot underlined the need to erect 'a *cordon sanitaire* against Bolshevism' until such time as its enemies inside the former Russian Empire were able to organise a credible military opposition.[9] Several weeks later the Quai d'Orsay produced yet another analysis based on the judgement that 'the reconstitution of Russia as it was in the time of the Tsars is not possible, not just and not desirable. From this fact flows important consequences for our policy.' Russian politics were compared to a brushfire raging out of control. The only short-term solution was to 'circumscribe its area of devastation' by 'tracing around it a security cordon'.[10]

Berthelot argued that intervention without substantial American, British or Japanese support threatened to 'drag us into commitments in both time and space that are well beyond both our means and the vital aims of our policy'. France must instead 'limit our action to our means'. In mid-January the DAPC judged Allied intervention a 'failure' and advocated instead construction of an 'armed barrage' based on Poland, Czechoslovakia and Romania. These judgements were further borne out by the mutiny of France's Black Sea fleet and the forced evacuation of Odessa.[11] Plans to construct a favourable balance of power in eastern Europe focused thereafter on the creation of strong 'successor states'.

This strategy, as we have seen, had long been present in French planning. It gained momentum after the armistice, however. A *tour d'horizon* prepared by the army staff in November envisaged a network of new states allied to France, each with enduring sources of enmity with either Germany or Italy. It recommended creating a powerful Yugoslavia, whose rivalry with Italy would allow France to bolster its influence by playing the role of arbitrator. It also welcomed the emergence of a Czechoslovakia that was 'clearly and necessarily anti-German' as a result of its intention to absorb the German population of Bohemia. This measure was judged indispensable to provide the new state

---

[7] MAE, *Série Z, URSS*, vol. 208, Clemenceau to Pichon, 23 Oct. 1918; much of this document is drawn word for word from the Georges memo cited above.
[8] K. Hovi, *Cordon Sanitaire or Barrière de l'Est? The Emergence of the New French European Alliance Policy, 1917–1919* (Turku, 1975), 168–74; D. Stevenson, *French War Aims against Germany, 1914–1919* (Oxford, 1982), 163–4.
[9] MAE, *Série Z, URSS*, vol. 224, 'Note sur l'action dans le sud de la Russie', 16 Nov. 1918.
[10] MAE, *Série Z, URSS*, vol. 210, 'Une Méthode d'action en Russie', 4 Dec. 1918.
[11] MAE, PA-AP 141, *Papiers Pichon*, vol. 5, Pichon (Berthelot) circular to Washington, London, Berne, the ministries of war, the *marine* and to Clemenceau, 29 Dec. 1918; MAE, *Série Z, Pologne*, vol. 68, 'Note pour le ministre', 14 Jan. 1919; see also Hovi, *Cordon Sanitaire*, 172–3 and A. Mayer, *The Politics and Diplomacy of Peacemaking: Containment and Counterrevolution at Versailles* (London, 1967), 481–3.

with defensible frontiers. But it would also constitute 'a permanent source of conflict with the Germanic world' and ensure Czechoslovak dependence on France. 'By its [geographic] position,' the study noted approvingly, 'this state threatens the heart of Germany.' It was therefore crucial to ensure 'the closest possible ties between the new Czech state and the anti-German powers of the west'. Romania was also allocated an important role in the nascent alliance bloc advocated by the general staff. Its population of 16 million made it 'the premier power in the Balkans' that 'must assume a preponderant place in all of our planning and initiatives in this region'.[12]

At the heart of the army general staff's vision was an assumption of permanent Franco-German tension. Eastern Europe would therefore need to be organised into an anti-German coalition that could offset, but never compensate fully, the loss of the Russian counterweight. The French naval staff concurred. Minister of the *marine* Georges Leygues summarised the views of his service when he observed in a note to the premier that 'we require, to assure our security in the future, not only positive guarantees on the Rhine, but also, and especially, guarantees that will result from the independence, the prosperity and the power of the nations that surround Germany to its north and east'.[13] This was also the judgement of a large number of parliamentarians. Before the chamber Franklin-Bouillon advocated the creation of a coalition of newly formed nation-states allied to France, which would function as 'the most solid barrier against Germany' as well as a vital tool to combat the spread of Bolshevism into Europe.[14]

The Quai d'Orsay continued to lead the way in arguing for an eastern counterweight. Foreign ministry officials were attracted by the prospect of close political and economic ties to an enlarged Romania. Its population and significant oil reserves were considered an important strategic asset. It was also considered a useful potential outlet for French manufactures. A DAPC memorandum in early January outlined these considerations and advocated support for Romania's territorial claims at the peace conference. The quid pro quo would be Romanian participation in France's strategic designs in eastern Europe. It recommended that France cement its influence in Romania through a combination of loans, investment and cultural imperialism.[15]

Senior officials were equally supportive of close ties to a strong Czechoslovakia. In September 1918, at Berthelot's initiative, the government had pledged to support virtually all Czechoslovak territorial claims. A team of French military advisers travelled to Bohemia to help deal with Sudeten

---

[12] SHD-DAT, *Fonds Clemenceau*, 6N 72–1, 'Note pour le 3ème Bureau', 23 Nov. 1918; summarised in BDIC, *Archives Klotz*, vol. 4, 'Propositions de l'état-major de l'armée'.
[13] SHD-DAT, *Fonds Clemenceau*, 6N 72–1 Leygues to Clemenceau, 25 Apr. 1919.
[14] *JO*, Chambre, *Débats*, 1918, second *séance*, 29 Dec. 1918.
[15] See Hovi, *Cordon Sanitaire*, 177–9 and G.-H. Soutou, 'L'Impérialisme du pauvre: la politique économique du gouvernement français en Europe centrale et orientale de 1918 à 1929', *RI*, 7 (1976), 221–3.

German agitation for *Anschluss* with Germany. A DAPC study of 20 December envisaged Czechoslovakia as a crucial link in 'a coalition of new states extending from the Baltic to the Mediterranean oriented clearly against Germany'.[16] In early 1919 the Czech leadership in Paris placed all Czechoslovak troops under the supreme command of Marshal Foch and agreed to host a French military mission in Prague (led by Foch protégé General Maurice Pellé) charged with training a new national army. From this point forward the mission became a symbol of Franco-Czechoslovak political and military cooperation.[17]

Poland was the most important member of the eastern coalition as it took shape in post-war planning. A foreign ministry memorandum of 4 December 1918 asserted that:

Since the reign of François I, France, in need of security, has always searched for an alliance with the power situated on the other side of Germany. But this power, for us, can now no longer be Russia. It must today be Poland and Bohemia. It is our interest to sponsor the creation of a greater Poland.[18]

Planning towards Poland was conceived squarely within the balance-of-power tradition in French strategy and diplomacy. A note by Georges Degrand entitled 'The need for a strong Poland' began with the observation that 'Germany will be definitively vanquished only if it loses its Polish provinces'; Degrand then invoked the tradition of an eastern counterweight to bolster French security on the Rhine. This function could only be properly fulfilled by a strong Poland allied to Bohemia and Romania. 'The stronger we make Poland at the expense of Germany,' Degrand advised, 'the greater the certainty that it will remain [Germany's] enemy.'[19] There is no purer expression of the traditional approach to security in all of the memoranda produced by the French policy machine in the era of the First World War than this memorandum by Degrand.

A reconstituted Poland with a large population, with possession of the rich coalfields of Upper Silesia (not part of its frontiers before the First Partition of 1772) and access to the sea, became a central pillar of the French peace programme. It was ranked second only to the issue of France's eastern frontiers in various lists of priorities produced by the foreign ministry in November and December 1918.[20] The army high command shared this assessment of Poland's importance. In early January Foch advised Clemenceau that the

---

[16] BDIC, *Archives Klotz*, vol. 14, untitled DAPC study of 20 Dec. 1918.
[17] Stevenson, *French War Aims*, 112, 137; A. Marès, 'Mission militaire et relations internationales: l'exemple franco-tchécoslovaque, 1918–1925', *Revue d'Histoire moderne et contemporaine*, 30 (1982), 559–86; and Hovi, *Cordon Sanitaire*, 156–9.
[18] MAE, *Série Z, URSS*, vol. 210, 'Une Méthode d'action en Russie', 4 Dec. 1918.
[19] MAE, *Série A*, vol. 61, 'Nécessité d'une Pologne forte', 20 Dec. 1918.
[20] MAE, PA-AP 141, *Papiers Pichon*, vol. 6, 'Préliminaires de paix avec l'Allemagne', undated Cambon note; 'Note sur les règlements de la paix', Berthelot note, 23 Déc. 1918; MAE, *Série A*, vol. 59, 'Mission militaire franco-polonaise', undated war ministry memo; BDIC, *Archives Klotz*, vol. 24, 'Eléments de la paix avec l'Allemagne', 13 Jan. 1919.

future of Poland was 'a question of the highest importance' for European security and must be given priority in the territorial settlements. He reiterated this judgement in subsequent notes to the premier and in conversations with other Allied officials.[21]

Two ad hoc committees met to hammer out France's position towards the frontiers of Czechoslovakia and Poland. The former, which included both Tardieu and Berthelot, underlined the political and strategic importance of Czechoslovakia in the 'anti-German barrage' the French government aimed to establish in the east. It therefore reaffirmed the government's earlier decision to support Czechoslovak claims to the frontiers of historical Bohemia. Special importance was attached to ensuring that the frontiers of the new state were viable in military terms. This meant giving it possession of predominantly (Sudeten) German areas in northern and southern Bohemia. In order to increase the new state's meagre reserves of raw materials, it was also decided to award it the largely Polish mining area of south-western Teschen. These measures created enduring sources of tension with both Germany and Poland.[22]

The subcommittee on Poland's frontiers, which included Tardieu, Degrand and Aubert as well as Foch's chief of staff General Auguste Le Rond, identified two central, if largely incompatible, principles. The first was to 'respect, *as much as possible*, ethnographical limits'.[23] The second was to 'organise a strong Poland' which would serve as a 'counter-weight to German ambitions' and a 'screen between Germany and Russia'. Significantly, access to the sea and defensible frontiers, particularly along the planned corridor through East Prussia, were given top priority. Also important, however, was the need to 'arbitrate as justly as possible the disputes that exist between Poland and its neighbours' so that they would together 'mass their forces more effectively against the *Deutschtum*'.[24] Improving relations between Poland and Czechoslovakia would remain an unfulfilled priority of France's eastern policy for the next twenty years.

To craft a case for this highly traditional policy conception, foreign ministry officials set to work addressing the implications of the principle of self-determination for a settlement in eastern Europe. There was no suggestion that the principle should be ignored, but there were arguments that it could not

---

[21] SHD-DAT, *Fonds Clemenceau*, 6N 53-3, Foch memoranda to Clemenceau, 9 Jan. and 18 Feb. 1919; HLRO, *David Lloyd George Papers*, F/89/2/24, note on a conversation between Foch and a British General du Cane, 18 Jan. 1919; *FRUS: PPC*, IV, 28-67: Council of Ten minutes for 24 and 25 Feb. 1919.

[22] MAE, PA-AP 166, *Papiers Tardieu*, vol. 314, 'Les Frontières de la Tchécoslovaquie', undated summary; see also P. Wandycz, *France and her Eastern Allies, 1919-1925: French-Czechoslovak-Polish Relations from the Paris Peace Conference to Locarno* (Minneapolis, 1962), 23-56.

[23] MAE, *Série Z, Pologne*, vol. 68, 'Pologne: conférence du 29 janvier 1919' (emphasis added).

[24] Ibid.; see also a DAPC memo entitled 'Le Territoire de la Pologne' in the same volume.

be applied systematically in a region characterised by centuries of migration and intermingling of ethnic groups. One study of this problem produced by the DAPC lamented the lack of any rigorous method for applying self-determination and advanced a critique that echoed Ernst Renan's reflections on nationalism and national identity:

> The worst thing is that there is no agreement as to the general principles to follow when undertaking the task of repartition. Indeed it must be admitted that scientific rules are of little value when it comes to determining the true nationality of a population, whether one should follow the language it uses or instead give priority to the nationality to which it imagines itself to belong and to which it remains attached.[25]

There was general agreement, in the end, that language must inevitably serve as the ultimate guide to nationality. But this was not ideal for the project to create strong successor states. Berthelot, drawing on a paper by Ernest Denis of the Comité d'études, pointed out that the 'language principle' provided Germans and Austrians with an unfair advantage because German had been the language of education and administration in the Hohenzollern and Habsburg empires. He argued that France must emphasise this factor when pressing for generous territorial settlements for new states.[26]

If the overriding aim was to create a network of states capable eventually of constituting a traditional counterweight to German power, the hope was also that Poland and Romania, in particular, could provide a 'screen' to prevent military cooperation between Germany and Bolshevik Russia. Jules Cambon described Poland as 'a rampart against Russian barbarism and a counterweight to German power'.[27] French officials pursued this policy assiduously during the peace conference. In subcommittees established to consider the frontiers of Poland, Czechoslovakia, Romania and Yugoslavia, they argued consistently that strategic factors must not be ignored in favour of self-determination.[28] Clemenceau pursued the same line of argument in the Council of Four. 'We must accept inevitable infringements to the principle of self-determination', he argued, 'if we wish to safeguard the principle itself.'[29]

---

[25] MAE, *Série A*, vol. 61, 'Note sur la délimitation entre eux des états Balkaniques et Danubiens et sur les dispositions accessoires qu'elle comporte', n.d. but certainly Dec. 1918 or early Jan. 1919.

[26] MAE, PA-AP 141, *Papiers Pichon*, 'Note sur les règlements de la paix', 23 Dec. 1918, drawing on MAE, *Série A*, vol. 288, untitled Comité d'études analysis, 1 Dec. 1918.

[27] Quoted in J. Baillou et al., *Les Affaires étrangères et le corps diplomatique français*, 2 vols. (Paris, 1984), II, 279; see also Hovi, *Cordon Sanitaire*, 154–217.

[28] See the dossiers produced by the Commission des affaires polonaises and the Commission des affaires tchèques in SHD-DAT, *Fonds Clemenceau*, 6N 74; see also *FRUS: PPC*, IV, 414–19 and 448–51: Council of Ten, 19 and 22 Mar. 1919 (Discussion of Poland) and 536–47, 601–12: Council of Ten, 1 and 23 Apr. 1919 (concerning Czechoslovakia); see also H. I. Nelson, *Land and Power: British and Allied Policy on Germany's Frontiers* (London, 1963), 282–311.

[29] Mantoux (ed.), *Conseil des quatre*, I, 42: 27 Mar. 1919.

This strategy was remarkably successful. Czechoslovakia obtained the important coal and industrial resources in the German-inhabited regions of historical Bohemia as well as defensible frontiers with both Germany and Austria. Romania was awarded large swathes of territory at the expense of Hungary, Bulgaria and Russia, and thus doubled both its territory and population. The frontiers of Yugoslavia were created to include key coastal areas on the Adriatic (including Fiume) coveted by Italy. A reconstituted Poland obtained nearly all of the former Prussian province of Posen and a substantial corridor to the Baltic Sea that cut East Prussia off from the rest of Germany. The port city of Danzig was internationalised under League of Nations protection, but with a customs union with Poland. Plebiscites were to determine the fate of Upper Silesia and the important strategic region of Marienwerder. The Polish settlement, in particular, was negotiated in the face of fierce opposition from Lloyd George, who warned against creating areas of '*Germania Irredenta*' that would trouble the future peace.[30] French negotiators persisted, however, and Poland emerged from the peace conference as a major regional power. Clemenceau and his advisers established the foundations for a potential anti-German coalition stretching from the Baltic to the Adriatic seas.[31]

Another issue where traditionally conceived French interests were in fundamental opposition with the doctrine of self-determination was the prospect of union between Germany and the ethnically German Austrian rump of the Habsburg Empire. The army general staff warned that such a development would establish a common frontier between Italy and Germany. Should the two states ever make common cause, this would 'render possible the creation of a single anti-French front stretching from the North Sea to the Mediterranean'.[32] Paul Cambon observed that Austria was a crucial intermediary state whose existence was necessary for the general effort to limit and contain German power.[33] Tardieu agreed, adding that an *Anschluss* would increase Germany's existing demographic superiority over France and place Czechoslovakia in an impossible strategic situation.[34]

Traditional considerations again trumped self-determination. French negotiators obtained a guarantee that Austro-German union could only take place if

---

[30] *FRUS: PPC*, IV, 414–19 and 448–51: Council of Ten, 19 and 22 Mar. 1919; quote from 417.
[31] Wandycz, *Eastern Allies*, 29–131; A. Sharp, *The Versailles Settlement: Peacemaking in Paris, 1919* (London, 1991), 130–58; M. MacMillan, *Paris 1919* (New York, 2001), 109–35, 207–56; Z. Steiner, *The Lights that Failed: European International History, 1919–1933* (Oxford, 2005), 51–5.
[32] BDIC, *Archives Klotz*, vol. 4, 'Propositions de l'état-major de l'armée', 23 Nov. 1918.
[33] MAE, *Série A*, vol. 110, 'Note au sujet de l'établissement d'une frontière commune entre l'Italie et l'Allemagne', 26 Feb. 1919.
[34] SHD-DAT, *Fonds Clemenceau*, 6N 75-2, 'Note relative à l'Autriche allemande', 17 Mar. 1919; see also Poincaré's views on the issue in MAE, PA-AP 141, *Papiers Pichon*, vol. 7, 'Textes relatif aux alliances', 23 Apr. 1919.

it was approved by the League Council. This gave France an effective veto over an *Anschluss* under the emerging treaty regime.[35] French policy towards Austria, as in other aspects of the settlement east of the Rhine, was largely successful in establishing the foundations of a pro-French security network. But the business of transforming the 'successor states' from a theoretical eastern counterweight to a united bloc of states cooperating effectively to maintain the status quo would prove much more challenging.

II

Post-war planning regarding the extra-European settlement rested to an even greater extent on traditional balance-of-power assumptions. If the peace settlement marked 'the climax of French imperial expansion', colonial issues were never central to the premier's vision of post-war security. On the one hand, this allowed the foreign and colonial ministries to exert decisive influence over policy in this domain. On the other, it meant that their planning could be ignored or dismissed by a premier whose priorities lay overwhelmingly in Europe.

The intellectual inspiration for the colonial programme came from an array of civil society associations aiming to promote French imperial interests such as the Société de géographie, the Comité de l'Afrique française and the Congrès français de la Syrie. Political patronage for this movement came from the Parti coloniale alliance in parliament. But neither movement possessed the necessary influence to shape the government's larger strategic designs.[36] The premier recognised that the war effort had benefited significantly from the resources drawn from 'greater France'. More than 555,000 colonial soldiers were mobilised after 1914 and more than 78,000 died during the war. Another 223,000 colonial workers had been employed in France's war industries. The premier had also come to understand that oil was an increasingly important source of industrial power and therefore national security.[37] But his overwhelming priority remained the frontier settlement between France and

---

[35] MAE, PA-AP 166, *Papiers Tardieu*, vol. 315, 'Indépendance de l'Autriche allemande', 20 Apr. 1919; Mantoux (ed.), *Conseil des quatres*, I, 461–2: 2 May 1919; Stevenson, *French War Aims*, 182–3; Nelson, *Land and Power*, 304–11.

[36] Pichon was a colonial enthusiast but failed to convert Clemenceau to the cause: C. Andrew and A. S. Kanya-Forstner, *France Overseas: The Great War and the Climax of French Imperial Expansion* (London, 1981), 164–79; see also M. Thomas, *The French Empire between the Wars: Imperialism, Politics, Policy* (Manchester, 2006), 93–124.

[37] The chief architects of French oil policy at this stage were Clémentel and Senator Henry Berenger, but there was inter-ministerial consensus on the strategic importance of oil; see R. Nayberg, 'Une Stratégie pétrolière pour la France: la défense des intérêts nationaux dans les conférences interalliées de 1918', *RH*, 590 (1994), 459–91; R. Nayberg, 'La Politique du française du pétrole à l'issue de la première guerre mondiale: perspectives et solutions', *GMCC*, 224 (2006), 111–33.

Germany, to which all other considerations were subordinated in his calculations.[38]

Plans drawn up by French officials considered the German and Ottoman Empires in essentially the same terms as colonial possessions in the peace settlements of the eighteenth and nineteenth centuries. Spoils were to be divided up according to the long tradition of imperial horse-trading. Despite the adjurations of Woodrow Wilson to consult the wishes of colonial subjects, the level of 'civilisation' in the German and Ottoman Empires was in general deemed insufficient for the application of self-determination. This was certainly the view of Gaston Doumergue, the most influential figure in the interministerial committee appointed to draft France's colonial aims. Doumergue's vision of the post-war imperial order departed little in substance from the long tradition of French colonial expansion stretching back more than three hundred years.[39]

Colonial minister Henry Simon, meanwhile, insisted that demanding sovereignty over German West Africa was a prerequisite for achieving the 'definitive unification of [France's] African empire' which constituted 'one of the best guarantees of political and economic power for future generations'.[40] A study by Emmanuel Peretti de la Rocca, of the Quai d'Orsay's Sous-direction d'Afrique, advocated exchanging some French interests in the Middle East for control of the entire West African coastline.[41] Planning for the Middle East envisaged implementing the Sykes–Picot Agreement of 1916 – an archimperialist arrangement that divided Ottoman Arab territories into zones of French and British domination – and cementing French influence in the region through the familiar strategy of cultural imperialism. Such a policy, submitted Robert de Caix, would ensure French power in the Levant for decades to come.[42]

The core attitudes and assumptions upon which French policy towards colonial repartition was based are distilled in a memorandum on the future of the Ottoman Empire written by Berthelot in mid-December 1918.[43] For Berthelot, Ottoman conduct with its 'exploitation of peoples of different race

---

[38] C. Carlier and G. Pédroncini (eds.), *Les Troupes coloniales dans la Grande Guerre* (Paris, 1997); M. Michel, *L'Appel à l'Afrique: contributions et réactions à l'effort de guerre en AOF, 1914–1919* (Paris, 1982); C. Andrew and A. S. Kanya-Forstner, 'France, Africa and the First World War', *Journal of African History*, 19, 1 (1978), 11–23; D. Watson, *Georges Clemenceau: A Political Biography* (London, 1974), 366–72.

[39] Andrew and Kanya-Forstner, *France Overseas*, 28–9, 56–63, 146–50.

[40] Quoted in ibid., 168; Thomas, *French Empire*, 38–9.

[41] MAE, *Série K (Afrique 1918–1940)*, vol. 116, 'Note de la sous-direction d'Afrique', 1 Dec. 1918, cited in Andrew and Kanya-Forstner, *France Overseas*, 169–70.

[42] BDIC, *Archives Klotz*, vol. 13, 'Note sur la liquidation de l'Empire ottoman et la constitution d'un état turc', n.d.; D. K. Fieldhouse, *Western Imperialism in the Middle East, 1914–1958* (Oxford, 2006), 44–66; G. Khoury, *Une Tutelle coloniale, écrits politiques de Robert de Caix* (Paris, 2006).

[43] SHD-DAT, *Fonds Clemenceau*, 6N 72, 'Plan de règlement des question d'Orient (Empire ottoman)', 12 Dec. 1918.

and superior civilisation' and its 'periodic massacre of its subjects' had demonstrated that it was 'the most diametrically opposed of all belligerents to the principles for which the Allies have fought'. It would therefore need to be dismantled and reorganised into various distinct polities. But this reorganisation could not be undertaken 'according to the same method adopted for Europe'. Since antiquity the populations of the region had been living side by side, and territorial division according to religion or ethnicity was impossible. Nor had they ever known political independence, having lived under Persian, Macedonian, Roman and then Turkish rule. A prolonged period of 'European tutelage and control' would thus be necessary before the peoples of the empire were ready to govern themselves. Berthelot advocated the internationalisation of the Dardanelles 'under the naval control of the Mediterranean powers' (by which he meant Britain and France). Constantinople and its environs would be established as a neutral state under the protection of the Great Powers until such time as the League of Nations was ready to assume responsibility for its administration. Berthelot even suggested that it be considered as a potential seat for the League.[44]

Turkey, meanwhile, would be reduced to the territory of Asia Minor and transformed into a virtual colony, without an army or navy and occupied by 'an international gendarmerie' recruited from the colonies of the European Great Powers. Armenia would be liberated and eventually become an independent state. In the interim 'a certain European surveillance' would be necessary as 'in these lands, riven by ethnic and religious hatred, only European commissioners can guarantee impartiality and security'. Berthelot evidently did not see the irony in this view, expressed as it was by a European in the aftermath of the greatest bloodletting in the history of the world.

The Arab territories would not be established as independent states but would be governed either directly or indirectly by Britain and France according to the stipulations of the Sykes–Picot accord, with both states sharing the profits arising from the oil extracted from the Mosul region in northern Mesopotamia. Berthelot advised that a crucial means of consolidating French power and influence was the establishment of French as the principal language of the cultured classes in the region stretching from southern Armenia and Cilicia in the north to the upper reaches of Palestine in the south. In this project for the future of the Middle East, Berthelot observed, France's 'moral interests' were 'in solidarity with its material interests'. Priority must be accorded to 'the extension of the benefits of civilisation' that would 'maintain the influence in the region that is an important part of the hereditary patrimony of France'.[45] When it came to the colonial settlement, Berthelot and his colleagues saw little need to engage with self-determination. In this domain,

[44] Ibid.   [45] Ibid.

France's 'civilising mission' was inseparable from the traditional pursuit of power and influence.[46]

Although Berthelot's careful argumentation provides compelling insight into the imperialist mindset of senior officials, it had little or no impact on government policy. The fact was that Clemenceau had already bargained away French 'rights' in Mosul and Palestine during a secret meeting with Lloyd George in London in early December. In exchange, he assumed that Britain would recognise French control of Cilicia, Syria and what is now Lebanon. Even more importantly, he believed that Lloyd George had undertaken to support French designs for Germany's western frontier. The Quai d'Orsay was neither consulted nor informed. When Lloyd George later failed to honour these alleged commitments (nothing was written down), the result was a series of violent confrontations that threatened to ruin Franco-British cooperation on wider issues.[47] The Ottoman settlement would continue to poison relations between the two states well into the next decade.

Ultimately, French and Allied plans to dominate Asia Minor and create a 'European' state based on Constantinople came to nothing as Turkey rebelled successfully against the terms of the Treaty of Sèvres. In the end German and Ottoman imperial possessions were divided into 'mandates' under the formal aegis of the League of Nations, but attributed in 'trusteeship' to Britain, France, Belgium, Australia, New Zealand, South Africa and Japan. Although these mandates were classified according to the supposed level of civilisation of their inhabitants, in practice the mandatory Great Powers were responsible for the administration and military security of the areas placed under their trusteeship. Mandates were governed in effect as colonies. France received control of present-day Syria and Lebanon, the majority of Cameroon and part of Togoland. Even this arrangement did not satisfy the imperialist predispositions of many policy elites, who tried to resist the mandate principle and argued instead for the concept of 'protectorates'. French officials lost this argument but were more successful in refusing to accept any restriction on France's right to raise a '*force noire*' from its African mandates should war return to Europe.[48]

In sum, if division of the colonial spoils was placed under the auspices of the League, the process was understood by French participants essentially as an exercise in traditional imperialism. Even Clemenceau found himself 'cynically disposing of people whose interests he did not understand and for whose fate he did not care'. Ironically, the power-political assumptions at the heart of the imperial idea meant that Clemenceau, an implacable opponent of French imperial expansion in the late nineteenth century, 'ended his career engaged

---

[46] Ibid.
[47] Andrew and Kanya-Forstner, *France Overseas*, 174–5; MacMillan, *Paris 1919*, 381–95.
[48] MAE, *SDN*, vol. 7, report on the mandate system by Hanotaux prepared for the 24th session of the CISDN commission; see also MacMillan, *Paris 1919*, 98–107; Thomas, *French Empire*, 17–89.

in one of the more disreputable episodes in the diplomacy of imperialism'.[49] The consequences of the settlement, and in particular the arbitrary and military-dominated political system put in place by the French in Syria and Lebanon, are still reverberating through the Middle East today.[50]

III

Planning for post-war economic security is best understood as part of a wider strategic conception aimed at constructing a transatlantic community of democratic Great Powers. This link between economic planning and overall policy has not been appreciated in the historiography. The same is true of the importance attributed to enmeshing and constraining Germany in the multilateral commercial regime advocated by the Clemenceau government. Ambiguity flowed through economic security planning as it did through other dimensions of the Clemenceau government's security strategy.

Historical writing about economic issues at the peace conference has been dominated by the reparations settlement with Germany.[51] Yet reparation was only part of the larger project to recalibrate the world economy and expand France's industrial base that had been under development in France since late 1915. Some scholars have interpreted this project as an attempt to overturn the pre-war Franco-German economic balance by imposing a settlement that placed the Reich in a situation of permanent commercial and industrial inferiority in relation to France.[52] Others stress the relative moderation of a programme that aimed at including rather than excluding Germany.[53] A look at this debate from the perspective of contending conceptions of security provides

---

[49] Andrew and Kanya-Forstner, *France Overseas*, 207.
[50] See esp. M. Thomas, *Empires of Intelligence? Security Services and Colonial Disorder in North Africa and the Middle East, 1914–40* (Berkeley, 2007); J.-D. Mizrahi, *Genèse de l'état mandataire* (Paris, 2003).
[51] A point made by Elisabeth Glaser in 'The Making of the Economic Peace' in M. Boemke, G. Feldman and E. Glaser (eds.), *The Treaty of Versailles: A Reassessment after 75 Years* (Cambridge, 1998), 371–99.
[52] J. Bariéty, 'Le Traité de Versailles et l'ambition d'industrialiser la France', *Revue d'Allemagne*, 30, 1 (1998), 41–52; J. Bariéty, *Les Relations franco-allemandes après la première guerre mondiale* (Paris, 1977), 134–48; G.-H. Soutou, *L'Or et le sang: les buts de guerre économiques de la Première Guerre mondiale* (Paris, 1989), 765–804; Stevenson, *French War Aims*, 136–60; D. Stevenson, 'France and the German Question in the Era of the First World War' in S. Schuker (ed.), *Deutschland und Frankreich Vom Konflikt zur Aussöhnung: Die Gestaltung der westeuropäischen Sicherheit 1914–1963* (Munich, 2000), 4–17; and P. Cohrs, *The Unfinished Peace after World War I* (Cambridge, 2006), 48–60.
[53] M. Trachtenberg, *Reparation in World Politics: France and European Economic Diplomacy, 1916–1923* (New York, 1980), 1–97; W. McDougall, 'Political economy versus national sovereignty: French structures for German economic integration after Versailles', *JMH*, 51 (1979), 4–23; S. Marks, 'Smoke and Mirrors: In Smoke-filled Rooms and the Galérie des Glaces' in Boemke et al. (eds.), *Treaty of Versailles*, 337–69; S. Marks, 'The myths of reparations', *Central European History*, 11, 3 (1978), 231–55.

a new perspective. The fact is that both impulses were present in French policy conceptions.

There were three interrelated strands to economic security planning in 1918–19. The first was the commerce ministry's conception of a post-war commercial order based on cooperation rather than competition. The second was the post-war financial settlement with Germany, and in particular the reparations payments that would be demanded from that country. The third was an ambitious project to expand France's iron and steel industry that included provisions to ensure access to the energy sources required to feed this expansion. Priority was given in the first instance to plans for a new international commercial regime.

Preparations for the post-war peace conference began in earnest within the ministry of commerce in late July 1918. Henri Hauser was again a central figure in this process. Responding to a request from Clémentel, Hauser produced a study of the 'principal economic questions' facing France at the end of the war.[54] His analysis rested on the assumption that German ambitions for continental economic dominance, as expressed in the peace treaties with Soviet Russia and Romania, would continue after the war. Fear that the war's end would provide Germany with favourable conditions in which to fashion a *Mitteleuropa* out of the ruins of central Europe haunted every aspect of French economic planning.[55] Hauser stressed that France, saddled with huge levels of external and internal debt and with its richest industrial departments in ruins, would be incapable of meeting this threat on its own. If a new economic order favourable to French recovery was not established at the peace conference, Germany would emerge victorious from the economic struggle despite having been defeated on the battlefield.[56]

Hauser therefore prescribed the creation of a 'West European Economic Union' as 'the only means of counter-balancing the homogenous force of *Mitteleuropa*'. At the heart of this union was the familiar concept of an international consortium for controlling the price of raw materials and regulating transport costs. On the 'vital condition' that it included the USA, such a consortium held out the possibility of using access to raw materials as a 'weapon' to force Germany to renounce its hegemonic economic ambitions.

---

[54] AN, F12 8106, 'Principales questions d'ordre économique dont le ministère de commerce aura à se préoccuper lors de la conclusion du traité du paix', n.d. but certainly early Aug. 1918.

[55] For these fears see also AN, F12 8104, 'La "Paix Allemande" de l'est et des avantages que l'Allemagne esperait en retirer', Aug. 1918; F12 8106, 'Ce que sera la tactique allemande à la Conférence de la paix en matière économique', Hauser memo, 25 Mar. 1918 and 'Introduction à l'étude de la conception allemande de la paix économique', versions from Jul. and Nov. 1918 and Feb. 1919 and 'Appendice à l'étude de la conception allemande de la paix économique', marked 'fin juillet 1918'.

[56] AN, F12, 8106, 'Principales questions d'ordre économique dont le ministère de commerce aura à se préoccuper lors de la conclusion du traité du paix', n.d. but certainly early Aug. 1918.

It would also free France's iron and steel industry from its dependence on German coal, coke and potash. Germany, in Hauser's vision, would retain the 'means' to 'live and prosper' within this system, but it would be deprived of the ability to dominate its smaller neighbours.[57]

This project would need to be combined, however, with a punitive commercial settlement that would remove the threat of German dumping and place restrictions on the Reich's ability to export during the period of France's recovery. It would also be necessary to ensure access to the German market for French exports (and in particular for raw materials and finished goods from Alsace and Lorraine). The final essential element of the economic panoply recommended by Hauser was the establishment of an international fund for reparation to make up the difference between what Germany and the other Central Powers owed and what they could pay. This system of reparation could be presented as a major concession on the part of the Allies and thus serve, in Hauser's words, as yet another 'useful mechanism of pressure' that could be used to induce German good behaviour.[58]

A familiar tension runs through Hauser's recommendations, which advocated a post-war economic order organised *against* Germany, on the one hand, but also a longer-term strategy aimed at *integrating* the Reich into a system that would constrain it, on the other. This tension was more pronounced in the programme for economic security developed by the commerce ministry in September 1918. This programme, drafted by Hauser and revised by Clémentel, was forwarded to Clemenceau in a bid to secure ministry control over economic planning for the peace conference.[59] Yet, where the emphasis of Hauser's July 1918 paper was on the construction of an anti-German economic system whose centre of gravity would be in Europe, the proposal forwarded to the premier was an ideologically charged vision of a transatlantic commercial consortium dominated by the victorious democracies operating under the umbrella of a league of nations.

The language used to articulate the commerce ministry's programme was internationalist. But a traditional aim to alter the economic balance also runs through the document. The chief strategy mooted was the imposition of a discriminatory commercial regime that would remain in place at least through the period of France's reconstruction. This regime would make a post-war *Mitteleuropa* impossible and remove the threat of German commercial dumping. Interestingly, there was also reference to the danger of an Anglo-Saxon-dominated global economy. To counter this, the recommendation was to create a new institutional framework for inter-Allied economic coordination. The solution proposed was an 'Atlantic Economic Union' within which France

---

[57] Ibid. [58] Ibid.
[59] AN, F12 8104, Clémentel to Clemenceau, 19 Sept. 1918; also published in Clémentel, *Politique économique*, 337–48. For insightful but fundamentally divergent analyses see Trachtenberg, *Reparation*, 15–22 and Soutou, *L'Or et le sang*, 766–9.

and Belgium would have the right to 'privileged treatment' (and thus Most Favoured Nation status). The envisaged union would not only exclude Germany but, in the first instance, would be directed against the Reich. The anti-German dimension to this system would function chiefly through use of the raw materials as an 'economic weapon' against German imperialism.

The commerce ministry's programme hinged on a system in which the victorious powers would collaborate in a rational distribution of their raw materials at fixed prices and arrange for transport at standard rates. This system would constitute a 'durable cement' that would bind France, the British empire and the USA in a post-war 'alliance'. It acknowledged that the American government was initially hostile to 'all measures of economic coercion aimed at Germany'. But there was optimism that this hostility could be overcome to secure the Wilson government's participation in French schemes.[60]

The strategy proposed for overcoming American opposition was to embed French plans within the future League of Nations. Clémentel embraced Tardieu's advice to 'present France's economic proposals under aegis of Wilson's principles'.[61] The first step was to construct an inter-Allied system of cooperation which could then be expanded and placed under the auspices of the League. Clémentel linked his programme explicitly to the regime of economic sanctions envisaged for the League. He also made repeated references to the need for an 'Atlantic Economic Union' or a 'Democratic Economic Union' that would, in turn, be part of the future League of Nations.[62]

On one level, deploying this language was an attempt to co-opt the principles of the League to promote a French programme. But to dismiss this connection as mere window dressing is to miss the crucial point that, to a significant degree, the 'Clémentel Plan' was inspired by an essentially internationalist vision of cooperation and interdependence. Its prescription for future economic security was the creation of a multilateral system based on economic cooperation. This cooperation would be restricted to the wartime Allies in the first instance. But it was not intended to remain a closed grouping. And its central purpose was not to destroy German power but instead to reintegrate Germany into a system that would constrain its aggressive economic impulses. 'Assuredly', Clémentel observed, 'it would be entirely foreign to the spirit of the Allies, once a just peace is concluded and the threat of German militarism removed, to deprive Germany of the means to live and get back to work.' Use of

[60] AN, F12 8104, Clémentel to Clemenceau, 19 Sept. 1918.
[61] AN, F12 8104, 'Réunion chez le président du conseil de MM. Clémenel, Pichon and Tardieu', 28 Sept. 1918.
[62] AN, F12 8104, Clémentel to Clemenceau, 19 Sept. 1918; Clémentel to Clemenceau, 31 Dec. 1918; MAE, *Série A*, vol. 59, 'Clauses économiques des préliminaires de paix: principes généraux', foreign ministry summary of commerce ministry proposals, n.d. but early Jan. 1918.

Towards a post-war security order 251

the 'economic arm' was envisaged as 'an effective means of recalling to Germany the need to respect its obligations as a civilised power'. The aim was to 'constrain German industry to collaborate peacefully with other nations'.[63] The multilateral character of this conception, and especially its aim to socialise Germany into a reconstructed world economy, was a significant departure from the traditional approach to security.

At the same time, balance-of-power calculations were undeniably important to the commerce ministry's programme. The participation of the USA, as 'the world's greatest economic power', was deemed a 'primordial factor' for the success of the French scheme. The growing importance of American power to French policy was clear at a meeting called to discuss Clémentel's proposals on 28 September 1918. In attendance, in addition to Clémentel, were Clemenceau, Pichon and Tardieu. Here it was agreed to adopt the programme as French economic policy. But Clemenceau and Pichon judged that priority must be given to securing American agreement before discussing the plan in London. Tardieu's very presence at this meeting testifies not only to his growing influence in policy making but also to the transatlantic focus of French thinking about post-war security.[64]

Economic planning within the policy establishment thereafter coalesced around the commerce ministry programme. The blockade ministry endorsed Clémentel's proposals in their entirety.[65] The Bureau d'études judged that a system of inter-Allied control and cooperation over raw materials provided a means of establishing 'a system of international security'. Former enemy states would only be granted membership in the envisaged economic consortium if they provided 'guarantees of sincerity and in particular the economic loyalty required to maintain the peace of the world'. The threat of economic sanctions could be used to socialise miscreant states into responsible behaviour and thus constituted 'a substantial guarantee of the new international order that is to be founded'.[66] Fernand Pila, from the Quai d'Orsay, characterised the machinery for inter-Allied wartime economic coordination as the League of Nations in embryo. Formalising a system of raw-material distribution during the 'transition period' was a step towards the creation of this institution. It would

---

[63] AN, F12 8104, Clémentel to Clemenceau, 31 Dec. 1918; as Marc Trachtenberg has pointed out, 'the aim was not to crush Germany' but instead to construct a 'system [that would] restrain German ambitions – both political and economic – up to the point where they no longer posed a threat': *Reparation*, 15–16.
[64] AN, F12 8104, 'Réunion chez le président du conseil de MM. Clémenel, Pichon and Tardieu', 28 Sept. 1918.
[65] MAE, *Série A*, vol. 59, 'Ministère du blocus: études et textes susceptibles d'être utilisés en vue de la préparation du traité de la paix', Dec. 1918; see also S. Jeannesson, 'La France et la levée de blocus interallié, 1918–1919', *GMCC*, 189 (1998), 51–73.
[66] MAE, *Série A*, vol. 59, 'Résumé des voeux et avis du Bureau d'études de la Presidence du Conseil concernant les dispositions à insérer dans les accords avec les Alliés', n.d. but certainly Dec. 1918.

minimise the effects of price instability and prevent the emergence of rival commercial blocs whose existence would 'imperil the peace of the world'.[67]

The great problem was that these plans hinged on American participation that was not forthcoming. On 27 September 1918 Wilson declared publicly that he opposed 'special economic combinations within the League' as well as 'any form of economic boycott' apart from the sanctions imposed by that organisation.[68] Even worse for the French scheme, Herbert Hoover, Wilson's chief economic adviser, was implacably hostile to 'any programme that even looks like inter-Allied control of our economic resources after peace'.[69] The French embassy in London warned that the Clémentel Plan would not fly in Washington. Cambon recommended a shift from advocating the creation of new inter-Allied commercial machinery to focus instead on maintaining and internationalising existing institutions such as the Inter-Allied Maritime Transport Commission. The aim was to maintain a framework in place to facilitate economic coordination in the short term that could eventually be transformed and made permanent under the auspices of the League.[70]

The commerce minister and his chief advisers were loath to abandon their vision of a new architecture for international commerce. Jean Monnet, serving as an army lieutenant on secondment as Clémentel's representative in London, warned that an immediate transition of the Allied economies from wartime state direction to unfettered market liberalism would cause severe economic and social problems and place Germany in a position to dominate European commerce after the war.[71] This scenario was at the heart of the more pessimistic set of proposals forwarded to Clemenceau by Clémentel in late December 1918.[72] In this document Clémentel articulated two visions of post-war economic security. The first was based on multilateral cooperation; the second on more traditional measures to alter the balance of industrial and commercial power. 'The Allies', Clémentel insisted,

> must decide if they will institute, thanks to measures taken in common accord, an economic organisation destined to assure the world, in the aftermath of its torment, a recovery with security; or if they envisage the only guarantee of this security a peace of reprisals and punishment.

---

[67] MAE, PA-AP 029, *Papiers Bourgeois*, vol. 14, 'Note pour M. Léon Bourgeois: clauses économiques des préliminaires de paix', 31 Oct. 1918.

[68] AN, F12 8104, 'Les Cinq conditions de Monsieur Wilson', n.d. but early Oct. 1918; speech reprinted in Scott, *Official Statements of War Aims*, 399–405.

[69] Cited in Trachtenberg, *Reparation*, 23.

[70] MAE, *Série A*, vol. 305, 'Note au sujet du rôle des organismes interalliés économiques après la cessation des hostilités', 3 Nov. 1918; see also Soutou, *L'Or et le sang*, 817–21.

[71] Monnet to Clémentel, 2 Nov. 1918, reprinted in E. Roussel, *Jean Monnet* (Paris, 1996), 73–5; see also J. Monnet, *Mémoires* (Paris, 1976), 83–4.

[72] AN, F12 8104, Clémentel to Clemenceau, 31 Dec. 1918; reprinted in Clémentel, *Politique économique*, 337–48.

Clémentel concluded with the warning that if the Allies chose an abrupt return to the competitive practices of the pre-1914 world economy, the result would be 'the return of national customs barriers and economic coalitions, both of which will be fearful for the peace of the world'.[73]

A peace based on 'economic organisation' was therefore essential and a necessary foundation for the League of Nations. Invoking the 'common mission of the Atlantic democracies', Clémentel argued for a post-war economic architecture based on 'principles of economic fairness' to create 'a regime of social balance based on democratic rights and duties'. Such a structure would rest on two key pillars: a system of raw-material sharing and a commercial regime that favoured those states engaged in post-war reconstruction. The former would provide the organisational framework for an 'economic league of nations' and eventually a 'society of nations' that would include Germany and the other Central Powers. The latter would establish a system of discrimination against Germany that would endure through the 'transition period' when the French economy would be rebuilt and recalibrated.[74]

The commercial regime outlined in Clémentel's 31 December memorandum was intended to establish the conditions necessary not only for French recovery but for a new commercial balance of power in Europe. Germany would lose its right to Most Favoured Nation status 'in general'. But it would grant this status to both France and Belgium unilaterally during the period of reconstruction. The Allies would also preserve the right to create 'favourable commercial combinations' from which Germany would be 'in principle' excluded. For French planners this meant creating a commercial zone that would include both Belgium and Luxembourg (the latter had been bound in a *Zollverein* with Prussia since the mid-nineteenth century). The aim was to deprive Germany of these two markets by creating a Franco-Belgian–Luxembourgeois customs area.[75] A Commission pour la rive gauche du Rhin was created within the Quai d'Orsay in early January 1919 to develop commercial links with the territories of the Left Bank. It was placed under the direction of Jacques Seydoux, a confidant of Berthelot's who was in the process of displacing Pila as the ministry's recognised expert on economic issues.[76]

Clémentel insisted that these measures were aimed at restoring the European economic balance. But he added that it was essential to build flexibility into the system so that the punitive measures envisaged could be 'attenuated' at the Allies' discretion. The clear expectation was that Germany

---

[73] AN, F12 8104, Clémentel to Clemenceau, 31 Dec. 1918; MAE, *Série A*, vol. 59, 'Clauses économiques des préliminaires de paix: principes généraux', foreign ministry summary of commerce ministry proposals, n.d. but early Jan. 1918.
[74] AN, F12 8104, Clémentel to Clemenceau, 31 Dec. 1918 (annex).
[75] See esp. E. Bussière, *La France, la Belgique et l'organisation économique de l'Europe, 1918–1935* (Paris, 1992), 19–21; and Soutou, *L'Or et le sang*, 794–800.
[76] S. Jeannesson, *Jacques Seydoux diplomate, 1870–1929* (Paris, 2013); Bariéty, *Relations franco-allemandes*, 39–40.

and other ex-enemies would eventually be included in the new economic order. 'We have no wish to ruin [Germany],' Clémentel stressed. 'There can be no question of revenge.' Once Germany provided 'evidence that it has embraced conceptions similar to those of the community of free nations', the punitive commercial regime imposed by the Allies could be withdrawn.[77] The long-term aim remained to enmesh Germany in a multilateral system that would constrain its aggressive economic impulses. The terms of enmeshment, however, would favour France.

A preference for an international solution based on cooperation between the Atlantic democracies also shaped initial reparations policy.[78] Commerce ministry officials cast doubt on both the feasibility and desirability of demanding huge sums in reparations from Germany after the war. Hauser stressed that Germany and its allies were incapable of paying for the full costs of war damage in France, Belgium and Italy. He also warned that large cash transfers from Germany would threaten France with 'enormous monetary inflation'. Extensive reparation in kind, meanwhile, might ultimately undermine France's industrial recovery by providing the Reich with a 'captive market' for its raw materials and manufactured goods. At the same time, however, if the economies of France and its allies were not compensated for the devastations they had suffered, Germany would enter the post-war period with decisive economic advantages.[79]

The solution Hauser proposed provides insight into the internationalist dimension to initial French policy towards reparations. A detailed accounting would be done to determine total war damages. The Central Powers would be declared liable for this sum, but not be required to pay the entire amount. A significant portion of the total figure would be financed by 'a sort of worldwide pool' to which all Allied states would contribute. The remainder would be charged to Germany and its allies in annuities to be paid over a lengthy term.[80] This multilateral solution to the reparation issue was linked to the League in Clémentel's 19 September memorandum to Clemenceau. Here the commerce minister acknowledged that '[financial] charges proportional to the damage caused would destroy the defeated party, reducing it to a state of economic servitude that would deprive humanity of all hope for a durable peace'. Germany, after accepting responsibility for causing the war, would instead pay a substantial portion of the reparation bill, mainly in shipments of coal, potash

---

[77] The proposed commercial regime is outlined in an 'introductory note' and an appendix to Clémentel's 31 Dec. missive to Clemenceau: see AN, F12 8104, 'Avant projet des clauses économiques des préliminaires de la paix: note introductive', Clémentel to Clemenceau, 31 Dec. 1918.

[78] For a comprehensive study of reparation see the studies by Marks, Kent and esp. Trachtenberg cited above; see also P. M. Burnett (ed.), *Reparation at the Paris Peace Conference from the Standpoint of the American Delegation*, 2 vols. (New York, 1940).

[79] AN, F12 8106, 'Principales questions d'ordre économique ...', Aug. 1918; F12 7985, 'Esquisse d'une politique économique de l'Europe occidentale', n.d. but Aug. 1918.

[80] AN, F12 8106, 'Principales questions d'ordre économique ...', Aug. 1918.

and other raw materials in annuities lasting twenty-five years. The remainder would be charged to a global reparations fund – with France and Belgium being given priority in the allocation of its resources. This fund would be represented as 'a moral advance conceded to Germany'.[81] Underpinning this logic, significantly, was the assumption that Germany would eventually be integrated into the post-war economic architecture to be created by the Allied states.

A final element in the French economic programme linked reparations to war debts. This aspect of French planning, which paralleled and may even have been inspired by thinking in London,[82] envisaged Britain and the USA annulling the war debts owed to them by France and Italy. The USA, in turn, would write off at least part of its loans to Britain. The objective was to reduce the strain that debt repayment would place on international economic recovery. Clémentel observed that the logical corollary to accepting relatively modest reparations payments from Germany was a 'commonly agreed revision and reduction' of France's war debts.[83] This linkage between reparations and war debts raised another issue that would bedevil France's relations with its wartime allies in the decade to come.

The commerce ministry's plans were endorsed by Clemenceau and Tardieu.[84] But they did not reflect a consensus view among the French political and industrial elite. Extensive state control over the nation's economic life was a permanent feature of Clémentel's vision of the future. Yet, as early as mid-December 1918, a group of parliamentarians led by the influential Radical senator Alfred Mascuraud demanded an end to such controls. The same demand was made by regional and national chambers of commerce.[85] The idea of demanding relatively modest reparations, meanwhile, was utterly at odds with public expectations that Germany would pay the full cost of the war. The strength of this feeling made it all but impossible for the Clemenceau government to agree to a definitive final reparations sum that recognised limitations on Germany's ability to pay. Equally important, by late December it was absolutely clear that the USA would refuse the French programme for a post-war trans-Atlantic raw-material and transport consortium.[86]

Clémentel and his advisers responded to the American refusal to participate by advocating a strategy of brinkmanship. Should the Wilson administration

---

[81] AN, F12 8104, Clémentel to Clemenceau, 19 Sept. 1918.
[82] MAE, PA-AP 029, *Papiers Bourgeois*, vol. 14, 'Mémorandum sur le développement de l'organisation interalliée actuellement existante'. This is a memo by British blockade minister Robert Cecil forwarded to Paris and marked 'proposé au War Cabinet', 31 Oct. 1918.
[83] AN, F12 8104, Clémentel to Clemenceau, 31 Dec. 1918.
[84] In addition to the meeting of 28 Sept. (cited above), see MAE, PA-AP 166, *Papiers Tardieu*, vol. 296, 'Préliminaires de paix: clauses économiques', Tardieu note, 10 Jan. 1919.
[85] Soutou, *L'Or et le sang*, 835–6.
[86] Trachtenberg, *Reparation*, 38–9; on the 'explosive importance' of reparations in public opinion see Marks, 'Smoke and Mirrors', 342; P. Miquel, *La Paix de Versailles et l'opinion publique française* (Paris, 1972), 433–60; and Stevenson, *French War Aims*, 138–9, 151–2, 168–9 and 175–7.

maintain its opposition, France must insist on a harsh peace that would render Germany incapable of defending itself in either military or economic terms. This would inevitably mean a demand for enormous reparations, including compensation not only for all war damages on land and at sea, but also for the industrial production that was lost to the need to shift the economy on to a war footing. But Clémentel made it clear that the demand for 'full reparations' would be subject to change if France secured 'in the form of Allied cooperation, corresponding guarantees of its economic recovery'.[87] This emphasis on reparations as bargaining leverage helps explain why French negotiators resisted specifying a final sum to be imposed on Germany. Clémentel argued that it would be a mistake to 'settle Germany's account' before a decision was made on 'the kind of economic order the Allies intend to establish'.[88]

In the end, American unwillingness to contemplate either a global consortium for natural resources or a link between reparations and war debts undermined the influence of the commerce minister. By mid-February Klotz and especially Loucheur had taken effective control of reparations negotiations.[89] The 'Clémentel Plan' had become a dead letter – and with it the aim to enmesh Germany in a transatlantic commercial system on terms favourable to France.

This did not mean that French policy aimed exclusively at crippling Germany, however. In fact, the strategy of using high reparations demands as leverage to obtain other concessions was retained. As Marc Trachtenberg has shown, Klotz and Loucheur appear to have worked in tandem in reparations negotiations, with the former making formal demands for large sums and the latter adopting a much more moderate position in private. Loucheur sat on both of the principal committees where reparations were debated during the peace conference. Throughout negotiations he demonstrated a moderation that placed him closer to the American position than to that of British officials who demanded that war pensions be included in the calculation of Germany's liability. A crucial objective from the French point of view was that Germany's reparations debt could be mobilised through the sale of bonds on the international money markets. This would ensure that all actors had a stake in Germany's fulfilment of its liabilities. Loucheur was intransigent only over the question of the percentage of reparations payments to be allotted to each of the Allied states.[90]

---

[87] AN, F12 8104, 'Avant projet ... note introductive', 31 Dec. 1918; Marc Trachtenberg was the first to identify this strategy in 'Reparation at the Paris Peace Conference', *JMH*, 51 (1979), 24–55.

[88] MAE, *Série A*, vol. 59, 'Préliminaires de paix: propositions du ministre des Finances', 27 Dec. 1918; AN, F12 8104, Clémentel to Clemenceau, 31 Dec. 1918.

[89] Trachtenberg, *Reparation*, 32–55; Sharp, *Versailles Settlement*, 99–100.

[90] SHD-DAT, *Fonds Clemenceau*, 6N 74, 'Règlement des réparations: matérialisation de la créance alliée', 5 Apr. 1919; L. Loucheur, *Carnets secrets, 1908–1932*, ed. J. de Launay (Paris, 1962), 14, 26 Mar. 1919: 69–70 and 73–4; Trachtenberg, *Reparation*, 40–72; B. Kent, *The Spoils of War: The Politics, Economics and Diplomacy of Reparations, 1918–1932* (Oxford, 1989), 70–6.

Loucheur's strategy, like that of Clémentel, did not take sufficient account of the strength of French public feeling over the question of reparations. In the end, Clemenceau refused to announce a relatively modest total figure that would enrage public opinion. In tandem with Lloyd George, he insisted that calculation of a final sum be put off until 1921. Wilson, who wanted to agree on a figure before presenting final terms to the Germans, was forced to give way. The peacemakers agreed on the creation of a reparations commission whose membership would be limited to France, Britain, the USA, Italy and either Japan or Yugoslavia (depending on the issue at hand). The commission would be charged with both determining Germany's total liability by May 1921 and managing procedures for payment. In the interim the Reich would make a payment of 20 billion gold marks to the Allies.[91] The difficult questions connected to reparations were therefore put off.

Whatever the merits of this decision not to decide, it cannot be attributed to a traditional aspiration to ruin Germany in a bid for French economic hegemony in Europe. As Tardieu acknowledged in an internal note of 5 April, the operating assumption among policy makers was that Germany would be forced to pay only a fraction of the final sum when it was finally determined. The French public was not ready to accept this hard reality in early 1919.[92] For both Clemenceau and Tardieu, reparations were at least as important for their leverage value as for their financial benefit. If this study has separated various themes of peace making for the sake of analytical focus, it is important to remember that negotiations over territorial and financial issues took place simultaneously in Paris. A crucial link existed in the French negotiating strategy between reparations payments and the occupation of the Rhine (discussed in the next chapter).

But this was not the only form of bargaining capital the premier and his team intended to use. There was also hope that reparations would provide useful leverage in secret bilateral negotiations with Germany. Direct dialogue with German officials, like other aspects of French plans for economic security, does not fit with the standard picture of a traditional bid for domination. Clandestine discussions concerning future economic relations were first undertaken in February 1919 through the offices of François-Émile Haguenin, professor of French literature at the University of Berlin and a prominent advocate of Franco-German cooperation before the war. Haguenin had spent much of the conflict as head of the French secret intelligence station in Berne, where he had at times served as a useful conduit for

---

[91] Mantoux (ed.), *Conseil des quatre*, I, 26, 28 Mar. 1919: 24–40, 58–62; Stevenson, *French War Aims*, 168–9, 175–7; and Sharp, *Versailles Settlement*, 33–5 and 87–95.

[92] SHD-DAT, *Fonds Clemenceau*, 6N 74, 'Règlement des réparations', marked 'De la part de M. Tardieu', 5 Apr. 1919. It was envisaged that Germany would make up to half its annual payments in paper marks, which reduced any total sum by up to half: see Mantoux (ed.), *Conseil des quatre*, I, 26 Mar. 1919: 24–40; Marks, 'Myths of reparations'; and Sharp, *Versailles Settlement*, 90–1.

deniable communications with the Germans.[93] In February 1919 he was sent to Berlin with instructions to report on the situation and to make unofficial contact with leading German politicians and industrialists. Here Haguenin became an early advocate of cooperation with Germany to facilitate France's economic reconstruction. Invoking the authority of both Clemenceau and Poincaré, he broached the subject with German officials in April–May 1919. Although his initiatives were unsuccessful, Haguenin continued to recommend collaboration with a reformed Germany as an important pillar of post-war security.[94]

A second secret channel of communication was opened by the junior diplomat René Massigli. A *normalien* and an academic historian who specialised in Germany, Massigli was recruited into the Quai d'Orsay during the war and posted with Haguenin in Berne. A perceptive and independent-minded *protégé* of Berthelot, Massigli would forge a glittering career at the Quai d'Orsay and become one of the most celebrated diplomats of his generation.[95] In the spring of 1919 he was attached to the peace conference secretariat. It was during this period that he became the key French interlocutor in secret communications with the German delegation. In May he met with Fritz Thyssen, an expert on iron and steel in the German delegation and a member of the Thyssen industrial dynasty in the Ruhr. Thyssen suggested that a 'true community of interests' existed between France and Germany over coal and iron ore. Massigli, in turn, observed that certain treaty stipulations could be revised if an understanding was reached over German cooperation in France's post-war reconstruction.[96]

In the end these conversations came to nothing. German officials were interested mainly in securing revision of the territorial aspects of the treaty. But the episode provides further evidence of a disposition within the Clemenceau government towards engagement with Germany. Massigli was at this stage far too junior to undertake such an initiative without the approval of senior officials. His

---

[93] J.-C. Montant, 'Émile Haguenin, "un homme d'influence"' in J.-J. Pollet and A.-M. Saint-Gille (eds.), *Écritures franco-allemandes de la Grande Guerre* (Arras, 1996), 114–26; M. Aballea, 'Une Diplomatie de professeurs au coeur de l'Allemagne vaincue: la mission Haguenin à Berlin (mars 1919–juin 1920)', *RI*, 150 (2012), 23–36.

[94] Haguenin's reports can be consulted in MAE, *Série Z, Allemagne*, vols. 7–17; see also Stevenson, *French War Aims*, 143, 189–90; G.-H. Soutou, 'The French Peacemakers and their Homefront' in Boemke et al. (eds.), *Treaty of Versailles*, 179–80; P. Krüger, *Deustchland und die Reparationen 1918/19: die Genesis des Reparationsproblems in Deutschland zwischen Waffenstillstand une Versailles Friedensschluss* (Stuttgart, 1973), 134–7; and Glaser, 'The Making of the Economic Peace', 393–4.

[95] See the excellent R. Ulrich-Pier, *René Massigli (1888–1988): une vie de diplomate*, 2 vols. (Brussels, 2006).

[96] MAE, PA-AP 217, *Papiers René Massigli*, vol. 13, untitled report, 12 May 1919; MAE, *Série Z, Sarre*, vol. 1, untitled report, 15 May 1919; see also Ulrich-Pier, *Massigli*, I, 63–6 and Trachtenberg, *Reparation*, 86–7. Bitter experience during the period 1935–45 would make Massigli much less enthusiastic about Franco-German collaboration in the post-1945 era.

activity should therefore be understood as expressing a wider current in official thinking. The strategy of direct engagement to facilitate economic cooperation would be taken up by both Loucheur and Seydoux in the aftermath of the peace conference and again by the Briand government in 1921. Massigli, meanwhile, would remain an advocate of collaborating with Germany from a position of strength through to the mid-1930s.

Clandestine discussions with German officials were connected to a final important strand in planning for economic security: the need to expand France's industrial base while at the same time ensuring access to the energy resources required to drive this expansion. The aim to alter the Franco-German industrial balance, particularly in iron and steel production, was at the heart of this project. With the return of Alsace-Lorraine it was expected that France would need to import more than 40 per cent of its coal and nearly 65 per cent of its requirements in metallurgical coke. These considerations, combined with the damage done to France's coal industry by the Germans, underpinned the French case for annexing the Saar coalfield. Laroche argued that German control of the Saar would leave France in a situation of 'unacceptable economic dependence' that would 'render its security precarious'.[97] Berthelot concurred that coal from this region was

indispensable for the prosperity of our metallurgical industries, which are, it must be emphasised, a vital element in the general organisation of a great power and form one of the pillars of its defence ... The security of the frontier and the economic independence of France militate equally for the return to our country of the mining district of the Saar.[98]

Access to energy was a core consideration in calculations of power and security.

Yet, because the Saar produced almost no surplus coke, it was critical that German reparations in kind included a steady flow of this crucial material. The commerce ministry called for Germany to make annual deliveries of 35 million tonnes of coal for twenty-five years, half of which was to be in coking coal.[99] The general staff went much further to advocate seizing control of German mines in Westphalia as compensation for the damage done to French industry and as a guarantee for reparations.[100] Loucheur, who was in charge of these

---

[97] MAE, *Série A*, vol. 289, 'La Frontière de l'Alsace-Lorraine et le statut de la rive gauche du Rhin', 1 Nov. 1918.
[98] MAE, *Série A*, vol. 289, 'Note sur la future frontière entre l'Alsace-Lorraine et l'Allemagne: raisons stratégiques, économiques et politiques', 10 Nov. 1918; see also Bariéty, *Relations franco-allemandes*, 126–71.
[99] AN, F12 8106, 'Principes économiques généraux pour la préparation du traité de paix', undated note; F12 8104, Clémentel to Clemenceau, 31 Dec. 1918 (annex). The finance ministry endorsed these figures: ibid., 'Dispositions à inscrire dans les préliminaires de paix', 30 Nov. 1918 and AN, F12 8036, Klotz to Pichon, 13 Dec. 1918. See also Soutou, *L'Or et le sang*, 779–80 and J.-N. Jeanneney, *François de Wendel en république: l'argent et pouvoir 1914–1940* (Paris, 1976), 118–20.
[100] MAE, *Série A*, vol. 59, 'Question du charbon', 30 Nov. 1918.

negotiations and did not wish to rule out Franco-German industrial cooperation, eventually settled for annual German coal deliveries of 20 million tonnes for five years and then 7–8 million tonnes for the next fifteen years, with up to three-quarters of this amount in coking coal. France also received ownership of the mines and infrastructure of the Saar. Taken together, these treaty benefits – virtually all of which were obtained at the expense of Germany – freed France from its wartime dependence on British coal and coke, and would play an important role in the extraordinary recovery and expansion of French heavy industry in the post-war decade.[101]

The importance attached to post-war energy policy must be understood in conjunction with the project to reduce and, if possible, end German dominance in European iron and steel.[102] The return of Lorraine, along with an end to German economic control of Luxembourg and the occupation of the Saar, were all central to this project. As a result of these treaty arrangements Germany lost 80 per cent of its pre-war iron ore and 36 per cent of its steel production.[103] Moreover, with French control of the Saar and the eventual cession of most of Upper Silesia to Poland, German coal production was reduced by nearly half.[104] By 1926 France's steel production had more than doubled and its share of west European iron and steel output increased from 13 to 32 per cent. Germany's share, meanwhile, fell from 65 to 41 per cent.[105]

Yet behind this overall strategy of improving the relative position of France's heavy industry were interesting divergences among French elites. A significant number of policy and political elites, in particular Hauser at the commerce ministry, Berthelot and Laroche at the Quai d'Orsay and many nationalists within the chamber, hoped to establish conditions that would enable France's metallurgical industry to surpass that of Germany. German iron and steel production, it was assumed, would suffer greatly if deprived of a steady flow of iron ore from Lorraine.[106] Against this traditional aim of overthrowing the Franco-German industrial balance was the preference among many industrialists to return to pre-1914 practices of industrial cooperation based on 'natural' commercial arrangements in which France sold its iron ore to Germany and purchased coal and coke in return.[107] A third current envisaged state

---

[101] Bariéty, *Relations franco-allemandes*, 138–40; Soutou, *L'Or et le sang*, 779–80; C. Feinstein, P. Temin and G. Toniolo, *The European Economy between the Wars* (Oxford, 1997), 55–62.
[102] Key studies are Bariéty, *Relations franco-allemandes*, 140–9 and Soutou, *L'Or et le sang*, 801–6.
[103] J. Bariéty, 'France and the Politics of Steel, 1919–1926' in R. Boyce (ed.), *French Foreign and Defence Policy, 1918–1939: The Decline and Fall of a Great Power* (London, 1998), 33–5; Soutou, *L'Or et le sang*, 801–2.
[104] Bariéty, *Relations franco-allemandes*, 138–40.
[105] Bariéty, 'France and the Politics of Steel', 44.   [106] Soutou, *L'Or et le sang*, 802–3.
[107] Bariéty, *Relations franco-allemandes*, 141–4. The Comité des forges was attacked by the right of the chamber for lacking patriotism and by the left for its self-interested perspective. Perhaps for this reason it was not consulted officially by the government: see Miquel, *Opinion publique*, 505–7; Soutou, 'French Peacemakers', 168–70; Jeanneney, *L'Argent et le pouvoir*, 120–2.

intervention to create a vast iron and steel cartel that would include France, Belgium, Luxembourg and Germany. This was the strategy eventually pursued by Loucheur in the summer of 1919 and again in 1921. As one eminent scholar of the economic peace has observed, the inspiration for this project was 'not to crush or to boycott Germany' but instead to construct a new industrial relationship that would if anything be 'closer than those that existed before the war'. The key difference would be that France would be negotiating from a much stronger position thanks to the military victory of 1918.[108] Loucheur's ultimate aim, like that of Clémentel, was to enmesh and constrain Germany.

The commercial and financial stipulations of the Treaty of Versailles left the way open for pursuit of all three approaches. Under the final treaty terms France had the right to deny Germany access to iron ore from Lorraine and Luxembourg, to resume the commercial arrangements of the pre-war era or to use access to iron ore to put pressure on German industry to agree to a larger cartel.[109] And this ambiguity and flexibility was characteristic of the commercial regime imposed by the treaty as a whole. Germany was forced to accord the Allies Most Favoured Nation privileges without reciprocity (Arts. 264–6 of the Treaty of Versailles) and was prevented from dumping and other unfair practices (Arts. 274–5). This was without doubt a punitive regime. But it was intended to restore balance to European commerce and to establish favourable conditions for recovery and reconstruction in France and Belgium. It was not aimed at crippling the German economy permanently. The economic clauses were not the subject of acrimonious debate among the peacemakers. Indeed, US officials were just as uncompromising in their determination to punish Germany as were their French and British counterparts. The intention was to impose temporary restrictions that would encourage the Reich to abandon future commercial aggression. The commercial regime imposed by the treaty was therefore to remain in effect for five years with the possibility of its prolongation at the discretion of the League Council (Art. 280).[110]

French policy for economic security, to sum up, was an interesting combination of traditional and internationalist currents. The impulse to overthrow the economic balance of power existed alongside visions of ensnaring Germany in a transatlantic commercial system that would constrain its aggressive impulses and provide favourable conditions for French economic recovery. Both of these currents are discernible in the financial and commercial terms imposed by the Versailles Treaty. Georges-Henri Soutou is certainly right to characterise the treaty as 'an essentially dynamic ensemble' that opened the

---

[108] Quote from Soutou, *L'Or et le sang*, 804; G.-H. Soutou, 'Une Autre politique? Les Tentatives françaises d'entente économique avec l'Allemagne, 1919–1921', *Revue d'Allemagne*, 8, 1 (1976), 21–34.
[109] See Soutou's succinct but penetrating analysis in *L'Or et le sang*, 804–6.
[110] See the analyses of Glaser, 'The Making of the Economic Peace'; Soutou, *L'Or et le sang*, 839–43; and Steiner, *Lights that Failed*, 61–2.

way for strategies of either punishment or engagement.[111] French policy makers would be tempted by both alternatives in the immediate post-war era.

IV

Policy towards the League of Nations is the least well-understood aspect of French security conceptions at the peace conference. The prevailing judgement that 'the French idea [for the League] was in essence an enlarged defensive alliance against a revived Germany' ignores the important distinction between the more traditional conceptions of mainstream officials and the juridical internationalist vision of the French delegates on the League of Nations Commission.[112]

It is true that few government officials placed much hope in a 'society of nations' as a source of security in itself. Most instead hoped to use the project as a means of cementing cooperation with Britain and especially the USA. Clemenceau and Tardieu were resolved to use the negotiations concerning the creation of the League as bargaining leverage to obtain British and American concessions in other aspects of the peace settlement. But Léon Bourgeois and Ferdinand Larnaude, the French representatives on the League Commission, pursued a highly juridical conception of the League that was much more than a de facto alliance of Great Powers.[113] They aimed to implement the CISDN programme and make the new institution a vehicle for imposing a binding regime of international law backed up by robust sanctions and an international armed force.

Bourgeois had outlined his vision of a future international organisation in a series of public interviews and published writings in late 1918. At the heart of his conception was the solidarist notion of a society of individuals joined by common cultural values as well as mutual obligations set down in law. He maintained the conviction that, although the League must have a 'universal tendency', its membership would be restricted initially to democratic states who acknowledged 'the reign of law'. Germany could only become a member of this society once it had demonstrated its democratic credentials.[114]

---

[111] Quote from Soutou, *L'Or et le sang*, 839.

[112] Quote from Steiner, *Lights that Failed*, 43; see also Miquel, *Opinion publique*, 167; P. Yearwood, *Guarantee of Peace: The League of Nations in British Policy, 1914–1925* (Oxford, 2009), esp. 114–15; D. Stevenson, *The First World War and International Politics* (Oxford, 1988), 266; D. Stevenson, 'Britain, France and the origins of German disarmament, 1916–1919', *JSS*, 29, 2 (2006), 204–5; A. Williams, *Failed Imagination? New World Orders of the Twentieth Century* (Manchester, 1998), 54–7.

[113] Excellent syntheses are Sharp, *Versailles Settlement*, 42–64; MacMillan, *Paris 1919*, 83–97; D. Armstrong and L. Lloyd, *From Versailles to Maastricht: International Organisation in the Twentieth Century* (London, 1996), 7–32.

[114] Quoted in Bourgeois, *Pacte de 1919*, 50 and 51–2; see also M. Sorlot, *Léon Bourgeois: un moraliste en politique* (Paris, 2005), 274–82.

The theoretical underpinnings of this vision of the League are evident in Bourgeois' inaugural address to the AFSDN on the eve of the armistice.[115] Here he deployed the quintessentially French argument that a society could not exist without a constitution. Invoking the Declaration of the Rights of Man, he asserted that the history of international relations, like the political history of states, was the story of a progressive campaign to assure the rights of individuals in a true society: 'The universal war of the present has demonstrated to all nations the need to have between them a constitution that guarantees the rights of all.' Peace could not be achieved without an established body of public law.[116]

This *solidarité*-inspired theory of international relations would gain few adherents among policy elites in 1919. Bourgeois was aware that his vision would prove anathema to traditionally minded advocates of a new balance of power. He was therefore at pains to reject charges of utopianism: 'I do not ignore the dangers of selfishness, of interests, of the unhealthy passions that are a permanent feature of humanity.' Nor, he continued, did he believe in 'the perfectibility of mankind, and still less of groups of men'. Yet he stressed the distinction between his ideas and traditional methods based on the balance of power:

Will the world continue to subject itself to further suffering by looking for security in the methods of the past? Even today many believe that they prove their patriotism in searching to establish the conditions of a durable peace solely in the destruction of the enemy. For them, it is sufficient to secure rigorous territorial guarantees and to establish powerful new military frontiers ... these practices have never brought peace and security to humanity.

The only way to control 'violent and aggressive human impulses', Bourgeois concluded, was to 'contain them in a regime of law'.[117]

This emphasis on law as the key to international peace did not rest on a more sanguine interpretation of the short-term challenge posed by Germany. Bourgeois and the majority of his internationalist colleagues shared the bleak assessment of Germany that dominated the French public sphere in 1918–19. Where they diverged was in the solution they advocated for dealing with this problem in the longer term. Germany, for Bourgeois, represented the antithesis of the ideal member of a society based on mutual rights and obligations. It was in the Reich, conversely, where 'the tragic doctrine of force over law' had become 'a sacred tenet of state policy'. Before it could become eligible for membership in the new international organisation, Germany would have to undergo 'a moral revolution much more far reaching than mere cosmetic changes to its political system'. The most reliable evidence that such a

---

[115] MAE, *SDN*, vol. 7, 'Discours prononcé à l'Assemblée générale constitutive du 10 novembre 1918 par M. Léon Bourgeois' (Paris, 1918).
[116] Ibid.   [117] Ibid.

revolution had taken place would be fulfilment of the peace terms to be imposed by the Allies, in particular reparation of war damages and the dismantling of its military and defence industry.

Bourgeois and other internationalists departed from the mainstream most radically in their belief that membership in the League could eventually have a positive socialising effect on German behaviour. Such membership would give the German people a stake in the society of mutual rights and obligations to which it would belong. Germany would, for example, submit to 'a regime of international verification' to give assurance that it had complied with its disarmament obligations. But it would not be singled out in this regard. Instead, 'all nations will submit to the same system of inspection'.[118] The idea that Great Powers would agree to international surveillance of their armaments policies was certainly naïve. It highlights the contradiction at the heart of a juridical conception of the League. On the one hand, French internationalists assumed that League members would willingly agree to obey the rule of international law. On the other, they decried any intention of creating an overarching sovereignty for the League that would threaten the individual rights of its members. The fact that most did not see the contradiction in their position reflects the centrality of codified law in the juridical internationalist position.

Bourgeois was unequivocal in his conviction that the only way to establish a stable world order was to establish a powerful international legal regime. 'It is not a matter of denying force,' he argued, once again invoking Pascal, 'it is a matter of making it the servant and guardian of international justice.' This, he insisted, was to develop the work begun by the two Hague Peace Conferences. The 'two primordial tasks' facing a new international organisation were, first, to make the arbitration of international disputes compulsory and, second, to provide the resulting international legal regime with powerful collective force to impose sanctions on recalcitrant states.[119] This conception of the League was much more than a mere prolongation of the wartime alliance. It envisaged a revolution in international politics no less radical than that advocated by Woodrow Wilson and other proponents of a new global order.

There were warning signs, however, that neither the Americans nor the British shared the legalist assumptions underpinning the French conception. A study of British thinking by Henri Fromageot observed that, although they attributed a prominent role to arbitration, British projects did not 'conceive of a truly international jurisdiction' and allotted no apparent role to the Permanent Court of Arbitration at the Hague. Just as importantly, the British version of a League Council of Great Powers would not have executive powers. It would have authority only to deliberate and recommend action to its members.[120]

---

[118] Ibid.   [119] Ibid.
[120] MAE, *SDN*, vol. 5, 'Observations concernant les travaux de la Commission britannique sur la Ligue des nations', 18 Sept. 1918.

Another warning sign was the publication of *The League of Nations: A Practical Suggestion* by Jan Christiaan Smuts in late 1918. Smuts, the South African foreign minister and a member of Lloyd George's war cabinet, advocated a League whose chief functions would be to provide Anglo-American moral leadership to the world and to consolidate the British Empire. This approach to international organisation, as one unidentified member of the CISDN observed, was 'entirely foreign' to the French conception.[121] Robert Cecil, another prominent British advocate of the League, initially favoured the more conservative notion of a resurrection of the Concert of Europe. But his views evolved after the armistice to end up much closer to those of Smuts.[122]

Across the Atlantic a number of prominent voices in American civil society advocated a 'legalist–sanctionist' conception of the League that was close to the juridical internationalist model in France.[123] The aim was to create an organisation that would have as its core a clearly defined contract to defend the rule of international law with organised collective force.[124] But Woodrow Wilson had little time for such legalist conceptions. Law, for him, was a momentary codification of social circumstances that were evolving constantly. It could not serve as a basis for politics. Wilson advocated instead a more open-ended approach to facilitate the moral regeneration of international politics by 'responding to the collective aspirations of humanity'. For Wilson the overriding sanction of the League would be 'the great force of common conscience'.[125] His initial draft of a covenant for the League made no mention of

---

[121] MAE, *SDN*, vol. 6, 'Tableau des différents systèmes de "Société des nations"', n.d. but certainly late Jan. or early Feb. 1919.

[122] On British approaches see G. W. Egerton, *Great Britain and the Creation of the League of Nations: Strategy, Politics and International Organisation, 1914–1919* (Chapel Hill, 1978); J. Morefield, *Covenants without Swords: Idealist Imperialism and the Spirit of Empire* (Princeton, 2005); Yearwood, *Guarantee of Peace*, 8–87; and 'Jan Smuts and Imperial Internationalism' and 'Alfred Zimmern and the Empire of Freedom' in M. Mazower, *No Enchanted Palace: The End of Empire and the Ideological Origins of the United Nations* (Princeton, 2009), 28–65 and 66–103.

[123] S. Wertheim, 'The league that wasn't: American designs for a legalist–sanctionist League of Nations and the intellectual origins of international organization, 1914–1920', *Diplomatic History*, 35, 5 (2011), 797–836; W. F. Kuehl, *Seeking World Order: The United States and International Organizations to 1920* (Nashville, 1969), 215–40; C. Bouchard, *Le Citoyen et l'ordre mondial (1914–1918): le rêve d'une paix durable au lendemain de la Grande Guerre* (Paris, 2008), 156–74.

[124] Stephen Wertheim has underlined important divergences within the 'legalist–sanctionist' movement between more conservative internationalists who stressed the importance of sanctions but refused to admit an international jurisdiction and advocates of such a jurisdiction who were wary of a robust sanctions regime: 'League that wasn't', 804–28.

[125] Quoted from Wilson's address to the second plenary session of the peace conference on 25 Jan. 1919 in *PV-SDN*, 8; see also Wertheim, 'League that wasn't'; T. J. Knock, *To End All Wars: Woodrow Wilson and the Quest for a New World Order* (Princeton, 1992), 44, 126–7, 149–53, 207; and L. Ambrosius, *Wilsonianism: Woodrow Wilson and his Legacy in American Foreign Relations* (London, 2002), 51–64.

an international court of any kind. 'I don't want lawyers drafting this treaty,' he insisted.[126] Bourgeois could expect little support for the CISDN programme from the American president.

In truth there was very limited support for the programme even among French officials. In early December Berthelot sketched out a very different conception of the League:

> The League of Nations exists. It has proven itself during the war, it is consecrated by a series of accords, not only political but military, financial and economic. It is essential to first reorganise and regulate it with a view to the post-war period... It is under the authority of the League that we can best monitor the neutrality of the Left Bank of the Rhine, Eastern Prussia and make ourselves the gendarmes of Europe. For these practical political and military goals, the League of Nations is *a necessity*.[127]

Berthelot's vision was echoed in a proposal by Klotz to establish a 'financial section' of the League that was in reality little more than a machine to collect reparations payments from Germany.[128] Paul Cambon was more dismissive. He complained that the League should have 'nothing to do with the peace settlement'. The whole idea, he concluded, amounted to nothing more than 'amateur silliness' and it was 'dangerous to waste time discussing such abstract nonsense when Germany has not been disarmed and issues of fundamental importance remain to be resolved'.[129]

Similar convictions prevailed among military elites. The most sympathetic view of the League within the army high command, expressed by General Pellé, envisaged it as 'a democratic version of the Holy Alliance but with an army and equal rights for all'.[130] Marshal Foch, however, was privately hostile to the entire project. 'Foch has a hatred of Wilson and a supreme contempt for ... such idiotic ideas as the League of Nations,' noted his colleague and friend General Sir Henry Wilson (the chief of the British Imperial General Staff).

---

[126] Quoted in Knock, *To End all Wars*, 205; see also R. Lansing, *The Peace Negotiations: A Personal Narrative* (Ebook, 2003), 39–40; Baker (ed.), *World Settlement*, III, 88–93; R. Kennedy, *The Will to Believe: Woodrow Wilson, World War I, and America's Strategy for Peace and Security* (Kent, Ohio, 2009), 182–202.

[127] SHD-DAT, *Fonds Clemenceau*, 6N 72, 'Société des nations', 18 Dec. 1918 (emphasis in original).

[128] MAE, *Série A*, vol. 67, 'Projet d'une "section financière" de la Société des nations', 1 Feb. 1919; this idea was roundly criticised by both the British and the Americans: see MAE, PA-AP 029, *Papiers Bourgeois*, vol. 14, 'Memorandum de M. Montagu sur le projet de M. Klotz concernant la Section financière de la Ligue des Nations', Feb. 1919 and 'Remarques de la délégation amércain sur le projet de M. Klotz', Feb. 1919.

[129] MAE, PA-AP 008, *Papiers Barrère*, vol. 1, Paul Cambon to Barrère, 7 Mar. 1919; P. Cambon, *Correspondance, 1870–1924*, vol. III: *(1912–1924) Les Guerres balkaniques. La Grande Guerre. L'Organisation de la paix* (Paris, 1946), P. Cambon to Xavier Charmes, 23 Jan. and 10 Feb. 1919: 298 and 307–9; P. Cambon to Aimé de Fleuriau, 27 Jan. 1919: 298–9.

[130] MAE, *Série A*, vol. 280, General Maurice Pellé, commander of fifth army corps, to Foch, 28 Oct. 1918.

'I cordially agree with him.'[131] Foch used different language in public, however. In a note to Allied leaders, drafted with the help of Tardieu, he observed that:

It is doubtless the case that we can, in the indeterminate future, count on the sufficient development of civilisation and of the moral sense of peoples to be able to look to a powerfully organised Society or a League of Nations as an effective obstacle to wars of conquest. But until this newborn society acquires the necessary authority to constitute by itself a guarantee that of peace, it is necessary that it receives a sufficient support and in particular the force that alone can assure its development. It is essential to know the situation of the peoples of yesterday in order to fix the situation of tomorrow and to take into account the material guarantees of peace that victory has placed in the hands of the Allies.[132]

Real security must rest on traditional practices and 'material guarantees'. This note, interestingly, was part of a systematic effort to incorporate the League into a negotiating strategy aimed at securing more traditional guarantees. This tactic was mooted by both Tardieu and Berthelot. The latter, in late November, judged that France 'must not fight this new idea of a League of Nations that has seduced popular opinion, we must instead use it to our advantage'.[133] The strategy was to use concessions to the Anglo-American conception of the League in exchange for agreement to France's security demands on the Rhine.

To the extent that he gave the issue much consideration at all, Clemenceau's thoughts on the role of an international organisation were in some ways closer to those of Smuts or Wilson than to those of Bourgeois and French juridical internationalists. Before the chamber he argued that the chief aim must be to create a new moral order:

If we really wish to create a League or Society of Nations – call it whatever you please – it is not enough to create, in black and white, texts to which each member must conform. What is really necessary is that there exists in every state the spiritual dispositions that will permit this Society that will be established to live and function.[134]

Wilson's adviser Colonel House met Clemenceau on 7 January to persuade him to agree to the American vision of a league of nations. The premier ended

---

[131] Quoted in W. R. Keylor, 'Versailles and International Diplomacy' in Boemke et al. (eds.), *Treaty of Versailles*, 483; see also J.-C. Notin, *Foch* (Paris, 2008), 428–44 and S. Schuker, 'The Rhineland Question: West European Security at the Paris Peace Conference of 1919' in Boemke et al. (eds.), *Treaty of Versailles*, 280–4.

[132] SHD-DAT, *Fonds Privés* (DITEEX), 1K 129, *Papiers Foch*, carton 1, dr. 7, 'Note', 10 Jan. 1919; an earlier draft of Foch's note, along with Tardieu's revisions, is in MAE, PA-AP 166, *Papiers Tardieu*, vol. 422.

[133] MAE, *SDN*, vol. 6, 'Société des nations: impossible d'y admettre de suite les états ennemis', 22 Dec. 1918.

[134] MAE, *SDN*, vol. 6, 'Extrait du discours prononcé par M. Clemenceau devant la Chambre des Députés le 16 janvier 1919'.

the meeting by placing his hands on the American's shoulders and intoning, 'You have convinced me. I am for this League of Nations as you have described it, and you may count upon me to work with you to establish it.'[135]

But House had not converted Clemenceau. The League was never central to French government policy. It was not until 17 January, in fact, that Bourgeois was informed of his appointment as French delegate on the League of Nations Commission. The news came in a two-line note that did not provide further instructions and did not suggest a meeting to discuss aims and strategy.[136] In reality, Clemenceau's prior commitment to House had already largely undermined any chance that Bourgeois might secure approval for the CISDN programme on the League Commission.

This became apparent when the League Commission first convened. The British and Americans had been meeting in secret throughout January to exchange drafts of what would become the League Covenant. Their aim was to impose an Anglo-American vision of the League. The result was the 'Hurst–Miller draft' of the Covenant, which was agreed between the two delegations on 2 February and presented without translation at the first meeting of the Commission the next day.[137] The French delegates were then railroaded into accepting this document as the 'basis for discussion' by the concerted efforts of Wilson (in the chair) and British delegate Robert Cecil. The CISDN programme was not even discussed.[138] From this point forward Bourgeois and Larnaude were in the invidious position of trying to insert the core principles of the CISDN plan as amendments to the Anglo-American proposal.

They would fail. The Hurst–Miller Draft envisaged the creation of an International Court of Justice but did not establish a jurisdiction for this court; although it referred to arbitration as a means of dispute settlement, recourse to arbitration was not made compulsory for any category of dispute. There was no mention whatever of the work of the Hague court (which Wilson considered an abject failure). Nor, crucially, was there any provision for imposing the will of either the International Court or the League Council

---

[135] SLYU, MSS 466, *Papers of Col. Edward Mandell House*, Series II (Diary), vol. 7: 7 Jan. 1919.

[136] MAE, PA-AP 198, *Papiers Georges Clemenceau*, Président du conseil (Mandel) to Bourgeois, 17 Jan. 1919.

[137] The document is named after the British legal expert Cecil Hurst and his American counterpart David Hunter Miller. For details see esp. Robert Cecil's diary in British Library (hereafter BL), *Lord Cecil of Chelwood Papers*, MSS 51131, 'Lord Cecil's Diary of the British Delegation: Formation of the League of Nations, 1919', entries for 8–31 Jan. 1919; see also S. Blair, 'La France et le pacte de la Société des nations: le rôle du gouvernement français dans l'élaboration du pacte de la Société des nations, 1914–1919', thèse de doctorat, Université de Paris I (Sorbonne), 1991, 418–31; P. Raffo, 'The Anglo-American preliminary negotiations for a League of Nations', *JCH*, 9, 4 (1974), 153–76.

[138] Though the minutes of the meeting were later doctored to indicate that both the French and Italians had also tabled proposals: S. Bonsal, *Unfinished Business* (New York, 1944), 31–3; and Blair, 'La France et le Pacte', 422–7.

Towards a post-war security order 269

with a regime of sanctions.[139] The Anglo-American document, in sum, advanced a radically different vision of the League based on a much more optimistic set of judgements about the power of public opinion and moral leadership to transform world politics.

Bourgeois and Larnaude responded by fighting hard for a series of amendments aimed at transforming the dispute settlement and collective security provisions of the Hurst–Miller Draft. Although historians have focused on their proposal to establish an international armed force, a close look at the documentary evidence reveals that they were much more concerned to secure a League based on the rule of international law. As Bourgeois observed, the 'most serious flaw' in the Anglo-American version of the League was that it was 'not legally required to enforce its decisions'.[140] Arbitration was neither compulsory nor binding, and the imposition of sanctions was not automatic. The Council would instead merely recommend actions to be taken by League members. French delegates further doubted that such a league would be able to make decisions effectively given that the International Court had no jurisdiction and Council decisions would need to be unanimous.[141] As Larnaude later recalled, the core problem was that the French approached collective security with assumptions that were profoundly different from those of Wilson:

> In reality, when it comes to the *nature of the obligation resulting from the Covenant*, there was a serious divergence between the American doctrine and the French doctrine. Devoted to clarity and precision, we have always feared that we have not *bound* states sufficiently to the dispositions of the Covenant. The US delegation, conversely, and I mean by this president Wilson, who alone spoke for his delegation, consistently rejected clear and trenchant formulations of the sort we demanded. The American position was that engagements *that we would consider moral* are superior to legal engagements. This is because, as president Wilson was fond of saying, the weight and modality of legal engagements can be debated, but one cannot debate a moral engagement ... It is impossible to understand the dynamics of the debates on the League of Nations Commission without taking into account this problem of mentality.[142]

The result, Larnaude later observed, was a Covenant that left the League's core missions 'vague and precarious'.[143]

---

[139] Lansing refers to Wilson's 'contempt' for the Hague Court in *Peace Negotiations*, 69; for the Hurst–Miller Draft see Baker (ed.), *World Settlement*, III, 144–51.
[140] Quote from Bourgeois in MAE, PA-AP 029, *Papiers Bourgeois*, vol. 18, 'Notes et propositions remises à la séance du 11 février par M. Léon Bourgeois'; also 'Textes provisoirement adoptés par la Commission de la SDN', 5 Feb. 1919.
[141] MAE, *SDN*, vol. 10, 'Interventions de M. Léon Bourgeois à la Commission de la SDN du 3 février 1919' and 'Exposé des motifs des amendements français au projet du Pacte', n.d.
[142] MAE, PA-AP 141, *Papiers Pichon*, vol. 8, 'Observations sur la discussion du traité devant la Chambre: séance du 3 septembre', 8 Sept. 1919 (emphasis in original).
[143] Ibid., 'Observations sur la discussion du traité devant la Chambre: séance du 2 septembre – discours de M. Tardieu', 7 Sept. 1919.

Bourgeois was particularly exercised by the lack of reference to The Hague and the Permanent Court in the Anglo-American document.[144] This has been attributed to his vanity. In fact, it was rooted in his conviction that peace could only be assured through the creation of a regime of compulsory arbitration. This of course was the project initiated at The Hague.[145] Bourgeois made his opposition to 'a purely political or moral idea of the League of Nations' clear both during League Commission debates and in public. 'The League of the future', he insisted, 'is above all a juridical question.'[146] In a note to Clemenceau he identified two 'primordial difficulties' with the Anglo-American conception. The first was the 'voluntary' (as opposed to legal) character of the commitment demanded of League members. The second was the 'lack of clear procedures' for executing arbitration as well as the verification that states had complied with their obligations.[147]

The first priority, however, was to secure clear wording to make arbitration compulsory and the imposition of sanctions as automatic as possible. To this end Larnaude pressed the case for a clear jurisdiction for the International Court to pass judgment on violations of the Covenant and decide on sanctions. Wilson replied that the court of world opinion would be the principal forum for such judgements:

Each public declaration constitutes a moral obligation; and the judgement of the tribunal of public opinion will be much more effective [in this regard] than that of any other tribunal in the world, because it is more powerful and can impose itself without technical subtleties.

'Surely', Larnaude responded with evident sarcasm, 'there must exist some technical questions that only a qualified jurisdiction is competent to interpret.' He pointed out that 'even in the most advanced countries such as America or Britain' legal rulings were not always beholden to the judgement of public opinion.[148] The gulf between this approach and that of the French delegates could scarcely have been wider. 'Tell me, my friend,' Larnaude said, turning to Bourgeois in despair, 'am I at a peace conference or in a madhouse?'[149]

French efforts to make arbitration binding and sanctions automatic met consistently with polite indifference from the rest of the commission.[150]

---

[144] See esp. *PV-SDN*, 'Procès-verbal No. 4: séance du 6 février 1919', 144–7.

[145] MAE, PA-AP 029, *Papiers Bourgeois*, vol. 18, 'Textes provisoirement adoptés par la Commission de la SDN', 5 Feb. 1919.

[146] L. Bourgeois, 'Le Fondements indispensables d'une Société des nations' in *Pacte de 1919*, 126–53.

[147] MAE, PA-AP 029, *Papiers Bourgeois*, vol. 18, Bourgeois to Clemenceau, 7 Feb. 1919.

[148] *PV-SDN*, 'Procès-verbal No. 7: séance du 10 février 1919', 157–8.

[149] Quoted in Bonsal, *Unfinished Business*, 52 (not in official minutes).

[150] See the *procès-verbaux* and *annexes* for the fourth, fifth and seventh meetings of the League Commission in *PV-SDN*, 145–7, 149–50 and 156–62; see also MAE, PA-AP 029, *Papiers Bourgeois*, vol. 18, 'Notes et propositions remises à la séance du 11 février par M. Léon Bourgeois'.

Towards a post-war security order 271

Their proposed amendments were either severely diluted or were 'reserved' for future consideration. The draft version of the Covenant that was released to the press and published on 14 February articulated a thoroughly Anglo-American conception of the League.[151]

The French CISDN reconvened to consider this draft in late February 1919. Paul Matter produced a study emphasising that sanctions must be automatic to have any deterrent effect.[152] Jean Gout and Jules Basdevant, in a critique of the 'political organisation' of the League outlined in the draft Covenant, observed that:

> The French commission sought to provide the means to obtain a jurisdictional solution to international disputes and to guarantee this solution. The proposed Covenant project takes a different view ... It seeks to establish a dilatory process in the hope that this will appease international tensions. If this dilatory system was preferred to a decisive system, this is in all likelihood because it marks the limit of the possible at this moment and that a more radical project has little chance of being approved.[153]

Gout and Basdevant's characterisation of the juridical alternative advocated by French delegates as 'a more radical project' is telling. Far from seeking to return to the traditions of the balance of power and alliance politics, the French delegates sought to establish a robust legal regime at the core of the League. As Larnaude observed, 'It would have been logical that an arbitral sentence be executed as is that of a tribunal in the national context; but it is not the juridical conception that prevailed, it was the political conception.'[154] The problem, as Gout and Basdevant pointed out, was that the 'juridical conception' required unacceptable sacrifices to national sovereignty. The contradiction at the heart of the CISDN programme, between the aim to ensure the effective rule of international law and the desire to protect sovereignty of League members, was once again laid bare.

The tensions inherent in the juridical internationalist approach emerged in the full glare of League Commission debates when Bourgeois pressed home his two amendments to Article 8. The first called for the creation of an international armed force 'more powerful than that of any individual nation'. This force would be endowed with a permanent military staff that would be responsible for its equipment and training as well as plans for its deployment.[155] The second called for 'the institution of a system of international surveillance and

---

[151] See Baker (ed.), *World Settlement*, 163–73.
[152] MAE, *SDN*, vol. 6, 'Nécessité de la promptidue dans les interventions de la Ligue', 28 Feb. 1919.
[153] MAE, *SDN*, vol. 6, 'Organisation politique de la Société des nations', 8 Mar. 1919.
[154] MAE, *SDN*, vol. 7, 'Procès-verbal du 24ème séance de la Commission de la SDN', 26 Feb. 1919.
[155] *PV-SDN*, 'Procès-verbal No. 8: séance du 11 février 1919', 166–7; in arguing for this amendment Bourgeois invoked one of Wilson's public declarations to the effect that the League must possess a force greater than that of any single nation. As Larnaude later

verification for both manpower and armaments' to which 'all League members would submit in good faith'.[156]

The British and Americans opposed these proposals as violations of the principle of national sovereignty. 'We must make a distinction between what is possible and what is not,' Wilson responded, adding that the amendments violated the US constitution. Cecil agreed that 'no country will accept an international general staff that would have the right to interfere in its own naval and military plans'.[157] Bourgeois was isolated on the Commission but continued to insist on his amendments even after they were rejected repeatedly. He obtained only two concessions. The Commission agreed to revise the language of Article 13 to attribute greater importance to arbitration. It also approved the creation of a permanent commission to provide expert advice on military questions (which became Article 9). But the Covenant remained an expression of the Anglo-American approach to international organisation.[158]

It is important to acknowledge that there was virtually no chance that other French policy elites would have accepted the limitations on France's sovereignty mooted by Bourgeois. Throughout the post-war decade the military establishment would prove implacably hostile to any outside interference in French defence policy.[159] The government, meanwhile, continued to use policy towards the League as bargaining leverage to obtain its larger strategic design. Although Clemenceau backed Bourgeois publicly, in private Tardieu distanced the government from his proposals and hinted that it would adopt a more 'reasonable' position if it obtained satisfaction regarding the Left Bank of the Rhine.[160] 'Go down fighting,' Clemenceau exhorted Bourgeois. 'Your failure will allow me to demand supplementary guarantees on the Rhine.'[161]

It is nonetheless essential to distinguish between the attitudes of Clemenceau, his advisers and security professionals, on the one hand, and that of Bourgeois, on the other. If the government was not inspired by the juridical internationalist approach to security, there is no doubt that Bourgeois pursued this agenda on the League Commission. Germany remained the

observed, however, Wilson was almost certainly referring to its moral force rather than its fighting power: MAE, PA-AP 141, *Papiers Pichon*, 'Observations sur la discussion du traité devant la Chambre: séance du 2 septembre 1919', 7 Sept. 1919.

[156] *PV-SDN*, 'Procès-verbal No. 8: séance du 11 février 1919', 168; see also MAE, PA-AP 029, *Papiers Bourgeois*, vol. 18, 'Notes et propositions remises à la séance du 11 février par M. Léon Bourgeois' and 'Note sur l'addition à l'Article 8 du Pacte', 24 Mar. 1919.

[157] *PV-SDN*, 'Procès-verbal No. 8: séance du 11 février 1919', 170–3; 'Procès-verbal No. 10: [deuxième] séance du 13 février 1919'; see also D. H. Miller, *The Drafting of the Covenant*, 2 vols. (New York, 1928), II, 290–3 and I, 247–8.

[158] Yearwood, *Guarantee of Peace*, 104–37; Blair, 'La France et le pacte', 485–579; MacMillan, *Paris 1919*, 86–97; Sharp, *Versailles Settlement*, 55–76.

[159] P. Jackson, 'France and the problems of security and disarmament after the First World War', *JSS*, 29, 2 (2006), 247–80.

[160] Cecil recounted that Tardieu considered Bourgeois' proposals 'quite useless': BL, *Cecil Papers*, MSS 51131, 'Diary', 28 Feb. 1919; see also Blair, 'La France et le pacte', 508–20 and Yearwood, *Guarantee of Peace*, 92–3.

[161] Poincaré, *Au Service de la France*, vol. XI: *À la recherche de la paix*, 27 Mar. 1919: 283–4.

Towards a post-war security order 273

overwhelming preoccupation, but the proposed solution aimed at enmeshment and constraint rather than power politics. The idea of *contrôle* (inspection and verification) was rooted in the solidarist conception of the social debt of all members of international society. Crucially, Bourgeois insisted that *all* League members must submit to this regime and to the machinery of arbitration and enforcement at the centre of his vision of the League. 'France, which is willing to accept inspection, considers that in doing so it relinquishes none of its national dignity ... [what we have proposed is] ... a common measure of mutual guarantee that must apply to equally even to great powers.'[162]

The proposed international force, similarly, was a mechanism of *collective* enforcement aimed at supporting the machinery of the League. It was based on the principle of mutual guarantee rather than the traditional aim of a preponderance of military power. It was an expression of the solidarist assumption that states must accept duties and obligations, and thus give up a measure of their sovereignty, in a system where security risks were mutualised. There were no less than eleven references to the need for a 'mutual' approach to security in Bourgeois' defence of his position before the plenary session of the peace conference on 14 February 1919.[163]

The distinctive character of the juridical internationalist vision is further illuminated in the position taken by Bourgeois regarding German admission to the League. Nearly all senior policy makers – including Berthelot, Tardieu, Poincaré and Clemenceau – assumed that eventual German entry was inevitable. Their priority was to make treaty fulfilment a cast-iron prerequisite. Significantly, the judgement that Germany was unfit for immediate membership was by no means an extreme position. It was shared even by President Wilson.[164] Bourgeois went further than most of his colleagues, however, to argue that German membership could one day constitute a *source* of security. If he was as convinced as any of his colleagues that Germany remained an inherently militarist and aggressive society, he held out greater hope that, once the Reich had adopted democratic political institutions and demonstrated a commitment to abide by the rule of international law, it could become a responsible member of the League.

This hope was rooted in Bourgeois' vision of the League as a society of states bound together by common political cultures and shared obligations. This was why he opposed the decision, taken in the Council of Four, to impose an

---

[162] *PV-SDN*, 'Procès-verbal No. 8: séance du 11 février 1919', 173.
[163] MAE, PA-AP 029, *Papiers Bourgeois*, vol. 18, 'Séance plenière de la Conférence de la paix: 14 février 1919'.
[164] MAE, *SDN*, vol. 6, 'Société des nations: impossible d'y admettre de suite les états ennemis', 22 Dec. 1918 (Berthelot); Poincaré: see his *Messages, discours, allocutions, lettres et télégrammes*, vol. II: *13 novembre 1918–2 août 1919* (Paris, 1920), 18 Jan. 1919: 143; Tardieu, *La Paix*, 135; Blair, 'La France et le pacte', 497; Miquel, *Opinion publique*, 196–8; Knock, *To End all Wars*, 221–47; Kennedy, *Will to Believe*, 196–200; and French embassy reports in SHD-DAT, *Fonds Clemenceau*, 6N 138, Jusserand to Pichon, 15, 27 Nov. and 1 Dec. 1918.

inspection regime on Germany alone (in Art. 213 of the Treaty of Versailles) rather than opt for his proposal of a universal system of verification. He characterised this system of 'individual inspection' as 'illusory' and 'dangerous' and predicted that it would lead to 'continual conflict'. The principle of inspection and verification should be embedded in a regime of 'mutual obligation' accepted by all states. Bourgeois stressed the socialising benefits of such a system which, he argued, held out the possibility of accelerating German entry into the League.[165]

Bourgeois summed up his conception of the League of Nations in an impassioned address to the fifth plenary session of the Peace Conference on 28 April 1919. Here he acknowledged that any attempt to establish the rule of law would require states to sacrifice a small measure of their sovereignty:

For us, state sovereignty is not an absolute notion ... like the liberty of individuals inside states, the sovereignty of each state must be limited in the eyes of the law by the sovereignty of others. The role of the international institution is to specify these limits, to fix them equitably on the basis of mutuality and reciprocity and to include, for all, certain guarantees and certain sanctions in a convention freely accepted by all and faithfully executed by all.[166]

States, like individuals, should willingly accept limitations on their sovereignty in exchange for increased security.

This juridical internationalist vision of the League was rejected in favour of the Anglo-American alternative. The final version of the Covenant did not make arbitration compulsory and did not attribute an international jurisdiction to either The Hague or the newly constituted International Court. Nor did it put in place a robust system of automatic sanctions to punish aggression. The muscular vision of the League advocated by Bourgeois was not supported even by the Clemenceau government, which, at the same plenary session, accepted the Covenant as it stood.[167]

Yet, despite their ultimate failure, the efforts of Bourgeois and Larnaude merit more consideration than they have hitherto received. Their proposals were an expression of the juridical internationalist current in French thinking that would become ever more influential during the post-war decade. Their critique of the Covenant would be taken up by a succession of French governments after 1919 and constitute a central element of French security policy from 1924 onward.

---

[165] MAE, PA-AP 029, *Papiers Bourgeois*, vol. 18, 'Résumé de la conversation avec M. Clemenceau', n.d. but marked 'Je lui ai lu cette note', and 'Séance plenière de la Conférence de la paix: 14 février 1919'; SHD-DAT, *Fonds Clemenceau*, 6N 74, Bourgeois and Larnaude to Clemenceau, 18 Apr. 1919; *PV-SDN*, 'Procès-verbal No. 11: séance du 22 mars 1919'; Miller, *Drafting of the Covenant*, II, 508–11.
[166] *PV-SDN*, 'Cinquième séance plenière', 28 Apr. 1919: 396.
[167] Blair, 'La France et le pacte', 555–7.

To conclude, there can be no doubt that French planning and policy towards the eastern European and colonial settlements was dominated by balance-of-power calculations. The traditional instincts of France's soldiers and diplomats were brought to bear with decisive effect in negotiations for a new political order in the east. French officials secured favourable strategic frontiers for Poland, Czechoslovakia, Romania and Yugoslavia in the hope that these states would support the larger strategic design of balancing German power in cooperation with France. Yet even together the new states could not replace Imperial Russia in the European strategic balance. The same was true of French colonial expansion in Africa and the Middle East. Colonial power had been of limited value during the war when compared to the contributions of France's Great Power coalition partners. Of more tangible benefit were the restrictions on German power imposed by the terms of the economic settlement. But even this aspect of the peace highlighted the limitations of a traditional approach directed *against* Germany. The vast majority of the economic measures imposed on the Reich were temporary and left that state's long-term economic advantages over its neighbours largely intact.

The Clemenceau government's response was to try to anchor France in a transatlantic community of democratic Great Powers. A departure from traditional power balancing, this was the strategy underpinning the Clémentel Plan. The aim was to enmesh and constrain Germany. Although its plan was rejected, the Clemenceau government continued to explore the option of post-war economic cooperation with Germany. In the summer of 1919 France's future economic relations with the Reich remained as undefined as the precise details of the reparations settlement.

Alternative currents are also evident in policy towards the League of Nations. Although they were never central to the French peace programme, the proposals advanced by Bourgeois and Larnaude called for a league that would bind Germany in a regime of international law backed up by powerful collective sanctions. This vision of international organisation was sacrificed on the altar of close relations with Britain and the USA. Interestingly, however, a common theme in both planning for economic security and internationalist projects for the League of Nations was the hope that membership in a wider system would not only constrain Germany but also have a positive effect on that state's behaviour. This more optimistic perspective on the socialising power of international regimes is part of the great fracture between 'realism' and most other theories of international politics. It was also central to the conceptual divide between internationalist calls for cooperation under the rule of law, on the one hand, and traditional conceptions of security through strategic preponderance, on the other.

8 The Rhineland settlement and the security of France

André Tardieu described the future political and military status of the Left Bank of the Rhine as 'the essential problem which dominates all others in our preparations'.[1] The swathe of territory stretching west of the Rhine from the Netherlands in the north to the Saar coal basin in the south was a traditional highway for European armies. Denying Germany the right to use the Left Bank as a staging ground for yet another invasion of France was an undisputed security priority for the vast majority of French political and policy elites. No issue took up more time or generated greater tensions during the peace conference.[2] French demands for a strategic frontier brought negotiations with the British and Americans to the point of complete breakdown. The compromise negotiated to end this impasse caused a civil–military crisis in France. No aspect of the peace settlement better illuminates the varied and dynamic character of elite conceptions of national security than that of France's eastern frontiers.

The Clemenceau government's policy towards France's 'eastern marches' underwent significant changes from the heady post-armistice period of mid-November 1918 to the difficult negotiations leading to a final agreement the following April. The initial French programme demanded that the Left Bank of the Rhine be detached from Germany and reconstituted as a buffer state under permanent occupation. This proposal was unacceptable to the British and the Americans. Lloyd George and Wilson offered instead to guarantee France against future German aggression. Unwilling to destroy Allied solidarity, Clemenceau and his advisers chose to accept this guarantee on the condition that the Rhineland remained demilitarised for all time.

Most historians have interpreted this French policy as a classic expression of realist power politics.[3] This judgement misses important dimensions to French

---

[1] MAE, PA-AP 166, *Papiers Tardieu*, vol. 412, 'Congrès de la paix: plan général', 5 Jan. 1919; Tardieu, *La paix*, 97–101.
[2] Stephen Schuker describes the Rhineland settlement as 'the cornerstone of the whole diplomatic edifice' under construction at the peace conference: 'The Rhineland Question: West European Security at the Paris Peace Conference of 1919' in M. Boemke, G. Feldman and E. Glaser (eds.), *The Treaty of Versailles: A Reassessment after 75 Years* (Cambridge, 1998), 275.
[3] G.-H. Soutou, 'La France et les marches de l'est, 1914–1919', *RH*, 528 (1978); H. I. Nelson, *Land and Power: British and Allied Policy on Germany's Frontiers* (London, 1963), 204–8;

planning and decision making. While the initial project to detach and occupy the Left Bank was a traditional bid to overthrow the European strategic balance, a closer look at this episode reveals the importance of ideological factors that were only indirectly connected with calculations of military advantage on the Rhine. The decision to accept the Anglo-American guarantee cannot properly be understood without taking into account the importance of both self-determination and conceptions of a North Atlantic security community to the Clemenceau government's policy.[4] The French peace programme, as it emerged in February–March 1919, was a complex combination of power-political calculation and an ideological commitment to a democratic peace based on new principles of international politics. The great difficulty was that this vision was not shared by the majority of the policy elite in 1919. Most security professionals and many parliamentarians favoured security through domination of the Rhineland.

I

As we have seen, a desire to assert French control over the territories west of the Rhine had been a central theme in French internal discourse since the beginning of the war. This highly traditional prescription for security was even more prominent as the war drew to a close and French officials began to draft memoranda on the post-war order in western Europe.

The foreign ministry, typically, took the lead in this process. A new balance of power was at the heart of a pair of widely circulated memoranda by Gabriel Hanotaux the day the armistice was signed. Hanotaux called for a 'grand peace' of 'European organisation'. By this he meant ending German unity, detaching the Left Bank and 'the occupation of Germany to the line of the Elbe River'. He also called for 'a vast strategic glacis' to be created to protect northern France from eastern Germany. Most of the Left Bank, including Luxembourg, would be ceded to France. Belgium and Holland would be 'compensated' for these French gains with annexations of their own (albeit on a much smaller scale). Hanotaux observed that these measures would return France to its 'natural limits'.[5] Germany, meanwhile, would be reorganised into a loose federation of

---

R. McCrum, 'French Rhineland policy at the Paris Peace Conference, 1919', *HJ*, 31, 3 (1978), 623–48; W. McDougall, *France's Rhineland Diplomacy, 1914–1924: The Last Bid for a Balance of Power in Europe* (Princeton, 1978), 33–96; D. Stevenson, *French War Aims against Germany, 1914–1919* (Oxford, 1982), 140–93; D. Stevenson, 'French War Aims and Peace Planning' in Boemke et al. (eds.), *Treaty of Versailles*; Schuker, 'West European Security', 275. Partial exceptions include P. Renouvin, 'Les Buts de guerre du gouvernement français, 1914–1918', *RH*, 516 (1966); P. Renouvin, *L'Armistice de Rethondes: 11 novembre 1918* (Paris, 1968), 217–18; D. Watson, *Georges Clemenceau: A Political Biography* (London, 1974), 352–3; J.-B. Duroselle, *Clemenceau* (Paris, 1988), 721–9.

[4] Georges-Henri Soutou alludes to the role of ideology in 'The French Peacemakers and their Homefront' in Boemke et al. (eds.), *Treaty of Versailles*, 169–72 but does not develop the notion of a transatlantic community of democratic power.

[5] MAE, *Série A*, vol. 60, 'De la future frontière', 11 Nov. 1918.

states, each with its own legislature and foreign policy. 'We must dismantle the empire of Bismarck [in order] to have a solid strategic peace,' he concluded.[6]

Hanotaux's outline for the future territorial settlement was the most radical and ambitious advocated by any senior French official after the armistice. Other foreign ministry officials recognised that France must proceed more carefully on the question of western territorial revision.[7] The most common objective was a neutralised and demilitarised Left Bank. Jules Laroche, for example, judged that the central aim of French policy must be 'to forbid Germany all of the military attributes of sovereignty on the Left Bank'. An inter-Allied military occupation would deliver this solution. Laroche added, however, that the Left Bank should be given privileged commercial relations with France which would establish the conditions 'for its eventual political detachment from Germany'.[8] His aim was not only to deny Germany use of the Left Bank for military purposes, but eventually to deprive it of this region altogether.

This gradualist solution to strategic transformation was adopted in most foreign ministry policy recommendations. Berthelot also argued that France must secure a military frontier on the river through the neutralisation and occupation of the Left Bank. From London, Paul Cambon declared that a 'defensive system on the Rhine' was an 'indispensable cornerstone of the European settlement'.[9]

Both Laroche and Berthelot also advocated abolishing the 1815 settlement that gave Prussia the Saar basin. Laroche combined economic and military arguments for returning this region to France. Its inhabitants would be given a choice between retaining their German nationality or becoming French citizens. Such an arrangement, he acknowledged, would involve 'modest violations' of the principle of self-determination (in fact, it would mean the annexation of more than one million Germans). But he argued that it would be impossible to apply this principle in all regions in any case given the need to provide France, its allies and new states under construction with defensible frontiers.[10]

It was at this early stage that Marshal Foch intervened. Foch would play a central role in the formulation of the French programme through late February

---

[6] MAE, *Série A*, vol. 60, 'De la future frontière' and 'Du sort de l'Allemagne unifiée', both dated 11 Nov. 1918; also in BDIC, *Archives Klotz*, dr. 18, 'Du sort de l'Allemagne unifiée', 11 Nov. 1918 and in SHD-DAT, 4N 92, *État-major du maréchal Foch*, dr. 1; see also MAE, PA-AP 166, *Papiers Tardieu*, vol. 417, 'Deux notes de M. Hanotaux', n.d.
[7] McDougall, *Rhineland Diplomacy*, 69.
[8] MAE, *Série A*, vol. 289, 'La Frontière de l'Alsace-Lorraine et le statut de la rive gauche du Rhin', 1 Nov. 1918.
[9] MAE, *Série A*, vol. 289, 'Note sur la future frontière' (Berthelot), 10 Nov. 1918; MAE, *Série Z, Grande Bretagne* (hereafter *GB*), vol. 36, 'Conditions de paix' (Cambon), 21 Nov. 1918.
[10] MAE, *Série A*, vol. 289, 'La Frontière de l'Alsace-Lorraine et le statut de la rive gauche du Rhin', 1 Nov. 1918 and 'Note sur la future frontière entre l'Alsace-Lorraine et l'Allemagne: raisons stratégiques, économiques et politiques' (Berthelot), 10 Nov. 1918.

1919. His staff, led by the indefatigable General Auguste Le Rond, produced a barrage of memoranda on the strategic importance of the Rhine, the ethnic make-up and political views of the Rhenish population and strategies for drawing the territories of the Left Bank into France's political orbit.[11] The drafting of these memoranda was assisted by a steady flow of information from Berthelot and the staff at the foreign ministry. There were also constant exchanges with Tardieu and his team at the war ministry during the months of December and January.[12] But, as the focus of government policy retreated from demanding an independent strategic buffer on the Rhine and moved towards an Anglo-American guarantee and a temporary occupation, the marshal and his military colleagues were progressively marginalised.

On 21 November 1918 Foch endorsed the recommendations of Laroche and Berthelot to annex the Saarland.[13] He turned to the question of 'a definitive regime for the Rhineland and the bridgeheads' in a lengthy missive to Clemenceau the following week. Here he stressed that, even after the return of Alsace-Lorraine, France and Belgium would be in a situation of demographic inferiority in relation to Germany. This would be compounded by the fact that there was no longer a Russian counterweight. Foch argued that the primordial requirement for European security must therefore be the formation of a coalition of states west of the Rhine that would include not only France, Belgium, Luxembourg and Britain but also the states along the Left Bank. The provinces of the Left Bank should be constituted as nominally independent states. But each would be obliged to provide conscript soldiers for the defence of western Europe. Foch concluded that only such a grouping of states 'protected by the natural barrier of the Rhine' could assure peace and security in Europe.[14] He made no mention of the United States.

American power was incorporated into another assessment of European security requirements drafted by Foch with Tardieu's assistance and forwarded to Allied leaders on 10 January 1919. In this note the marshal retreated from the idea of incorporating the Left Bank into a western defensive alliance. He argued instead for the creation of a new state or states that would be

---

[11] SHD-DAT, 4N 92, *État-major Foch*, 'Étude sur le régime futur des pays de la rive gauche du Rhin', 17 Nov. 1918; 'Étude sur la situation déficitaire actuelle des pays de la rive gauche du Rhin en Houille et Coke', 19 Nov. 1918; 'Le Rhin frontière militaire', 3 Déc. 1918; 'Note sur la rive gauche du Rhin: importance que lui ont attribuée les allemands – rôle qu'elle a joué en 1870 et en 1914', n.d.; 'Note sur l'organisation militaire des pays de la rive gauche du Rhin', 19 Déc. 1918.
[12] See the voluminous documentation in SHD-DAT, 4N 92, *État-major Foch* and MAE, PA-AP 166, *Papiers Tardieu*, vols. 421 and 422.
[13] SHD-DAT, *Fonds Clemenceau*, 6N 70–1, 'Note', 21 Nov. 1918; also in English in SHD-DAT, *Fonds Clemenceau*, 6N 73–1, 'Note by Marshal Foch'.
[14] SHD-DAT, *Fonds Clemenceau*, 6N 73–2, 'Note', 27 Nov. 1918 (forwarded to Clemenceau on 28 Nov.); Foch outlined this argument to Lloyd George during a visit to London on 1 Dec. 1918: see 'Conversation entre M. Lloyd George et le maréchal Foch, 10 Downing Street' in the same carton.

neutralised, placed under Allied occupation and granted a favourable customs regime with the 'states of the west' with whom they might eventually 'desire to attach themselves as they had in the past'. The USA would join with the other Allied states in the military occupation of the Left Bank. The Rhine would thus constitute 'the military frontier of the western democracies'.[15]

The inspiration for virtually all post-armistice memoranda generated by the policy machine was the traditional approach to security. In keeping with wartime treatment of this question, both history and the ideology of France's 'natural frontiers' were mobilised in support of a programme for permanent strategic preponderance over Germany. The 'Gallic' or 'Celtic' character of the Rhenish population was asserted, along with the fact that the region had been part of Germany for only forty-five years. The myth of Rhineland solidarity with Revolutionary France was also deployed to support claims that the Rhineland was a distinct political space with historical ties to France.[16] The Saarland was represented, in familiar language, as a territory that had been 'seized from France by force' as part of the settlement of 1815.[17]

Hanotaux asserted that Germany 'can be contained in its true place' only if France obtained its 'historic and natural frontier' on the Rhine.[18] Berthelot referred to the 'old European tradition' in which the Rhine functioned as 'the ancient frontier of Gaul and the natural limit of France'.[19] Military officials were most seduced by the romance of France's natural frontiers, however. As Stephen Schuker has observed, France's army commanders on the Rhine, Generals Charles Mangin and Augustin Gérard, 'envisioned themselves as latter-day proconsuls destined to rekindle the glorious traditions of Hoche, Beugnot and Napoleon'.[20] For Mangin 'France on the Rhine' was 'the immortal France, become once again the "grand nation"'.[21] Foch returned obsessively to the 'historic' role played by France's 'natural barrier'. He warned that the Rhine had 'constituted the western frontier of the German peoples for

---

[15] SHD, Fonds Privés (DITEEX), *Archives du maréchal Foch*, 1K 129, carton 1, dr. 7, 'Note', Foch to Allied plenipotentiaries, 10 Jan. 1919; see also Soutou, 'Marches de l'est', 384; Stevenson, *French War Aims*, 156; and Schuker, 'West European Security', 290–1.

[16] MAE, PA-AP 166, *Papiers Tardieu*, vol. 417, 'Note sur le statut politique des pays de la rive gauche du Rhin', 20 Jan. 1919; also 'Note sur le rôle international du Rhine comme "Frontière de la Liberté"', 20 Jan. 1919.

[17] SHD-DAT, *Fonds Clemenceau*, 6N 73–4, 'Note sommaire sur la frontière de 1814 et le Bassin de la Sarre', n.d.; MAE, PA-AP 166, *Papiers Tardieu*, vol. 415, 'Bassin de la Sarre' (Lavisse), 11 Jan. 1919 and 'Titres de la France à la frontière de 1814', n.d.

[18] MAE, *Série A*, vol. 60, 'De la future frontière', 11 Nov. 1918.

[19] MAE, *Série A*, vol. 289, 'Note sur la future frontière', 10 Nov. 1918.

[20] Schuker, 'West European Security', 289; see also Mangin's historical musings in *Des Hommes et des faits: Hoche, Marceau, Napoléon, Gallieni* (Paris, 1923).

[21] Quoted in L. E. Mangin, *France et le Rhin, hier et aujourd'hui* (Geneva, 1945), 42; see also J. Nobécourt, 'Mangin et les mythes du Rhin' in *Une Histoire politique de l'armée*, vol. I: *De Pétain à Pétain* (Paris, 1967), 77–94.

centuries' and that only 'a return to this state of affairs' could 'provide a reliable guarantee of security for the West'.[22]

These allusions to France's historical limits were combined with the familiar picture of Germans as aggressive and violent, united by a hatred of France. Prussian–German policy was represented as a 'systematic programme of domination' aimed at destroying French power.[23] The wars of 1914, 1871 and even 1815 had all been caused by 'the Prussian spirit of economic and military aggression'.[24] From London, Paul Cambon submitted that 'the Prussianised Germans, that we know all too well, will neither forget nor pardon their defeat in 1918'.[25] Foch indulged in frequent and dire warnings about the 'Germanic mass of 70–75 millions' on France's eastern frontier. 'The German nation', he predicted, 'will always be bellicose and envious ... as it was formed by war and is inspired above all by the notions of force and conquest.'[26] Pétain's chief of staff, General Edmond Buat, was more blunt; Germany, he advised, should be treated like a dangerous animal: 'If one holds such an animal by its most sensitive part, one can control its behaviour ... and in the case of Germany, the sensitive part is the Left Bank of the Rhine.'[27]

The corollary to these pessimistic assessments of the German character was deep scepticism concerning prospects for German democratisation. The German people were deemed unsuited for democracy. Nor would a change in political constitution transform this mentality. The evolution of a true democratic sensibility would take many years.[28] General Fayolle dismissed the idea that Germany would 'change its mentality' by changing its political constitution as a 'fantasy'. 'The German will remain that which he has been for 2,500 years ... He will not change because the characteristics of race do not change, no more than do the laws of nature.'[29] The overarching lesson was that

---

[22] Quotations from SHD-DAT, *Fonds Clemenceau*, 6N 73-2, 'Note', 27 Nov. 1918 and 6N 73-2, 'Conversation entre M. Lloyd George et le maréchal Foch, 10 Downing Street, 1.12.18 à 5h' respectively.

[23] MAE, *Série A*, vol. 289, 'Note sur la future frontière entre l'Alsace-Lorraine et l'Allemagne: arguments historiques et moraux', 10 Nov. 1918.

[24] MAE, PA-AP 166, *Papiers Tardieu*, vol. 415, 'Titres de la France à la Fontière de 1814', n.d.

[25] SHD-DAT, *Fonds Clemenceau*, 6N 73-2, Cambon to Pichon, 2 Apr. 1919.

[26] SHD-DAT, *Fonds Clemenceau*, 6N 70-1, 'Note', Foch to Clemenceau, 21 Nov. 1918; 6N 73-2, 'Note' by Foch, 27 Nov. 1918; SHD-DAT, Fonds Privés (DITEEX), *Archives Foch*, 1K 129, carton 1, dr. 7, 'Note', 10 Jan. 1919; MAE, PA-AP 166, *Papiers Tardieu*, vol. 418, 'Note' (Foch to Council of Four), 31 Mar. 1919.

[27] Institut de France, *Souvenirs du Général Edmond Buat*, MS 5391 (1918–20), cahier 1 (9), 6 Oct. 1918.

[28] MAE, *Série A*, vol. 60, 'Du sort de l'Allemagne unifiée', 11 Nov. 1918; MAE, PA-AP 166, *Papiers Tardieu*, vol. 415, 'Note de M. Lavisse', 11 Jan. 1919; SHD-DAT, *Fonds Clemenceau*, 6N 73-2, Foch 'Note' to Clemenceau, 27 Nov. 1918; and SHD-DAT, Fonds Privés (DITEEX), *Archives Foch*, 1K 129, carton 1, dr. 7, Foch 'Note' to Allied leadership, 10 Jan. 1919.

[29] MAE, PA-AP 166, *Papiers Tardieu*, vol. 417, 'Note relative à la paix', 14 Feb. 1919.

future conflict was inevitable unless Germany was so weakened that it would be permanently deterred from aggression.

One means of weakening Germany was to impose legal limitations on its military power. Part V of the Versailles Treaty restricted the German army to an internal and border security force. Its size was limited to 100,000 long-term volunteers organised into three cavalry and seven infantry divisions. Germany was forbidden heavy artillery, tanks, combat aircraft and chemical weapons. The institutions of conscription and the army general staff were outlawed and the army was prohibited from large-scale field manoeuvres. The German navy was restricted to six battleships, six light cruisers, twelve destroyers and 15,000 total personnel. It was forbidden from building any warships displacing more than 10,000 tonnes and prohibited from possessing submarines. These restrictions on German sovereignty were to be permanent. Three inter-Allied control commissions were established to monitor German compliance with the land, air and sea provisions in the treaty.[30]

Few French policy makers considered these legal restrictions on German armed forces an important source of security. Enforced disarmament of Germany was never a significant war aim or a prominent element in peace planning.[31] A series of memoranda produced by the army staff during and after the peace conference warned that any programme of enforced disarmament would be difficult to impose and impossible to monitor. Clemenceau's staff predicted that, whatever limitations were imposed on its military power, 'Germany will find a way to evade the restrictions that are imposed and create the cadres for a great army'. The example of Prussian evasion of the disarmament measures imposed by Napoleonic France was invoked in support of this judgement. As long as Germany retained its heavy industry and the geographical advantage of the Rhineland, Part V of the Versailles Treaty could never be considered an important source of security.[32] Foch was characteristically blunt: 'Disarmament, one cannot repeat too often, gives us only a temporary, precarious, fictitious security ... Weakness in your adversary,' he warned, 'does not create strength in you.'[33]

Pessimistic judgements about the German national character and prospects for democracy across the Rhine, along with the expectation that Germany would subvert the disarmament provisions of the treaty, are hardly surprising

---

[30] See the online version of Articles 159–213 of the Versailles Treaty at www.lib.byu.edu/index.php/Articles_159_-_213; see also D. Stevenson, 'Britain, France and the origins of German disarmament', *JSS*, 29, 2 (2006), 195–224.
[31] Stevenson, 'Britain, France and the Origins of German Disarmament'.
[32] SHD-DAT, *Fonds Clemenceau*, 6N 73-1, 'Observations concernant le projet d'imposer à l'Allemagne le système d'une force permanent recrutée pour un service à long terme, et strictement destinée à assurer l'ordre à l'intérieur', n.d.; see also SHD-DAT, 7N 3529-2, 'Note au sujet du désarmement de l'Allemagne', Feb. 1919 and 'Historique du project de désarmement de l'Allemagne', 30 Sept. 1919.
[33] Quoted in J. King, *Foch versus Clemenceau: France and German Dismemberment, 1918–1919* (Cambridge, Mass., 1960), 22.

given the intensity of the conflict that had just ended. What is important is that they reinforced a tragic vision that was all but impossible to reconcile with widespread calls for a new basis for international politics.

II

Normative arguments invoking self-determination were employed to argue for a 'Rhenish Peace'. The hope was that the application of self-determination, when combined with the introduction of democratic liberties, would weaken the political sinews of the German Reich. There were interesting tensions between the various discursive strategies deployed in support of an independent Left Bank. Representations of the Reich as an artificial creation imposed by Prussian brutality sat uneasily alongside historical constructions of a highly cohesive and incorrigibly aggressive German national character.

To make the argument that the bonds of political unity between the Left Bank and the rest of Germany were fragile, national feeling in the region was represented as in its essence materialistic and self-interested. Laroche submitted that the 'sense of attachment' to Germany in the Rhineland was 'relatively recent and appears to be more a result of the material interests of its inhabitants than a profound and durable patriotic sentiment of the kind that attaches the immense majority of French people to their country'.[34] Berthelot pointed to 'particularist and federalist currents' within the Reichstag and concluded that 'it is in our interest to favour [German] federalism by furnishing it with the opportunity to express itself through elections based on universal suffrage'. He recommended what was essentially a strategy of economic bribery to facilitate the 'gradual evolution of popular sentiment on the Left Bank in favour of France'. A 'special military regime' would be put in place on the Left Bank. But Berthelot made no mention of annexing that territory or unilaterally altering its political status in the peace terms. The ultimate aim was to convince the Rhinelanders over time that their political future lay with France.[35] Tardieu endorsed this gradualist solution. He judged that the 'creation of a different economic orientation' on the Left Bank would 'create the *eventual* conditions for a political reorientation'. The region could then be drawn into the French orbit.[36]

Military officials lobbied for a much more aggressive strategy of detaching and dominating the Rhineland. A Contrôle-général des territoires rhénans was created under Foch's authority only weeks after the armistice. Paul Tirard was

---

[34] MAE, *Série A*, vol. 289, 'Les Frontières de l'Alsace-Lorraine et le statut de la rive gauche du Rhin', 1 Nov. 1918; see also Stevenson, *French War Aims*, 140–1.
[35] MAE, PA-AP 141, *Papiers Pichon*, vol. 6, 'Note sur les règlements de la paix', 23 Dec. 1918; see also Hanotaux's observations on the 'artificial' political character of Germany in MAE, *Série A*, vol. 60, 'Du sort de l'Allemagne unifiée', 11 Nov. 1918.
[36] MAE, PA-AP 166, *Papiers Tardieu*, vol. 417, 'Note sur l'organisation des provinces rhénanes', 26 Jan. 1919 (emphasis added).

appointed as controller-general of this new authority. Tirard was another graduate of the École libre who had made his reputation as a colonial administrator in Morocco before the war. He worked closely with Foch and other military elites to establish political and administrative conditions favourable to Rhenish separatism in the region. His strategy was economic and political associationalism in a regime akin to self-government for a colony.[37] But self-determination was also invoked. Foch insisted that the constitution of one or more buffer states was 'in accordance with the principle of the liberty of peoples that is acknowledged by all'.[38] From mid-December the Contrôle-général provided a steady stream of intelligence reports indicating goodwill towards France and support for separation from Germany. Foch and Pétain used this reporting to agitate for a more forward policy aimed at encouraging the industries of the Left Bank to 'turn towards France'.[39]

These assessments of opinion in the Rhineland were greeted with scepticism in Paris, however. The picture they painted was at odds with analyses of the situation prepared by the Quai d'Orsay's Service de documentation pour le Congrès de la paix. While this organ identified widespread antipathy for Prussia, it also judged the Catholic Rhinelanders to be 'just as patriotic as other Germans'. Although they wished to end Prussian domination of their region, the vast majority had 'no thought of becoming independent and no desire to become closer to France'.[40] Tardieu and his team, which included the exceedingly able Lieutenant Colonel Édouard Réquin as military adviser, expressed increasing scepticism of military intelligence reports of widespread enthusiasm for separatism on the Left Bank.[41]

This judgement cast doubt on the argument that an autonomous Left Bank was an exercise in self-determination and the extension of democratic liberties. Aubert, who worked at the nerve-centre of the policy machinery set up by Tardieu, underlined this fact. He warned that 'moral arguments based on the

---

[37] McDougall, *Rhineland Diplomacy*, 44; French planning for an occupation regime in the Rhineland is detailed in G.-H. Soutou, *L'Or et le sang: les buts de guerre économiques de la Première Guerre mondiale* (Paris, 1989), 788–94; Stevenson, *French War Aims*, 133–59; King, *Foch versus Clemenceau*; J. Bariéty, *Les Relations franco-allemandes après la première guerre mondiale* (Paris, 1977), 14–45; and P. Tirard, *La France sur le Rhin: douze années d'occupation rhénane* (Paris, 1930).

[38] SHD-DAT, Fonds Privés (DITEEX), *Archives Foch*, 1K 129, carton 1, dr. 7, Foch 'Note' to Allied leadership, 10 Jan. 1919.

[39] Many of these reports (along with voluminous other intelligence on the situation in Germany) can be consulted in SHD-DAT, *Fonds Clemenceau*, 6N 81, 112–20, 249 and 6N 261–8 as well as in MAE, PA-AP 166, *Papiers Tardieu*, vols. 426 and 427 (with a greater concentration on the Rhineland) and vol. 420, Pétain to Foch, 30 Dec. 1918 (forwarded by Foch on 3 Jan. 1919; see also McDougall, *Rhineland Diplomacy*, 51–66.

[40] MAE, Série Z, *Rive Gauche du Rhin* (hereafter *RGR*), vol. 1 (entitled 'République rhénane'), 'Le Projet d'une République Rhéno-Westphalienne', 17 Feb. 1919; this report was forwarded to Clemenceau, Tardieu and Foch.

[41] See esp. McDougall, *Rhineland Diplomacy*, 66 and Schuker, 'West European Security', 289–90.

principle that peoples have the right to determine their own political future have little force in relation to the immediate status of the Rhineland'. Berthelot acknowledged the same problem in relation to French claims to the Saar.[42]

The significance of these judgements should not be underestimated. Two key figures within the security policy hierarchy judged the principle of self-determination incompatible with imposing autonomy on the Left Bank as part of the peace settlement. This posed a serious challenge for policy calculations. A buffer state was central not only to Foch's 10 January note to Allied leaders, but also to the government's memorandum on west European security distributed to France's allies on 25 February 1919.[43]

Another example of this kind of normative engagement on the part of policy elites was a consistent emphasis on democracy as a force for peace and security in both internal and external correspondence. Growing importance was attributed to the democratic bonds uniting France with its allies in a transatlantic political and cultural community. This was in one sense only a continuation of familiar discourses depicting the forces of 'liberty' and 'civilisation' as locked in mortal combat with German 'barbarism' that had pervaded the public sphere since 1914. But it also reflected geo-political developments during the war.

The centre of gravity in world politics was moving slowly but inevitably away from Europe. The importance both Tardieu and Aubert attached to this seismic geo-political change is reflected in the frequency with which they referred to the importance of an 'Atlantic' or 'North Atlantic' grouping of powers.[44] One of their most common rhetorical strategies was to elide the specific interests of France with those of the western allies as a whole by representing the 'western' or 'Atlantic' powers as a coherent political and cultural unit. The Rhine could thus be depicted as 'the international frontier of liberty' dividing the 'civilised democracies of the west' from German barbarism and autocracy.[45] In rhetoric that anticipated the propaganda battles of the Cold War, power-political security aims were dressed up as vital to the future of freedom and democracy.

---

[42] AN, 324 AP 51, *Archives André Tardieu*, 'Rhin', handwritten note by Aubert, undated but drafted the first week of March; MAE, PA-AP 141, *Papiers Pichon*, vol. 7, 'Sarre: note B', 20 Jan. 1919.

[43] SHD-DAT, *Fonds Clemenceau*, 6N 73-2, 'Mémoire du gouvernement français sur la fixation de la frontière occidentale de l'Allemagne et l'occupation interalliée des ponts du fleuve', 25 Feb. 1919 (reprinted in Tardieu, *La Paix*, 165–84 and Cmd. 2169, *Negotiations for an Anglo-French Pact*, 41–57).

[44] MAE, PA-AP 166, *Papiers Tardieu*, vol. 417, 'Rive gauche de Rhin: la neutralisation militaire', 2 Feb. 1919. David Stevenson notes this strategy in *French War Aims*, 155, but he does not reflect upon its significance; Georges-Henri Soutou goes further in 'French Peacemakers', but does not link Clemenceau's ideological affinities to the views of other members of the policy and political elite.

[45] MAE, PA-AP 166, *Papiers Tardieu*, vol. 417: 'Note sur le rôle international du Rhine comme "Frontière de la Liberté"', 20 Jan. 1917 (note drafted by Tardieu with assistance from Aubert and Réquin).

It was Aubert who first sketched the broad outlines of an Atlantic alliance in a memorandum of 2 January 1919 when he argued that:

The Rhine, which for centuries has been considered as the natural frontier between France and Germany, must, as a result of this war, be considered as the natural frontier between the democracies of the North-Atlantic and Germany.[46]

The concept of a transatlantic security community was taken up by Tardieu in his revision of Foch's note to Allied leaders one week later. Tardieu inserted the phrase 'co-operation between all democratic powers' into Foch's text. He also anticipated the course of negotiations to come when he advocated 'an engagement of reciprocal assurance and military assistance ... in the case of a new German aggression'.[47] This would be the core security requirement of the Clemenceau government.

Linked to the discourse of democratic peace were efforts to co-opt the themes of the League of Nations and the rule of law into traditional arguments for a favourable balance of power. The impulse for this engagement again came from Aubert and Tardieu. A memo entitled 'The Rhine Frontier and the League of Nations', drafted by Aubert to serve as part of the government's official memorandum on the Rhineland, asserted that Allied domination of the Left Bank was an essential precondition for the effective functioning of the League. Aubert deployed the criticisms of the draft covenant advanced by Bourgeois on the League of Nations Commission to support the case for a strategic buffer. He argued that the legal guarantees and collective security provisions envisaged for the League were too cumbersome and ambiguous to provide immediate material assistance in the event of another German invasion. The only such guarantee available was the occupation of the Left Bank and control of the Rhine bridgeheads. This 'physical guarantee' was represented as 'in the interest of the League of Nations no less'.[48]

This line of argument ultimately only served to highlight the contradiction between desire for a favourable balance of power, on the one hand, and the need to adapt to new international norms, on the other. The result was a considerable muddle that did not strengthen the French case. In order to co-opt the normative authority of the League, for example, Aubert tried to argue that it required a violation of the principle of self-determination to function effectively. These tensions would surface in glaring fashion once negotiations for a west European settlement began in earnest. The Clemenceau government would be forced to make difficult choices in pursuit of long-term security.

---

[46] MAE, PA-AP 166, *Papiers Tardieu*, vol. 417, 'Rive gauche de Rhin', Aubert note, 2 Feb. 1919.

[47] Compare the final draft forwarded by Foch with Tardieu's revisions in MAE, PA-AP 166, *Papiers Tardieu*, vol. 422.

[48] MAE, PA-AP 166, *Papiers Tardieu*, vol. 420, 'La Frontière du Rhin et la Ligue des nations', n.d. but late Feb. 1919.

III

Tardieu and his staff drew the French programme together in two lengthy memoranda, the first on the Rhine frontier (25 February) and the second on the future of the Saarland (8 March).[49] A central aim of both documents was to overthrow the European strategic balance.

The 'French government memorandum on the fixing of the Rhine as the western frontier of Germany and the occupation of its bridges' called for establishing the Left Bank as an autonomous region and for a permanent inter-Allied occupation of the Rhine bridgeheads. The precise political status of the region was left open. These measures were justified by an uncompromising survey of the strategic situation. Germany's population was twice that of France. Even if it was deprived of Posnania, Schleswig and the provinces of the Left Bank, the Reich's population would still outnumber that of France, Belgium and Luxembourg combined. The same held true of Germany's industrial infrastructure, which remained intact while that of France lay in ruins. Nor could this 'dangerous imbalance of power' be counterbalanced with support from Russia, as it had been before the war.[50]

From these observations flowed the logic of creating a strategic buffer – a measure that Tardieu equated with British and American desires to retain significant naval power. France had no sea to protect it against the chief threat to its existence. It was therefore vital to 'create a zone of security' on its eastern frontier that would 'close off the historic invasion route' that Germany had used in 1815, 1871 and 1914. The French industrial heartland was within easy striking distance of German troops concentrated on the Left Bank. As a result, France had lost 90 per cent of its mineral production and 86 per cent of its cast iron output during the opening phase of the war. To leave Germany in control of the Left Bank, Tardieu warned, would be to assure it the most favourable conditions for future aggression aimed at 'crushing the western democracies'.[51]

The majority of the French political and policy elite was united behind the Rhineland memorandum. Foch endorsed it without hesitation. Clemenceau approved it with only very marginal changes. Poincaré described it as 'absolutely remarkable'. His only suggestion was to stipulate that the Left Bank would not be annexed 'against the will of its population'. This would give a nod

---

[49] SHD-DAT, *Fonds Clemenceau*, 6N 73–2, 'Mémoire du gouvernement français sur la fixation de la frontière occidentale de l'Allemagne et l'occupation interalliée des ponts du fleuve', 25 Feb. 1919 (reprinted in Tardieu, *La Paix*, 165–84 and Cmd. 2169, *Negotiations for an Anglo-French Pact*, 41–57); MAE, PA-AP 166, *Papiers Tardieu*, vol. 415, 'Mémoire du gouvernement français sur le frontière septentrionale de l'Alsace-Lorraine', 8 Mar. 1919 (reprinted in part in Tardieu, *La Paix*, 279–89).

[50] SHD-DAT, *Fonds Clemenceau*, 6N 73–2, 'Mémoire du gouvernement français sur la fixation de la frontière occidentale de l'Allemagne et l'ocupation interalliée des ponts du fleuve', 25 Feb. 1919.

[51] Ibid.

to self-determination but also leave open the possibility that the inhabitants might someday voluntarily opt for union with France.[52] David Stevenson has rightly concluded that the memorandum provides a window into 'the French elite's innermost thinking'.[53] There was a widespread desire to transform the geo-political situation in Europe to France's advantage.

Improving the balance of power was also the chief aim of the 'French government memorandum on the northern frontier of Alsace-Lorraine'. In this document Tardieu outlined three categories of claim for the Saar, resulting in three distinct territorial settlements.[54] The first was based on the principle of 'military security' and demanded the 'natural strategic frontier' recommended by Foch the previous November. Strategic priorities were invoked to argue for a frontier that would entail the annexation of over one million German nationals by France.[55] The second order of claim came under the rubric of 'juridical restitution' and demanded the restoration of France's frontier of 1814. The final category was based on the principle of 'economic reparation': Germany must compensate France for the systematic destruction of its mines and industrial infrastructure in 1918. If it did not, 'France would become an economic tributary of Germany, which, through its coal, would control the price of all our metallurgical production and thus dominate our entire policy'. Cession of the entire Saar coalfield was therefore 'indispensable from a general point of view'.

The memo then mooted a combination of military, legal and economic claims in a solution that conformed to the principle of self-determination. Stressing the 'profound unity' of the region's industrial, commercial and social infrastructure, it proposed that France regain its 1814 frontier plus ownership of the mines of the entire Saar basin and the industrial infrastructure linked to them. Citing France's commitment to 'respect the rights and interests of the people', it was proposed that after twenty years the inhabitants of the region be given the right to choose their citizenship 'whether this be French, German or Rhenish'. The mines and infrastructure, however, would remain under the ownership of the French state, their value set against the German reparations account.[56]

---

[52] This suggestion was ignored, however. This was doubtless because Tardieu and his team realised that invoking self-determination would undermine the case for Left Bank autonomy. See Poincaré, *Au service de la France*, vol. XI: *À la recherche de la paix*, Poincaré to Pichon and Poincaré to Tardieu, both from 25 Feb. 1919, 182–4.
[53] Stevenson, *French War Aims*, 158–9.
[54] MAE, PA-AP 166, *Papiers Tardieu*, vol. 415, 'Mémoire du gouvernement français sur le frontière septentrionale de l'Alsace-Lorraine', 8 Mar. 1919.
[55] The tricky question of self-determination in the Saar was dealt with by arguing that in 1793 the Saarlanders had manifested a 'passionate desire for union with France' and that this sentiment endured in 1919.
[56] MAE, PA-AP 166, *Papiers Tardieu*, vol. 415, 'Mémoire du gouvernement français sur le frontière septentrionale de l'Alsace-Lorraine', 8 Mar. 1919.

Taken together the two memoranda provide ample testimony to the powerful current of traditional thinking in French policy. The objective was a transformation of power relations in western Europe. The Left Bank would be detached and neutralised; the Rhine bridgeheads would be occupied by France and its allies; and the coal-rich Saarland would come under French control for the foreseeable future.

And yet there was more to the French programme than calculations based on power and strategic advantage. France's position towards the Saarland, for example, was represented as a rectification of historical injustice that reflected the imperative of self-determination. The bid for a Left Bank buffer state, meanwhile, was couched in the language of common interest and democratic solidarity. There are no less than fifteen references to the 'western democracies' as a single political and cultural entity in the Rhineland memorandum. The following passage is indicative of the ideologically charged language used throughout:

The common security of the western and overseas democracies requires that Germany be deprived of the means to once again mount the sudden attacks of 1870 and 1914 ... [we must] ... take from Germany not only the Left Bank but also the bridgeheads of the Rhine – so that its western frontier is once again fixed on the Rhine ... the history of the past century demonstrates the need for this protection. The common security of the Allies demands that the Rhine must become, in the words of president Wilson, 'the frontier of Liberty'.

The memo also deployed Aubert's argument that the proposed 'physical guarantee' would be a boon for the League of Nations. An Allied military presence on the Rhine, it added, would also permit the League to intervene in support of the successor states in eastern Europe in the event that Germany attempted to 'strangle' them before they could establish themselves. The French proposal was thus 'animated by the spirit of the League of Nations' and therefore 'in the general interest of humanity'. 'France', the Allies were assured, 'demands nothing for itself, not one inch of territory nor any right of sovereignty ... What it proposes instead is the creation, in the general interest, of a common protection for all pacific democracies, for the League of Nations, for liberty and for peace.'[57]

Great emphasis was also placed on the extent to which the French programme was a break with past practices. 'Our solution is a liberal solution,' Tardieu insisted. 'It is clearly different to the old solutions of the past.'[58] Such claims were more than mere rhetoric. They flowed from a realisation that close post-war relations

---

[57] SHD-DAT, *Fonds Clemenceau*, 6N 73–2, 'Mémoire du gouvernement français sur la fixation de la frontière occidentale de l'Allemagne et l'occupation interalliée des ponts du fleuve', 25 Feb. 1919.
[58] MAE, PA-AP 166, *Papiers Tardieu*, vol. 421, 'Conversation du 11 mars 1919': this is Tardieu's account of his meeting with Sidney Mezes and Philip Kerr (who Tardieu erroneously identifies as 'M. Carr').

with the Anglo-Saxon democracies were incompatible with a return to exclusively traditional practices. The attractions of a north Atlantic community, moreover, were based on more than power-political considerations. They rested also on the belief that political and cultural affinities made the United States and Britain the most reliable allies for France in the long term. When put to the test, this conviction would prove decisive.

IV

France's Great Power allies were not willing to break up Germany. The British and Americans instead took the unprecedented step of offering to guarantee France's security from unprovoked aggression. French negotiators were asked to give up the claim to an autonomous buffer state in return.

From the American perspective, measures imposed on Germany could only be justified either as an application of self-determination or as temporary measures to ensure German compliance and preserve peace until the League of Nations was working effectively. The French proposal to detach the Left Bank fulfilled neither of these criteria.[59] Wilson was highly critical of French attempts to 'interpret the principle of self-determination with a lawyer's cunning'. He judged French ambitions 'stupid' and 'insane' and vowed that he would 'rather be stoned in the streets' than give in to them.[60]

The British, who had long been aware of French designs for the Rhineland, interpreted them as a threat to Britain's interests and to prospects for a durable peace settlement.[61] Philip Kerr, private secretary to Lloyd George, described the French scheme as a 'shell shock proposition' that should be resisted 'to the end'.[62] Balfour lamented that French policy was based on 'a lurid picture of Franco-German relations'. He judged that

> if international relations and international methods are, as the French assume, going to remain in the future what they have been in the past ... no manipulation of the Rhine frontier is going to make France anything more than a second-rate power, trembling at the nod of its great neighbours to the East and depending from day to day on the changes and chances of a shifting diplomacy and uncertain alliances.[63]

---

[59] House, *Intimate Papers*, IV, 345: 9 Feb. 1919; see also M. MacMillan, *Paris 1919* (New York, 2001), 174.
[60] Quoted in Schuker, 'West European Security', 302 and 290 respectively.
[61] HLRO, *Lloyd George Papers*, LG F/3/3/35, Balfour to Lloyd George, 29 Nov. 1918; LG F/52/2/52, Derby to Balfour, 14 Dec. 1918; LG F/3/4/2, Cecil to Balfour (forwarded to Lloyd George), 8 Jan. 1919; Cmd. 2169, *Negotiations for an Anglo-French Pact*, 10: 'Extract from French proposals for the preliminaries of peace with Germany communicated by the French Ambassador, Nov. 26 1918'.
[62] Cmd. 2169, *Negotiations for an Anglo-French Pact*, 68–9: 'Minute from Mr P. H. Kerr to prime minister and Mr Balfour', 13 Mar. 1919; HLRO, *Lloyd George Papers*, F/89/2/40, 'Notes of a discussion with M. Tardieu and Dr Mezes', 12 Mar. 1919.
[63] HLRO, *Lloyd George Papers*, F/3/4/19, Balfour note to Lloyd George, 18 Mar. 1919.

What was needed instead, Balfour submitted, was 'a change in the international system of the world'.[64]

Lloyd George, for his part, suspected a French bid for continental pre-eminence. He resolved to oppose any Allied occupation of the Left Bank.[65] To convince the French to renounce their plan, he proposed an Anglo-American military guarantee. This idea, which probably originated with Kerr, was first mooted to the British cabinet on 4 March 1919. Lloyd George predicted that the Clemenceau government would renounce its plan for dismembering and occupying Germany in return for a promise of immediate British and American military assistance in the event of a German attack.[66] The idea was first raised with the French by Kerr in a meeting with Tardieu on 11 March.[67] Lloyd George did the same in a conversation with Clemenceau the following day, sweetening the offer with disingenuous talk of a channel tunnel to expedite future British military intervention. The proposal of British and American treaties of guarantee, which were to remain in force until the League was capable of providing France with security, was extended formally in a meeting between Lloyd George, Wilson and Clemenceau on the afternoon of 14 March.[68]

The guarantee offer was the pivot upon which the entire German question turned. It forced the French government to define its 'bottom line' in terms of security in Europe. Would France continue to insist on the highly traditional solution of a strategic buffer in the Rhineland? Or would it renounce this claim in favour of the more innovative guarantee formula proposed by the other great 'North Atlantic democracies'?

A close look at the evidence suggests that Clemenceau and his advisers had all along anticipated that such an offer might be made. What is more, the French government made it clear that it was willing to discuss this issue. In December, Jean Monnet met with American treasury official Norman Davis in London. Monnet advised Davis that France's territorial demands would be uncompromising unless it received an Anglo-American guarantee against a

---

[64] Ibid.
[65] M. G. Fry, *And Fortune Fled: David Lloyd George: The First Democratic Statesman, 1916–1922* (New York, 2011), 195–6, 200, 218–23; MacMillan, *Paris 1918*, 144–5, 170–4, 194–8.
[66] TNA-PRO, CAB, 23/15/541A, War Cabinet minutes, 4 Mar. 1919.
[67] The British and French records of this meeting differ. In Tardieu's account, the idea of a guarantee is outlined clearly by Kerr on 11 Mar. 1919. According to Kerr's record, he made no mention of the idea on 11 Mar. but hinted at a guarantee the following day. See MAE, PA-AP 166, *Papiers Tardieu*, vol. 421, 'Conversation du 11 mars 1919' and Cmd. 2169, *Negotiations for an Anglo-French Pact*, 59–62: 'Notes of a discussion between Mr P. H. Kerr, M. Tardieu and Dr Mezes'.
[68] Fry, *Fortune Fled*, 218–19 and 235–6; A. Lentin, 'Several types of ambiguity: Lloyd George at the Paris Peace Conference', *D&S*, 6, 1 (1995), 223–51; House, *Intimate Papers*, IV, 356–60 and 392–4; Nelson, *Land and Power*, 219–28.

German attack on France.[69] There were also hints in the Rhineland memo that the 'physical guarantee' on the Left Bank could be temporary rather than permanent.[70] Tardieu assured the British that France was 'ready to consider anything which the Allies thought reasonable' as long as the Left Bank was closed for all time to the German military.[71] He later admitted that the 25 February memorandum was an 'instrument of discussion' drafted at a time when France had no peacetime commitment from its allies.[72]

Tardieu's claim is supported by a fascinating note on the strategic importance of the Rhine prepared by Aubert at the beginning of March. Aubert began by listing, in their order of importance, the key arguments for staying on the Rhine as they had been presented to France's allies: first, the Rhine constituted an excellent defensive position to protect French soil from another German attack; second, it would also serve as a base of offensive operations in support of the newly formed eastern states; third, the Rhine provided the Allies with an excellent *gage* to ensure German treaty compliance. But Aubert went on to argue that Germany's weakened state, and in particular the rising levels of political disorder in that country, meant that 'this order of importance must be reversed'. A position on the Rhine was foremost a means to compel German compliance, then a means of supporting the eastern successor states and finally a defensive position. German weakness combined with the principle of self-determination to force a reconsideration of French policy. 'We must recognise', Aubert observed,

that for the moment the danger of a resurgence of the German peril is assuming an ever more academic character that does not justify great political decisions such as the permanent detachment from Germany of five million Germans of the Left Bank ... Our allies can, not without a strong case, offer us a substitute in the form of an alliance.

If such an offer was made, 'it would be wise to recognise the temporary character of our case for a watch on the Rhine ... and envisage an occupation for as long as Germany remains a threat'.[73] In Aubert's judgement, a temporary but prolonged occupation, if supplemented by a strategic commitment

---

[69] *FRUS, PPC*, I, Report of a conversation between Norman Davis and Jean Monnet, 3 Dec. 1918: 334–6; see also D. H. Miller, *My Diary at the Peace Conference of Paris: With Documents*, 21 vols. (New York, 1928), I, 3 Dec. 1918: 25.
[70] 'It is essential to reinforce, at least temporarily, the legal guarantees [in the Covenant] with a guarantee of a physical character': SHD-DAT, *Fonds Clemenceau*, 6N 73-2, 'Mémoire du gouvernement français sur la fixation de la frontière occidentale de l'Allemagne et l'ocupation interalliée des ponts du fleuve', 25 Feb. 1919.
[71] BL, *Cecil Papers*, MSS 51131, 'Diary', 28 Feb. 1919.
[72] MAE, PA-AP 166, *Papiers Tardieu*, vol. 421, 'Réponse du gouvernement' to a questionnaire submitted by the chamber foreign affairs commission, 29 Jul. 1919.
[73] AN, 324 AP 51, *Papiers Tardieu*, 'Rhin', Aubert note; the subject matter and tense used in this document leave little doubt that it dates from the first week in March.

from Britain and the USA, was preferable to permanent occupation and political isolation.

Aubert's observations provide an important window into the thinking of Clemenceau's inner circle as French policy evolved away from security based on traditional military preponderance towards security based on treaty enforcement underwritten by Great Power co-operation. The importance attached to self-determination was also evident in the position taken by Tardieu in conversations with British and American officials in late February and early March. He assured Cecil, for example, that, as long as the Rhine bridgeheads were occupied, the Left Bank could remain 'in all other respects German'.[74] He went further in conversations with House and Balfour to suggest that neither the Allied occupation nor the Rhineland buffer need necessarily be permanent. Once Germany was no longer a threat to peace, 'in five, ten or some other number of years', France would 'have no objection to [the Left Bank] going where the inclination of the people might lead them'.[75] Tardieu reiterated this offer in meetings with Kerr and Mezes on 11 and 12 March.[76] These hints convinced Lloyd George that the French government was not 'really behind' its Rhineland proposal. He judged that the programme had been adopted to appease Foch and other hardliners.[77]

Lloyd George was only partly correct. The Clemenceau government would almost certainly have welcomed an independent or autonomous Rhineland. But it was unwilling to impose such a solution on the population of the Left Bank. Such a policy would have lacked legitimacy both abroad and at home. It would also have provoked a rupture with France's most powerful allies. The gradualist solution based on temporary occupation, conversely, satisfied the principle of self-determination, would not alienate the British and Americans, and yet still held out the prospect of luring the Rhinelanders into a closer relationship with France in the longer term.

'We must thus choose', Clemenceau observed to his closest advisers on the evening of 14 March, 'either France alone on the Left Bank of the Rhine or France with the return of the 1814 frontier, that is to say with Alsace-Lorraine and part, if not all, of the Saar, and America and Britain allied to us.' The fact that the premier framed the choice in this way leaves little doubt as to his thinking. The following morning Tardieu and Pichon raised doubts about giving up a physical guarantee for a promise of assistance. But Louis Loucheur and Clemenceau both argued forcefully for engagement with the

---

[74] BL, *Cecil Papers*, MSS 51131, 'Diary', 28 Feb. 1919.
[75] House, *Intimate Papers*, IV, 346–7: 23 Feb. 1919; TNA-PRO, FO/608/142, 'Summary of a conversation with M. Tardieu: an independent republic on the west bank of the Rhine', n.d. but late Feb. 1919; see also Stevenson, *French War Aims*, 167 and McCrum, 'French Rhineland policy', 628.
[76] Cmd. 2169, *Negotiations for an Anglo-French Pact*, 59–65: 'Notes of a discussion between Mr P. H. Kerr, M. Tardieu and Dr Mezes', 11, 12 and 13 Mar. 1919.
[77] TNA-PRO, CAB, 23/15/541A, cabinet minutes, 4 Mar. 1919.

Anglo-American proposals. France, they argued, could not manage a permanent occupation of the Rhineland on its own. All agreed that the guarantee offer was impossible to refuse. Tardieu and Pichon were instructed to draw up a note accepting the proposition with demands for supplementary guarantees.[78] Forced to choose, the Clemenceau government opted for membership in a North Atlantic alliance over a bid to transform the balance of power.

There was also agreement, however, that the Anglo-American proposal could only be accepted if it was accompanied by a series of supplementary guarantees. Tardieu outlined six conditions for accepting the guarantee offer.[79] First, the Left Bank, along with a strip of territory fifty kilometres wide on the right bank, would be demilitarised permanently (this stipulation had already been agreed in principle[80]). Second, an inter-Allied force would occupy the Left Bank and bridgeheads for a period to be set by the treaty – the initial French suggestion was thirty years – as a guarantee of German reparations payments. Third, any German violation of the demilitarisation or the disarmament clauses of the treaty would be defined as an act of aggression against all signatories. The aim was to delineate an unambiguous *casus foederis* for the operation of the guarantee. Fourth, France must be granted the right to reoccupy the Left Bank and bridgeheads in the event such a case was established. Fifth, acknowledging the legitimacy of the League, the French proposed that its Council be granted a permanent right to inspect German compliance with the disarmament and demilitarisation clauses of the treaty. Finally, France would gain the frontier of 1814 with the right to occupy the entire Saar basin.[81]

These demands met with stiff resistance. Lloyd George remained opposed to any occupation of German territory. Wilson, meanwhile, refused to define all German disarmament violations as acts of aggression. He was also against making the League a vehicle for punishing Germany.[82] The deadlock was eventually broken by bilateral exchanges between the French and Americans in which Wilson accepted a temporary occupation as a means of ensuring German compliance. Clemenceau and Wilson agreed in mid-March to a fifteen-year occupation with a three-stage evacuation contingent on German

---

[78] The only primary source record of the two crucial meetings is Loucheur's diary: *Carnets secrets*, 71–2: entries for Friday 14 and Saturday 15 Mar. 1919.
[79] MAE, PA-AP 166, *Papiers Tardieu*, vol. 418 (also in vol. 421), 'Note sur la suggestion présentée le 14 mars (Remise le 17 mars au P. Wilson et à M. Lloyd George)'; the French position was further developed in SHD-DAT, *Fonds Clemenceau*, 6N 73–2, 'Note sur la conversation du 18 mars', 19 Mar. 1919 and MAE, PA-AP 166, *Papiers Tardieu*, vol. 419, 'Amendements proposés par la France', 2 Apr. 1919.
[80] Cmd. 2169, *Negotiations for an Anglo-French Pact*, 58–9: 'Extract from Draft Conditions to be imposed on Germany, presented to the Supreme War Council', 17 Mar. 1919.
[81] On 2 April Tardieu tried briefly to argue for doubling the width of the demilitarised zone on the right bank: MAE, PA-AP 166, *Papiers Tardieu*, vol. 419, 'Amendements proposés par la France', 2 Apr. 1919.
[82] A. Sharp, *The Versailles Settlement: Peacemaking in Paris, 1919* (London, 1991), 106–13; McCrum, 'French Rhineland Policy', 634–42; McDougall, *Rhineland Diplomacy*, 60–72.

execution of the treaty. Clemenceau further obtained the right to reoccupy in the event of German default in reparations payments as well as agreement that any violation of the demilitarised status of the Rhineland would be defined as a *casus foederis*. He dropped the demand to interpret German violation of the disarmament clauses in the same way. The League, however, would be given the right to inspect and verify German compliance. Lloyd George, who had been away from Paris, had little choice but to accept these arrangements upon his return.[83]

The issue of the Saar coalfield proved almost as difficult to resolve. Lloyd George and especially Wilson were unwilling to agree to the French claim to this region. Both, however, were persuaded that France had at least a temporary right to Saar coal as reparation. Clemenceau, on the other hand, believed that the frontier of 1814 represented historical justice for France. He had broached this question with House even before the armistice was signed.[84] He pressed the claim again in March, this time against the advice of both Tardieu and Berthelot. They pointed out that the 1814 boundary had limited strategic value and was impossible to justify in terms of self-determination. Tardieu went so far as to describe insisting on it as 'stupidity'.[85] Berthelot deployed the logic of a gradualist solution to argue for a future plebiscite. Such an outcome, he pointed out, would provide France with immediate economic advantages while retaining the long-term prospect of drawing the entire region into its orbit.[86]

Clemenceau was not persuaded, and insisted on the 1814 frontier. The result was an acute crisis that threatened a complete breakdown in Allied solidarity. Compromise was reached roughly along the lines of Berthelot's proposal. A plebiscite was to decide the political status of the Saarland after fifteen years. During that time France would have ownership of the coalfield and its infrastructure. The region would be administered by a League of Nations commission but would form part of the French monetary and fiscal area.[87] The episode demonstrates yet again the difficulties inherent in

---

[83] MAE, PA-AP 166, *Papiers Tardieu*, vol. 419, 'Résumé sommaire d'une conversation avec le Colonel House', 3 Apr. 1919; 'Memorandum on the Amendments proposed by France to the Agreement suggested by P. Wilson regarding the Rhine frontier', 12 Apr. 1919; 'Projet: Mémorandum en réponse à la note du P. Wilson', 15 Apr. 1919; 'Clauses du traité franco-américain (arrêtées par MM. Wilson et Clemenceau)', 16 Apr. 1919; 'Articles relatifs à la garantie d'exécution du traité', 20 Apr. 1919; Nelson, *Land and Power*, 232–45.

[84] SLYU, MS 466, *Papers of Col. Edward Mandell House*, Series II (Diary), vol. 6, 9 Nov. 1918; MAE, PA-AP 166, *Papiers Tardieu*, vol. 415, 'Note présenté à M. Clemenceau par M. Tardieu au sujet du Bassin de la Sarre', Jan. 1919.

[85] Poincaré, *À la recherche de la paix*, 310: 3 Apr. 1919; MAE, PA-AP 166, *Papiers Tardieu*, vol. 415, 'Note présenté à M. Clemenceau par M. Tardieu au sujet du Bassin de la Sarre', Jan. 1919: the 1814 boundary left Germany in possession of the richest portion of the coalfield and the strategically valuable terrain to the north of the Saar basin: see also Schuker, 'West European Security', 302.

[86] MAE, PA-AP 141, *Papiers Pichon*, vol. 7, 'Sarre: note B', 20 Jan. 1919 and 'Note sur la question des pays rhénans', Berthelot, 31 Mar. 1919.

[87] Sharp, *Versailles Settlement*, 113–18; Nelson, *Land and Power*, 255–81.

categorising the French peace programme exclusively in terms of a bid for strategic predominance. Clemenceau's thinking regarding the Saar was motivated more by a romantic notion of justice for France than by hard-headed 'realism'.[88]

The right to reoccupy the Rhineland in the event of German non-payment of reparations was another vexed issue. Clemenceau was forced to concede that reoccupation could only take place if the Reparations Commission judged Germany to be in default of its financial obligations. He obtained an important final success, however, when an amendment was inserted into Article 429 of the treaty which stipulated that

if [at the end of the fifteen-year period] the guarantees against unprovoked aggression are not considered sufficient by the Allied and Associated Governments, the evacuation of the occupying troops may be delayed to the extent regarded as necessary for the purposes of obtaining the required guarantees.[89]

This preserved for France the right to prolong the occupation in the event of German non-compliance.

The significance of this and the other legal constraints imposed by the treaty is worth emphasising. Four of the six demands advanced by the French in response to the guarantee offer were what Tardieu described as 'contractual guarantees'.[90] Their value was based on their status as permanent elements of international public law. This gave French security policy a legal character that has not been recognised in the literature. The key demand for a clear *casus foederis* to trigger both the Anglo-American guarantee and the reoccupation of the Rhineland was based explicitly on the Clemenceau team's analysis of the insufficiencies of Articles 10 through 16 of the League Covenant.[91] 'It is essential above all', Tardieu insisted, 'that the *casus feoderis* be defined with the greatest clarity so that Germany can have no uncertainty as to the precise and immediate consequences of any aggression ... It is this prompt and automatic character that is presently missing in the dispositions inscribed in

---

[88] Stevenson, *French War Aims*, 179 observes that this was 'the closest to a French demand of sheer unreason, unsupported either by convincing arguments from national self-determination or by the logic of a broader strategic design'.

[89] MAE, PA-AP 166, *Papiers Tardieu*, vol. 419, 'Proposition remise à Clemenceau', 28 Apr. 1919; this is a revision of the key clause in ibid., 'Articles relatifs à la garantie d'exécution du traité', 24 Apr. 1919. See also Stevenson, *French War Aims*, 174.

[90] AN, 324 AP 51, *Archives Tardieu*, 'Question du Rhin', n.d. Tardieu also uses the term 'contractual guarantee' in a summary of the French position prepared for Clemenceau: MAE, PA-AP 166, *Papiers Tardieu*, vol. 419, 'Note pour M. Clemenceau: la question du Rhin', 23 Apr. 1919.

[91] SHD-DAT, *Fonds Clemenceau*, 6N 73-2, 'Question du Rhin: 2ème solution (engagement)', 19 Mar. 1919; MAE, PA-AP 166, *Papiers Tardieu*, vol. 418, 'La France et la question du Rhin', 29 Mar. 1919; MAE, PA-AP 166, *Papiers Tardieu*, vol. 419, 'Note pour M. Clemenceau: la question du Rhin', 23 Apr. 1919.

the League of Nations Covenant.'[92] This critique of the 'gaps' in the Covenant would be taken up by every post-war government through 1925 in pursuit of supplementary security guarantees.

The significance of the fact that these guarantees were legal in character, embedded in international public law, has been overlooked by most scholars of the peace settlement. They were far from classic mechanisms of traditional power politics. The same is true to an even greater degree of Article 429, which outlined conditions that would lead to an evacuation of the Rhineland and provided for a prolongation of the occupation in the event of German non-compliance. When defending the settlement, both Tardieu and Clemenceau characterised this stipulation as decisive insurance against either German non-compliance or refusal by the US congress to ratify the treaty. 'I insisted myself on the inclusion of this article,' the premier advised the chamber. 'As a result we are safeguarded against all scenarios.'[93]

The above emphasis on juridical safeguards embedded in international legal institutions should not obscure the fundamental importance of traditional balance-of-power considerations in the French peace programme. Berthelot's preference for a gradualist policy aimed at luring the occupied Left Bank in stages away from Prussia and towards France was an innovative strategy to achieve a traditional outcome.[94] Tardieu noted that 'the idea of an *autonomous* state remains conceivable'. An eventual customs treaty with the Left Bank, he speculated, would afford 'the opportunity of attracting into the French sphere a region that, of its own accord, would be situated on the margins of Germany'. Such a result would offer 'all the advantages of an independent state without the inconveniences [of violating the norm of self-determination]'.[95] France would secure a strategic buffer while at the same time benefiting from the Anglo-American strategic commitment. Hope remained that the balance of power could be altered in the name of self-determination.

The Clemenceau government had nonetheless given up the demand for a 'physical guarantee' in exchange for a temporary occupation. This would prove wholly unacceptable to those constituencies in France that remained committed to a traditional solution to the security question.

---

[92] MAE, PA-AP 166, *Papiers Tardieu*, vol. 418, 'La France et la question du Rhin', 29 Mar. 1919. Interestingly, however, the key phrase in this article 'not considered sufficient by the Allied and Associated governments' was open to legal interpretation; its application would depend on France making a strong legal case.
[93] *JO*, Chambre, *Débats*, 1919, 25 Sept. 1919.
[94] MAE, PA-AP 141, *Papiers Pichon*, vol. 7, 'Note sur la question des pays rhénans', Berthelot, 31 Mar. 1919; see also BDIC, *Archives Klotz*, dr. 18, 'Note sur la question rhénane (résumé de rapports et notes antérieurs)', 2 Apr. 1919.
[95] MAE, PA-AP 166, *Papiers Tardieu*, vol. 418, undated and untitled note drafted in late March or early April.

V

In late March and April 1919 government policy faced a direct challenge from advocates of a 'Rhenish peace'. It was at this juncture that Marshal Foch committed his formidable symbolic capital to a campaign for a permanent presence on the Rhine. While such a campaign could be useful to Clemenceau in negotiations in the Council of Four, in April 1919 opposition to his policy threatened to erupt into a full-blown constitutional crisis. A close look at this episode underscores the distinctions between the innovative character of the government's programme and the uncompromisingly traditional prescriptions of its most formidable opponents.

The traditional dispositions of most senior diplomats led them to dismiss the policy of guarantees and temporary occupation as ill-conceived and inadequate. Paul Cambon dismissed the arrangement as a 'bastard solution' based on 'a naïve conception of our national security requirements'.[96] His brother Jules despaired that 'nothing will remain of our victory, we will have lost everything'.[97] Barrère lamented that Clemenceau had lost 'the opportunity to achieve for his country that goal which its statesmen and men of war had pursued for centuries, the possession of an invulnerable frontier'. He characterised the guarantee treaties as an 'affront to France's status and traditions' that placed it 'in the same tributary situation as Portugal'.[98] Berthelot, who had a better understanding of the challenges facing the government, was nonetheless despondent. 'Everything is coming together,' he observed with characteristic irony, 'but badly.'[99]

Poincaré had been an early advocate of a traditional peace programme based on domination of the Rhineland. But by late March he had come to understand that projects for a buffer state were unworkable in the face of British and American opposition. This did not prevent him from criticising the nature of the occupation or questioning the value of the Anglo-American security guarantees. France, Poincaré argued, must 'conserve its territorial guarantee until Germany has executed all conditions of the peace treaty'. This would mean an occupation of thirty years or more.[100] Behind these legalistic critiques,

---

[96] MAE, PA-AP 008, *Papiers Barrère*, vol. 1, Cambon to Barrère, 2 Apr. 1919; see also P. Cambon, *Correspondance, 1870–1924*, vol. III: *(1912–1924) Les Guerres balkaniques. La Grande Guerre. L'Organisation de la paix* (Paris, 1946), 355: Paul to Henri Cambon, 20 Sept. 1919.

[97] P. M. H. Bell, *France and Britain, 1900–1940: Entente and Estrangement* (London, 1996), 162.

[98] MAE, PA-AP 008, *Papiers Barrère*, vol. 6, 'Traité de paix – Clauses du Rhin – Traité de garantie anglo-américain', 2 Aug. 1919; 'Au sujet de la conférence de la paix', Barrère testimonial written in Apr.–May 1919 but misdated 'March 1919'.

[99] J. Chastenet, *Quatre fois vingt ans, 1893–1973* (Paris, 1974), 118.

[100] MAE, PA-AP 141, *Papiers Pichon*, vol. 7, Poincaré to Pichon, 23 Apr. 1919; Poincaré to Clemenceau, 28 Apr. 1919, published in *Le Temps* on 12 Sept. 1921; Poincaré, *À la recherche de la paix*, 363–7; McDougall, *Rhineland Diplomacy*, 68; J. F. V. Keiger, *Raymond Poincaré* (Cambridge, 1996), 260–2.

however, Poincaré continued to hanker after German dismemberment and a buffer state. He stressed that a lengthy occupation would allow more time for French influence to shape political attitudes among the region's 'docile population'. The settlement as it stood, he warned, only reinforced German unity.[101]

Poincaré's critique of the guarantee treaties was also traditional in inspiration. Ignoring all arguments based on ideological affinity, he suspected that the British and Americans could not be counted upon to fulfil their commitments in the absence of a full military alliance. 'There is nothing in the text concerning the timetable, the extent and the conditions of the promised military assistance,' Poincaré observed. This, he insisted, rendered them 'illusory'. He also worried that the treaties might not be ratified. France, he maintained, must agree to a specified occupation regime 'only after the alliances have been voted and military conventions have been put in place'.[102] Traditional alliances reinforced by joint war planning were the only viable substitute for the physical guarantee offered by a frontier on the Rhine.

The most determined opposition came from the military establishment, and above all from Foch. The marshal warned Clemenceau that the constitution of a Rhenish buffer state was 'the primordial issue on which rests the political and military fate of Europe and even the existence of France as an independent power'.[103] From late March Foch mounted a campaign to reverse Clemenceau's policy, if necessary by overthrowing his government.

Frustrated by the secrecy surrounding negotiations and alarmed by news that a compromise was under consideration, Foch demanded an audience before the Council of Four. Appearing before the Allied leaders on 31 March, he presented a baleful vision of the future of European politics, predicting an invasion of France by 'a Germanic mass of around 70 millions' that might well be augmented by 'a Slavic mass of even greater proportions'.[104] He also dismissed all legal measures to limit German power: 'If we do not hold the Rhine permanently, there is no neutrality, disarmament or written clause of any kind that can prevent Germany from seizing the Rhine and mounting an attack under advantageous conditions.' Foch closed by denouncing the 'principles' animating the peace settlement, arguing that there was 'no higher principle' than a frontier on the Rhine.[105]

---

[101] Bibliothèque nationale de France (hereafter BNF), Nouvelle acquisitions françaises (hereafter NAF), *Papiers Poincaré*, 16033, Notes journalières, 30 Mar., 8, 28 Apr., 20 and 21 May 1919; Keiger, *Poincaré*, 257–61; and G. Wormser, *Le Septennat de Poincaré* (Paris, 1977), 176–94.
[102] MAE, PA-AP 141, *Papiers Pichon*, vol. 7, Poincaré to Pichon, 23 Apr. 1919.
[103] SHD-DAT, *Fonds Clemenceau*, 6N 53–3, 'Note', Foch to Clemenceau, 18 Feb. 1919.
[104] SHD-DAT, 4N 92–1, *État-major Foch*, Foch to Clemenceau, 30 Mar. 1919; on the crisis that ensued see also King, *Foch versus Clemenceau*, 44–72; and J.-C. Notin, *Foch* (Paris, 2008), 439–88.
[105] SHD-DAT, 4N 92–1, *État-major Foch*, 'Note' marked 'lu devant les Chefs de Gouvernement', 31 Mar. 1919; also in MAE, PA-AP 141, *Papiers Pichon*, vol. 7; see also

Foch's arguments made no impact on the Big Four. 'I admire and am very fond of Marshal Foch,' Lloyd George remarked, 'but when it comes to political questions, he is a child.'[106] Informed of the terms of the Rhineland settlement, Foch asserted that they would 'leave us in the most complete insecurity'. He insisted on a hearing with the French cabinet before 'irrevocable decisions' were taken.[107] Behind the scenes, he urged Poincaré to intervene and assume control of peace negotiations as president of the Republic. Poincaré refused on the grounds of established practice. Foch then demanded to take part in negotiations himself as a member of the French delegation. This Clemenceau refused, pointing out that the Allied generalissimo could hardly represent France at the conference.[108] The marshal then crossed the line between soldiering and politics, a line that had remained inviolate in France since the Boulanger Affair. He met with the presidents of both the senate and chamber to warn them that Clemenceau had become 'a danger to France' and recommend that the government be overthrown.[109] In addition to these meetings, Foch made contact with the 'war aims bloc' in parliament through the head of his civilian *cabinet*, Jacques Bardoux. The aim was to stir up parliamentary support for his rebellion.[110]

The marshal combined these back-channel manoeuvres with open insubordination. He gave sensational interviews to *Le Matin* and the *Daily Mail* in which he invoked every traditional argument for French cannon on the Rhine.[111] Despite these manoeuvres, Clemenceau agreed to grant him an audience before the cabinet on 25 April 1919. Here he described the Rhineland settlement as 'a crime of *lèse patrie*'. He also contrasted the 'solid reality' of military domination of the Left Bank with political and legal measures that lacked permanence. Interestingly, however, even Foch's prescription had changed slightly by late April. Before the cabinet he endorsed Poincaré's formula of occupation until all reparations were paid. He added, however, that the occupation should remain in some form 'as long as the situation of the German spirit does not leave us in complete security'.[112] Given Foch's

---

the ensuing discussion in Mantoux (ed.), *Conseil des quatre*, I, 46: 31 Mar. 1919; P. Jackson, 'Foch et la politique de sécurité française, 1919–1924' in F. Cochet and R. Porte (eds.), *Ferdinand Foch (1851–1929): apprenez à penser* (Paris, 2010), 337–8.

[106] Mantoux (ed.), *Conseil des quatre*, I, 92–5: 27 Mar. 1919.
[107] SHD-DAT, 4N 92-1, *État-major Foch*, Foch to Clemenceau, 15 and 17 Apr. 1919.
[108] SHD-DAT, 4N 92-1, *État-major Foch*, Foch to Clemenceau, 6 Apr. 1919; Clemenceau to Foch, 9 Apr. 1919.
[109] Poincaré, *À la recherche de la paix*, 337–40; Notin, *Foch*, 457–8. According to at least one account Foch even offered himself to head up a new government; see Schuker, 'West European Security', 307–9.
[110] P. Miquel, *La Paix de Versailles et l'opinion publique française* (Paris, 1972), 371–82.
[111] King, *Foch versus Clemenceau*, 57–8. Foch was identified only as a 'highly qualified military authority' in the *Le Matin* interview. The interview in the *Daily Mail* was not published in France.
[112] SHD-DAT, 4N 92-1, *État-major Foch*, 'Séance du 25 avril 1919: conseil des ministres, délégués de français à la Conférence de la paix, maréchal Foch' (typo-laden minutes taken by General Maxime Weygand).

doom-laden interpretation of the future, this recommendation would place France on the Rhine for generations to come.

There was considerable support for Foch's position in parliament and the press. On 10–11 April more than three hundred senators and deputies signed a manifesto demanding that Germany provide 'territorial guarantees'.[113] A delegation of Radical deputies asked the premier for reassurance that he would demand 'immediate and material guarantees of French security' based on 'the construction of a solid frontier'.[114] On 17 April Antonin Dubost and Jules Méline submitted a senate motion calling on the government to 'insert immediately into the treaty of peace the military guarantees indicated by the commander of the Allied armies'.[115] These moves were supported by a press campaign in centre-right and right-wing newspapers.[116]

Foch had made himself a lightning-rod for traditional opponents of Clemenceau's policy. His views reflected the convictions of nearly all his colleagues within the military. Mangin, for example, judged the Rhineland agreement as 'the worst of solutions'.[117] Fayolle concurred and resolved to take the initiative in forcing the issue of Rhenish separatism. On 10 March he instructed both Mangin and Gérard to 'go a step farther and prepare the solutions that we deem favourable'. This meant supporting autonomist politics in their respective regions. Contact was established with separatists on the Left Bank, who were encouraged to present the Allied leadership with a fait accompli in the Rhineland. This plotting, which gained momentum over the month of May 1919, culminated in proclamations of Rhenish and Palatine republics at the beginning of June. Both coup attempts failed miserably, however, underlining the extent to which senior French army officers misunderstood the political situation in the region.[118] The army's links with separatist agitation on the Left Bank succeeded only in provoking outrage among France's allies and brought Clemenceau under renewed pressure within the Council of Four to renounce a fifteen-year occupation.[119]

In the end Foch and his subordinates failed utterly to force a change in security policy. Poincaré did not support the marshal's argument before the cabinet in late April. The government's policy was instead approved unanimously at the end of this meeting.[120] Clemenceau, aware that the vast majority of French opinion was more concerned with financial security and a return to normality than with projects for dominating the Rhineland, ignored the

---

[113] Miquel, *Opinion publique*, 371; Stevenson, *French War Aims*, 187.
[114] McDougall, *Rhineland Diplomacy*, 64–5; Miquel, *Opinion publique*, 375.
[115] *Le Temps*, 19 Apr. 1919.   [116] Miquel, *Opinion publique*, 377–87.
[117] C. Mangin, 'Lettres de la Rhénanie', *Revue de Paris* (15 Apr. 1936), 501.
[118] King, *Foch versus Clemenceau*, 73–112; Bariéty, *Relations franco-allemandes*, 47–51; McDougall, *Rhineland Diplomacy*, 70–2.
[119] Mantoux (ed.), *Conseil des quatre*, II, 265–82: 2 and 3 Jun. 1919; Stevenson, *French War Aims*, 190–4.
[120] Keiger, *Poincaré*, 261; Bariéty, *Relations franco-allemandes*, 83.

marshal's parliamentary machinations.[121] He placated the uneasy Radical deputies with assurances of his patriotism and commitment to French security. He dealt more forcefully with the senate, responding that its motion was 'contrary to all principles of democratic government' because it 'subordinated peace treaty discussions to the desires of the military command'. He threatened to pose a question of confidence in parliament. Supporters of the motion retreated immediately.[122]

Nor did the episode become the press sensation hoped for by Foch's entourage. It did not receive front-page coverage in any of the major papers. In fact, it received more criticism than support in the majority of the mainstream press.[123] When it came to the crunch, Clemenceau's opponents realised they would lose a political showdown over the peace terms. Advocates of a traditional 'Rhenish peace' were out of step not only with international sentiment but also, to a significant degree, with French public opinion. Clemenceau was alive to this fact.[124]

Traditionally inclined critics of the government's security policy had a final opportunity to attack the government during the treaty ratification process the following summer. The outcome of the April confrontations dictated that the chamber and senate would not be able to reject the treaty. But traditionalists in parliament were determined to press the government rigorously over its Rhineland policy. The most effective means of doing so was through the parliamentary commissions. Peace treaty commissions were convened by both the senate and chamber to compile reports intended to inform ratification debates that were to begin in the chamber and senate in August.[125]

The chamber commission, which met almost daily through the month of July, was dominated by centre-right figures such as Viviani, Barthou, Benoist and Franklin-Bouillon. All favoured traditional solutions to France's security requirements. There were no Socialist deputies on this commission. The SFIO deputies nominated to serve in this capacity had all resigned in protest at the exclusion of Jean Longuet and Barthélémy Mayéras from the treaty commission on account of their 'defeatism' during the war.[126] The commission's first move was to demand copies of Marshal Foch's various missives pertaining to the Left Bank along with explanations as to why his prescriptions had been

---

[121] Miquel, *Opinion publique*, 377–402.
[122] AS, *CAES*, vol. 1893, 69S 266, 'Séance du vendredi 18 avril 1919'.
[123] Miquel, *Opinion publique*, 381–401.
[124] Tardieu invoked Clemenceau's judgement that reparations were far a greater preoccupation than the Rhineland: SHD-DAT, *Fonds Clemenceau*, 6N 79–3, 'Discours de Franklin-Bouillon', n.d.
[125] AN, C/7773, *Commission des affaires étrangères de l'assemblée nationale* (hereafter *CAEAN*), Commission du Traité de paix (hereafter CTP), observations by Barthou, Charles Benoist and Victor Augagner during the second and third *séances* on 8 and 9 Jul. 1919.
[126] E. Bonnefous, *Histoire politique de la Troisième République*, vol. III: *L'Après guerre* (Paris, 1959), 43–4.

ignored.[127] The commission also pressed the government on the nature of the British and American guarantee treaties and the reasons they had not been supplemented by military conventions.[128] The majority of its members expressed regret that German unity and power had not been broken as well as a belief in the doctrine of natural frontiers. The right-wing Catholic Jacques Piou dismissed all prospects of reforming Germany. 'I do not believe in the conversion of races,' he submitted. 'Wilson has not converted the Germans. They remain the Teutons of Tacitus.' Piou lamented that the Rhineland had not been transformed into 'a sort of Switzerland' under French patronage. Control of the Left Bank, he argued, had been 'a central theme in the entire history of France – of revolutionary France as well as monarchical France – Danton pursued this policy with the same energy as did Richelieu'.[129] Charles Benoist, the commission's *rapporteur* for frontier questions, agreed that 'to our east there is only one military frontier: the Rhine. We have had neither security or tranquillity without this frontier.'[130] 'It is a good thing that president Wilson has done away with the balance of power,' he observed ironically, 'because the treaty has left no prospect of providing security on such terms.'[131]

Members of the senate treaty commission shared this preoccupation with the balance of power and a frontier on the Rhine. On 31 July the commission forwarded a list of twenty-four questions to the premier's office. No less than sixteen of these addressed the issues of the balance of power and the Left Bank.[132] The *rapporteur* for the west European clauses of the treaty, the Radical senator Maurice Couyba, regretted that Prussia retained its position on the Rhine. 'Europe', he insisted, 'will never be at peace as long as this grotesque injustice is not rectified.'[133] A significant majority on both parliamentary commissions longed for a return to the time before German unity transformed the European balance of power.

Similar judgements were advanced in the nationalist press. Charles Maurras in the *Action française* lamented the 'superstitious respect for German unity'

---

[127] AN, C/7773, *CAEAN*, CTP, third séance, 9 Jul. 1919; MAE, PA-AP 166, *Papiers Tardieu*, vol. 419, 'Observations sur les notes du maréchal Foch', 17 Jul. 1919.
[128] MAE, PA-AP 166, *Papiers Tardieu*, vol. 421, Commission des Traités de paix to Clemenceau, 25 Jul. 1919; AN, C/7773, *CAEAN*, CTP, third, fifth and tenth séances, 9, 10 and 17 Jul. 1919.
[129] AN, C/7773, *CAEAN*, CTP, sixth séance, 12 Jul. 1919.
[130] The rapport is reproduced in C. Benoist, *Les Nouvelles frontières d'Allemagne et la nouvelle carte d'Europe* (Paris, 1920), quote from viii–ix.
[131] AN, C/7773, *CAEAN*, CTP, fifth séance, 10 Jul. 1919, Benoist during Clemenceau audition.
[132] MAE, PA-AP 029, *Papiers Bourgeois*, vol. 13, 'Questions relatives aux clauses militaires du Traité de la paix': marked 'Envoyé au président du conseil le 3–7-19', 31 Jul. 1919 and 'Présidence du conseil: réponse à 24 questions posées par la Commission du sénat', 9 Aug. 1919. Ten of the twenty-four questions were posed by Senator Doumer.
[133] MAE, PA-AP 029, *Papiers Bourgeois*, vol. 13, 'Rapport sur les clauses politiques du Traité de paix avec l'Allemagne concernant la Belgique, le Luxembourg et la rive gauche du Rhin'.

that had 'deformed' the peace settlement.[134] This theme was developed more systematically by Jacques Bainville in the same paper. Bainville's criticisms of the treaty were steeped in references to a bygone era of French predominance, when the France of Louis XIV or Napoleon dominated a divided collection of German principalities. He called for 'return to the principle that has animated French policy since the peace of Westphalia'. This was a determination 'to intervene by any means necessary, including the use of force, to prevent the political unity of the states of Germany'.[135] André Géraud ('Pertinax'), the influential diplomatic editor of *L'Echo de Paris*, joined Maurice Barrès in calling for a revision of the treaty. Similar criticisms were advanced in *La République française* and *Le Télégramme du nord*.[136]

Not all condemnation of the frontier settlement was from a traditional perspective, however. Vibrant criticism came from further left. Juridical internationalists for the most part refrained from criticising the treaty during ratification debates. Following the example of Bourgeois, they looked to the League of Nations as the great hope for a transformation of international politics.[137] French socialists were less resigned. 'This conception of the peace', proclaimed CGT leader Léon Jouhaux, 'gives satisfaction to no one in this country and misunderstands our true interests.'[138] Marcel Sembat expressed anger that calls for a new approach had been ignored:

Who among us does not see that this is a treaty like all those that have come before it? It does not establish a new justice ... It is the old justice that continues to prevail, a justice as usual imposed by the victor that, as usual, will be accepted as long as the vanquished feels weak.[139]

Sembat, along with other Socialists, advocated cooperation with democratic elements across the Rhine in a policy based on a 'universal' League of Nations.[140]

The fact that trenchant criticisms of the peace treaty came from both traditional and internationalist perspectives underlines the multifaceted and ambiguous character of the peace settlement, the defining feature of which was its flexibility. This was the crucial point missed by Bainville's much-quoted judgement that the treaty was 'too gentle for all that is in it which is harsh'.[141] The

---

[134] C. Maurras, 'La Politique', *Action française*, 24 Sept. 1919.
[135] Bainville, 'Ce qui a sauvé l'unité allemande', in *Conséquences politiques de la paix*, 52–3.
[136] See Miquel, *Opinion publique*, 377–87 and 401–12.
[137] J.-M. Guieu, *Le Rameau et le glaive: les militants français pour la Société des nations* (Paris, 2008), 53–62; S. Berstein, *Histoire du Parti Radical*, vol. I: *À la recherche de l'âge d'or* (Paris, 1980), 99–103; and esp. L. Bourgeois, *Le Traité de paix de Versailles* (Paris, 1919).
[138] Miquel, *Opinion publique*, 486.
[139] J.-J. Becker and S. Audouin-Rouzeau, *La France, la nation et la guerre: 1850–1920* (Paris, 1995), 350.
[140] *JO*, Chambre, *Débats*, 1919, 29 Aug. and 4, 18, 19, 25 Sept. 1919.
[141] J. Bainville, 'Une Paix trop douce pour ce qu'elle a de dur', *Action française*, 8 May 1919; this point made by Stevenson in 'France and the German Question in the Era of the First World

problem for the government was that such criticisms did not cancel one another out. Clemenceau did not depend on socialist support and could ignore internationalist criticism. The same was not true of the centre-right, however. The premier was obliged to defend its programme from traditionalists in the chamber and senate.

VI

The arguments prepared by Clemenceau's team illuminate the ambiguous character of the French peace programme in 1919. These arguments, it is worth emphasising, were for internal consumption. They were aimed above all at the centre and centre-right politicians who dominated the parliamentary peace treaty commissions and who constituted the preponderant bloc in both the chamber and senate. The government's defence of the Treaty of Versailles was emphatically not a case of *captatio benevolentiae*.

The government's case was an interesting combination of ideological arguments and an emphasis on the balance of power advantages of the Anglo-American guarantees. Aubert, who worked closely with Tardieu to prepare arguments for both the parliamentary treaty commissions and the ratification debates, stressed that a strategic commitment from the Anglo-Saxon Great Powers would 'provide our policy with the most persuasive threat that one could use against Germany to prevent another war'.[142] But he also laid great emphasis on political and cultural affinities binding France to its Great Power allies. An 'association of liberal great powers', Aubert argued, would establish the basis for 'a new era in international politics'. France, Britain and the USA, he pointed out, 'share more than one hundred years of democratic ideas'. This common ideological affinity was 'a more powerful bond than any combination of material interests one can find in the long tradition of our diplomacy'.[143] Many international political theorists would nowadays point to Aubert's language as evidence of a nascent 'security community': a grouping of states for whom shared interests combine with political and cultural affinities to make war between them 'unthinkable'. Aubert's call for cooperation among Atlantic liberal powers in many ways anticipated the 1947 North Atlantic Alliance.[144]

War' in S. Schuker (ed.), *Deutschland und Frankreich Vom Konflict zur Aussöhnung: Die Gestaltung der westeuropäischen Sicherheit 1914–1963* (Munich, 2000), 17.

[142] MAE, PA-AP 166, *Papiers Tardieu*, vol. 418, Aubert note marked 'Négociat. rive g. du Rhin' and dated 'fin mars'; the exact same phrase appears in an untitled document prepared for Tardieu's appearance before the chamber peace treaty commission on 29 Jul. 1919 that is in MAE, PA-AP 166, *Papiers Tardieu*, vol. 419.

[143] MAE, PA-AP 166, *Papiers Tardieu*, vol. 423, 'L'Alliance défensive franco-anglo-américain', 12 May 1919.

[144] The security community concept was first developed in K. Deutsch (et al.), *Political Community and the North Atlantic Area* (Princeton, 1957), 1–25; E. Adler and M. Barnett refined the term, stressing shared political identities and long-term interests in *Security Communities* (Cambridge, 1998).

Both Clemenceau and Tardieu would take up Aubert's language and his arguments in their defence of the Rhineland settlement. Both referred to the guarantees as 'alliances' and emphasised the strategic advantages they offered in terms of traditional power politics. But both also made repeated references to the 'moral authority' that an association of the world's most powerful democracies would provide. And they defended the decision not to demand an autonomous Rhineland with reference to the principle of self-determination.

Tardieu appeared before both parliamentary commissions in July and August 1919 before intervening in the chamber ratification debate the following September. On the question of the Franco-German military balance, he pointed out that the treaty reduced Germany's population by nearly twelve million, imposed strict limits on German land and sea power and demilitarised the Rhineland for all time. He underlined the fact that any violation of this last clause would trigger immediate British and American military aid. He emphasised that the treaty had also more than doubled the productive capacities of France's iron and steel industries, increased the size of its textile industry by one-third and ensured that its annual deficit of coal would be filled by production from the Saar. Nearly all of these increases in French industrial power, he added, had come at the expense of Germany.[145]

Moving on to defend the guarantees, Tardieu underlined the importance of British and American economic, maritime and military power. He provided a detailed inventory of the vast natural and economic resources controlled by France's Anglo-Saxon allies. He noted, by way of illustration, that the size of the US army had increased from less than 200,000 in 1916 to more than 3.6 million by November 1918. The size of the American merchant marine, meanwhile, had increased tenfold during the same period. British and American naval power were crucial not only for transporting vital troops, equipment and foodstuffs to Europe, but also for mounting an effective naval blockade. All of this made the strategic commitment embodied in the guarantees 'a decisive advantage in the European balance of power that no physical guarantee can replace'. Added to this was France's acute need for continued Anglo-American financial assistance during its reconstruction. Maintaining the demand for an independent Rhineland in defiance of the British and Americans, Tardieu argued, would have meant renouncing all of these strategic advantages and placing France 'in a position of political and military isolation facing a state that would remain larger and more populous ... with only Italy as a great power ally'.[146]

---

[145] AN, 324 AP 51, *Archives Tardieu*, 'Ce que la paix avec l'Allemagne apporte à la France', undated document (written in Tardieu's hand) that served as the basis for Tardieu's defence of the treaty; see also AN, C/7773, *CAEAN*, CTP, twentieth *séance*, 29 Jul. 1919; MAE, PA-AP 141, *Papiers Pichon*, 'Observations sur la discussion du traité devant la Chambre: séance du 2 septembre', 7 Sept. 1919.

[146] Quotations from AN, C/7773, *CAEAN*, CTP, twentieth *séance*, 29 Jul. 1919 and MAE, PA-AP 166, *Papiers Tardieu*, vol. 420, 'Réponse du gouvernement', 29 Jul. 1919 (note prepared

All of this was to emphasise the balance-of-power advantages of the settlement. Significantly, however, Tardieu also deployed a series of normative arguments. 'The treaty of peace', he asserted, 'in all of its articles ... conforms exactly, as far as France is concerned, to all of the declarations it has made concerning its war aims.' This gave the treaty a 'high moral authority' both in France and abroad. The alternative, to detach the Left Bank with its more than five million inhabitants, would have undermined this authority.[147] Before the full chamber Tardieu underlined the power of self-determination and the constraints it had placed on France during negotiations:

To break up the German empire would have meant only one thing: it would have been to say, following the principle of state self-interest, we will use our force as victors to impose on Germany a change in the constitution that it had reaffirmed continually in free votes since 1871. The Allied and Associated powers, having waged the war for the liberation of peoples, would not have accepted that their peace could result in damaging the internal liberties of even a defeated people ... We [therefore] considered German unity an established fact. In changing it we would have given the Germans arguments against the treaty that would have been powerful and, what is more, legitimate.[148]

Tardieu neglected to mention that the government had tried and failed to secure a suspension of self-determination in the Rhineland. Nor did he articulate lingering hopes that the fifteen-year occupation might still facilitate a gradualist strategy of luring the Rhinelanders into a closer association with France. His crucial point was that traditional schemes for breaking up Germany were fundamentally at odds with new standards of international legitimacy.

The French programme as it was outlined by Tardieu combined balance-of-power conceptions with normative arguments drawn from the discourse of a democratic international order after the First World War. Britain and America, he pointed out, were 'not only the world's two greatest financial, industrial and commercial powers', they were also 'the two greatest liberal powers with whom we are most certain to share a unity of democratic views'.[149] Shared ideology made the guarantees reliable and durable instruments of policy. 'The French government', Tardieu enthused, 'sees in this grouping of three free peoples, united by the League of Nations, a powerful source of security at the service of

---

for Tardieu's appearance at the above session); also vol. 419, 'Pièce 52', 28 Jul. 1919; and AN, 324 AP 51, *Archives Tardieu*, 'Note: gains de la France', n.d.

[147] AN, 324 AP 51, *Archives Tardieu*, 'Ce que la paix avec l'Allemagne apporte à la France', n.d.; MAE, PA-AP 166, *Papiers Tardieu*, vol. 420, 'Réponse du gouvernement', 29 Jul. 1919.

[148] *JO*, Chambre, *Débats*, 1919, 2 Sept. 1919, which draws on MAE, PA-AP 166, *Papiers Tardieu*, 'Réponse du gouvernement', 29 Jul. 1919; see also MAE, PA-AP 141, *Papiers Pichon*, 'Observations sur la discussion du traité devant la chambre: séance du 2 septembre', 7 Sept. 1919.

[149] AN, C/7773, *CAEAN*, CTP, twentieth *séance*, 29 Jul. 1919; almost identical language in *JO*, Chambre, *Débats*, 1919, 2 Sept. 1919.

shared ideals.'[150] Ideological affinity provided powerful cement for the envisaged North Atlantic alliance. Accepting the Anglo-American guarantees constituted a strategy of 'engagement' that would deliver 'a *democratic* alliance with Britain and the United States ... [that is] ... an advantage that *nothing* can replace'.[151] This ideological dimension to French security policy cannot be explained with reference to traditional approaches to peace and security.

Clemenceau joined Tardieu in defence of the juridical character of the peace settlement. Both stressed that the legal mechanisms for verification and enforcement of the treaty's disarmament and demilitarisation clauses would deliver French military superiority for the foreseeable future. Tardieu assured the senate treaty commission that French intelligence would monitor the situation in Germany carefully. Evidence of German non-compliance would be forwarded to the League Council. The Council would then impose sanctions by majority vote. Tardieu made a further normative argument when he insisted that, because the regime of *contrôle* would operate through the League, it would enjoy greater legitimacy than a system imposed by France and its allies independently of the new international organisation.[152] 'If Germany wishes to rearm,' Tardieu judged, 'it will be obliged to commit, not just a few isolated violations of minor aspects of the treaty, but a host of violations so evident and manifest that it would require a veritable will to suicide on the part of the Allies to close our eyes and do nothing.'[153] This faith in the collective resolve of the victorious powers to uphold the rule of law would prove badly misplaced.

The precise relationship between traditional and more innovative currents in Clemenceau's thinking is more difficult to assess. The premier wrote almost nothing down, and contradicted himself regularly. 'The British and Americans envisage an occupation of only one or two years,' he advised Poincaré in February 1919. 'For my part, I told them "In Infinitum". I will not give way.'[154] A few weeks later he accepted a compromise of fifteen years. Clemenceau's contributions to the Council of Four were characterised by alarmist assessments of the German national character and dire warnings about the danger Germany would continue to pose to Europe for the foreseeable future.[155] He struck a similar tone before his cabinet on 25 April: 'I shall make a prediction: Germany will default and we shall stay where we are, with

---

[150] MAE, PA-AP 166, *Papiers Tardieu*, vol. 419, 'Note pour M. Clemenceau: la question du Rhin', 23 Apr. 1919 – used by the premier during his 10 Jul. 1919 appearance before the chamber treaty commission.
[151] SHD-DAT, *Fonds Clemenceau*, 6N 73-2, 'Question du Rhin: 2ème solution (engagement)', 19 Mar. 1919, emphasis in original; MAE, PA-AP 166, *Papiers Tardieu*, vol. 418, 'Note sur la conversation du 14 mars', 15 Mar. 1919; SHD-DAT, *Fonds Clemenceau*, 6N 73-2, 'Note sur la suggestion présentée le 14 mars', 16 Mar. 1919.
[152] AS, *CAES*, vol. 1893, 69S 266, joint *audition* by Clemenceau and Tardieu, 25 Aug. 1919.
[153] *JO*, Chambre, *Débats*, 1919, 2 Sept. 1919, Tardieu *audition*.
[154] Poincaré, *À la recherche de la paix*, 122: 7 Feb. 1919.
[155] See, for example, Mantoux (ed.), *Conseil des quatre*, I, 41–6 and 147–58: 27 Mar. and 4 Apr. 1919.

the alliance.'[156] Yet he knew and approved of secret contacts with German officials to establish the basis for future economic cooperation and facilitate German reparations payments.

These various strands in government policy are best explained as a reflection of Clemenceau's flexible approach to peace making. Preoccupied with France's relative decline, he recognised the need for safeguards that would allow France to deal from a position of strength with a Germany that desired to overthrow the post-war order. But he understood the need for a settlement that could also accommodate gradual reconciliation and, eventually, Franco-German cooperation. A strategic relationship with the world's other two great liberal powers would provide a solid basis for France to deal with either a revisionist or a cooperative Germany. Such an arrangement could be defended in balance-of-power terms. But it also held open the possibility of a more internationalist future based on cooperation and the rule of law. All of this explains why Clemenceau emphasised the open-endedness of the Versailles Treaty before parliament, describing it as 'a collection of possibilities' that was 'not even a beginning, it is the beginning of a beginning'.[157]

What is most interesting about Clemenceau's defence of the peace settlement is the extent to which he invoked the changed international environment – and in particular the democratic principle of self-determination. Although he mocked Wilson's 'desire to resolve all the difficulties before us by applying the axiom of self-determination', Clemenceau's justification for renouncing a buffer state was framed entirely in terms of this axiom. 'On the Left Bank', he submitted, 'there is a German population, more German than many of us would like to admit.' This, he argued, 'is an inconvenient fact that nonetheless must have important implications for our policy'.[158]

Clemenceau did not deny that the dismemberment of Germany was a desirable end if it could be achieved. But he warned against the 'illusion' that the Rhinelanders were ready to embrace France. Nearly all the leading figures in the region, the premier reminded the members of the chamber treaty commission, were veterans of four long years of war. They had 'no sympathy whatever with France'. When consulted, their response was consistently 'We are Germans.' Clemenceau judged that French policy 'must be to help these people – though I would not want this repeated in the press – to shake off Prussia'. But he characterised this as a long-term goal that was undermined by open sponsorship of the separatist fringe on the Left Bank. What was needed instead was 'a policy of prudence and good will' as opposed to the 'imprudences' committed by 'several of our generals who do not understand the nuances

---

[156] Bariéty, *Relations franco-allemandes*, 83.
[157] *JO*, Chambre, *Débats*, 1919, 25 Sept. 1919; see also Emmanuel Beau de Loménie, *Le Débat de ratification du traité de Versailles à la chambre des députés et dans la presse en 1919* (Paris, 1945), 173–202; Duroselle, *Clemenceau*, 765–73; and Watson, *Clemenceau: A Political Biography*, 359–65.
[158] AS, *CAES*, vol. 1893, 69S 266, Clemenceau *audition*, 25 Aug. 1919.

of politics in the Rhineland'.[159] Attempts to stir up separatist feeling on the Left Bank, the premier argued, were 'a policy that weakens us morally and physically'.[160]

Before the senate Clemenceau delivered a powerful critique of the traditional argument for German dismemberment. 'A signature at the bottom of a treaty does not suffice to obtain the dissolution of a nation,' he observed. '[National] unity does not spring from the protocols of diplomacy.'[161] Violation of the principle of self-determination, he warned, would create permanent tensions with Germany, deprive France of its Great Power allies and 'damage our moral standing in the world'.[162] This position is entirely consistent with the premier's instructions to Foch the previous January, which stressed that the Marshal should 'under no circumstances interfere in the internal politics of Luxemburg'.[163] It also underpinned his rebuke of General Mangin in May: 'We will put no obstacle in the way [of an independent Left Bank], but we do not have the right either to incite it or to furnish it with material support.'[164] After the ratification debates he sacked Fayolle, Mangin and Gérard and forced through a presidential decree that imposed strict limitations on the authority of Tirard's Rhineland commission, removed it from Foch's command and placed it under the authority of the foreign ministry.[165] Berthelot summarised the premier's policy as 'sympathetic' to Rhenish separatism but nonetheless 'resolved to abstain from any intervention in the internal affairs of Germany having the character of pressure on the sentiments of the population'.[166] Clemenceau's 'Rhenish policy', to the extent that it existed at all, was cautious, long-term and sharply circumscribed by the norm of self-determination.

France's relationship with Britain and especially the United States remained the dominant consideration in Clemenceau's thinking. The British and American guarantees, he believed, would allow France to deal with Germany from a position of strength. He referred often to 'the two countries that came to our aid' and sometimes even 'the two countries that saved us'. Although he

---

[159] AN, C/7773, *CAEAN*, CTP, twentieth *séance*, 29 Jul. 1919.
[160] *JO*, Chambre, *Débats*, 1919, 25 Sept. 1919.
[161] Quoted in Beau de Loménie, *Débat de ratification*, 220.
[162] Quotes from AS, *CAES*, vol. 1893, 69S 266, Clemenceau *audition*, 25 Aug. 1919; and *JO*, Chambre, *Débats*, 1919, 25 Sept. 1919 respectively.
[163] Cited in Soutou, *L'Or et le sang*, 797.
[164] Cited in G. Wormser, *La République Clemenceau* (Paris, 1961), pp. 504–7; see also SHD-DAT, *Fonds Clemenceau*, 6N 73–2, Clemenceau to Mangin, 31 May 1919. Several weeks later Mangin claimed that Clemenceau 'appreciated the advantages' of separatist sentiment in the Rhineland. But he also acknowledged the premier's insistence that French authorities remain 'rigorously impartial': MAE, *Série Z, RGR*, vol. 1, 'Conversation avec le général Mangin', Berthelot note, 16 Jul. 1919.
[165] MAE, *Série Z, Allemagne*, 'Haut-comissariat des Territoire Rhénans', 25 Nov. 1919 and telegram from Pichon to Tirard, 5 Jan. 1920; MAE, *Série A*, vol. 166, untitled memo, 31 Dec. 1919.
[166] MAE, *Série Z, RGR*, vol. 1, 'Note pour la sous-direction des relations commerciales: République rhénan', 10 Jun. 1919.

made few direct allusions to common ideological bonds, Clemenceau emphasised that the ties between France and the USA, in particular, transcended traditional diplomatic practices. 'As we counted on America during the war, so we will be able to count on America in peacetime ... If you want my innermost thoughts, there is no written treaty that I would count on in this way.'[167]

The premier assured his parliamentary colleagues that he had taken Marshal Foch's arguments very seriously:

But when he declared 'I would rather have the Rhine than Britain and America I said to myself 'This is the view of a military official and not a politician.' After having waged war with these two powers, if you lose this political, economic and military union, I put it to you, what do you have left?[168]

Clemenceau's preference for the North Atlantic alliance was based on this admixture of power politics, ideological conviction and cultural affinity.

The need to come to terms with a reformed Germany also figured prominently in the Tiger's defence of the settlement. 'Our central challenge', he insisted to the senate commission,

consists in demilitarising Germany, and all of our efforts must focus on this objective. I would not go so far as to use the word 'conciliation', but all the same, we must find an accommodation with Germany and its 60 million inhabitants while we have only 40 million.[169]

Before the chamber commission he stressed the need to transform German political culture: 'For us it is not a matter of destroying the German people. To give you my entire thoughts, civilisation would gain nothing by this ... I propose instead to destroy the Germany that lusts for conquest and domination.'[170]

The premier returned to this theme before the entire chamber in late September. France could not seriously propose the destruction of a nation of more than sixty million inhabitants. 'We must live with them, support them even, endeavour to find an accommodation. This is a problem that cannot be resolved in any other sense than that of accommodation.'[171] French policy was based on the assumption that German unity was an established fact. It followed from this that some form of Franco-German reconciliation and cooperation was essential for the future.

Clemenceau embedded this argument in a wider set of observations about the changed character of international relations after 1918 that bear citing at

---

[167] Quoted in Beau de Loménie, *Débat de ratification*, 190.
[168] AN, C/7773, *CAEAN*, CTP, twentieth *séance*, 29 Jul. 1919.
[169] AS, *CAES*, vol. 1893, 69S 266, Clemenceau *audition*, 25 Aug. 1919.
[170] AN, C/7773, *CAEAN*, CTP, twentieth *séance*, 29 Jul. 1919.
[171] *JO*, Chambre, *Débats*, 1919, 25 Sept. 1919.

length. 'Our European situation has in effect changed dramatically,' he observed.

We must reconstruct France, but not in the fashion of the past; we must rebuild a France that understands that world politics have changed, that the eras of domination are gone and must never return, and that our chief task is to destroy all attempts to use violence in the world with the aid of our allies and of those countries that have been liberated.

The premier made these arguments, it is worth noting, before the chamber treaty commission, the vast majority of which was highly critical of his failure to deliver a traditional settlement based on German dismemberment. They cannot therefore be dismissed as disingenuous eyewash and a tactical effort to sell the government's programme to his audience. Indeed, he went on to argue for a new approach less constrained by the traditional conceptions of security professionals:

It is a strange thing that the mentality of the people adapts more easily to a new psyche – if you will permit the use of this word – than that of governments. Governments are like bureaucrats, they are restricted by the girdle of tradition. We are surrounded by officials who are steeped in traditions. They are respectable, traditions; they must be observed; but sometimes it is essential to know when to break with them ... the strength of our treaty is its orientation towards the future that I have just described ... the ideas it contains will grow and bear fruit.[172]

In his inspired final defence of the settlement before the chamber, Clemenceau exhorted his colleagues to adopt a more self-confident vision of the future unencumbered by obsessive fears of German revenge. The treaty, he acknowledged, demanded both vigilance and resolve from France. But these were necessary at all times in politics and could not be eliminated by a treaty. He ended his dramatic defence of the treaty by stressing the open-ended character of a peace settlement: 'Do not forget that this complex treaty will be worth only what you are worth; it will be what you make of it.'[173]

From London Paul Cambon denounced Clemenceau and his team for having 'sacrificed everything to the need to maintain the alliance with the Americans'. The result, he judged, was to place France 'in a state of virtual domesticity' without the advantages of 'true security'.[174] The course of international politics over the ensuing twenty years appears to confirm the merits of this and other traditional criticisms of French policy, including and especially Foch's famous characterisation of the Versailles Treaty as a 'twenty-year truce'. When evaluating the Clemenceau government's peace programme, however, it is essential to remember that purely traditional solutions to the security problem were

---

[172] AN, C/7773, *CAEAN*, CTP, twentieth *séance*, 29 Jul. 1919.
[173] *JO*, Chambre, *Débats*, 1919, 25 Sept. 1919.
[174] Cambon, *Correspondance*, III, Paul to Jules Cambon, 4 Feb. 1919: 304.

impossible to obtain in 1919. Wilson and Lloyd George opposed the idea of an autonomous Rhineland and rejected Poincaré's call to transform guarantees into traditional military alliances.[175] Foch's haughty disregard for the complexities of France's diplomatic position in 1919 seems prescient with the benefit of hindsight. But his security prescription would have left France isolated, without critically important Anglo-American financial assistance and with no guarantee of much-needed reparations from Germany.

When viewed from the perspective of divergent conceptions of national security, the Clemenceau government's policy towards the eastern frontier is most notable for its ambiguity and flexibility. The initial programme expressed in Tardieu's Rhineland memorandum was in many ways a classic expression of the traditional conception of national security. It aimed to transform the balance of power to the advantage of France. And yet, upon close examination, it is clear that even this programme was a fusion of traditional concepts such as the balance of power and 'physical guarantees' with normative references to an 'Atlantic' political and cultural entity united in defence of democracy and international justice.

Internal discussions within the French policy machine reflected the influence of the changed structural environment in which French policy was made. Even early plans for an autonomous Left Bank acknowledged the power of self-determination. Annexation was rejected explicitly when the French programme was presented to the Allies. Hope certainly remained that an autonomous Left Bank could be drawn gradually into the French political sphere. As Berthelot observed, such an eventuality would be 'a solution equally acceptable to those of our Allies who wish to apply Wilsonian principles to the Rhineland as has been done elsewhere'.[176] Georges-Henri Soutou has dismissed references to democracy and self-determination as a tactic to cover traditional strategic claims 'in Wilsonian clothing'.[177] This is in some respects true. But the fact remains that, by invoking the principle of self-determination, French officials were acknowledging its legitimacy and power.

If the doctrine of self-determination conditioned planning for France's eastern frontier, so, too, did a commitment to establishing a transatlantic security regime binding France, Britain and the USA together in a democratic 'community of power'. Underpinning this commitment, to be sure, was a reading of the global strategic balance that attributed decisive importance to the rise of American power. Equally important, however, was an ideological vision of a

---

[175] Lloyd George dismissed Poincaré's proposal as 'a serious provocation to fresh tension and even war in Europe': Cmd. 2169, *Negotiations for an Anglo-French Pact*, 104: Lloyd George to Clemenceau, 6 May 1919. Clemenceau recalled that 'President Wilson made clear that, if I proposed such a [military] convention, he would refuse to even discuss the question': AN, C/7773, *CAEAN*, CTP, tenth *séance*, 17 Jul. 1919.

[176] MAE, PA-AP 141, *Papiers Pichon*, vol. 7, 'Note sur la question des pays Rhénans', Berthelot, 31 Mar. 1919.

[177] Quote from Soutou, *L'Or et le sang*, 776.

democratic international order in which Germany would be enmeshed and constrained. When forced to choose between this conception of an Atlantic security community and a traditional arrangement based on dominating the Rhine, Clemenceau and his advisers opted with little hesitation for the Atlanticist alternative. They justified this decision, significantly, with reference to both the balance of power and the ideological and cultural bonds uniting France to its Anglo-Saxon allies.

The normative and ideological dimensions to French policy have not been given the attention they deserve in the existing literature. Tardieu pointed out that:

For each of the [Versailles] treaty's chapters – whether relating either to frontiers or to new states, or to reparations or to the constitution of populations – one can, if one holds to the Bismarckian style and its preference for imperialist solutions, regret and criticise the character of the treaty. But one cannot claim to be surprised. Over the entire course of the war all Allied governments, without exception and in entire accord with their populations, had constantly announced that, once victory had been achieved, the peace would be fashioned in the manner that it was.[178]

It is impossible to understand French policy strictly within the conceptual parameters of realpolitik and the traditional approach to security. The forward-looking and optimistic character of Clemenceau's defence of the settlement before parliament jars with the image of a cynical and pessimistic statesman that dominates the literature on the Paris Peace Conference.

This argument should not be pushed too far. The traditional concern for a favourable strategic balance was central to the importance Clemenceau and his team attached to the British and American guarantees. If the Clemenceau peace programme was much more ambiguous than is typically understood, it was by no means a juridical internationalist project to revolutionise international politics by imposing the rule of law. It was instead a cocktail of traditional strategic calculation, commitment to liberal democracy and misplaced faith in the political and cultural bonds linking France to its Anglo-Saxon allies. Clemenceau and Tardieu badly misread the political dynamics in the United States. America was not yet ready to assume the global leadership role allotted to it in French policy. Yet both at least understood that France was no longer a first-rank power. It is not a simplification to say that the premier and his advisers looked to the future. Traditionally minded critics of government policy, conversely, wanted to turn back the clock to an era of French predominance.

Clemenceau later summarised the crossroads facing the peacemakers in 1919 in a passage that captures the two approaches to peace and security that flow through this book:

There were for us only two sorts of peace to be contemplated: the maintenance of the military domination that our coalition possessed after the defeat of Germany

---

[178] Tardieu, *La Paix*, 94.

or a marshalling of those core elements of European justice capable of forming an insurmountable barrier against the vagaries of conquest. *A Europe of justice* in place of a dismembered Europe, that was the truly beautiful *coup de théâtre*.[179]

This is a very long way from Clemenceau the narrow-minded nationalist of historiographical legend. A true understanding of national security policy at this pivotal moment in France's history must account for Clemenceau the committed democrat as well as Clemenceau the hard-boiled realist.

---

[179] Quoted in Duroselle, *Clemenceau*, 721 (emphasis in original).

Part IV
Imposing security

'Remember this, young man,' Jules Cambon advised Jacques Chastenet, a junior official at the foreign ministry in 1921, 'in the years to come the chief difficulty will be to slide France as smoothly as possible into the ranks of the second-order powers where she belongs.'[1] Cambon was articulating an objective fact. French power was in relative decline, and this process had been accelerated by the First World War. Yet his advice cut against the grain. For centuries the conviction that France was a first-rank power had been central to the belief systems of French soldiers, diplomats and statesmen. The challenge of adapting to the profound international changes wrought by the war was compounded by the fact that, in the early 1920s, France found itself in a situation of artificial predominance in Europe. The USA had retreated into relative political isolation, Russia was in turmoil and Germany was reeling from the consequences of military defeat and the peace terms imposed at Versailles. France and Britain were the only major powers on the European continent. This situation was temporary, however. In every key category of long-term national power, France remained, after Italy, the weakest of the European Great Powers.

The tension and uncertainty created by this situation were captured in a survey of the post-war European political landscape prepared by foreign ministry mandarin Jacques Seydoux in November 1920. Seydoux observed that, while European international relations were dominated for the moment by Great Britain and France, the current situation was necessarily temporary and, to a certain extent, artificial:

Two states scarcely figure in the foregoing analysis: Russia and the United States. When these powers again make their appearance in international assemblies, the order of things will be profoundly changed ... The world is not yet complete and the factors that are missing, by their active or latent power and by their economic and social structure, will introduce transformations to the precarious balance of the moment that are still impossible to foresee.

---
[1] J. Chastenet, *Quatre fois vingt ans, 1893–1973* (Paris, 1974), 121.

European politics, in other words, were in a transitory phase. The emergence of American and Russian power would inevitably transform the international system. Implicit in Seydoux's analysis was the assumption that France's days as a major global power were numbered. French policy should be adjusted accordingly. Two consistent themes in his policy prescriptions were first that France must concentrate its efforts on playing a leading role in European reconstruction and second that this reconstruction was impossible without German participation.[2] Seydoux would become the most influential voice within the policy establishment calling for a flexible approach to interpreting and implementing the Treaty of Versailles. The aim, he insisted, must be to secure maximum German collaboration in the task of post-war reconstruction.

The judgement that France must scale back its ambitions was far from the consensus view within the French policy elite. A number of influential members of this elite were convinced that France must use the temporary advantages built into the peace settlement to achieve a permanent transformation of the European balance of power. For most of the post-war period, this current of thought took the form of pressure for a forward policy in the Rhineland aimed at promoting the cause of autonomy for that region and closer ties with France. This policy vision was ultimately incompatible with the argument of Seydoux (and others) that Germany should be incorporated into the wider project of European reconstruction.

The flexibility built into the Versailles Treaty left open the possibility of pursuing either of the above strategies. This explains why there was near consensus within the political mainstream that the peace treaty must be enforced. The phrase 'execution of the treaty' quickly became an omnipresent mantra in public and parliamentary discourse. All heads of government from 1920 through 1924 (Alexandre Millerand, Georges Leygues, Aristide Briand and Raymond Poincaré) assured the chamber of deputies of their determination to execute the treaty.[3] Even Seydoux, perhaps the most far-sighted and imaginative official within the French policy machine, acknowledged that the Versailles Treaty 'must serve as the political and economic charter of Europe'.[4] This did not mean enforcing every clause of the treaty to the letter, however. What was essential for Seydoux was that Germany acknowledged the legitimacy of the new order and thus its obligations under the treaty. Maurice Barrès expressed the same view when he warned that 'there has been no moral

---

[2] MAE, PA-AP 261, *Papiers Seydoux*, vol. 19, 'Situation respective des états à la conférence financière de Bruxelles', 16 Nov. 1920; see also S. Jeannesson, *Jacques Seydoux diplomate, 1870–1929* (Paris, 2013), 149–78.

[3] N. Roussellier, *Le Parlement d'éloquence: la souveraineté de la délibération au lendemain de la Grande Guerre* (Paris, 1997), esp. 71–2, 84–5, 89–91.

[4] MAE, PA-AP 261, *Papiers Seydoux*, vol. 18, 'Note: problème des réparations', 15 Oct. 1920; see also the overview of French policy in MAE, PA-AP 217, *Papiers Massigli*, vol. 13, 'Historique des négociations interalliées d'où est sorti le projet de conférence de Genève', 11 Oct. 1920.

Imposing security 319

disarmament in Germany ... France cannot breathe freely until Germany accepts its legal and moral obligations to fulfil the treaty'.[5] This emphasis on the legitimacy of the peace settlement left considerable room for disagreement over its precise interpretation and implementation. The meaning of treaty enforcement was understood very differently by different actors in the policy process.

This lack of consensus over the meaning of enforcement, and thus the proper orientation of foreign and security policy, has not been recognised in the existing literature. The foreign policy of the Bloc national is typically characterised as a traditional effort to impose the 'integral execution' of the Versailles Treaty on a recalcitrant Germany and, if possible, to revise the settlement to establish French 'hegemony' through domination of the Rhineland.[6] 'France alone', Professor Schuker has insisted, 'remained committed to the integral defence of the European political structure established at Versailles.'[7] This conclusion underpins wider interpretations of French policy as inspired exclusively by traditional concerns for power politics. Maurice Vaïsse describes French security policy during the 1920s as 'animated by a realist conception of international life' in which 'peace is not a normal state of affairs' and 'conflict is the rule between states'.[8] Anthony Adamthwaite similarly characterises the period from 1919 to 1924 as one in which 'a near-great power overreached itself by trying to turn the artificial predominance of Versailles into real hegemony'.[9] Patrick Cohrs refers to France's 'uncompromising position', which he argues caused Europe's 'regression to old-style power politics after Versailles'.[10] The presence of alternative currents within the policy machine is rarely acknowledged and virtually never placed within the context of the increasing influence of internationalist doctrines.[11]

A more accurate picture of French policy during this period would identify two general approaches to the challenge of treaty enforcement. The first conceived of enforcement as a means to maintain and if possible enhance the

---

[5] *JO*, Chambre, *Débats*, 1920, 6 Feb. 1920.
[6] Quotes from J. Bariéty, *Les Relations franco-allemandes après la première guerre mondiale* (Paris, 1977), 193 and J.-J. Becker and S. Berstein, *Victoire et frustrations, 1914–1929* (Paris, 1990), 210; see also S. Schirmann, *Quel ordre européen? De Versailles à la chute de IIIème Reich* (Paris, 2006), 44–59.
[7] S. Schuker, *The End of French Predominance in Europe: The Financial Crisis of 1924 and the Adoption of the Dawes Plan* (Chapel Hill, 1977), 384.
[8] M. Vaïsse, *Sécurité d'abord: politique française en matière de désarmement, 1930–1934* (Paris, 1981), 28.
[9] A. Adamthwaite, *Grandeur and Misery: France's Bid for Power in Europe, 1914–1940* (London, 1995), 91 and 230 respectively.
[10] Quotes from P. Cohrs, *The Unfinished Peace after World War I* (Cambridge, 2006), 69, and see more generally 68–75; W. McDougall, *France's Rhineland Diplomacy, 1914–1924: The Last Bid for a Balance of Power in Europe* (Princeton, 1978), 97–313; R. Boyce, *The Great Interwar Crisis and the Collapse of Globalization* (London, 2009), 91–134.
[11] Soutou, Trachtenberg, Jordan and Jeannesson (cited below) are partial exceptions; none of these, however, detects the influence of internationalist currents in French policy.

strategic advantages accorded to France under Versailles. Sanctions, the most important of which was the occupation of the industrial basin of the Ruhr, occupied a central place within this fundamentally traditional conception of security through enforcement. But so too did the continued military and political support of Britain. Applying the treaty provided the only sure way to construct and maintain a favourable balance of power against Germany. The most extreme variant of this approach went further, seeing treaty enforcement as an opportunity to overthrow the 1919 territorial settlement to France's advantage. This was the solution advocated most notably by senior military officials, the French occupation authority in the Rhineland and a minority within the Quai d'Orsay. The strategy was to use France's occupation of German territory to encourage and provide financial support for the cause of autonomist and federalist movements. The holy grail of an autonomous or independent Rhineland could thus be achieved through a gradual weakening of the political bonds of the Reich.

A contending perspective envisaged enforcement not only as a means to secure reparations and German disarmament, but also to lay the foundations for a stable political order that could eventually include Germany. Advocates of this alternative were open to the idea of cooperation with Germany both in the execution of the treaty and in the wider effort to restore economic prosperity. France could be flexible as to the precise manner in which the treaty was executed and could accept even a modest revision of its terms as long as it obtained fulfilment of its central elements. Planning for economic security embraced the idea of economic and industrial collaboration with Germany to accelerate the reconstruction of France's devastated regions and facilitate German treaty fulfilment. An influential constituency within the policy elite came to view economic cooperation as a necessary first step towards more confident political relations based on the consolidation of democracy across the Rhine.

It would be misleading to describe this alternative current within the policy elite as internationalist in its inspiration. Very few policy makers at this time understood international institutions as a source of security. Internationalist advocates of peace through law and the League of Nations remained confined to the margins of public and parliamentary discourse in the immediate aftermath of the war. But there were fundamental affinities between internationalist visions of security between interdependent democracies and official planning for economic and political cooperation in a wider system that included a democratising Germany. These affinities were not lost on French internationalists.

The two general approaches described above are best understood as positions on a continuum. Millerand, Briand and Poincaré all at one time or another espoused the traditional language of sanctions to impose the treaty by force. At the same time all three at different times contemplated engagement with Germany. When engagement failed to produce results, Millerand and

Poincaré returned to traditional methods based on the balance of power. Interestingly, the ultimate sanction – occupation of the Ruhr industrial basin – was compatible with both approaches. The threat of occupation was a useful tool for encouraging a reasonable attitude on the part of successive German governments. The threat could be used in conjunction with incentives to cooperate with France. The Ruhr was even more central to balance-of-power strategies aiming at German dismemberment. An occupation of the Ruhr would effectively cut the Rhineland off from the rest of Germany, increasing its dependence on France and vulnerability to French influence. A move against the Ruhr, justified with reference to paragraph 18 in Annexe II of Part VIII (reparations) of the Versailles Treaty, loomed in the background of Franco-German relations from the outset of this period.

Contending approaches to treaty enforcement within the policy establishment reflected wider divisions of opinion within the public sphere. As Professor Kedward has put it, responses to victory in 1919 had 'a Janus-like quality', which helped define attitudes towards international politics in the 1920s in ways that have not always been well understood:

> Public opinion no less than political leadership fell into binary opposites; either returning to pre-war structures or building new ones; either making Germany pay or creating a new Franco-German understanding; either stressing nationalist values or searching for internationalism.[12]

Distinctions between 'the two Germanys' became commonplace in political discourse on the centre-left. The 'good' Germany was democratic and associated most often with the common people. The 'bad' Germany was militarist and associated with the Prussian aristocracy and state apparatus. This development has not been sufficiently integrated into the international history of the post-1919 period. Nor has the growing strength of anti-war sentiment in postwar France.

These trends would underpin arguments for a less confrontational policy towards Germany that would gain in influence as more traditional methods failed to deliver durable security. Growing popular support for the League of Nations, for example, led to the beginnings of a policy of engagement with Geneva. Most importantly, over the course of 1921 the government of Aristide Briand altered its priorities and began to seek security through the creation of a multilateral system that would include Germany. These initiatives anticipated the much more radical changes in security policy that emerged in 1924.

The next three chapters argue that there was much more ambiguity in French security policy than has hitherto been understood. The policy of 'integral execution' was largely a myth. From the outset of the post-war period French policy makers found it necessary to adopt a flexible strategy that left open the

---

[12] R. Kedward, *La Vie en bleu: France and the French since 1900* (London, 2005), 104.

possibility of engagement and cooperation with Germany in the reconstruction of Europe. At the same time, French policy towards eastern Europe consistently pursued the familiar goal of constructing a counterweight to German power. This highly traditional strategy in the east complemented the bid to transform the balance of power with the creation of an autonomous buffer state on the Rhine by the Poincaré government in 1923.

9 Post-war dilemmas: enforcement or engagement?

On 16 November 1919 French national elections delivered a majority for a Bloc national coalition that promised to continue the Union sacrée in peacetime. National security had been a dominant theme in the Bloc's electoral programme, which pledged that:

> External peace will be maintained and the territory protected against any aggression by the strict execution of the Treaty of Versailles, vigilant monitoring of its application, the development of our alliances and the sincere orientation of all peoples towards the ideal of the League of Nations which must be made into a reality.[1]

The traditional conception of security was in the ascendant. The League of Nations, significantly, came last in the above list of priorities. It was all but dismissed as an 'ideal' that must one day 'be made into a reality'. The chief priority was to maintain the strategic advantages won at such cost during the war. 'Let us tear the sword from German hands and not tolerate her picking up the pieces,' exhorted Poincaré in a much-publicised speech at Verdun in early 1920.[2]

Putting rhetoric into practice would prove difficult, however. Support for an uncompromising policy towards Germany was less solid than it appeared in the immediate aftermath of the war. The Bloc national was not a unified ideological project and its majority was subject to sharp fluctuations. And Britain, still France's chief ally, was unwilling to support a policy of coercing Germany to comply with the letter of the Versailles Treaty. A more flexible strategy, based on cooperation with those elements in Germany willing to engage with the treaty regime, gained adherents within the policy elite. A re-examination of the course of security policy during this period provides a new perspective on international politics in Europe immediately after the First World War.

---

[1] 'Programme du Bloc national républicain' in O. Wieviorka and C. Prochasson (eds.), *La France du XXème siècle: documents d'histoire* (Paris, 1994), 243.
[2] Quoted in J. F. V. Keiger, *Raymond Poincaré* (Cambridge, 1996), 268.

I

The war did not end in 1918. Military conflict and paramilitary violence continued in the territories of the four great European empires for more than four years after the armistice was signed. Central and eastern Europe, Russia and the western regions of the former Ottoman Empire experienced inter-state war, civil war and deadly ethnic conflict at least until 1923. Revolution, civil war and foreign intervention in Russia were followed by a more traditional conflict between the Soviet Union and Poland. The aftermath of the Ottoman collapse witnessed a widening conflict between Turkish nationalists and Greeks who, with Allied support, aimed to impose the Treaty of Sèvres to their advantage. Vast swathes of territory from the Balkans to the Baltic Sea, meanwhile, were stricken by the political disorder and ethnic violence that inevitably followed after the far-reaching territorial readjustments imposed by the Paris settlement.[3]

Just as the war did not come to a neat conclusion in 1918, the *culture de guerre* that helped bind the French population to the war effort did not disappear after the fighting ceased. It instead culminated in a 'patriotic explosion' that continued to shape both official and popular responses to questions of domestic and international politics into the early 1920s.[4] It is within this context that victory for the nationalist politics of the centre-right Bloc national coalition should be understood. Alongside the politics of patriotism and national unity at the heart of the Bloc national project, there emerged a very different system of representations of the meaning of the war, the significance of which has been neglected in the international history of this period. Annette Becker and others have argued persuasively that a 'national liturgy of mourning and commemoration' evolved after 1918 to constitute an important structural element in the discursive landscape of post-war France.[5]

Fifty-two months of struggle and sacrifice had shattered pre-1914 visions of war as glorious and heroic. In the 1920s the predominant themes in representations of war were those of suffering and loss. This is evident not least in the character of the more than 35,000 monuments to the war dead raised in almost every village and *commune* in France. The vast majority of these monuments

---

[3] The historical literature on this issue is large and growing; for an overview see A. Sammartino, *The Impossible Border: Germany and the East, 1914–1922* (London, 2010), 45–119 and R. Gerwath and J. Horne, 'Vectors of violence: paramilitarism in Europe after the Great War, 1917–1923', *JMH*, 83, 3 (2011), 489–512; see also the special issue of *Contemporary European History* devoted to 'Aftershocks: violence in dissolving empires after the First World War', 19, 3 (2010).

[4] J.-J. Becker and S. Audoin-Rouzeau, *La France, la nation, la guerre: 1850–1920* (Paris, 1995), 302–3; see also J.-J. Becker, *La France en guerre, 1914–1918: la grande mutation* (Brussels, 1999), 123–35.

[5] A. Becker, *La Guerre et la foi: de la mort à la mémoire* (Paris, 1998), 119; see also S. Tison, *Comment sortir de la guerre: deuil, mémoire et traumatisme (1870–1940)* (Rennes, 2011), 155–207, 275–91.

were erected between 1920 and 1924. Most either contained no statue at all or simply an anonymous *poilu*. Although relatively few were overtly anti-militarist, martial themes were strikingly absent. The predominant symbolism was one of mourning and civic commemoration.[6] The emergence of a more realistic discourse around the meaning of the war is evident in the organisation of the Verdun battlefield as a commemorative space. During the conflict the battlefield occupied a central role in dominant narratives of courage and heroism. Soon after the war, however, it became a symbol of sacrifice in France's 'pacific' struggle to beat back the German invader. The most prominent manifestation of this process was the gigantic ossuary at Douaumont, on the Verdun battlefield. Here the remains of thousands of French and German soldiers were placed together in a site of collective mourning. The battlefield of Verdun came to be commemorated not as a space of heroic sacrifice for the nation, but rather as 'a transgression of the limits of the human condition'.[7]

The impact of these changing representations of the war manifested itself only gradually, and initially remained overshadowed by the patriotic nationalism that had underpinned the war effort. Yet the Bloc's victory was not a straightforward endorsement of the traditional conservative–nationalist approach to international relations by the French electorate. Indeed, the term *bloc* is itself misleading as a description of the loose electoral alliance that prevailed in 1919. The only truly modern political party at this time was the SFIO. A diverse array of parties and political groupings made up the remainder of the political spectrum. Party affiliations were fluid, voting discipline was almost non-existent and ideological divisions cut across group membership. Just as important was a return to pre-war parliamentary practices where discussion and debate returned to the centre of the governing process as the chamber took back the authority it had relinquished under Clemenceau. The result was a profound instability that characterised the parliamentary majority of the twelfth legislature (1920–4). Support for government policy depended on the strength of the arguments put forward by ministers before the chamber and senate.[8]

The Bloc national was in any case much more of an electoral strategy than a coherent political movement. It aimed at a coalition stretching from the Radicals and Independent Socialists on the centre-left to the conservative Nationalist Republicans on the right. This project divided the Radical Party.

---

[6] See, among others, A. Prost, 'Les Monuments aux morts' in P. Nora (ed.), *Lieux de mémoire*, 3 vols. (Paris, 1997), I, 199–223; A. Becker, *Les Monuments aux morts: mémoire de la Grande Guerre* (Paris, 1988); J. Winter, *Sites of Memory, Sites of Mourning* (Cambridge, 1995), esp. 13–117; D. Sherman, *The Construction of Memory in Interwar France* (Chicago, 1999), 13–103, 143–213, 281–308.

[7] A. Prost, 'Verdun' in Nora (ed.), *Lieux de mémoire*, II, 1775 and generally 1755–80; Sherman, *Memory in Interwar France*, 311–14.

[8] N. Roussellier, *Le Parlement de l'éloquence: la souveraineté de la délibération au lendemain de la Grande Guerre* (Paris, 1997), 49–152.

On the one hand, the Radicals were in disarray in the aftermath of the war. The party had suffered a series of debilitating setbacks during the war, including the arrest of several of its leading figures on charges of treason. Adhering to the Bloc national would restore the party's patriotic credentials. On the other hand, many Radicals feared losing their party identity in an alliance that included centre-right Catholics. In the end the Radicals participated in the Bloc alliance, but internal divisions and misgivings meant that this participation was ambiguous and incomplete.[9] Behind the surface rhetoric of national unity and anti-Bolshevism, therefore, the Bloc national was compromised by fundamental ideological differences. Its campaign strategy was characterised above all by vague but evocative references to the dangers of revolution and the need for a peacetime *union sacrée*. Any attempt to fashion a more detailed programme in the realms of international, internal and financial policy would only have exposed the ideological fissures in the Bloc coalition.[10]

The elections nonetheless marked a decisive parliamentary victory for the Bloc national. A new system introduced in 1919 favoured electoral alliances within individual lists. Because the centre and right were more disciplined than the Radicals in adhering to Bloc lists, centrist and centre-right deputies won 400 seats in the new chamber. It is important to note, however, that they achieved this stunning success without any significant increase in their share of the overall vote (which remained just under 41 per cent). The Radicals, who were less disciplined, suffered a terrible setback. The Radical share of seats dropped from 172 to 86 even though its share of the total vote diminished only marginally. The number of SFIO deputies also fell from 102 to 68, despite the fact that the party's share of the popular vote actually increased from 17 to 23 per cent. Although the Bloc secured a large number of seats in the chamber in 1919, its success did not reflect a decisive shift to the right in political attitudes.[11] Nor, finally, was its majority as imposing as it first appeared. The ambivalence of many Radical and left-leaning centrist deputies compromised its parliamentary coherence. The ability of the Bloc to govern thus depended on the continuing cooperation of a significant proportion of Radicals. This was not straightforward because at the outset of the new assembly the Radicals were badly divided over fundamental issues of foreign and security policy.[12]

There were important issues of relative consensus.[13] The need to move past pre-war political divisions and to emphasise unity was one such issue. The

---

[9] J.-J. Becker and S. Berstein, *Victoire et frustrations, 1914–1929* (Paris, 1990), 181–94; S. Berstein, *Histoire du Parti Radical*, vol. I: *À la recherche de l'âge d'or* (Paris, 1980), 97–135.
[10] Roussellier, *Parlement de l'éloquence*, 53–87.
[11] E. Bonnefous, *Histoire politique de la Troisième République*, vol. III: *L'Après-guerre* (Paris, 1959), 69–73.
[12] Roussellier, *Parlement de l'éloquence*, 72–84; S. Berstein and P. Milza, *Histoire de la France au XXème siècle*, vol. I: *1900–1930* (Paris, 1999), 471–91.
[13] This paragraph is drawn from Roussellier, *Parlement de l'éloquence*, 50–103 and Bonnefous, *Après-guerre*, 69–72.

political debt owed to war veterans was another. Nearly 60 per cent of the deputies elected in 1919 were new to parliament; and the vast majority of these were war veterans. When the new legislature convened, nearly three hundred deputies (44 per cent) were wearing military uniforms in what has ever since been described as the *Chambre bleu horizon*. A final area of consensus pertained to Germany's obligation to comply with the Versailles Treaty. The only political constituency that called openly for treaty revision was the SFIO; but even Socialists supported France's reparations claim.

Yet beneath this exterior consensus there existed a range of views on how best to obtain German treaty compliance. Roussellier's indispensable analysis of parliamentary discourse demonstrates that the intransigent mood of early 1920 had evolved even by mid-1921 as an increasingly narrow majority in the chamber remained committed to an unbending 'policy of firmness' to enforce the letter of the treaty. A growing number of deputies, mainly but not exclusively from the centre-left, accepted the need for flexibility and engagement with democratic elements inside Germany. When he succeeded Clemenceau as premier on 20 January 1920, Alexandre Millerand was a strident advocate of strict enforcement. As head of government, however, he revised his position in favour of a more flexible policy that he described as 'realisation'.[14]

Clemenceau discovered the extent of parliamentary resentment of his methods when he failed to win the support of the chamber and senate for his election as president of the Republic in January 1920. He lost to chamber president Paul Deschanel in what was clearly a protest vote. Deschanel's fragile mental state soon ended his tenure at the Élysée Palace. He was replaced by Millerand in September 1920. Millerand was by no means willing to surrender his influence. In much the same manner as Poincaré had done before the advent of Clemenceau, he remained a central figure in the elaboration of French foreign and security policy until he resigned as president after the elections of 1924.[15]

Two of the most pressing problems confronting France in early 1920 were linked directly to the war and the peace settlement. The first was the black hole left in France's finances by the war. Overall indebtedness had only increased in 1919–20. By 1920 France's short-term public debt totalled nearly 65 per cent of total national income (compared to a corresponding figure of less than 5 per cent for Britain). Between 1919 and 1924 the cost of servicing this debt accounted for as much as 44 per cent of total public expenditure.[16] The war that had destroyed France's relatively strong global financial position of 1913 introduced an era of financial instability that endured through to the second half

---

[14] *JO*, Chambre, *Débats*, 1920, 20 Jul. 1920; see also AN, C/14632, *CAEAN*, 27 Jul. 1920.
[15] M. M. Farrar, *Principled Pragmatist: The Political Career of Alexandre Millerand* (Oxford, 1991), 215–362.
[16] K. Mouré, *The Gold Standard Illusion: France, the Bank of France, and the International Gold Standard, 1914–1939* (Oxford, 2002), 42; B. Eichengreen, *Golden Fetters: The Gold Standard and the Great Depression, 1919–1939* (Oxford, 1992), 81; D. Artaud, *La Question des dettes*

of the 1920s. A succession of Bloc national governments failed utterly to deal with the debt problem. This failure was rooted in a determination to return the French economy to the liberal practices of the pre-war period, combined with powerful opposition to introducing either a modern system of income tax or cutting back on public spending.

Efforts to balance the national budget were deeply unpopular in an atmosphere in which the pervasive conviction was that Germany should pay for the restoration of France. Modest tax increases introduced in 1920 were not accompanied by cuts in expenditure, and did not even dent France's rising public debt. Until 1924 successive governments put off dealing with France's debt crisis by borrowing and by printing money (which allowed the government to pay down the internal debt in depreciated currency). In 1919, in order to disguise the scale of the problem, finance minister Klotz was forced to divide the budget into 'ordinary' and 'extraordinary' accounts. The latter were described as 'recoverables' tied to reconstruction and pensions. It was assumed that they would eventually be recovered by reparations from Germany. The foundations were thus laid for the full-blown financial meltdown that would threaten national solvency in early 1924.[17]

The second major challenge facing France's governing elite was that of social order. The tensions generated by demobilisation and disappointed hopes for far-reaching social change within the workers' movement produced a highly fraught political atmosphere in 1919. Mainstream anxiety was exacerbated by the spread of revolutionary unrest in central and eastern Europe and by the mutiny of France's Black Sea Fleet in March of that year. In 1919–20 thousands of official and unofficial reports of revolutionary activity in Europe reached the highest levels of the government and state security apparatus. The Socialist Party and trade unions were placed under heavy surveillance. Intelligence concerning links between revolutionary socialists in France and agents of the Bolshevik regime in Russia were a source of constant anxiety among political and security elites.[18]

While much of this reporting, particularly on the situation in Russia and eastern Europe, was of dubious reliability, the anxieties they generated among France's political elites were real enough. Social agitation and the possibility of revolution constituted a central element in popular discourse in 1919. The

---

interalliées et la reconstruction de l'Europe, 1917–1929, 2 vols. (Paris, 1978), II, 63; S. Schuker, *The End of French Predominance in Europe: The Financial Crisis of 1924 and the Adoption of the Dawes Plan* (Chapel Hill, 1977), 31–47.

[17] A. Leménorel, *L'Économie libérale à l'épreuve* (Paris, 1997), 5–29, 55–65, 90–2; J.-C. Asselain, *Histoire économique de la France*, vol. II (Paris, 1984), 13–25; Mouré, *Gold Standard Illusion*, 44–69.

[18] See, for example, MAE, *Série Y (Internationale)*, vol. 378, dossier entitled 'Action pacifiste et révolutionnaire, 1919–1920'; *Série Z, URSS*, vols. 90–8, 129–36, 391–6, 865–88; PA-AP 118, *Papiers Alexandre Millerand*, vol. 67; AN, 470 AP 62, *Archives Alexandre Millerand*, 'USSR'; SHD-DAT, *Fonds Clemenceau*, 6N 81, 'Bolchevisme, 1918–1920'; see also T. Stovall, *Paris and the Spirit of 1919: Consumer Struggles, Transnationalism and Revolution* (Cambridge, 2012), 142–81.

revolutionary peril and the need for a 'return to political order' were central themes of the Bloc national campaign strategy in 1919. It was in the lead-up to this election that the infamous poster of the hirsute Asiatic with a knife between his teeth first made its appearance in the French public sphere.[19] The CGT, which claimed a membership of more than two million, became more assertive in its relations with government. There was hope within the radical wings of both the CGT and SFIO that demonstrations on 1 May 1919 would lead to violence that could spark a revolution. The Clemenceau government responded by introducing legislation for an eight-hour working day in an attempt to head off further unrest.[20]

In the end, May Day violence was limited and revolutionary conditions failed to materialise. They did contribute to a long-running debate over the future of the workers' movement, however. Disagreement centred on the issues of revolutionary violence and relations with the Bolshevik regime in Russia. Moderate Socialists such as Marcel Sembat, Pierre Renaudel, Paul Faure and Léon Blum remained committed to the reformist tradition and a democratic route to power. They were opposed by a younger generation of Socialists inspired by events in Russia who preferred immediate revolution. The moderates were dealt a blow by the results of the 1919 election, which was amplified by the ferocious response of the Millerand government to more strikes in May 1920. These strikes were denounced by Bloc interior minister Théodore Steeg as 'an illness from the east'. More than 6,000 strikers were arrested and more than 15,000 rail workers were fired.[21]

It was in this atmosphere that the SFIO and the CGT debated the question of relations with the Third International (Comintern). The Soviet leadership imposed twenty-one conditions for membership. These included demands that French Socialists abandon reformism entirely for a strategy of revolutionary violence. Accordingly, all dissidents must be expelled and clandestine cells must be established to promote subversion. The SFIO would be required to change its name to 'Communist Party' and submit to all directives emanating from the executive committee of the Comintern. There was also a reference to the need for 'periodic purges' to ensure total commitment to the revolutionary project among party members.[22] These conditions were unacceptable

---

[19] C. Maier, *Recasting Bourgeois Europe: Stabilization in France, Germany and Italy in the Decade after World War I* (Princeton, 1975), 19–108; S. Berstein and J.-J. Becker, *Histoire de l'anticommunisme en France*, vol. I (Paris, 1987), 14–89; S. Couré, *La Grande lueur à l'est: les Français et l'Union soviétique 1917–1939* (Paris, 1999), 21–54; F. Monier, *Le Complot dans la République: stratégies du secret de Boulanger à la Cagoule* (Paris, 1998), 89–129.

[20] L. Robert, *Les Ouvriers, la Patrie et la Révolution, Paris, 1914–1919* (Paris, 1995), 291–403; Stovall, *Spirit of 1919*, 184–282.

[21] S. Courtois and M. Lazar, *Histoire du Parti communiste français*, 2nd edn (Paris, 2000), 33–45.

[22] These are reproduced as an appendix in A. Kriegel (ed.), *Le Congrès de Tours (1920): naissance du Parti communiste français* (Paris, 1975), 249–53; see also P. Robrieux, *Histoire intérieure du Parti communiste*, 4 vols. (Paris, 1984), I, 555–66.

to the majority of the senior leadership of the SFIO. Enthusiasm for joining the Third International was strongest within the rank and file, and especially the leading voices within the younger generation that included Paul Vaillant-Couturier and Fernand Loriot.[23]

The question of adherence to the Comintern dominated the SFIO party congress at Tours in December 1920. Nearly 75 per cent of the party voted to join the Comintern and accept Soviet domination. The result was that the SFIO fractured and a French Communist Party (PCF) was born. The CGT went through a similar process the following year. Support for revolutionary politics was weaker within the trade unions, however. Léon Jouhaux managed to maintain control and exclude the extreme revolutionary element from the CGT. A much smaller Confédération générale du travail unitaire (CGTU) was established by these dissidents.[24]

The French left was badly fractured. This was a particular blow to the internationalist movement. The SFIO had provided outspoken support to internationalist causes ever since the advent of Jaurès. Socialist deputies continued to argue that the Versailles Treaty must be revised and that the League of Nations must function as the prime vehicle for both French and international security. But their ranks were depleted by the schism and they were often marginalised in chamber debates and on the chamber's foreign affairs commission. The PCF, meanwhile, opposed virtually all aspects of government foreign policy, was regarded as an 'internal enemy' and had no impact on security policy decisions.

All of this meant that political support for an internationalist alternative to the traditional prescriptions of the Bloc national government was weaker than it had been at any time since 1916. Only when traditional practices failed to deliver either German treaty compliance or a Great Power alliance did support begin to coalesce for an alternative policy towards Germany. In many respects decision makers led the way in recognising that policies based on the balance of power, military alliances and strict treaty enforcement were out of step with changed international conditions. Adjustments would be necessary.

II

The policies of other states were central to this perception. German non-compliance posed the most immediate and intractable challenge to French security at this juncture. There were two central aspects to this challenge. The first was the persistent refusal of both popular and elite opinion inside Germany to acknowledge the decisive character of the Reich's military defeat and accept the legitimacy of the Versailles Treaty. Returning German troops marched

---

[23] Courtois and Lazar, *Histoire du Parti communiste*, 46–67.
[24] Kriegel (ed.), *Congrès de Tours*, 139–248; M. Dreyfus, *Histoire de la CGT* (Paris, 1995), 100–50.

under banners proclaiming that 'the *Heimat* greets its undefeated heroes'.[25] Newly elected president Friedrich Ebert's famous 'salute' to German soldiers returning 'unvanquished from the field of battle' was symptomatic of a society that could not come to grips either with the result of the war or the realities of the peace.[26] The conviction that Allied demands were both unjust and unrealistic became an article of faith that extended from political elites to industrial magnates, petty-bourgeois shopkeepers and the working class. 'We signed the peace treaty', observed Weimar Republic war minister Gustav Noske, 'knowing we could never fulfil the terms and believing no nation would ever expect us to do so.'[27]

Another important factor shaping politics and policy in Germany was the power of Ruhr industrial magnates such as Gustav Krupp von Bohlen und Halbach, Fritz Thyssen and Hugo Stinnes. Together they controlled a significant proportion of German industrial production. Nearly all were opposed to any form of treaty compliance.[28] Their opposition made it difficult, if not impossible, for the Weimar government to adopt the fiscal reforms necessary to place Germany in a position to pay reparations. Indeed, the belief that Germany could not and should not make such payments was one of the few issues upon which all Weimar parties could agree. Even moderate Weimar politicians such as Walther Rathenau or Carl Bergmann pursued *Erfüllungspolitik* (a policy of fulfilment) only to demonstrate the impossibility of making reparations payments on the scale expected by France and its allies.[29] When one considers that Millerand's policy of 'realisation' was aimed at encouraging gradual German acceptance and compliance, the abyss separating the French and German positions was almost unbridgeable.

German outrage over the territorial settlement in eastern Europe was just as pervasive. No German statesman could admit the legitimacy of a settlement that left nearly seven million Germans living in Poland and Czechoslovakia. When a League of Nations judgment on the plebiscite in Upper Silesia left the majority of the coal mines in this region to Poland, this was perceived as yet another injustice imposed upon the German people. Obtaining a revision of the post-war territorial settlement was an objective of virtually every German government during the inter-war period. This made French patronage of the 'successor

---

[25] R. Bessel, *Germany after the First World War* (Oxford, 1993), 85.
[26] P. Jardin, *Aux racines du mal: 1918, le déni de la défaite* (Paris, 2005); R. J. Evans, *The Coming of the Third Reich* (London, 2003), 66.
[27] Quoted in J. Edmonds, *The Occupation of the Rhineland, 1918–1929* (London, 1987), 184; see also Jardin, *Racines du mal*; Bessel, *Germany after the First World War*.
[28] G. Feldman, 'The French Policies of Hugo Stinnes' in S. Schuker (ed.), *Deutschland und Frankreich vom Konflikt zur Aussöhnung: Die Gestaltung der westeuropäischen Sicherheit 1914–1963* (Munich, 2000), 43–64; G. Feldman, *The Great Disorder: Politics, Economics and Society in the German Inflation, 1914–1924* (Oxford, 1997), 255–307; H. A. Turner, *German Big Business and the Rise of Hitler* (New York, 1985), 3–30.
[29] M. Trachtenberg, *Reparation in World Politics: France and European Economic Diplomacy, 1916–1923* (New York, 1980), 213–15; Feldman, *Great Disorder*, 309–82.

states' in the east was a source of permanent tension in post-war international relations.[30] The grim paradox for French policy makers after 1918 was that forcing the Weimar regime to acknowledge the legitimacy of the Treaty of Versailles (and thus become a responsible member of the international community) tended to undermine the domestic legitimacy of that regime and thus the hopes for a democratisation of German society (another key criterion for international acceptance).

Italy had intervened in the war chiefly to complete its unification and to strengthen its strategic position in southern Europe and the Balkans. But the impact of the war destabilised society and polarised Italian politics. A wave of intense nationalism generated widespread support for the much more ambitious policy of expansion into the Balkans, Africa and the Mediterranean basin advocated by the foreign ministry and the military services. Italian foreign policy took on a revisionist character that would only intensify once Mussolini and the Fascist Party took power in 1922.[31]

Soviet Russia posed a different set of problems for French policy. By late 1919 the Red Army had defeated all of the most significant White Russian factions. Allied efforts to intervene on behalf of the Whites had lacked both coordination and conviction. By late 1920 the Soviets had defeated the twin threats of internal resistance and foreign intervention. The chief result of intervention was to reinforce the belief that the USSR was encircled by hostile powers that desired its destruction. On 21 November 1920, however, Lenin observed that the Soviet regime had 'won conditions enabling us to co-exist side by side with capitalist powers, who are now compelled to enter into commercial relations with us'.[32] The time had come for a 'New Economic Policy' in which 'normal' diplomacy and commercial relations were accepted as necessary to obtain capital investment. Tentative commercial negotiations had opened between the Entente and the Soviets in spring 1920 and continued through 1921. But the Communist regime remained isolated and vulnerable until it signed a tentative alliance with Germany at Rapallo in April 1922.[33]

At the same time, however, the Bolshevik regime continued to promote an international workers' revolution as 'the only sure victory' that would guarantee the USSR's existence.[34] This clandestine dimension of Soviet foreign policy was managed by Grigory Zinoviev in his role as chairman of the executive committee of the Comintern. Conventional diplomatic relations were the

---

[30] P. Krüger, *Die Aussenpolitik der Republik von Weimar* (Munich, 2013), 17–147; P. Cohrs, *The Unfinished Peace after World War I* (Cambridge, 2006), 60–2.
[31] M. Knox, 'Fascism and Italian Foreign Policy: Continuity and Break' in *Common Destiny: Dictatorship, Foreign Policy and War in Fascist Italy and Nazi Germany* (Cambridge, 2000), 113–28.
[32] V. I. Lenin, 'Our Foreign and Domestic Position and Party Tasks' in *Lenin: Collected Works*, trans. J. Katzer, vol. XXXI (Moscow, 1965), 410.
[33] R. W. Davies, *Soviet Economic Development from Lenin to Kruschev* (Cambridge, 1998), 17–37; J. Jacobson, *When the Soviet Union Entered World Politics* (Berkeley, 1994), 81–105.
[34] Lenin, 'Our Foreign and Domestic Position', 410; A. Kocho-Williams, *Russian and Soviet Diplomacy, 1900–1939* (London, 2011), 45–76.

responsibility of Georgy Chicherin, a former Tsarist diplomat and newly appointed head of Narkomindel. Although Chicherin described Soviet policy as an 'experiment in peaceful co-existence with bourgeois states', another aim was to export revolution to every corner of the globe. The unique internal and external challenges posed by Soviet policy would endure throughout the inter-war period.[35]

Prospects for a League-based collective security strategy suffered a major blow when the US Congress refused to ratify the Versailles Treaty for the second time in March 1920. The USA did not join the League of Nations and the American guarantee of French security evaporated.[36] American rejection of the treaty also undermined hopes for US financial assistance to Europe. The American representative was withdrawn from the reparations commission created by the treaty.[37] The new Republican administration of Warren Harding insisted that future loans to Europe would be contingent on Allied repayment of war debts. This obliged French governments to turn to private American capital, giving US investment banks a voice in debates about the European financial order. Meanwhile, suspicion of France became a significant factor in US policy making. American commerce secretary Herbert Hoover blamed France for maintaining the 'whole economic and political life' of Europe 'in an atmosphere of war'.[38] Allegations of French militarism would reach a crescendo during the Washington Naval Disarmament Conference in late 1921 and play an important role in convincing a number of senior policy makers that a change in tactics was necessary.

Another crucial consequence of American withdrawal from the Versailles system was the retraction of Britain's guarantee to France. The Lloyd George government refused to extend a unilateral guarantee.[39] This deprived France of the key pillar of Clemenceau's security policy at the peace conference. French policy makers would spend the entire inter-war period attempting to fashion replacements for the lost Anglo-American guarantee. Efforts to secure

---

[35] C. Read, 'The View from the Kremlin: Soviet Assumptions about the Capitalist World in the 1920s' in S. Casey and J. Wright (eds.), *Mental Maps in the Era of Two World Wars* (London, 2008), 38–57; Jacobson, *Soviet Union*, 32–127; A. Hogenhuis-Seliverstoff, *Les Relations franco-soviétiques 1917–1924* (Paris, 1981), 54–143.

[36] J. Milton Cooper, *Breaking the Heart of the World: Woodrow Wilson and the Fight for the League of Nations* (Cambridge, 2001), 109–414; L. Ambrosius, *Woodrow Wilson and the American Diplomatic Tradition: The Treaty Fight in Perspective* (Cambridge, 1987), 80–106, 135–289.

[37] F. Costigliola, *Awkward Dominion: American Political, Economic and Cultural Relations with Europe, 1919–1933* (Ithaca, 1984), 25–110; Z. Steiner, *The Lights that Failed: European International History, 1919–1933* (Oxford, 2005), 185–91.

[38] Quote from Cohrs, *Unfinished Peace*, 69; see also M. Hogan, *Informal Entente: The Private Structure of Co-operation in Anglo-American Diplomacy, 1918–1928* (Columbia, 1977), 38–65; R. Boyce, *The Great Interwar Crisis and the Collapse of Globalization* (London, 2009), 78–85.

[39] A. Lentin, 'Several types of ambiguity: Lloyd George at the Paris Peace Conference', *D&S*, 6, 1 (1995), 223–51.

a British 'continental commitment' were complicated by divergent perceptions of the nature of the German problem in Paris and London. British policy inclined towards a swift reintegration of Germany into the international political and economic system. The hope was that the Reich could serve as an engine of European recovery. The trauma of war, moreover, had produced very different attitudes towards the Entente in Britain and France. A central legacy of the wartime experience in Britain was an aversion to future military adventures in Europe. The pervasive conviction, held by British political elites as well as the general public, was that Britain had been drawn into making imprudent and unnecessary commitments to the French before 1914. This proved a powerful obstacle to any such commitment in the future. Another such obstacle was a lingering suspicion of France. 'We have been brought, for reasons of national safety, into an alliance with the French which I hope will last,' soon-to-be foreign secretary Lord Curzon observed, 'but their national character is different from ours ... I am afraid that the Great Power from whom we most have to fear in the future is France.'[40]

Lloyd George was not a Francophobe, but he was inclined to see designs for European hegemony in French policy. He also wrongly identified a collapse in trade as the source of Britain's economic ills.[41] He gave priority to the restoration of the German economy and a resumption of commercial relations with Russia. Millerand and his successors came under increasing British pressure to adopt a moderate line over German treaty compliance (especially reparations payments) and to agree to commercial negotiations with Bolshevik representatives. A final area of Franco-British tension was policy towards Turkey. British policy aimed to impose the harsh terms of the Treaty of Sèvres signed with the Ottoman Empire. The Quai d'Orsay favoured coming to terms with the Turkish nationalists in order to concentrate scarce military resources on establishing French control in Syria.[42] French and British 'conflicting strategies of peace' would play an important role in shaping the course of European politics through to the end of the 1930s.[43]

---

[40] Curzon quoted in M. Dockrill, *British Establishment Perspectives on France 1936–1940* (London, 1999), 2; see also M. Howard, *Continental Commitment: The Dilemma of British Defence Policy in the Era of the Two World Wars* (London, 1972), 18–96.

[41] The deflationary measures imposed by the Lloyd George government were more damaging: Eichengreen, *Golden Fetters*, 107–24.

[42] AN, 470 AP 56, *Archives Millerand*, 'Note sur la paix avec la Turquie', DAPC study, 20 Feb. 1920; M. Thomas, 'Anglo-French imperial relations in the Arab World', *D&S*, 17, 1 (2006), 1–28.

[43] A. Wolfers, *Britain and France between Two Wars: Conflicting Strategies of Peace since Versailles* (New York, 1968); G. Bennett, *British Foreign Policy during the Curzon Period, 1919–1924* (London, 1995); J. Ferris, *The Evolution of British Strategic Policy, 1919–1925* (London, 1987), 48–101; Steiner, *Lights that Failed*, 193–203; P. M. H. Bell, *France and Britain, 1900–1940: Entente and Estrangement* (London, 1996), 72–158; Boyce, *Great Interwar Crisis*, 23–76.

III

Alexandre Millerand was the most influential figure in security policy making during the early 1920s. When he succeeded Clemenceau as premier on 20 January 1920, Millerand had more than thirty-five years' experience of parliamentary politics.[44] He rose from lower-middle-class origins to become secretary of the Conférence des avocats before being elected to the chamber in 1885. A defender of workers' rights, Millerand was one of the most prominent socialists of the late nineteenth century. He refused to recognise the logic of party politics, however, and was excluded from Socialist ranks after he agreed to serve as minister in the Waldeck-Rousseau government of 1899. This led to his exclusion from the SFIO when it was founded in 1905 and set him on an altered political trajectory that saw him become preoccupied with the problem of political authority under the Third Republic and join the ranks of the moderate right. He served as minister of public works in Briand's first cabinet and as minister of war during the initial stages of the First World War. By 1919 Millerand was a central figure of the Bloc national coalition and was identified with the nationalist right.[45]

The newly constituted Millerand government faced formidable international challenges. Germany failed to comply with its obligations to make preliminary reparations payments either in hard currency or gold; it did not deliver the significant quantities of coal and coke required under the treaty; nor, finally, did it adhere to the restrictions placed on its armed forces and defence industries by the treaty.[46] This generated widespread anxiety, and Millerand was pressed constantly on these issues in parliament and in the nationalist press. Non-compliance was a headline item at meetings of the Allied Supreme Council and the conference of ambassadors during the first half of 1920.[47] The symbolic importance attached to maintaining the integrity of the Treaty of Versailles was a key feature of post-war parliamentary discourse across the political spectrum, from the extreme right to the moderate Socialists. Millerand, for example, insisted that the Versailles Treaty was 'the only possible framework' for international relations in Europe. 'If we go down the road of saying that Germany has signed an engagement that it cannot fulfil and that it is therefore best to dispense with it, where will we end up?' he warned Lloyd

---

[44] The following sketch is drawn from his unpublished memoirs, 'Mes souvenirs' in AN, 470 AP 1, *Archives Millerand*; L. Derfler, *Alexandre Millerand: The Socialist Years* (The Hague, 1977); and Farrar, *Principled Pragmatist*.

[45] AN, 470 AP 42, *Archives Millerand*, 'Les Leçons de la guerre', speech at Versailles, 19 Jan. 1919.

[46] AN, 470 AP 56, *Archives Millerand*, 'Questions concernant l'exécution par l'Allemagne du traité de Versailles', Apr. 1920; 470 AP 57, 'Note pour le président du conseil: manquements de l'Allemagne à l'exécution du traité de paix', 12 May 1920.

[47] See, for example, AN, C/14632, *CAEAN*, sessions of 4, 17, 20 Feb., 4 Mar. and 10 Jun. 1920; see also *JO*, Chambre, *Débats*, 1920, 6 Feb., 26 Mar. and 26 Jun. 1920.

George.[48] French policy officials were advised that the treaty regime must not be compromised. The size of Henri Fromageot's legal department at the Quai d'Orsay was increased threefold to cope with requests for advice on different aspects of the treaty.[49]

Yet it was much easier to proclaim the need for integral treaty enforcement than to obtain compliance. Millerand and his successors all found it necessary to scale back the inflexible rhetoric and seek *modi vivendi*. Millerand had insisted initially that the terms of the Versailles Treaty 'are not, and cannot be, a matter of negotiation'. Dealings with the Germans must take the form of 'precise and clearly formulated demands that they fulfil their engagements ... for me the question is very simple: I have a treaty that outlines a procedure for obtaining from the Germans what they owe me. I will hold to it.'[50] Briand similarly argued for absolute inflexibility: 'Any modifications to the contract however slight, even on secondary or tertiary issues, will compromise our position when it comes to executing core elements of the treaty.' This, he insisted, would 'leave us with an instrument that is fundamentally weakened'.[51] When it came to putting this rhetoric into practice, however, Briand also proved willing to make compromises to achieve some German compliance.

In terms of diplomatic practices, the post-war period saw a continuation of summit diplomacy. Millerand had face-to-face meetings with Lloyd George in San Remo, Hythe, Boulogne, Brussels and Spa.[52] Allied heads of government met directly with their German counterparts for the first time at the Spa Conference in July. Policy formulation in peacetime thus remained concentrated in the hands of the premier and his permanent advisers. The result, in the French case, was further tension between permanent officials in the foreign ministry and senior diplomats posted abroad. Poincaré lamented this trend towards 'casino politics', which he associated with endless concessions. He called in vain for a return to the traditional practices of European diplomacy.[53]

The core aims of the Millerand government's policy of enforcement were twofold. The first was to construct a common Allied front – and especially a

---

[48] Ministère des affaires étrangères, Commission des archives diplomatiques, *Documents diplomatiques français* (hereafter *DDF*), Série 1920–1932, *Annexes (10 janvier 1920–31 décembre 1921)* (Paris, 2005), #1, 'Conférence de Londres, 12–13 février 1920: P.V. no. 1', 12 Feb. 1920; see also AN, 470 AP 56, *Archives Millerand*, 'Procès-verbal d'une entrevue entre M. Millerand et M. Lloyd George, samedi matin 24 avril à San Remo'.

[49] See MAE, Service juridique, *Fonds Fromageot*, vols. 1–6.

[50] AN, 470 AP 56, *Archives Millerand*, 'Compte-rendu d'une entrevue entre MM. Lloyd George, Millerand et Nitti à San Remo', 18 Apr. 1920.

[51] AN, C/14632, *CAEAN*, XIIème Législature, Millerand *audition*, 17 Feb. 1920.

[52] Reasonably complete French records for these various summit conferences can be consulted in *DDF, Annexes (1920–1921)*, #1–57.

[53] Quote from Steiner, *Lights that Failed*, 183; see also Poincaré, 'Sous le ciel bleu de San Remo', *Le Matin*, 19 Apr. 1920; É. Weill-Raynal, *Les Réparations allemandes et la France*, vol. I: *Des Origines jusqu'à l'institution de l'état des payements* (Paris, 1947), 547–8.

Franco-British front – in the face of German defiance. This included agreement on the size, nature and modalities of German annual payments as well as on the portion of the total sum that each member of the Entente would receive. The second aim was to secure Allied agreement on the application of sanctions to punish non-compliance. Millerand pressed, in particular, for Allied agreement on the principle of an occupation of the Ruhr basin. Such an occupation would cut off the Left Bank of the Rhine from the rest of Germany, leaving it more dependent on commerce with France and, it was hoped, more receptive to French influence. Behind the threat to occupy the Ruhr, therefore, lurked the prospect of a forward policy in the Rhineland and an attempt to transform the European strategic balance along the lines advocated by Foch in 1919.[54]

The results obtained were mixed. France's chief allies were generally more sympathetic to German protestations that fulfilment was impossible. Lloyd George argued for patience. He pressed Millerand repeatedly to agree to direct meetings with German leaders. And he consistently opposed an occupation of the Ruhr. The French premier, under intense pressure to take strong action against Germany, was forced to choose between unilateral action and possible isolation, on the one hand, and concessions and a common front with Britain, on the other. This dilemma came to a head in early April, when the Weimar government sent troops into the Ruhr during the Kapp Putsch. The Millerand government responded to this violation of the demilitarised zone by occupying Frankfurt, Darmstadt and three other towns in the Main area of Germany. The move provoked angry protests from London and Washington as well as Berlin, but failed to compel the Germans to disarm or send more coal.[55] Millerand was forced to retreat. Two weeks later at San Remo he agreed to evacuate the Maingau and pledged in future to act only in accord with France's allies. The episode demonstrated that limited punitive operations were costly, provoked opposition among France's allies and would not compel Germany to fulfil its obligations. The chief lesson drawn was that future unilateral action must secure control of the coal mines of the Ruhr basin.[56]

Millerand opted for Allied solidarity. This choice was based predominantly on balance-of-power calculations. France and Britain together constituted an unchallengeable power bloc. 'There can be no balance of power in Europe and thus no security for France without close Franco-British cooperation,' Millerand observed before the chamber's foreign affairs commission. 'The maintenance of our alliances must therefore be the basis of our entire external

---

[54] J. Bariéty, *Les Relations franco-allemandes après la première guerre mondiale* (Paris, 1977), 61–89; W. McDougall, *France's Rhineland Diplomacy, 1914–1924: The Last Bid for a Balance of Power in Europe* (Princeton, 1978), 97–147.
[55] See the tense exchanges in MAE, PA-AP 118, *Papiers Millerand*, vol. 41; see also A. Sharp, 'Enforcement of the Treaty of Versailles, 1919–1923', *D&S*, 16 (2005), 424–8.
[56] AN, 470 AP 57, *Archives Millerand*, Berthelot note of 22 May 1920; McDougall, *Rhineland Diplomacy*, 110–12.

policy.'[57] In the end, this Entente-based strategy succeeded in securing British, Belgian and Italian commitments to threaten Germany with military occupation of the Ruhr. The threat to use force was made explicit before Allied chiefs met with the German delegation at Spa.[58] Germany responded by pledging to disarm to the level stipulated by the treaty and to increase deliveries of coal and coke to France. To obtain these results, however, Millerand was forced to make important concessions over the deadline for disarmament and over the amount and terms for German coal delivery to France. He came under particularly heavy criticism in the chamber's foreign affairs commission for assenting to this de facto treaty revision. But his policy did secure a measure of German compliance over the final six months of 1920.[59]

IV

The background to French policy choices in 1920 was an interesting series of debates concerning France's strategic options. Although the traditional conception of security dominated these internal discussions, they were also characterised by implicit, and sometimes explicit, disagreements over both the meaning of security and the ultimate objectives of a Ruhr occupation.[60]

Millerand raised the issue of the Ruhr at the first post-war meeting of the CSG in late January, noting that an occupation held the dual advantage of securing reparations and 'adjusting the balance of forces at least temporarily in our favour'.[61] He returned to the issue when the CSDN met in mid-March, noting that an alleged German violation of the demilitarised zone 'presents us with a new opportunity to address the questions of an occupation of the Ruhr'.[62] Interestingly, the most prominent voices urging caution at this stage were from the military. Army chief of staff General Buat warned that a Ruhr occupation would require partial mobilisation.[63] Marshals Foch and Pétain were equally cautious. But there was more to this than prudence on the part of France's military chiefs. Their assessments were part of a political dogfight over

---

[57] AN, C/14632, *CAEAN*, XIIème Législature, Millerand *audition*, 20 Feb. 1920; see also P. Jackson, 'British Power and French Security, 1919–1939' in K. Neilson and G. Kennedy (eds.), *The British Way in Warfare: Power in the International System* (London, 2010), 101–34.

[58] MAE, PA-AP 217, *Papiers Massigli*, vol. 13, 'Historique des négociations interalliées ...', 11 Oct. 1920.

[59] Trachtenberg, *Reparation*, 148–52; on German disarmament see C. Metzger, 'L'Allemagne: un danger pour la France en 1920?', *GMCC*, 193 (1999), 5–22; and R. Shuster, *German Disarmament after World War I: The Diplomacy of International Arms Inspection* (London, 2006), 33–127.

[60] AN, 470 AP 57, *Archives Millerand*, Berthelot note of 22 May 1920; McDougall, *Rhineland Diplomacy*, 110–12.

[61] SHD-DAT, 1N 23–1, 'Procès-verbal de la séance du CSG du 31 janvier 1920'.

[62] SHD-DAT, 2N 5–1, 'Conseil supérieur de la Défense nationale: séance tenue au Palais de l'Élysée le vendredi 19 mars 1920'.

[63] SHD-DAT, 1N 23–1, 'Procès-verbal de la séance du CSG du 31 janvier 1920'.

Post-war dilemmas: enforcement or engagement? 339

cuts to the defence budget and the size of France's standing army. 'To occupy the Ruhr,' Foch observed, 'we must be a military power. At this moment we are not ready.'[64]

This judgement can only be understood within the context of pressure from the finance ministry for cuts to military spending and a reduction in the length of military service.[65] Military leaders were determined to resist this pressure, and deployed their substantial symbolic and cultural capital in order to do so. The German military threat was massively exaggerated as part of this effort. In March 1920 the Deuxième bureau judged that Germany could mobilise between sixty and seventy-five infantry divisions.[66] The following December its assessment was only slightly less alarming. Although it was acknowledged that large numbers of military units and heavy equipment had been dismantled after the Spa Conference, huge importance was attached to the military significance of special police and paramilitary units. The Deuxième bureau also warned that German heavy industry remained capable of equipping up to forty-five divisions after three months.[67] Pétain cited this intelligence at the March CSDN meeting and observed that France would have great difficulty dealing with Germany on its own, should war break out.[68]

This was an absurd distortion of the military balance that ignored the formidable complexities of industrial mobilisation and wildly exaggerated the combat effectiveness of various police and paramilitary units.[69] A more honest assessment was provided by General Henri Niessel, who advised the chamber's army and foreign affairs commissions that 'it will take years for Germany to reconstitute the *matériel* necessary for another war'. He reckoned that a significant military threat from Germany would not emerge for another fifteen years.[70] During a confrontation with French military chiefs on the CSDN, finance minister Frédéric François-Marsal pointed out that Germany's finances were 'in chaos' and that it was in 'no position to fight'. Foch's response is highly revealing:

Financial issues must not be allowed to obstruct military policy ... military decisions brought about the end to the war when all else failed; our current security problem must be understood in the same terms. It will be determined by our military

---

[64] SHD-DAT, 2N 5–1, 'Conseil supérieur de la Défense nationale: séance tenue au Palais de l'Élysée le vendredi 19 mars 1920'.
[65] See esp. M. Vaïsse and J. Doise, *Diplomatie et outil militaire: politique étrangère de la France, 1871–1991* (Paris, 1992), 335–9.
[66] SHD-DAT, 7N 2610–2, 'État d'esprit en Allemagne', 17 juin 1919; 2N 5–1, 'Note sur les conditions générales de la mobilisation', Mar. 1920.
[67] SHD-DAT, 2N 5–3, 'Résumé de la situation allemande', 13 Dec. 1920.
[68] SHD-DAT, 2N 5–1, 'Conseil supérieur de la Défense nationale: séance tenue au Palais de l'Élysée le vendredi 19 mars 1920'.
[69] Metzger, 'Danger?' argues that Germany posed a credible threat in 1920, but deploys decisive evidence to the contrary; see also Shuster, *German Disarmament*, 5–22.
[70] AN, C/14632, *CAEAN*, XIIème Législature, Niessel *audition*, 12 Feb. 1920.

possibilities. We must have a military situation that assures minimum security for our country. We cannot count on the weakness of our adversary.[71]

Foch's analysis of the situation made no distinction between conditions of peace and those of war. His setback at the peace conference had in no way altered either his deeply pessimistic understanding of international politics or his highly traditional conception of national security.

German dismemberment remained central to the geo-political vision of Foch and other members of his *maison*. If the marshal did not press for a move against the Ruhr in early 1920, this was only to make a stronger argument against defence cuts. In fact, from April 1920, Foch and his lieutenants advocated a move against the Ruhr with increasing urgency. Such a move, crucially, was always conceived as more than a means to obtain German treaty compliance. It held out the prospect of realising the strategic aims of a frontier on the Rhine and of German dismemberment that France had failed to secure at the peace conference.[72]

Two prominent advocates of this traditional prescription of France's security were General Joseph Degoutte, commander of the French army of the Rhine, and Paul Tirard, France's high commissioner in the Rhineland and head of the Inter-Allied Rhineland High Commission. Both were close allies of Foch. Both advocated support for separatist and autonomist movements inside Germany, and particularly the Left Bank. Both were consistent advocates of a Ruhr occupation. An occupation of the Ruhr, Degoutte argued, was 'the most effective guarantee of our security'. It would provide control of over 40 per cent of the German economy, including the vast majority of its war industry. More importantly, it would isolate the Rhineland and trigger the dissolution of the German Reich of 1871. This was Degoutte's core security prescription:

To obtain a durable peace we must transform Germany; we must destroy the work of the Hohenzollern [and] suppress its Prussian armature forged by war and for war. Only the reconstitution of Germany on a federalist basis and the disappearance of the formidable machine of war that is Prussian Germany will deliver peace for Europe.

Degoutte therefore urged close coordination between the policies towards the Rhineland and the Ruhr, security and reparations: 'The federalist policy on the one hand and the policy of guarantees on the other must never be considered strategies of imperialism or annexation. Together they are simply a preventative policy of security.'[73]

---

[71] SHD-DAT, 2N 5-1, 'Conseil supérieur de la Défense nationale: séance tenue au Palais de l'Élysée le vendredi 19 mars 1920'; also 4N 92-2, 'Note' by Foch on the reduction of military charges, 26 Oct. 1920.

[72] J.-C. Notin, *Foch* (Paris, 2008), 489–511.

[73] SHD-DAT, 7N 2656, Degoutte commentary on an intelligence report forwarded to the war ministry, 24 Dec. 1921; see also S. Jeannesson, *Poincaré, la France et la Ruhr (1922–1924)* (Strasbourg, 1998), 39–40.

Although he was less forthright in his prescriptions, Tirard shared the traditional vision of Foch and Degoutte.[74] From early March he took part in planning for sanctions aimed at Germany. His preferred strategy was to create a new customs barrier that closed off the Left Bank from the rest of the Reich. This, Tirard pointed out, would establish the conditions for drawing the region into the French economic orbit.[75] Tirard was also centrally involved in all discussion and planning for an occupation of the Ruhr. An occupation, he observed, would provide the opportunity to 'intensify our economic action in the Rhineland'.[76] This, he argued, would stimulate pre-existing support for breaking away from Germany in order to obtain better political and economic conditions: 'By demonstrating a determination to exercise our rights ... we will accentuate the desire of the Rhinelanders to free themselves from the clutches of Prussia.'[77]

Altering the political make-up of Germany was also the preferred strategy of Maurice Paléologue, the newly appointed secretary general of the Quai d'Orsay. Paléologue was a controversial figure who was widely detested by the centre-left and left. He owed his appointment to lobbying on his behalf by Poincaré, who wished to thwart the influence of Philippe Berthelot within the foreign ministry.[78] Paléologue's appointment was greeted with approval by the traditionally minded old guard within the diplomatic corps. 'Our new chief has chosen his *éminence grise* well,' observed Jusserand from Washington. 'We cannot return too soon to our austere and classical ideals of order.'[79] Paléologue's chief policy initiative towards Germany was an ill-advised flirtation with federalist movements in Bavaria and Hesse. From early 1919 the foreign ministry received reports on support for separatism or autonomy in these regions. Haguenin in Berlin, among others, recommended discreet contacts with the various Catholic politicians in Bavaria who were reported to favour breaking with Berlin.[80] Paléologue, whose expertise lay in central and

---

[74] Jacques Bariéty has argued that an independent Left Bank was 'the raison d'être' of the French high commission in the Rhineland: *Relations franco-allemandes*, 68.
[75] *DDF, 1920*, III, #78, Tirard to DAPC summarising his strategy, 15 Oct. 1920; see also Bariéty, *Relations franco-allemandes*, 51–67; McDougall, *Rhineland Diplomacy*, 89–96, 113–36; Jeannesson, *Ruhr*, 36–9.
[76] MAE, PA-AP 261, *Papiers Seydoux*, vol. 19, 'Note pour le ministre: étude sur les moyens de représailles économiques à titre de "l'occupation" en cas d'inexécution du traité de paix par l'Allemagne', Tirard note, 30 Mar. 1920; MAE, PA-AP 118, *Papiers Millerand*, vol. 41, Tirard to Briand, 10 and 18 Feb. 1921.
[77] MAE, PA-AP 261, *Papiers Seydoux*, vol. 19, 'L'Occupation envisagée comme gage de l'exécution du traité de paix', Tirard note, 8 Nov. 1920.
[78] Armand Fallières, a former French president, characterised Paléologue as 'the Black Prince' of French diplomacy: 'Introduction' to Paléologue, *Crépuscule des tsars*, 24; Keiger, *Poincaré*, 167–77.
[79] MAE, PA-AP 93, *Papiers Jusserand*, vol. 37, Jusserand to Paléologue, 29 Jan. 1920; also cited in McDougall, *Rhineland Diplomacy*, 100.
[80] MAE, Série Z, *Allemagne*, vol. 352, 'La Situation en Bavière', Haguenin note, 28 Jun. 1919; AN, 470 AP 57, *Archives Millerand*, 'Représentation à Munich', Paléologue to Millerand, 18 Jun. 1920.

eastern Europe, envisaged uniting Bavaria, Austria and Hungary in a southern power bloc that would counterbalance Prussian-dominated northern Germany. This ambitious design crumbled, however, when it became clear that federalist sentiment was much weaker than had been imagined and that most of those sympathetic to federalism remained virulently anti-French. With his grand strategic project in tatters, Paléologue was replaced as secretary general by Berthelot in September 1920.[81]

The vision of post-war security promulgated by Foch, Degoutte, Tirard and Paléologue was an attempt to return to a period of imagined French predominance before 1871. The extent to which Millerand approved of links with federalists and separatists across the Rhine is impossible to know. He was aware of contacts with these various movements and probably approved modest sums to subsidise them. Like Clemenceau, however, he was wary of policy initiatives that could undermine France's negotiating position on more pressing issues. 'It goes without saying that we must not discourage the federalists,' he instructed. He added, however, that 'I cannot overstate how important it is for French officials to do absolutely nothing that might lead to accusations of interference in German internal affairs.'[82]

Millerand's judgement reflected the preponderant view within the Quai d'Orsay, which favoured pursuing security through an *entente* with Britain. Jules Laroche recalled that Paléologue's complicated project for the political reordering of Europe – which envisaged the restoration of monarchical rule in both Hungary and Bavaria – was 'in complete opposition' to majority opinion within the foreign ministry.[83] Berthelot pointed out in September 1920 that, despite its inevitable tensions, 'the Franco-British Entente remains the most solid foundation for our security'. Berthelot, like the vast majority of his colleagues, would have welcomed an upsurge of separatist or autonomous sentiment across the Rhine. As long as this sentiment failed to materialise, however, he argued that France 'must work with the reality that presents itself to us, and that reality is our difficult alliance with the British'.[84]

The majority of mainstream parliamentary discourse remained fixated on the holy grail of integral treaty execution. From his position as chair of the chamber's foreign affairs commission, Louis Barthou exerted unrelenting pressure on both Millerand and his successor Georges Leygues to obtain full execution of the Treaty of Versailles.[85] Tardieu was another hardliner, not least because the best way to defend a treaty that he had played such an

---

[81] *DDF*, *1920*, I, #385, Paléologue to Millerand (San Remo), 20 Apr. 1920; see esp. the perceptive analysis in McDougall, *Rhineland Diplomacy*, 116–22; J. L. Barré, *Philippe Berthelot: l'éminence grise, 1866–1934* (Paris, 1998), 354–5.
[82] *DDF*, *1920*, I, #36, 'Particularisme allemand', Millerand to Lefèvre, 22 Jan. 1922.
[83] Laroche, *Quai d'Orsay*, 111–14.
[84] MAE, PA-AP 72, *Papiers Aimé de Fleuriau*, vol. 3, Berthelot to de Fleuriau, 2 Aug. 1920; see also MAE, *Série Z, GB*, vol. 45, Leygues (Berthelot) to Paul Cambon, 6 Nov. 1920.
[85] *JO*, Chambre, *Débats*, 1920, 26 Feb. 1920.

Post-war dilemmas: enforcement or engagement? 343

important role in negotiating was to criticise the government's failure to enforce it.[86] War minister André Lefèvre was particularly uncompromising on this issue. In December 1920 he resigned from the cabinet rather than agree to any reduction in military service while German disarmament remained incomplete. Before the chamber he painted an apocalyptic picture of the strategic situation: 'Think of what our situation will be tomorrow if 60 million Germans and 80 million Russians collaborate to launch an offensive west of the Rhine.' To protests that France could not keep one million men under arms indefinitely he responded, 'This is exactly the dilemma that I fear! ... Let us make war now!'[87] Lefèvre's alarm, like plans to dismember Germany, underlines both the anxiety generated by German non-fulfilment and the power of the traditional approach to security in French policy conceptions in 1920.

If the majority of parliamentary and press opinion continued to adopt a hardline position over German compliance, it is interesting to note the emergence of support for an alternative strategy of engagement and cooperation with Germany. Marc Trachtenberg has remarked that 'one of the more perplexing features of French policy towards Germany in 1920' was 'the coexistence of harsh and moderate strains of policy'.[88] From Berlin, Professor Haguenin, who had established an impressive network of contacts that included Walther Rathenau and Gustav Stresemann, was the source of a series of interesting missives along these lines.[89] Haguenin had from the beginning recommended a subtle strategy of treating Germany with a firmness that did not rule out eventual economic and even political cooperation. By early 1920 he had come to see such cooperation as an urgent necessity for France. 'If Germany does not reconstitute itself under our surveillance and with our assistance,' he warned, '*it will reconstitute itself nonetheless by other means and against us.*'[90] In early March Haguenin forwarded a long note that urged a very different approach:

If we want that which is essential in the treaty to be executed we must work with those elements inside Germany with whom we have common interests, individuals as well as parties. Methods of external coercion are ineffective; they expose us to the hatred of neutrals and the betrayal of our allies ... It is not a matter of abdicating, revising or renouncing any of our rights. It is a matter of changing not our objectives, but our method.[91]

---

[86] MAE, PA-AP 217, *Papiers Massigli*, vol. 13, 'Réponse au questionnaire de M. Tardieu', 29 Jun. 1920; 'Résultats des accords de Spa', 19 Nov. 1920; see also Roussellier, *Parlement de l'éloquence*, 56, 67–8, 89–94.
[87] Quotes from Bonnefous, *Après-guerre*, 197–8; see also J. Hughes, *To the Maginot Line: The Politics of French Military Preparation in the 1920s* (Cambridge, Mass., 1971), 112–19.
[88] Trachtenberg, *Reparation*, 121.
[89] Bariéty, *Relations franco-allemandes*, 214–15; J.-C. Montant, 'Émile Haguenin, "un homme d'influence"' in J.-J. Pollet and A.-M. Saint-Gille (eds.), *Écritures franco-allemandes de la Grande Guerre* (Arras, 1996), 124–5.
[90] AN, 470 AP 59, *Archives Millerand*, Haguenin note, 27 Feb. 1920 (emphasis by Millerand in original).
[91] AN, 470 AP 59, *Archives Millerand*, Haguenin note, 8 Mar. 1920.

Haguenin developed this proposition in a subsequent note where he argued that victory in 1918 had 'rendered victors and vanquished interdependent, and this solidarity will be a partnership of misery and ruin if we refuse to accept its implications and use it to our advantage'. It was essential that France cooperate with the Reich while it was weak in order to 'shape its development as a democracy in a positive sense'.[92]

It is difficult to assess the significance of Haguenin's policy prescriptions. His analysis was sometimes contradictory, if not confused. Two things are not in doubt, however. First, Haguenin's views reached the highest echelons of government. They almost certainly influenced an interview with the *Daily Chronicle* on 20 March in which Millerand declared that 'in our future relations with Germany we have never excluded the possibility of economic cooperation'. Six days later the premier made a similar statement before the chamber of deputies.[93] Second, Haguenin's analysis complemented in interesting ways that of Jacques Seydoux, the increasingly influential head of the *sous-direction* of Commercial Relations at the Quai d'Orsay.

Seydoux's vision of European political and economic reconstruction was fundamentally multilateral. He understood, even at this early stage, that French economic recovery was dependent on a wider European reconstruction that must necessarily involve Germany. He argued consistently that reparation was a problem of European reconstruction that could not be resolved without German economic recovery and political participation.[94] As early as the previous June, Seydoux had lamented the 'utterly selfish' economic policies of both Britain and the USA. To maintain its independence in relation to both powers, he judged, France could not afford to exclude 'the idea of a resumption of economic cooperation with Germany, whose role will again become ever important for Europe'.[95] Seydoux remained an advocate of this cooperation through to his retirement in 1927.

In late April 1920 the German government suggested meetings between French and German economic experts to discuss 'all economic questions that might be studied in common'. Seydoux, who was charged with organising this meeting, observed that such commercial negotiations could 'establish the conditions for a larger entente', envisaging not only the reconstruction of France, but also 'the general restoration of healthy economic life in Europe'.

---

[92] AN, 470 AP 59, *Archives Millerand*, 'Action en Allemagne', Haguenin, 18 Mar. 1920; Haguenin note (forwarded to Millerand), 11 Apr. 1920.

[93] *JO*, Chambre, *Débats*, 1920, 26 Mar. 1920; AN, 470 AP 59, *Archives Millerand*, 'Les Rapports franco-allemands' (interview with *Daily Chronicle* that was also published in *Le Temps*, 20 Mar. 1920).

[94] S. Jeannesson, 'Jacques Seydoux et la diplomatie économique dans la France de l'après-guerre', *RI*, 121 (2005), 15–17; N. Jordan, 'The reorientation of French diplomacy in the 1920s: the role of Jacques Seydoux', *EHR*, 117, 473 (2002), 870–3.

[95] MAE, RC, Série B40, vol. 1, Seydoux note, 19 Jun. 1919; also cited in G.-H. Soutou, *L'Or et le sang: les buts de guerre économiques de la Première Guerre mondiale* (Paris, 1989), 285.

While the Versailles Treaty must serve as the basis for future cooperation, Seydoux argued that emphasis must shift towards 'coming to agreement on its application rather than its interpretation'.[96] Seydoux's analysis was close to that of Joseph Avenol, then a finance ministry official attached to the French embassy in London. In a widely circulated study of the reparations issue, Avenol argued that the best means to achieve German treaty compliance was to 'pursue a policy of community of interests', not only among the Allied states but also with Germany. This would mean 'a loosening of some of the political and juridical guarantees expressed in the treaty'. The end result would be a measure of German fulfilment.[97]

The policy recommendations of Seydoux and Avenol marked an important departure from more traditional solutions based on coercion. Both advocated a practical and more flexible approach to treaty fulfilment, recognising that de facto revision of the letter of the treaty was necessary to secure some measure of its fulfilment. They also advocated German participation in the economic and thus the political reconstruction of Europe. Calls for the integral fulfilment of the treaty, conversely, envisaged organising European politics against Germany.

The arguments of Seydoux and Avenol found an increasingly receptive audience with Millerand. In late March Millerand advised the chamber that treaty fulfilment must be informed by 'a sense of realities'.[98] In conversation with Lloyd George in May 1920 Millerand hinted at a willingness to be flexible in interpreting the treaty: 'I attach an extreme importance to sticking to the treaty *as closely as possible* and to applying *as much as possible* all of its clauses.'[99] Underneath his surface rhetoric of firmness was a clearly implied willingness to negotiate. 'If we will not accept any revision of the treaty,' Millerand argued before the chamber the following July, 'we are nevertheless obliged to interpret it in order to draw tangible realities from it.' This, he argued, constituted a 'policy of realisation'.[100] By the following October Millerand had moved even further in this direction. 'The literal execution of the treaty is a chimera,' he observed in a high-level meeting on the reparations problem. 'France can, in accordance with the treaty, use coercion to obtain payment. But we must understand that such a procedure is dangerous and will lead to grave trouble

---

[96] *DDF*, *1920*, I, #419, 'Négociations commerciales avec l'Allemagne: démarche de M. Göppert', Millerand (Seydoux) to Berlin, 29 Apr. 1920; #466, 'Note pour M. Millerand, président du conseil: négociations avec l'Allemagne', 12 May 1920; the talks took place in May but went nowhere.

[97] AN, 470 AP 57, *Archives Millerand*, 'Note Avenol', 6 May 1920.

[98] *JO*, Chambre, *Débats*, 1920, 26 Mar. 1920; see also G.-H. Soutou, 'Problèmes concernant le rétablissement des relations économiques franco-allemandes après la première guerre mondiale', *Francia*, 2 (1974), 580–96; Trachtenberg, *Reparation*, 99–153.

[99] AN, 470 AP 57, *Archives Millerand*, 'Conversation entre les premiers ministres de la France et de la Grande-Bretagne à Belcaire, Lympne, Kent, le samedi 15 mai à 10.15hrs du matin', 15 May 1920 (emphasis added).

[100] *JO*, Chambre, *Débats*, 1920, 20 Jul. 1920.

with Britain.' He therefore argued for a flexible approach aimed at creating structures of cooperation to encourage Germany to accept treaty compliance and participate in general reconstruction.[101]

In sum, by the autumn of 1920 a limited number of senior officials, including president Millerand, were considering alternatives to the traditional focus on coercion and the balance of power. 'France and Germany live in the same building,' Millerand observed in his instructions to the first French ambassador posted to Berlin since 1914. 'They cannot destroy one another and it is therefore essential that they render their house habitable.'[102] This multilateral policy orientation, which aimed at enmeshing and constraining Germany on terms favourable to France, underpinned the strategy to achieve economic security through direct Franco-German economic collaboration developed by Seydoux in late 1920.

V

Jacques Seydoux followed a standard path to a position in the foreign ministry but fashioned an extraordinary career thereafter.[103] The son of a Bonapartist who resigned from the Quai d'Orsay in 1871, he was a committed republican with a powerful intellect and an independent cast of mind. After obtaining a *licence* in law, he took the preparatory course for diplomats at the École libre before passing the *concours* of 1895.[104] Evaluations of Seydoux's 'general aptitude' praised his 'excellent intellectual preparation', but also noted 'a certain exuberance of spirit' that was 'happily counterbalanced' by his 'good practical sense and sound judgement'. These latter qualities were attributed to his having been 'raised in the traditions of the department of foreign affairs'.[105]

After postings in Athens and Berlin, Seydoux returned to the central administration in Paris in 1905, where he remained until his retirement in 1927. From the early 1900s he suffered from crippling rheumatoid arthritis that, by the opening of the First World War, had confined him permanently to a wheelchair. He nonetheless distinguished himself at the head of the foreign ministry's Service de la guerre économique. This role was fundamental to the future

---

[101] MAE, PA-AP 261, *Papiers Seydoux*, vol. 18, 'Note no. 12: question des réparations', 24 Oct. 1920.
[102] MAE, PA-AP 261, *Papiers Seydoux*, vol. 1, 'Instructions à l'Ambassadeur de France à Berlin', 26 Jun. 1920; this note was first drafted by Seydoux, significantly.
[103] F. Seydoux, 'Hier au Quai d'Orsay: Jacques Seydoux, mon père', *RDDM* (15 Jan. 1964), 179–92; S. Jeannesson, 'L'Europe de Jacques Seydoux', *RH*, 299 (1998), 124–43; Jordan, 'Reorientation of French diplomacy'.
[104] S. Jeannesson, *Jacques Seydoux diplomate, 1870–1929* (Paris, 2013), 14–66; MAE, *Dossiers de personnel*, 2ème série, vol. 1426: Charles Louis Auguste Jacques Seydoux, de Courcels to Jules Develle, 14 Oct. 1893; Messimy to Delcassé, 30 Jan. 1905; 'Notes du Chef de Poste' (Legrand), 1894.
[105] MAE, *Dossiers de personnel*, 2ème série, vol. 1426, 'Notes du Chef de Poste' (de Courcels in London), 1895; note from the cabinet du ministre to Seydoux, 26 Dec. 1895.

course of his career. It forced him to acquire a command of commercial and financial issues and placed him in daily contact with Allied colleagues working on questions of economic warfare (Seydoux was awarded an OBE by the British government in early 1921). This gave him a broader perspective on the great economic challenges facing post-war Europe as well as a better feel for the policy orientations of France's allies. He was therefore the natural choice to take charge of the new Sous-direction des relations commerciales forged out of the Service de la guerre économique with Berthelot's support in May 1919.[106]

Seydoux's intellectual gifts, expertise and independent temperament combined to produce a distinctive approach to France's economic security. Among the first to underline the attractions of Franco-German economic collaboration, he was also willing to discuss policy in the public sphere. Seydoux had close ties with the internationalist-leaning journal *L'Europe nouvelle* and published an influential essay as early as 1921 in the *Revue d'économie politique*.[107] From late 1918 to his illness-induced retirement in 1927 he was unquestionably the most influential voice on international economic issues within the policy establishment. And few officials rivalled his influence over European policy more generally. His direct style, courage and commitment to French interests earned the esteem of such vastly different personalities as Poincaré, Briand and Clemenceau. This esteem extended well beyond France. In Whitehall Seydoux was described as 'the guiding spirit of the French F[oreign] O[ffice]' and 'a man of great knowledge and moderate disposition who is well disposed towards us'.[108]

In late 1920 Seydoux devised a programme for the payment of reparations in kind that aimed explicitly at establishing a community of economic interest with Germany. Franco-German economic cooperation would serve as the foundation for European recovery. Seydoux derived this fundamentally internationalist perspective not out of pro-German sympathies, but instead as a result of his conviction that 'as long as the Allies limit themselves to waiting for the benevolent execution of the peace treaty from Germany, they will get nothing'. Seydoux did not advocate fundamental revision of the treaty. What was needed, he argued, was a flexible and imaginative strategy for its application. 'The treaty is executable,' he insisted. What was needed was 'determination' along with 'practical measures' in the way it was put into effect. When

---

[106] S. Jeannesson, 'La Sous-direction des relations commerciales du Quai d'Orsay' in L. Badel, S. Jeannesson and P. Ludlow (eds.), *Les Administrations nationales et la construction européenne: une approche historique* (Berne, 2005), 37–56.

[107] Seydoux's writings are assembled in his posthumous *De Versailles au Plan Young: réparations, dettes interalliées et reconstruction européenne* (Paris, 1932).

[108] TNA-PRO, *James Ramsay MacDonald: official papers*, 30/69/16, Henry Wickham-Steed to Ronald Waterhouse, 10 Jun. 1924; see also the lengthy preface by François Charles-Roux in *De Versailles au Plan Young*, i–xxi.

all attempts to find such measures failed and Germany remained defiant, he advocated occupying the Ruhr.[109]

Under Seydoux's direction the newly created Commercial Relations *sous-direction* assumed responsibility for managing all aspects of international financial and commercial policy. This expansive remit led to tensions with what Seydoux described as 'the technical ministries' involved in commercial and financial policy.[110] Relations with the commerce ministry were particularly difficult. After the failure of Clémentel's project for economic cooperation, commerce officials retreated to a default position of negotiating bilateral commercial accords with other states. This reflex was in complete opposition to the multilateral approach favoured by Seydoux. Under his direction the commercial relations department prioritised European reconstruction and cooperation with the Anglo-Saxon powers. Within the foreign ministry, and the policy establishment more generally, Seydoux's team was considered a vital repository of expertise on economic issues and an essential cog in the machinery of post-war foreign policy.[111]

In early 1920 the prospect of German economic recovery was widely perceived as a potential threat to France. This view, which was rooted in the assumption of long-term Franco-German enmity, underpinned the instructions given to the French *chargé d'affaires* in Berlin in January 1920:

The peace treaty has tied German economic recovery to the reparations it owes for war-time damage. For this reason we must look with favour on a resumption of economic activity, which will permit the restoration of our devastated regions. But we can legitimately fear that Germany will very rapidly resume the place it occupied in the world before the war. We must therefore seek to obtain the maximum in reparations with the minimum of [German] economic power.[112]

Germany was expected to strive to regain the economic predominance it had enjoyed before 1914.[113]

This fundamentally pessimistic assessment of the future of Franco-German economic relations was much less prominent in the instructions given six months later to Charles Laurent, France's first post-war ambassador to Berlin. Laurent had been head of the Union des industries métallurgiques et minières de France. His

---

[109] AN, 470 AP 57, *Archives Millerand*, 'Note pour le président du conseil: manquements de l'Allemagne à l'exécution du traité de paix', 12 May 1920; Trachtenberg, *Reparation*, 163–4.
[110] MAE, PA-AP 261, *Papiers Seydoux*, vol. 18, 'Note: services de la sous-direction des relations commerciales', 22 Oct. 1920.
[111] J. Baillou et al., *Les Affaires étrangères et le corps diplomatique français*, 2 vols. (Paris, 1984), II, 384–407; M. Vaïsse, 'L'Adaptation du Quai d'Orsay aux nouvelles conditions diplomatiques (1919–1939)', *Revue d'histoire moderne et contemporaine*, 32 (1985); Jeannesson, 'Relations commerciales', 40–2.
[112] MAE, PA-AP 261, *Papiers Seydoux*, vol. 1, 'Instructions', 13 Jan. 1920.
[113] AN, 470 AP 57, *Archives Millerand*, Berthelot note of 22 May 1920; McDougall, *Rhineland Diplomacy*, 110–12.

appointment to Berlin was rightly interpreted as an expression of the Millerand government's willingness to engage with Germany in the economic realm.[114] Laurent was advised that economic cooperation was 'the only area of understanding that exists at the moment between France and Germany; it is in this domain that we have the best chance of obtaining compliance with a treaty whose political clauses are particularly humiliating for [German] pride'. He was therefore encouraged to seek opportunities for industrial cooperation and cross-investment. German economic growth was no longer represented as a threat in and of itself. It was instead considered desirable as long as it took place within the context of German treaty compliance.[115]

A willingness to envisage economic cooperation with Germany shaped responses to the two most pressing challenges to French economic security: a quest for reliable supplies of energy and the need to reconstruct France's devastated industrial regions. France was desperately short of coal and coke in early 1920. This shortage combined with a spike in coal prices on the world market to create a full-blown energy crisis in spring 1920.[116] The original terms of the peace treaty required Germany to provide France with 2 million tonnes of coal and coke per month for ten years. This figure had been reduced to 1.66 million tonnes in an accord negotiated by Loucheur on 19 August 1919 (an early de facto revision of the treaty).[117] During the first six months of 1920, however, Germany delivered less than half of the coal required under this accord. In order to increase these shipments, Millerand agreed in the Spa Protocol both to reduce the monthly amount to 1.6 million tonnes and to pay a surcharge of five gold marks for every tonne of coal delivered in order to subsidise wages and infrastructure in the German coal industry. This arrangement was a genuine success. German coal deliveries increased in the ensuing six months to nearly 2 million tonnes per month.[118]

Greater flexibility also characterised French policy towards reparations more generally. At the heart of discussions was the vexed issue of fixing a total sum for the German debt (not necessary under the treaty until May 1921). The British argued that setting a total sum would help stabilise the German economy and improve prospects for mobilising at least a substantial portion of the reparations debt on the international money market. Following Avenol's advice, the Millerand government indicated a willingness to agree a fixed sum but insisted on obtaining concrete assurances in return that this debt

---

[114] Trachtenberg, *Reparation*, 158–9.
[115] MAE, PA-AP 261, *Papiers Seydoux*, vol. 1, 'Instructions à l'Ambassadeur de France à Berlin', 26 Jun. 1920.
[116] Maier, *Recasting Bourgeois Europe*, 194–214.
[117] AN, C/14632, *CAEAN*, Millerand *audition*, 4 Feb. 1920; Trachtenberg, *Reparation*, 122–3.
[118] MAE, PA-AP 217, *Papiers Massigli*, vol. 13, 'Note: résultats des accords de Spa', 19 Nov. 1920; 'Après Spa', 12 Oct. 1920; PA-AP 261, *Papiers Seydoux*, vol. 19, 'Note pour le président du conseil: protocoles de Spa', 18 Nov. 1920.

would be commercialised in London and New York.[119] Allied leaders tentatively agreed to an arrangement in which the German debt was set at approximately 100 billion gold marks to be paid over thirty-three years in annuities rising from 3 to 7 billion gold marks. Crucially, however, Germany would also be given the option of paying off a reduced sum of 65 billion gold marks in one payment funded by the commercialisation of its debt on the international financial market. All of these calculations, importantly, were based on the assumption that Britain and the USA would write off the vast majority, if not all, of the war debts owed them by France.[120]

As Marc Trachtenberg has argued, France's position during these negotiations was far more flexible and conciliatory than most historians have recognised. In effect, provided that the entire German debt could be mobilised, Millerand was willing to settle for a one-off total payment of approximately 35 billion gold marks. This was a far cry from the figures of 200–230 billion that were bandied about in the French press.[121] It was for this reason that the French premier came under heavy criticism. Among his most vocal critics were Tardieu and Loucheur, both of whom, as we have seen, had been willing to accept relatively low final figures in 1919. Poincaré was also highly critical. He objected to the fact that negotiations on a final figure were taking place in private conversations between heads of government rather than in the reparations commission stipulated in the Versailles Treaty. To protest Millerand's concessions, he resigned as president and French delegate on the commission on 18 May.[122]

Millerand's flexibility before and during the Spa Conference was inspired mainly by the attractions of commercialising Germany's reparations debt. This project can be traced to ideas put forward by John Maynard Keynes during the peace conference in 1919. It was attractive mainly because it held out the prospect of securing a substantial lump-sum payment for France at a time when the long-term prospects of German fulfilment were at best uncertain. It was thus the preferred solution of finance minister François-Marsal and other influential officials within the finance ministry such as Avenol and Alexandre de Cellier.[123] But the prospect of reducing the German reparations debt created a firestorm in the French press. The German government of Constantin Fehrenbach was in any case too

---

[119] *DDF, 1920*, I, #468, Avenol to Millerand and Marsal, 13 May 1920.
[120] MAE, PA-AP 217, *Papiers Massigli*, vol. 13, 'Historique des négociations interalliées ...', 11 Oct. 1920; AN, 470 AP 57, *Archives Millerand*, 'Conversation entre les premiers ministres de la France et de la Grande-Bretagne à Belcaire, Lympne, Kent, le Samedi 15 mai à 3:45 heures de l'après-midi'; and MAE, PA-AP 118, *Papiers Millerand*, vol. 43, François-Marsal to Millerand, 12 May 1920.
[121] Trachtenberg, *Reparation*, 138–46.
[122] See, for example, correspondence between Millerand and Tardieu in AN, 470 AP 59, *Archives Millerand*; Poincaré, 'Chronique de la quinzaine', *RDDM* (May–June, 1920), 712–14; F. Roth, *Raymond Poincaré: un homme d'état républicain* (Paris, 2006), 393–8.
[123] MAE, PA-AP 118, *Papiers Millerand*, vol. 43, François-Marsal to Millerand, 12 May 1920; on the origins of plans to commercialise the debt see Schuker, *End*, 175–6.

weak to negotiate a fixed sum and payment schedule. As a result, plans to establish the conditions for mobilising the German debt came to nothing at the Spa Conference.[124]

It is nevertheless worth pausing to consider affinities between the project to commercialise the German debt on the international market and the internationalist approach to security. Stephen Schuker has dismissed this project as a plot to ensure that 'America would be left holding the bag' in the event of a German default.[125] There is another dimension to French thinking on this issue, however. An international mobilisation of the reparations debt would mutualise the risk assumed by Germany's creditors in the same way that internationalist solutions envisaged a mutualisation of traditional threats to territorial security. In such a scenario France would no longer bear the main responsibility for enforcing the financial clauses of the peace treaty. This burden would be transferred to the international community as a whole, which would have a vital interest in ensuring German repayment. This is the sense in which the question was framed by both Avenol and de Cellier.

The parallels between the aim to mobilise the German debt and the principles of mutualisation and international cooperation at the heart of internationalist theories of peace and security are striking. With the benefit of hindsight it is clear that this project, with its blurring of the distinctions between public and private finance, was unrealistic. It hinged on the willingness of private bankers to assume risks that the American government refused to contemplate. But this should not obscure the fact that the internationalisation of Germany's reparation debt remained the preferred option for all Millerand's successors from Briand to Poincaré to Édouard Herriot.

The success of the Spa Protocol in obtaining coal deliveries inspired Seydoux to tackle the issue of reparations in kind as a means of securing German assistance in French reconstruction. The core principles of the resulting 'Seydoux Plan' were threefold. The first was that the fundamental obstacles to German payment were political rather than economic. Although he acknowledged that Germany would be unable to make payments in hard currency for the next few years, Seydoux was convinced that it could make reasonable payments *in kind* if it had the political will to do so.[126] A second key assumption was that French efforts must shift from theoretical arguments about the interpretation of the treaty to practical plans for its application. Seydoux reckoned that the strength of public opinion in both countries made agreement on a fixed sum impossible for the foreseeable future. He was convinced, moreover, that no final settlement of the reparations issue was possible

[124] Maier, *Recasting Bourgeois Europe*, 172–3, 203–9; Trachtenberg, *Reparation*, 144–7.
[125] Schuker, *End*, 176.
[126] AN, 470 AP 57, *Archives Millerand*, 'Note pour le président du conseil: manquements de l'Allemagne à l'exécution du traité de paix', 12 May 1920; MAE, PA-AP 261, *Papiers Seydoux*, vol. 18, 'Note pour le secrétaire général: réparations et négociations avec l'Allemagne', 8 Oct. 1920.

without US intervention.[127] Focus should therefore shift to medium-term solutions aimed at facilitating reparations in kind. The third core principle was that German industry and labour must be given an interest in treaty fulfilment. As things stood, neither constituency had such an interest. 'We must find a way to give them a stake in the process,' Seydoux argued.[128]

There were two central aims to Seydoux's plan. The first was to establish Franco-German economic cooperation as a driver for both French reconstruction and the wider restoration of the European economy. The second was to put an end to France's utter dependence on Britain to obtain German treaty compliance.[129] At the heart of the plan was the creation of a revolving fund on which French agents could draw to purchase German goods or services for reconstruction. The Weimar government would finance the fund with paper marks, which would be paid out to those private German concerns providing reparation in kind. The Germans, in turn, would agree to open their own market to French goods in exchange for the opportunities provided to German business by the revolving fund.[130]

Seydoux's project had two important advantages. First, it placed French and German private business in direct contact, and thus established conditions for ongoing cooperation. The hope was that supplementary commercial arrangements and eventually a wider commercial accord would emerge out of this contact. Second, it gave German industry an interest in treaty compliance and French public and private concerns an interest in German economic recovery. To provide further incentive to German business, Seydoux's department proposed a system based on the Spa Protocol whereby part of the purchase price for German payments in kind (between 30 and 50 per cent) would be met with French currency. Finally, to make the system more flexible and intensify links between private industry in both countries, French agents were to be able to use the paper marks in the revolving fund to invest in German business.[131]

There was considerable opposition to the Seydoux project. Many among the French elite remained reluctant to depart from a strict interpretation of the treaty provisions. At a meeting to discuss the project on 23 October, Seydoux's ideas were rejected by Émile Ogier (minister for liberated territories); by Louis Dubois (who replaced Poincaré as French delegate and chair of the reparations

---

[127] Quoted in Trachtenberg, *Reparation*, 183.
[128] MAE, PA-AP 261, *Papiers Seydoux*, vol. 18, 'Note: problème des réparations', 15 Oct. 1920.
[129] AN, 470 AP 59, *Archives Millerand*, 'Note pour le président du conseil: état d'esprit de la finance anglaise à l'égard du traité de paix', 1 May 1920; G.-H. Soutou, 'Die deutschen Reparationen und das Seydoux-Projekt, 1920–1921', *Vierteljahrschaft für Zeitgeschichte*, 23 (1975); Trachtenberg, *Reparation*, 155–92; Jeannesson, 'Diplomatie économique', 19–23.
[130] See esp. MAE, PA-AP 261, *Papiers Seydoux*, vol. 18, 'Note: problème des réparations', 15 Oct. 1920.
[131] See esp. MAE, PA-AP 261, *Papiers Seydoux*, vol. 19, 'Conférence de Bruxelles', 11 Dec. 1920.

Post-war dilemmas: enforcement or engagement? 353

commission); and by François-Marsal.[132] All three objected that departing from the processes outlined in the treaty would undermine France's legal position.[133] The project was rejected in even stronger terms by commerce minister August Isaac. 'We must not be tempted by an over-indulgent interpretation of the peace treaty to deal with Germany as equal to equal,' Isaac warned. France should obtain German compliance 'through the unilateral rights that the peace treaty confers'. Departing from the treaty 'would be a breach in the edifice of our guarantees'.[134] Isaac's position was moderate, however, when compared to more radical prescriptions for economic security such as that proposed by nationalist deputy Léon Daudet. 'It is more important than ever to bridle Germany,' Daudet proclaimed in the chamber, 'and there is only one way to do that, namely by bridling her economic development with the aid of a military policy.'[135]

Seydoux responded that opponents of his plan 'do not sufficiently understand the situation in which we find ourselves'. A strict application of the treaty was impossible, he argued, without giving Germans a stake in its execution. Alternative schemes to seize control of tax revenues in the occupied territories, meanwhile, would only reinforce widespread suspicion of French designs on the Left Bank.[136] 'It is essential to be reasonable, to face reality, at least if we wish to avoid a return to tensions and conflict, as much with our allies as with the Germans.' An arrangement with German state and private interests, Seydoux argued, was

the only reasonable solution if we wish to achieve not a new global disruption but a restoration of peace and an effective economic collaboration with Germany. There remains, of course, the option of seizing possession of the Ruhr Basin. This is the violent solution that will settle everything and render us masters of Germany, independent of Britain and an industrial power of the first order. I know that in France a substantial current of opinion considers this the necessary solution. But it comes with such risks, in the internal domain as well as the external domain, that I believe it is indispensable to exhaust all possibility of conciliation before taking this step.[137]

For Seydoux reparation was never purely an economic question. It was always understood as part of the wider problem of achieving political stability in Europe. 'The problem of reparations dominates the economic life of Germany, of France, and, as a consequence, of Europe,' Seydoux observed

---

[132] MAE, PA-AP 261, *Papiers Seydoux*, vol. 18, 'Note no. 12: question des réparations', 24 Oct.; this is a summary of the 23 Oct. meeting forwarded to Millerand's secretary Pierre Vignon; see also Jeannesson, 'Diplomatie économique', 19–20.
[133] MAE, PA-AP 261, *Papiers Seydoux*, vol. 18, François-Marsal to Leygues, 8 Nov. 1920.
[134] MAE, *RC*, Série B81–82, vol. 28, Isaac to Seydoux, 11 Jan. 1921.
[135] Quoted in Trachtenberg, *Reparation*, 159.
[136] MAE, PA-AP 261, *Papiers Seydoux*, vol. 18, Seydoux to Vignon, 25 Oct. 1920; vol. 19, 'Note pour le président du conseil: situation respective des états à la Conférence financière de Bruxelles' (Seydoux and Berthelot), 16 Nov. 1920.
[137] MAE, PA-AP 261, *Papiers Seydoux*, vol. 18, Seydoux to Vignon, 25 Oct. 1920.

in early 1921. 'As long as there is no solution to this problem Germany cannot borrow, nor can it take its moral, political and economic place among other nations.'[138] The need to integrate Germany into a stable economic and political order would be a consistent theme in Seydoux's policy proposals over the next five years.

Seydoux's project was supported by the foreign ministry, President Millerand and a significant cross-section of elite opinion. The left-wing *Information ouvrière et sociale* was enthusiastic. So too, however, was Tardieu writing in *Le Temps*, Poincaré in the *Revue des deux mondes* and Pertinax in *L'Écho de Paris*.[139] The project was adopted as official policy and presented to German and Allied experts at the Brussels Conference in mid-December 1920. German representatives recognised the political implications of the French plan: 'The French', observed one Reich official, 'are evidently striving for an interlocking of German and French industry, out of which a political compromise between the two countries will arise.'[140]

The Seydoux Plan was never adopted. German negotiators tried to link their participation in the project to concessions over Upper Silesia and other unacceptable revisions to the treaty regime. It was opposed by the British, who felt threatened by closer Franco-German relations that they could not control. The plan also generated considerable alarm among business and industrial interests inside France, worried about losing a portion of their internal market to Germany.[141]

Professor Trachtenberg has argued that French sponsorship of Seydoux's project provided 'a real opportunity for putting European politics on a fundamentally different footing'.[142] This almost certainly underestimates the profound structural challenges to genuine stabilisation and ignores American unwillingness to write off war debts. But it does underline the fact that French economic security policy was much more dynamic and open-ended than is generally recognised. Senior figures within the French governing elite sought to engage Germany in a system that would secure reparations payments while at the same time promoting economic cooperation as an engine of European economic and political reconstruction. This was an important departure from more traditional schemes that sought to use the mechanisms of the treaty to compel German compliance.

---

[138] MAE, *RC*, Série B81–82, vol. 28, Seydoux to Haguenin, 8 Jan. 1921.
[139] Trachtenberg, *Reparation*, 174–5; Seydoux's project did not contravene the demand for a huge final sum advocated by both Poincaré and Tardieu.
[140] Quoted in Trachtenberg, *Reparation*, 184.
[141] MAE, PA-AP 118, *Papiers Millerand*, vol. 19, 'Esquisse sommaire des grandes étapes de la politique des réparations au cours de l'année 1921', 1 Dec. 1921; Soutou, 'Seydoux-Projekt', esp. 264–9; Trachtenberg, *Reparation*, 186–98; Bariéty, *Relations franco-allemandes*, 61–90; Jeannesson, 'Diplomatie économique', 22–4.
[142] Trachtenberg, *Reparation*, 172.

The extent to which French security policy aimed at collaboration with Germany should not be exaggerated. The traditional approach continued to dominate thinking about political and territorial security within the policy elite. At the same time that Millerand was moving towards economic cooperation with Germany, for example, he was also involved in negotiating a highly traditional military alliance with Belgium. High-level Franco-Belgian discussions began in late January 1920 with Marshal Foch as the lead French negotiator.[143] At the heart of the agreement that resulted was a secret military convention directed explicitly against Germany. This convention, which would not have been out of place in 1890 or even 1790, envisaged joint war planning to be conducted in ongoing staff conversations. It also provided for the coordination of French and Belgian defensive systems and mobilisation procedures once the occupation regime in the Rhineland ended.[144] Britain declined to participate either in the accord itself or in the envisaged staff conversations. The Franco-Belgian arrangement ran against the prevailing post-war normative current. This is clear from subterfuge in which the Quai d'Orsay engaged in order to conform to Article 18 of the Covenant (which required that all treaties signed by member states be registered with the League). In the event, the exchange of letters between governments approving the accord was registered, but the content of the military convention remained secret.[145]

The traditional approach to security maintained the status of a 'practical logic' when it came to west European political order. Pervasive assumptions of Germany's bad faith and aggressive tendencies underpinned widespread support for security through traditional diplomatic practices and strict enforcement of the Versailles Treaty. An important current within the policy elite, moreover, continued to advocate German dismemberment as the fundamental requirement of France's security. Conceptions of economic security, however, were far more diverse and ambiguous. While a number of senior officials maintained that France should stick to the treaty regime in pursuit of a favourable economic balance of power, a contending approach advocated a strategy of engagement with Germany in the economic reconstruction of Europe.

Strategies for economic cooperation remained some way from a true internationalist position. Neither Millerand nor Seydoux considered international

---

[143] D. Stevenson, 'Belgium, Luxemburg and the defence of Western Europe, 1914–1920', *IHR*, 4, 4 (1982), 514–23; N. Fleurier, 'Entre partenariat et alliance: rapports diplomatiques et militaires de la Belgique avec la France', *GMCC*, 193 (1999), 23–38.

[144] *DDF, 1920*, II, #440, 'Accord militaire défensif franco-belge approuvé par les états-majors français et belge pour le cas d'une agression allemande non-provoquée', 7 Sept. 1920; an earlier version, the language of which was judged too aggressive by the Belgian government, can be consulted in SHD-DAT, 4N 93–2, *État-major Foch*, 'Accord militaire franco-belge', 29 Jul. 1920.

[145] *DDF, 1920*, III, #58, 'Note du département pour le secrétaire général' (Laroche), 11 Oct. 1920; #113, 'Note au sujet de la communication de l'accord militaire à la Société des nations', 25 Oct. 1920.

institutions as a key source of security for France. But there were unmistakable political implications to an approach that prioritised collaboration with France's recent enemy. 'My system', Seydoux explained, 'consists essentially in convincing the Germans of the importance of reparations and us, in turn, of the economic development of Germany.' The larger aim was to 'couple' the two economies to establish 'the only solid foundations of European reconstruction'.[146] For much of 1921 this conception of the post-war order was confined to economic security planning. Towards the end of that year, however, Aristide Briand would incorporate the constructive assumptions at the heart of Seydoux's vision in a bid to establish a Europe-wide security order that would include Germany.

[146] Quoted in Jeannesson, 'Diplomatie économique', 17.

10 Briand and the emergence of a multilateral alternative, 1921

Speaking before the chamber of deputies on 21 October 1921, premier Aristide Briand lamented that 'too many of our compatriots continue to think that France has merely to state its case with firmness in international counsels in order to obtain the reparations and security that are due to us'. He stressed the fundamental changes that had taken place in the international sphere since the war. 'Any experience of international negotiations', Briand argued, 'demonstrates the reality of our situation ... we must pursue security in cooperation with the rest of Europe, with our ally Britain and, yes, even with Germany.' Briand then went on to argue that peace in Europe could last only if it came to constitute 'a state of mind' and thus 'an atmosphere'. To achieve this, he insisted, it was essential to 'encourage the evolution of a Germany with whom we can live'.[1] This language marked a decisive departure from the tone employed by Briand upon assuming the premiership the previous January, when he had proclaimed that 'the sanction of the Great War, and the consequence of victory, is execution of the treaty ... we have force at our disposal, we can and we will make use of it if necessary to impose respect for all engagements undertaken'.[2]

Historians have concluded that Briand's 'conversion' was in response to a 'sea change' in international relations over the course of 1921, which led him to give absolute priority to an *entente* with Britain.[3] The chapter that follows attributes greater importance to developments inside France in explaining the evolution of foreign and security policy in 1921. It also identifies a

---

[1] *JO*, Chambre, *Débats*, 1921, 21 Oct. 1921.   [2] *JO*, Chambre, *Débats*, 1921, 20 Jan. 1921.
[3] Quote from J. Bariéty, *Les Relations franco-allemandes après la première guerre mondiale* (Paris, 1977), 68–76 (quote on p. 75); see also J. Bariéty, 'Aristide Briand et la sécurité de la France en Europe, 1919–1932' in S. Schuker (ed.), *Deutschland und Frankreich vom Konflikt zur Aussöhnung: Die Gestaltung der westeuropäischen Sicherheit 1914–1963* (Munich, 2000), 123–5; W. McDougall, *France's Rhineland Diplomacy, 1914–1924: The Last Bid for a Balance of Power in Europe* (Princeton, 1978), 140–6; G. Suarez, *Briand: sa vie, son oeuvre, avec son journal et de nombreux documents inédits*, 6 vols. (Paris, 1938–52), vol. V: *Artisan de la paix, 1918–1923* (Paris, 1941), 97–238; B. Bibes, C. Defrance, A. Hogenhuis-Seliverstoff and J. de Lespinois, 'Le Retour de Briand aux affaires en 1921' in J. Bariéty (ed.), *Aristide Briand, la Société des nations et l'Europe, 1919–1932* (Paris, 2007), 41–59.

predisposition to engage with Germany within the policy elite that helped shape policy making under Briand. The result, by late 1921, was a significant departure from the traditional emphasis on the balance of power. At the Cannes Conference in early 1922 Briand advocated enmeshing Germany in a Europe-wide security system underwritten by France and Britain.

I

Leygues was unable to manage the mercurial majority within the chamber, and his government fell on 12 January 1921.[4] To form a new government Millerand turned to Briand, who took the portfolio of foreign minister for himself and assembled a ministerial team that included the respected nationalist Louis Barthou as war minister. Notably absent from Briand's cabinet was Raymond Poincaré, who coveted the post of foreign minister and refused to accept any other role. The press remarked that the new government was less representative of the Bloc national coalition than its predecessors. Briand, it was observed, would need to manage parliament with care to preserve his position.[5]

Few politicians have ever been better equipped for this task. Briand is impossible to categorise in ideological terms. He belonged to no party and represented no political majority within the chamber or the senate. At fifty-eight years of age, he retained his two great political gifts. The first was his unparalleled eloquence, which Nicolas Roussellier characterises as 'the condition of his political survival'.[6] The second was his ability to adjust to the prevailing winds of parliamentary and public opinion. 'Briand's superiority', observed his contemporary Charles Benoist, was due above all to his 'acute sense of the rhetorical possibilities of the moment'.[7] These qualities make it difficult to identify a consistent line of policy for Briand's government based on his public declarations. The challenge is compounded by the fact that he never committed anything substantial to paper. One is forced instead to focus on decisions taken at key moments and relate these, whenever possible, to the advice he received from his advisers and, just as importantly, to the wider political context in which they were made. And the political context was undergoing important transformations beneath the surface of mainstream parliamentary discourse.

---

[4] N. Roussellier, *Le Parlement de l'éloquence: la souveraineté de la délibération au lendemain de la Grande Guerre* (Paris, 1997), 132–6; E. Bonnefous, *Histoire politique de la Troisième République*, vol. III: *L'Après-guerre* (Paris, 1959), 205–6.
[5] Suarez, *Briand*, V, 99–116; S. Unger, *Briand: le ferme conciliateur* (Paris, 2005), 418–20; Bonnefous, *Après-guerre*, 207–10.
[6] Roussellier, *Parlement de l'éloquence*, 134; on Briand's parliamentary position see also J. Wright, 'Aristide Briand et les problèmes d'un socialiste indépendant' in Bariéty (ed.), *Briand*, 440–7.
[7] Benoist, *Souvenirs*, III, 159.

Two developments were particularly important for the future evolution of national security policy. The first was the liberating effects of the Tours schism on Socialist attitudes towards international politics. No longer constrained by the need to placate extreme-left hostility to bourgeois party politics after 1920, Socialists were able to make common cause with Radical internationalists over foreign policy questions in the chamber.[8] The second was the slow recovery of the Radical Party and the increasing willingness of its leadership to distance itself from the Bloc national over foreign policy issues.[9] These developments remained in their early stages in 1921. But the second half of that year saw the beginning of what would evolve into an electoral coalition between the two political constituencies most sympathetic to juridical internationalism and the League of Nations. It was towards this nascent parliamentary concentration that Briand would gravitate during the final months of his tenure as premier and foreign minister.

Over the course of 1921 the foreign ministry regained much of its influence over the making of foreign and security policy. This was due not least to the effective partnership of Briand and Philippe Berthelot. These two very different characters renewed the close working relationship first established during the war. Berthelot briefed the premier, offered counsel on every substantive policy issue and resumed the practice of drafting nearly all of the circulars and instructions that went out in Briand's name.[10] Briand and Berthelot formed the central axis of foreign policy making. Berthelot appreciated Briand's native intelligence and gift for negotiation. He contrasted these qualities with the more inflexible approach of Briand's chief rival. 'Poincaré', he observed, 'says "no, because" ... Briand says "yes, but".' Berthelot saw his role as providing substance to Briand's 'but'.[11] In the public sphere, and even within the Quai d'Orsay, Berthelot and Poincaré came to represent two opposing styles of statecraft.[12]

Berthelot believed that France must eventually come to terms with Germany if Europe was to experience any lasting peace and stability. But he was also convinced that a workable Franco-German understanding could only be obtained within the context of a solid Franco-British front. 'We are too often surprised when the British pursue their interests with the same conviction that

---

[8] P. Buffotot, *Le Socialisme français et la guerre: du soldat-citoyen à l'armée professionelle, 1871–1998* (Paris, 1999), 91–4.
[9] Roussellier, *Parlement de l'éloquence*, 147–52; Bonnefous, *Après-guerre*, 237–9; S. Berstein, *Histoire du Parti Radical*, vol. I: *À la recherche de l'âge d'or* (Paris, 1980), 339–47.
[10] J. L. Barré, *Philippe Berthelot: l'éminence grise, 1866–1934* (Paris, 1998), 356–60.
[11] Quoted in Laroche, *Quai d'Orsay*, 136; see also A. Bréal, *Philippe Berthelot* (Paris, 1937), 206–10.
[12] There was also considerable personal animus between Poincaré and Berthelot. The former was suspicious of the latter's empire-building and personal authority within the ministry: F. Seydoux, 'Aux Affaires étrangères: de Jules Cambon à Geoffroy de Courcel', *RDDM* (Feb. 1973), 382–3; Laroche, *Quai d'Orsay*, 132–8, 189–92; Barré, *Berthelot*, 355–8, 375–9; Claudel, *Accompagnements*, 199–204.

we would like to demonstrate in our own policy,' Berthelot observed. 'Tensions of second order will always manifest themselves in our relations with Britain. But we will never succeed in obtaining German good faith if the Reich sees any hope in dividing the two dominant powers in Europe at the moment.' Without British support, moreover, it would be difficult if not impossible to mobilise the German debt.[13]

Cooperation with Britain paid early dividends. In meetings with Lloyd George in early 1921 Briand accepted the principle that reparations must be calculated according to Germany's capacity to pay (a point already conceded by Millerand). In return he secured British support for applying a range of sanctions to force Germany to comply with the treaty. The sanctions mooted included the occupation of further German territory and the imposition of an Allied customs regime on the Left Bank.[14] This development set in train the machinery of sanctions planning in Paris. Within the foreign ministry there was general consensus that the preparation and implementation of sanctions should be coordinated with the British. The successful coercion of the Germans at Spa the previous summer was attributed to the fact that Britain and France had presented a united front. Internal correspondence in 1921 was replete with references to 'the experience of Spa'.[15] In mid-January Jules Laroche, head of the Sous-direction d'Europe, drafted an important memorandum on the nature and role of sanctions. Laroche advocated a strategy that would now be described as 'coercive diplomacy'.[16] He stressed that the threat of sanctions must be credible. All measures envisaged would need to be 'outlined with precision in advance' and it must be made clear that 'the sanction in question will be implemented *automatically*'. The character of the sanction applied, Laroche advised, should suit the nature of the infraction. The Ruhr occupation could be undertaken only in the event of egregious violations of core elements of the treaty. Laroche's entire analysis, significantly, was based on the assumption of joint Franco-British action. He added that the need for Allied solidarity meant that France must take care to avoid exacerbating British suspicions of its intentions towards the Left Bank.[17] The objective was German compliance rather than a forward policy in the Rhineland.

---

[13] MAE, *Série Z, Allemagne*, vol. 230, 'Note pour le président du conseil', 22 Jan. 1921.
[14] *DDF, 1921*, I, #51, Peretti de la Rocca circular, 29 Jan. 1921; #53, 'Note au sujet des décisions de la conférence interalliée', 30 Jan. 1921; #54, 'Note au sujet des sanctions prévues contre l'Allemagne', 30 Jan. 1921.
[15] Bibes et al., 'Retour de Briand', 44–5.
[16] T. Schelling, *Arms and Influence* (New Haven, 1966), 69–91; P. Jackson, 'Deterrence, Coercion and Enmeshment: French Grand Strategy and the German Problem after World War I' in J. Taliaferro, S. Lobell and N. Ripsman (eds.), *The Challenge of Grand Strategy* (Cambridge, 2012), 39–47.
[17] MAE, *Série Z, Allemagne*, vol. 230, 'Note au sujet de la question des sanctions', 21 Jan. 1921; also vol. 232, 'Réponse aux questions posées par M. Poincaré dans sa lettre du 12 mars 1921', Berthelot, 12 Mar. 1921 and *DDF, 1921*, I, #19.

Jacques Seydoux agreed with Laroche that the threat of force against the Ruhr must be part of France's negotiating position. He also concurred that a common front with Britain was the most effective means of coercion. He added, however, that British self-interest and suspicion of French motives complicated the situation:

Since the armistice the British government ... has very naturally sought to shackle French policy, striving to prevent not only a Franco-German accord, but also the employment of force by France ... The British aim is to maintain sufficient points of friction between France and Germany to make any conversation impossible but to intervene each time that this friction becomes too serious.

France faced a choice, according to Seydoux. It could pursue 'a policy of force' and occupy the Ruhr to extract reparations directly from the German economy. This might lead to 'the destruction of the Reich'. But it might also destroy the Entente. The alternative was to cooperate with Britain to secure German treaty compliance and lay the foundations for European reconstruction. Seydoux plainly favoured the latter approach. But he argued that British suspicions must be allayed to achieve this. 'The British must sense that France pursues no other goal in Europe beyond the conservation of its security.'[18] Like Laroche, Seydoux urged restraint in the Rhineland.

This was not the perspective of the military establishment. Foch produced two studies of the sanctions issue in early 1921. The first insisted that military control of the Left Bank was 'the lone guarantee of the execution of the treaty' and must therefore be prolonged. Foch warned that the timetable for Allied withdrawal from the Cologne region (January 1925) was unacceptable as it would deprive the Allies of the necessary concentration point for an occupation of the Ruhr.[19] Foch's second note focused on the Ruhr. 'Control of the Ruhr', he advised, would allow France to 'dominate the life of Germany from an economic point of view'. But Foch conceived of a Ruhr occupation as more than a mere punitive expedition:

From the political point of view, the separation of Berlin from the region of the Left Bank of the Rhine will give new force to Rhenish separatist elements. We could thus anticipate, with greater probability than we can at the moment, the constitution of an independent Rhenish state that could be attracted to our zone of influence.[20]

The two defining features of Foch's approach to foreign policy during the peace conference, a pessimistic view of international politics and an indifference to France's diplomatic position, remained central to his analysis of the situation in 1921. The marshal continued to place power and strategic advantage over the

---

[18] MAE, PA-AP 261, *Papiers Seydoux*, vol. 22, 'Note au sujet de la politique de la France à l'égard de l'Angleterre et de l'Allemagne', 1 Aug. 1921.
[19] SHD-DAT, 4N 92–2, *État-major Foch*, Foch to Briand, 16 Feb. 1921.
[20] SHD-DAT, 4N 92–2, *État-major Foch*, 'Note sur l'application des sanctions', 19 Feb. 1921.

political, legal and moral guarantees that were the preferred international currency of the post-war decade.

From the Left Bank, high commissioner Tirard and General Degoutte both supported Foch's analysis. On 10 February 1921 Tirard forwarded two notes on the subject of sanctions. The first, drafted with cooperation from Seydoux as well as officials from the ministries of finance and commerce, was a carefully worded document intended for inter-Allied consumption. It suggested an Allied customs barrier on the Rhine that could be extended to the Ruhr basin in the event that it was occupied.[21] The second note was of a different character. It proposed securing political control of the Left Bank for the Rhineland High Commission through a 'purge' of the local administrative apparatus and an extension of the High Commission's legislative and budgetary authority. Higher tariffs for exports from the Rhineland to unoccupied Germany would be accompanied by lower rates for exports into France. Tirard's aim, as Bariéty has observed, was to 'use the economic lever to engineer a political solution in the Rhineland'.[22] Degoutte endorsed Tirard's project but added that 'economic sanctions in the Rhineland make sense from a French point of view only if they are aimed at first economic and then political autonomy for the region'.[23] Tirard and Degoutte, like Foch, understood sanctions less as a means of coercing German compliance than as a tool to overthrow the balance of power established at Versailles.

To what extent was Briand attracted to a highly traditional policy conception recommended by the '*maison* Foch'? Briand provided frequent public assurances of his willingness to use force against the Ruhr in the event of German defiance. He famously declared before the senate that Germany would 'feel a firm hand on its collar' if it continued to flout its obligations. But he qualified this hard talk with *sotto voce* allusions to a need for Allied support for sanctions.[24] In conversations with Lloyd George on 23–24 April, Briand pressed for occupation in the event of German defiance. The class of 1919 was called up to prepare for the operation.[25] At the moment of decision, however, Briand opted for Allied solidarity over a policy of force. He envisaged an occupation only as an Allied operation undertaken with British cooperation.[26]

The first step towards occupation of the Ruhr took place after the German government refused to come up with a serious programme of reparations

---

[21] MAE, PA-AP 118, *Papiers Millerand*, vol. 41, Tirard to Briand, 10 Feb. 1921.
[22] MAE, PA-AP 118, *Papiers Millerand*, vol. 41, Tirard 'Note personnelle' to Briand, 10 Feb. 1921; Bariéty, *Relations franco-allemandes*, 71.
[23] SHD-DAT, 7N 2655, 'Répercussions des sanctions économiques sur la question rhénane', 19 Mar. 1921; also in MAE, *Série Z, RGR*, vol. 63.
[24] Bonnefous, *Après-guerre*, 234.
[25] *DDF, 1921*, I, #316, Saint-Aulaire to Berthelot, 25 Apr. 1921; #342, Berthelot (London) to Paris, 1 May 1919; Bariéty, *Relations franco-allemandes*, 72–4.
[26] See also S. Jeannesson, *Poincaré, la France et la Ruhr (1922–1924)* (Strasbourg, 1998), 53–67 and M. Trachtenberg, *Reparation in World Politics: France and European Economic Diplomacy, 1916–1923* (New York, 1980), 204–10.

payments in early March. In response the Allies agreed to occupy the port towns of Ruhrort, Duisburg and Düsseldorf on the right bank of the Rhine and to impose a customs barrier on the Rhine. This measure placed French troops on the front porch of the Ruhr.[27] The ensuing weeks witnessed another round of planning for the occupation of the industrial basin. An interministerial committee was established to plan the operation. Members included Seydoux, Tirard, Foch and Louis Loucheur, minister of liberated regions in Briand's cabinet. The committee met only twice and did not consult the views of any constituency outside government. The result was the lengthy 'Loucheur Plan', which defined the core objective of the occupation as 'to bring the enemy to their knees'. It focused on procedures for extracting payment in kind from the Ruhr, with particular emphasis on coal and coke. It also envisaged extending the new customs barrier in the Rhineland to include the Ruhr basin.[28]

Two aspects of the Loucheur Plan are particularly significant. First, it was conceived as an Allied operation based on close cooperation between Britain and France. The British ambassador Charles Hardinge was assured that 'whatever action is taken against Germany ... it should be with the co-operation of the Allies'.[29] Second, as one recent study has observed, the Loucheur Plan was 'above all an instrument of economic pressure' to seize a 'productive guarantee'. No changes were envisaged for the occupation regime on the Left Bank, nor were there any plans to fashion a single economic or political entity out of the two regions.[30] The aim in 1921 was to coerce rather than to dismember Germany.

In the end military coercion proved unnecessary. At the end of April Germany was presented with the 'London Schedule of Payments' that included a final reparations bill for 132 billion gold marks. After German protests, Lloyd George insisted on a final ultimatum, giving Berlin one week to agree to the Allied terms. Briand agreed. The German government, threatened with the immediate occupation of the Ruhr if it did not accept the London Schedule, capitulated on 10–11 May 1921.[31]

There were important differences between the two dominant currents in French policy at this stage. The strategy of Foch and his chief collaborators, which enjoyed widespread support from conservative nationalist parliamentary and popular opinion, sought to use force to revise the treaty and transform the European political and strategic order. It was wholly inspired by the traditional

---

[27] *DDF, 1921*, I, #161 and #177, Berthelot (London) to Paris, 1 and 7 Mar. 1921; Trachtenberg, *Reparation*, 205–6; Jeannesson, *Ruhr*, 55–8.
[28] MAE, RC, Série B81–82, vol. 68, 'Projet d'occupation de la région industrielle de la Ruhr', 22 Apr. 1921; see also Jeannesson, *Ruhr*, 59–61; Bariéty, *Relations franco-allemandes*, 71–3; and L. Zimmermann, *Frankreichs Ruhrpolitik* (Göttingen, 1971), 73–7.
[29] Cambridge University Library (hereafter CUL), *Sir Charles Hardinge Papers*, GB 12, Hardinge MSS. Add. 1.27, *Diary*, 17 Apr. 1921; see also Zimmermann, *Frankreichs Ruhrpolitik*, 73–4. I am very grateful to Keith Neilson for sharing his notes on Hardinge's diary with me.
[30] Jeannesson, *Ruhr*, 59–60.   [31] Ibid., 61–7; Trachtenberg, *Reparation*, 206–12.

approach to security. There was also a strong traditional component to the alternative policy advocated by the pro-Entente lobby within the foreign ministry and adopted by Briand. Germany was compelled to accept Allied demands by the threat of an immediate occupation of the Ruhr. The difference was that the latter strategy was multilateral, based on inter-Allied cooperation. It was also more open-ended. As Seydoux observed in early June 1921, the logical corollary of Germany's capitulation was a 'complete modification of the situation of France vis-à-vis Germany' that held out the possibility of mutually beneficial arrangements for reparations in kind, expanded trade and industrial cooperation between the two countries.[32] The multilateral strategy pursued by Briand left open the possibility of integrating Germany into a new European economic and political order.

II

If there were ambiguities in the French pursuit of German treaty compliance, virtually all strands of policy towards eastern Europe were inspired by the traditional aim of creating a traditional counterbalance to German power. In December 1919 Clemenceau had defined the role of eastern European states as a 'barrier to the eternal pan-German dream of *Mitteleuropa*' and an 'indispensable source of support against German designs for hegemony in Europe'.[33] One of the key advantages France possessed was its substantial military presence in the region. In July 1920 more than two thousand French officers were posted to military missions located from the Baltic to the Aegean Sea. Most were charged with assisting (and in many cases leading) the organisation and training of the armed forces of their host states. France's network of military missions played a central role in all efforts to fashion a French-sponsored security system in the east.[34]

There were formidable obstacles to this strategy, however. The frontier settlements in eastern Europe were uneasy compromises between conflicting principles that left a host of territorial disputes unresolved. Indeed, as Professor Soutou has pointed out, the creation of the 'successor states' transformed what had once been internal disputes between the nationalities of empires

---

[32] MAE, PA-AP 261, *Papiers Seydoux*, vol. 21, 'Note au sujet des réparations en nature', 9 Jun. 1921; see also Jeannesson, *Ruhr*, 64–7.

[33] Quoted in P. Jackson, 'La Faillite de la dissuasion française en Europe centrale' in M. Vaïsse (ed.), *Bâtir une nouvelle sécurité: la coopération militaire entre la France et les États d'Europe centrale et orientale de 1919–1929* (Vincennes, 2001), 153–4; also K. Hovi, *Alliance de revers: Stabilization of France's Alliance Politics in East Central Europe, 1919–1921* (Turku, 1984), 85–8, 110–14, 122–4; T. Sandu, 'La Roumanie et l'impossible articulation d'un système de sécurité français en Europe centre-orientale, 1920–1921', *GMCC*, 193 (1999), 51–68.

[34] F. Guelton, 'Typologie des missions militaires françaises dans l'Est européen' in Vaïsse (ed.), *Nouvelle sécurité*, 51–67; A. Marès, 'Mission militaire et relations internationales: l'exemple franco-tchécoslovaque, 1918–1925', *Revue d'Histoire moderne et contemporaine*, 30 (1983), 559–86.

into international problems often requiring Great Power mediation. No state in eastern Europe was strong enough to stand on its own. The two largest and most industrially advanced countries in the region, Poland and Czechoslovakia, were divided by a bitter frontier dispute over Teschen and by conflicting policies towards both Germany and Russia.[35]

The Piłsudski government in Poland feared the revival of a strong Russia on its border. In an effort to create a Polish-dominated federation along its eastern marches, it initiated a full-scale war with the Soviet Union in April 1920. The result was calamity as the Red Army regrouped and drove the Poles back to the outskirts of Warsaw. France sent Poland military expertise but only limited material support. In the end the Poles managed to turn back the Red Army and force it to retreat. An armistice was agreed on 12 October. The resulting Treaty of Riga left Poland with more territory than the Paris settlement. But the sources of Polish–Soviet tension remained.[36]

In Czechoslovakia foreign minister Edvard Beneš pursued a complicated strategy that combined traditional practices with a growing emphasis on the internationalist machinery of the League. Beneš had four key aims. The first was strong bilateral relations with France. The second was cooperation with Romania and Yugoslavia against Hungary. The third was 'normal' relations with the USSR. The fourth was an ongoing commitment to collective security under the umbrella of the League of Nations. Prospects of cooperation between Czechoslovakia and Poland were limited by mutual suspicion and by the Czechoslovak desire for good relations with the Soviet Union. This, in turn, compromised French plans for the construction of an 'eastern barrier' to German expansion.[37]

The outline of French policy towards the eastern states emerged in an influential memorandum by Laroche in January 1920. He recommended a public declaration that 'the Allied powers have no intention of interfering in internal Russian affairs' and that, as a result, 'they will give no assistance to states adopting an offensive policy towards the Soviet government or any other government in Russia'. In other words, France and its allies renounced intervention in Russia but did not recognise the Soviet regime. Laroche also emphasised that the states in the region could only ensure their security 'if they

---

[35] G.-H. Soutou, 'L'Ordre européen de Versailles à Locarno' in G.-H. Soutou and C. Carlier (eds.), *1919: Comment faire la paix?* (Paris, 2001), 301–31; see also S. Sierpowski, 'La Société des nations et le règlement des conflits frontaliers de 1920 à 1924' in C. Baechler and C. Fink (eds.), *L'Établissement des frontières en Europe après les deux guerres mondiales* (Berne, 1996), 55–69; Z. Steiner, *The Lights that Failed: European International History, 1919–1933* (Oxford, 2005), 80–125.

[36] N. Davies, *White Eagle, Red Star: The Polish–Soviet War, 1919–1920* (London, 1972); R. Debo, *Survival and Consolidation: The Foreign Policy of Soviet Russia, 1918–1921* (Montreal, 1992), 191–284; Steiner, *Lights that Failed*, 142–52.

[37] P. Wandycz, *France and her Eastern Allies, 1919–1925: French–Czechoslovak–Polish Relations from the Paris Peace Conference to Locarno* (Minneapolis, 1962), 135–311; Steiner, *Lights that Failed*, 256–309.

can be convinced to establish between them a strictly defensive entente' based on 'the principle of mutual assistance'. It was the responsibility of France, he argued, to take the initiative in the creation of such an entente.[38]

Despite its reckless foreign policy, Poland remained central to all plans for an eastern counterweight. French army intelligence judged that it would eventually be capable of fielding an army of sixty divisions on condition that it received French material and financial assistance. Such a force, when combined with those of the other eastern states, could be 'a decisive factor in the European balance of power'. The destruction of Poland, warned the Deuxième bureau, would 'render a great part of the Entente's victory vain'.[39] 'We sincerely desire a strong Poland,' Millerand added several weeks later. 'Our policy in eastern Europe depends on the evolution of a modern and responsible Polish state.' Instructions given to the French minister in Warsaw emphasised 'the need to promote cooperation between Poland and another of our allies, Czechoslovakia'.[40] This was a project that French policy elites would pursue for the rest of the inter-war period.

The first soundings for a formal Franco-Polish alliance were made by the Poles in late September. The question divided the security establishment. Foch and Berthelot both argued that such an alliance was premature. Foch characterised Poland as a 'young state, whose organisation is far from complete, with a relatively weak army only recently formed, in a difficult economic situation'. He added that more than 60 per cent of its 3,500-kilometre frontier was with potentially hostile powers.[41] He judged that common action between France and Poland was not feasible without the cooperation of Czechoslovakia and Romania.[42] Berthelot, long a critic of Polish ambitions under Piłsudski, agreed with Foch. He acknowledged that Poland 'must be part of our larger aims in central Europe'. But in the circumstances of late 1920 he reckoned that an alliance with Poland would be more of a burden than a strategic asset.[43]

---

[38] *DDF, 1920*, I, #32, 'Les États limitrophes de la Russie et les bolcheviks' (Laroche), 20 Jan. 1920. Michael Carley has argued that France encouraged the Polish offensive into Russia in April 1920. This thesis, which is based almost entirely on negative evidence, has been rejected persuasively by Anne Hogenhuis-Seliverstoff and Kalervo Hovi: see M. Carley, 'The politics of anti-Bolshevism: the French government and the Russo-Polish War', *HJ*, 19, 1 (1976), 163–89; A. Hogenhuis-Seliverstoff, *Les Relations franco-soviétiques 1917–1924* (Paris, 1981), 159–78; and Hovi, *Alliance de revers*, 44–53.

[39] SHD-DAT, 7N 3009, 'Situation militaire de la Pologne', 11 Jul. 1920.

[40] MAE, *Série Z, Pologne*, vol. 130, Millerand to de Panafieu, 16 Apr. 1920; see also AN, C/14632, *CAEAN*, XIIème Législature, Millerand's *auditions* of 4 and 17 Feb. 1920.

[41] SHD-DAT, 7N 3006–1, 'Note sur la situation de la Pologne', 24 May 1920, circulated by Millerand to French posts in Warsaw, Prague, Bucharest, London, Rome and Berlin, 25 May 1920.

[42] SHD-DAT, 7N 3006–1, 'Note', 4 Jan. 1921; see the similar assessment prepared by Weygand: SHD-DAT, 4N 93–1, *État-major Foch*, 'Note du général Weygand', 14 Jan. 1921.

[43] MAE, *Série Z, Pologne*, vol. 130, Leygues (Berthelot) to de Panafieu, 7 Nov. 1920; see also Laroche, *Quai d'Orsay*, 136–7.

From within the Quai d'Orsay Laroche and Emmanuel Peretti de la Rocca (newly promoted to political director) argued that such an alliance would provide French policy with the leverage with which to press the Polish government to cooperate with Czechoslovakia. They also judged that France could take advantage of Poland's search for political and financial assistance to negotiate a favourable commercial arrangement.[44] These arguments were endorsed by General Buat and Marshal Pétain from the army general staff, and accepted by both Millerand and Barthou. In December Marshal Piłsudski was invited to Paris to discuss an alliance.[45]

The broad lines of the political accord that resulted were negotiated directly by Millerand and Piłsudski. Both states agreed to 'concert' with one another over political, economic and defence issues of mutual interest. The secret military convention was longer, more detailed, and directed explicitly against Germany.[46] Ongoing staff conversations were to prepare coordinated military operations in the event of German aggression against either party. Polish armaments policy would be brought in line with that of France to ensure the interoperability of the armaments used by both states. To facilitate the construction of a strong Polish army, France extended a 400-million-franc line of credit to be spent on French armaments.[47] On 19 February both accords were signed and France was tied to Poland in a classic military alliance aimed at Germany.

The traditional impulse to weaken Germany and strengthen Poland inspired French policy on the issue of Upper Silesia. French officials agreed with Bismarck's judgement that the mines and heavy industry of Silesia and Pomerania constituted the 'vital muscle' of the Prussian body. Their aim was to weaken this muscle by ensuring that the industrial area of Upper Silesia was attributed to Poland. The results of the plebiscite of March 1921 were inconclusive. An overall majority opted for Germany, but a majority within the most heavily industrialised areas chose Poland. The result was a standoff in which Britain supported returning the entire region to the Reich and France argued for attributing the industrial region to Poland. When the issue was referred to the League Council, French diplomacy successfully engineered a settlement in

---

[44] MAE, *Série Z, Pologne*, vol. 131, 'Affaires polonaises', dossier prepared for Berthelot and Briand, 4 Feb. 1921; see also *DDF, 1921*, I, #76, 'Note du département', 4 Feb. 1921; #14, 'Note de M. Laroche', 19 Jan. 1921; #45, 'Affaires de Pologne' (Laroche), 28 Jan. 1921.

[45] T. Schramm and H. Bulhak, 'La France et la Pologne, 1920–1922: relations bilatérales ou partie d'un système européen de sécurité?', *GMCC*, 193 (1999), 39–51.

[46] Foch, who led the conversations on the French side, rejected a Polish proposal to extend this arrangement to the Soviet Union. The final document committed France to support Poland only in the event of unprovoked aggression by the Soviet Union and even then mainly by keeping Germany 'in check'.

[47] *DDF, 1921*, I, #126, 'Accord politique franco-polonais', 19 Feb. 1921; #127, 'Accord militaire franco-polonais', 19 Feb. 1921; see also Hovi, *Alliance de revers*, 102–10; Schramm and Bulhak, 'La France et la Pologne', 42–7; Wandycz, *Eastern Allies*, 211–25; Hovi, *Alliance de revers*, 102–7.

which nearly the whole of the industrial area was awarded to Poland when Upper Silesia was partitioned the following October.[48]

The issue of Upper Silesia was settled under Briand. Like Berthelot, however, Briand was not enthusiastic about the alliance with Poland. The premier and foreign minister did not take an active part in the final negotiations leading to the agreement. Berthelot instead took the lead and insisted that the alliance would not come into effect until Poland signed a series of commercial, industrial and financial accords with France. This stipulation, combined with the fact that the question of Upper Silesia remained unresolved, provided the Briand government with a pretext to put off the implementation of the alliance. In fact, the agreement was not ratified until Poincaré replaced Briand as premier and foreign minister nearly twelve months later.[49] Scepticism concerning the traditional alliance with Poland would characterise the thinking of Berthelot and Briand through to the end of the 1920s.

The operating assumption during the peace conference had been that Czechoslovakia would provide the hub around which a French-sponsored east–central European order would turn. This became less certain with the appointment of Maurice Paléologue as secretary general. The deeply conservative former ambassador to Russia was appointed on the advice of Poincaré, who wanted to counterbalance the influence of Berthelot within the foreign ministry.[50] During the spring and summer of 1920 Paléologue explored the possibility of constructing a Danubian confederation centred on Hungary rather than Czechoslovakia. Hungarian agents met with Paléologue and Millerand to offer France extensive commercial and industrial concessions in Hungary. In return they asked for French support in revising the peace settlement, which had left more than 3 million ethnic Hungarians in neighbouring states. The Hungarian head of government, Admiral Nicholas Horthy, was reportedly willing to 'place 500,000 fit and experienced soldiers at France's disposal'.[51]

Paléologue was receptive to these overtures. Although his precise vision for eastern Europe remains obscure, it is clear that he envisaged the authoritarian Horthy regime as the pivot of a bloc of states under French political, cultural and especially economic influence.[52] This provoked determined opposition,

---

[48] See esp. R. Boyce, *The Great Interwar Crisis and the Collapse of Globalization* (London, 2009), 106–7 and F. Dessberg, 'Enjeux et rivalités politiques franco-britanniques: le plébiscite de haute Silésie', *RHA*, 254 (2009), 53–66; see also Laroche, *Quai d'Orsay*, 128–44.

[49] SHD-DAT, 7N 3006–1, Briand circular, 19 Feb. 1921; H. Bulhak, 'L'Alliance militaire franco-polonaise: son développement et ses crises' in Vaïsse (ed.), *Bâtir une nouvelle sécurité*, 223–34.

[50] Barré, *Berthelot*, 347–54.

[51] *DDF, 1920*, I, #373, 'Note de Halmos', 13 Apr. 1920; also #281, 'Note de M. Paléologue', 23 Mar. 1920 (and n. 2 in same doc.); #397, Halmos to Paléologue, 23 Apr. 1920; #465, 'Note remise par M. Halmos à M. Paléologue', 12 May 1920.

[52] *DDF, 1920*, I, #470, Paléologue to French High Commission, Budapest, 13 May 1920; Wandycz, *Eastern Allies*, 198.

not only from successor states in the region who were threatened by Hungarian ambitions, but also from Berthelot and the pro-Czech lobby within the Quai d'Orsay. The formation of the 'Little Entente' grouping of Czechoslovakia, Romania and Yugoslavia was a direct response to France's flirtation with Hungary.[53] Berthelot, Peretti, Paul Cambon and Laroche successfully opposed Paléologue in internal debates. The Millerand government rejected the extensive revision of the Treaty of Trianon (signed officially only on 4 June 1920). The project for a Danubian confederation foundered.[54] Briand's return allowed Berthelot to effectively bury the project in favour of support for the Little Entente.[55]

The episode is most interesting for what it reveals about the ideological divide between pro-democratic and more traditional elements within the Quai d'Orsay and the impact of this divide on security policy in eastern Europe. Paléologue's policy conception echoed the project for a separate peace and political arrangement with the Habsburgs during the war. It was blocked by the same alliance of foreign ministry officials that had resisted the general staff project in 1917. Subsequent French policy initiatives focused on the newly constituted Little Entente and aimed above all at linking this group of states with Poland in a multilateral system based on military cooperation against Germany.[56]

Alongside French efforts to construct a military bloc in eastern Europe there was an ambitious programme of commercial, industrial and financial expansion in the region. The overriding aim of this 'imperialism of the poor' was to replace Germany as the dominant economic power in east–central Europe. Tools provided by the peace settlement were deployed to promote the interests of French finance, heavy industry and commerce. In Czechoslovakia the French company Schneider secured control of a vast mining, manufacturing and steel-producing empire that included the strategically important Skoda Works. Significant concessions were also obtained for French companies in the mines of Upper Silesia and in oilfields in Poland and Romania. The programme fell short of the grand design envisaged by the Quai d'Orsay, however. Post-war French governments lacked financial resources, a competitive export industry and the financial resources for direct investment. These shortcomings left France unable to compete with Germany or even Great Britain for economic dominance in eastern Europe.[57]

---

[53] M. Ádám, *The Versailles System and Central Europe* (London, 2004), 29–112; Hovi, *Alliance de revers*, 53–64; Wandycz, *Eastern Allies*, 186–207.
[54] Hovi, *Alliance de revers*, 63–4, 110–15; Ádám, *Versailles System*, 77–9.
[55] *DDF, 1921*, I, #1, Berthelot circular, 16 Jan. 1921; Ádám, *Versailles System*, 77–9; Hovi, *Alliance de revers*, 63–4, 110–15.
[56] Y. Lacaze, 'Simple coopération militaire ou signature d'une convention militaire contraignante? Le Dilemme franco-tchécoslovaque (1919–1924)'; J. Nouzille, 'La Politique de coopération militaire française dans l'Est et le Sud-Est européen' in Vaïsse (ed.), *Nouvelle sécurité*, 345–72 and 403–22 respectively.
[57] G.-H. Soutou, 'L'Impérialisme du pauvre: la politique économique du gouvernement français en Europe centrale et orientale de 1918 à 1929', *RI*, 7 (1976), 219–23; G.-H.

All French policy initiatives in eastern Europe were traditional in inspiration. The overriding aim was to create a bloc of states capable of replacing Russia as a counterweight to German power. 'France has, and will continue to have, need of a power base to the east of Germany,' observed General Maurice Pellé in Prague. A young French captain posted to the French mission in Warsaw agreed: 'A strong Poland is in our national interest,' observed Charles de Gaulle. 'Germany is defeated, but it will recover just as the Anglo-Saxon forces withdraw from the Rhine.'[58] Balance-of-power calculations determined virtually every aspect of security policy in the east.

III

Traditional predispositions also shaped French policy towards the League of Nations. From the outset policy makers exhibited a clear tendency to treat the League more as a threat to France's interests than as a potential source of security. Berthelot responded to criticism of the League in the chamber by expressing the views of many of his colleagues: 'We did not come up with an ideal League because it was impossible to do so, and we will not for a long time obtain this pacifist dream.'[59]

Official attitudes, and the policies that flowed from them, were a source of considerable frustration for French internationalists. To understand their reactions, it is important to place French civil society activists within the wider context of a global movement intent on persuading international public opinion of the need for greater international cooperation. The traditional methods of the peacemakers had drawn heavy criticism from this constituency both internationally and inside France.[60] Jean Hennessy, who controlled the key centre-left press organs *L'Oeuvre* and *Le Quotidien* and was a tireless advocate of the League, noted that 'these outdated methods of secret diplomacy were condemned roundly when it was necessary to galvanize public support'. Traditional diplomacy, Hennessy argued, had 'long been proved worthless ... it is the source of the insecurity in which we find ourselves in at the moment'.[61] The character of the League was a subject of even greater disappointment. Alphonse Aulard observed that 'the admirable picture sketched by President Wilson led us to expect an organic conception very

Soutou, 'La Politique économique de la France en Pologne, 1920–1924', *RH*, 509 (1974), 85–116; C. Laforest, 'La Stratégie française et la Pologne, 1919–1939: aspects économiques et implications politiques', *Histoire, économie et société*, 22 (2003), 395–411; P. Segal, *The French State and French Private Investment in Czechoslovakia, 1918–1938: A Study of Economic Diplomacy* (New York, 1987).

[58] SHD-DAT, 7N 3103-1, Pellé to Paris, 20 Jul. 1920; de Gaulle quoted in Guelton, 'Typologie', 59.
[59] MAE, PA-AP 141, *Papiers Pichon*, vol. 8, 'Observations sur la discussion du traité devant la Chambre: séance du 3 septembre', 8 Sept. 1919.
[60] D. Gorman, *The Emergence of International Society in the 1920s* (Cambridge, 2012), passim.
[61] J. Hennessy, 'De la Nécessité d'un nouveau Congrès pour donner au monde une paix durable', *Progrès civique*, 31 Jan. 1920.

different to the inadequate system that finally prevailed'. For Célestin Bouglé the lack of both an international force and compulsory arbitration were 'the two most striking and most troubling weaknesses' of the League.[62] 'The creation of the League is a triumph for the rule of law,' proclaimed Théodore Ruyssen, 'and yet how frail and imperfect remains its design!' There was general agreement that the Covenant must be revised.[63]

The chief target for revision was the collective security provision of the Covenant (Arts. 10 to 16). Ruyssen judged that 'the procedures adopted to settle disputes and prevent armed conflict are slow, complicated and are likely to prove inoperable'. He called for a general tightening of the articles in question, making mutual assistance to oppose unprovoked aggression both immediate and compulsory for all member states.[64] He also advocated an international force. 'Security', he argued, invoking Pascal, 'cannot rest simply on "spiritual transformation" and the rule of law ... it must also rest on force.'[65] These criticisms and recommendations were central to the campaign to strengthen the Covenant mounted with increasing vigour by the French internationalist movement over the course of the 1920s. Georges Scelle invoked the need to oppose the 'idealistic and utopian pacifism of the Anglo-Saxons' with a 'constructive and realist vision that is French in inspiration'.[66] This campaign would gain in strength and influence in the mid-1920s.

If there was general agreement on the need to revise and strengthen the Covenant, there was less unity among internationalists over the proper character of the League. Debate was particularly vibrant over the issue of German membership in the League. At war's end most internationalists endorsed the official view that Germany must be denied membership until it demonstrated good faith by executing the treaty. This position was challenged, however, by an alternative vision of a League that would enmesh and constrain the Reich. 'The most effective means to control the behaviour of dangerous states', Scelle argued, 'is to force their activity to develop within the society of peaceful nations and under the League's regime of public diplomacy.' Admitting Germany would 'entangle it so effectively within the restraining ties of law and solidarity that it will find it impossible to break free'.[67] Aulard agreed,

---

[62] C. Bouglé, 'Une Chose vivante', *La Dépêche*, 5 Jul. 1919.
[63] T. Ruyssen, 'Appel programme', *PPD*, Jan.–Feb. 1922; J.-M. Guieu, *Le Rameau et le glaive: les militants français pour la Société des nations* (Paris, 2008), 54–68; C. Birebent, *Militants de la paix et de la SDN: les mouvements de soutien à la Société des nations en France et au Royaume-Uni, 1918-1925* (Paris, 2007), 59–69.
[64] Quoted in J.-M. Guieu, 'Les Apôtres français de "l'esprit de Genève": les militants pour la Société des nations dans la première moitié du XXe siècle', thèse de doctorat, Université de Paris I (Sorbonne), 2004, 135.
[65] T. Ruyssen, 'On ne réalisera le désarmement moral des peuples que s'ils se sentent défendus par une force internationale', *Progrès civique*, 15 Dec. 1923.
[66] Quoted in Guieu, *Rameau et glaive*, 73.
[67] G. Scelle, 'Feuilletons ensemble le dossier du conflit franco-allemand', *Progrès civique*, 27 May 1922.

adding that the socialising effect of League membership would strengthen 'the democratic spirit, the spirit of cooperation and peace, inside Germany'.[68] By the early 1920s German admission had become an objective of the majority of French internationalists, who argued that it must be enmeshed in a web of legal and moral restraints that would condition its future behaviour.

This analysis, significantly, flowed from the conviction that there were two distinct political currents across the Rhine. The first was constituted by the imperialist and militarist traditions that were responsible for the war. The second was democratic in character and could be oriented towards peace and international cooperation. Ruyssen argued that German democrats must be 'encouraged, supported, aided' because 'they alone, supported by the western democracies, can open the way to a more peaceful and secure future'.[69] This was the thesis of the 'two Germanys' that had long been a pillar of Socialist Party doctrine. It would eventually be embraced by the political mainstream to become a central element in foreign and security policy making.

In the immediate aftermath of the war, however, French internationalism remained marginal in French politics. The SFIO was divided. So, too, were juridical internationalists. The creation of the Fédération française des associations pour la Société des nations (FFSDN) in May 1920 was a façade behind which thirteen different associations and committees pursued their own agendas. Within this federation the AFSDN under Bourgeois remained the most influential. But it failed to coordinate the efforts of 'old-style' pacifists within the Bureau international de la paix and the energetic but impatient militants of a new generation of activists epitomised by the Groupement universitaire français pour la Société des nations (GUSDN). There was no French equivalent of the British League of Nations Union (LNU) that could speak for the internationalist movement as a whole. Pacifist and pro-League associations in France lacked the mass membership of the LNU.[70]

The lack of widespread public enthusiasm for internationalism was a source of concern for French activists during the early 1920s. Yet there was great optimism that the tide of history favoured the internationalist cause. 'A new world is taking shape,' Scelle enthused. 'We are witnessing a revolution in the traditional conception of international law; we are in the early stages of the disintegration of that metaphysical construction that is known as state sovereignty.'[71] The great problem was that states remained in control of foreign and security policy. The divided and marginal character of the French internationalist movement made it easy for ministers and security professionals to ignore its prescriptions.

---

[68] Quoted in Guieu, 'Les Apôtres', 277–81; Guieu, *Rameau et glaive*, 69–72.
[69] T. Ruyssen, 'L'Allemagne et la Société des nations', *PPD*, Feb. 1921.
[70] Birebent, *Militants*, 151–84; N. Ingram, *The Politics of Dissent: Pacifism in France, 1919–1939* (Oxford, 1991), 2–3.
[71] G. Scelle, 'Une Ère juridique nouvelle', *PPD* (Jul.–Aug. 1919); see also Guieu, *Rameau et glaive*, 82–115.

The execution of state policy towards the League was concentrated within the Quai d'Orsay's Service français de la Société des nations (SFSDN). Officially constituted on 23 December 1919 the SFSDN, like Seydoux's Relations commerciales, was created at Berthelot's initiative to ensure that the foreign ministry retained control over this new realm of policy.[72] Its core function, Berthelot insisted, was 'the defence of French interests within this international institution'. This required an 'absolute cohesion in both doctrine and direction' between the Quai d'Orsay and French delegates in Geneva.[73] The first head of the SFSDN was Jean Gout, a veteran of the ministry's central administration who had been deputy director of the blockade service and a member of the CISDN during the war. An unusually large proportion of SFSDN staff was drawn from outside the Quai d'Orsay. Its offices were originally across the Seine on the rue François 1er before it moved in 1922 to the Hôtel des Invalides. These physical locations of the SFSDN outside the ministry reflected its marginal status within the policy machine.[74]

From the outset senior policy makers expressed frustration with the constraints the Covenant imposed on traditional practices of statecraft. Berthelot characterised Article 18, which stipulated that all international engagements by member states must be registered for publication by the League secretariat, as 'absurd' and 'a threat to the military security of [League members]'. He was also hostile to the League-based project to extend compulsory arbitration to the settlement of all political disputes. 'No state worthy of its name could agree to this,' Berthelot insisted. Recourse to arbitration could be envisaged 'only over issues where our vital interests are not at stake'.[75] The secretary general had no faith in the internationalist doctrine of peace through law.

It was the League-sponsored campaign for international arms reduction, however, that posed the most serious threat to traditional security practices.[76] A commitment to disarm was built into the peace settlement. Article 8 of the Covenant stipulated that the maintenance of peace required the reduction of national armaments to 'the minimum level compatible with national security'.

---

[72] M.-R. Mouton, *La Société des nations et les intérêts de la France (1920–1924)* (Berne, 1995), 13–14, 39–45; M. Marbeau, 'Un Acteur des nouvelles relations multilatérales: le Service français de la Société des nations, 1919–1940', *Matériaux pour l'histoire de notre temps*, 36 (1994), 11–20; R. Ulrich-Pier, 'Le Service français de la Société des nations et les questions européennes dans l'entre-deux-guerres' in L. Badel, S. Jeannesson and P. Ludlow (eds.), *Les Administrations nationales et la construction européenne: une approche historique* (Berne, 2005), 15–36.
[73] Quoted in Mouton, *Société des nations*, 40.
[74] Marbeau, 'Un Acteur', 12–18; Ulrich-Pier, 'Service français', 19–24; J. Baillou et al., *Les Affaires étrangères et le corps diplomatique français*, 2 vols. (Paris, 1984), II, 326–7, 350.
[75] MAE, *Série Z, GB*, vol. 37, 'Ordre du jour de la Société des nations', Leygues (Berthelot) circular, 6 Nov. 1920.
[76] T. Davies, *The Possibilities of Transnational Activism: The Campaign for Disarmament between the Two World Wars* (London, 2007), 55–71; A. Webster, 'The transnational dream: politicians, diplomats and soldiers in the pursuit of international disarmament, 1920–1938', *CEH*, 14, 4 (2005), 493–518.

The Preamble to Part V of the Versailles Treaty, meanwhile, pledged that the disarmament of Germany was the first step towards 'a general limitation of the armaments of all nations'.[77] Tremendous popular support for the cause of disarmament, particularly in Britain and the neutral countries, ensured that arms reductions were a prominent item on the agenda for the first League Assembly. Léon Bourgeois, the Assembly's first president, identified disarmament as the 'great task' of the League. 'To postpone the discussion of so important a problem would be to disappoint the most confident hopes of the peoples of the world.'[78] A resolution from the Danish, Swedish and Norwegian representatives in the Assembly called for immediate action in implementing Article 8, with the preparation of a universal programme for arms limitation.[79]

The wording of Article 8 was ambiguous, however. To protect national sovereignty, the authors of the Covenant had left judgements concerning the 'minimum level' of armaments required for national security to individual states. This allowed French officials in Geneva to link disarmament to the prior fulfilment of security requirements, a position to which they adhered through the remainder of the inter-war period.[80] French officials argued that there could be no disarmament before Germany had fulfilled its obligations under the Versailles Treaty. International disarmament policy must focus first on enforcing German disarmament.[81]

These arguments shaped the policy adopted toward the creation of the Permanent Advisory Commission on Military, Naval and Air Questions (PAC) decreed by Article 9 of the Covenant. The key French delegate on this commission was Lieutenant Colonel Édouard Réquin, an exceptionally able soldier-diplomat who had been military adviser to the French delegation in Washington. There he had developed an excellent working relationship with Tardieu and Aubert that had continued through the peace conference. In late 1919 he was seconded to the foreign ministry as chief military adviser to the SFSDN. Intelligent, industrious and collegial, Réquin gradually assumed a pivotal role in the formulation of disarmament and security policy. His personnel file overflows with praise from the political, military and diplomatic elite of the Third Republic.[82] Salvador de Madariaga, director of the Disarmament Section of the League Secretariat, praised him as 'one of the clearest brains,

---

[77] Quoted in A. Webster, 'Making disarmament work: the implementation of the international disarmament provisions in the League of Nations Covenant', *D&S*, 16, 3 (2005), 551.
[78] Ibid., 551–69. [79] Mouton, *Société des nations*, 192–3.
[80] M. Vaïsse, *Sécurité d'abord: politique française en matière de désarmement, 1930–1934* (Paris, 1981).
[81] P. Jackson, 'France and the problems of security and disarmament after the First World War', *JSS*, 29, 2 (2006), 252–8; J. L. Hogge II, 'Arbitrage, Sécurité, Désarmement: French Security and the League of Nations, 1920–1925', Ph.D. dissertation, New York University, 1994, 13–36.
[82] SHD-DAT, Dossiers et états de service, *Dossier personnel du general Édouard Réquin*, 13Yd 753, 'Feuillet du Personnel de M. Réquin', includes glowing assessments from Tardieu, Briand, Berthelot and Foch.

most determined wills and most commanding presences which the peculiar world of Geneva experts has ever known'.[83]

Réquin's first task at the SFSDN was to draft a proposal for the organisation and functioning of the PAC. The project he came up with envisaged the PAC essentially as a sort of international general staff responsible for enforcing German disarmament.[84] General disarmament was scarcely mentioned, aside from the warning that 'contrary to the stated goal of providing international security ... by reducing armaments, the members of the League of Nations could in reality bring about the triumph of force over law'.[85] Réquin's proposal reflected the military establishment's opposition to the very idea of multilateral arms reductions. Yet it was his conception that served as the basis of the PAC adopted by the League Council. The commission that resulted was staffed exclusively by military officials. It reported to the Council (where France had veto rights) rather than the Assembly (where it did not). Bourgeois explained to colleagues in Paris that the central aim was to pre-empt naïve calls for immediate and total disarmament in Geneva.[86] When the commission met it predictably exhibited little interest in general disarmament. As de Madariaga observed, 'It was as foolish to expect a disarmament convention from such a commission as a declaration of atheism from a commission of clergymen.'[87]

Yet the issue would not go away. Pressure from the Assembly meant that execution of Article 8 would remain one of the chief items on the League agenda in the years to come. Requests for guidance from French officials in Geneva prompted a round of interdepartmental discussions and disagreements which illuminate the way questions of disarmament and security were understood in Paris. The foreign ministry asked the armed services for their views on how France should respond to international pressure for reductions in armaments. Neither the army nor the navy offered positive suggestions, however. The army staff, in fact, responded with an alarmist assessment of German and Soviet military potential and warned of the possibility of 'common German–Bolshevik action' against Poland.[88]

---

[83] S. de Madariaga, *Disarmament* (Oxford, 1929), 82.
[84] MAE, *SDN*, vol. 13, 'Note au sujet de la constitution, du rôle et du fonctionnement de la Commission Permanente (militaire, navale et aérienne) prévue par l'article IX du pacte de la SDN', 22 Jul. 1919.
[85] Quoted in a later draft: MAE, PA-AP 118, *Papiers Millerand*, vol. 4, 'Note sur la constitution de la Commission permanente militaire, navale et aérienne prévue par l'article IX du Pacte de la SDN', 29 Oct. 1921; also in SHD-DAT, 7N 3529-3, marked 'Texte révisé' to take into account the views of Foch and Pétain.
[86] Jackson, 'Security and disarmament', 252–3.   [87] De Madariaga, *Disarmament*, 78–9.
[88] SHD-DAT, 2N 5-3, 'Résumé de la situation allemande' and 'Situation de l'armée Bolchevique', 13 Dec. 1920; see also A. Barros, 'Disarmament as a weapon: Anglo-French relations and the problems of enforcing German disarmament, 1919–1928', *JSS*, 29, 2 (2006), 301–21.

It was nonetheless evident that the politics of international disarmament clearly had the potential to affect French military policy. This was especially true in the light of charges of French militarism that gathered momentum in the international sphere after 1919. 'From the external point of view,' premier Leygues demanded, 'how can we announce to the world that, after its victory, France intends to maintain an army of 900,000 men, keeping more soldiers under the colours than in 1914? How can we explain this?'[89] These were internal debates, however, and they were not aired in the international arena. The official French position in Geneva through to the summer of 1922 remained that general disarmament could not be discussed until Germany had complied fully with its treaty obligations.

The chief tactic employed was to focus the attention of the PAC on Germany's failure to disarm and on the need for permanent surveillance mechanisms for monitoring German compliance after the last Allied occupation forces left the Rhineland in 1935.[90] The problem was that the French delegation could not prevent proposals for freezing all military spending from gaining significant support within the League Assembly. Such proposals provoked implacable opposition in Paris. War minister Lefèvre responded that 'as long as the League of Nations is not able to enforce the treaty itself, [France] must conserve complete liberty to maintain our armaments at the level we deem fit'. He then went on to reject the very idea of internationalist schemes for security: 'No measure of our defence policy can ever be left to the League without making it a super-state and thus abdicating all political freedom of action.'[91] From the foreign ministry Berthelot insisted that France must conserve complete liberty over defence policy and dismissed League arms-reduction schemes as 'pure illusion'.[92]

The French position was entirely negative. France would not consider disarmament until it received concrete security guarantees. But the question of the form 'minimum guarantees' might assume was never addressed, much less outlined, in any of these discussions. Instead, virtually all French initiatives were aimed at stifling any discussion of disarmament in Geneva. This trend continued through to the summer of 1921, when French delegates were confronted with a fresh challenge in the form of the newly constituted Temporary Mixed Commission (TMC). This new organ was created by the Assembly to jump-start the disarmament process by circumventing the PAC. The new commission was to be staffed mainly by private citizens rather than military officials. And it was charged explicitly with producing proposals for generalised arms reductions.[93]

[89] SHD-DAT, 2N 5–2, CSDN procès-verbal, 27 Oct. 1920.
[90] SHD-DAT, 7N 3530–1, 'Note sur le réduction des armements', 9 Nov. 1920.
[91] SHD-DAT, 7N 3530–2, 'Proposition faite à la Sous-commission des armements de la Société des nations', 11 Dec. 1920 and 'Article 8 du Pacte de la Société des nations', 10 Nov. 1920.
[92] MAE, *SDN*, vol. 72, Berthelot to SFSDN, 11 Dec. 1920.
[93] Webster, 'Making Disarmament Work', 554–5.

The chair of the TMC went to René Viviani, however, who was just as opposed to general arms reductions as any French soldier. Viviani used his position to limit the activities of the commission. The other French official on the TMC was Réquin (who was an omnipresent figure in disarmament discussions in Geneva).[94] Réquin argued that the TMC must focus its initial efforts on establishing a permanent inspection regime inside Germany.[95] He also warned that discussions in Geneva might prejudice the conference on security and disarmament in the Pacific, scheduled to take place in Washington later in 1921.[96] Above all, however, he insisted that arms reductions could not be considered without prior security guarantees.[97]

Despite the best efforts of Viviani and Réquin to limit its effectiveness, the TMC emerged from the Second League Assembly with its authority enhanced. A resolution was passed charging the TMC with preparing a draft treaty for arms reduction for consideration at the next Assembly. Réquin was appalled that the 'irresponsible amateurs' on the TMC were to negotiate a treaty pertaining to France's military status.[98] The fact of the matter was that it was increasingly difficult in public relations terms for French representatives to continue to obstruct disarmament negotiations. Proposals by the TMC could be voted down in the League Council, where France had the veto, but this would further undermine France's moral authority and provide ammunition for those who denounced French militarism. The archival record testifies to the increasing sensitivity of both politicians and diplomats to such accusations. Pressure to engage with the discourse of disarmament would become impossible to resist in the months to come.[99]

Through to the end of 1921, however, the attitudes of senior policy officials towards the League were characterised chiefly by scepticism concerning its aims and suspicion of its practices. The enthusiasm and efforts of French internationalists had little or no impact on fundamental policy calculations.

---

[94] See the summary of French participation in the TMC in SHD-DAT, 7N 3529–1, Pétain (chief of army staff) to André Maginot (war minister), 28 Dec. 1922.
[95] MAE, *SDN*, vol. 826, 'Note au sujet de l'échange des renseignements prévu par l'Article 8 du Pacte', 6 Jul. 1921.
[96] MAE, *SDN*, vol. 706, 'Le Problème de la réduction des armements devant la Société des nations', SFSDN note, 1 Jan. 1921; SHD-DAT, 7N 3530–2, 'La Société des nations et la limitation des dépenses militaires', 3 Apr. 1921; 7N 3530–3, 'Résolution approuvée par la sous-commission le 19 juillet 1921'; 7N 3529–3, 'Rapport de M. le Maréchal Fayolle', 4 Nov. 1921.
[97] Cited from SHD-DAT, 7N 3530–2, 'La Société des nations et la limitation des dépenses militaires', 3 Apr. 1921; 7N 3530–2, 'La SDN et la limitation des dépenses militaires', 18 Apr. 1921; and MAE, *Série Y*, vol. 435, Briand instructions, 9 Sept. 1921.
[98] MAE, PA-AP 029, *Papiers Bourgeois*, vol. 37, Réquin to Monnet (forwarded to Bourgeois).
[99] A. Webster, '"Absolutely irresponsible amateurs": the Temporary Mixed Commission on Armaments, 1921–1924', *Australian Journal of Politics and History*, 54, 3 (2008), 380–5; Hogge, 'Arbitrage', 128–33; R. J. Young, *Marketing Marianne: French Propaganda in America, 1900–1914* (London, 2004), 71–92.

No faith was placed in generalised arms reductions because armaments were one of the few reliable sources of national security. French delegates in Geneva were saddled with the difficult task of refuting charges of militarism while at the same time doing everything they could to kill any initiative tending towards international arms reductions. Bourgeois, the head of the French delegation, expressed frustration at what he considered to be exaggerated fears of disarmament discussions that were damaging France's standing in Geneva. 'In Paris', he lamented, 'they have evidently not understood the character of the question.'[100]

IV

Economic security policy under Briand was less forthrightly traditional in its inspiration and execution. The key objective of this policy remained to establish the necessary conditions for an international mobilisation of the German debt. The primary authors of this strategy, Loucheur and Seydoux, also revived projects for German payment of reparations in kind that, it was hoped, would open the way for a wider commercial and industrial entente. This strategy appeared to hold genuine promise during the summer and early autumn of 1921. When it collapsed, both Loucheur and Seydoux advocated imposing financial controls on the German economy. The former approach aimed at engagement with Germany and a measure of independence from British policy. The latter was a strategy of coercion requiring British cooperation.

Flexibility and moderation were inherent in the terms of the London Schedule of Payments accepted by Germany on 11 May 1921. Although total reparations were set nominally at 132 billion gold marks, Germany's 'real' debt under the agreement was far less onerous. A system of variable bond issues was adopted in which only 50 billion gold marks (in 'A' and 'B' category bonds) were to be mobilised in the first instance. Payment of the remainder was put off until such time as the reparations commission judged Germany able to pay. This translated into annuities of 2 billion gold marks plus 20 per cent of the value of German exports over thirty-six years. Even John Maynard Keynes recommended that Germany accept the accord.[101]

Two key policy objectives underpinned the relative moderation in France's position. The first was a desire to secure some form of German payment in 1921. The second was to come up with a fixed sum that would be interpreted as reasonable by international opinion. This is clear from a meeting of senior policy makers on 24 January 1921. Millerand stressed the need to obtain 'tangible results' that year. Briand agreed. Louis Dubois then mooted a figure of 212 billion gold marks. Both Briand and Millerand dismissed this figure as

---

[100] Mouton, *Société des nations*, 1999.
[101] Trachtenberg, *Reparation*, 210–11; Steiner, *Lights that Failed*, 196–202.

far too high, predicting that it would destroy prospects for international cooperation in mobilising the German debt. Loucheur proposed a compromise solution where a significant portion of the reparations debt would be held in abeyance pending Germany's future economic recovery. This would establish the conditions for more realistic annuities in the short term.[102] Loucheur's proposal anticipated the terms of the London Schedule.

Almost immediately after the Weimar government submitted to the London terms, Seydoux began arguing for a recalibration of French policy to focus on reparations in kind. Such a strategy, he argued, implied a reconsideration of the sanctions imposed in April and a willingness to discuss economic cooperation with the new German government of Joseph Wirth.[103] Seydoux's proposal was challenged by the more hardline Peretti, who argued that sanctions must be left in place pending further evidence of German treaty compliance. Tirard went further to demand greater administrative powers on the Left Bank and a more generous regime of French commercial preference for the Rhineland.[104]

But enthusiasm for an ambitious Rhineland policy was at a low ebb in Paris. There was little evidence that the customs barrier imposed in April had accomplished anything beyond stoking resentment of France among the population on the Left Bank. Seydoux argued that the customs sanction was entirely out of step with the new political and economic context of the London Schedule: 'At a moment when any payment of reparations depends on future German prosperity, there is no logic in shackling that prosperity with an internal barrier.'[105] Seydoux submitted that priority must be attached to stimulating Franco-German economic collaboration. The only sanction that should remain in place, he concluded, was the occupation of the port towns that were 'the key to the Ruhr' and thus allowed France to maintain the implicit threat of force in its dealings with Germany.[106]

Seydoux's arguments prevailed. On 24 May 1921 Briand praised German policy before the chamber and declared that his government placed 'confidence in chancellor Wirth'. Tirard was instructed to observe 'an attitude of absolute disinterest' in politics on the Left Bank.[107] French confidence appeared to be rewarded when Germany made its first payment under the

---

[102] MAE, *Série Z, Allemagne*, vol. 457, 'Réunion du 23 janvier chez le président de la République', 24 Jan. 1921; Loucheur advocated the creation of a 'compte d'attente'.

[103] MAE, *RC*, Série B81–82, vol. 41, 'Réparations: maintien des sanctions de Londres' (Seydoux), 13 May 1921.

[104] MAE, *Série Z, Allemagne*, vol. 234, 'Réparations: sanctions de Londres' (Peretti), 17 May 1921. See esp. McDougall, *Rhineland Diplomacy*, 158–63.

[105] MAE, PA-AP 261, *Papiers Seydoux*, vol. 22, retrospective 'Note au sujet des sanctions de Londres', 18 Oct. 1921.

[106] MAE, *RC*, Série B81–82, vol. 41, 'Réparations: maintien des sanctions de Londres' (Seydoux), 13 May 1921; *DDF, 1921*, I, #458, 'Note au sujet des réparations en nature', 9 Jun. 1921; #513, 'Note au sujet des sanctions', Seydoux to Berthelot, 29 Jun. 1920.

[107] MAE, *Série Z, RGR*, vol. 26, Briand to Tirard, 29 Jul. 1921; Bonnefous, *Après-guerre*, 242; McDougall, *Rhineland Diplomacy*, 161–5.

London Schedule on 1 June. This was followed several days later by an overture from the German reconstruction minister Walther Rathenau suggesting a meeting to discuss reparations.[108]

The cabinet approved the idea of such a meeting. Seydoux prepared a long analysis of the reparations issue that stressed the advantages of payments in kind. Such a system, he argued, would ease the 'transfer problem', relieve the French treasury of the costs of reconstruction, provide German industry with a vested interest in treaty fulfilment and, finally, lay the foundations of more extensive commercial and industrial collaboration between the two economies:

> French industry cannot live if it does not export its iron ore and if it cannot import a sufficient quantity of coal. An understanding with Germany is indispensable to achieve a re-balancing of French and German iron and steel production. Such understandings can only be fashioned between representatives of the two industries and are possible only once the political atmosphere has been clarified and improved.[109]

Seydoux envisaged an economic and political entente with Germany that would be based on pre-1914 structures of industrial cooperation and would drive forward west European economic reconstruction.

Loucheur met with Rathenau three times between June and October 1921. The result was the 'Wiesbaden Accords', which, had they ever been implemented, would have gone a long way to establishing the conditions for collaboration outlined by Seydoux. Rathenau suggested an arrangement whereby Germany would deliver huge quantities of reparations in kind to speed up the reconstruction of France's devastated areas. A programme of this sort, he observed, 'could serve as the basis for Franco-German economic relations'.[110] The accords initialled by both parties on 27 August envisaged the creation of bureaucratic machinery to manage the delivery of raw materials and manufactured goods destined for the reconstruction of northern France. The aim was to deliver a maximum of 7 billion gold marks in reparations in kind between October 1921 and May 1926 (Rathenau initially offered 9–10 billion). No more than 1 billion gold marks per year, between 35 and 45 per cent of the total worth of the goods delivered, would be credited to Germany's annual reparations payment. The remaining value would be set against interest on payments after 1926.[111] These arrangements, which were remarkably generous to France, were supplemented by an accord to increase German coal deliveries to France at internal German prices (a tremendous boon to French

---

[108] Loucheur, *Carnets secrets*, 4, 5, 7 and 8 Jun. 1921, 84–5; S. Carls, *Louis Loucheur and the Shaping of Modern France, 1916–1931* (Baton Rouge, 1993), 228–9.
[109] *DDF, 1921*, I, #458, 'Note au sujet des réparations en nature', 9 Jun. 1921.
[110] Loucheur, *Carnets secrets*, 12 Jun. 1921, 88.
[111] See the rich file on Wiesbaden in MAE, *RC*, Série B84, vol. 3; see also Loucheur, *Carnets secrets*, 12–13 Jun. 1921, 84–92; Bariéty, *Relations franco-allemandes*, 82–9; Trachtenberg, *Reparation*, 214–18; and Carls, *Loucheur*, 228–35.

industry, which was obliged to pay much higher prices for coal from Britain and North America).[112]

The Wiesbaden Accords were never ratified, however. French coal producers and local chambers of commerce objected that they would be disadvantaged by a flood of German goods into northern France. The Lloyd George government, meanwhile, claimed that the accords would weaken Germany and were in violation of the London Schedule. The British mobilised opposition to Wiesbaden on the reparations commission, which would need to approve the agreement before it could come into effect. Franco-German economic cooperation again failed to materialise.[113]

Historians disagree over the extent to which both sides were truly committed to the Wiesbaden project.[114] There is considerable doubt that Germany could ever have financed it.[115] On the French side, conversely, there is considerable evidence suggesting that the Briand government was inclined to pursue the accords despite internal opposition. On 7 September Briand observed to the German ambassador that the moment had come for 'a comprehensive entente on all reciprocal interests' between France and Germany.[116] He defended the Wiesbaden meetings before the chamber by arguing for the political benefits of economic cooperation: 'These accords of an economic order are of a character liable to create an atmosphere of peace ... to reduce the risks of war, to encourage the evolution in the heart of Germany of a Germany with which we can live.'[117] This was an early iteration of the 'two Germanys' discourse to which Briand would return frequently during the Locarno era.

There were limits to French conciliation, however. Looming over the Wiesbaden negotiations was the vexed issue of Upper Silesia and France's support for Poland in this dispute. Rathenau had tried repeatedly to use payment in kind as leverage to obtain a French attitude favourable to German claims to this region. Loucheur and other French negotiators refused categorically to admit any relationship between German fulfilment and Upper Silesia.[118] The traditional strategy of weakening Germany and strengthening the eastern counterweight would not be sacrificed for tentative initiatives to reach détente and economic cooperation with the Reich.

When the League-adjudicated settlement proved favourable to Poland, German policy moved decisively away from cooperation with France to focus on obtaining British support for a revision of the London Schedule. By

[112] Bariéty, *Relations franco-allemandes*, 85.
[113] Trachtenberg, *Reparation*, 217–18; Boyce, *Great Interwar Crisis*, 109–15; Steiner, *Lights that Failed*, 202–3.
[114] Bariéty concludes that both sides were sincere; Trachtenberg, Boyce and Steiner judge that neither was committed fully (see citations above).
[115] G. Feldman, *The Great Disorder: Politics, Economics and Society in the German Inflation, 1914– 1924* (Oxford, 1997), 358–404.
[116] Quoted in Bariéty, *Relations franco-allemandes*, 87.
[117] *JO*, Chambre, *Débats*, 1921, 21 Oct. 1921.
[118] See esp. Loucheur, *Carnets secrets*, 12 Jun. 1921, 86–8.

mid-November it was clear that Germany had neither the will nor the capacity to make its January 1922 payment under the London Schedule. The Wirth government, with British support, requested a reparations moratorium. Seydoux and Loucheur both responded to the apparent collapse of German 'fulfilment' by advocating the imposition of a series of financial controls on the German economy. Both had mooted this option previously as an alternative to a policy of force in the Ruhr.[119] Loucheur and his team prepared a programme aimed at 'a complete reform of the finances of the Reich' in which Germany stabilised its currency, blocked the flight of German capital abroad and embraced budgetary discipline in order to secure foreign lending to facilitate reparations.[120]

Such coercive measures required British cooperation on the reparations council. But the British opposed the idea of financial controls and pressed instead for a moratorium. Lloyd George advised Loucheur of the British position in early December. He added that a French occupation of the Ruhr in response to a German default would destroy the Entente.[121] Lloyd George met with both Loucheur and Briand in mid-December and reiterated that he was not willing to violate German sovereignty by imposing controls on the Reich's economy. He proposed instead that Britain extend a military guarantee to France. In exchange France must agree to renounce the use of military force to coerce German payments and participate in an ambitious project to reintegrate Russia into the European economy at a large economic conference he proposed to convene in the spring.[122]

The British offer presented the Briand government with a fundamental choice that would shape the course of French security policy for the foreseeable future. Would France agree to renounce force, accept a moratorium and participate in an economic conference to which the Germans, and even the Soviets, would be invited as equals? Or would it refuse a moratorium, maintain the option of occupying the Ruhr and scuttle British hopes for a general conference on economic reconstruction? The policy elite was deeply divided. Loucheur was open to the idea of a general conference and advocated a flexible

---

[119] MAE, PA-AP 118, *Papiers Millerand*, vol. 19, 'Esquisse sommaire des grandes étapes de la politique des réparations au cours de l'année 1921' (Seydoux), 1 Dec. 1921 and vol. 18, 'La Faillite de l'Allemagne' (Loucheur), 10 Sept. 1921; see also Trachtenberg, *Reparation*, 221–6 and Boyce, *Great Interwar Crisis*, 110–12.

[120] *DDF, 1921*, I, 'Réunion tenue le 7 décembre 1921, chez M. Briand, relative aux réparations et au voyage de M. Loucheur à Londres', 7 Dec. 1921.

[121] Loucheur, *Carnets secrets*, 'Conversation "aux Chequers"', 8 Dec. 1921, 185–8; D. Artaud, *La Question des dettes interalliées et la reconstruction de l'Europe, 1917–1929*, 2 vols. (Paris, 1978), I, 374–80.

[122] *DDF, 1921 (Annexes)*, #1245, 'Notes sur un entretien à Downing Street le lundi 19 décembre 1921'; #126, 'Notes sur un entretien à Downing Street le mardi 20 décembre 1921'; #127, 'Notes sur un entretien à Downing Street le mercredi 21 décembre 1921, 12h'; see also C. Fink, *The Genoa Conference: European Diplomacy, 1921–1922* (Syracuse, 1993), 18–28.

posture aimed at preserving the Entente while seeking further financial controls on Germany.[123] Millerand, whose relations with Briand had deteriorated badly since the previous May, and who had from the beginning expressed serious misgivings about the merits of 'confidence' in the Wirth government, was steadfastly opposed to further concessions. Others within Briand's cabinet, including Barthou, shared this view, as did Peretti within the foreign ministry.[124] Briand, true to form, responded with an attempt to alter the conditions of choice. The result was an imaginative plan to link the various strands of security policy together in the construction of a Europe-wide system of multilateral guarantees, at the heart of which would be a Franco-British alliance.

V

Briand's belief in the importance of the Franco-British Entente was only reinforced by the experience of the Washington conference on arms limitation. The premier led the French delegation to Washington with two main objectives. The first was to protect the French navy from unacceptable limitations on its right to rebuild. Planning was underway within the *marine* for what would become the Statut naval of 1924 – an ambitious programme aimed at restoring the navy's ability to protect France's global imperial interests. The second was to protect the French army from serious limitation to its size. The French delegation was resolved to reject any limitation whatsoever without concrete security commitments from Britain and the USA.[125]

French negotiators achieved both goals, but at a high cost. Briand used the absence of an Anglo-American guarantee to argue successfully that land armaments could not be discussed. In the ensuing weeks the French delegation agreed to restrictions on the tonnage of capital ships France could build but resisted intense pressure to accept similar restrictions on lighter classes of warships or on its right to build submarines. The consequence, however, was a crescendo of vitriolic denunciations of French militarism, particularly in the British and American press. The conference was a disaster for the French government's campaign to influence world opinion in favour of its need for long-term security.[126]

The Washington Conference also underlined the danger of political isolation. The common Anglo-American front over naval armaments had placed

---

[123] Carls, *Loucheur*, 234–7; Jeannesson, *Ruhr*, 72–3.
[124] Loucheur, *Carnets secrets*, 29 Jul. 1921, 94; Bariéty, *Relations franco-allemandes*, 88–90; R. J. Young, *Power and Pleasure: Louis Barthou and the Third French Republic* (Montreal, 1991), 167–8; Suarez, *Briand*, V, 340–51.
[125] MAE, *Série Y*, vol. 503, 'Note pour la sous-direction d'Europe' (Laroche), 22 Sept. 1921; ibid., 'Note: programme de Washington', 18 Oct. 1921; ibid., vol. 504, 'Pour l'Amiral de Bon', 18 Nov. 1921; P. Masson, 'La Politique navale française de 1919–1939', *Revue maritime*, 252 (1968), 286–95.
[126] Concerns over the portrayal of France are in MAE, *Série Y*, vols. 504–5 and SHD-DAT, *Fonds Clemenceau*, cartons 6N 138 and 139; see also D. Birn, 'Open diplomacy at the

French negotiators in an extremely difficult position. British sympathy for the German position threatened to do the same in Europe. Relations with Britain had suffered successive hammer blows over the resolution of the issue of Upper Silesia, disagreement over the fate of Tangier and especially France's decision to make peace with the Turkish nationalists on 20 October (which destroyed what was left of the Treaty of Sèvres).[127] 'We cannot be at peace in Europe', observed Seydoux, 'if we are not in accord with Great Britain.' The alternative was political and economic isolation. 'It is French policy in Europe that is at stake at the moment,' he warned.[128]

Briand and his team responded with an attempt to remake French security policy. A number of fine studies have examined the ensuing negotiations for a Franco-British security pact.[129] None have recognised the novelty and significance of the French negotiating position, however. The strategy that emerged in early January 1922 departed from purely traditional practices in two distinct ways. First, it aimed at enmeshing Germany in a multilateral system that would provide political and legal constraints on its freedom of action. At the heart of this system would be a bilateral agreement with Britain. Second, it did not demand a full-blown military alliance with Britain. Importance was instead attached to a British political commitment. Both of these innovations were responses to the changed international atmosphere after 1918. Neither would meet with the approval of domestic advocates of a more traditional approach to security, who held a majority not only in parliament but also within Briand's cabinet.

The conceptual architecture of the French programme was inspired by the multilateral four-power treaty for Pacific security agreed at Washington. The Briand government aimed to construct a European equivalent anchored by a bilateral treaty with Britain. The early outlines of the new French approach are evident in the minutes of the Franco-British summit in London on 21 December 1921. Here Briand stressed the need for a 'solid entente' that would allow his government to reduce its military expenditures. This would ease British anxieties about French militarism. Such an entente, he argued,

Washington Conference, 1921–2: the British and French experience', *Comparative Studies in Society and History*, 12, 3 (1970), 297–319; J. Blatt, 'France and the Washington Conference', *D&S*, 4, 3 (1993), 192–219; Young, *Marketing Marianne*, 75–93.

[127] Correspondence between Hardinge (Paris) and foreign secretary Curzon is replete with references to French 'treachery' and 'lies' over the Turkish issue: see BL, India Office Library (hereafter IOL), F112, *Papers of Marquess Curzon of Kedleston*, vol. 200A, 22 Oct., 6, 12, 18 Nov. 1921.

[128] MAE, PA-AP 261, *Papiers Seydoux*, vol. 23, Seydoux to Laroche, 29 Nov. 1921.

[129] S. Marks, 'Ménage à trois: the negotiations for an Anglo-French–Belgian Pact in 1922', *IHR*, 4, 4 (1982), 475–627; S. Marks, 'Mésentente Cordiale: The Anglo-French Relationship, 1921–1922' in M. Petricioli (ed.), *A Missed Opportunity? 1922 and the Reconstruction of Europe* (Berne, 1995), 33–45; J. Bariéty, 'Le Projet de pacte franco-britannique, 1920–1922', *GMCC*, 193 (1999), 83–99; Boyce, *Great Interwar Crisis*, 115–19; J. Keiger, 'Aristide Briand et Lloyd George, 1921–1922: entre entente et mésentente cordiale', in Bariéty (ed.), *Briand*, 60–73; A. Orde, *Great Britain and International Security, 1920–1926* (London, 1978), 6–36.

must take the form of 'a substantial alliance in which the two powers guaranteed one another's reciprocal interests across the globe and would come to the aid of one another when necessary'. This essentially traditional arrangement would facilitate the creation of 'a broader security pact' to include France, Britain, Belgium and other interested states. 'Germany', Briand observed, 'must be part of this pact.'[130]

The significance of this innovation in French thinking should not be underestimated. In Briand's conception, Germany would be bound up in a multilateral system that would not only deter it from using violence to revise the peace settlement, but also help shape its future behaviour as a responsible state. 'Within this system of guarantees', the French premier predicted, 'the Germans are likely to renounce their warlike designs.' This was because the character of the system would 'aid German democracy, prepare the return of Germany to the community of nations and thus have a stabilising effect on Europe'.[131] This was a very different approach to European security from anything attempted by France since the summer of 1919.

Lloyd George responded that British public opinion would not countenance a military alliance. He added that the price for a political guarantee would be French participation in his proposed economic conference. It was clear that not only would Germany be granted a moratorium, but the reparations payment schedule would also be up for renegotiation. These were the quid pro quos for British participation in a security arrangement with France. It was agreed that the details of the arrangement and preparations for the economic conference would be elaborated at another summit meeting in Cannes in early January.[132]

The prospect of negotiations for a security pact prompted a round of consultations within the foreign ministry. The most original contribution was that of Seydoux, who evoked the stabilisation of Europe after the Napoleonic Wars to argue for a multilateral solution to security that would include Germany. Seydoux compared the project outlined by Briand in London to the strategy of the 'Holy Alliance' at Aachen in 1818, in which France was invited to 'unite its councils' to the efforts of Austria, Britain, Prussia and Russia to 'work together to maintain existing treaties'. Aachen had laid the foundations for the European 'concert' that endured through to the middle of the nineteenth century.[133] Seydoux suggested that a similar level of stabilisation might be achieved by granting Germany a moratorium and obtaining, in return, collaboration in the creation of a wider European system of security. If such collaboration could be secured, Seydoux predicted in a revealing passage, it would,

---

[130] MAE, *Série Z, GB*, vol. 69, 'Notes prises au cours d'une conversation entre M. Lloyd George et M. Briand le mercredi 21 décembre 1921'.
[131] Ibid.   [132] Ibid.
[133] MAE, *Série Z, GB*, vol. 69, 'Alliance', Seydoux note, 26 Dec. 1921; Sally Marks notes Seydoux's meaning without dwelling on its significance in 'Mésentente Cordiale', 35–6; on the Aachen Conference see P. W. Schroeder, *The Transformation of European Politics 1763–1848* (Oxford, 1994), 592–3 and 598–9.

'by rehabilitating Germany from a moral point of view, engage it all the more in the execution of the treaty. There would then be no problem in agreeing to German entry into the League of Nations.'[134] This constructive prescription for stability and security was a far cry from the uncompromising approach typically attributed to French policy at this juncture.

Seydoux was ahead of most of his colleagues, however. The majority of senior diplomats preferred an exclusive alliance with Britain to a multilateral pact including Germany. Laroche agreed that an 'entente' of four or more states would be useful to provide reassurance to Britain and Germany. But he argued that such an arrangement must 'necessarily be rather vague and general' and preceded by a treaty with Britain.[135] Fromageot, now chief legal counsellor, extolled the deterrent value of a Franco-British alliance but made only passing reference to a wider entente.[136] Paul Cambon's replacement in London, the comte de Saint-Aulaire, drafted terms for an exclusive alliance which he forwarded to Paris in the expectation that they would serve as the basis for French policy. His draft was a veritable distillation of the traditional approach to security. It contained only one clause relating to 'cooperation' with third parties committed to 'maintaining the political status quo'. It envisaged not only regular Franco-British staff talks and a military convention but also provisions aimed at French and British support for Rhenish separatism.[137] This was a vision to which most military elites would readily have subscribed. Significantly, however, France's military leadership does not seem to have been consulted at all before the Cannes summit.

Frustratingly, it is impossible to know the views of Briand's chief adviser because Berthelot was caught up in a parliamentary row over his alleged role in the collapse of the Banque industrielle de Chine (his brother André Berthelot was director of the bank). When the scandal placed Briand under severe pressure in the chamber in late December, Berthelot resigned and was not replaced.[138] This left the policy machine without its chief engineer. Briand, as a result, went to Cannes in early January 1922 without the raft of documentation that would normally constitute the sinews of security policy making.

The resulting paucity of evidence has led historians to assume that Saint-Aulaire's project represented the French negotiating position. The multilateral strategy advocated by Seydoux and articulated by Briand in London, conversely, is either ignored or dismissed as window dressing for the core aim of a military

---

[134] MAE, *Série Z, GB*, vol. 69, 'Alliance', Seydoux note, 26 Dec. 1921.
[135] MAE, *Série Z, GB*, vol. 69, 'Observations sur la rédaction du projet', Laroche note, 28 Dec. 1921; see also Laroche's marginal comment at the top of Seydoux's 26 Dec. note cited above.
[136] MAE, *Série Z, GB*, vol. 69, Fromageot note, 27 Dec. 1921.
[137] MAE, *Série Z, GB*, vol. 69, 'Projet Saint-Aulaire', n.d. and 'Projet d'alliance franco-anglaise', Saint-Aulaire to Paris, 28 Dec. 1921.
[138] Berthelot's letter of resignation appeared in *Le Temps*, 27 Dec. 1921; see also MAE, PA-AP 335, *Papiers Aristide Briand*, vol. 10; Barré, *Berthelot*, 375–83.

alliance.[139] This is unfortunate. Briand's commitment to a new strategy is evident in the stenographic records of the Cannes meetings. Saint-Aulaire's draft treaty was relegated to the files – as, eventually, were hopes to add staff talks and a military convention to the bilateral pact with Britain.

There was no hope that any British government would agree to a pact along the lines suggested by Saint-Aulaire. Foreign secretary Curzon observed that the changed international atmosphere ruled out any policy that might be interpreted as 'an attempt to revive the old politics of State alliances dominating and controlling the future of Europe'. A military alliance was impossible, he argued, 'at a time when such arrangements are believed to have been superseded by the newer conceptions embodied in the League of Nations, in international courts and conferences, and in the theory of corporate action as opposed to the rival grouping of powers'.[140] Briand, with his acute political antennae, recognised the limits beyond which the British could not go.

The French premier further developed his commitment to a multilateral security system in interviews with the French and British press before Cannes. To the *Daily Mail* he emphasised that a Franco-British 'alliance pact' would 'constitute the kernel of a wider arrangement' modelled on the Pacific four-power pact. Two days later an editorial was placed in *Le Temps* characterising a Franco-British pact as 'the sole means of restoring prosperity and bringing Germany ... back into the family of nations'.[141]

Briand outlined this policy conception at the first meeting with Lloyd George at Cannes on 4 January 1922.[142] French insecurity was at the heart of Europe's 'malaise', he argued. Other challenges could not be tackled without bolstering the post-war order with a Franco-British pact. This pact would serve as the foundation for a 'larger conception' that would bind the states of Europe together. Briand argued in essence for a regional security system in which

> France and Great Britain, united in some kind of arrangement which remains to be found, would be surrounded by all of the peoples who had signed the Treaty of Versailles in a general entente. All of these nations would engage to consult together in the event of trouble and to examine the causes of conflict in a manner permitting their amiable settlement. In the event that this proves impossible, the arbitration [of the disagreement] will be guaranteed by Great Britain and France. It will thus be possible to maintain the peace in any circumstances.

---

[139] The multilateral dimension of Briand's conception is dismissed as 'rather nebulous' by Marks and ignored altogether by Bariéty: see P. Jackson, 'French security and a British "continental commitment" after the First World War', *EHR*, 126, 519 (2011), 345–85.
[140] BL, IOL, F112, *Curzon Papers*, vol. 242, 'Memorandum on the Question of an Anglo-French Alliance', 28 Dec. 1921; see also TNA-PRO, FO 371, 7000, W13420/12716/17, 'Notes respecting the possible conclusion of an Anglo-French alliance', 26 Dec. 1921 (permanent undersecretary Sir Eyre Crowe).
[141] *Daily Mail*, 3 Jan. 1922; *Le Temps*, 5 Jan. 1922.
[142] The analysis that follows is based on the French records of the summit meetings between Briand and Lloyd George that are in MAE, *Série Z, GB*, vol. 69.

Arbitration, crucially, would underpin interlocking political commitments. Germany, Briand added, could be admitted on the conditions that it renounced aggression and accepted the principle of compulsory arbitration. The same offer could be extended to Soviet Russia. A regional system of this kind, Briand insisted, would strengthen the League and therefore gain the wholehearted support of the mainstream left-wing parties in both France and Britain.[143]

The French produced proposals for both accords on 8 January 1922. The proposed Franco-British pact included a provision for joint war planning between the French and British general staffs and reaffirmed German violation of Rhineland demilitarisation as a *casus belli*. It further stipulated that the Franco-British entente would underpin a wider regional pact that would provide security 'in a still more precise manner than that of the stipulations of the Covenant'.[144] Briand and his advisers could not have been surprised when Lloyd George rejected references to staff talks and military collaboration as 'precisely the sort of engagement that the British public loathes the most'. The British prime minister offered instead a pledge to come to France's assistance in the event of unprovoked aggression. Even this promise, he made clear, was dependent on French agreement to extend a payment moratorium to Germany and participate in an international economic conference.[145]

Briand, supported by Laroche, immediately indicated a willingness to sacrifice staff conversations. He assured Lloyd George that all mention of military collaboration could be excised from the proposed bilateral pact. He pressed forward with the idea of regional mutual assistance, however, insisting that such a system need not entail precise measures of military coercion. Lloyd George observed that such an engagement 'would bind together all of the powers that posed a danger to European peace: Russia, Germany, Poland, Hungary and Bulgaria'. Briand agreed, responding that 'this is precisely the goal that must be achieved'. If a Franco-British entente could be placed alongside the wider arrangement, he argued, 'we will have fashioned a solid political system that can usefully support the League of Nations'.[146]

The prevailing historiographical judgement is that the multilateral dimension was a throwaway appendix to the French negotiating position, the true focus of which was a bilateral alliance.[147] This ignores the fact that Briand

---

[143] MAE, *Série Z, GB*, vol. 69, 'Compte-rendu de la conversation ayant eu lieu à Cannes, Villa Valetta, entre MM. Briand et Loucheur et M. Lloyd George, le 4 janvier 1922 à 16.15' and 'Compte-rendu de la conversation ayant eu lieu, le jeudi, 5 janvier 1922 entre MM. Briand et Loucheur et M. Lloyd George'.
[144] TNA-PRO, FO 371, 8249, W343/50/17, 'Statement of the French Government on Anglo-French Relations', 8 Jan. 1922.
[145] MAE, *Série Z, GB*, vol. 69, 'Résumé d'une conversation entre M. Briand et M. Lloyd George (Cannes, Villa Valetta, 8 janvier 1922, 18h)'.
[146] Ibid. [147] See the references to Marks, Bariéty, Keiger and Boyce in note 129 above.

returned to this theme repeatedly in three subsequent meetings in Cannes on 4, 5 and 8 January 1922. The multilateral dimension of Briand's project was more than a sop intended to lure the British into what was essentially an old-fashioned alliance. It was an ambitious effort to secure British participation in a Europe-wide security regime intended to buttress the collective security provisions of the League Covenant. British participation in a regional security regime held out the possibility of engaging and constraining Germany.

The focus of the French delegation shifted to securing a bilateral pact with Britain only after Briand came under intense pressure to deliver such an agreement from President Millerand, the nationalist press and his own cabinet. These efforts were doomed to failure, however. The British were utterly opposed to the kind of power-political arrangement demanded by Millerand, Barthou and traditionalists in the cabinet. The draft treaty of guarantee proposed by Lloyd George's negotiating team contained no provisions for military cooperation.[148] This project would never have satisfied Briand's opponents in Paris. Millerand was also opposed to an economic conference and to a moratorium on reparations payments. Keen to assert a controlling influence on foreign policy, the president took the extraordinary measure of convening a meeting of the cabinet without Briand. Here it was decided that no Franco-British agreement could be signed without prior cabinet debate and approval.[149] This virtually ruled out an arrangement of any kind. Briand was left little choice but to resign, which he did in dramatic fashion before the chamber on 12 January 1922.[150]

Briand's effort to change the course of French security policy is instructive in three respects. First, it represents an early attempt to come to terms with changes in the normative environment of the 1920s. Briand and several of his key advisers proved willing to eschew military conventions and staff conversations in pursuit of a political entente with Britain that would allow France to engage with Germany from a position of strength. Second, the episode reveals the extent to which multilateral thinking had penetrated the highest levels of the French policy establishment nearly four years before the Locarno Accords. The concept of regional assistance accords that would include Germany and be underwritten by Franco-British cooperation would assume an increasingly central role in French thinking. Seydoux, along with two of Briand's chief collaborators in Cannes, Jules Laroche and René Massigli, would play an important role in resurrecting this approach in 1924.

---

[148] MAE, *Série Z, GB*, vol. 69, Laroche and Loucheur to Paris, 11 Jan. 1922; 'Draft of Treaty Between the Governments of the British Empire and the French Republic', 11 Jan. 1922 in Cmd. 2169, *Negotiations for an Anglo-French Pact* (although misdated 12 Jan. 1922).
[149] Millerand's pressure is clear in AN, *Archives Millerand*, 470 AP 81, 'Conférence de Cannes, 1922'; see also MAE, PA-AP 118, *Papiers Millerand*, vol. 58, Millerand to Briand (in Cannes), 8 Jan. 1922; MAE, *Série Z, GB*, vol. 69, Millerand to Briand, 11 Jan. 1922.
[150] Suarez, *Briand*, V, 406.

Finally, parliamentary debates concerning national security in late 1921 and early 1922 illuminate growing fault lines over the issue of national security within the chamber of deputies and public opinion more broadly. By late 1921 an increasing number of Radicals, led by party leader Édouard Herriot, adopted a more confident and forthright tone, rejecting the confrontational politics advocated by the nationalist–conservative bloc. The similarities between Briand's plan to enmesh Germany and the strategies for peace advocated by internationalists such as Aulard, Scelle and Ruyssen are striking. The SFIO, meanwhile, remained consistent in advocating an internationalist agenda. Party leader Léon Blum argued that a League that included Germany would constitute 'the juridical expression of the civilised world' and provide France's best hope for lasting security.[151]

Herriot expressed the views of a growing number of centre-left deputies when he stated:

> We must choose between the policy of Tardieu and that of the premier. The policy of Tardieu we know well: it is the one that goes on the attack each time a foreign policy issue arises ... Against this policy, absolute, magnificent on paper, which promises everything without ceding anything, we have another policy, one that I would call liberal, mindful of the interests of France, guaranteeing its rights, but more human and as a result more French. I choose this latter policy.[152]

Divisions within the chamber were becoming more pronounced. Briand did not undergo a sudden 'conversion' in 1921. He was no St Paul and he did not travel on the road to Damascus. He was a politician to the ends of his fingertips and was attuned to the limits of political possibility in the international environment of the post-war era. He was always more likely to opt for a policy that maximised France's negotiating options, minimised its political isolation and retained the support of its only Great Power ally. Briand was also attuned to the evolution of opinion on the centre-left. Part of his strategy in resigning was almost certainly to position himself to play a leading foreign policy role in a Radical-dominated government after the next national elections. In the mean time the Bloc national majority clamoured for a return to coercion, the balance of power and the politics of confrontation.

---

[151] Guieu, *Rameau et glaive*, 129–31; L. Blum, 'Le Bilan', *Le Populaire*, 16 Aug. 1921.
[152] Quoted in J.-B. Duroselle and A. Kaspi, *Histoire des relations internationales de 1919 à 1945* (Paris, 2001), 56.

11 The politics of confrontation

Raymond Poincaré replaced Briand as premier and foreign minister on 15 January 1922 amid expectations that he would take firm action to defend France's rights and vital interests. His return to high office was therefore welcomed by the centre and right. In the British press, conversely, it was greeted with dismay. And in Germany the reaction was so hostile that ambassador Laurent was instructed to make a formal protest to the Weimar government. The 'France first' theme of the political programme Poincaré outlined to the chamber on 19 January only reinforced widespread expectations of a return to a more traditional approach to security.[1]

These expectations would prove well founded. Balance-of-power calculations were more influential in foreign and security policy under Poincaré than at any time since the era of the Cambon Letter and Doumergue Agreement in early 1917. The rhetoric of '*gages*' returned to shape both internal and public discourse on national security. The central event of Poincaré's premiership, the occupation of the Ruhr, has long divided historians. Until recently a consensus had emerged that the occupation was in its inception a last-ditch effort to force Germany to pay reparations.[2] There can now be little doubt, however, that the Ruhr occupation was conceived as a bid to transform the European balance of power with the creation of a Rhenish or Rheno-Westphalian state. The strategy of German dismemberment gained ascendancy in late 1922.[3]

---

[1] *JO*, Chambre, *Débats*, 1922, 19 Jan. 1922; see also E. Bonnefous, *Histoire politique de la Troisième République*, vol. III: *L'Après-guerre* (Paris, 1959), 284–5; J. F. V. Keiger, *Raymond Poincaré* (Cambridge, 1996), 274–6; N. Roussellier, *Le Parlement de l'éloquence: la souveraineté de la délibération au lendemain de la Grande Guerre* (Paris, 1997), 179–82; Z. Steiner, *The Lights that Failed: European International History, 1919–1933* (Oxford, 2005), 210–11.

[2] J. Jacobson, 'Strategies of French foreign policy after World War I', *JMH*, 55 (1983), 87–9; Keiger, *Poincaré*, 294–311; S. Marks, 'Poincaré-la-peur: France and the Ruhr Crisis of 1923' in M. Alexander and K. Mouré (eds.), *Crisis and Renewal in France* (Oxford, 2002), 28–45; François Roth is more ambiguous but generally follows this interpretation in *Raymond Poincaré, un homme d'état républicain* (Paris, 2006), 419–30.

[3] G.-H. Soutou, 'L'Année 1922 et les ambiguïtés économiques du Traité de Versailles' in M. Petricioli (ed.), *A Missed Opportunity? 1922 and the Reconstruction of Europe* (Berne, 1995), 197–214; S. Jeannesson, *Poincaré, la France et la Ruhr (1922–1924)* (Strasbourg, 1998); see also R. Boyce, *The Great Interwar Crisis and the Collapse of Globalization* (London, 2009), 126–9.

At the same time, however, other aspects of security policy were less traditional in their inspiration. Poincaré and his civilian advisers remained convinced that the ultimate resolution of the reparations issue must be a mobilisation of the German debt through a vast system of international loans. This, crucially, required the participation of British and American capital and thus the cooperation of the governments in London and Washington. In Geneva, meanwhile, French representatives adopted a strategy of engagement with the discourse of arms limitation in a process that laid the groundwork for a new direction in security policy making. Even at this juncture, therefore, there were interesting tensions and contradictions in national security policy. In general terms, however, the period 1922–4 marked a return to traditional power politics. The outcome of the Franco-German struggle in the Ruhr would determine the future structure of European international politics.

I

Recent scholarship has tended to represent the differences between the policies of Briand and Poincaré as more of style than substance.[4] A detailed look at negotiations for a Franco-British pact does not support this interpretation. There were fundamental differences in the political conceptions of the two leaders. Although both attached great importance to strategic support from Britain, Poincaré sought a traditional military alliance and was not interested in Briand's idea of including Germany in a wider European security system. Poincaré was willing to cooperate with Germany on a bilateral basis only after it accepted its obligations under the Versailles Treaty. Britain's role was to be a loyal partner in this process and to support France with a military alliance.[5]

The obstacles confronting this strategy should have been clear when the French and British premiers met for the first time on 14 January 1922. Poincaré insisted that any pact take the form of a reciprocal alliance and include a military convention. He invoked pre-1914 Franco-British staff talks with approval. He was either unaware of or indifferent to the fact that in Britain these arrangements were widely considered an important cause of the war. Poincaré lectured the British prime minister that 'a guarantee pact that is not accompanied by a document indicating the number and quality of troops to be placed at the disposition of France in case of need would be, in a word, ineffective'. Lloyd George responded that if Britain promised to come to the

---

[4] Keiger, *Poincaré*, 274–86; J. F. V. Keiger, 'Raymond Poincaré' in S. Casey and J. Wright (eds.), *Mental Maps in the Era of the Two World Wars* (London, 2008), 1–21; J. Bariéty, *Les Relations franco-allemandes après la première guerre mondiale* (Paris, 1977), 91–2; Marks, 'Poincaré-la-peur', 29–30; Boyce, *Great Interwar Crisis*, 141.

[5] See esp. R. Poincaré, 'Chronique de la quinzaine', *RDDM*, 81 (May–Jun. 1921), 709–20; P. Jackson, 'French Security and a British "continental commitment" after the First World War', *EHR*, 126, 519 (2011), 362–5.

aid of France, the French government 'must have confidence in her word and this must suffice'. If France demanded more, he warned, a pact was impossible.[6]

Poincaré misinterpreted this as an initial bargaining position. With Peretti's assistance, he drafted a nineteen-page memorandum outlining 'Conditions for a Franco-British pact' that called for joint military planning and a pledge to 'concert together' in the event of German aggression in eastern Europe.[7] This memo formed the basis of a new draft treaty forwarded to the British government in late January.[8] Saint-Aulaire, who never mastered English during his time in London and badly misjudged British attitudes towards an alliance, compounded Poincaré's ill-judged initiative by suggesting that the military convention could take the traditional form of a secret exchange of letters appended to the treaty.[9]

These moves marked a major departure from previous policy. Where Briand understood that a full-blown military alliance was impossible, Poincaré aimed at an arrangement similar to the Franco-Belgian agreement. Where Briand was typically vague about the structure and functioning of the multilateral security regime he proposed, Poincaré demanded detailed arrangements for military collaboration. Where Briand sensed the need to adapt French security strategy to the prevailing norms of the early 1920s, Poincaré refused to accept anything less than a traditional alliance accompanied by a military convention.

Poincaré's strategy had no hope of succeeding. No British government would or could accept a pre-1914-style bid to organise the European balance of power against Germany. Lloyd George was willing to offer at best a limited guarantee to induce France's cooperation in a revision of the international economic order and an international disarmament regime. The British prime minister vowed to oppose 'handing over Europe to the tender mercies of M. Poincaré and the French militarists'. His cabinet colleagues agreed.[10] Negotiations for a security pact sputtered along until the end of June 1922. The Poincaré government decided eventually, on the recommendation of the war ministry, to drop the formal demand for a military convention in favour of a

---

[6] MAE, *Série Z, GB*, vol. 69, 'Compte-rendu d'une conversation entre M. Poincaré et M. Lloyd George à l'ambassade d'Angleterre, le 14 janvier 1922'; British record in TNA-PRO, FO 371, 8249, W528/50/17, 'Meeting between M. Lloyd George and M. Poincaré at British embassy, Paris'.
[7] MAE, *Série Z, GB*, vol. 70, 'Conditions d'un pacte franco-britannique', 23 Jan. 1922 (with Poincaré's annotations); also 'Au Sujet des pactes franco-anglais et franco-belge' (Peretti de la Rocca for Poincaré), 28 Jan. 1922 and 'Alliance franco-anglaise' (Poincaré), 29 Jan. 1922.
[8] TNA-PRO, FO 371 8250, W963/50/17, 'French Draft of Proposed Anglo-French Treaty', 26 Jan. 1922 and TNA-PRO, CAB/24/132, 'Memorandum concerning the amendments to be made in the British draft treaty', circulated to the British cabinet 1 Feb. 1922.
[9] MAE, *Série Z, GB*, vol. 70, 'Négociations relatives à l'alliance', 1 Feb. 1922.
[10] TNA-PRO, CAB/23/30, CC 44/22, 10 Aug. 1922; CAB/24/133, CP3760, 'The Anglo-French Agreement' (Curzon), 17 Feb. 1922.

tacit understanding that staff conversations would take place as a matter of course.[11] But intractable differences remained, and were exacerbated by mutual recriminations over the failure of the Genoa Conference, the Rapallo Treaty between Germany and Soviet Russia and a mounting crisis in Turkey. The window of opportunity for a Franco-British security pact had long passed when Saint-Aulaire observed that British public opinion considered 'our version of the pact to be a war machine'. By the end of April 1922 he judged that 'a veritable psychological divorce' existed between France and Britain'.[12] The Poincaré government continued its pursuit of a British commitment even after formal exchanges on the subject ceased. From mid-1922, however, the forum for this effort shifted from bilateral negotiations through traditional diplomatic channels to debates over disarmament in Geneva.

A storm was gathering in Franco-British relations. From the French perspective, the British government seemed intent on destroying the architecture of the peace treaty. Britain refused to agree to meaningful measures of control over German finances, but instead placed unrelenting pressure on the French government to agree to a lengthy moratorium.[13] French policy makers were further aggrieved by the Balfour Note, which stipulated that Britain would not write off the war debts it was owed by France and other Allies unless the USA did the same. The French pointed out the incongruities in a British policy that placed enormous pressure on France to agree to a reduction in the German reparations debt while at the same time demanding payment in full for monies loaned in a common war effort against that country.[14] From the point of view of the Lloyd George government, however, French policy makers seemed unwilling or unable to acknowledge that the treaty system was unworkable and in need of revision. Hopes that the Genoa Conference could launch the process of revision and stimulate European recovery were to be stymied by the suffocating conditions the Poincaré government attached to French participation. Bitter disagreements over policy towards Turkey led to a full-blown crisis in September 1922 and to the fall of Lloyd George. But the advent of a Conservative government changed the form rather than the substance of the Franco-British *mésentente*.[15] The progressive radicalisation of French foreign

---

[11] SHD-DAT, *Fonds Clemenceau*, 6N 82–2, 'Note sur les clauses militaires du pacte franco-anglais', Maginot (war ministry) to Poincaré, 9 Feb. 1922; MAE, *Série Z, GB*, vol. 70, 'Alliance franco-britannique: arrangements entre les état-majors', 21 Feb. 1922 and vol. 71, 'Négociations relatives au pacte franco-britannique (1921–1922)', 19 Nov. 1923.
[12] MAE, *Série Z, GB*, vol. 71, 'Au Sujet du pacte franco-anglais' (citing Jacques Bardoux), 30 Apr. 1922.
[13] Boyce, *Great Interwar Crisis*, 126–7; M. Trachtenberg, *Reparation in World Politics: France and European Economic Diplomacy, 1916–1923* (New York, 1980), 244–7.
[14] MAE, PA-AP 118, *Papiers Millerand*, vol. 6, 'Note: position de la France à l'égard de la Note Balfour', 17 Aug. 1922.
[15] C. Fink, *The Genoa Conference: European Diplomacy, 1921–1922* (Syracuse, 1993), 69–105; P. M. H. Bell, *France and Britain, 1900–1940: Entente and Estrangement* (London, 1996), 137–9.

and security policy over the course of 1922 can only be fully understood within the context of the deterioration of relations with Britain.

II

This radicalisation was not inevitable when Poincaré took power. His vision of future security did not initially rule out either flexibility over reparations or future industrial collaboration with Germany. He advocated using the legal options built into the treaty to give Germany the opportunity to demonstrate its good faith. In terms of reparations, Poincaré had long distinguished between the Reich's 'theoretical debt' (the total sum demanded) and a final sum and payments schedule based on its ability to pay:

> I would, for my part, be ready to say to Germany that I will examine with 'benevolence' its capacity to pay in order to fix the sums that the Allies will in reality demand. But I would nonetheless conserve the theoretical claim against the possibility of German non-execution of its obligations. The claim could constitute a precious weapon in relation to both Germany and our Allies.[16]

The above quotation illuminates two key aspects of Poincaré's policy conception. First, he understood Germany's 'theoretical debt' as a source of leverage in obtaining treaty compliance. Once the German government demonstrated the will to comply with the treaty, France could discuss its capacity to fulfil its obligations. Crucially, however, Poincaré would prove willing to use force to create the will to comply.[17] Second, the French premier understood that any final resolution of the reparations issue would depend on multilateral negotiations with Britain and the USA in which France would need whatever leverage it could secure. His aim was to mobilise the German debt in a vast international credit operation that linked reparations with war debts.

Yet there was more to the premier's vision of security than a legalistic commitment to treaty fulfilment and the internationalisation of the reparations problem. Poincaré, it is worth remembering, had supported the idea of a buffer state in 1919. He had also criticised the decision to set the deadline for evacuating the Rhineland at 1935, which he argued would leave France without a *gage* to ensure German reparations payments. These concerns remained central to his approach to security in 1922. Poincaré and others among the senior policy elite were haunted not only by the 1935 deadline for Rhineland evacuation but also by the fact that German coal and coke shipments to France under the treaty regime were scheduled to cease in 1930. After this date French iron and steel would be in a situation of dependency. The German steel

---

[16] MAE, PA-AP 118, *Papiers Millerand*, vol. 46, 'Conversation de Cheysson avec M. Poincaré, le 8 janvier 1921' and 'Vignon note: M. Poincaré a dit à Cheyson il y a 12 jours', 20 Jan. 1921.
[17] See also S. Jeannesson, 'Pourquoi la France a-t-elle occupé la Ruhr?', *VS*, 51 (1996), 57–8.

industry, meanwhile, had managed to free itself of its pre-war dependency on Lorraine iron ore with purchasing arrangements in Scandinavia.[18] When Britain proved unwilling to support French projects to impose financial controls on Germany, officials in Paris began to consider alternative strategies that would secure control over Ruhr coal and a military presence on the Left Bank beyond the deadlines established by the treaty. The link between extracting reparations from Germany and a forward policy in the Rhineland re-emerged in the second half of 1922 to become a central pillar of French policy.

If the steady erosion of the Entente was an essential precondition for France's Ruhr policy, even more important was the evaporation of all indications of German good will. Almost from the moment it had accepted the London Schedule, the Weimar government had embarked on a policy of destroying its currency. Unwilling to cut spending or raise taxes, the only way it could stay afloat was through a vast increase in the amount of paper marks in circulation. Rich industrialists were protected from the effects of inflation, however, because the government also failed to apply exchange controls or restrict the flow of capital from Germany. From the French perspective, this exercise in bad faith was compounded by repeated demands for a lengthy moratorium on reparations payments.[19]

The result was a growing sense that a Franco-German showdown was inevitable. 'Whether it is in the realm of reparations or military clauses, the Treaty of Versailles is currently defunct,' noted the DAPC. 'Germany has placed itself in a position where it will be materially impossible for us to gain satisfaction of our rights under the treaty for years to come.' Planning for a move into the Ruhr began to gather momentum again in the spring of 1922.[20] By May of that year internal correspondence began to refer to 'our future operation in the Ruhr' as if it were a foregone conclusion. In July Poincaré ordered the creation of an inter-ministerial committee under Seydoux's chairmanship to plan the operation.[21] Even relative moderates concluded that a trial of force was necessary to reset Franco-German relations by forcing Germany to accept its treaty obligations. 'We have at last moved beyond the false position of the last two years,' Seydoux observed in mid-August, 'and rather than continue to pursue a policy of empty threats and weakness towards Germany, we can

---

[18] MAE, PA-AP 261, *Papiers Seydoux*, vol. 26, 'Question des réparations', 24 Jul. 1922; see also Jeannesson, *Ruhr*, 21–33, 411–12 and Bariéty, *Relations franco-allemandes*, 150–71.

[19] MAE, PA-AP 261, *Papiers Seydoux*, vol. 26, 'Note: question des réparations', 24 Jul. 1922; 'Emprunt international allemand', 8 Aug. 1922; 'La Question des réparations pendant l'année 1922', 28 Nov. 1922.

[20] MAE, RC, Série B81–82, vol. 141, 'Note' (DAPC), 20 Nov. 1922; vol. 69, 'Rapport sur les modalités d'exploitation de la Ruhr', 2 May 1922 and 'Accord entre les mesures militaires et économiques à prendre dans la Ruhr', Maginot (war minister) to Poincaré, 17 Jun. 1922; Jeannesson, *Ruhr*, 75–107.

[21] MAE, RC, Série B81–82, vol. 69, 'Mesures économiques à prendre dans la Ruhr', Poincaré circular, 12 Jul. 1922 and 'Conférence relative aux mesures économiques et financières éventuelles à envisager en cas d'occupation du Bassin de la Ruhr', 9 Aug. 1922.

now mark our determination to act if necessary by force.' But he also observed that the ultimate goal must be 'energetic collaboration' once 'normal relations' were re-established with Germany.[22]

Planning for the Ruhr inevitably stimulated enthusiasm for a forward policy in the Rhineland. Under Briand the aim was to maintain the threat of a 'Rhenish solution' to compel German treaty compliance and to maintain pressure on Britain for a Franco-British security pact.[23] Under Poincaré, however, plans for an autonomous buffer state became a central feature of an ambitious strategy to transform the strategic balance in Europe.

There were three central pillars to French policy as it evolved over the course of 1922. The first was an ambitious programme of international loans to restore German solvency and guarantee reparations payments. The second was the seizure of 'productive *gages*' in the Ruhr and Rhineland to ensure payment in the interim. The third was an alteration of the political and territorial make-up of Germany with the creation of an autonomous polity on its western frontier with France and Belgium. The premier and his advisers seemed unwilling to recognise that the first pillar was fundamentally incompatible with the second and third.

One of Poincaré's first policy initiatives was to request that the reparations commission 'study the question of a large-scale operation based on international loans, which will provide a positive and practical solution to the problem of reparations'.[24] The strategy, inherited from Poincaré's predecessors, remained to embed Germany's reparation debt in a wider system of international credit. France, it was assumed, would receive either a large lump-sum payment from Germany or priority in payments after order had been restored to the German economy. As Trachtenberg has noted, the commercialisation of German reparations obligations on the international markets remained 'a constant and central aspect of Poincaré's policy right down to the eve of the Ruhr occupation'.[25] Poincaré's finance minister, Charles de Lasteyrie, argued repeatedly that commercialisation of the German debt was 'the only practical solution to the reparation problem'.[26] On 4 April Poincaré approved the participation of French financiers in a 'committee of bankers' enlisted to discuss conditions for an international loan to Germany. The results of this consultation were not promising. The committee, which included Americans Charles Dawes and J. P. Morgan, recommended a reduction of the German

---

[22] MAE, PA-AP 261, *Papiers Seydoux*, vol. 26, 'Note pour le président du conseil: rapports franco-allemands et entretiens Stinnes-Lubersac', 17 Aug. 1922.
[23] Loucheur explained this to Foch: see *Carnets secrets*, 'Entrevue avec Foch vers le 12 octobre 1921', 95–6.
[24] MAE, PA-AP 118, *Papiers Millerand*, vol. 20, Poincaré to Dubois, 2 Feb. 1922.
[25] Trachtenberg observes that 'in the archival sources there are continued references to a loan scheme throughout 1922': *Reparation*, 237 and 390n3.
[26] MAE, PA-AP 261, *Papiers Seydoux*, vol. 25, de Lasteyrie to Seydoux, 23 Mar. 1922; *DDF, 1922*, II, #105, 'Note de M. de Lasteyrie', 13 Aug. 1922.

reparations debt, the stabilisation of Germany's currency and a realistic policy of tax rises and spending cuts. But it also insisted that lending institutions must have priority over reparations when it came to German repayment.[27]

The French response to this news was similar to that of Clémentel in 1918: mounting evidence that a loan strategy was unworkable was ignored and planning remained unchanged. The premier refused to consider any reduction in Germany's 'theoretical debt' without the guarantee that France would receive immediate and substantive payments in return. 'I am counting on an international loan,' Poincaré advised British leaders at a summit meeting where the bankers' conclusions were discussed.[28] The fact that such an arrangement was impossible does not seem to have affected the calculations of senior policy makers. Both Poincaré and de Lasteyrie consistently reiterated the need for international credit in any durable resolution of the reparations over the remainder of 1922. 'Sanctions are not a long-term solution to the problem of reparations,' the premier acknowledged before the senate on 29 June. 'An international loan [to Germany] constitutes the only means to bring about a final and satisfactory resolution to this question.'[29] At a gathering of senior officials on 13 October, de Lasteyrie argued that 'France can only get out of the present situation by means of an [international] loan'. Poincaré underlined the importance of mobilising Germany's external debt again on 23 November and returned to this theme on 3 December.[30]

Emphasis on the need for 'productive guarantees', meanwhile, increased as frustration grew with the Allied and especially British refusal to agree to rigorous financial controls on Germany. By May 1922 planning was under way for a programme to extract payments directly from the German economy. Measures envisaged included requisitioning certain types of government revenue as reparations payment, collecting taxes on coal production and re-establishing the customs barrier on the Rhine but extending it to encompass the industrial basin of the Ruhr.[31] These measures were of limited value, however, because they would produce increasingly worthless paper marks. To secure more tangible benefits, Seydoux and his long-time friend Émile Coste,

---

[27] *DDF, 1922*, I, #429, 'Notes prises au cours d'une conversation entre M. Poincaré et M. Lloyd George à 10 Downing Street', 19 Jun. 1922; MAE, PA-AP 261, *Papiers Seydoux*, vol. 26, 'Emprunt international allemand', 8 Aug. 1922; Bariéty, *Relations franco-allemandes*, 94–5.

[28] *DDF, 1922*, I, #429, 'Notes prises au cours d'une conversation entre M. Poincaré et M. Lloyd George à 10 Downing Street', 19 Jun. 1922.

[29] *JO*, Sénat, *Débats*, 29 Jun. 1922.

[30] MAE, PA-AP 118, *Papiers Millerand*, vol. 23, 'Réunion tenue chez M. le Président du conseil le 13 octobre 1922'; vol. 24, 'Réunion chez le Président du Conseil, 23 Nov. 1922 and 'Réunion tenue le 3 décembre 1922 dans le cabinet du président du conseil: préparations des réunions de Londres et Bruxelles'; Jeannesson, *Ruhr*, 117–21; Trachtenberg, *Reparation*, 237–8.

[31] MAE, *RC*, Série B81–82, vol. 69, 'Accord entre mesures militaires et économiques à prendre dans la Ruhr', 17 Jun. 1922; Trachtenberg, *Reparation*, 249–65.

The politics of confrontation 399

inspecteur général des mines at the ministry of public works, elaborated plans for the direct seizure of Prussian state mines and the forests in the Ruhr. They also advocated securing controlling interests in chemical and even aviation firms in both the Ruhr and the Left Bank. All planning was aimed at grouping the occupied Left Bank and the Ruhr basin together as a single economic space in order to minimise economic disruption and maximise the exploitation of the region.[32]

The project drawn up by Seydoux and Coste were approved at the first meeting of the inter-ministerial planning committee for the Ruhr on 9 August 1922.[33] The most important economic objective was unquestionably control of coal and coke production in the Ruhr. Ruhr state mines were estimated to produce 12.6 million tonnes of coal and 3 million tonnes of coke annually. Possession of these mines, Seydoux noted, would 'singularly facilitate the long-term resolution of the question of metallurgical coke for France'.[34] Seydoux's commitment to Franco-German economic cooperation was giving way to a more pessimistic vision of the future and the conviction that France must take permanent measures to redress the imbalance in industrial power in relation to Germany.

Such measures would not overcome the problem of Germany's plummeting currency, however. Unless this situation was rectified, the sums raised in customs duties and taxes would be worthless. The initial solution envisaged was for the French ministry of finance to print and guarantee paper marks that would not lose their value in the occupied territories.[35] This project was superseded first by plans to introduce the franc into the region and then to create a Rhenish currency. The latter project was eventually taken in hand by Jean Tannery, the head of the German section at the finance ministry.[36] There was thus a radicalising logic to French planning for *gages productifs*: for an occupation to be effective, the Ruhr and Left Bank would need to be grouped

---

[32] MAE, *RC*, Série B81–82, vol. 69, 'Note pour M. de Peretti: question de la Ruhr' (Seydoux note), 30 May 1922 and 'Études entreprises en mai 1922 en vue de l'occupation éventuelle de la Ruhr' (Coste), 15 Jun. 1922.

[33] MAE, *RC*, Série B81–82, vol. 69, 'Conférence relative aux mesures économiques et financières éventuelles à envisager en cas d'occupation du Bassin de la Ruhr', 9 and 10 Aug. 1922 and 'Note au sujet des mesures financières envisagées en cas d'occupation de la Ruhr', 11 Aug. 1922.

[34] MAE, PA-AP 261, *Papiers Seydoux*, vol. 26, 'Note sur la Ruhr' (summarising conclusions of the inter-ministerial Ruhr committee), 19 Aug. 1922.

[35] MAE, *RC*, Série B81–82, vol. 69, 'Conférence relative aux mesures économiques et financières éventuelles à envisager en cas d'occupation du Bassin de la Ruhr', 9 and 10 Aug. 1922; 'Note au sujet des mesures financiers envisagées en cas d'occupation de la Ruhr', 11 Aug. 1922; 'Plan schématique d'action militaire et économiques en cas de carence de l'Allemagne', 16 Aug. 1922; and esp. PA-AP 261, *Papiers Seydoux*, vol. 26, 'Note sur la Ruhr', 19 Aug. 1922.

[36] MAE, PA-AP 118, *Papiers Millerand*, vol. 24, 'Note pour le président du conseil: question des réparations', 21 Nov. 1922; MAE, *RC*, Série B81–82, vol. 141, 'Note pour le ministre. Occupation de la Ruhr: conséquences au point de vue financier', 23 Dec. 1922.

together in a single bloc; for this bloc to be stable and productive, it would need its own currency; these measures, in turn, pointed towards the economic and political separation of the Rhenish and Westphalian regions from the rest of Germany. If France's avowed aims in occupying the Ruhr were short term, internal planning envisaged long-term control of the economic life of the occupied regions and a revision of the political status quo.

This rationale was identified and endorsed by General Degoutte in the Rhineland. Degoutte stressed the possibilities a Ruhr occupation would open up if it could be combined with his gradualist strategy for Rhenish autonomy. He urged that the initial stage of the operation must be 'a simple seizure of a "gage"' and that 'for the moment no political consequences should be drawn from it'. Precipitate action, such as an attempt to introduce a Rhenish currency, would 'provoke the immediate hostility of Rhenish parties and create an anti-French agitation among workers that would otherwise remain neutral'. Degoutte recommended instead the gradual approach that French authorities had pursued since 1919: 'It is only later and as a result of a prolonged occupation of the Ruhr that we can exercise an effective action, implemented slowly, prudently, with a view to the political reorganisation of Germany on a federalist basis.'[37] For Degoutte, such a reorganisation remained the fundamental condition for France's security. 'Let us complete this occupation with a series of administrative, financial and economic measures ... And we will not fail to achieve our goal: the Rhineland will separate from Prussia, perhaps from the Reich, as a ripe fruit falls from a tree.'[38] The long-term aim was to overturn the European strategic balance. 'From the point of view of our security,' Degoutte judged, 'an occupation would be preferable to [an international] loan.'[39]

Tirard, predictably, endorsed Degoutte's assessment and recommended a strategy of 'progressive penetration' beginning with a modest and unobtrusive presence in the first instance. He predicted that German authorities would resist any French measures. More extensive and intrusive steps could then be taken to assume control of the local administration and purge the existing civil service. 'In this way the total autonomy of these regions will come about as a result of the actions of the German government.'[40] Tirard's conception of progressive penetration was central to the final plan for the Ruhr occupation developed by Foch's staff on 20 November 1922. This plan envisaged a three-phase operation, with the second and third phases being triggered by German defiance. It is interesting that at this point Marshal Foch counselled caution. He warned that an occupation would be difficult and would be unlikely to pay dividends in

---

[37] MAE, RC, Série B81–82, vol. 69, Degoutte to Foch, Maginot and Tirard (forwarded to Poincaré by Tirard), 19 May 1922.
[38] Quoted in Trachtenberg, *Reparation*, 266.
[39] MAE, RC, Série B81–82, vol. 69, Degoutte to Foch, 19 May 1922.
[40] MAE, RC, Série B81–82, vol. 141, 'Note' (Tirard), 24 Nov. 1922.

the short term. 'We must not undertake the execution of this programme', he warned, 'unless we are resolved to see it through to the end.' Foch, who never attributed the same importance to the Ruhr as he did to the Left Bank, feared a lack of resolve.[41]

There was an undeniable hardening of views elsewhere within the policy establishment. Minister of public works Yves Le Trocquer reminded his colleagues that German coke deliveries under the treaty would end in less than ten years. Once freed of its treaty obligations, he warned, Germany's central aim would be 'to destroy our metallurgical industry by refusing to sell us coke or providing it at a prohibitive price'.[42] France must therefore 'remove Germany's ability to annihilate the fruits of our victory'. For Le Trocquer it was 'absolutely essential' that France secure 'independent access to coke beyond the period fixed by the treaties'. This could be accomplished either by taking direct possession of state mines in the Ruhr or gaining a controlling interest in this industry under the rubric of reparation.[43] War minister André Maginot approved of Degoutte's analysis. He consistently advocated the occupation and comprehensive exploitation of both the Ruhr and the Rhineland.[44] Although Millerand's role has almost certainly been exaggerated by historians relying on contemporary accounts and his unpublished memoirs, it is clear that the president favoured occupying the Ruhr to overturn the economic and territorial terms of a peace settlement he had long considered unenforceable.[45]

Even Seydoux now admitted that a more traditional response might be necessary, even if he continued to prefer a multilateral solution. Along with Tannery, he recommended reducing the total German reparations debt from 132 to 75 billion gold marks. This would facilitate an international loan to restore order to German finances and pave the way for future reparations payments.[46] But he recognised that his scheme was impossible without German cooperation. If this was refused Seydoux advised that

> it would be useless and even dangerous to pursue such a programme. We have essentially no interest in strengthening the German economy if it is not tied to reparations in such a manner that will ensure that we will not be threatened with

---

[41] MAE, PA-AP 118, *Papiers Millerand*, vol. 96, 'Note' (Foch's plan for the occupation), 20 Nov. 1922; see also Jeannesson, *Ruhr*, 114–16; and esp. J.-C. Notin, *Foch* (Paris, 2008), 512–15.
[42] Quoted in Jeannesson, *Ruhr*, 91.
[43] MAE, PA-AP 118, *Papiers Millerand*, vol. 96, 'Occupation de la Ruhr', Le Trocquer to Poincaré, 4 Dec. 1922.
[44] MAE, PA-AP 118, *Papiers Millerand*, vol. 96, Maginot to Poincaré, 17 Jul. 1922; 'Dossier concernant la Ruhr', n.d.; 'Notes de Millerand', 27 Nov. 1922.
[45] For Millerand's account see AN, 470 AP 1, 'Mes souvenirs (1859–1941)', 112–15; see also M. M. Farrar, *Principled Pragmatist: The Political Career of Alexandre Millerand* (Oxford, 1991), 338–40; and Jeannesson, *Ruhr*, 93–5, 115–17, 242–3.
[46] MAE, PA-AP 261, *Papiers Seydoux*, vol. 26, 'Note pour le président du conseil: question des réparations', 21 Nov. 1922; also PA-AP 118, *Papiers Millerand*, vol. 24, 'Note' (Seydoux and Tannery), 30 Nov. 1922.

future bids for economic or political hegemony. If we do not receive such guarantees we must, on the contrary, disinterest ourselves in the fate of Germany.

Seydoux predicted that, if Germany descended into political and economic chaos, 'the population of the Left Bank of the Rhine will be happy to accept our assistance'. Control of coal and coke in the Ruhr, meanwhile, would provide effective leverage for France to shape the political future of the region.[47] In November 1922 even Seydoux was willing to contemplate the traditional strategy of security based on the destruction of German power.

Poincaré's commitment to this strategy is no longer in doubt. The premier had been preparing parliamentary and public opinion for the possibility of a Ruhr operation since April 1922. In public speeches and before parliament he insisted on France's resolve to act alone if need be.[48] The principle of independent French action was approved at a cabinet meeting in Rambouillet on 16 August. Dubois, who had been reluctant to court isolation on the reparations commission, was replaced as French delegate by the more hardline Barthou.[49] As detailed plans for the exploitation of the Rheno-Westphalian economic space evolved, the emphasis of French policy shifted gradually towards constructing a strong legal and public-relations case for an occupation, as well as convincing the Belgian government to take part. Meeting with the Belgian premier and foreign minister on 23 November, Poincaré insisted that a German default, or a decision to grant Germany a moratorium, must be accompanied by guarantees. 'Ultimately,' he observed, 'there is only one true guarantee and that is coal.' This meant occupying the Ruhr. Belgian premier Theunis asked point blank if a move against the Ruhr was a cover for 'an annexationist or separatist policy towards Germany'. Poincaré denied that French policy was in any way annexationist. 'But it would be another thing to have a Rhineland without Prussians,' he added. 'Such an entity would once again constitute a neutral zone in its sympathies, whose population would become attached to us.'[50]

A French bid to transform the strategic balance emerges clearly from the record of a high-level meeting convened at the Élysée Palace on 27 November 1922. Millerand's notes on this meeting, held back from researchers for almost ninety years, reveal that the Ruhr occupation was understood as an opportunity to alter the political status of Germany.[51] In attendance were Poincaré, de Lasteyrie, Maginot, Le Trocquer, Barthou, Foch, Degoutte, Coste, Tirard and Charles Reibel. Foch's relatively cautious occupation plan was adopted.

---

[47] MAE, PA-AP 261, *Papiers Seydoux*, 'Note pour le président du conseil: question des réparations', 21 Nov. 1922.
[48] Keiger, *Poincaré*, 288–94; Bonnefous, *Après-guerre*, 300–42.
[49] Jeannesson, *Ruhr*, 94–6.
[50] MAE, PA-AP 118, *Papiers Millerand*, vol. 24, 'Réunion chez le président du conseil', 23 Nov. 1922.
[51] Ludwig Zimmermann accessed this material during the Second World War and used it in *Frankreichs Ruhrpolitik* (Göttingen, 1971); see also Jeannesson, *Ruhr*, 115–16.

Poincaré stressed his desire to avoid a break with the British. Tirard then raised the issue of Germany's response to an occupation of the Ruhr. He outlined two possibilities: Germany would either accept the occupation or mount a campaign of resistance based on strike action. In the first case Germany would continue to pay public expenditure and the occupation could be limited to the fiscal and industrial exploitation anticipated in French plans. In the second case, the outcome Tirard clearly anticipated, France would need to assume responsibility for public expenditure and 'the operation would become profitable only little by little'. The outcome, he predicted, would be that 'the occupied zones would become an autonomous state: threats would doubtless force the Reich to accept this. The Left Bank of the Rhine represents one-tenth of the entire Reich, more with Essen.' Poincaré concluded the meeting with the observation that 'by March or April we will witness the disaggregation of Germany'.[52]

There was a fundamental tension between the traditional character of this strategy and the long-term aim of resolving the reparations problem with an ambitious programme of international loans. De Lasteyrie underlined this tension in his criticisms of planning for the Ruhr. He warned that plans to introduce a new currency into the occupied territories would 'provoke protests from all over the world' and thus 'undermine prospects for mobilising the German debt through a series of external loans'.[53] De Lasteyrie held to this line of argument consistently over the final months of 1922. The commercialisation of German reparations, he insisted, would be possible only after France had withdrawn from the Ruhr. He also pointed out the contradiction between granting a moratorium and seizing 'productive guarantees': 'we cannot do everything at once, accord Germany a moratorium so that it can recover while at the same time depriving it of its principal resources'.[54]

De Lasteyrie's criticisms underline the incoherence of security policy at this juncture. The international mobilisation of reparations and the attenuation of inter-Allied war debts were central features of the French programme presented to the Allied conference in Paris on 2 January 1923. This plan presented financial controls as a 'collateral' that the Allies would be obliged to demand in return for loans to Germany.[55] This fundamentally internationalist solution to the reparations problem was incompatible with traditional plans to create an

---

[52] MAE, PA-AP 118, *Papiers Millerand*, vol. 96, 'Notes de Millerand', 27 Nov. 1922. This volume was recently integrated into the Millerand papers; the French word Poincaré used was 'désorganisation', which Jeannesson (citing from the same document) translates into English as 'disintegration': see S. Jeannesson, 'French Policy in the Rhineland', *D&S*, 16, 3 (2005), 483; see also his comprehensive analysis in *Ruhr*, 115–17.
[53] MAE, RC, Série B81–82, vol. 69, de Lasteyrie to Poincaré, 24 Aug. 1924.
[54] MAE, PA-AP 118, *Papiers Millerand*, vol. 24, 'Réunion tenue chez le président du conseil le 17 décembre 1922'; also 'Réunion tenue le 3 décembre dans le cabinet du président du conseil: préparation des réunions de Londres et Bruxelles' and 'Réparations', 4 Dec. 1922.
[55] *DDF*, *1923*, I, #1, 'Note du département: programme de la conférence', 2 Jan. 1923; On the British position see E. O'Riordan, *Britain and the Ruhr Crisis* (London, 2001), 13–36.

autonomous buffer state. It is likely that Poincaré and many of his closest advisers hoped that this incoherence would be resolved by the looming trial of strength. The decision to move against the Ruhr was much more than an exercise in treaty enforcement. Its objective was to bring about the long-awaited showdown that would determine the true victors of the First World War.

III

The Ruhr episode began when engineers of the Franco-Belgian Mission interalliée de contrôle des usines et des mines (MICUM) entered Essen to impose Allied supervision of the local coal industry. The MICUM officials were accompanied by French and Belgian troops charged with ensuring their security. The occupation almost immediately encountered determined resistance from industrialists, miners and railway workers, who refused to cooperate. Waves of strikes led to the extension and militarisation of the operation, which eventually saw more than 47,000 French soldiers deployed around the industrial basin. The German government declared a policy of 'passive resistance', which it attempted to fund by printing billions of increasingly worthless paper marks.[56]

'We are going in search of coal and that is all,' Poincaré declared disingenuously before the chamber as French engineers and soldiers moved into the Ruhr on 11 January 1923. 'We have no desire to strangle Germany or to bring about its ruin.'[57] This and other misleading public declarations made by the premier in early 1923 serve to highlight one of the most striking aspects of France's Ruhr policy: the extent to which it was undertaken in relative isolation from parliamentary and public opinion.

Planning and decision making for the Ruhr occupation were concentrated within a surprisingly small group of civil servants and elected officials. Discussion of public attitudes was almost absent in this process. Nor indeed was there systematic consultation with France's industrial elites. This constituency was divided in any case between the iron and steel magnates on the Comité des forges who were broadly favourable to the occupation and the coal producers on the Comité des houillères who were predictably hostile to any project that threatened to flood France with relatively inexpensive energy.[58] Poincaré claimed that the overwhelming majority of French opinion supported a policy of firmness – a claim that seemed to be validated when the chamber

---

[56] C. Fischer, *The Ruhr Crisis, 1923–1924* (Oxford, 2003); Jeannesson, *Ruhr*, 151–85.
[57] Quoted in Bonnefous, *Après-guerre*, 347–8; see also Poincaré's *audition* before the chamber's foreign affairs commission: AN, C/14635, *CAEAN*, 19 Feb. 1923.
[58] Jeannesson, 'Pourquoi', 62–4; Jeannesson, *Ruhr*, 141–3 and 366–71; see also J.-N. Jeanneney, *François de Wendel en république: l'argent et pouvoir 1914–1940* (Paris, 1976), 111–15 and 148–69; Bariéty, *Relations franco-allemandes*, 171.

approved the occupation of the Ruhr by a margin of 452 to 72 in a vote of confidence on 11 January 1923.[59]

Yet behind the veneer of parliamentary support, fissures were emerging within the electoral majority of the Bloc national. Poincaré was a controversial figure. Praised on the right as the 'inventor' of the Union sacrée, on the left and in the international press it was alleged that he bore a heavy responsibility for the outbreak of war in 1914.[60] From the outset, moreover, Poincaré's parliamentary style differed sharply from that of his predecessor. Where the rhetoric of Briand had aimed at drawing a line under the war, Poincaré returned to the discourses of national struggle and sacred union. France, he warned, 'must not blindly believe in the existence of two Germanys'. He invoked 'the sacred character of the peace treaty' which had been 'signed in the blood of our soldiers'.[61]

These arguments had no impact on French Socialists. The SFIO denounced nearly all aspects of the Versailles Treaty and bitterly opposed an occupation of the Ruhr. Over the course of 1922 both Léon Blum (the party's leader and chief spokesperson on foreign affairs) and Vincent Auriol (an expert on financial issues) had warned that financial collapse in Germany posed a threat to democracy in that country and thus to European peace. They argued for a reduction of Germany's reparations debt and an international programme of loans to stabilise its currency. These were presented as vital preconditions for a wider programme of European political and economic reconstruction that was the only solid foundation for security.[62]

Poincaré's rhetorical strategy was not aimed at Socialists, however. Patriotic Radicals were his target. The premier's discursive strategy presented a significant challenge for Radical Party leader, Édouard Herriot. Like a growing number of Radicals, Herriot was uncomfortable with the confrontational posture France had assumed since the advent of Poincaré. He believed that Imperial Germany was responsible for causing the war and deserved to be punished. But he also favoured multilateral solutions to the problem of European security, and argued consistently that peace and security depended on the democratic transformation of Germany. Like Briand, Herriot distinguished between the democratic 'good Germany', on the one hand, and the 'holy alliance of coal, iron, electricity and paper' that made up the 'imperialist Germany', on the other. 'We must do everything we can', he judged, 'to

---

[59] Bonnefous, *Après-guerre*, 347–8; Keiger, *Poincaré*, 295–7.
[60] A. Barros and F. Guelton, 'Les Imprévus de l'histoire instrumentalisée: le livre jaune de 1914 et les Documents diplomatiques français sur les origines de la Grande Guerre', *RHD*, 1 (2006), 7–23.
[61] Quotations from Roussellier, *Parlement de l'éloquence*, 182 and 200 respectively.
[62] L. Blum, 'Le Change et les réparations' and 'En Allemagne', *Le Populaire*, 5 Oct. 1921 and 12 Jul. 1922 respectively; see also R. Gombin, *Les Socialistes et la guerre: la SFIO et la politique étrangère entre les deux guerres mondiales* (The Hague, 1970), 22–44; T. Judt, *La Reconstruction du parti socialiste, 1921–26* (Paris, 1976), 114–21; S. Berstein, *Léon Blum* (Paris, 2006), 233–49.

support the consolidation of democracy [in Germany] and declare peace to all Germans of good will.'[63] A member of the AFSDN Council, he consistently argued for a greater role for the League of Nations in international politics. 'There are two general trends,' he observed before the Radical Party's executive committee in January 1922, 'the trend towards force and the idealist trend towards international solidarity ... we must not forget our tradition, we must not forget that we are Jacobins.' Herriot's approach to peace and security was a classic Radical combination of patriotism and internationalism.[64]

Herriot's problem was that the internationalist contingent within his party, although growing in both confidence and influence, remained a minority. And yet, if two-thirds of Radical deputies (including Herriot) abstained in the vote of investiture for Poincaré's government on 19 January 1922, most were unwilling to go further to assume a position of outright opposition that might compromise France's position in international negotiations. Herriot's caution was due mainly to a preoccupation with party unity. He was committed to rebuilding the Radicals into a party of government and was unwilling to alienate an important contingent within the Radical movement that continued to favour a more traditional approach to security.[65]

The result was that the Radical position towards the prospect of a Ruhr occupation was much more equivocal than that of the SFIO. Herriot recommended that Radical deputies abstain in the vote of confidence on 11 January. In the end thirty-three Radical and six Republican Socialist deputies (led by Paul Painlevé) either abstained or voted against the government.[66] Herriot defended the strategy by arguing that to vote against the government would be to 'provide a weapon to Germany'. To vote for the occupation, however, would be 'to deny our doctrine, to which we must one day return'.[67] The ambiguities in the Radical response to the Ruhr were echoed in the pages of *L'Europe nouvelle*, the internationalist-leaning weekly to which Radicals often contributed. As the occupation began, editor-in-chief Philippe Millet insisted that it was legal and should not be opposed inside France. One week later, however, he stressed the need to 're-establish inter-Allied cooperation in order to prepare not only the terms of a moratorium but the settlement of the entire reparations issue'. This could only be accomplished 'with the mediation of America and Britain'.[68] The contradictions in this position reflected wider

---

[63] Quoted in R. Bournazel, *Rapallo: la politique de la peur dans la France du Bloc national* (Paris, 1974), 84–5; see also S. Berstein, *Édouard Herriot ou la République en personne* (Paris, 1985), 89–95.
[64] Berstein, *Herriot*, 90; J.-M. Guieu, *Le Rameau et le glaive: les militants français pour la Société des nations* (Paris, 2008), 101–5; Jacques Bariéty claims that Herriot was not an internationalist, but then provides powerful evidence to the contrary: *Relations franco-allemandes*, 327–38.
[65] S. Berstein, *Histoire du Parti Radical*, vol. I: *À la recherche de l'âge d'or* (Paris, 1980), 356–65; Jeannesson, *Ruhr*, 209–10.
[66] Roussellier, *Parlement de l'éloquence*, 199–200.   [67] Berstein, *Herriot*, 91–2.
[68] P. Millet, 'Que ferons-nous de la Ruhr?', 'Le Nouveau conflit franco-allemand' and 'Après la Ruhr' in *L'Europe nouvelle*, 20, 27 Jan. 1923 respectively.

tensions among Radicals over the Ruhr occupation. Opposition to Poincaré's policy of force on the centre-left would not develop into a decisive factor in the French internal situation until the run-up to the national elections of May 1924.

IV

By mid-February 1923 the Ruhr operation had become a trial of strength that favoured France. Seydoux observed that:

The situation established by the Treaty of Versailles has been altered completely. For the first time we possess a *gage*, the continual and gradual exploitation of which will exert pressure that Germany will find difficult, if not impossible, to withstand in the long term.[69]

French policy elites correctly judged that Germany would eventually capitulate – although they underestimated both the time this would take and the lengths to which the Weimar government would go to support passive resistance. The result was destructive hyperinflation that did lasting damage to the social and political fibre of democracy in Germany.[70]

By early February resistance spread to the Rhineland and forced the occupying powers to seize control of the regional rail network and create their own administration to remove coal and coke from the industrial basin. The Ruhr basin and the Left Bank were cut off from the rest of Germany by a customs barrier that also served as a blockade of coal and manufactured goods. In late January the French began sacking and expelling uncooperative civil servants (a measure advocated without success by Tirard since early 1920). By the following October nearly 139,000 individuals were expelled from the occupied territories in what was essentially a programme of systematic 'deprussification' mounted by France.[71]

There were limits to the confrontation. There was no general strike and violence was generally limited. French authorities exercised relative restraint during the first few months of the operation. A separate currency was not imposed on the occupied territories; existing German law was not abrogated and officials kept their distance from separatist politics in the region. This initial restraint was in line with gradualist logic adopted by the occupation authorities since 1919. The aim was to weaken the German economy to help convince the population in the region that its material interests were better served by a closer economic relationship with France.[72] Nor did the Poincaré

---

[69] MAE, PA-AP 261, *Papiers Seydoux*, vol. 7, 'Note de M. Seydoux', 16 Feb. 1923.
[70] G. Feldman, *The Great Disorder: Politics, Economics and Society in the German Inflation, 1914–1924* (Oxford, 1997), 631–97.
[71] Jeannesson, *Ruhr*, 203–4; Bariéty provides a higher figure of 147,000: *Relations franco-allemandes*, 114, which is cited by Fischer in *Ruhr Crisis*, 86.
[72] Trachtenberg, *Reparation*, 291–4, 305–6; Jeannesson, *Ruhr*, 205–8, 221–2.

government want to alienate international opinion with projects for a Rhenish currency. Indeed, Poincaré harboured illusions that Britain might eventually acquiesce to an alteration of the status of the Left Bank if it was presented as an issue of self-determination. He also needed to maintain a measure of 'national concord' over the occupation. The Radicals, in particular, were opposed to any effort to overturn the territorial settlement established by the Versailles Treaty. The government was therefore obliged to tread carefully.[73] Behind the scenes, however, the year 1923 saw a recrudescence of French ambitions to overturn the political order in Europe.

A meeting of the inter-ministerial Ruhr committee was convened by Seydoux on 6 March 1923. Present were representatives from the ministries of finance and public works, Foch's staff and the head of the general secretariat of the CSDN (the SGDN), General Bernard Serrigny (a close ally of Marshal Pétain). Serrigny's presence illustrates the growing importance of this planning section within the CSDN.[74] Seydoux acknowledged that 'our security would be complete if we could be assured of an effective neutralisation of the Left Bank'. But his ideal solution was an arrangement in which 'the entire Left Bank, including the Saar, could become an autonomous state with local representation and administration and thus detached from the Reich and placed under the control of the League of Nations'.[75] On 10 March Poincaré instructed the SGDN to prepare a comprehensive study of the question of autonomy for the Left Bank from the Belgian occupied zone in the north to the Saarland in the south. Serrigny duly circulated a secret questionnaire concerning the military, political and economic requirements of a Rhenish state. Familiar myths concerning the region's distinct character and links to France were dusted off and deployed in the preamble.[76] Attached 'for information' was a lengthy study prepared by Tirard's high commission that emphasised the need to maintain the military occupation 'for several generations' in order to 'permit us to shepherd the Rhenish population towards a solution that will guarantee the security of France'. Tirard's goal remained a polity that would

---

[73] W. McDougall, *France's Rhineland Diplomacy, 1914–1924: The Last Bid for a Balance of Power in Europe* (Princeton, 1978), 264–6; Trachtenberg, *Reparation*, 300–11; Jeannesson, *Ruhr*, 117–21, 221, 229–33, 239–46, 253–8; Steiner, *Lights that Failed*, 226–9.

[74] SHD-DAT, 2N 237-1, 'Procès-verbal du comité interministériel du 6 mars 1923 (58ème séance): propositions de paix à faire à l'Allemagne' (dossier labelled 'Projet de création d'un État rhénan autonome'); on Serrigny's background and role see T. Imlay, 'Preparing for total war: industrial and economic preparations for war in France between the two World Wars', *War in History*, 15, 1 (2008), 45–50 and Serrigny's memoir: *Trente ans avec Pétain* (Paris, 1959).

[75] SHD-DAT, 2N 237-1, 'Propositions de paix à faire à l'Allemagne', 6 Mar. 1923.

[76] SHD-DAT, 2N 237-1, Serrigny forwarding a questionnaire entitled 'Organisation de la Rhénanie', 26 Mar. 1923 (also in MAE, *Série Z, RGR*, vol. 29) and Serrigny to Poincaré, 16 Mar. 1923. The analysis that follows is drawn from the various responses to this questionnaire but has also benefited from the interpretations in Jeannesson, *Ruhr*, 222–7 and P. Jardin, 'Le Conseil supérieur de la défense nationale et les projets d'organisation d'un état rhénan (mars 1923)', *Francia*, 19, 3 (1992), 81–96.

initially remain 'nominally under German sovereignty' but evolve gradually and of its own accord into the orbit of France.[77]

Responses to the SGDN questionnaire illustrate the extent to which Rhenish dreaming had once again become central to security planning in Paris. Raymond Brugère, from Poincaré's cabinet at the foreign ministry, endorsed Tirard's conception.[78] General Degoutte, meanwhile, insisted that the question of Rhenish autonomy could not be studied in isolation from 'the problem of the political evolution of Germany as a whole'. France, he argued, 'must pursue the transformation of the Reich in a federalist sense'.[79] Army chief of staff General Buat insisted that France must secure permanent control of the Rhine. He recommended extending the frontier of the new state to include the Maingau cities of Frankfurt and Darmstadt as well as the construction of an extensive system of rail and canal transportation to facilitate commerce with France.[80] General Mangin, who was also consulted, put forward a typically grandiose vision, replete with pseudo-historical analysis, that called for a reconstitution of the Napoleonic Confederation of the Rhine.[81]

Two striking aspects of this internal correspondence are, first, the general consensus on the need to overturn the territorial settlement of 1919 and, second, the prominent role of the military in planning for future security. Military elites had been marginalised from policy debates during the latter stages of Briand's premiership but had regained a key voice under Poincaré. The result was a recalibration of security planning and a return to centuries-old ambitions to dominate the Rhine. Mangin warned that 'it would be an error to assume that a Rhenish republic will emerge on its own, in the sense desired by us... An excellent solution is there for the taking, one that offers us both security and reparations. But we must act swiftly, very swiftly.'[82] Foch's staff, meanwhile, reiterated every argument for dominating the Rhine that the marshal had made during the peace conference. 'As long as the reparations question is not settled,' the note began, 'our security is not threatened because we will continue to occupy the Ruhr and the Rhineland. If French troops were to withdraw, however, France and Belgium will have *no security*.' Allied occupation of the Rhine bridgeheads would need to remain in place 'until the issues of security and reparations are entirely resolved (a minimum of several generations) ... If in this way we weaken the links that unite the

---

[77] SHD-DAT, 2N 237–1, 'Note relative aux mesures à imposer à l'Allemagne en ce qui concerne la rive gauche du Rhin', 24 Mar. 1923; Jeannesson, *Ruhr*, 224–6.
[78] MAE, *Série Z, RGR*, vol. 29, 'Note préparée par M. Brugère pour le président du conseil: organisation rhénane', 30 Mar. 1923.
[79] SHD-DAT, 2N 237–1, Degoutte to Serrigny (untitled), 2 Apr. 1923.
[80] SHD-DAT, 2N 237–1, 'Organisation éventuelle des pays Rhénans', 12 Apr. 1923.
[81] SHD-DAT, 2N 237–1, 'Note sommaire sur l'établissement de la République rhénane' and 'Note au sujet d'un programme de l'Union populaire rhénane', 5 Apr. 1923.
[82] MAE, PA-AP 118, *Papiers Millerand*, vol. 97, 'Lettre du général Mangin à M. de Peretti' marked 'Remis par Seydoux', 21 Apr. 1923.

Rhineland with Berlin,' the study concluded, 'is this not to the profit of general peace?'[83]

The most fantastic project to emerge in 1923, however, was a scheme for the transformation of Germany into a federation of small states, conceived by General Degoutte in July. Degoutte's plan recalled the conception advocated by Hanotaux in November 1919. The Rhineland would become one of eleven distinct states, each with a population of between 4.5 and 8 million. 'It is in our interest that these new states constitute homogenous blocs as different from one another as possible with abundant religious, political, economic differences between them.' Degoutte predicted that the constituent states of a federal Germany would become absorbed with internal rivalries and present no threat to France. The ultimate aim, as Stanislas Jeannesson has observed, was to return to the eighteenth century.[84]

These plans were all based on the expectation of a complete political collapse in Germany. This seemed increasingly likely after the government of Gustav Stresemann brought an effective end to passive resistance on 26 September 1923. Poincaré responded by refusing to negotiate with Berlin. De Margerie, who had succeeded Laurent as ambassador in Berlin in October 1922, was instructed to cease all communications with the German government. The aim was to maintain political and economic pressure on the Reich in the hope that it would begin to come apart at the seams. Always careful to cover his tracks, Poincaré did not commit his intentions to paper. Instead, he sent a verbal message to de Margerie that 'the French government possesses the most serious reasons to believe in the imminent disaggregation of the Reich'. This, he explained, was 'the real reason' why France refused to negotiate with the Stresemann government. From his command post in the Rhineland, Degoutte judged that 'the policy we have pursued thus far is beginning to bear fruit'.[85]

Preparations to introduce a separate currency in the occupied territories were finally set in train.[86] The situation came to a head from 21 October when a series of separatist coups in various towns on the Left Bank forced France's hand. Tentative negotiations had been ongoing with political and industrial elites in the Ruhr and Rhineland since the summer. On 24 October, however, Poincaré decided to go much further and give support to the separatist insurgents. The details of this episode are well known.[87] The key aspect of the affair, for the purposes of this study, is the fact that French policy under

---

[83] MAE, PA-AP 118, *Papiers Millerand*, vol. 97, 'Note du Comité Militaire Allié', 21 Jul. 1923.
[84] SHD-DAT, 7N 3489–1, 'Note: le fédéralisme allemand', 11 July 1923; Jeannesson, *Ruhr*, 227–9.
[85] Poincaré quoted in Jeannesson, *Ruhr*, 302–3; Degoutte in Trachtenberg, *Reparation*, 321.
[86] MAE, PA-AP 118, *Papiers Millerand*, vol. 98, 'Banque d'émission pour la Rhénanie', 12 Nov. 1923; Trachtenberg, *Reparation*, 322–4; Jeannesson, *Ruhr*, 315–18.
[87] See esp. McDougall, *Rhineland Diplomacy*, 299–359; Bariéty, *Relations franco-allemandes*, 247–66; Fischer, *Ruhr Crisis*, 243–57; and Jeannesson, *Ruhr*, 333–71.

Poincaré aimed at the break-up of the German Reich and the constitution of a buffer state on the Left Bank and, if possible, in the Ruhr.

On 25 October a gathering of senior officials debated France's response to the turmoil in western Germany. Seydoux, Laroche, Victor de Lacroix (head of the Quai d'Orsay's European desk) and even Tirard all counselled caution. They were sceptical of the separatist movement and recommended maintaining close contacts with the more conservative political and economic notables in the region. Both Poincaré and Peretti, however, 'objected that if we do not obtain an independent Rhenish state we will have neither security nor reparations'.[88] Tirard responded that autonomy must remain the objective of French policy. 'Neither M. Barrès nor general Mangin have demanded that the Rhineland leave Germany,' he argued. 'Even Richelieu was content with less.'[89]

There were concerns that opposition from Britain and Belgium would undermine the chances of German decomposition. From London the government of Stanley Baldwin warned that the decomposition of Germany would render the Treaty of Versailles invalid and require the negotiation of an entirely new settlement. The DAPC was duly instructed to prepare a study of 'the maximum regime of autonomy that would give us satisfaction but would not be in contradiction with the treaty'.[90] Poincaré produced his own analysis of this question, judging that 'the dissociation of a state bound by a treaty with other states, and having been the object of treaties between those other states, has never put an end to the validity of these treaties'.[91] The premier did not view the prospect of German disintegration as a threat either to France's treaty rights or its security interests.

And yet there was another dimension to French policy conceptions at this stage. Alongside the traditional bid to destroy German power there remained the assumption that the long-term resolution of the reparations issue required an international programme of loans. Poincaré had all along insisted that Britain must be part of any final reparations settlement. And French planning for such a settlement continued to project that war debts to both Britain and the USA would be written off in exchange for a renunciation of the 'C' category reparation bonds under the London Schedule.[92] All of this assumed a significant level of cooperation with the British and Americans. De Lasteyrie again

---

[88] MAE, PA-AP 118, *Papiers Millerand*, vol. 98, notes taken at this meeting by Millerand's secretary, Pierre Vignon.
[89] MAE, PA-AP 118, *Papiers Millerand*, vol. 98, 'Visite de Hermant', 27 Oct. 1923.
[90] MAE, PA-AP 118, *Papiers Millerand*, vol. 98, 'Conversation avec M. Peretti', 1 Nov. 1923.
[91] MAE, PA-AP 118, *Papiers Millerand*, vol. 98, 'Mouvement rhénan: note anglaise', 31 Oct. 1923; 'Lettre à l'ambassadeur d'Angleterre', 1 Nov. 1923; 'Coup de téléphone de M. Herbette à M. Peretti', 2 Nov. 1923.
[92] MAE, PA-AP 261, *Papiers Seydoux*, vol. 7, 'Note de M. Seydoux', 16 Feb. 1923; Trachtenberg, *Reparation*, 315–16.

underlined the evident contradiction in the French position when he pointed to 'a certain antimony' between the aim to obtain reparations, which in the long run required the cooperation of both the Germans and 'our Anglo-Saxon allies', and ambitions to overturn the balance of power by dismembering the Reich, which would alienate those same allies and undermine prospects for international collaboration.[93]

In fact, that international financial cooperation had been on offer for some time. American secretary of state Charles Hughes had proposed the creation of an international committee of financial experts to be charged with examining Germany's situation and providing suggestions to resolve the issue of reparations payments. He pledged official support for the intervention of private American capital to underwrite a programme of loans. He stressed that all parties must agree in advance to abide by the findings of this committee, however. This suggestion was taken up first by the German government on 7 June and then in a British note of 11 August 1923. Each time, the idea was rebuffed by the French government.[94] The French response was different when the British and Americans, concerned at the possible break-up of Germany, renewed the proposal on 19 October 1923. This time Poincaré accepted the idea almost immediately.[95]

The reasons for this sudden reversal, which was to have far-reaching consequences for the future of both French policy and European international relations, have long puzzled historians. The most plausible explanation for Poincaré's decision is that he aimed to take advantage of the acute political crisis in Germany to resolve both the economic and financial dimensions of France's security problem. The premier and his advisers hoped that the political disintegration of the Reich would present France's allies with a fait accompli that they would have little choice but to accept, given their commitment to self-determination. France would then be in a strong position from which to negotiate a settlement of the reparations issue. This optimistic reading of the situation can only be understood within the context of soaring hopes that the Reich of 1871 was about to disappear.[96]

If the notion that Britain would have acquiesced in the break-up of Germany now seems far-fetched, there were, at least in the mind of the French premier, some grounds for optimism. In official correspondence and in its public declarations, the Baldwin government issued dire warnings about the consequences of a German break-up. In a face-to-face discussion on 11 November 1923, however, British ambassador Lord Crewe appears to have agreed with

---

[93] MAE, PA-AP 118, *Papiers Millerand*, vol. 25, 'Note' (de Lasteyrie), 11 Apr. 1923.
[94] O'Riordan, *Britain and the Ruhr*, 28–9, 125–36; Steiner, *Lights that Failed*, 219–29.
[95] Trachtenberg, *Reparation*, 331–3.
[96] This analysis is close to that of Jeannesson in *Ruhr*, 336–8; for different perspectives see Roth, *Poincaré*, 435–8 and 442–50 and Keiger, *Poincaré*, 294–311.

The politics of confrontation 413

Poincaré's assertion that 'a German confederation [would present] advantages from the point of view of peace'. After this meeting the premier noted that 'Lord Crewe left me with the very clear impression that his government believed the work of Bismarck to be destroyed'.[97]

This impression, like so much of French policy at this time, was based on an excessively optimistic reading of the situation. Hopes for the collapse of Germany withered in late 1923. The resulting disillusion was exacerbated by a serious deterioration in France's diplomatic and financial position. Severe pressure on the franc combined with political isolation to leave the Poincaré government with much less leverage than it had anticipated when it had agreed to accept the intervention of a committee of experts. 'It is no longer possible', Seydoux observed in late December, 'for us to deal with Germany in terms of victor and vanquished.'[98] A new approach would be necessary. The Ruhr standoff would help bring about a fundamental reordering of post-war Europe, but not on the terms hoped for by Poincaré and many of his advisers.

V

Traditional power politics continued to be at the heart of French policy towards eastern Europe. Persistent uncertainty concerning the future of Russia complicated all efforts to integrate central and eastern Europe into French security policy. The challenge this posed for policy making was amplified by the disagreement within both elite and popular opinion over the proper policy to follow towards the USSR. The left argued that the Soviet Union must be admitted into international society. The leadership of the PCF served as a conduit for Soviet attempts to negotiate an economic and possibly even a political rapprochement with the Bloc government.[99] The SFIO, despite its opposition to the practices of the Comintern, advocated establishing diplomatic relations with Moscow. Blum and other leading Socialists argued that the reintegration of Russia into the European economy must be a central aim of the Genoa Conference planned for April 1922.[100] This was also the position of most Radicals. Party leader Herriot predicted that improved political and commercial relations with the rest of Europe would moderate Soviet behaviour. In 1922 Herriot undertook a much-publicised visit to Russia. He returned

---

[97] MAE, PA-AP 118, *Papiers Millerand*, vol. 98, 'Note écrite par M. Poincaré après une visite que Lord Crewe a faite ce matin', 11 Nov. 1923.
[98] MAE, PA-AP 118, *Papiers Millerand*, vol. 33, 'Emprunt en Amérique: premières réflexions', 27 Dec. 1923; Seydoux, *De Versailles au Plan Young*, 304–9.
[99] Bournazel, *Rapallo*, 89–92.
[100] *JO, Chambre, Débats*, 3 Apr. 1922; L. Blum, 'Lénine ou Poincaré?', *Le Populaire*, 25 Feb. 1922; J. Longuet, 'Notre isolement à Gênes', *Le Populaire*, 29 Mar. 1922; S. Grumbach, 'Principes communistes et diplomatie soviétique', *Le Populaire*, 14 Feb. 1922; Bournazel, *Rapallo*, 87–9.

convinced that the USSR could play a central role in the political and economic reconstruction of Europe.[101]

This was not the mainstream view within the Bloc national. Many conservative elites agreed with Clemenceau's judgement that the Soviet regime was 'the most atrocious, most barbaric government ever to devastate any territory of the known world'.[102] This ideological repugnance limited any role the USSR might play in security planning. Another factor was the Soviet regime's repudiation of the debts of its Tsarist predecessor. Millerand, in particular, was convinced that the USSR could not be admitted into the society of states until it acknowledged its responsibility for these debts.[103] But not all Bloc politicians agreed with a strategy of cordon sanitaire. Louis Barthou, for example, argued that a unilateral commercial boycott only damaged French interests. This argument, which complemented the case made on the left, was taken up by a diverse cross-section of parliamentary and press opinion.[104] The worry was that France's allies – or, worse yet, Germany – would steal a march on French commerce inside Russia. Instructions to ambassador Laurent in Berlin urged him to 'think always of Russia' and report all evidence of Russo-German political and economic cooperation.[105] The Millerand government settled on a position of permitting (even encouraging) French private business to pursue economic interests in the Soviet Union while at the same time refusing to restore formal diplomatic ties as long as the debt question remained unresolved. This remained the French position when Lloyd George proposed to create a 'European consortium' for the reconstruction of the Russian economy at the Genoa conference in April 1922.[106]

Genoa was a failure. Indeed, the most notable outcome of the conference was the signature of the Rapallo Accords between Germany and the USSR. Rapallo appeared to confirm the fear of German–Bolshevik collusion that had been a constant since 1917. The result was a 'veritable security psychosis'.[107] The official response was to renew efforts to weld the smaller states in eastern Europe into a coherent bloc capable of resisting Soviet–German pressure in the short term and counterbalancing German power in the long term. Foch and the military played a central role in this policy.

---

[101] A. Hogenhuis-Seliverstoff, *Les Relations franco-soviétiques 1917–1924* (Paris, 1981), 163–73, 234–7; S. Couré, *La Grande lueur à l'Est: les Français et l'Union soviétique 1917–1939* (Paris, 1999), 64–8; see also Herriot's *La Russie nouvelle* (Paris, 1922).

[102] *Le Temps*, 25 Dec. 1929.

[103] MAE, Série Z, URSS, vol. 156, 'Note: paix avec les bolcheviks', 10 Feb. 1920; AN, C/14632, *CAEAN*, XIIème Législature, Millerand *auditions* of 4 and 17 Feb. 1920; AN, 470 AP 57, *Archives Millerand*, 'Notes d'une conversation tenu à Lympne', 20 Jun. 1920.

[104] Hogenhuis-Seliverstoff, *Relations franco-soviétiques*, 165–72.

[105] MAE, PA-AP 261, *Papiers Seydoux*, vol. 1, 'Questions économiques', 13 Jan. 1920 and 'Instructions à l'ambassadeur de France à Berlin', 26 Jun. 1920.

[106] Fink, *Genoa Conference*, 177–257; Hogenhuis-Seliverstoff, *Relations franco-soviétiques*, 193–214.

[107] Jeannesson, 'Pourquoi', 65; see also Bournazel, *Rapallo*, 117–41.

One of Poincaré's first actions as foreign minister was to take up ratification of the Franco-Polish alliance that had been left dormant under Briand. Peretti argued that the chief purpose of the alliance was to 'constitute a military force to the east of Germany [capable of] preventing the Berlin government from attempting to destroy Poland and thus overthrow the territorial balance created by the Treaty of Versailles'. Until the alliance was ratified, however, the Franco-Polish military cooperation at the heart of this project could not take place. Poincaré resolved to press ahead with ratification, which was finalised in June 1922. Poland began placing orders for armaments in France the following winter.[108]

Foch's staff took the lead in developing the sinews of the Franco-Polish military alliance. Weygand was dispatched to Warsaw with a series of recommendations for the organisation of Poland's national defence, and Polish army chief of staff Władysław Sikorski was invited to Paris.[109] The first round of joint military planning took place the following September. Sikorski was advised that Poland could count on 'the immediate intervention of France' in the event of an attack by Germany but only 'remote aid' in the event of Soviet aggression. In the event of war against a German–Soviet combination (considered a likely scenario after Rapallo) it was agreed that the principal effort of both Poland and France must come against Germany, which retained the trained soldiery, industrial capacity and political motivation to mount a successful invasion of Poland. The turmoil in Russia, conversely, reduced the threat posed by the Red Army. 'The soul of the German–Soviet threat', it was agreed, 'will remain, for a long time, Berlin.' Joint planning extended to French naval assistance in the defence of the Polish Corridor, detailed timetables for mobilisation and offensive operations, arrangements for intelligence sharing and even the coordination of French and Polish policy towards disarmament initiatives in Geneva.[110]

One of the chief preoccupations for French participants in these talks was Poland's relative isolation from its neighbours. In the event of a two-front war, Poland could count on only limited support from Romania and none whatsoever from Czechoslovakia. If a coalition could be constructed, however, the demographic resources of the eastern states, estimated at nearly 100 million, would outweigh those of Germany (estimated at 65 million). This was the

---

[108] *DDF, 1922*, I, 'Note du Département pour le Président du conseil', 29 Jan. 1922; SHD-DAT, 7N 3006–1, 'Accord politique entre la France et la Pologne', n.d.; 7N 3006–2, 'Note historique sur la question de fourniture de matériel de guerre par la France à la Pologne', 1928; P. Wandycz, *France and her Eastern Allies, 1919–1925: French–Czechoslovak–Polish Relations from the Paris Peace Conference to Locarno* (Minneapolis, 1962), 217–24, 256–64.
[109] SHD-DAT, 7N 3006–1, 'Note remise par le général Weygand', 3 Jun. 1922.
[110] Quotation from SHD-DAT, 7N 3006–1, 'Résumé des entretiens du M. Foch, du général Buat et du vice-amiral Grasset avec le général Sikorski', 13 Nov. 1922; also 'Procès-verbal sommaire de la conférence tenue par MM. les généraux Sikorski, Buat et Weygand le 9 septembre 1922' and 'Note: conférences tenues avec le général Sikorski', Maginot to Poincaré, 18 Sept. 1922.

central theme of an important *tour d'horizon* prepared by Deuxième bureau chief Lieutenant Colonel Charles Fournier in July 1922. Fournier began with the observation that 'Germany, humiliated by its defeat, thinks only of revenge, but must wait for a favourable occasion to act'. He considered that:

> We have before us a respite of at least ten years [before the evacuation of the Rhineland] during which time we can form against our future adversary, with Belgium and Britain on one side and Poland, Romania, Czechoslovakia and Yugoslavia on the other, a true coalition, closely encircling Germany and capable of removing its taste for revenge; or, if it persists in its blindness, to drive it once again to disaster.

Fournier then went on to emphasise the military potential of the eastern states. Poland's population of nearly 30 million, he noted, was animated by an 'elevated patriotic sentiment' and constituted a rich source of raw soldiery. Strength in numbers, when combined with the 'undeniable intellectual qualities' of the Polish officer class, formed a promising basis for the construction of 'a solid modern army capable of fulfilling the task defined for it [in French strategy]'.[111]

Fournier was equally enthusiastic about Czechoslovakia's modern heavy industry and 'advanced political culture'. He judged that the twelve-division-strong Czech army, commanded by Foch protégé General Eugène Mittelhauser, 'represents even now a force that cannot be ignored'. The Czechoslovaks, moreover, were the only state in the region to understand the importance of aviation to modern war and had devoted considerable resources to the development of an independent aircraft industry. Fournier acknowledged that Czechoslovakia's geographical situation, surrounded on three sides by Germany and Austria, was 'very unfavourable from a defensive point of view'. He argued that it was well placed, on the other hand, for a swift offensive into Bavaria and an air campaign against Berlin. Fournier recommended that Czechoslovakia be designated as the pivot of the combined offensive operations of a coalition that must also include Romania and Yugoslavia.[112]

Fournier concluded his assessment by stressing the deterrent value of such an eastern bloc:

> The lone means that we possess to avoid a new war – for which Germany is even now preparing – is to threaten it openly with a coalition including Poland and the Little Entente. It is often repeated that if Britain had placed itself clearly at France's side on 25 July 1914, war would not have broken out. Why should the encirclement that we are trying to construct around Germany not prevent it from letting loose a second such catastrophe?[113]

---

[111] SHD-DAT, 7N 2520–1, 'Nécessité d'une coalition contre l'Allemagne', 13 Jul. 1922.
[112] Ibid.   [113] Ibid.

Fournier was advocating a traditional strategy of deterrence: peace would be preserved by threatening Germany with military force.[114] His analysis was embraced by Foch, who forwarded it to Poincaré, recommending that it serve as the basis of French policy towards eastern Europe. The premier responded by suggesting that France sponsor detailed staff conversations involving all Little Entente states on the model of the pre-1914 Franco-British arrangements.[115]

Over the next two years French policy pursued construction of an eastern barrier along these lines. Foch was central to this effort. In 1923 he embarked on a tour of central Europe, visiting both Warsaw and Prague and urging the governments of both countries to cooperate with one another against Germany. Foch lamented that Czechoslovak policy, in particular, was not oriented towards an inevitable war with Germany. 'The existence of the states of central Europe', he observed in a note to Mittelhauser, 'is entirely conditioned by that of Germany ... the first preoccupation of Czechoslovakia must be to confront Germany and to collaborate in its ruin, which will settle everything.'[116] French diplomacy placed pressure on Prague to agree to a Franco-Czechoslovak military alliance. But Czechoslovakia had secured a prominent role in Geneva (where it had obtained a seat on the League Council) and foreign minister Beneš was reluctant to agree to a traditional alliance that could be interpreted as an attempt to encircle Germany – particularly when the French army was in the Ruhr. In the end the Franco-Czechoslovak 'Treaty of Alliance and Friendship' of January 1924 was a political agreement to consult and cooperate against common threats to European security. It did not include a military convention.[117]

The absence of such a convention did not preclude intimate joint planning between the French and Czechoslovak military establishments. Indeed, the Treaty of Alliance was accompanied by a secret exchange of letters between Poincaré and Beneš that referred to the need to 'maintain and intensify' contacts between the general staffs of the two countries with a view to 'establish concerted plans to meet aggression directed against either of the two countries by a common enemy'.[118] This exchange was hardly necessary in any case. Throughout this period Mittelhauser remained in command of the Czechoslovak army. This ensured that Czechoslovak strategic plans

---

[114] P. Jackson, 'La Faillite de la dissuasion française en Europe centrale' in M. Vaïsse (ed.), *Bâtir une nouvelle sécurité: la coopération militaire entre la France et les États d'Europe centrale et orientale de 1919–1929* (Vincennes, 2001), 151–9.

[115] SHD-DAT, 4N 93-2, *État-major Foch*, 'Note' (Foch), 13 Jul.1922 and 'Études militaires avec les États-majors de la Petite Entente' (Poincaré), 25 Jul. 1922.

[116] SHD-DAT, 4N 93-2, *État-major Foch*, Foch to Mittelhauser, 5 Jun. 1923; see also Notin, *Foch*, 515–17.

[117] P. Wandycz, *The Twilight of French Eastern Alliances* (Princeton, 1988), 9–10; Steiner, *Lights that Failed*, 303–5.

[118] P. Wandycz, 'L'Alliance franco-tchécoslovaque: un échange de lettres Poincaré-Beneš', *RHD*, 3–4 (1984), 328–33.

complemented the French mobilisation-and-concentration Plan P and its successor Plan A. Both plans envisaged an offensive into western Germany in coordination with Poland and Czechoslovakia. An air-power convention between the two states stipulated that France would send two fighter squadrons and a bomber group to Czechoslovakia at the outset of hostilities.[119]

The great weakness in French plans for a traditional eastern counterweight remained the refusal of Czechoslovakia and Poland to collaborate with one another. Mutual suspicion, along with sharply divergent strategic priorities, continued to all but rule out effective cooperation between the two states.[120] After the Cartel des gauches came to power in May 1924, moreover, a French-sponsored power bloc in the east ceased to be a priority for the foreign ministry. Although the army staff continued to press for Polish–Czechoslovak cooperation, the Quai d'Orsay was drawn increasingly into projects for a continental security system that would include Germany and have the Rhine as its centre of gravity. The traditional strategy of an eastern counterweight would not be a priority until it was taken up again by the foreign ministry in the mid-1930s. Focus shifted instead to western Europe, a British continental commitment and an internationalist agenda centred on the League of Nations.

VI

Under Poincaré French policy towards the League evolved gradually towards cautious engagement with projects for collective security and arms limitation. French representatives in Geneva took the initiative to shape the tone and parameters of negotiations. This strategy had two aims. The first was to improve public perceptions of French policy both inside France and abroad. The second was to ensure that France's interests were represented in key discussions. By mid-1923 the Poincaré government had begun to contemplate disarmament negotiations as a means of obtaining a security guarantee from Britain.

France's delegates to the League played an important role in this process. And from the beginning juridical internationalists had been prominent within the French delegation. In addition to Bourgeois, who served as leader through 1923, the French mission also included Henry de Jouvenel, Jean Hennessy,

---

[119] SHD-DAT, 7N 3605, 'Étude sur les bases du Plan P', 23 Nov. 1922; 7N 3446-2, 'Procès-verbal de la conférence tenue à Prague, le 11 janvier 1924, entre les officiers représentant les États-majors généraux français et tchéco-slovaques'; 7N 3111, 'Rôle de la Tchécoslovaquie dans une coalition contre l'Allemagne', Jun. 1923 and 'Signature de la convention aérienne franco-tchécoslovaque', 11 Jan. 1923; P. Hauser, 'La Désignation du général Pellé comme chef de la mission militaire française en Tchécoslovaquie et ses conséquences' in Vaïsse (ed.), *Bâtir une nouvelle sécurité*, 323–31.

[120] Y. Lacaze, 'Simple coopération militaire ou signature d'une convention militaire contraignante? Le Dilemme franco-tchécoslovaque (1919–1924)' in Vaïsse (ed.), *Bâtir une nouvelle sécurité*; Wandycz, *Twilight*, 203–21.

Joseph Barthélemy and Louis Aubert (who became an active member of the AFSDN after the peace conference). De Jouvenel played an increasingly important role. A Radical senator, he was also editor-in-chief of *Le Matin* and would serve as a minister in several centre-left and centrist governments. As the health of Bourgeois declined, de Jouvenel became the most prominent French representative in Geneva – though his influence over policy never rivalled that of Lieutenant Colonel Réquin.[121]

Relations between internationalists and the Bloc national were far from straightforward, however. While leading Bloc politicians such as Millerand, Barthou and Poincaré expressed public support for the League, they were much less enthusiastic about the internationalist cause in private.[122] The Quai d'Orsay, for its part, was determined to control the activities of French representatives in Geneva. The French delegation to the League was financed by the foreign ministry. The SFSDN provided the policy expertise and administrative support necessary to its effective functioning. On Berthelot's instructions, the Quai d'Orsay also subsidised a wide range of pro-League associations. It provided 10,000 francs per year to finance the travel of French internationalists to the annual conference of the International Union of League of Nations Associations. It also placed office space at the disposal of the groups such as the GUSDN.[123]

In return, delegates in Geneva were expected to follow policy laid down in Paris. Bourgeois complained that the foreign ministry issued policy edicts without consulting French delegates, who were often forced to adopt positions that were diametrically opposed to their personal opinions and expert judgements. 'The Quai d'Orsay', Bourgeois complained, 'struggled against [the League] from the first day, from ignorance and from political prejudice.'[124] Poincaré considered that the obligation to support official policy should extend even to academics. When Georges Scelle (then professor of international law at the University of Dijon) called publicly for German admission into the League, the premier wrote to the directorate of higher education to complain that this view was 'in absolute contradiction with the policy of the French government'. Poincaré demanded that measures be taken to 'open the eyes of M. Scelle to the

---

[121] De Jouvenel was also married to the novelist Colette, and moved in the same social circles as Berthelot and the coterie of writer-diplomats: see C. Manigand, *Les Français au service de la Société des nations* (Berne, 2003), 61–112; C. Manigand, *Henry de Jouvenel* (Paris, 2000); R. Cecil, *A Great Experiment: An Autobiography* (Oxford, 1941), 138–41; C. Birebent, *Militants de la paix et de la SDN: les mouvements de soutien à la Société des nations en France et au Royaume-Uni, 1918–1925* (Paris, 2007), 135–45.
[122] Guieu, *Rameau et glaive*, 121–4.
[123] J.-M. Guieu, 'Les Apôtres français de "l'esprit de Genève": les militants pour la Société des Nations dans la première moitié du XXe siècle', thèse de doctorat, Université de Paris I (Sorbonne), 2004, 204–9.
[124] Quoted in M.-R. Mouton, *La Société des nations et les intérêts de la France (1920–1924)* (Berne, 1995), 514; see also Guieu, 'Les Apôtres', 288–94.

dangers of his position'.[125] Poincaré's angry missive, written in October 1923, illustrates the extent to which internationalist views had become an issue of concern for policy officials.

Foreign ministry mandarins were therefore aware of internationalist criticisms. An important side effect of the government's preoccupation with the Franco-German confrontation, moreover, was that it left permanent officials in both Paris and Geneva with a measure of autonomy in the formulation of policy towards the League and disarmament. This autonomy, combined with growing internal discontent and an awareness of wider public misgivings with the government's hardline policy, created the conditions for a more constructive approach to multilateral disarmament and security negotiations. The result was the gradual emergence of a new policy line.

The first significant development in international disarmament in 1922 was the 'Esher Plan' to extend the scheme for levels of naval armaments laid down by the Washington Treaty to land forces. French officials hated this proposal, and it was dismissed out of hand by representatives in Geneva. 'It is in French councils and not elsewhere', Poincaré responded, 'that the question of our armaments must be settled.'[126] The Esher Plan did set in motion a process with significant consequences for French policy, however. Summarising French opposition to the plan during debates in Geneva, Réquin insisted that the central issue was not numbers of divisions or cannons but instead conditions of security. He argued that the TMC must devote its attention to the necessary political bases for disarmament.[127]

Réquin's arguments pointed the way towards constructive discussion of European security in Geneva. Jean Gout, still head of the SFSDN, had emphasised the potential value of 'a more positive approach' in a note to Millerand:

Instead of always playing the dog in the manger, would we not be better off and more prudent by proposing our own serious plan for general disarmament? Consider the effect if France, accused of militarism, were to put itself at the head of the disarmament movement, but naturally under conditions clearly determined to assure our security and that of our allies in eastern Europe.[128]

Gout's reflection coincided, significantly, with increased British pressure on France to agree to some measure of disarmament.[129]

---

[125] MAE, *SDN*, vol. 17, Poincaré to the Directorate of higher education at the ministry of public instruction and fine arts, 24 Oct. 1923; also cited in Guieu, 'Les Apôtres', 293.

[126] MAE, *SDN*, vol. 707, Réquin note of 20 Mar. 1922 and Poincaré note to Geneva, 1 Apr. 1922.

[127] MAE, *SDN*, vol. 707, 'Note pour M. Lebrun', 3 Apr. 1922; SHD-DAT, 7N 3529–3, 'Rapport de la Commission permanente consultative ... à la suite de la session de Genève (12–17 mai 1922)', 19 Apr. 1922.

[128] MAE, PA-AP 118, *Papiers Millerand*, vol. 3, Gout to Millerand, 25 Feb. 1922.

[129] J. L. Hogge II, 'Arbitration, Sécurité, Désarmement: French Security and the League of Nations, 1920–1925', Ph.D. dissertation, New York University, 1994', 182–3.

The politics of confrontation 421

This was the background against which French officials responded to Lord Cecil's July 1922 proposal for a 'treaty of mutual guarantee' intended to prepare the way for disarmament. There were four chief principles to the 'Cecil Plan': first, no arms-reduction project could be successful unless it was general; second, in acknowledgement of the French position, no government could agree to significant disarmament without receiving substantial guarantees for its national security in return; third, security requirements could be fulfilled through a general defensive accord based on immediate mutual assistance; finally, the ultimate objective was a general agreement for arms reductions.[130] Cecil's plan marked a watershed because it placed the onus on French policy makers to engage constructively with the discourse of disarmament in Geneva. The French response was drafted by Réquin and Gout and approved by Poincaré in late August 1922. It established the bases for a new policy towards both disarmament and security.

Réquin and Gout both welcomed Cecil's linkage of disarmament with security. But they argued that the general nature of Cecil's idea of mutual guarantee rendered it no more effective than the Covenant. They urged instead that 'effective mutual assistance' should serve as the departure point for the construction of a system of 'regional defensive accords' between states with 'similar vital interests'.[131] Regional accords would bind states more closely than the Covenant because they would allow states with common security concerns to make the kind of specific military commitments that they would not extend to all League members. Arrangements for immediate military assistance were thus embedded in a larger multilateral framework.[132] Regional defensive accords would function as the building blocks for a wider security system. Negotiations for a treaty of mutual guarantee had become a means to pursue the elusive military guarantee from Britain.

Most French officials undoubtedly continued to prefer a traditional alliance. But even Poincaré acknowledged that such an alliance was impossible 'under the prevailing political conditions in Europe'.[133] Réquin advised that engaging with the idea of regional mutual assistance held out other benefits. It would 'attract the sympathy of other nations by proving before world opinion that we are looking for a positive solution'. Interestingly, Réquin argued that the benefits that would accrue would be 'perhaps superior to the reductions of armaments that we make in return for security guarantees'.[134] This view was

---

[130] Cecil, *Great Experiment*, 138–40; Mouton, *Société des nations*, 287–9.
[131] SHD-DAT, 7N 3529-3, 'Rapport du Lt-Col. Réquin sur les travaux de la Commission temporaire des armements (session de Paris, 3 et 7 juillet 1922)', 7 Jul. 1922.
[132] MAE, *SDN*, vol. 709, 'Note du Lt. Colonel Réquin: conclusions auxquelles conduit l'examen du projet de Lord Robert Cecil', 24 Apr. 1922; SHD-DAT, 7N 3529-3, as 'Note sur les projets de Lord Esher et de Lord Robert Cecil', 23 Aug. 1922, and marked 'approuvée par le président du conseil'.
[133] MAE, *Série Z, GB*, vol. 71, Poincaré to Saint-Aulaire, 11 Aug. 1922.
[134] MAE, PA-AP 118, *Papiers Millerand*, vol. 4, Réquin note, 6 Sept. 1922.

endorsed by de Jouvenel, who pointed out that France could not prevent discussion in Geneva and should therefore adopt a forward policy in order to shape the course of debate. Gout added that such an approach offered 'important propaganda advantages'. Poincaré was persuaded, and Réquin was granted permission to adopt a constructive approach in Geneva.[135] Pursuit of a Franco-British security pact within a system of regional mutual assistance was therefore a response to the changed international norms of the post-war era.

The first tangible result of the new approach was League Assembly Resolution XIV. This resolution, which was voted through in September 1922, called for a general treaty of security and disarmament. While it stipulated that arms reductions must be general in order to be effective, it also recognised that security must precede disarmament and, most importantly, that the conditions of security would best be realised in defensive agreements providing 'immediate and effective assistance in accordance with a pre-arranged plan'. This opened the way for regional accords with military conventions. Just as crucially, national governments would retain the right to determine the relationship between the security guarantees obtained from a future treaty and the level of arms reductions that could be undertaken.[136] Resolution XIV was a victory for the French position and a testament to Réquin's gifts as a negotiator.

Opinion among policy elites remained divided over its meaning, however. One current of thought, which included Réquin, the army high command, traditionalist diplomats and most Bloc politicians, saw it as an effective means of avoiding arms reductions without first achieving a British military commitment. An opposing view, which included the majority of centre-left political and public opinion as well as a number of League-minded officials at the foreign ministry, came to view the resolution as a bold new approach to obtaining security.[137] The SFSDN argued that a treaty of mutual assistance would 'put an end to the many fantasist projects for arms reductions' and contain 'wording that would not be illusory, but would provide us with real guarantees of security'.[138] But in 1922 the traditional approach remained ascendant. There was no hope that the Poincaré government would sign a general treaty without prior assurance of a British military guarantee.

The views of traditionally minded officials ensured that the idea of a general treaty was rejected. Peretti and chief legal counsel Henri Fromageot stressed that viable mutual assistance accords were impossible under the umbrella of

---

[135] MAE, PA-AP 118, *Papiers Millerand*, vol. 4, de Jouvenel to Poincaré, 14 Sept. 1922 and Gout to Millerand, 6 Sept. 1922.

[136] Quotes from A. Zimmern, *The League of Nations and the Rule of Law, 1918–1935* (London, 1936), 340; SHD-DAT, 7N 3531–1, 'Étude des conditions dans lesquelles des traités de garantie mutuelle pourraient permettre une réduction des armements', 19 Mar. 1923.

[137] Hogge, 'Arbitrage', 211–14.

[138] SHD-DAT, 7N 3529–3, 'Note au sujet de la Résolution XIV de l'Assemblée (Projet de traité de garantie mutuelle)', 8 Nov. 1922.

the League.[139] A long study of the issue by the SGDN concluded that 'the only immediate and truly effective means of assuring the security necessary for arms reductions is a series of very precise special conventions envisaging predetermined hypotheses for conflict ... the one power with the potential to provide effective and timely military assistance is Great Britain'.[140] In other words, the military demanded a more airtight version of the Franco-British military entente concluded before the First World War as the fundamental prerequisite to a wider treaty leading to arms reductions. Few policy makers harboured any illusions that such an entente was possible in 1923.

The French response was to attempt to close down all discussion of a general treaty.[141] But the issue would not go away. Lord Cecil submitted a draft mutual assistance treaty to the TMC in early 1923. Réquin advised both the foreign ministry and the premier that France must present a counter-proposal. His priority remained to shape the course of negotiations. Positive engagement, he argued, would 'serve France's ulterior policies' by putting an end to 'disarmament fantasies' and providing a means of answering criticism of its armaments levels. Poincaré, concerned with France's international image during the Ruhr Crisis, agreed.[142]

In the end Réquin's negotiating skills secured yet another victory for the French position. A French counter-proposal became the basis for a compromise 'Draft Treaty of Mutual Assistance'. This document combined Cecil's grandiose but vague ambitions for a general agreement with Réquin's insistence on precise (and unobtainable) security guarantees. The two core principles of the French position – security through immediate, prearranged military assistance and the state's right to judge what arms reductions might be made in accordance with security guarantees obtained – were embedded in the draft treaty. What was more, the draft treaty had no official status. French representatives could insist on whatever further clarifications they deemed necessary when the treaty was discussed in the Assembly and in the League Council. If need be, moreover, France could also veto the treaty in the Council.[143]

---

[139] MAE, PA-AP 118, *Papiers Millerand*, vol. 5, 'Note sur le projet d'assistance mutuelle', 21 Aug. 1923.

[140] SHD-DAT, 7N 3531-1, 'Étude des conditions dans lesquelles des traités de garantie mutuelle pourraient permettre une réduction des armements', 19 Mar. 1923 and 2N 5-9, 'Rapport fait au Conseil supérieur de la défense nationale au nom de la Commission d'études', 30 May 1923.

[141] P. Jackson, 'France and the problems of security and disarmament after the First World War', *JSS*, 29, 2 (2006), 262–5.

[142] MAE, *SDN*, vol. 716, Réquin note (forwarded to Poincaré), 5 May 1923; SHD-DAT, 7N 3531-1, 'Rapport du Lt. Colonel Réquin', 23 May 1923 and 'Note pour M. le Président du conseil', 24 May 1923.

[143] SHD-DAT, 7N 3531-1, 'Rapport du Lt. Colonel Réquin', 12 Jun. 1923 and 'Analyse du Rapport sur les travaux du Comité spécial de la Commission temporaire des armements de la SDN (session de juillet 1923)'.

Réquin's success did not satisfy deep misgivings about the whole enterprise among the traditional elements of the French policy machine. From the military came another round of criticisms aimed more at the ideas of multilateralism and arms reductions than at the contents of the draft treaty. Maginot refused to consider any agreement that 'admits *even the possibility* of future restrictions on our sovereignty over defence policy'.[144] Poincaré concurred with this view and instructed the French delegation in Geneva to avoid any further discussion of the draft treaty.[145]

There were thus clear limits to engagement with the League under Poincaré. The decision to break off negotiations in Geneva coincided, it is worth remembering, with the end of passive resistance in Germany and the resurgence of plans for an autonomous buffer state on the Left Bank. This conjuncture of events, when combined with determined opposition from the military and many professional diplomats, all but ensured that the draft treaty would be rejected.[146] At the same time, the extent to which French policy had evolved should not be underestimated. What French officials consistently termed 'a positive approach' marked an important departure from earlier strategies aimed at using the lack of security guarantees as a reason not to engage with initiatives from Geneva. From early 1922 this strategy shifted towards using disarmament negotiations as a means to obtain security guarantees, and in particular to secure a British commitment to underwrite the European status quo.

The return of Poincaré to power in early 1922 also marked a return to traditional security practices. From autumn 1922 French strategy focused increasingly on a bid to overturn the European strategic balance by transforming the political character of the Reich and creating an autonomous buffer zone on the Rhine. The traditional approach to national security was reinstated as a practical logic that shaped the choices of policy elites. Power politics became more central to foreign and security policy making than at any time since the political upheavals of 1917.

Yet there remained a significant counter-current to this trend. Resistance to the confrontational politics of the Poincaré government grew steadily on the left of the political spectrum. There were also contending perspectives within the policy machine. Deputy political director Laroche, for example, recommended as early as March 1923 that France's ultimate priority must be to 'hasten the return of normal relations with Germany'. This, he judged, would

---

[144] SHD-DAT, 7N 3531-1, 'Note au sujet du projet de traité d'assistance mutuelle' (SGDN note), 15 Aug. 1923; 'Note: Considérations générales sur le projet d'assistance mutuelle' (general staff note), Aug. 1923; 'Pacte de garantie et réduction des armements' (general staff note), 1 Sept. 1923; 'Pacte de garantie et réduction des armements', Maginot to Poincaré, 7 Sept. 1923 (emphasis in original).
[145] SHD-DAT, 7N 3531-1, Poincaré to the French delegation in Geneva, 12 Sept. 1923.
[146] Jackson, 'Security and disarmament', 264–5.

open the way to reconstituting the Entente, which was 'the pivot around which European politics must turn'.[147] Seydoux had from the beginning taken such an international perspective on the Ruhr Crisis and was consistently sceptical of the strategy of destroying German power. 'We must always keep in mind', he had advised Poincaré in early February, 'that our true objective is the moral disarmament of Germany ... treaty revision must be envisaged eventually but can only take place once Germany has accepted her obligations to participate in the construction of a durable peace settlement.'[148]

Both Seydoux and Laroche were frustrated by Poincaré's refusal to negotiate after Germany ended passive resistance. Neither approved of the aggressive strategy adopted the following autumn.[149] In a conversation with Millerand's private secretary in November 1923, Seydoux expressed the deep misgivings that he shared with Laroche over the direction of French policy:

Is it wise to destroy German unity? Who knows what will happen in twenty years. We must not pursue a short-sighted policy. After a crisis Germany will pick herself back up and a reconstitution of her unity in a spirit of revenge might result in a Reich more dangerous to us than the one whose ruin we had sought.[150]

Laroche and Seydoux favoured cooperation with Germany from a position of strength. This view, significantly, corresponded almost exactly to the judgement of Philippe Berthelot expressed in a note to Briand at the opening of the Ruhr Crisis:

It should not be forgotten that, even if we are stronger today and will remain so for another decade, in twenty to fifty years the weight of 70 million organised and hardworking Germans will ultimately overcome that of 38 million Frenchmen. If therefore we do not succeed in the creation of a German republic hostile to war, we are doomed. Far from gaining ground among democratic opinion, we ceaselessly attract its hatred. In the event that we succeed in forcing Germany to give in through our pressure in the Ruhr, our immediate policy thereafter will have to be very generous and very probably sacrifice the original objective of our action.[151]

Two aspects of this diagnosis are particularly interesting. The first is its ideological dimension: crucial importance is attributed to the development of democracy in Germany. The second is its implicit assumption that long-term security rested on some form of durable Franco-German reconciliation. Both elements of Berthelot's analysis were compatible with the internationalist

---

[147] MAE, PA-AP 008, *Papiers Barrère*, vol. 3, Laroche to Barrère, 8 Mar. 1923.
[148] MAE, PA-AP 261, *Papiers Seydoux*, vol. 7, 'Note de M. Seydoux: occupation de la rive gauche du Rhin', 16 Feb. 1923.
[149] Laroche, *Quai d'Orsay*, 89, 190; Trachtenberg, *Reparation*, 305–16; B. Auffray, *Pierre de Margerie et la vie diplomatique de son temps, 1861–1942* (Paris, 1976), 428–9.
[150] AN, 470 AP 71, *Archives Millerand*, 'Conversation avec Seydoux et avec Laroche', 7 Nov. 1923.
[151] Quoted in G. Suarez, *Briand: sa vie, son oeuvre, avec son journal et de nombreux documents inédits*, 6 vols. (Paris, 1938–52), vol. V: *Artisan de la paix, 1918–1923* (Paris, 1941), 429–30.

agenda for European reconstruction. They were very different from the aims that inspired the Poincaré government's occupation of the Ruhr.

Berthelot expressed this view from exile. He had been officially suspended from the diplomatic service after a humiliating disciplinary hearing conducted at Poincaré's insistence in March 1922.[152] The episode created considerable tension within the Quai d'Orsay, where Berthelot remained popular and influential (particularly with the younger generation of officials now rising to positions of greater responsibility within the ministry). Most agreed with Berthelot's call for a new approach to security.[153]

Discontent within the Quai d'Orsay would prove crucial. As Professor Jeannesson has argued, 'the occupation of the Ruhr, by its failure, put an end to a certain conception of Franco-German relations founded on bi-lateral force'.[154] Growing support for an alternative strategy among professional diplomats provided Édouard Herriot with a constituency with which he could work to implement his agenda for a new direction in foreign and security policy after the elections of May 1924.

---

[152] MAE, *Dossiers de Personnel*, 2ème série, vol 15: *Philippe Berthelot*, dossier marked 'Réservé', untitled transcript of the disciplinary hearing dated 13 Mar. 1922; see also J. L. Barré, *Philippe Berthelot: l'éminence grise, 1866–1934* (Paris, 1998), 375–83.

[153] P. Jackson, 'Tradition and adaptation: the social universe of the French foreign ministry in the era of the First World War', *French History*, 24, 2 (2010), 184–6.

[154] Jeannesson, *Ruhr*, 414.

Part V

The Cartel des gauches and the 'internationalisation of security'

'The objective of my policy', explained premier Édouard Herriot to the chamber's foreign affairs commission in early 1925, 'is the internationalisation of security.' This, Herriot observed, required greater faith in international cooperation and strengthening the collective security machinery of the League of Nations.[1] Herriot was summarising the reorientation of French security policy put in place by the Cartel des gauches after its electoral victory in May 1924.

This decisive shift in policy practices has gone virtually unnoticed in the historiography of inter-war international relations. Historians have ignored the ideological commitment to internationalism on the part of the Cartel. Nor has the existing literature considered the impact of Cartel politics on those security professionals responsible for the formulation and execution of policy. The tendency has instead been to try to force the Cartel security policy into a traditional framework. Professor Soutou, for example, has recently argued that the security policy of the Herriot government 'consisted overwhelmingly of an effort to contain Germany more by a geo-strategic balance of traditional inspiration than by collective security'.[2] Walter McDougall judged that the years 1924 to 1926 marked the utter defeat of French efforts to achieve 'a stabilization based on material guarantees of a balance of power'.[3] Even those scholars that allow for a measure of change over time do not see the impetus for that change coming from inside France. Patrick Cohrs, for example, assumes that only British and American statesmen underwent a 'learning process' and responded to the changed normative context of the post-1918 international environment. Changes in French policy were the product of British and American pressure and, when they emerged, were based on 'Anglo-Saxon' conceptions of international security. Cohrs goes so far as to assert that 'de facto French policy... gravitated towards Anglo-American principles and rules

---

[1] AN, C/14762, *CAEAN*, XIIIème Législature, Herriot *audition*, 11 Mar. 1925.
[2] G.-H. Soutou, 'Le Deuil de la puissance (1914–1958)' in *Histoire de la diplomatie française*, vol. II: *De 1815 à nos jours* (Paris, 2005), 321.
[3] W. McDougall, *France's Rhineland Diplomacy, 1914–1924: The Last Bid for a Balance of Power in Europe* (Princeton, 1978), 374.

of pacific settlement'.[4] Specifically French principles, according to this view, either did not exist or had no impact on the evolution of French policy.

There are two general reasons why historians have failed to understand the dynamic changes at work in French security policy. The first is a preoccupation with economic and especially financial questions that characterises the historiography. In his impressive study of international politics in 1924, for example, Stephen Schuker begins with the assumption that reparations were 'the pivotal issue in European diplomacy during the years after the war'.[5] Financial questions were similarly at the heart of the analyses of Denise Artaud and Marc Trachtenberg. Key works by McDougall and Jacques Bariéty deployed a broader approach but nonetheless end with the London Conference. Clemens Wurm's detailed study of French security policy during this period, meanwhile, scarcely mentions the negotiations surrounding the Geneva Protocol, passing directly from the London Conference to the diplomatic exchanges leading up to Locarno.[6] The result of this preoccupation is the judgement that foreign and security policy was determined overwhelmingly by economic considerations. Nicole Jordan, for example, concludes that the 'reorientation' in French policy during this period came about 'not for ideological reasons' but instead 'as a function of French reparations policy, which increasingly worked to define national security in economic terms'.[7]

A second factor contributing to the skewed picture that prevails is a widespread unwillingness to take seriously the influence of internationalist conceptions of peace and security. Most scholars tend to depict Herriot, who became premier and foreign minister after the electoral victory of the Cartel des gauches, as a well-meaning but naïve figure who lacked a coherent policy programme or any clear idea of how to achieve national security.[8] Little importance is attributed to Herriot's pronouncements on foreign and security policy before he became premier. Cartel security policy is instead interpreted either as a confused attempt to continue Poincaré's policy or as an empty vessel with no motivating principles or pre-existing doctrine. Even those scholars who acknowledge the importance of internationalist ideas do not recognise the importance of a specifically French variant of internationalism. Serge Berstein, for example, rightly points out that the security policy of the Herriot government is based on

---

[4] P. Cohrs, *The Unfinished Peace after World War I* (Cambridge, 2006), 606–12.
[5] S. Schuker, *The End of French Predominance in Europe: The Financial Crisis of 1924 and the Adoption of the Dawes Plan* (Chapel Hill, 1977), 6.
[6] C. Wurm, *Die Französische Sicherheitspolitik in der Phase der Umorientierung, 1924–1926* (Frankfurt, 1979), 190–8.
[7] N. Jordan, 'The reorientation of French diplomacy in the 1920s: the role of Jacques Seydoux', *EHR*, 117, 473 (2002), 877.
[8] A. Adamthwaite, *Grandeur and Misery: France's Bid for Power in Europe, 1914–1940* (London, 1995), 102–6; Jordan, 'Reorientation of French diplomacy', 876–9; J. Bariéty, *Les Relations franco-allemandes après la première guerre mondiale* (Paris, 1977), 348–9, 680–4, 703–22; Schuker, *End*, 126–9, 232–7; J.-N. Jeanneney, *La Faillite du Cartel, 1924–1926: leçon d'histoire pour une gauche au pouvoir*, 2nd edn (Paris, 1981), 50–4.

'an alternative philosophy of international relations'. But he wrongly characterises this philosophy as 'Wilsonian in inspiration'.[9]

The book's final two chapters challenge the standard narrative of French foreign and security policy in the mid-1920s. They argue that Herriot's government did have a reasonably coherent foreign policy programme. The core objectives of this programme were guarantees embedded in international public law and backed up by binding commitments of mutual assistance under the wider umbrella of the League of Nations. This international approach to France's security was expressed in the formula 'arbitration–security–disarmament' that was introduced at the Fifth League Assembly in September 1924. French negotiators succeeded in placing this formula at the heart of international efforts to bolster the collective security provisions of the Covenant in a process that resulted in the Geneva Protocol. The Protocol was a Europe-wide system based on the principle of mutual assistance and resting on binding arbitration that was underwritten by Britain and France. It marked a decisive transition from security based on traditional practices of the balance of power, exclusive alliances and the Rhine.

This transition cannot be properly understood without taking into account the seismic changes in French attitudes towards the issues of peace and security towards the middle of the 1920s. This period saw a dramatic rise in support for the League of Nations. This development proceeded hand in hand with the emergence of an increasingly large and well-organised pacifist movement in France as dominant narratives of the war as a heroic struggle for the *patrie* were gradually displaced by discourses of suffering and sacrifice at the front and national mourning on the home front. These trends provided the crucial political context for growing disillusion with the confrontational style of foreign and security policy under Poincaré and increased support for a strategy based on international cooperation advocated by the political leadership of the Cartel des gauches electoral coalition. By mid-1924 even André Tardieu, who had been a prominent advocate of a hardline policy based on strict treaty enforcement, was moved to observe that 'there is no longer any room for anyone's hegemony'.[10]

The Protocol foundered in the face of opposition from a new British government elected in November 1924. Britain's refusal to ratify the agreement was a blow for French foreign and security policy under Herriot. But the Protocol nonetheless served as a template for French policy in the difficult discussions that led to signature of the Locarno Accords in October 1925. Herriot's government fell in April of that year. But the essentials of its negotiating strategy were taken up by Aristide Briand, who succeeded him as foreign minister in another Cartel government led by Paul Painlevé. Although

---

[9] S. Berstein, *Histoire du Parti Radical*, vol. I: *À la Recherche de l'âge d'or* (Paris, 1980), 398.
[10] Quoted in McDougall, *Rhineland Diplomacy*, 369.

Briand was forced to make important sacrifices to secure a British guarantee of the Rhineland frontier, the core elements of the Protocol, and in particular the principles of arbitration and interlocking mutual assistance, remained central to the Locarno Treaties. A focus on this internationalist dimension to French policy provides a fresh perspective on the road to Locarno.

12 A new approach: arbitration, security, disarmament

The Geneva Protocol is one of the most neglected episodes in the history of twentieth-century international relations. Historians of this period have focused overwhelmingly on the Dawes Plan and the London Conference of July–August 1924. The international effort to devise a new security architecture for Europe undertaken in Geneva in September 1924, however, has been treated as an afterthought, when it has not been ignored altogether. The result has been a general failure to recognise the revolution in French foreign and security policy implemented by the Radical-dominated government of Édouard Herriot. From the outset Herriot was resolved to pursue an internationalist vision of security based on strengthening both international law and the coercive power of the League of Nations. The French programme provided the conceptual architecture for the Geneva Protocol. The foreign policy of the Cartel des gauches thus marked a decisive break from the traditional aims of the Poincaré government. Taking account of the internationalist current in French thinking about peace and security provides a new perspective on both the foreign policy of France and European international relations in 1924.

I

Édouard Herriot was fifty-one years of age when he assumed the portfolios of premier and foreign minister in the first Cartel government, established in June 1924. The son of an impoverished army officer, Herriot was a brilliant student whose rise to the pinnacle of French political life has led Serge Berstein to characterise his career as the 'personification' of the Third Republic.[1] Herriot was a *normalien* who ranked first in the *agrégation* for his year. He taught rhetoric at a *lycée* in Lyons (where his pupils included future Radical luminaries Édouard Daladier and Yvon Delbos) while completing a doctorate in French literature. The Dreyfus Affair was pivotal to Herriot's political evolution. Herriot was one of the founders of the Lyons branch of the Ligue des droits de l'homme. A gifted orator with immense personal charm, he was also a

---

[1] S. Berstein, *Édouard Herriot ou la république en personne* (Paris, 1985); see also É. Herriot, *Jadis*, 2 vols. (Paris, 1952).

passionate defender of parliamentary republicanism. After joining the Radical Party he rose rapidly in local politics, replacing his patron Victor Augagneur as mayor of Lyons in 1905 (a post he would hold for more than fifty years). Herriot entered national politics in 1912 when he was elected senator for the Rhône *département*. His political rise was confirmed in 1919 when, almost unexpectedly, he was elected president of a Radical Party seeking to revive its fortunes.[2]

Herriot's credentials as a republican of the centre-left were by this time well established. His attitude towards international politics was less well developed, however. During the war he had been both a prominent figure within the Comité de la rive gauche du Rhin and a passionate campaigner for a society of nations to establish the rule of international law. His initial preoccupations as Radical Party president were to establish his personal authority and to maintain party unity in preparation for a shift back to the left that would culminate in an electoral alliance with the SFIO. By late 1921, as we have seen, Herriot had developed a more clearly defined position on foreign policy that emphasised international cooperation and championed the League of Nations. And yet, as we have also seen, he was loath to alienate traditionalists on the right of his party by assuming a position in direct opposition to the Ruhr occupation. It was only after Herriot assumed control of foreign policy as head of government that the extent of his commitment to internationalism became clear.

Historians have been little impressed with Herriot's performance as a statesman in 1924. Anthony Adamthwaite describes Herriot as 'wet and weak'. Jordan, meanwhile, refers to him as 'the hapless Radical-Socialist Édouard Herriot'. The interpretations of Bariéty, Schuker and Jean-Noël Jeanneney echo these judgements.[3] Much of this criticism is deserved. Herriot's literary background and experience in provincial politics left him ill prepared for the formidable financial problems confronting his Cartel government when it assumed power in mid-June. He did not possess good contacts within either industrial or banking circles. From the very beginning these two constituencies manifested a profound lack of confidence in Cartel finance policy. Nor was the new premier inclined to put in the time and effort required to understand the complex interrelationship between domestic fiscal policy, diplomacy and international finance. Herriot, unlike Poincaré, was not an *homme de dossiers*. He preferred grand designs to detailed plans.

All of these factors contributed to the Cartel's comprehensive failure to deal with France's ongoing financial crisis. At the same time, many of the criticisms

---

[2] S. Berstein, *Histoire du Parti Radical*, vol. I: *À la recherche de l'âge d'or* (Paris, 1980), 139–62.
[3] A. Adamthwaite, *Grandeur and Misery: France's Bid for Power in Europe, 1914–1940* (London, 1995), 102–3; Jordan, 'Reorientation of French diplomacy', 877; J. Bariéty, *Les Relations franco-allemandes après la première guerre mondiale* (Paris, 1977), 348–9; S. Schuker, *The End of French Predominance in Europe: The Financial Crisis of 1924 and the Adoption of the Dawes Plan* (Chapel Hill, 1977), 126–9, 232–7; J.-N. Jeanneney, *La Faillite du Cartel, 1924–1926: leçon d'histoire pour une gauche au pouvoir*, 2nd edn (Paris, 1981), 50–1.

of foreign and security policy under Herriot are based on fundamental misunderstandings of the nature of that policy. Herriot is often censured for failing to secure essentially traditional objectives – most notably lasting military preponderance over Germany – that were impossible to obtain, and were never core objectives of his security policy in any case. It must also be acknowledged that the Cartel inherited a terrible financial legacy from the Bloc national. France's chronic indebtedness had only worsened under Poincaré, who, like his predecessors, had failed to implement a creditable fiscal policy. The result, by early 1924, was an exchange crisis that threatened to undermine national solvency and placed powerful restrictions on foreign and defence policy options.

To understand the dynamics of the financial crisis it is important to remember that in the aftermath of the Great War, France's political elites were grappling with the challenge of devising a modern system of taxation and public expenditure. The chief consequence of their failure to agree on such a system was that the national deficits of the post-war period exceeded those of wartime.[4] As it became increasingly evident that German reparations payments would not solve the debt question, observers both inside and outside France became concerned that lack of a coherent fiscal policy could destroy the value of the franc. Towards the end of 1922 France had reached the limits of its domestic borrowing capacity. An increasing proportion of government spending had therefore to be financed through the sale of short-term bonds with maturities of between one month and one year. The result was an ever larger 'floating debt' (76 billion francs by late 1922) that left the government in a highly vulnerable position should investors take fright and not renew bonds as they became due. Should the government be forced to print money to cover any shortfall, this might provoke a run on the franc.[5]

The danger this situation posed to French finances was underlined in memoranda by de Lasteyrie and Jean Parmentier, the director of the Mouvement général des fonds at the finance ministry. Both stressed the need to take action to reduce the budget deficit by raising taxes and cutting expenditure. Parmentier, in particular, urged drastic reductions in government spending on pensions and reconstruction. The measure finally introduced was the *double décime*: a 20 per cent increase in nearly all taxes, aimed at covering the deficit for the financial year. In presenting the *double décime* to parliament, de Lasteyrie described it as a temporary expedient to be scrapped once reparations began to arrive from Germany. Even so, the new tax was resisted vigorously in the national press, in the chamber and in the senate. Poincaré proved unwilling to press too hard

---

[4] Schuker, *End*, 38; my analysis of the financial crisis of 1924 relies heavily on Schuker's indispensable study.
[5] Ibid., 37–9; J.-J. Becker and S. Berstein, *Victoire et frustrations, 1914–1929* (Paris, 1990), 227–9.

over the issue at a time when he was seeking to build a national consensus in favour of the Ruhr operation. And so the *double décime* languished in parliamentary committees for the whole of 1923. Public and parliamentary opinion were not ready to do away with the fiction of 'recoverable expenses' and the hope that reparations payments would restore the nation's financial health.[6]

The exchange crisis of early 1924 forced political elites to give up this fantasy and accept that France would have to rely on its own resources to reduce its debt. The franc had begun to lose ground on the international exchange in mid-1922, falling from 10.80 to the dollar in April of that year to 14.62 in November. Over the course of 1923 its value declined by a further 31 per cent. This decline became precipitous in January 1924, when a 'bear raid' on the franc caused its value to drop to 28.74 to the dollar by 8 March. For the first time the front pages of French newspapers quoted the exchange rate.[7] In the end France was forced to turn to Wall Street for help in saving its currency. With the blessing of the American government, the French treasury was able to secure from JP Morgan a large dollar credit that was used to turn the tables and rout international speculators. To obtain this loan, however, the Poincaré government was forced to give assurances that it would implement a credible programme of taxation and spending cuts. Although Poincaré had often pledged that he would never 'entrust the destinies of France to international bankers', the exchange crisis highlighted France's vulnerability and dependence on international foreign capital.[8] The fact that the exchange crisis coincided with the massacre of remaining separatist elements in the Palatinate only underlined the extent to which France's international position had changed since the previous spring.[9]

This was the international context in which the committees of international financial experts began their work in January 1924. The most important of these, chaired by the American banker and politician Charles Dawes, was officially charged with formulating proposals to restore Germany's finances. Its remit expanded steadily, however, as a result of American and British pressure to include a comprehensive plan for reparations payments.[10] Poincaré, who had accepted the proposal for an expert committee during the heady period the previous autumn when Prussian Germany seemed on the verge of breaking apart, struggled from the beginning to restrict its purpose and powers. The French premier argued that the scope of the enquiry should be

---

[6] Schuker, *End*, 44–50; N. Roussellier, *Le Parlement d'éloquence: la souveraineté de la délibération au lendemain de la Grande Guerre* (Paris, 1997), 239–42.

[7] Figures from Schuker, *End*, 53–5 and Becker and Berstein, *Victoire et frustrations*, 228.

[8] Schuker, *End*, 89–123 and 171–231 (quotation at 110); K. Mouré, *The Gold Standard Illusion: France, the Bank of France, and the International Gold Standard, 1914–1939* (Oxford, 2002), 71–6; and A. Sauvy, *Histoire économique de la France*, 4 vols. (Paris, 1967), I, 45–57.

[9] A point made forcefully by Seydoux in MAE, PA-AP 261, *Papiers Seydoux*, vol. 1, 'Possibilités de négociations avec l'Allemagne et l'Angleterre' (a retrospective analysis), 25 Aug. 1924.

[10] Bariéty, *Relations franco-allemandes*, 307–14; P. Cohrs, *The Unfinished Peace after World War I* (Cambridge, 2006), 137–41; and esp. Schuker, *End*, 180–4.

limited to evaluating German capacity to pay and proposing means to obtain payment.[11] Poincaré was just as adamant that the final sum fixed in May 1921 could not be revised, nor could the occupation of the Ruhr be discussed. Neither the British nor the American governments were willing to accept these restrictions, however. Both threatened to refuse to take part if the investigative committee was not given the power to recommend a new payments programme. In the end Poincaré was forced to give way and accept a committee with the power to recommend a new system of reparations payments.[12] When the Dawes Committee eventually reported on 9 April 1924, its proposals amounted to a far-reaching revision of the entire reparations regime established under the London Schedule.

The Dawes Plan did not offer a definitive solution to the reparations issue. Nor did it address the question of Germany's total liability directly. But its terms implied a significant de facto reduction of the German debt and an end to the Ruhr occupation. It proposed a payment programme to last a maximum of sixty-four years, with initial annuities set at 1 billion gold marks that would rise to 2.5 billion by 1928–9. Thereafter annual payments would be adjusted upwards in accord with an 'index of prosperity' linked to German economic growth. Annuity payments would cover not only reparations payments but also the maintenance of the occupation forces and, importantly, interest on the foreign loan that would be raised to launch the plan. Half of the annuity would be drawn from the government budget, with the remainder coming from interest on bond issues set against German industry and railway assets.[13]

Two aspects of the Dawes Plan merit particular consideration. First, the plan recommended what was in effect a major reduction in Germany's total liability. Assuming payments continued for the maximum sixty-four years (until 1988–9), the value of German debt was worth 39–40 billion gold marks. But this schedule was not expected to remain in place. It was widely recognised at the time that the plan was an interim arrangement that would sooner or later be revised further (as indeed it was under the Young Plan of 1929). Second, the Dawes Committee's proposals for the economic and financial restoration of Germany assumed the fiscal and commercial unity of the Reich. France would relinquish its 'productive guarantees' in exchange for an 800-million goldmark financial stimulus to Germany (financed by American and British private capital) designed to establish conditions for future reparations payments.[14]

---

[11] MAE, RC, Série B84, vol. 20, Poincaré to André de Laboulaye (chargé d'affaires in Washington), 6 Nov. 1923.
[12] S. Jeannesson, 'La Sous-direction des relations commerciales du Quai d'Orsay' in L. Badel, S. Jeannesson and P. Ludlow (eds.), *Les Administrations nationales et la construction européenne: une approche historique* (Berne, 2005), 49–50; Schuker, *End*, 171–3.
[13] HMSO, Cmd. 2105, *Reports of the Expert Committees appointed by the Reparation Commission* (London, 1924); R. W. Boyden, 'The Dawes Report', *Foreign Affairs* (June 1924), 583–97; Schuker, *End*, 180–6; Bariéty, *Relations franco-allemandes*, 308–11.
[14] Boyden, 'Dawes Report', 588–91; Schuker, *End*, 185–6.

Crucially, the report ruled out the future seizure of any such guarantees except in the event of a 'flagrant failure to fulfil the conditions accepted'. In this case it was anticipated that the 'creditor governments' would take collective action.[15] The Dawes Plan was a thoroughly internationalist solution to the reparations impasse that left the related issues of war debts and security very much up in the air.

International reaction to the Dawes Committee report was in general favourable.[16] Although it continued to insist on its political neutrality, the American government gave the project enthusiastic support and indicated its willingness to sanction the private loans from Wall Street at the heart of the programme.[17] The Belgian government, desperate to get out of the Ruhr, also embraced the Dawes proposals. British officials judged the payments regime still too harsh. Ramsay MacDonald, the newly elected Labour prime minister who also assumed the role of foreign secretary, was resigned to acceptance of the plan but aimed to place maximum pressure on France to accept it without revision. The German government, led by Wilhelm Marx with Stresemann as foreign minister, expressed disappointment that the Dawes proposals did not include a straightforward reduction in Germany's total reparations debt and protested that the annuities were too high. But it also recognised that the plan would restore German economic sovereignty in the Ruhr and Rhineland and leave open the possibility for further payment reductions in the future. Stresemann stipulated that German opinion could accept the Dawes programme only if France and Belgium ended the occupation of the Ruhr.[18]

In Paris senior policymakers initially considered the Dawes Report as a starting point for a lengthy process of negotiation. The Poincaré government hoped to avoid having to relinquish any of the *gages* France had seized. Particular importance was attached to maintaining the Franco-Belgian *régie*, which provided control of German railways on the Left Bank and in the Ruhr. Poincaré further sought to link any reduction of the German reparations obligation to a similar reduction in French war debts owed to Britain and the USA. And he refused to renounce France's right to impose unilateral sanctions until a detailed procedure was put in place for automatic collective action in the event of a German default.[19] In the end France was the last state to accept the Dawes Report, on 25 April 1924. Nor was its acceptance unconditional. 'It is for governments to determine the guarantees necessary for the implementation

---

[15] Schuker, *End*, 186.
[16] Where not otherwise indicated, this paragraph is drawn from the excellent synthesis in Z. Steiner, *The Lights that Failed: European International History, 1919–1933* (Oxford, 2005), 241–3.
[17] Cohrs, *Unfinished Peace*, 139–42.
[18] Schuker, *End*, 190–1; E. O'Riordan, *Britain and the Ruhr Crisis* (London, 2001), 145–60; J. Wright, *Gustav Stresemann: Weimar's Greatest Statesman* (Oxford, 2002), 270–80.
[19] MAE, Série Z, GB, vol. 57, Poincaré to Saint-Aulaire, 17 Apr. 1924; PA-AP 118, *Papiers Millerand*, vol. 32, Poincaré to de Laboulaye, 8 Nov. 1923; Schuker, *End*, 205–16; Bariéty, *Relations franco-allemandes*, 309–13.

of the experts' programme,' asserted the official French note to the Reparations Commission. Poincaré sought, in other words, to retain control of the occupation regime in the Ruhr until France obtained satisfaction over the questions of sanctions, war debts and the wider security regime to be imposed.

Poincaré's opposition to the conditions outlined in the Dawes Plan was by no means the majority view within the foreign ministry. Seydoux viewed the implementation of the plan as another opportunity to launch his programme for industrial and commercial collaboration with Germany. He had raised this possibility in a meeting with the influential German banker Hjalmar Schacht in late January. Seydoux's abiding preoccupation was to ensure a steady flow of coal and coke to the steel mills in Lorraine. This could best be guaranteed, he argued, if it was embedded in industrial and commercial accords that were linked to reparations but would be profitable for both parties. He added that it was time to move beyond the economic structures established in 1919 to set Franco-German relations on a new footing. 'I am opposed to the continuation of the economic system [created by] the peace treaty,' he informed Schacht, 'which prevents the resumption of normal economic life and, as a consequence, peaceful relations between France and Germany.'[20]

Seydoux developed a programme for economic cooperation in two important memoranda drafted in spring 1924. Both stressed European economic interdependence and the importance of concerted action between Britain, France and Germany. Seydoux argued in mid-February that

> It is essential to establish a general programme of European reconstruction that will reopen markets. But such a programme makes sense only if Britain forges a close economic understanding with France, Belgium and Germany. Europe, for its part, needs the financial power of Britain; it is only by way of such an understanding that the states of the continent can recover financially and that Britain can obtain the markets it needs for its economic recovery.[21]

Seydoux's prescriptions for a Europe-wide programme for economic recovery, which anticipated post-1945 structures of European cooperation, were based on an internationalist conception of economic security. This dimension of Seydoux's analysis is even more pronounced in a note of 30 May 1924, where he observed that the central objective to be attained was

> essentially a matter of us coming to terms with Britain on a formula that will allow Germany to find its place in the Europe of today and to pursue, in concert with the Allies, the work of economic and financial reconstruction that alone can heal the wounds of the war and avoid new conflicts in the future.

---

[20] MAE, PA-AP 261, *Papiers Seydoux*, vol. 1, 'Visite de M. Schacht à M. Seydoux', 24 Jan. 1924.
[21] MAE, PA-AP 261, *Papiers Seydoux*, vol. 30, Seydoux note forwarded to Saint-Aulaire, 18 Feb. 1924.

Seydoux was alive to the political dimension of this project. 'If French and German industries do not collaborate to pool their resources of coal and iron ore and to share foreign markets,' he warned, 'they will soon be obliged to wage a merciless war with one another.'[22]

II

Seydoux's prescriptions were part of a wider reconsideration of France's foreign and security policy begun within the Quai d'Orsay. In late January Leopold von Hoesch, the acting head of the German embassy in Paris, had raised the possibility of a Franco-German security agreement as a means of improving relations between the two states and ending the Ruhr occupation. This prompted Seydoux to set down his views on the need to set any security arrangement with Germany in a wider multilateral scheme anchored by a close Franco-British *entente*. For such an *entente* to succeed, he judged, France would need to 'cease all practices that give the impression that we are pursuing a policy of encirclement or dislocation of Germany'.[23] Political director Peretti de la Rocca, a solid ally of Poincaré's, agreed that France 'must reassure the British entirely concerning our intentions in the Ruhr and the Rhineland'. But he did not approve of multilateral schemes that would include Germany.[24]

Poincaré at this time recognised the need to reconsider the bases of French security policy. He instructed Jules Laroche, now the second-ranking official within the foreign ministry, to prepare an analysis of the security problem for wider consideration. In a lengthy document first circulated on 21 February 1924, Laroche began with the observation that France had two choices: it could either continue to aim for permanent strategic predominance through control of the Rhineland or it could pursue security through a multilateral strategy based on the principle of mutual assistance rather than exclusive alliances. The first option, he asserted, had been tried and had failed.[25] Laroche therefore recommended 'a pact or a system of pacts between interested nations providing security guarantees in the form of automatic sanctions that would extend to the use of armed force'. Such a solution, he argued, 'would be an improvement on the League of Nations, which, while its moral force is bound to grow, will continue for a long time to remain rather inoperable in its actions and especially slow to put these into motion'. The initial phase of this system would be the

---

[22] MAE, *RC*, Série B84, vol. 24, Seydoux note, 30 May 1924, also cited in Jeannesson, 'Relations commerciales', 50–1.

[23] MAE, PA-AP 118, *Papiers Millerand*, vol. 35, 'Note', 4 Feb. 1924.

[24] MAE, PA-AP 118, *Papiers Millerand*, vol. 9, handwritten note by Peretti dated 5 Feb. 1924; also cited in Bariéty, *Relations franco-allemandes*, 294.

[25] This study evolved over three months in an interesting process that can be traced in MAE, PA-AP 118, *Papiers Millerand*, vol. 41, 'Étude des garanties de sécurité', 21 Feb. 1924; 'Envoi d'une note sur le problème de la sécurité' (Poincaré directive instructing the foreign ministry to collaborate with the general staff), 29 Mar. 1924; 'Note sur les garanties de sécurité', 14 Apr. 1924; 'Garanties de sécurité', 20 May 1924.

construction of a Franco-British–Belgian pact 'inspired by the old treaties of guarantee, but more precise and more clearly adapted to prevailing circumstances'. This tripartite pact constituted the chief deterrent element in Laroche's scheme. It was also a strategy to bind Britain to the wider European status quo. France and Britain would together underwrite an interlocking system of regional pacts that included Germany and extended to eastern Europe.[26]

Laroche noted that France would need to incorporate the new states of eastern Europe in this strategy. The British, he recognised, were sure to object to any military commitment to the new states of eastern Europe. He argued that the best way to answer British objections would be to erect 'a wider security system' alongside the Franco-British–Belgian agreement. Such a system would be constituted by a series of reciprocal non-aggression agreements and, crucially, would include Germany. In adhering to such an arrangement, Germany would commit itself to a 'regime of collective and individual guarantees against aggression'. This would provide France with 'a legal right to take military action against Germany through the demilitarized zone in the event it attacks any other states adhering to the pact'.[27] Laroche may well have been trimming his sails to the prevailing electoral winds in anticipation of a Cartel government. Whatever the case, his memoranda placed the idea of including Germany in a multilateral security system back on the agenda.

It was for this reason that Laroche's ideas met with sharp criticism. Regional security pacts, military officials argued, could be effective only if they included detailed joint planning for military assistance. 'In order to impose our will on Germany in wartime as well as peacetime,' insisted General Marie-Eugène Debeney (who replaced General Buat as army chief of staff in 1923), 'it is essential that we secure arrangements with powers allied to the west.' Assistance pacts could only function as worthwhile security guarantees, argued the chief of staff, 'on the condition that it is made absolutely clear that each pact will be followed by a military convention'.[28] There was also determined opposition to any arrangement that included Germany as an equal participant. 'It is imperative', asserted an army general staff assessment, 'that all supplementary guarantees be linked to the Treaty of Versailles.' This would 'enable us to maintain our position as victors and to avoid engaging in negotiations with Germany on a level of equality'.[29] Marshal Pétain, commander-in-chief

---

[26] MAE, PA-AP 118, *Papiers Millerand*, vol. 41, 'Étude des garanties de sécurité', 21 Feb. 1924 and 'Garanties de sécurité', 20 May 1924.
[27] SHD-DAT, 7N 3531-2, 'Étude des garanties de sécurité', 21 Feb. 1924.
[28] SHD-DAT, 7N 3531-2, 'Observations au sujet de la note des Affaires étrangères sur les Garanties de sécurité', 4 Apr. 1924; see also General Debeney's *Sur la Sécurité militaire de la France* (Paris, 1930), 106–30.
[29] SHD-DAT, 7N 3531-2, 'Au Sujet des garanties de sécurité', 1 May 1924.

designate, also insisted on the need to ensure 'automatic military sanctions'.[30] Foch, for his part, accepted that regional pacts might bolster the position of the eastern European successor states in relation to Germany and Soviet Russia. But he warned that France's security could be assured only by a permanent occupation of the Rhineland or by a military alliance with Britain.[31]

Military officials, in sum, were willing to contemplate regional pacts and mutual assistance only to the extent that they provided cover for traditional alliances directed against Germany. Opposition was not limited to the military establishment, however. From London, ambassador Saint-Aulaire described the idea of treating Germany as an equal as 'monstrous' and 'a negation of the very idea of a Franco-British alliance'.[32] From Rome, ambassador Barrère endorsed Saint-Aulaire's assessment, characterising all projects to 'place France on the same footing as Germany' as 'shocking' and 'intolerable'.[33] The traditional approach continued to enjoy extensive support within the French security policy establishment.

Laroche's memorandum was redrafted several times in an effort to incorporate the military point of view. But there was a fundamental theoretical divergence between the approach emerging within the Quai d'Orsay and that of the military services.[34] Laroche's arguments were based on the assumption that the guarantees of the Versailles Treaty provided only temporary security. It acknowledged the need to build a new system to meet the challenge France would face once the Rhineland was evacuated. Military officials, conversely, focused on adding a military alliance with Britain to the guarantees already embedded in the treaty. Meanwhile, an international arms-limitation agreement (something Britain was sure to demand in exchange for any security commitment to France) was opposed by virtually all senior military and naval officials.[35]

Poincaré almost certainly sensed that the military prescription for security was out of step with both external possibilities and the mood inside France. On 1 May, the eve of what would be his electoral defeat, the premier personally set out a revised security policy advocating a system of pacts between Germany's neighbours 'with the adhesion of Britain' as its chief objective.[36] Some change

---

[30] MAE, PA-AP 118, *Papiers Millerand*, vol. 41, 'Garanties de sécurité', 20 May 1924, note by Laroche recounting Pétain's views.
[31] SHD-DAT, 7N 3531-2, 'Note du Maréchal Foch', 15 Apr. 1924; SHD-DAT, 4N 92-2, État-major Foch, 'Pactes de garantie mutuelle', 30 May 1924; P. Jackson, 'Foch et la politique de sécurité française, 1919–1924' in F. Cochet and R. Porte (eds.), *Ferdinand Foch (1851–1929): apprenez à penser* (Paris, 2010), 333–47.
[32] SHD-DAT, 7N 3531-2, 'Au Sujet de la sécurité', Saint-Aulaire to Poincaré, 7 Apr. 1924.
[33] MAE, *Série Z, GB*, vol. 71, Barrère to Poincaré, 4 Apr. 1921.
[34] See the material in MAE, PA-AP 118, *Papiers Millerand*, vol. 41 and SHD-DAT, 7N 3531.
[35] P. Jackson, 'France and the problems of security and disarmament after the First World War', *JSS*, 29, 2 (2006), 261–6.
[36] SHD-DAT, 7N 3531-2, 'Analyse succincte de la note sur le garanties de sécurité', 1 May 1924.

in the orientation of foreign and security policy was therefore under way before the advent of the Cartel des gauches the following June. But the extent and significance of this change should not be exaggerated. While the principle of regional security pacts had been approved, such pacts were understood by Poincaré and his advisers primarily as a means of obtaining a military alliance with Britain. Opposition to any commitment to future disarmament, moreover, remained as powerful as ever. High-ranking military and diplomatic officials such as SGDN chief Serrigny and Peretti de la Rocca continued to speak out against the inclusion of Germany in any new security system.[37] The Poincaré government continued to adhere to a fundamentally traditional conception of French security. The commitment to a multilateral security system that included Germany was an innovation put in place by the Herriot government.

III

The innovative character of French policy under Herriot must be understood against the background of Radical Party attitudes towards security and foreign affairs. The wider context within which security policy was made has not been integrated into the existing literature on French strategy and diplomacy. Jacques Bariéty, for example, rightly points out that Radicals and Socialists remained divided by the discourse of international class struggle. But he wrongly argues that, because Herriot and other Radicals rejected the doctrine of class struggle, they were not internationalists. This judgement ignores the strength of juridical internationalism within the party as well as the central place of the League of Nations in Radical foreign policy doctrine.[38] The reality is that Herriot had been criticising the confrontational character of French policy under Poincaré consistently since mid-1922. Without international cooperation, he warned, the economic recovery of Europe was impossible. And without economic recovery 'all initiatives for our security will prove illusory'.[39] Herriot attributed priority to a restoration of the Entente and engagement with democratic Germany. His vision of international security was indisputably much closer to that advocated by Blum and the SFIO than to the traditional power politics of the Bloc national. These arguments for multilateral engagement were rooted firmly in the internationalist tradition of the Radical Party.[40]

---

[37] The SGDN remained equally opposed to Russian participation in any new security order. For Serrigny's views see SHD-DAT, 7N 3531-1, 'Note: considérations générales sur le projet d'assistance mutuelle' (general staff note), Aug. 1923 and 'Pacte de garantie et réduction des armements', 1 Sept. 1923; for those of Peretti see MAE, PA-AP 029, *Papiers Bourgeois*, vol. 22, Peretti, 'Note sur l'entrée de l'Allemagne dans la SDN', 26 Jul. 1922.
[38] Bariéty, *Relations franco-allemandes*, 324–52 (esp. 351).
[39] *JO*, Chambre, *Débats*, 1922, 2 Jun. 1922.
[40] Berstein, *Herriot*, 91; Berstein, *Recherche de l'âge d'or*, 332.

Radical disenchantment with Bloc security policy emerged clearly during parliamentary debates over the term of military service and thus the size of the standing army. A government project to lower the term of service from twenty-four to eighteen months occasioned the longest debate of the entire legislature (running from 28 February to 29 June 1922). The proposed reform aimed to reduce the total size of the national army to 660,000.[41] The programme was opposed by Radical and Socialist calls for one-year and eight-month service respectively.[42] But there was more at stake in this debate than the term of military conscription. The Radical and Socialist proposals envisaged a fundamentally defensive role for the army. Even a one-year military service regime would make it almost impossible for France to mount and sustain an ambitious occupation of the Ruhr. The government's plan, conversely, left the army of the Rhine with the capability to mount such an operation. Also at stake was the symbolic power of the army. An eighteen-month term of military service was accepted only reluctantly by both the army high command and nationalist right as the absolute minimum requirement for national security. In the end the eighteen-month law passed in the chamber. But it was opposed by many Radicals. For the first time in the post-war period arguments invoking the Union sacrée failed to rally the centre-left over a key issue related to national security.[43] The Radical Party was moving to the left.

The evolution of Radical attitudes is important for two reasons. First, the ultimate result of the leftward shift of the Radical Party would be an alliance with the Socialists and victory in the elections of May 1924. Second, the mood of the party reflected a growing disenchantment with the politics of confrontation among a French population that emerged from the war traumatised, exhausted and desiring above all a 'return to normalcy'.[44] The emergence of war veterans as a political and cultural force for which there was no precedent in French history was an important element in this process. France's *anciens combattants* were a mass movement with tremendous symbolic power. Between 1919 and 1936 veterans made up roughly one-half of the electorate (women were still denied the right to vote) and were universally acknowledged to

---

[41] J. Hughes, *To the Maginot Line: The Politics of French Military Preparation in the 1920s* (Cambridge, Mass., 1971), 123–43.

[42] F.-A. Paoli, *L'Armée française de 1919 à 1939*, vol. I: *La Phase de fermeté* (Vincennes, 1971), 105–12; P. Buffotot, *Le Socialisme français et la guerre: du soldat-citoyen à l'armée professionnelle, 1871–1998* (Paris, 1999), 91–7; Hughes, *Maginot Line*, 136–41.

[43] The final vote was 365–204: Roussellier, *Parlement d'éloquence*, 187–9; E. Bonnefous, *Histoire politique de la Troisième République*, vol. III: *L'Après-guerre* (Paris, 1959), 309–13.

[44] S. Tison, *Comment sortir de la guerre: deuil, mémoire et traumatisme (1870–1940)* (Rennes, 2011), 275–303; B. Martin, *France and the Après Guerre, 1918–1924* (Baton Rouge, 1999), 20–39; R. Kedward, *La Vie en bleu: France and the French since 1900* (London, 2005), 93–5; B. Cabanes and G. Pikett, *Retour à l'intime au sortir de la guerre* (Paris, 2009); T. Stovall, *Paris and the Spirit of 1919: Consumer Struggles, Transnationalism and Revolution* (Cambridge, 2012), 1–23; J. Winter, *Sites of Memory, Sites of Mourning* (Cambridge, 1995), 145–221; G. Thomas, *Treating the Trauma of the Great War: Soldiers, Civilians and Psychiatry in France, 1914–1940* (Baton Rouge, 2009).

possess inalienable rights over the rest of society. During the 1920s the political organisation of the veterans' movement was dominated by three large national associations: the Union nationale des mutilés et réformés, the Union fédérale (UF) and the Union nationale des combattants (UNC).[45] Antoine Prost demonstrated that anti-militarism and support for internationalist ideas were central features of veteran politics during this period. The left-leaning UF advocated a policy of reconciliation with Germany from the early 1920s. The UNC tended more to the right and was in general more sceptical of projects for Franco-German cooperation. But both organisations opposed large armaments expenditure and supported the cause of the League of Nations.[46] The 'Message to the French People' issued by the UF on 11 November 1922 expressed the complex mixture of patriotism and internationalism that characterised the veterans' movement in France:

Citizens! The men of the war wish to celebrate 11 November. The date 11 November 1918 marked the end of the most dreadful butchery ever to desolate the modern world ... Republican and pacific France battled for justice, for liberty and for the rule of law ... The men of the war desire that their victory consecrates an end to war. They desire that guilty Germany pay for the destruction it has unleashed. They desire that victorious France remain the homeland of justice and the soldier of peace. They desire that the present anarchy between peoples is replaced by the reign of law among nations.

The UF declaration concluded with an endorsement of the internationalist vision of peace and security:

War Veterans! In memory of the titanic struggle that we have endured, and in the name of our dead brothers, we are the pacific servants of the Society of Nations.[47]

Interestingly, a number of the key tropes of the patriotic–nationalist discourse are deployed in this passage. Germany is held responsible for the war and accountable for the damage done to France. But the prescription for future peace emphasises the rule of law and the League of Nations rather than the use of military force.

The politics of schoolteachers and the women's movement were characterised above all by a commitment to pacifism and internationalism. Nearly half of all teachers mobilised during the war were killed. These losses help explain the

---

[45] A. Prost, *Les Anciens combattants et la société française, 1914–1939*, 3 vols. (Paris, 1977), abridged in English as *In the Wake of War: Les Anciens combattants and French Society* (Oxford, 1992); see also Becker and Berstein, *Victoire et frustrations*, 165–9; and F. Monier, *Les Années 20* (Paris, 1999), 42–8.

[46] Prost, *Anciens combattants*, vol. III: *Mentalités et idéologies*, 35–151; A. Prost and J. Winter, *René Cassin* (Paris, 2011), 79–80, 94–105; C. Birebent, *Militants de la paix et de la SDN: les mouvements de soutien à la Société des nations en France et au Royaume-Uni, 1918–1925* (Paris, 2007), 107–12.

[47] 'Appel des mutilés et des combattants', reprinted in A. Prost, *Les Anciens combattants, 1914–1940* (Paris, 1977), 100–2; see also Prost and Winter, *René Cassin*, 43–78.

profound strength of pacifism among the teaching profession during the 1920s.[48] Women had also paid a heavy price for victory. The war had created more than 600,000 widows, and many more women had lost a son or a brother. A Ligue des femmes contre la guerre was founded in 1921. It forged links with similar anti-war groups within the worldwide women's movement. Both of these constituencies provided fertile ground for internationalist doctrines of peace and cooperation. Both were active in shaping public discourse in the post-war decade.[49]

The political influence of anti-militarist responses to the Great War gathered momentum only gradually after 1919. Nicolas Roussellier has traced this process in his brilliant study of parliamentary discourse in the post-war period. By 1923–4, he argues, the war 'had become above all a source of affliction rather than a means of political mobilization'.[50] The legacy of the conflict was a subject for mourning rather than a source of nationalist intransigence. The implications of this gradual but profound change in attitudes for national security policy would not be apparent until the electoral victory of the Cartel des gauches in 1924. But the process was well under way when French troops occupied the Ruhr in early 1923.

The left of the political spectrum embraced the politics of peace and cooperation from the outset. The SFIO had consistently opposed the Ruhr occupation as both immoral and impractical.[51] Blum criticised Poincaré relentlessly for basing France's security on 'calculations of power and the use of force that are from a bygone era'. The Ruhr strategy had failed to provide either economic or political security but had alienated France from Britain and closed down all prospects for meeting France's security requirements through international cooperation. These requirements, Blum argued, could not be resolved through 'traditional methods that have produced only war and suffering over the last two centuries'.[52]

It was the SFIO's position that in the end forced the Radical leadership to clarify its stance towards international affairs in general and the Ruhr in particular. Concerned to preserve party unity, Herriot had resisted pressure from Radical internationalists to oppose the occupation openly. But Socialist

---

[48] O. Loubes, *L'École et la patrie: histoire d'un désenchantement, 1914–1940* (Paris, 2001); M. Siegel, *The Moral Disarmament of France: Education, Pacifism and Patriotism, 1914–1940* (Cambridge, 2004). Loubes doubts the patriotic commitment of most teachers after 1919; Siegel makes a convincing argument to the contrary.

[49] C. Bard, *Les Filles de Marianne: histoire des féminismes, 1914–1940* (Paris, 1995), 135–41; S. Reynolds, *France between the Wars: Gender and Politics* (London, 1996), 181–94; Kedward, *Vie en bleu*, 105–6.

[50] Roussellier, *Parlement d'éloquence*, 98.

[51] L. Blum, *L'Oeuvre de Léon Blum, 1924–1928* (Paris, 1972), 259–330; see also T. Judt, *La Reconstruction du parti socialiste, 1921–26* (Paris, 1976), 121–2.

[52] R. Gombin, *Les Socialistes et la guerre: la SFIO et la politique étrangère entre les deux guerres mondiales* (The Hague, 1970), 55–62; *JO, Chambre, Débats*, 1923, 27 Dec. 1923; S. Berstein, *Léon Blum* (Paris, 2006), 238–44.

leaders made opposition to the occupation a condition for an electoral alliance. Herriot finally condemned the government's Ruhr policy before the Radical Party Congress in October 1923. Some historians have judged that this step was taken less out of conviction than out of a desire to ally with the SFIO.[53] This is to misread Herriot's personal position along with the strength of internationalism among the younger and more dynamic elements of the Radical movement. Before the chamber on 28 December 1923 Herriot stressed the importance of 'an international solution to the problem of reparations' based on 'the substitution of juridical guarantees for the military guarantees'. Two weeks later he sketched out the broad lines of a 'Radical policy' that would be based on 'the values of international solidarity' and 'an engagement with the democratic forces inside Germany'.[54]

By autumn 1923 the size and influence of the internationalist movement had increased along with public support for the League. Virtually all significant veterans' organisations, including the UF, the UNC, the Fédération nationale des anciens prisonniers de guerre and the Union nationale des mutilés et réformés, had allied themselves to the AFSDN. Union fédérale president René Cassin, who would serve as a French delegate in Geneva from 1924 to 1938, led the way in arguing that veterans must support the League's project to 'substitute the rule of law among nations for the existing state of anarchy in international politics'.[55] The pro-League movement was further bolstered by support from other elements of French civil society. The Union féminine pour la Société des nations was formed in 1920 and affiliated to the AFSDN, as was the Ligue des mères et éducatrices pour la paix. A prominent group of Catholic internationalists led by centre-right deputy Marc Sangnier endorsed the League as a force for progress and for the 'disarmament of hatred'.[56] The most dynamic civil society support for the League, however, came from French students. The first public meeting of the GUSDN took place in March 1923 with Robert Cecil, Henry de Jouvenel and Paul Painlevé in attendance. Although the GUSDN was not a mass organisation, it included an impressive cohort of activists, including René Pleven, Pierre Brossolette, Bertrand de

---

[53] D. Artaud, *La Question des dettes interalliées et la reconstruction de l'Europe, 1917–1929*, 2 vols. (Paris, 1978), I, 555–6; Bariéty, *Relations franco-allemandes*, 324–52; S. Jeannesson, *Poincaré, la France et la Ruhr (1922–1924)* (Strasbourg, 1998), 210–11.

[54] *JO*, Chambre, *Débats*, 1923, 28 Dec. 1923; *JO*, Chambre, *Débats*, 1924, 11 Jan. 1924.

[55] Cassin quoted in J.-M. Guieu, *Le Rameau et le glaive: les militants français pour la Société des nations* (Paris, 2008), 83.

[56] Reynolds, *Gender and Politics*, 186–92; T. Davies, *The Possibilities of Transnational Activism: The Campaign for Disarmament between the Two World Wars* (London, 2007), 49–50; G. Barry, *The Disarmament of Hatred: Marc Sangnier, French Catholicism and the Legacy of the First World War, 1919–1945* (London, 2012), 42–126; see also the various essays in M. Perticioli and D. Cherubini (eds.), *For Peace in Europe: Institutions and Civil Society Between the World Wars* (Berne, 2007).

Jouvenel, Georges Pompidou and Pierre Cot, who would play prominent roles in French political and intellectual life for the next half-century.[57]

All of this translated into a significant surge in civil society support for the League. Between 1922 and 1924 the collective membership of the AFSDN rose from 88,200 to 347,468. During the same period, the number of its provincial branches increased sixfold, so that by 1926 it boasted no less than fifty-six member associations based outside Paris. The evolution of public support was increasingly difficult for the government to ignore.[58] The British embassy in Paris reported 'a distinct advance in certain sections of French public opinion towards the League, so much so that even M. Poincaré himself has felt constrained to give it lip service'.[59]

Growing enthusiasm for the internationalist cause gave greater prominence to the long-standing campaign to reform the League. The 'Anglo-Saxon' character of the League of Nations, and in particular its lack of a robust machinery of enforcement, was a unifying theme in this discourse. Articulating the French conception of international organisation that predated the Great War, activists stressed the need to strengthen the League's capacity to deploy swift and decisive collective force against aggression. Scelle attributed the League's lack of teeth to the 'mystical pacifism practised by old women and Anglo-Saxons' which 'consists mainly of imploring the sky to change the hearts of men'. What was needed, Scelle argued, was a comprehensive legal regime and powerful tools of enforcement.[60] The Socialist deputy Joseph Paul-Boncour agreed with Scelle. He deployed arguments (first formulated by Léon Bourgeois during the peace conference) for the creation of an international armed force under League control. Such a measure, he argued, was the only means to prevent the return of arms races and alliance blocs.[61]

Disenchantment with the Bloc national's traditional national security policy combined with growing support for the League to play an important role in the elections of May 1924. It provided both Socialist and Radical internationalists with an opportunity to propose a new conception of security based on the League. Socialist pronouncements on foreign policy during the election campaign were virtually identical to those of Radical internationalists. Vincent

---

[57] C. Birebent, 'Le Groupement universitaire pour la Société des nations', *Matériaux pour l'histoire de notre temps*, 74 (2004), 14–19; Guieu, *Rameau et glaive*, 84–6.

[58] J.-M. Guieu, 'Les Apôtres français de "l'esprit de Genève": les militants pour la Société des nations dans la première moitié du XXe siècle', thèse de doctorat, Université de Paris I (Sorbonne), 2004, 186–8; see also Davies, *Transnational Activism*, 55–84.

[59] Churchill College Archives, Cambridge (hereafter CCAC), *Sir Eric Phipps Papers*, PHPP 1/2, Phipps to Ramsay MacDonald, 16 Mar. 1924.

[60] Ibid.; see also Guieu, *Rameau et glaive*, 127–30.

[61] J. Paul-Boncour, 'Armez-la!', *L'Oeuvre*, 21 Sept. 1923; Paul-Boncour would try to implement this conception the following decade when, as foreign minister, he presented a 'constructive plan' for an international force to the World Disarmament Conference: see M. Vaïsse, *Sécurité d'abord: politique française en matière de désarmement, 1930–1934* (Paris, 1981), 297–318.

A new approach: arbitration, security, disarmament 447

Auriol, for example, called for an end to the 'formalist conception of international politics held by diplomats'. He argued that French policy must adopt 'an economic and humane conception' that would mean evacuating the Ruhr but would, in turn, unlock the 'mechanism of credits' that would 'assure the complete payment of reparations'.[62]

Herriot, for his part, deplored the meagre financial return from the Ruhr operation and urged Poincaré to 'give a free hand to the committee of experts' and 'devote French policy to strengthening the League of Nations'. The League, Herriot argued, offered the best means to 'restore peace to a troubled Europe'. One of the few leading Radicals to oppose the electoral strategy of the Cartel, significantly, was Henry Franklin-Bouillon, a committed proponent of a more traditional approach to national security.[63]

Support for the League was a central feature of the Radical electoral platform. A 'sincere and loyal adherence to the League of Nations' was one of the four 'barrages' established by Herriot in February 1924 as conditions for adherence to the Cartel. These 'barrages' were a means to distinguish the Cartel clearly from the politics of the Bloc national.[64] As Berstein rightly emphasises, more than any other issue, foreign affairs provided the 'glue' that held an otherwise shaky Cartel electoral alliance together. Beyond the importance of the League as a source of security, Radicals and Socialists also agreed on the principle of establishing formal relations with the USSR once that state provided assurances that it would assume responsibility for Tsarist debts.[65] Virtually all of the programmes put forward by the candidates in Cartel electoral *listes* in 1924 pledged to place the League at the centre of national security policy. The vast majority called for measures to strengthen the new organisation along the lines proposed by Bourgeois at the peace conference.[66] The foreign policy proposed by the Cartel coalition was unquestionably internationalist in inspiration.

IV

The same is true of the policy pursued by the Herriot government once in power. The elections of 11 May 1924 restored the Radical Party to its pre-war role as the party of government. But the majority that resulted was even more unstable than that of the Bloc national after 1919. The electoral alliance between the centre-left and left (excluding the Communists) delivered decisive major gains for both of the main parties of the Cartel. The number of Radical deputies rose by more than 70 per cent from 86 in 1919 to 139 in 1924; that of

---

[62] Quoted in Schuker, *End*, 76.
[63] 'La Politique extérieure: discours de M. Herriot' and 'Bulletin du jour: discours de M. Herriot', *Le Temps*, 13 Jan. 1924; Berstein, *Recherche de l'âge d'or*, 377.
[64] Berstein, *Herriot*, 102–3.
[65] S. Couré, *La Grande lueur à l'est: les Français et l'Union soviétique 1917–1939* (Paris, 1999), 70–4.
[66] Berstein, *Recherche de l'âge d'or*, 384–5.

the SFIO increased from 68 to 104. At the same time, the distribution of votes remained relatively unchanged. Radical, Republican Socialists and SFIO candidates obtained just under 3.4 million votes as compared to well over 4 million for the constituent elements of the Bloc national. The core membership of the Cartel in the chamber, meanwhile, comprised only 287 deputies. To ensure itself a majority (in a 610-seat chamber) Herriot's government would need to secure the support of the forty deputies from the centrist Républicains de gauche. Finally, in the aftermath of the elections it became clear that the Socialists would not participate in government. Socialist leader Blum summed up the majority view of his party when he observed that the central aim of the electoral Cartel alliance had been to defeat the Bloc. But his party would not participate in a government it did not control. The best the Herriot government could hope for was support for its policies from SFIO deputies.[67]

The fragility of his government's parliamentary majority did not prevent Herriot from declaring his intention to break decisively with the foreign policy of Poincaré. In negotiations aimed at securing SFIO participation in his government Herriot had stressed that 'one duty dominates all others: to construct peace'. In a letter to Blum dated 2 June he outlined an essentially internationalist set of foreign and security policy aims. These included a reduction in the length of military service, a central role for a reinforced League of Nations in French policy, the transfer to the League of responsibility for enforcing German disarmament, an end to diplomatic relations with the Vatican, implementation of the Dawes Plan and evacuation of the Ruhr after the arrangements recommended by the plan were in operation. Herriot concluded by reaffirming his conviction that France could not achieve peace and security until 'the role of the League of Nations has been strengthened and enlarged along with that of other international institutions such as the Hague Tribunal and the International Labour Bureau'.[68]

Herriot outlined this programme before the chamber on 17 June 1924. In his ministerial declaration he stressed the need for a 'new international order based on the rule of law'. Although France would defend its right to reparations under the treaty, 'as soon as Germany observes the stipulations of the treaty from the point of view of reparations and security, it will be welcome to enter the League of Nations'. As he had done in his letter to Blum, Herriot stressed his commitment to the solutions proposed by the Dawes Plan as the best means to obtain German compliance. And he explicitly repudiated the unilateral use of force employed by his predecessor. He stated that his government was

> hostile to the policy of isolation and force that led to occupations and the seizure of territorial guarantees. Given the present state of Germany, given the need to protect not only France but all peoples from a return of aggressive pan-Germanism, we do

---

[67] Becker and Berstein, *Victoire et frustrations*, 241–8; Berstein, *Blum*, 264–80.
[68] Letter cited in G. Glasgow, *MacDonald as Diplomatist: The Foreign Policy of the First Labour Government in Britain* (London, 1924), 109–10.

not believe it will be possible to evacuate the Ruhr before the guarantees devised by the Experts, whose report we accept without condition, have been put in place along with guarantees for their equitable execution and vested in the international organisations qualified to administer them.[69]

France would pursue reparations through the international machinery recommended by the Dawes Committee. The enforcement of German disarmament would also be internationalised. 'We believe', Herriot continued, 'that it is essential to oversee the disarmament of Germany by a common effort with our allies and, as soon as possible, by the action of the League of Nations.'[70] The importance attributed to working through the League was an entirely new departure in security policy.

All sections of the French press underlined the gulf between the policy conceptions of the Cartel and those of its Bloc predecessor. Pro-Radical newspapers such as *L'Oeuvre* and *Le Quotidien* heralded the beginning of a new era in international politics.[71] The extent to which the Cartel intended to change course was evident in the presidential crisis that followed the elections. President Millerand had broken with established custom when he openly endorsed the foreign and domestic policies of the Bloc national in a much-publicised speech at Évreux in October 1923. The centre-left and left-wing press inevitably called for his resignation immediately after the elections. Cartel deputies made it clear that they would refuse to form a government while Millerand remained as president. Millerand finally resigned on 11 May 1924.[72] As president he had been one of the most strident advocates of a traditional approach to security. His removal created space for the alternative vision of the Cartel leadership.

This episode stimulated an already strident campaign for a purge of senior civil servants in the Cartel press. *Le Quotidien* called for 'les places, toutes les places et tout de suite' for Cartel-sponsored officials with unimpeachable republican credentials.[73] Quai d'Orsay mandarins were a prominent target of this campaign. In the pages of *Le Quotidien* and *Progrès civique* senior foreign ministry officials were painted as reactionary figures incorrigibly hostile to the new diplomatic practices of the post-war era. Their alleged lack of confidence in the League of Nations, in collective security and compulsory arbitration was attributed to their insufficient commitment to democracy and republicanism.[74] Radical senator François-Albert called for a 'freshening of the air at the Quai d'Orsay'.[75]

---

[69] *JO*, Chambre, Débats, 1924, 17 Jun. 1924.   [70] Ibid.
[71] Berstein, *Recherche de l'âge d'or*, 396–9; Schuker, *End*, 217–18.
[72] Jeanneney, *Faillite du Cartel*, 4–9.
[73] E. Bonnefous, *Histoire de la Troisième République*, vol. IV: *Cartel des gauches et Union nationale (1924–1929)* (Paris, 1960), 7–8.
[74] G. Scelle, 'Les Erreurs de notre politique extérieure', *Progrès civique*, 21 May 1924; V. Vivier, 'De la Suppression de la diplomatie secrète', *Progrès civique*, 2 Aug. 1924; both also cited in Schuker, *End*, 234.
[75] A. François-Albert, 'Vous devrez bien, ô Marianne, rafraîchir un peu l'air du Quai d'Orsay', *Progrès civique*, 21 Apr. 1923.

Much of this criticism was ill informed and unjust. In fact, a number of career diplomats had been active in cultivating relationships with the Cartel politicians since the previous autumn. It was through the good offices of René Massigli, for example, that British diplomats Orme Sargent and Eric Phipps first met Léon Blum in January 1924. The conversation, Phipps reported, was 'of a distinctly anti-Poincaré tendency ... even Massigli himself occasionally chipped in'.[76] Laroche, Seydoux and Massigli were all on good terms with both Herriot and Painlevé. All frequented the high-powered political salon hosted by Comtesse Élisabeth Greffulhe. After the Cartel victory, rumours abounded that Peretti would be replaced as political director by either Laroche or Seydoux. Massigli, for his part, confided to Sargent that he expected to be appointed as Herriot's *chef de cabinet*.[77] In the end, however, Herriot chose Gaston Bergery for this post – an outsider known for his criticisms of traditional diplomatic practices and his advocacy of closer relations with Soviet Russia.[78] But the premier was otherwise cautious. There were no immediate purges or large-scale reassignments during the early months of his premiership.

In choosing his cabinet Herriot also exercised prudence. Like all previous post-war premiers, he assumed the foreign minister's portfolio. For the finance ministry he opted for his Radical colleague Étienne Clémentel. As war minister he appointed General Marie Édouard Nollet, former head of the Inter-Allied Control Commission in Germany. Nollet had a reputation as an independent-minded soldier and a committed republican. His candid view that Germany did not present an immediate military threat to France had drawn the ire of the high command in Paris (and of Foch in particular).[79] Nollet was convinced, however, that Germany posed a serious threat for the future. His tenure as head of the Control Commission had convinced him that efforts to permanently suppress German war production were ultimately futile. Germany would regain its status as a great military power. Nollet judged that the most effective means of limiting the threat it posed in the long term was through international negotiations and a thorough reorganisation of France's armed forces.[80] Neither aim was incompatible with Herriot's internationalist agenda. In a conversation with the German ambassador, the premier observed that having a professional soldier as war minister would not only leave his government less

---

[76] CCAC, *Phipps Papers*, 2/3, Phipps to Eyre Crowe, 5 Jan. 1924.

[77] CCAC, *Phipps Papers*, 2/3, Phipps to Eyre Crowe, 19 May 1924 and 2/4, Phipps to Eyre Crowe, 12 Jun. 1924.

[78] Bergery, the illegitimate son of a Jewish German financier, married one of the daughters of the first Soviet ambassador in Paris, Leonid Krassine: see his file in AN, F7 13498; on his eventful political career see P. Burrin, *La Dérive fasciste: Doriot, Déat, Bergery* (Paris, 2003), 35–40 and D. Labrosse, 'Gaston Bergery and the politics of late Third Republic France and the early Vichy state', *Historical Reflections*, 34, 2 (2008), 66–87.

[79] AN, 470 AP 59, *Archives Millerand*, undated note from spring 1921.

[80] [General] C. Nollet, *Une Expérience de désarmement: cinq ans de contrôle militaire en Allemagne* (Paris, 1932).

A new approach: arbitration, security, disarmament   451

open to charges of weakness over the question of security, it would also 'permit him to make concessions if the circumstances allowed'.[81]

Immediately after introducing his government to the chamber, Herriot offered to travel to Britain to meet with MacDonald. He revealed his inexperience by failing to develop a detailed negotiating strategy before leaving for London. A meeting convened the evening before his departure revealed deep divisions between Nollet, who argued that France must retain its right to act unilaterally, and Bergery, who stressed the power of 'international guarantees' for France's economic and military security.[82] Peretti did not have a chance to brief Herriot until the two met on the railway platform. In the event, the political director ended up accompanying the premier to the summit in London without his pyjamas, toothbrush or dinner jacket. Upon its arrival in London, the French entourage avoided the ambassador's residence and travelled directly to the British prime minister's country house at Chequers. Saint-Aulaire was not invited.[83] The first meeting of Herriot and MacDonald was by no means a classic diplomatic encounter.

Before leaving for London, Herriot had received a 139-page analysis of the Treaty of Mutual Assistance from the SGDN. This report reiterated all of the criticisms of the draft treaty that had been made by the military the previous autumn. It concluded, predictably, that only regional accords including detailed military commitments could provide the security necessary for an arms-limitation agreement. The report also referred with contempt to what it termed 'transactions' in Geneva that had 'undermined' the utility of mutual assistance. The SGDN, articulating the view of the entire military establishment, continued to insist on a military alliance with Britain as the only reliable security guarantee for France. The premier was exhorted not to let his 'spirit of conciliation' lead him to 'mistake illusions for certainties'.[84]

Herriot was not persuaded by the anti-League argument of the SGDN report. But he did accept the need for a substantive strategic commitment from Britain. While on the train to London he prepared a 'plan' for negotiations with the British. Significantly, all of the objectives outlined in this document, which Herriot drafted himself in pencil, were oriented towards international cooperation.[85] Under the rubric 'guarantees for execution' (of the Dawes Plan) the premier included internationalising the Franco-Belgian railway *régie* in the occupied territories 'with American participation'. Another aim was the

---

[81] Quoted in Bariéty, *Relations franco-allemandes*, 365.
[82] G. Suarez, *Herriot, 1924–1932* (Paris, 1932) (rev. edn of *Une nuit chez Cromwell* (Paris, 1930)), 36–40; Schuker, *End*, 235–7.
[83] Saint-Aulaire, *Confession*, 708–15; Jeanneney, *Faillite du Cartel*, 44–51; Bariéty, *Relations franco-allemandes*, 373–6.
[84] SHD-DAT, 7N 3531-1, 'Étude sur le projet d'assistance mutuelle de la Société des nations', 12 Jun. 1924.
[85] MAE, PA-AP 089, *Papiers Édouard Herriot*, vol. 16, 'Plan Herriot, 21 juin 1924'. It is extraordinary that the only document remotely resembling an overall French programme for the Chequers summit is a barely legible set of general aims that was obviously drafted in

'synchronisation of the military evacuation [of the Ruhr]' with both the international loan and the commercialisation of the industrial and railway bonds. The procedure for responding to any German defaults would be for the Reparations Commission to raise with 'the financial committee of the League of Nations' and an 'American arbiter'. The sanctions to be imposed if a default was declared would be outlined in a 'cooperation pact with a written general guarantee'. Under the rubric of 'security guarantees' Herriot's chief aims were to establish inter-Allied military cooperation to control the *régie*, to maintain the Allied occupation of the Cologne zone, to maintain the activities of the Inter-Allied Control Commission 'until they are passed to the League of Nations' and, crucially, 'a security pact, to be extended eventually to Germany, along the lines envisaged by the League of Nations'. The issues of inter-Allied debts and coal, meanwhile, were listed under the heading 'subsidiary questions'.[86]

Herriot's tentative programme has been characterised as a 'continuation' of Poincaré's strategy.[87] But this judgement does not square with the evidence. The most striking aspect of his ideas is the importance attributed to international solutions to economic and military security requirements. This is not to say that Herriot intended to forgo all traditional safeguards. As the negotiations of the ensuing three months demonstrated, his central aim, like that of Briand in 1921–2, was to construct a wider League-based security system around the core element of a Franco-British security pact. His preference for this combination is clear from the negotiations that took place at Chequers on 21–22 June 1922.

The chief British aims at this summit were first to secure a French commitment to withdraw from the Ruhr once the mechanisms proposed by the Dawes Plan were implemented, and second to obtain assurances that France would not undertake unilateral action in the future.[88] MacDonald and his aides were successful on both counts. Herriot opened the first meeting with MacDonald by stating that he wanted a security commitment from Britain and was prepared to make concessions on reparations issues to achieve this. To demonstrate his commitment he agreed at the outset to link the evacuation of the Rhineland to the implementation of the Dawes Plan. He also agreed, in general terms, to a procedure whereby disagreement over a German default would go before an arbitration panel rather than rest exclusively on a decision by the Reparations Commission. Finally, Herriot accepted the British suggestion of a conference in London to finalise the implementation of the Dawes Plan. The

haste by the premier himself. Almost as extraordinary is the fact that this document is squirrelled away in an untitled envelope glued to the first page of this volume of Herriot's papers.

[86] Ibid.
[87] V. Pitts, *France and the German Problem: Politics and Economics in the Locarno Period, 1924–1929* (New York, 1987), 4–7; Bariéty, *Relations franco-allemandes*, 377–8. Bariéty also attributes a coherence to Herriot's 'plan' that is difficult to identify in the document itself.
[88] O'Riordan, *Britain and the Ruhr*, 157–60.

A new approach: arbitration, security, disarmament 453

head of the foreign office, Eyre Crowe, initially proposed to invite a German delegation to negotiate on an equal footing from the outset, but Herriot insisted that the Germans should be invited only after the Allies had agreed a common position.[89]

The issue of France's territorial security was addressed only briefly at Chequers. Herriot and Peretti proposed a new security architecture based on Laroche's blueprint for combining deterrence and multilateralism. The French plan was a three-tier system. The first tier was a general pact open to all. The second was a series of arbitration agreements between Germany and its neighbours that would supplement the general pact. The third tier was a bilateral mutual assistance pact between Britain and France that, it was suggested, might include a military convention. The French could not have been surprised when MacDonald rejected this proposal. The British prime minister promised only to renew discussion of security arrangements after final agreement was reached on the implementation of the Dawes Plan. The French were forced to settle for 'a moral pact of continuous collaboration'.[90]

Herriot and his advisers returned to the issue of security when MacDonald came to Paris on 7–8 July 1924.[91] In meetings at the Quai d'Orsay Herriot again proposed a multi-tiered security system, at the heart of which was a Franco-British pact. He stressed that precautions must be taken for the 'transition period' during which Germany would need to demonstrate the good faith necessary for full admission into the community of nations. 'Germany is a country where the individual political sensibility is underdeveloped,' the French premier warned. 'If a new Bismarck emerges there is a great danger of a return to a warlike policy.' France therefore had no choice but to 'take measures to ensure that the peace will be guaranteed during this intermediary period'. Hence the need for a Franco-British pact to anchor the wider security system. Peretti made it clear that 'France would not insist on a military alliance if this appears impossible to the British government'. MacDonald remained unmoved, however. The furthest he would go was to pledge that the security question would be taken up in negotiations after the reparations question was settled at the London Conference.[92]

The stage was thus set for the London Economic Conference that opened on 16 July 1924. This gathering marked the return of the USA to European politics. For the first time since the peace conference, an American delegation took full part in proceedings. It also marked the first time German officials were

---

[89] The French minutes of the Chequers meetings are in MAE, *Série Y*, vol. 691; see also O'Riordan, *Britain and the Ruhr*, 160–2; Bariéty, *Relations franco-allemandes*, 390–415.
[90] Quoted in Jeanneney, *Faillite du Cartel*, 54; see also Schuker, *End*, 237–45; Suarez, *Herriot*, 99–148; and A. Cassels, 'Repairing the Entente Cordiale and the New Diplomacy', *HJ*, 23, 1 (1980), 133–53.
[91] CCAC, *Phipps Papers*, 1/3, Phipps to MacDonald, 6 Jul. 1924.
[92] MAE, PA-AP 089, *Papiers Herriot*, vol. 22, 'Notes prises au cours d'une conversation entre M. Herriot et M. MacDonald', 8 Jul. 1924.

invited to international negotiations as equals rather than as representatives of a defeated power. Although the invitation was officially issued only after preliminary agreement had been reached among the former Allies, the Germans were unofficially involved from the outset. The analysis that follows does not seek to add substantively to the excellent and detailed interpretations of the London Conference by Schuker, Bariéty and Cohrs.[93] It aims instead to set the negotiations in London within the wider context of Cartel foreign and security policy.

In London French negotiators came under intense pressure to evacuate the Ruhr, to agree to a new system for establishing German reparations default and to renounce the right to impose unilateral military sanctions in the event of a default. British treasury secretary Philip Snowden and Bank of England governor Montagu Norman took the lead in turning the screws on French negotiators. Both were opposed to the very principle of reparations and determined to ensure that another Ruhr occupation was impossible. MacDonald appeared moderate in comparison, but was also determined to deprive France of the right to act independently to enforce the new settlement. Senior American policy makers, many of whom were present in London in an unofficial capacity, generally followed the British line. One of the chief levers employed to force concessions from the French were the conditions laid down by Anglo-American private bankers for raising the loan to kick-start the Dawes Plan. Failure to achieve these conditions, Herriot and his team were warned, would end all prospects of American loans to Europe and force France to find alternative means to shore up its currency.[94]

Herriot was not the man to withstand such pressure. It did not help that France's finances were near collapse or that his team was badly divided and had failed to agree on a coherent plan.[95] War minister Nollet, for example, argued that the evacuation of the Ruhr must be linked to German compliance with the disarmament clauses of the Versailles Treaty. He brushed aside the fact that there was no legal basis for linking the Ruhr occupation and disarmament. Marshal Foch, conversely, advised that withdrawal from the Ruhr should be calibrated in response to German reparations payments and that Herriot should refuse all pressure to set a definitive timetable for this procedure. Finance minister Clémentel, supported by Seydoux, insisted initially on linking an end to the Ruhr occupation to the negotiation of a wide-ranging Franco-German commercial treaty. This position was opposed by the commerce ministry, however, which argued instead that France must seek to prolong

---

[93] Artaud, *Dettes interalliées*, I, 356–7; Schuker, *End*, 293–382; Bariéty, *Relations franco-allemandes*, 507–732; Cohrs, *Unfinished Peace*, 154–226.

[94] O'Riordan, *Britain and the Ruhr*, 165–9; Schuker, *End*, 304–8, 315–16, 325, 344–5, 349–52.

[95] The closest the French delegation came to developing such a plan was Seydoux's 4 August memo 'L'Évacuation de la Ruhr', which is in MAE, PA-AP 089, *Papiers Herriot*, vol. 24; even this document reflects the contradictory positions adopted by various officials.

A new approach: arbitration, security, disarmament 455

the commercial regime established by the Treaty of Versailles (which was due to expire in January 1925).[96]

The London Conference, in sum, was not the finest hour for the French policy machine. Such disorder and division would have been unthinkable under Poincaré, Tardieu or Berthelot. Herriot did not provide effective leadership.[97] Among the most significant concessions made in London was a revision of procedures to give Britain and the USA an effective veto over any declaration of a flagrant German default. Under the new regime all disputes over sanctions were to go to arbitration before the Permanent Court of International Justice. Herriot also conceded that the timetable of the Rhineland occupation had begun in January 1920 (the French position had previously been that German treaty violations meant that the clock had not yet started to run). British and American negotiators refused to link either war debts or security to the negotiations concerning evacuation of the Ruhr. Nor were any commercial concessions obtained from Germany in exchange for withdrawal from the Ruhr basin. Under intense pressure during the final stages of the conference, Herriot agreed that the evacuation would take place one year from the signature of the conference protocol (on 16 August 1924). French negotiators thus failed to obtain any major concessions in return for the evacuation of the Ruhr.[98]

Much of the criticism of French policy at the London Conference is therefore merited. There is nonetheless a need for greater nuance when assessing Cartel policy at this stage. It should be remembered that Herriot's room to manoeuvre was limited by the official justification advanced by Poincaré for the Ruhr operation. As Seydoux pointed out, 'it is difficult to see how we can tie the question of our security to that of the Ruhr occupation because we have always said that we are occupying the Ruhr over the issue of reparations and not over that of security'.[99] Nor was Herriot in a position to demand a link between war debts and the Ruhr given France's desperate need for an infusion of British and American capital to prop up the franc.

Just as important as these considerations were the internationalist convictions of senior Cartel political leaders. Herriot, it is worth recalling, had never been in favour of the Ruhr occupation. He had abstained in the chamber vote of confidence on the issue in January 1923, and by the end of that year was openly opposed to the occupation. It is worth remembering that a pledge to end the

---

[96] MAE, PA-AP 089, *Papiers Herriot*, vol. 24, 'Sécurité' (Nollet), 3 Aug. 1924; vol. 23, 'Note Foch' (Foch's telephone instructions to his chief of staff), 30 Jul. 1924; 'Note de M. Seydoux: Évacuation militaire de la Ruhr', 30 Jul. 1924. On the issue of future commercial relations with Germany see esp. Schuker, *End*, 368–73.
[97] The premier confirmed the British perception of his weakness by weeping in front of MacDonald and Eyre Crowe: Schuker, *End*, 298.
[98] In addition to the sources in note 93 (above), useful syntheses are Steiner, *Lights that Failed*, 242–8 and S. Marks, *The Illusion of Peace: International Relations in Europe, 1918–1933*, 2nd edn (London, 2003), 121–6.
[99] MAE, PA-AP 089, *Papiers Herriot*, vol. 23, 'Note de M. Seydoux: évacuation militaire de la Ruhr', 30 Jul. 1924.

occupation was a central plank of the Cartel electoral platform. Those who criticised Herriot for agreeing to evacuate the Ruhr tended to forget that this is exactly what he had promised to do.

Two further aspects of the London negotiations underline the growing importance of the internationalist current in French policy. The first is the role attributed to arbitration in the process of declaring default and agreeing on sanctions. French negotiators had called for arbitration agreements as part of the architecture of the new security system they had proposed at Chequers the previous June. In subsequent negotiations in Paris, Herriot had admitted the possibility of a role for arbitration in the process of declaring a German default. All of this was in keeping with the importance attributed to arbitration, and the rule of law more generally, in Radical Party international doctrine. It was entirely consistent with Cartel policy prescriptions, therefore, when French negotiators 'expressed keen interest' in the idea of using arbitration to resolve future disputes on the reparations commission. Henri Fromageot, the chief *jurisconsulte* at the Quai d'Orsay, indicated to his British colleagues that his political superiors favoured such a solution.[100] Historians who attribute this decision to lack of organisation or foresight within the French delegation have ignored the influence of juridical internationalism within the Cartel leadership.[101]

The second internationalist dimension to French policy in London was the pursuit of a wide-ranging commercial and industrial accord with Germany by Clémentel and Seydoux. The aim here was to implement the first stage of Seydoux's grand design by replacing the Versailles Treaty regime with an agreement based on cooperation and mutual benefit. At stake was the future viability of France's steel industry, which depended on a steady supply of coke at a reasonable price from Germany. Seydoux argued that 'guaranteeing access to coke is infinitely more important for us than the occupation of the Ruhr'. He recommended bilateral discussions to lay the foundations for a multilateral system of industrial collaboration. Seydoux dismissed commerce ministry proposals to use the Ruhr evacuation as leverage to prolong the punitive commercial system imposed by the peace treaty. 'The time for dealing with Germany as victor to vanquished has passed,' he repeated. 'From now on we must pursue commercial and industrial relations that are of mutual benefit. The reconstruction of Europe depends on our ability to negotiate such arrangements.'[102] Clémentel endorsed this line of reasoning. Together with Seydoux he outlined an ambitious programme of Franco-German economic collaboration to Stresemann on 11 August.[103] Pursuit of economic

---

[100] Schuker, *End*, 311–12.
[101] Bariéty, *Relations franco-allemandes*, 550–2; Schuker, *End*, 311–12.
[102] MAE, PA-AP 089, *Papiers Herriot*, vol. 23, 'Note de M. Seydoux: évacuation militaire de la Ruhr', 30 Jul. 1924 and vol. 24, 'L'Évacuation de la Ruhr', 4 Aug. 1924; PA-AP 261, *Papiers Seydoux*, vol. 1, 'Possibilités de négociation avec l'Allemagne et l'Angleterre', 25 Aug. 1924.
[103] Schuker, *End*, 371–2; Bariéty, *Relations franco-allemandes*, 646–51.

A new approach: arbitration, security, disarmament 457

collaboration was a forward-looking strategy that envisaged Franco-German cooperation as a pillar of future European stability. It was in keeping with the general internationalist orientation of Cartel policy at the London Conference that has not received the attention it deserves in the historiography.

V

While negotiations were taking place in London over the Ruhr and reparations, officials in Paris were laying the foundations of a new bid for security based on multilateral pacts and compulsory arbitration. Joseph Paul-Boncour played a leading role in this process. By 1924 Paul-Boncour had already established himself as the expert on defence issues within the Socialist Party. He had worked as a lawyer before entering political life first as private secretary to the moderate premier Waldeck-Rousseau and then as head of René Viviani's staff at the labour ministry. First elected to the chamber as an Independent Socialist in 1909, he joined the SFIO after being elected as a deputy for the Seine in 1919. A decorated war veteran, he served with distinction on the chamber's army and foreign affairs commissions. Paul-Boncour was on the right of the Socialist Party and favoured SFIO participation in the Cartel government. He was also a long-standing supporter of the League of Nations, whose understanding of international politics was very close to that of Bourgeois and other juridical internationalists within the Radical Party.[104] In the summer of 1924 he worked closely with Herriot to fashion a new course for French security policy.

Aware of the need to shape the security agenda from inside the machinery of national defence, Herriot appointed Paul-Boncour vice-president and chair of the CSDN Commission d'études. The first of a series of difficult battles to bring the CSDN (and thus the French security establishment) into line with the government's new policy took place when the commission met in July to pass judgement on the Treaty of Mutual Assistance (TMA). The British government had rejected the TMA on 5 July, suggesting instead that another general disarmament conference along the lines of Washington should be convened.[105] In a note that illuminates the extent to which multilateral solutions were becoming central to thinking within the Quai d'Orsay, Laroche warned Herriot that

---

[104] J. Paul-Boncour, *Entre-deux-guerres: souvenirs de la IIIème République*, 3 vols., vol. II: *Les Lendemains de la victoire, 1918–1934* (Paris, 1946), 4–97; J. Wright, 'Joseph Paul-Boncour: regionalism, syndicalism and the Third Republic', *Nottingham French Studies*, 44, 1 (2005), 66–81.
[105] MAE, *SDN*, vol. 710, 'Note pour la Direction politique' (Réquin), 21 Jul. 1924; Réquin denounced this decision as 'taking international negotiations on security and arms limitations back to the situation of 1920'.

It is no longer merely the question of the Treaty of Mutual Assistance that is at stake, it is all future negotiations with Britain over the question of security guarantees. The British prime minister seems opposed to the idea of a defensive pact even within the structures of the League. But he also refuses to admit even the principle of a general treaty aimed at giving greater precision, and thus life, to Article 10 of the Covenant, the terms of which are so general as to render them useless.

Laroche then paraphrased Pascal, asking:

How can Justice impose itself without material force? However great the moral authority of the League, it is insufficient to prevent or to punish aggression ... The Treaty of Mutual Assistance project is far from perfect, and will need to be revised, but it is essential that the two great democracies support its principles.[106]

Herriot responded that France must champion the TMA at the League Assembly. The first step, however, was to secure CSDN approval for the treaty. This would enable the Cartel government to pose as the champion of multilateral cooperation at the League's Fifth Assembly in September.[107]

The military establishment had dug in its heels, however. The SGDN prepared a summary of its earlier negative assessment of the TMA that highlighted the difficulty in defining aggression and identifying aggressor states (which would trigger the operation of regional mutual assistance pacts) as one of the 'insuperable obstacles' to its effective functioning.[108] But Herriot was determined to secure approval for the TMA. He instructed the service ministers and his own foreign minister to make it clear to senior military officials that the TMA must be approved at the next meeting of the Commission d'études. Laroche was designated by Herriot to speak for the foreign ministry, and was given specific instructions to support Paul-Boncour.[109] When the commission was reconvened on 23 July, Generals Debeney, Serrigny and Mangin all indulged in tirades against the principle of multilateral mutual assistance. Yet all ultimately gave in and approved the treaty. Paul-Boncour declared that the vexed question of defining aggression 'will be studied at a later date, perhaps after the treaty is adopted'. He afterwards wrote to Herriot that 'you now have, with the assent of the army, navy and foreign ministry, a free hand to adopt a position in Geneva that contrasts favourably with that of the British government'.[110]

A foreign ministry communiqué of 21 August expressed approval in principle for the TMA. But it also noted that the 'general character' of Article 10 of

---

[106] MAE, *SDN*, vol. 710, 'Note', 6 Jul. 1924.
[107] Jackson, 'Security and disarmament', 271–4.
[108] SHD-DAT, 7N 3531–2, 'Note pour la réunion de la Commission d'études (1ère section) du 9 juillet 1924 (Examen du Projet de Traité d'assistance mutuelle de la SDN)', 7 Jul. 1924.
[109] MAE, *SDN*, vol. 710, Laroche note, 21 Aug. 1924.
[110] SHD-DAT, 7N 3531–1, 'Délibérations de la 1ère section de la Commission d'études du Conseil supérieur de la défense nationale dans sa séance du 23 juillet 1924'; MAE, PA-AP 089, *Papiers Herriot*, vol. 23, Paul-Boncour to Herriot, 25 Jul. 1925.

A new approach: arbitration, security, disarmament   459

the Covenant rendered it 'insufficient as a guarantee of security'. This raised the need for 'the further legal and military guarantees' provided by the 'particular defensive accords that are an indispensable component of the Treaty of Mutual Assistance'. 'These accords', the foreign ministry observed, 'are impossible to confuse with old-style alliances.' The communiqué highlighted two further 'gaps' in the Covenant that needed to be filled. The first was 'the need to define, if not all, at least the most flagrant cases of aggression'. The second was the fact that the League Council was required to agree unanimously on the application of sanctions by member states. This point pertained to 'general' mutual assistance as opposed to the regional defensive pacts. Once these questions were resolved, the French government would 'approve without reservation the proposed combination of defensive accords and a general treaty in the effort to prevent wars of aggression'.[111]

The next step in the evolution of a new approach was a 5 August note by Laroche outlining France's security requirements. Asking his colleagues for their views, he observed that 'we know the British do not want a pact, but we must put their backs to the wall and force them to tell us why'.[112] Laroche's revised conception, which served as the basis for an official note sent to the British government on 11 August, called for three 'supplementary permanent guarantees'. The first was the 'organisation' of European security around 'the nucleus of a Franco-British defensive pact'. The pact between France and Britain would be 'completed' by a series of defensive pacts with those states neighbouring Germany. The second guarantee was a network of reciprocal non-aggression agreements to be signed by these same states and Germany. The third was the 'reinforcement of the authority of the League of Nations' by the 'effective organisation of mutual assistance' against states guilty of aggression.[113] The strategy of placing mutual assistance arrangements under, rather than parallel to, the legal umbrella of the League was a significant innovation that reflected the ideological commitment of the Cartel to internationalism. But it was also a strategy to take advantage of the widespread legitimacy the League enjoyed across the Channel to obtain a substantial continental commitment from Britain. British liberalism would in this way be outflanked by French proposals to bolster the League of Nations.[114]

The final girder in the conceptual architecture of a new security policy for the Cartel was the decision to employ compulsory arbitration as a mechanism to

---

[111] MAE, *SDN*, vol. 710, 'Avis du gouvernement français sur le projet de traité d'assistance mutuelle de la SDN', 21 Aug. 1924.
[112] MAE, *Série Z, GB*, vol. 71, Laroche handwritten note to Peretti, 5 Aug. 1924; see also SHD-DAT, 7N 3531-2, 'Garanties inscrites dans le traité de Versailles', 4 Aug. 1924 and 'Remise à M. MacDonald d'une note sur la sécurité', 11 Aug. 1924.
[113] SHD-DAT, 7N 3531-2, 'Remise à M. MacDonald d'une note sur la sécurité', 11 Aug. 1924.
[114] MAE, *SDN*, vol. 710, 'Note pour la Direction politique', 21 Jul. 1924; Jackson, 'Security and disarmament', 270-1.

define aggression. The Quai d'Orsay had been contemplating a more substantial role for arbitration in French policy since the previous spring (hence the alacrity with which Fromageot had greeted British proposals in London to use arbitration to resolve disputes over reparations).[115] In August 1924, with the approval of Herriot, the DAPC embraced the principle of introducing binding arbitration as a means to trigger mutual assistance. This development was stimulated by an unofficial American proposal sponsored by James Shotwell and Tasker Bliss to link a general security and disarmament treaty to a system of compulsory arbitration. Foreign ministry officials approved the project in principle but pointed out that the idea could only be effective if all states agreed to submit to arbitration.[116] Consensus emerged among Herriot's chief advisers that arbitration could provide security only if it was combined with regional pacts. Any state involved in a dispute that did not agree to a ceasefire and submit to arbitration by the International Court would automatically be declared an aggressor. This, in turn, would trigger the operation of defensive mutual assistance pacts. The operation of mutual assistance would in this way be made as automatic as possible. 'These accords will be registered with the [League] Council, which will recognise their defensive character; but they must remain the armature of the system.'[117]

The principle of compulsory arbitration as a means to define aggression complemented the legalist reflexes of the French political and foreign policy establishment. But it was also an expression of the fundamental French aim to construct a security system that would cement the status quo in a binding regime of international public law. The policy that was emerging was thus a hybrid that incorporated the goal of a British pledge of immediate assistance within a multilateral framework that reflected the internationalist orientations of the new Herriot government. Arbitration was in this way combined with 'security' and 'disarmament' to constitute the three conceptual pillars of French security policy for the next decade.

Herriot introduced the new French security conception in his celebrated 5 September 1924 speech before the Fifth Assembly of the League in Geneva,

---

[115] SHD-DAT, 7N 3532–1, 'Origine du protocole d'arbitrage, de sécurité et de réduction des armements': misdated 9 Sept., this document was drafted by the SFSDN after the protocol was agreed.

[116] MAE, *SDN*, vol. 710, 'Projet de traité de désarmement et de sécurité présenté par le "Groupe Américain"', 5 Jul. 1924; 'Note du Col. Réquin [on the Shotwell–Bliss Plan]', 23 Aug. 1924; and esp. 'Étude comparative sur le projet américain, le projet de la 5ème Commission de la 4ème Assemblée et les avis de la Commission d'études du CSDN', Sept. 1924; vol. 711, 'Note pour le président du conseil: projet américain de traité d'assistance', 2 Sept. 1924; see also C. Bouchard, 'Le "Plan Américain" Shotwell–Bliss de 1924: une initiative méconnue pour le renforcement de la paix', *GMCC*, 202–3 (2002), 203–25.

[117] MAE, *SDN*, vol. 711, 'Réunion du 1er septembre après-midi': this was a strategy meeting to prepare for the League Assembly; SHD-DAT, 7N 3532–1, 'Origine du protocole'; A. Webster, 'International arbitration, the pacific settlement of disputes and the French security-disarmament dilemma (1919–1931)', *French History*, 24, 2 (2010), 242–51.

where he outlined the triple formula of 'arbitrage, sécurité, désarmement'. The French aim was to draw the MacDonald government into talks for a multilateral security system that would incorporate compulsory arbitration into existing schemes for regional pacts. The Herriot government's determination to reach an agreement is clear from the team of political heavyweights that was sent to negotiate in Geneva. Briand, Paul-Boncour, de Jouvenel, René Cassin and Louis Loucheur were named France's delegates to the Fifth Assembly. Significantly, while the army staff was kept abreast of the course of negotiations, neither Réquin nor any other senior French military official was given a direct role in the proceedings.[118]

Herriot was the first French head of government to appear before the League Assembly. His address followed that of MacDonald the previous day. The British prime minister had warned that an excessive concern over national security among some member states threatened a return to the arms races that had characterised the pre-1914 era. 'International security', he insisted, 'must not be viewed as a military problem.' He urged that states embrace the principle of arbitration as the means to define aggression and ensure peace. MacDonald argued in effect that disarmament and the rule of law constituted sufficient sources of security on their own. His speech was rightly interpreted by the French press as a rejection of the French argument for supplementary security arrangements.[119]

Herriot defended the French thesis that disarmament was a consequence rather than a cause of security. He declared openly that France could assent to German entry into the League only if the Reich could be enmeshed in a robust security system capable of restraining its revisionist impulses. He also claimed the concept of arbitration as part of the French internationalist tradition: 'In accepting the idea of arbitration,' the French premier argued, 'we are doing nothing more than following in the juridical tradition of our country that was so nobly articulated at the Hague conferences by Léon Bourgeois.'[120] He added, however, that arbitration could provide the security necessary for disarmament only if it was supported by a robust regime of automatic mutual assistance. The French premier invoked Pascal in his rebuttal of MacDonald:

My dear friend Mr MacDonald has said that arbitration provides justice without prejudice or passion ... Yes, but justice must not be without force. Force cannot be left at the cruel service of injustice ... Justice without force is impotent; force without justice is tyranny ... it is essential to speak clearly and directly and to consider the problem of peace in all of its aspects. Arbitration is necessary but it is not sufficient on its own. It is a means rather than an end.

---

[118] 'Bulletin du jour', *Le Temps*, 5 Sept. 1924; Prost and Winter, *René Cassin*, 101–3; J. L. Hogge II, 'Arbitrage, Sécurité, Désarmement: French Security and the League of Nations, 1920–1925', Ph.D. dissertation, New York University, 1994, 360–7.
[119] 'Désarmement et sécurité', *Le Temps*, 5 Sept. 1924.
[120] 'Le Discours de M. Édouard Herriot', *Le Temps*, 6 Sept. 1924.

Herriot then articulated a muscular internationalist vision of peace and security:

> Peace must not be an abstract notion, an empty wish. To truly create [peace] requires determination and virility, more virility and determination, perhaps, than war. Arbitration, security, disarmament, are the three master pillars of the edifice of peace we must construct ... There can be no community of international peace without these core pillars of international solidarity.[121]

This security conception was rooted in the solidarist international doctrine developed by Bourgeois and Théodore Ruyssen before the First World War.

France's key eastern allies supported the French position. Polish foreign minister Aleksander Skrzyński endorsed Herriot's call for a combination of binding arbitration and regional defensive accords. Czechoslovak foreign minister Edvard Beneš, in a move that had been prearranged with the French delegation, went further to propose a working programme to revise the TMA into a protocol containing concrete security guarantees, based on arbitration and sanctions, that would prepare the way for arms limitations.[122] Beneš played a key role in all of the negotiations that followed. He chaired the important committee on security and worked especially closely with Paul-Boncour to link arbitration with diplomatic, economic and military sanctions. The end result was that the French formula 'arbitration, security, disarmament' remained at the heart of the resulting protocol to the League Covenant.[123]

The Protocol for the Pacific Settlement of International Disputes was therefore a significant triumph for the French vision of international security. The Protocol was in essence a European security arrangement (though it was in theory open to all League members) placed under the auspices of the League Council. It provided additional security guarantees, as well as additional obligations, for all participating states. Its guiding principle was to use compulsory arbitration to close the 'gaps' in the Covenant in order to make functioning of collective security as automatic as possible. Sanctions would apply automatically to any state that refused to submit to arbitration. Decision making within the League Council was streamlined so that a two-thirds majority rather than the unanimity required by the Covenant – would suffice to impose sanctions and trigger mutual assistance pacts. Also important was the fact that European security under the terms of the Protocol was conceived as an indivisible whole. All participants assumed more precise and binding obligations than those laid down in Articles 10 to 16 of the Covenant. Crucially, this implied an extension of British obligations

---

[121] Ibid.
[122] 'Le Discours de M. Benès [sic]', *Le Temps*, 7 Sept. 1924; MAE, *SDN*, vol. 710, 'Visite de M. Benes', 31 Aug. 1924; SHD-DAT, 7N 3532–1, 'Origine du protocole'.
[123] Detailed French records of the proceedings can be found in MAE, *SDN*, vols. 711 and 712 as well as SHD-DAT, 7N 3532, dossiers 1–3.

towards eastern European states. French negotiators further succeeded in including a clause declaring that any violation of the Rhineland demilitarised zone must automatically be judged an act of aggression. Finally, the Protocol provided for the negotiation of 'particular accords' between signatory states designed to maximise the speed and effectiveness of mutual assistance. This aspect of the accord was particularly important for France as a means to secure a regional defensive pact with Britain.[124]

Three further aspects of the Protocol terms illustrate the evolution of security policy under the Cartel. First, conventions for military assistance were no longer integral components of regional accords. Second, the accord was intended to provide the security necessary to negotiate a far-reaching arms-limitation agreement. Indeed, the Protocol was not to come into effect until an international conference was convened to prepare such an agreement. A preliminary date of 1 June 1925 was set for the opening of this conference. Although individual states retained the right to determine the relationship between armaments levels and their specific national security requirements, the commitment to disarmament was much more prominent in the new accord than it had been in the TMA.[125] Third, Germany was expected to sign the Protocol, be admitted into the League of Nations and be granted a permanent seat on the Council. The Reich would thus gain readmission into the European political community. In return it would have to accept the obligations and constraints imposed by both the League Covenant and the Protocol. League membership would also give Germany the right to pursue peaceful revision of the Versailles Treaty as envisaged by Article 19 of the League Covenant.[126] Where French policy under Poincaré sought to balance against German power with exclusive alliances, the Cartel's strategy was to enmesh the Weimar Republic in a legal regime aimed at ensuring that any revision of the treaty would be peaceful and under conditions tolerable to France.

VI

The Geneva Protocol marked the zenith of international attempts to preserve peace through binding legal commitments. In adhering to the Protocol France also committed itself to accepting the 'Optional Clause' recognising the

---

[124] MAE, PA-AP 089, *Papiers Herriot*, vol. 18, 'Arbitrage, sécurité et réduction des armements: documents relatifs au Protocole pour la règlement pacifique des différends internationaux et la Conférence pour la réduction des armements', 14 Oct. 1924; see also P. J. Noel-Baker, *The Geneva Protocol* (London, 1925), 215–24; Webster, 'International arbitration', 242–54; and S. Schirmann, *Quel ordre europeen? De Versailles à la chute de IIIème Reich* (Paris, 2006), 119–20.

[125] Jackson, 'Security and disarmament', 272–3.

[126] Herriot, *Jadis*, vol. II: *D'une guerre à l'autre*, 178–9; P. Jackson, 'Deterrence, Coercion and Enmeshment: French Grand Strategy and the German Problem after World War I' in J. Taliaferro, S. Lobell and N. Ripsman (eds.), *The Challenge of Grand Strategy* (Cambridge, 2012), 54–7.

compulsory jurisdiction of the Permanent Court of International Justice for fifteen years.[127] The extent to which this marked a decisive departure from previous security policy is clear from the fierce opposition to the Protocol among traditionally minded soldiers and diplomats.

Military opposition to the Protocol increased as the accord took shape and focused inevitably on the commitment to disarm. The SGDN approved of compulsory arbitration and demilitarised zones but expressed strident opposition to any disarmament conference. Claiming to represent the views of both the general staff and Marshal Foch, General Serrigny repeated the mantra that the only real value of any security lay in immediate and prearranged military assistance. He insisted that the lack of military conventions in the regional accords envisaged in the Protocol must rule out any commitment to participate in a conference on arms reductions. 'Otherwise', he warned, 'we risk ... the disappearance, to our great loss, of the hopes invested by our government in its complete adherence to the ideas of justice and international solidarity.'[128] The army general staff condemned the Protocol in the most uncompromising terms. It asserted that a lack of precision concerning military sanctions (as opposed to the provisions for economic and financial sanctions) rendered the accord of little value as a deterrent.[129] Réquin, who had spent years establishing a link between security and prearranged military assistance, also denounced the Protocol arrangements. The accord 'might increase the *sense of security*', he observed, 'but *it is not a guarantee* upon which a nation's defence can be based'. He understood that concessions were made in order to secure a political commitment from Britain. He warned, however, that the Protocol was a 'manoeuvre ... inspired [by] Britain's policy of ruining all European political systems that might constitute a counterweight to its own maritime power'.[130] The perspective of military elites on the problem of security had scarcely evolved.

The case of foreign ministry officials is more complicated. The Protocol, with its emphasis on strengthening the collective security machinery of the

---

[127] MAE, *SDN*, vol. 731, 'Note pour M. le président du conseil: position de la France à l'égard de l'Article 36 du statut de la Cour permanente de justice internationale', 2 Sept. 1924 and 'Signature de la France de la Disposition Facultative', 17 Oct. 1924. The Optional Clause was Article 36, Paragraph 2 of the Statute of the Permanent Court of International Justice. France adhered under the important condition of reciprocity and provided that the Protocol was ratified by the French parliament and that it was implemented by other signatories. These conditions did not prevail, however, and in the event France did not sign the Optional Clause formally until 1929. On the Optional Clause see L. Lloyd, *Peace through Law: Britain and the International Court in the 1920s* (London, 1997).

[128] SHD-DAT, 7N 3532–3, 'Questions à examiner à la demande des délégués français', 16 Sept. 1924; marked 'Copie de note remise de la main à la main par le général Serrigny à M. Laroche'.

[129] SHD-DAT, 7N 3532–3, 'Observations sur les textes examinés le 23 septembre 1924 dans les bureaux de M. Laroche' and 'Note du général Debeney', n.d.

[130] SHD-DAT, 7N 3532–1, 'Mémorandum au sujet du programme de la Conférence projetée sur la réduction des armements', 20 Oct. 1924 (emphasis in original).

A new approach: arbitration, security, disarmament 465

League, posed a fundamental challenge to traditional practices within the Quai d'Orsay. Senior officials were forced to choose between adapting their practices and joining with the military establishment in open opposition to Cartel policy. The choices made by these officials, interestingly, tended to reflect the generation gap that had opened up within the ministry during the First World War.

There was widespread discomfort within the Quai d'Orsay about the swift evolution of French foreign policy under Herriot, not least because the Cartel's recognition of the Soviet Union was unpopular with many diplomats.[131] Among the premier's most important critics from within the ministry were Peretti de la Rocca, Camille Barrère, Jules Jusserand and Saint-Aulaire. Peretti had been Poincaré's chief collaborator throughout the Ruhr occupation. He had also accompanied Herriot to London in June 1924 and had taken part in negotiations at the London Conference later that summer. But he did not participate in drafting the policy memoranda that underpinned the Geneva Protocol. Nor did he take part in the defence of the policy of the Protocol mounted by foreign ministry officials within the crucial subcommittees of the CSDN in September and November. Barrère in Rome and Jusserand in Washington, the two remaining *grands* of the pre-1914 era, both discreetly indicated their preference for a more traditional policy.[132] Saint-Aulaire in London was less circumspect. Angered at being excluded from the first Herriot–MacDonald summit, he had leaked the minutes of the Chequers meeting to Pertinax at *L'Écho de Paris* in an attempt to undermine the premier's policy.[133]

In contrast to this opposition, however, were the views of the newer generation of Quai bureaucrats. Nearly all of these were protégés of Berthelot. All were convinced of the supreme importance of *entente* with Britain. All, moreover, had disapproved of the politics of confrontation under Poincaré. Although most remained sceptical of the value of the League as a source of national security, they were amenable to embracing legalist and multilateral solutions, provided a Franco-British entente remained at the heart of all policy conceptions. This enabled them to cooperate with the new Cartel regime. The most senior among this cohort were Laroche and Seydoux, who had both played central roles in developing an alternative policy conception in spring–summer 1924. Also important was Fromageot, who, as chief legal counsel, embraced the concept of compulsory arbitration. It was at this stage, moreover, that a group of younger officials that included Massigli, Alexis Léger, Charles Corbin and Paul Bargeton emerged to take a hand in the elaboration of security policy. All would rise to prominence as technicians of Briandist multilateralism

---

[131] A. Hogenhuis-Seliverstoff, *Les Relations franco-soviétiques 1917–1924* (Paris, 1981), 278–94.
[132] P. Jackson, 'Tradition and adaptation: the social universe of the French foreign ministry in the era of the First World War', *French History*, 24, 2 (2010).
[133] Schuker, *End*, 257–61.

into the 1930s. All assisted Laroche as he took the lead in defending the Protocol in a series of robust engagements with senior military officials in the autumn of 1924.

The military establishment mounted an intense last-ditch effort to resist the new direction in French policy. Instructed by the premier's office to prepare a programme of study for implementing the Protocol, the SGDN responded with a list of theoretical and practical arguments against multilateralism and disarmament.[134] In meetings of the Commission d'études on 22 October and 7 November 1924, senior service chiefs insisted, one after another, that the Protocol offered no new guarantees and that further arms reductions were therefore impossible. Generals Debeney and Mangin objected with particular vehemence to the need for the Council to identify aggression before regional pacts could be put into operation.[135] The core obstacle was a fundamental refusal to recognise anything other than a classic military alliance as a basis for security. General Mangin, for his part, was unable to let go of the Rhenish dream: 'Against a Germany that is not federalist but is instead unified under Prussia', he warned, 'all present measures will prove impotent and we will never be able to take too many precautions.' Only an independent Rhineland could provide 'absolute security'.[136]

Laroche and Fromageot joined Paul-Boncour in defence of the Protocol. Paul-Boncour stressed the 'near automatic' character of the process of defining aggression. The divergent perspectives on the role of Germany that surfaced during these exchanges are particularly illuminating. Debeney opposed any accord that would include Germany, arguing that there remained 'too many uncertainties' surrounding its status in Europe. Fromageot responded that arbitration accords offered substantial benefit only vis-à-vis states with whom they had been signed. Laroche then added, 'in the case in point our security would be assured if we were bound with Britain, Spain, Italy and Germany'. A multilateral arbitration regime, in other words, would place further legal constraints on German revisionism.[137]

Such arguments, which rested ultimately on the power of law, international legitimacy and the threat of collective action to condition state behaviour, did little to reassure military elites. Another report prepared by the SGDN was replete with thinly veiled criticisms of the accord. It observed, for example, that:

[134] SHD-DAT, 7N 3532–4, 'Cadre Général des études à entreprendre en vue de la réunion du Comité du conseil de la Société des nations le 17 novembre 1924 (Application du protocole de Genève et travaux préparatoires à l'établissement du programme général de la Conférence sur la réduction des armements)', 18 Oct. 1924.
[135] SHD-DAT, 7N 3532–4, 'Délibération de la 1ère section de la Commission d'études du CSDN dans sa séance du 7 novembre 1924'.
[136] SHD-DAT, 7N 3532–4, 'Délibération de la 1ère section de la Commission d'études du CSDN dans sa séance du 22 octobre 1924'.
[137] SHD-DAT, 7N 3532–4, 'Délibération de la 1ère section de la Commission d'études du CSDN dans sa séance du 7 novembre 1924'.

A new approach: arbitration, security, disarmament

The compulsory peaceful settlement of all international differences, or more briefly arbitration, which is the base of the protocol, will increase as an element of security only to the extent that it enters genuinely in the practice of international moral standards and replaces the warrior spirit that continues to animate certain peoples partisan to the 'right of force'.[138]

The position of the military establishment was clear. French policy must rest on the coercive and deterrent power of military alliances rather than on a strategy of enmeshing Germany in a web of legal commitments under the aegis of the League of Nations.

The issue was only finally settled at a meeting of the full CSDN on 15 November 1924. In a 'bruising encounter' Herriot, Paul-Boncour and especially Briand defended the accord from broadsides by senior military figures.[139] Debeney again raised objections to the role of the Council in triggering regional accords. Using the hypothesis of a German attack on Poland, he argued that France's right to come to the latter's assistance was an issue of 'legitimate self-defence' that must not be impaired by cumbersome procedures in Geneva. Pétain seconded these views and underlined the difficulties in determining the meaning of military preparations within the context of identifying the aggressor. Both insisted that, as a result of these imperfections, the Protocol added no substantial benefits to French security. Their objections were overridden by a forceful response from Briand stressing the deterrent effect of the Protocol. Briand argued that had such a system been in place in 1914, the position of Britain would have been clarified and Germany would not have dared to resort to war. When objections to German participation were raised, Briand brushed these aside as well. He asserted bluntly that there would be no hope of security pacts with Britain, Spain or Italy 'if these powers suspected that such pacts contained the slightest offensive character towards Germany'. The only way to remove such suspicions, he insisted, was to open up the Protocol to German participation. It was agreed that a pact including Britain must be the 'absolute priority' of French policy.[140] Objections to disarmament were met with assurances that negotiations for a programme of arms reduction would start only after a 'balance sheet of guarantees' had been established. The link between security and arms reduction would be preserved. But France's military leadership was forced to accept the Protocol and the new direction in which France's civilian leadership was taking national security policy.

---

[138] SHD-DAT, 2N 6–3, 'Étude au sujet des travaux préparatoires à l'application du Protocole de Genève', 4 Nov. 1924 and 'Resumé du rapport fait, au nom de la commission d'études, au sujet des travaux préparatoires à l'application du Protocole de Genève', 15 Nov. 1924.
[139] SHD-DAT, 2N 6–3, 'CSDN: Procès-verbal de la séance du 15 novembre 1924'; Hogge, 'Arbitrage', 395–7.
[140] SHD-DAT, 2N 6–3, 'CSDN: Procès-verbal de la séance du 15 novembre 1924'; 7N 3532–1, 'Avis émis par la réunion du CSDN dans sa séance du 15 novembre 1924' and 'Note au sujet d'un accord éventuel entre la France et l'Angleterre sur les bases du Protocole de Genève', Nov 1924.

In the end the Geneva Protocol was never implemented. While British representatives in Geneva had played a central role in drafting the accord, they did so in an unofficial capacity. This fact was not sufficiently understood in Paris, and led to intense disappointment when a new Conservative government led by prime minister Stanley Baldwin declined to ratify the Protocol in early 1925. Yet the ultimate failure to implement the accord should not obscure its fundamental importance. By late 1924 the conceptual underpinnings to France's Locarno policy were already in place. First, multilateral pacts had replaced traditional alliances and joint preparations for war as the chief means by which France sought to bolster its strategic position. Second, political and legal guarantees from Britain had replaced a military commitment from that country as the central objective of security policy. Third, the inviolable status of the Rhineland was established as a cornerstone of a multilateral system. Finally, French policy elites accepted that Germany must be integrated into the new security regime under construction.

When French delegate Aristide Briand proclaimed France's adherence to the Protocol before the Assembly on 1 October 1924 he signalled a revolution in French security policy. France renounced its quest for a British military guarantee and agreed to integrating Germany into a multilateral system for security in Europe. Strangely, this revolution is almost entirely absent in the relevant literature. Most accounts of the international history of this period either ignore or pass quickly over the events of autumn 1924. Professor Schuker, for example, dismisses the programme for security developed during the summer of 1924 as one of the 'lingering illusions' to which the Herriot government clung in the aftermath of the London Conference. Zara Steiner and Patrick Cohrs both characterise the international processes leading to the Protocol as driven by a British desire to address France's 'malaise'.[141]

The reality is that the Geneva Protocol was the culmination of a fundamental reorientation in French foreign and security policy introduced by the Herriot government. British officials recognised that the accord was an attempt to reintroduce the more muscular vision of the League advocated by Bourgeois at the peace conference. British cabinet secretary Maurice Hankey observed that the heart of the Protocol was 'the French conception of a League of Nations that was rejected by the British and the [American] delegations at the Peace Conference'.[142] Hankey was correct. Cartel foreign policy was rooted in a long tradition of internationalist thought in France that can be traced back to the late nineteenth century and the emergence of a juridical internationalist conception of peace and security.

[141] Schuker, *End*, 354–7 (quote at 354); Steiner, *Lights that Failed*, 380–1 (quote at 380); Cohrs, *Unfinished Peace*, 202–3.
[142] TNA-PRO, CAB, 21/289, CID Paper no. 559-B, 'Reduction of Armaments, Protocol on the Pacific Settlement of International Disputes', Jan. 1925 (memo by Hankey).

13 Locarno

The Locarno Accords of October 1925 are usually represented as the end point of a process of rebuilding European security after the First World War.[1] This is not how they were understood and represented in France, however. For most French policy elites, Locarno constituted an important waypoint in an ongoing project to establish the foundations of a new European security system. This system would be based on Franco-German conciliation and cooperation, guaranteed by Great Britain and embedded within the wider structures of the League of Nations. Germany would be enmeshed in a political, legal and economic regime that would contain its aggressive instincts and ensure that any future treaty revision would be peaceful and take place under conditions favourable to France. This project endured through to the mid-1930s, when it was destroyed by the effects of economic crisis and by the rise of the Nazi regime in Germany, whose central purpose was to prepare a new European war.

It is a testament to the extraordinary flexibility of the Treaty of Versailles that French policy makers were able to pursue this new security programme without renouncing any of France's core treaty rights. The most important of these remained the occupation of the Left Bank of the Rhine, but the disarmament clauses of the treaty were also defended by the Herriot government. The crucial difference was that where Poincaré had imposed the treaty in an attempt to secure a British alliance and achieve strategic preponderance for France, for Herriot, and for his successor Aristide Briand, treaty enforcement was a means to secure British and German participation in a Europe-wide security system. This effort was only partially successful. Neither Britain nor Germany was willing to accept the French programme in the long term. But the Locarno Accords, which were a system of interlocking mutual assistance commitments

---

[1] Most recently by the majority of the contributions in G. Johnson (ed.), *Locarno Revisited: European Diplomacy, 1920–1929* (London, 2004); Cohrs characterises Locarno as the 'second "real" peace settlement' after the First World War: P. Cohrs, *The Unfinished Peace after World War I* (Cambridge, 2006), 259–86; Boyce, meanwhile, argues that the Locarno system brought about the 'emasculation of European security': R. Boyce, *The Great Interwar Crisis and the Collapse of Globalization* (London, 2009), 77–141.

with compulsory arbitration agreements, owed much more to the French conception of international security than is commonly understood.

There were two distinct stages in the evolution of France's Locarno policy. The first was a challenging series of essentially bilateral negotiations leading to the creation of a common Franco-British front. The second was characterised by multilateral exchanges that included Germany and culminated in the signature of a western European security pact at the Locarno Conference. The first stage was by far the most important. It was in negotiations with the British that French officials were forced to make crucial concessions and sacrifices to their original policy conception based on the Geneva Protocol. It was at this stage, moreover, that it is possible to identify the emergence of a new 'practical logic' among senior French political and policy elites. This logic would shape the policy reflexes of foreign ministry officials well into the 1930s.

I

The aftermath of the Geneva Protocol witnessed important changes within the French policy establishment. From mid-1924 rumours circulated of an impending purge of France's senior diplomats.[2] Herriot was determined to impose his policy on permanent officials within the foreign ministry. The result was that the senior leadership of the Quai d'Orsay was transformed by the removal of virtually all of the most prominent advocates of traditional foreign and security policy practices. Saint-Aulaire was removed from his post in December and forced to retire. He would spend the remainder of the 1920s railing against multilateral diplomacy and the League of Nations in the pages of *Le Figaro*.[3] Jules Jusserand and Camille Barrère, meanwhile, were eased more gracefully into permanent retirement. Peretti, who had been on 'holiday' during the Protocol negotiations, was replaced as political director by Laroche upon his return. Other senior foreign ministry officials who were able to adapt to Cartel foreign policy were promoted. One such official was Seydoux, who since 1919 had advocated engagement with Germany within a wider multilateral political and economic context. He was appointed deputy political director.[4]

These moves were part of a major shake-up within the foreign service that included as many as 150 personnel changes. At the mid-career level, meanwhile, a number of younger figures emerged to take on increased responsibility

---

[2] CCAC, *Phipps Papers*, 1/3, Phipps to MacDonald, 13 Jun. and 17 Jul. 1924; R. J. Young, *An American by Degrees: The Extraordinary Lives of French Ambassador Jules Jusserand* (Montreal, 2009), 203–4.

[3] Saint-Aulaire, *Confession*, 704–62; Saint-Aulaire's editorial work in *Le Figaro* is published as *La Mythologie de la paix* (Paris, 1930).

[4] P. Jackson, 'Tradition and adaptation: the social universe of the French foreign ministry in the era of the First World War', *French History*, 24, 2 (2010), 192–4; Young, *Jusserand*, 204–6; Laroche, *Au Quai d'Orsay*, 196–8.

in the formulation of policy. One of the most significant of these was René Massigli, who since 1920 had held the important post of general secretary of the Conference of Ambassadors. From mid-1924 he became more thoroughly integrated into the DAPC and played a central role in the evolution of France's Locarno policy.[5] But Massigli was only one of a substantial cohort of fast-rising permanent officials that also included Aimé de Fleuriau, Alexis Léger, Jean Giraudoux, Charles Corbin and Paul Bargeton. All of these officials were convinced of the fundamental importance of Britain to French security; all agreed on the need to adapt French policy to the post-war international political context and all were protégés of Berthelot. It was this generation that would become the chief implementers of 'Briandism' over the following decade.[6]

There was no such restructuring of the military establishment. The strategy of Herriot and Briand was to ignore senior military officials rather than remove them. Serrigny therefore remained at the head of the SGDN, Debeney retained his post as chief of army staff, and Pétain continued as inspector general of the army, vice-president of the CSG and commander-in-chief designate. Foch, meanwhile, remained president of the Allied Military Commission at Versailles.[7] But all were increasingly marginalised from security policy making. The archival record reveals that France's military chiefs were rarely even consulted as France's Locarno policy was hammered out over the course of 1925.

Foch was deeply frustrated by this state of affairs. 'I work constantly in a fog that seems to get thicker all the time,' he complained. He attributed this fog to a dearth of capable political leadership. 'A statesman,' Foch observed, 'like a great military chief, must have a doctrine, a method and a clear idea of the principal issues at stake.' He judged these qualities sorely lacking among France's post-war political class and thought that the Cartel government would undermine what was left of France's security. 'The victorious powers chase ceaselessly after peace without ever attaining it,' he lamented. 'The end result is a grim paradox: they seek an understanding with the defeated party and are unaware that this strategy marks the beginning of their own defeat.'[8] Foch remained an unyielding critic of multilateralism and engagement until his death in 1929.

---

[5] Massigli downplayed his contribution, but the archives reveal his deep involvement at this stage: see R. Ulrich-Pier, *René Massigli (1888–1988): une vie de diplomate*, 2 vols. (Brussels, 2006), I, 140–56.

[6] J. L. Barré, *Philippe Berthelot: l'éminence grise, 1866–1934* (Paris, 1998), 204–29; R. Meltz, *Alexis Léger dit Saint-John Perse* (Paris, 2008), 258–61; Ulrich-Pier, *Massigli*, I, 118–37; Jackson, 'Tradition and adaptation', 184–96.

[7] M. Vaïsse and J. Doise, *Diplomatie et outil militaire: politique étrangère de la France, 1871–1991* (Paris, 1992), 340–8.

[8] Quotations from J.-C. Notin, *Foch* (Paris, 2008), 512, 518–19 and M. Weygand, *Foch* (Paris, 1947), 286.

Not all senior military officers were as inflexible as Foch. Pétain and Debeney both proved willing to adapt the army to the changed domestic and international context of the mid-1920s. Although both opposed further reductions to the size of the standing army, they accepted that a move to one-year military service was inevitable. Such a reduction in the term of conscription had long been an aim of the left. It was first introduced into formal policy deliberations in late 1924 by war minister Nollet. Although the CSG rejected Nollet's initial proposal, it accepted a programme put forward by his successor, Paul Painlevé, the following summer that reduced the term of service to one year and the size of the standing army from thirty-two to twenty divisions. These reforms were the first step in what would be a thorough reorganisation of the French army in 1927–8.[9]

The lack of determined resistance to one-year service from the high command must be interpreted within the wider context of what even Nollet admitted was a generalised 'state of malaise' within the military in the mid-1920s.[10] Military professionals experienced difficulty adjusting to the changed political status of the army in the post-war decade. The army gradually lost its identity as the living embodiment of the French nation as popular sentiment became ever more critical of the discourses of patriotism and sacrifice that were central to the belief systems of professional soldiers. This process, when combined with the increasing strain placed on the army by the demands of occupying Germany and fighting full-scale colonial wars in Morocco and Syria, undermined morale and led to problems with recruitment and retention.[11] The army leadership sensed itself increasingly isolated and vulnerable as the 1920s wore on. This was the political and cultural context for the transformation of the French army from a powerful offensive force designed to act against Germany into a short-term training cadre for a mobilised nation-in-arms designed to defend French territory. The official history of the French army for this period is aptly entitled 'The time of compromises'.[12]

Military policy was reconfigured to reflect the new direction of the Herriot government's security policy. This is clear not least from the evolution of the SGDN's policy prescriptions in late 1924. After the tense meeting of the CSDN on 15 November resulted in victory for the government's position, the SGDN produced yet another highly critical assessment of the value of the

---

[9] F.-A. Paoli, *L'Armée française de 1919 à 1939*, vol. III: *Le temps des compromis* (Vincennes, 1974), 40–92; J. Hughes, *To the Maginot Line: The Politics of French Military Preparation in the 1920s* (Cambridge, Mass., 1971), 172–8.
[10] SHD-DAT, 1N 27-1, 'Procès-verbal de la séance du CSG du 30 Mars 1925'.
[11] R. Girardet, *La Société militaire de 1815 à nos jours*, 2nd edn (Paris, 1998), 237–49; Hughes, *Maginot Line*, 160–72.
[12] Paoli, *Temps des compromis*, 93–104; Vaïsse and Doise, *Outil militaire*, 339–53.

Geneva Protocol for French security.[13] Herriot and Laroche responded by instructing General Serrigny to reconsider the issue of a Franco-British pact under the Protocol.[14] The result was an SGDN proposal for a possible Franco-British security pact based explicitly on 'the essential principles of the Protocol'. 'The first principle to which we must remain attached', the SGDN observed in this document, 'is that of *arbitration*.' Compulsory arbitration offered 'a crucial advantage by providing the formal and automatic definition of aggression' and therefore must constitute 'the basis of any eventual Franco-British accord'.[15] It was also essential, the study noted, to retain the Protocol's provision that any violation of the demilitarised zone by Germany must also be defined as aggression. However reluctantly, the SGDN had come around to the idea of security guarantees embedded in international public law.

The SGDN study also addressed the great source of tension in French security policy at this juncture: the fact that the British were not willing to extend any commitment to eastern Europe. 'We must avoid at all costs', it recommended, 'a situation where we will be forced to choose between allowing Poland to be destroyed or intervening, only to see Britain refuse to honour its commitment with us because we have taken the initiative [against Germany].' Interestingly, the SGDN suggested a strategy of multilateral enmeshment in which the British military commitment would be embedded in a wider arrangement that was open to both Poland and Germany:

It is essential that the Franco-British accord be divested of any offensive character vis-à-vis Germany. This has always been the British point of view. If, in order to fulfil this condition, [the pact] must remain open to German participation, so must it also remain open to the participation of any other state and notably Poland and Czechoslovakia.

Germany would be included in a system of mutual assistance that extended across Europe. This was in fact the strategy adopted by the French government in the negotiations leading to Locarno the following spring and summer. Its prospects for success, however, hinged on Britain's willingness to make an indirect commitment to the states to the east of Germany.

II

There was no hope that Britain would make such a commitment. The advent of a Conservative government led by Stanley Baldwin sealed the fate of the Protocol. The British Committee of Imperial Defence (CID) rejected the

---

[13] SHD-DAT, 7N 3532–4, 'Le Point de vue français sur l'application du Protocole de Genève', 21 Nov. 1924, forwarded by Serrigny to the DAPC and Herriot, 22 Nov. 1924.
[14] MAE, *Série Z, GB*, vol. 71, 'Implémentation du Protocole de Genève', Laroche communicating Herriot's instructions to 'causer' with Serrigny, 24 Nov. 1924.
[15] MAE, *Série Z, GB*, vol. 71, 'Note au sujet d'un accord éventuel entre la France et l'Angleterre sur les bases du Protocole de Genève', 5 Dec. 1924 (emphasis in original).

Protocol decisively in mid-December 1924. British soldiers and diplomats were united in fierce opposition to the generalised yet automatic character of the sanctions envisaged in the Protocol.[16] The Baldwin government's decision to reject the Protocol was, in the words of new foreign secretary Austen Chamberlain, 'a simple and a necessary decision'.[17] The core issue, as Lora Gibson has observed, was that French and British policy elites held divergent views on the role of force in international politics: 'For the British government, any automatic obligation to enforce sanctions, particularly of the military variety, was dangerous ... [For the French government] only such an obligatory and automatic system of sanctions could compel states to abide by the arbitral decisions of the League Council.'[18] Pascal remained at the centre of French security conceptions.

European security was nonetheless a priority in London. One of the first memoranda prepared for Chamberlain upon his arrival at the foreign office was entitled 'The Necessity of the Early Consideration of the Question of French Security'. This document observed that

H[is]M[ajesty's]G[overnment], while not legally bound, are at least morally bound to see whether some satisfactory solution cannot be reached. For, whatever views may be held about the desirability or otherwise of giving a pact of guarantee to France, there can be no doubt that the great proportion of the trouble of the past five years is traceable to the failure to implement the guarantee treaties signed by this country and the United States and attached to the Treaty of Versailles.[19]

Chamberlain accepted this reasoning: 'It is time that we at the foreign office should attempt to develop a constructive policy.'[20] His preference was for an Anglo-Franco-Belgian security pact that would sit alongside a broader arrangement including Germany. This idea proved unacceptable to his cabinet colleagues, however, who on 2 March 1925 rejected the idea of a Franco-British pact or any other arrangement that did not include Germany.[21]

---

[16] TNA-PRO, CAB 2/4, minutes of the 192nd meeting of the CID, 16 Dec. 1924 and 21/289, CID paper no. 559-B, 'Reduction of Armaments, Protocol on the Pacific Settlement of International Disputes', Jan. 1925; see also J. Ferris, *The Evolution of British Strategic Policy, 1919–1925* (London, 1987), 144, 147–8, 152.

[17] TNA-PRO, FO 371, 11064, W25/9/93, 'French Ratification of the Geneva Protocol', 31 Dec. 1924, Chamberlain minute, 4 Jan. 1925.

[18] L. Gibson, 'The Role of International Sanctions in British and French Strategy and Diplomacy: A Comparative Perspective, 1919–1935', Ph.D. thesis, Aberystwyth University, 2007, 51–7, 44.

[19] TNA-PRO, FO 371, 9820, C16913/2048/18, 'Memorandum on the Necessity of the Early Consideration of the Question of French Security', 4 Nov. 1924.

[20] TNA-PRO, FO 371, 11064, W362/9/93, 'Minute by the Secretary of State', 4 Jan. 1925.

[21] MAE, *Série Z, GB*, vol. 74, 'Entrevue de M. Herriot avec M. Chamberlain', 16 Mar. 1925; E. Goldstein, 'The Evolution of British Diplomatic Strategy for the Locarno Pact, 1924–1925' in M. Dockrill and B. McKercher (eds.), *Diplomacy and World Power: Studies in British Foreign Policy, 1890–1950* (Cambridge, 1996), 115–35; J. Jacobson, 'Locarno, Britain and the Security of Europe' in Johnson (ed.), *Locarno Revisited*, 11–32.

Most French officials were slow to understand the direction in which British policy was moving. On 15 November 1924 Massigli prepared an optimistic assessment of prospects for Franco-British cooperation. 'In terms of the settlement of the security problem,' he submitted, 'at Geneva we witnessed the progressive coming together of French and British theses despite initial opposition.' He rightly judged that the prime minister and especially the foreign secretary were well disposed towards France. 'We can hope that the rapprochement achieved these last months between our two countries will subsist,' he advised. 'There is even hope that the new cabinet will be more inclined [than the Labour government] to make our security needs more of an immediate priority.'[22] Briand was even more optimistic. 'There is in Britain a strong tendency favourable to the conclusion of particular accords,' he had assured the CSDN. 'She seems to want them. If, as a result of this orientation, the Protocol is adopted in its three parts, it will constitute for France a near complete guarantee.'[23]

Senior French politicians had too much invested in the Protocol to readily accept its demise. 'The Protocol is regarded by the [French] government with a paternal feeling,' judged the British ambassador in Paris. 'I am of the opinion that M. Herriot sincerely regards it as the best possible solution, in all the circumstances, of the security problem.'[24] Nor did Herriot want to choose between the Protocol and a regional security pact with Britain. Indeed, the two were considered indispensable pillars of the security system under construction. 'Of course we are going to sign the Protocol,' Gaston Bergery advised Chamberlain in early December. 'It is going to establish our moral position in Europe; but we want as its natural concomitant a tripartite arrangement with Belgium and Great Britain.'[25]

The Herriot government's attachment to the Protocol as a framework for security endured even after the Baldwin government formally declined to ratify the accord. 'The Protocol is essentially a mechanism for the effective administration and implementation of the Covenant,' Herriot advised the chamber's foreign affairs committee in March 1925. 'As a consequence, Britain will one day or another come to understand this.'[26] Briand concurred. 'It is very possible', he insisted, 'that Great Britain will return to the spirit of the Protocol and make proposals under another name. The Church as well as the Labour and Liberal parties all, at the end of the day, support the spirit of the Protocol.'[27] This optimism was unfounded, but it would endure within the policy elite through to the mid-1930s. It reflected a strong commitment to

---

[22] MAE, *Série Z, GB*, vol. 71, 'Note sur les relations franco-anglaises (de Massigli)', 15 Nov. 1924.
[23] SHD-DAT, 2N 6–3, 'CSDN: Procès-verbal de la séance du 15 novembre 1924'.
[24] TNA-PRO, FO 371, 9820, C18465/248/18, Crewe to Chamberlain, 12 Nov. 1924.
[25] TNA-PRO, CAB 2/4, minutes of the 192nd meeting of the CID, 16 Dec. 1924.
[26] AN, C/14762, *CAEAN*, XIIIème Législature, Herriot *audition*, 11 Mar. 1925.
[27] AN, C/14762, *CAEAN*, XIIIème Législature, 'Délibérations' of 27 Mar. 1925.

the strategy of enmeshing both Germany and Britain in a multilateral security system. It is impossible to understand the dynamics of French policy during the Locarno negotiations without taking this commitment into account.

To procure the elusive security guarantee from Britain, the Herriot government developed a strategy based on advantages obtained by Clemenceau at the peace conference and written into the Versailles Treaty. German non-compliance with the treaty's disarmament clauses was used as justification for refusing to evacuate the Cologne occupation zone as scheduled on 10 January 1925. Laroche had identified two vital issues at stake in this question the previous summer. The first was the need to obtain a British security commitment to make good the guarantee extended to Clemenceau in 1919. The second was to ensure the permanent demilitarised status of the Rhineland after the Inter-Allied Control Commission completed its work. France must do everything in its power to achieve these objectives before any part of the Rhineland was evacuated.[28]

Laroche argued that France could use its rights under the peace treaty to achieve these aims. He attached particular importance to Article 429, which made evacuation of the Rhineland contingent on German treaty fulfilment and stipulated that the occupation could be prolonged 'if guarantees against unprovoked aggression by Germany are not considered sufficient'. Laroche collaborated with Fromageot to recommend using Article 429 first to insist on a permanent inspection regime for the demilitarised zone and second to press the British to make a concrete security commitment to France.[29] Defending the treaty remained as important under the Cartel as it had been under the Bloc national. The difference was that, where traditional strategic preponderance had been a central aim of treaty defence for Millerand and Poincaré, Herriot and his successors aimed to construct a Europe-wide security system under the auspices of the League.

The debate and discussion that resulted from Laroche's proposal provides further insight into the security conceptions of key actors. The SGDN studied the question of arms inspections and came to the predictable conclusion that it would be impossible to prevent German rearmament in the medium term. It advised that, although Article 213 of the peace treaty attributed to the League of Nations the permanent right of inspection inside Germany, there was no hope that such a regime would be effective. Serrigny's staff contended that this was a powerful argument for the permanent occupation of the Left Bank. But the SGDN did distinguish between preventing the rearmament of Germany as a whole and maintaining the demilitarised status of the Rhineland. The latter

---

[28] MAE, *Série Z, RGR*, vol. 79, untitled Laroche note, 8 Aug. 1924; *Série Z, GB*, vol. 71, 'Garanties inscrites dans le traité de Versailles', 4 Aug. 1924.

[29] MAE, *Série Z, GB*, vol. 71, 'Garanties inscrites dans le traité de Versailles', 4 Aug. 1924; *Série Z, RGR*, vol. 79, untitled Laroche note, 8 Aug. 1924; 'Note' (Laroche and Fromageot), 6 Sept. 1924; see also the run of documents on the question of League-sponsored inspection in PA-AP 089, *Papiers Herriot*, vol. 18.

was relatively easy to enforce under the occupation regime. If the Rhineland were to be evacuated according to schedule, however, the SGDN judged that a robust regime of League-sponsored inspection under Article 213 *could* prove effective in detecting German violations and bringing them to the attention of the Council.[30]

The SGDN's judgement was endorsed by both the Commission d'études and the foreign ministry. Laroche and Fromageot collaborated on another note which emphasised the advantages 'from a moral point of view' of inspection managed from the League of Nations. The legitimacy of the League, they argued, would make such a system 'easier for Germany to support than inspection imposed by the victorious powers alone in the name of the justice conferred only by victory'.[31] This was a long way from the position taken under the Bloc national. During the Fifth Assembly in Geneva the French delegation lobbied for a League-sponsored system of inspection for the Rhineland. Herriot, meanwhile, advised MacDonald that France could not assent to any evacuation of the Rhineland before some system for the surveillance of the demilitarised zone was assured.[32] The League Council duly agreed to study the issue in late November. British officials correctly judged that the French were angling to establish permanent inspection stations in the Rhineland.[33] Although the League Council approved the creation of a League-based inspection system the following March, the French plan for permanent inspection in the Rhineland foundered on the shoals of both German and British opposition.[34] The course of internal debates over this issue nonetheless illustrates an evolution among security professionals towards greater reliance on the League as a source of security.

The looming deadline for evacuating the Cologne zone prompted a similarly illuminating round of internal discussions. During the summer Herriot and MacDonald had agreed that Britain and France must assume a common

---

[30] SHD-DAT, 7N 3531–2, 'Note au sujet de l'exercise du droit d'investigation de la Société des nations', 28 Jul. 1924; this note drew on a previous SGDN study: 7N 3529–2, 'Sur le caractère de l'article 213 du Traité de Versailles', 28 Feb. 1924; see also 7N 3532–4, 'Note au sujet des zones démilitarisées', 19 Oct. 1924; see also R. Shuster, *German Disarmament after World War I: The Diplomacy of International Arms Inspection* (London, 2006), 104–27 and A. Barros, 'Disarmament as a weapon: Anglo-French relations and the problems of enforcing German disarmament, 1919–1928', *JSS*, 29, 2 (2006), esp. 315–18.

[31] MAE, *Série Z, RGR*, vol. 79, 'Note' (Laroche and Fromageot), 6 Sept. 1924; SHD-DAT, 7N 3532–1, 'Délibération de la 1ère section de la Commission d'études du 30 septembre 1924'.

[32] TNA-PRO, FO 371, 9819, C12870/2048/18, Herriot to MacDonald, 12 Aug. 1924.

[33] TNA-PRO, FO 371, 9820, C18874/2048/18, 'Supervision by the League of Nations of the Demilitarisation of the Rhineland', 17 Dec. 1924, with minutes by Harold Nicolson, Norman Lampson and Cecil Hurst (FO legal counsellor).

[34] See the overview in MAE, Service juridique, *Fonds Fromageot*, vol. 54, 'Allemagne et droit d'investigation', 29 Oct. 1926; see also A. Webster, 'Making disarmament work: the implementation of the international disarmament provisions in the League of Nations Covenant', *D&S*, 16, 3 (2005), 553 and Edmonds, *Rhineland*, 268–82.

position over the issue. There was also general agreement on both sides that it made little sense to evacuate the zone before all French troops left the Ruhr.[35] The Quai d'Orsay recommended using Cologne as leverage to press Britain for a security commitment. 'It is absolutely essential', Laroche wrote to Herriot, 'that we do not agree to withdraw from Cologne until we have something serious in hand as a guarantee.'[36] The pretext to be used was German non-fulfilment of the disarmament clauses of the Versailles Treaty as stipulated in Article 429. The Inter-Allied Military Control Commission (IMCC) had been prevented from performing its task from the autumn of 1922 to the aftermath of the Ruhr crisis. This meant that there was no chance it would be able to prepare a systematic report on the situation regarding German compliance before the Allies met to consider the issue of evacuating Cologne.[37]

Laroche convened a meeting to formulate policy towards the Cologne zone.[38] In attendance were representatives from Foch's staff, the army general staff, the SGDN, General Henri Guillaumat of the army of the Rhine, Tirard's Rhineland Commission staff, the finance ministry and Laroche, Fromageot and Massigli from the Quai d'Orsay. The resulting exchanges illuminate persistent divergences within the security establishment over the role of the Rhineland and acceptable conditions of security. Most military officials, supported by Tirard's staff, continued to argue that the Rhineland occupation was vital to French security and must be prolonged indefinitely. Foreign ministry officials, conversely, pointed out that the occupation was necessarily temporary. They stressed the need to coordinate eventual withdrawal with the 'organisation' of France's future security.

Foch and Tirard both forwarded position papers to inform debate. Foch, for his part, opposed all talk of withdrawal from the Cologne zone. He argued that Germany had failed to comply with the treaty. Its failure to disarm was patent. And the very existence of the Dawes Plan constituted proof of German non-execution of the financial clauses of the treaty. The marshal insisted that the Rhineland occupation constituted the sole reliable guarantee of France's security and must be prolonged under Article 429 'until the execution of the treaty is advanced to a point where we can have no doubt that the entirety of Germany's obligations will be fulfilled'. This of course was a prescription for

---

[35] MAE, *Série Z, RGR*, vol. 79, 'Evacuation de Cologne', 20 Sept. 1924; 'Evacuation de la rive gauche du Rhin', 20 Oct. 1924; 'Evacuation de la zone de Cologne', Herriot to Foch and French embassies in London, Rome, Brussels and Berlin, 28 Nov. 1924; TNA-PRO, FO 371, 9819, C15288/2048/18, 'French views on security', 29 Sept. and 12, 15 Nov. 1924; V. Pitts, *France and the German Problem: Politics and Economics in the Locarno Period, 1924–1929* (New York, 1987), 6–8.

[36] MAE, *Série Z, GB*, vol. 71, Laroche to Peretti (for Herriot), 5 Aug. 1924.

[37] MAE, *Série Z, RGR*, vol. 79, untitled Laroche note, 8 Aug. 1924 and 'Evacuation de la zone de Cologne', 13 Nov. 1924.

[38] MAE, *Série Z, RGR*, vol. 79, 'Evacuation de la zone de Cologne', 19 Nov. 1924 and 'Note' (DAPC), 21 Nov. 1924.

occupying the entire region indefinitely.[39] Tirard provided a detailed list of all German treaty violations. He echoed Foch's argument that the Dawes Plan constituted non-compliance and could be used as justification for not withdrawing from Cologne. He underlined the strategic importance of the rail hub at Cologne and recommended putting off evacuation by 'a minimum of three or four years'.[40] If, on the other hand, 'a transaction is necessary', he judged that

> the question must be put off to a later date, provided that this date is sufficiently far off to permit beforehand the general settlement of conditions of security through international accords. These accords must include detailed provisions for military co-operation in the event of any violation of [their] security clauses, with due care taken to ensure our ability to intervene to protect the states to the East.[41]

Tirard was arguing for a de facto military alliance with Britain linked to France's eastern security system.

The SGDN response was more interesting because it was more ambiguous. General Serrigny began by making it clear that any decision to evacuate Cologne in the near future would be 'political'. It could not be justified either in strict legal terms or from the perspective of national defence:

> It is only by entering into the reality of purely political considerations, which it is not my role to evaluate, that one might, for the sake of appeasement and détente, assent to a manifestation of goodwill towards Germany and judge it opportune to commence an eventual evacuation that the facts in themselves by no means justify.[42]

Serrigny in this way left no doubt that he opposed a decision to withdraw from Cologne in principle. Should the route of 'appeasement' be chosen, however, he stipulated that under no circumstances could it be envisaged for 10 January 1925. He recommended that it be put off until the summer at the earliest. In return, he argued, France must obtain three core guarantees. The first was satisfaction that Germany was complying with the most important military clauses. The second was 'a complete and permanent system of inspection organised by the League of Nations in the Rhineland'. The third was application of the Geneva Protocol supplemented by 'British participation in a "regional entente" with the other states in western Europe'.[43] Serrigny and his staff were by this time resigned to the eventual surrender of France's 'physical guarantee' on the Rhine in exchange for the political and legal guarantees embodied in the Protocol.

---

[39] MAE, *Série Z, RGR*, vol. 79, 'Note du Maréchal Foch', 28 Nov. 1924. Foch did acknowledge that the occupation was a 'guarantee of treaty execution'.
[40] MAE, *Série Z, RGR*, vol. 79, Tirard to Herriot (DAPC), 25 Nov. 1924; also Tirard's contribution to debate, 'Evacuation de la zone de Cologne (texte définitif)', 28 Nov. 1924.
[41] MAE, *Série Z, RGR*, vol. 79, Tirard to Herriot (DAPC), 25 Nov. 1924.
[42] MAE, *Série Z, RGR*, vol. 79, 'Note pour la réunion du vendredi 28 novembre au ministère des Affaires étrangères', 26 Nov. 1924.
[43] Ibid.

Foreign ministry officials did not circulate a preliminary study but were well prepared for the meeting that took place on 28 November 1924. Laroche, supported by Fromageot and by an official from the finance ministry, rejected the argument that the Dawes Plan constituted evidence of German non-compliance. Both insisted that any refusal to withdraw must rest on non-fulfilment of the disarmament clauses of the treaty. This, they added, would secure only a short-term postponement. Germany was almost certain to comply with the final report of the IMCC when it was filed the following spring. Massigli interjected that France must accept that the Rhineland occupation was temporary and 'anticipate the organisation of European security along different lines'.[44] Debeney disagreed, contending that:

> The occupied territories are a guarantee of security for France: in effect the clauses of the Treaty of Versailles relative to the line of the Rhine were accepted by the French delegation only in return for the promise, signed by the British and American delegates, of a guarantee pact. As this promise was not fulfilled, the French government has the legal right to demand that its Allies recognise its right to determine itself the conditions of the occupation.

Laroche and Fromageot both responded that, under the legal terms of the treaty, the occupation constituted 'a general guarantee of the execution of the treaty'. The treaty, in turn, guaranteed French security.[45] It is interesting to note that the fault lines between the security conceptions of Debeney, on the one hand, and foreign ministry mandarins, on the other, were very similar to those that had existed between Foch and Clemenceau in 1919. The former was rooted in traditional power politics and sought control of the Rhineland. The latter was a response to the changed normative context of the post-war period and sought political guarantees from other Great Powers that would be embedded in international public law.

The chief result of the interdepartmental meeting of 28 November was agreement that no date could be set for the evacuation of Cologne until the final IMCC report had been submitted. This, crucially, would allow the French government to use withdrawal from the region as leverage to obtain British acceptance of the Protocol or some similar commitment in future negotiations for a new security system.[46] This strategy was embraced by Herriot and approved by his cabinet. Before the chamber the following January he declared that 'at the present time the most important issue for our foreign policy is the evacuation of Cologne'.[47] But the premier's ultimate aim was unequivocally a regional pact with Britain under the wider umbrella of the

---

[44] MAE, *Série Z, RGR*, vol. 79, 'Evacuation de la zone de Cologne (texte définitif)', 28 Nov. 1924.
[45] Ibid.   [46] Ibid.; Pitts, *German Problem*, 12–14.
[47] *JO*, Chambre, *Débats*, 1925, 26 Jan. 1925; MAE, *Série Z, RGR*, vol. 79, 'Évacuation de Cologne', 10 Dec. 1924; 'Question de l'évacuation de la zone de Cologne', 15 Dec. 1924; 'Note: évacuation de Cologne', 17 Dec. 1924; 'Évacuation de Cologne', 21 Dec. 1924.

Protocol and the League of Nations. During his first meeting with Austen Chamberlain on 5 December, the premier made an explicit link between the questions of Cologne, a British security commitment and the Geneva Protocol. When Chamberlain asked whether France preferred a British guarantee or the Geneva Protocol, Herriot replied that he wanted both.[48] He instructed the new ambassador in London, Aimé de Fleuriau (yet another protégé of Berthelot), to hold to this line in all dealings with British policy elites. 'It will not be easy to get the French out of Cologne with the Protocol hanging fire,' Chamberlain remarked in late December 1924.[49] He was right.

III

The Geneva Protocol provided the conceptual framework for French policy in the crucial negotiations that followed a German offer of a Rhineland security pact, which arrived in early February 1925. This offer was a revised version of a previous proposal for a security pact by the Cuno government that was rejected by Poincaré in late 1922. It went further, however, in offering to guarantee the demilitarised status of the Rhineland and to conclude arbitration treaties with 'all other states' in order to 'guarantee the peaceful settlement of juridical and political conflicts'.[50] Germany was offering in effect to renounce the use of force in its pursuit of treaty revision in eastern Europe. In return, however, it demanded tacit acknowledgement that the rules for security in the east were different than those in the west.

The German proposals were not unexpected. On 24 January ambassador de Margerie in Berlin reported that the Luther government was contemplating a security proposal 'in the form of a guarantee of French frontiers and a promise never to attack France'. He recommended engagement with the German initiative. But he also warned that the German government was likely to propose a separate and very different arrangement for the Reich's eastern frontiers. Such a solution posed an evident threat to France's ties with Poland and Czechoslovakia.[51] Two days later rumours of a German proposal

---

[48] MAE, *Série Z, RGR*, vol. 79, 'Visite de M. Chamberlain à M. Herriot', 5 Dec. 1924 and 'Entretien avec M. Chamberlain', 6 Dec. 1924.
[49] TNA-PRO, FO 371, 9820, C18874/2048/18, Chamberlain minute, 21 Dec. 1924; see also MAE, *Série Z, RGR*, vol. 80, 'Évacuation de Cologne', Herriot to de Fleuriau, 12 Jan. 1925; MAE, *Série Z, GB*, vol. 72, de Fleuriau to Paris, 6 Jan. 1925; 'L'Évacuation de Cologne et la sécurité de la France', 25 Jan. 1925; 'La Grande-Bretagne et la sécurité de la France', de Fleuriau to Paris, 29 Jan. 1925.
[50] MAE, PA-AP 089, *Papiers Herriot*, vol. 18, 'Mémorandum (allemand)', 9 février 1925; reprinted in G. Stresemann, *Vermächtnis: der Nachlass*, 3 vols. (Berlin, 1932), II, 62–3 and Herriot, *D'Une guerre à l'autre*, 181–2; see also J. Wright, *Gustav Stresemann: Weimar's Greatest Statesman* (Oxford, 2002), 301–9.
[51] MAE, *Série Z, GB*, vol. 72, de Margerie to Paris, 24 Jan. 1925 (two telegrammes); 'Pacte de Garantie: article de la "Germania"', 26 Jan. 1925; de Margerie to Paris, 30 Jan. 1925; 'La Question de la sécurité et l'offre éventuelle d'un pacte de garantie', 5 Feb. 1925; de Margerie to Paris, 6 Feb. 1926.

broke in the European press. From London de Fleuriau reported that the Germans had raised the subject with Chamberlain and other officials at the Foreign Office. He judged that the British were contemplating some sort of multilateral arrangement that would guarantee French security.[52]

Officials at the Quai d'Orsay rightly saw in the German proposal an attempt to accelerate the evacuation of the Rhineland, pre-empt the Geneva Protocol (which would make the future revision of Germany's eastern frontiers much more difficult) and test the strength of the Entente. Seydoux noted that 'the Germans indicate their desire to modify their eastern frontiers, but they affirm that they are willing to undertake this by diplomatic means and will count on British support to achieve this'.[53] Herriot made a high-profile speech to the chamber in response to rumours of a German overture. He stressed the importance of the demilitarised zone and, following the strategy established the previous autumn, linked the continued occupation of Cologne to the absence of a British commitment. He added, however, that 'our security can only truly be guaranteed by the moral disarmament of Germany'. The Reich could demonstrate its progress along this road by fulfilling its obligations under the peace treaty and by embracing 'the spirit of the Protocol emanating from Geneva'.[54]

The fundamentals of the French negotiating position were hammered out in the weeks that followed. Herriot judged that the 'ideal solution' would be 'the combination of a direct accord [with Britain] and some variant of the Geneva pact'.[55] The crucial first step was to establish a preliminary understanding with Britain that would present Germany with a united front. Such an understanding would remain the overriding priority in virtually all of the negotiations leading to the Locarno Accords.[56] The strategy of the Herriot government was to try to combine the German suggestion with bilateral or trilateral security pacts with Britain and Belgium. This would bind security in eastern and western Europe in a system underwritten by Britain and France. A separate pact providing a British guarantee, the Quai d'Orsay observed, would provide the 'indispensable element of force without which the guarantee system would be

---

[52] Quote from MAE, *Série Z, GB*, vol. 72, 'La Grande-Bretagne et la sécurité de la France', 29 Jan. 1925; but see also de Fleuriau to Paris, 28 Jan. 1925; on press coverage see ibid., 'Les Rapports franco-allemands et la question de la sécurité' (press summary), 27 Jan. 1925.

[53] MAE, *Série Z, GB*, vol. 72, Seydoux's marginal comments on 'La Question de la sécurité et l'offre éventuelle d'un pacte de garantie', 5 Feb. 1925; also 'L'Évacuation de Cologne et la sécurité de la France', 29 Jan. 1925.

[54] *JO*, Chambre, *Débats*, 1925, 26 Jan. 1925.

[55] MAE, *Série Z, GB*, vol. 72, 'L'Évacuation de Cologne et la sécurité de la France', 29 Jan. 1925; 'Proposition allemande de garantie pour la sécurité de la France', Herriot circular (drafted by Bergery) for French embassies in London, Rome, Berlin and Brussels, 8 Feb. 1925; 'Sécurité', Herriot circular, 21 Feb. 1925.

[56] P. Jackson, 'French security and a British "continental commitment" after the First World War', *EHR*, 126, 519 (2011), 374–81; Pitts, *German Problem*, 22–36.

weakened in a fundamental sense'.[57] The deterrent power of a British continental commitment would be embedded in a multilateral strategy of enmeshment.

At the same time there was general agreement first that there could be no security without engaging Germany and second that the best means to achieve this would be within the wider structures of the League of Nations. An assessment drafted by Laroche in collaboration with Massigli and Fromageot observed that a German guarantee 'integrated into the structures of the League of Nations' would 'restrict Germany's freedom of action in other domains, which it would otherwise conserve if it remained outside [the League]'. This conclusion was endorsed by Seydoux.[58] The logic of the Protocol made German entry into the League an increasingly central element in French security policy.

In drafting a list of 'ideas' to serve as the basis for a French response, Laroche acknowledged the need to engage with Germany. While recognising the risks of such a policy, he argued that France had no choice but to 'facilitate any solution that will encourage the progress of democratic and pacifist ideas in Germany'.[59] Such an observation, from the pen of the senior permanent official at the foreign ministry, illustrates the extent to which alternative conceptions of security existed alongside more traditional convictions in the minds of key policy makers. Seydoux concurred with Laroche, reiterating his conviction that there could be no security and reconstruction in Europe without engaging Germany. He recognised German ambitions to revise the Polish and Czechoslovak frontiers. But he argued that these ambitions could best be contained within the framework of a regional security arrangement including France and placed under the League of Nations.[60] Herriot endorsed this judgement. 'German membership in the League of Nations', the premier asserted, 'constitutes a supplementary guarantee that must not be underestimated as it would impose the same obligations on Germany as on other members.'[61]

---

[57] MAE, PA-AP 217, *Papiers Massigli*, vol. 7, 'Note sur les propositions allemandes', drafted by Laroche, Fromageot and Massigli, 26 Feb. 1925; also 'La Grande-Bretagne et la sécurité de la France', 29 Jan. 1925.

[58] MAE, PA-AP 217, *Papiers Massigli*, vol. 7, 'Note sur les propositions allemandes' (Laroche, Fromageot and Massigli), 26 Feb. 1925; MAE, PA-AP 261, *Papiers Seydoux*, vol. 1, 'Sécurité', 28 Feb. 1925; 'Note: avant projet', 5 Mar. 1925; see also the astute analysis in N. Jordan, 'The reorientation of French diplomacy in the 1920s: the role of Jacques Seydoux', *EHR*, 117, 473 (2002), 880–3.

[59] MAE, *Série Z, GB*, vol. 73, 'Quelques idées en vue de la rédaction d'une note sur les propositions allemandes', 23 Feb. 1925.

[60] MAE, PA-AP 261, *Papiers Seydoux*, vol. 1, 'Sécurité', 28 Feb. 1925; 'Note: avant projet', 5 Mar. 1925; 'Etat de fait en présence duquel se pose le problème de la paix de l'Europe', n.d. but early Mar. 1925.

[61] MAE, *Série Z, GB*, vol. 73, 'Project d'instructions à Londres, Berlin, Rome, Bruxelles', 12 Mar. 1925 (marked 'Projet munis au Pt. du Conseil après revision avec MM. Laroche et Seydoux').

An emphasis on the constraining power of the League was now firmly entrenched in the conceptual architecture of French security policy. Herriot and Briand (now head of the French delegation in Geneva) resolved together that imposing the 'legal regime of the Covenant' on Germany must be 'a precondition to all future negotiations' with that country.[62] Herriot reiterated this conviction in an internal memorandum. 'German participation in a future guarantee system', he observed, 'presumes its prior or simultaneous entry into the League of Nations.' German membership in the League, the premier argued, 'would impose additional legal obligations on that country and oblige it to recognise that all future treaty revision through violence is impossible'.[63] On 11 March Herriot appeared before the chamber's foreign affairs commission to describe the wider objectives of French policy as the 'constitution of a security regime' and the establishment of a 'regime of arbitration'. France, he insisted, could not return to the 'isolation and insecurity' of the Poincaré era. 'We do not have an option,' he argued. 'We must engage both Britain and Germany in a durable system of security and such a system can only be achieved under the juridical regime of the League of Nations.'[64] The twin aims of a British security guarantee and a more robust League combined to produce a security policy that was an amalgamation of traditional and multilateral approaches to security.

There remained the problem of security east of the Rhine, however. Germany refused to guarantee its eastern frontiers and Britain was unwilling to make a strategic commitment to this region. There was general agreement that the Rhineland pact must not compromise France's right to fulfil its alliance obligations to Poland and Czechoslovakia. The best way to ensure this was to embed the western pact under the umbrella of the League Covenant. This would ensure that France retained the legal right to intervene under Articles 10 and 16 in the event of unprovoked German aggression. It would also, it was observed, reaffirm the obligations of both Britain and Germany towards Poland and Czechoslovakia as members of the League. Arbitration treaties between Germany and Poland, on the one hand, and Germany and Czechoslovakia, on the other, should further be guaranteed by both Britain and France. These treaties would have to be concluded at the same time as the accords between the western states to constitute an 'inseparable whole'.[65]

---

[62] MAE, PA-AP 089, *Papiers Herriot*, vol. 18, 'Entrevue avec M. Briand', 16 Mar. 1925; see also J. Wright and J. Wright, 'One Mind at Locarno? Aristide Briand and Gustav Stresemann' in S. Casey and J. Wright (eds.), *Mental Maps in the Era of the Two World Wars* (London, 2008), 58–76.
[63] MAE, PA-AP 089, *Papiers Herriot*, vol. 18, 'Mémorandum', n.d. but certainly Mar. 1925.
[64] AN, C/14762, *CAEAN*, XIIIème Législature, Herriot *audition*, 11 Mar. 1925.
[65] MAE, PA-AP 217, *Papiers Massigli*, vol. 7, 'Note sur les propositions allemandes', 26 Feb. 1925; MAE, *Série Z, GB*, vol. 73, 'Projet d'instructions à Londres, Berlin, Rome, Bruxelles', 12 Mar. 1925.

There was an uncomfortable corollary to bringing the various pacts and treaties under League auspices, however. The Franco-Polish alliance, with its secret military convention, was incompatible with the new security policy under construction. This fact had been acknowledged within the Quai d'Orsay the previous October, when Laroche had pressed for a revision of the 1921 alliance to bring it into line with the Geneva Protocol.[66] Laroche returned to this issue, recommending that the Franco-Polish treaty be subordinated to the Covenant: 'It will be essential to revise the treaty with Poland to eliminate any clause creating a *casus foederis* that would not also be justified, indeed commanded, by the Covenant of the League of Nations or by any protocol completing this pact.' The alliance with Poland would not be allowed to undermine chances of securing a binding commitment on the Rhine.[67]

The French strategy, in effect, was to integrate a Rhineland pact into a wider regime identical in almost every respect to the Geneva Protocol. 'For my part,' Herriot observed before the chamber's foreign affairs commission, 'I am convinced that France must remain firmly committed to the doctrine of the Protocol.'[68] Massigli, Laroche and Fromageot concluded that, if the general principles of the Protocol could be established in a system of Europe-wide security, 'the pact on offer could constitute a serious guarantee of peace'. To refuse to engage with Germany, on the other hand, would only give credibility to charges of French militarism in Britain and play into the hands of German efforts to split the Entente.[69]

IV

The foundations of this policy were shaken when Britain refused to sign a separate Franco-British or Franco-Belgian–British pact. Chamberlain advised Herriot of this decision on 6 March. Although he had been informed in advance, the French premier pretended to be shocked. He warned that France might be forced to stay in the Rhineland indefinitely.[70] This convinced Chamberlain that a major crisis was in the making. After threatening to resign, he was given permission by the Baldwin cabinet to pursue a four- or five-power agreement that included Germany. In making this offer he pledged that Britain and France would consult to fashion a preliminary accord before negotiations

---

[66] See the sub-dossier on this issue in SHD-DAT, 7N 3006–2; see also G.-H. Soutou, 'L'Alliance franco-polonaise 1925–1933 ou comment s'en débarrasser?', *RHD*, 2, 3–4 (1981), 297–302.
[67] MAE, PA-AP 217, *Papiers Massigli*, vol. 7, 'Note sur les propositions allemandes', 26 Feb. 1925.
[68] AN, C/14762, *CAEAN*, XIIIème Législature, Herriot *audition*, 11 Mar. 1925.
[69] MAE, PA-AP 217, *Papiers Massigli*, vol. 7, 'Note sur les propositions allemandes', 26 Feb. 1925.
[70] For Herriot's advance warning see MAE, *Série Z*, *GB*, vol. 73, 'La Question de sécurité, l'Allemagne et l'Angleterre' (de Fleuriau), 25 Feb. 1925; de Fleuriau to Laroche, 2 Mar. 1925.

with Germany were begun. He also pledged to oppose any German attempt to secure an early evacuation of the Rhineland.[71]

The British refusal to negotiate a separate pact was a debilitating blow, nonetheless. There was disagreement as to how France should respond. Massigli submitted that France must hold fast to the principles of the Protocol and refuse the British offer of a pact limited to western Europe. 'Each day', he argued, 'offers new proof that it is impossible to arrive at a durable solution if the western frontiers of Poland and Czechoslovakia are not guaranteed by the general accord.' He added that France should continue to insist on a separate pact with Britain and Belgium as 'a *sine qua non* condition of our adhesion to a general pact'.[72] From London de Fleuriau challenged this judgement. France, he insisted, had no choice other than a pact limited to western Europe. Such an arrangement, he argued, was the maximum it could hope to obtain from any British government for the foreseeable future.[73]

Herriot and Laroche accepted this argument. On 16 March 1925 they collaborated to draft two documents that laid down the essentials of French policy. France would accept a western mutual assistance pact. But this pact must preserve intact the occupation regime in the Rhineland as well as the demilitarised status of that region for all time. Germany, moreover, would need to join the League of Nations without preconditions and 'accept all of the engagements in the Covenant'. Great importance was attached to the arbitration treaties to be concluded between Germany and its eastern neighbours. These treaties would be guaranteed by Britain and France and be attached to the western guarantee to form a single general settlement. A western treaty must not open the way to treaty revision in the east. It was envisaged, finally, that negotiations for a western security pact would proceed in two stages. France, Britain and Belgium would agree on a memorandum which would then be presented to the German government as a joint negotiating position.[74]

The League of Nations was thus allotted a pivotal role in what had become a thoroughly multilateral strategy based on interlocking mutual assistance and arbitration pacts. Briand underlined its importance before the chamber's foreign affairs commission:

---

[71] MAE, *Série Z, GB*, vol. 74, 'Entrevue de M. Herriot avec M. Chamberlain' and 'Mémorandum', 16 Mar. 1925; Goldstein, 'Locarno Pact', 131–3; R. S. Grayson, *Austen Chamberlain and the Commitment to Europe* (London, 1997), 50–4.

[72] MAE, *Série Z, GB*, vol. 73, 'Note de Massigli: propositions allemandes', 6 Mar. 1925; see also C. Wurm, *Die französische Sicherheitspolitik in der Phase der Umorientierung, 1924–1926* (Frankfurt, 1979), 256–7.

[73] MAE, *Série Z, GB*, vol. 73, de Fleuriau to Laroche, 11 Mar. 1925 and vol. 74, 'Le Gouvernement britannique, le Protocole de Genève et la question de sécurité', 16 Mar. 1925.

[74] MAE, *Série Z, GB*, vol. 74, 'Memorandum', 16 Mar. 1925; 'Proposition de la part de l'Allemagne d'un Pacte de garantie', 16 Mar. 1925; 'Entrevue de M. Herriot avec M. Briand', 16 Mar. 1925.

The more I examine the situation, the greater is my certainty that the strongest guarantee of our security lies within the framework of the League of Nations ... German entry into the League would lay the foundations of a powerful system of security.[75]

Even if we allow for Briand's characteristic hyperbole, it is clear that key policy elites in Paris considered the League a useful vehicle with which to enmesh both Germany and Britain in a European security regime. Seydoux, for example, returned to the analogy of 1815 to argue that 'what we all desire in Europe is peace; to achieve this, it is essential to enlist Germany in our efforts by admitting her into the League of Nations'. Only full British participation could induce German good faith in this enterprise. 'We must profit from the German offers', he recommended, 'to engage both Germany and Great Britain to the furthest extent possible on the road to security.' Herriot agreed, writing in the margins that Seydoux's views 'accord exactly with my own' and that 'we must now prepare our own response and obtain the adhesion of Britain to our conception of the essential points of discussion'.[76]

Advocates of a more traditional vision of security mounted determined opposition to Herriot's policy from outside the policy machine. The two most prominent voices in this campaign, predictably, were Poincaré and Foch. Poincaré described the German offer of a pact as 'a detestable attempt to undermine the security of Europe'. He warned that Germany intended to 'swallow up Poland before turning on France in twenty years' time'.[77] Poincaré declared that the senate foreign affairs commission was 'almost unanimously' against a pact including Germany. He warned that 'most senators' would never ratify such an agreement. What was needed for the security of France, he reiterated, was a military alliance of the 1912 variety.[78] Foch remained convinced that the only formula for European security was 'France and her allies on the Rhine with uplifted weapons'. The marshal was furious at being excluded from security discussions and worked feverishly behind the scenes to undermine any chances for a pact that included Germany. He warned that under such an arrangement Austria, Poland and Czechoslovakia would disappear from the map of Europe.[79] France would then be faced with a Germany more powerful than it had been in 1914. He dismissed the League of Nations as 'an assembly of neutrals' and was contemptuous of the idea that it could provide security. But the marshal's symbolic power was on the wane by 1925. His warnings of the mortal threat posed by a resurgent Germany met

---

[75] AN, C/14762, *CAEAN*, XIIIème Législature, 'Délibérations', 18 Mar. 1925.
[76] MAE, *Série Z, GB*, vol. 74, 'Sécurité: Note de M. Seydoux – Visite de l'Ambassadeur de Belgique', 25 Mar. 1925 and Herriot's marginal comment on this document.
[77] CCAC, *Phipps Papers*, 1/4, Phipps to FO, 4 Mar. 1925.
[78] Quoted in Pitts, *German Problem*, 31; see also CCAC, *Phipps Papers*, 1/4, Phipps to FO, 18 Apr. 1925.
[79] MAE, *Série Z, GB*, vol. 76, 'Note du sous-directeur d'Europe' (Corbin), 27 May 1925; Pitts, *German Problem*, 34–8.

with ridicule. 'Save me, save me,' Briand implored his cabinet on one occasion, 'Marshal Foch is on the attack again.'[80] It is impossible to imagine Foch being treated with such disrespect under the Bloc national. It would be hard to find a better illustration of the extent to which the political context had changed since 1919.

What is perhaps most significant about these interventions, however, is their modest impact on public and parliamentary debate. At no point in 1925 was the Herriot government's majority in the chamber under threat over its foreign and security policy. Admittedly this was in part because parliamentary debates were dominated by the continuing financial crisis. But there had been an undeniable sea change in attitudes towards international politics. The election of the intransigent General von Hindenburg as president of Germany in April, for example, generated extensive press commentary but had no impact on negotiations for a pact including Germany.[81] Public and parliamentary opinion could no longer be stirred into a state of febrile anxiety by dire warnings of a German threat in the indeterminate future.

At the opposite end of the public spectrum were committed internationalists. This constituency had greeted the Geneva Protocol with unbridled enthusiasm. Jules Prudhommeaux articulated the view of the vast majority of League supporters when he described the Protocol as 'a vessel at full sail … carrying the League of Nations towards a future of light and joy'.[82] René Cassin was less lyrical but no less optimistic in his assessment of the Protocol as a 'product of a slow evolution' that constituted an indispensable 'instrument for the practical realisation of the Covenant'. He warned that failure to implement the accord would inevitably weaken the League and disappoint widespread hopes for increased international cooperation.[83] Even those League enthusiasts who felt the Protocol did not go far enough praised the fact that the machinery of the League had been integrated into state efforts to obtain international security.[84]

---

[80] Quoted in Notin, *Foch*, 520–2; see also P. Jackson, 'Foch et la politique de sécurité française, 1919–1924' in F. Cochet and R. Porte (eds.), *Ferdinand Foch (1851–1929): apprenez à penser* (Paris, 2010), 345–6; Pitts, *German Problem*, 40–4.

[81] Z. Steiner, *The Lights that Failed: European International History, 1919–1933* (Oxford, 2005), 392; J.-M. Mayeur, *La Vie politique sous la Troisième République* (Paris, 1984), 271–83; E. Bonnefous, *Histoire de la Troisième République*, vol. IV: *Cartel des gauches et Union nationale (1924–1929)* (Paris, 1960), 46–78.

[82] Quoted in J.-M. Guieu, *Le Rameau et le glaive: les militants français pour la Société des nations* (Paris, 2008), 139.

[83] A. Prost and J. Winter, *René Cassin* (Paris, 2011), 103; C. Birebent, *Militants de la paix et de la SDN: les mouvements de soutien à la Société des nations en France et au Royaume-Uni, 1918–1925* (Paris, 2007), 334–5.

[84] G. Scelle, 'Vue d'ensemble sur les résultats de la Vème Assemblée de la Société des nations', *Progrès civique*, 11 Oct. 1924; Guieu, *Rameau et glaive*, 138–44.

There was therefore considerable public-sphere support for a League-based approach to security. Herriot responded to critics by arguing that his strategy of prior consultation with Britain was 'a method of bringing us as close as possible to a Franco-Belgian–British pact'.[85] Great importance was attached to the Franco-British guarantee of the German–Polish and German–Czechoslovak arbitration accords. 'Given that Britain refuses to guarantee the frontiers of Poland and Czechoslovakia directly,' Herriot assured Czechoslovak foreign minister Edvard Beneš, 'my policy is to get [the British] to guarantee the arbitration treaties, which will guarantee these frontiers.'[86] Fromageot added that such a Franco-British guarantee would establish not only France's right to intervene in a conflict in eastern Europe, but also British moral and political support for French intervention terms less ambiguous than those of the League Covenant.[87] Laroche admitted to Beneš that 'the greatest interest that a pact with Germany holds for us is that it provides a means to obtain a British engagement of assistance'. Yet he also observed that the western pact held out the possibility of 'bringing Britain, little by little, into a wider policy of European solidarity'.[88] This aim would be central to French policy for the remainder of the inter-war period.

The fact that professional diplomats such as Laroche and Fromageot regularly used the language of arbitration and solidarity in their internal correspondence highlights the extent to which foreign ministry officials had adapted their practices to prevailing norms of statecraft in the mid-1920s.[89] Traditional prescriptions for security were no longer an automatic frame of reference for policy elites in 1925. Traditional and multilateralist currents instead coexisted in the policy conceptions of key officials. The role allotted to Britain, meanwhile, had evolved from military ally to joint 'underwriter' of a Europe-wide security system aimed at including, constraining and, if possible, reforming Germany. The threat of force remained a central element in this conception. But it was implicit and linked to the rule of law rather than explicit in an alliance directed against Germany. 'The chief attraction for us in this affair', Laroche observed on 24 March, 'is to have a document with the signature of Britain, which is indispensable to validate the signature of Germany.'[90] A new practical logic was emerging that combined the traditional predispositions of security professionals and the internationalist-inspired vision of multilateral cooperation under the rule of international law.

---

[85] AN, C/14762, *CAEAN*, XIIIème Législature, Herriot *audition*, 11 Mar. 1925.
[86] MAE, Série Z, *GB*, vol. 74, 'Conversation avec M. Beneš', 16 Mar. 1925.
[87] MAE, *Série Z, GB*, vol. 75, 'Note pour le président du conseil', 10 Apr. 1925; also untitled memo dated 17 Apr. 1925.
[88] MAE, *Série Z, GB*, vol. 74, 'Visite de Monsieur Benes à M. Laroche', 18 Mar. 1925.
[89] Jackson, 'Tradition and adaptation', 190–6.
[90] MAE, *Série Z, GB*, vol. 74, 'Note de M. Laroche', 24 Mar. 1925.

V

A comprehensive security strategy was thus already in place when Herriot's government fell in mid-April 1925 over its inability to resolve France's ongoing financial crisis.[91] Briand assumed the foreign minister's portfolio in a new ministry led by Paul Painlevé. Briand's first official act was to restore Philippe Berthelot to the foreign ministry as secretary general. Berthelot had kept in close touch with his allies at the ministry during his exile, and moved seamlessly back into his familiar role at the centre of the Quai d'Orsay policy machine.[92] But there were no fundamental changes to the foreign and security policy that had been developed under Herriot. If the Locarno Accords have long been associated with Briand, their foundations were laid down under Herriot.

The one significant modification made to French policy was forced on Briand when the British government refused to guarantee the arbitration treaties between Germany and its eastern neighbours. On 16 May 1925 Berthelot drafted a lengthy note outlining the French programme to the British government. This version retained the crucial term 'inseparable whole', which made the link between the western and eastern aspects of the general settlement.[93] In the difficult negotiations that followed, however, the British refused to guarantee the eastern arbitration treaties and objected to all language implying that the eastern and western treaties were part of the same accords.[94] The Quai d'Orsay responded by protesting that a British guarantee of the eastern arbitration accords had 'essentially a moral character' and was thus distinct from the commitment on the Rhine. The joint guarantee, it was suggested, could be watered down to a commitment to mediate to prevent hostilities.[95]

The British were unmoved. Chamberlain advised French statesman Henry de Jouvenel that the juridical and system-building aspects of the French proposal were antithetical to the most basic instincts of British policy makers:

> The French and the British tend to approach questions from very different perspectives, which is the natural result of their national characters and their history ... It is worth remembering that our common law and our constitution are not the result of legislative measures and are not integrated into a juridical system ... In seeking to

---

[91] J.-N. Jeanneney, *La Faillite du Cartel, 1924–1926: leçon d'histoire pour une gauche au pouvoir*, 2nd edn (Paris, 1981), 87–119; Bonnefous, *Cartel des gauches*, 75–80.

[92] Laroche, *Quai d'Orsay*, 209–12; Barré, *Berthelot*, 380–6.

[93] The French 'Projet de réponse' is reprinted in HMSO, Cmd. 2435, *Papers Respecting the Proposals for a Pact of Security Made by the German Government on February 9, 1925* (London, 1926), 5–10.

[94] MAE, *Série Z, GB*, vol. 75, 'Projet français: observations anglaises', de Fleuriau to Paris, 14 Apr. 1925; Cmd. 2435, *Proposals*, 'Memorandum communicated informally by Mr Austen Chamberlain to the French Ambassador', 19 May 1925, 11–12.

[95] MAE, *Série Z, GB*, vol. 75, Berthelot (for Briand) to de Fleuriau (London), 16 May 1925 and vol. 76, 'Suggestion de M. Fromageot', 27 May 1925.

engage us in obligations that are greater and more extensive than we are ready to accept [France] is in danger of rendering it impossible for us to make the contribution to general security than it would otherwise be in our power to give.[96]

The attempt to smuggle the principles of the Geneva Protocol into the guarantee treaties failed just as utterly as had every previous effort to secure a British commitment to eastern Europe. Convinced that British cooperation was crucial to any policy of engagement with Germany, Briand and his team sacrificed the Europe-wide character of the system envisaged under the Protocol in order to obtain a joint negotiating position with London. Briand and Chamberlain came to a final and full agreement on a joint response to the German guarantee proposal when they met in Geneva in early June. All references to a joint guarantee and a general accord were ultimately excised from the final text sent by Briand to Stresemann on 16 June.[97]

Briand and his policy advisers thus accepted the principle that European security was divisible. This was a massive blow to the 'doctrine of the Protocol'. The consequences of this step for French influence in east–central Europe were potentially far reaching. This price was deemed worth paying in return for a British commitment in the west. It is however worth emphasising that, in accepting the limits to Britain's European commitment, Briand was adhering to Herriot's driving principle of placing Franco-British cooperation at the heart of French security planning. No amount of obduracy on the part of France would have induced the British to extend their commitments to eastern Europe. There can be little doubt that Herriot, like Briand, would have been forced to accept the limited British commitment that was on offer. The alternative, as Briand pointed out, was a return to the politics of confrontation.

The absolute priority accorded to Britain by Briand reflected the views of senior diplomats. From London de Fleuriau unsurprisingly accorded supreme importance to the *entente* with Britain. Of the various accords under consideration, he argued, 'only the Rhineland pact offers us a durable guarantee ... we must [therefore] not tie its fate to that of supplementary conventions such as arbitration treaties'. He warned that such an attempt 'to fashion a new Geneva Protocol' would never be accepted in London. Proceeding in complete accord with the British, he added, would 'draw them ever closer to us in the event that negotiations with Germany fail'.[98] Laroche, who, at Berthelot's insistence, retained the functions and authority that he had exercised under Herriot, endorsed de Fleuriau's argument. France, he argued, could not risk the

---

[96] MAE, *Série Z, GB*, vol. 76, 'Compte-rendu d'une conversation entre le secrétaire d'état et M. de Jouvenel', 27 May 1925.
[97] France, Ministère des affaires étrangères, *Pacte de sécurité*, vol. I (Paris, 1925), docs. 7, 8 and 9, 22–31.
[98] MAE, *Série Z, GB*, vol. 76, de Fleuriau letters to Berthelot, 25 May and 8 Jun. 1925 and 'Note: Sécurité', 27 May 1925.

collapse of the *entente* that had been so painstakingly restored over the previous year.[99]

Berthelot agreed. During his time away from the ministry the secretary general had by no means abandoned the traditional policy instincts that had shaped his approach to security until 1921. But these instincts had always been combined with a pragmatic sense of the need to adapt to prevailing conditions. Berthelot's traditional inclinations made him highly sceptical of all diplomacy practised through the League. He was adamant that the meeting of legal experts that preceded the Locarno Conference must not take place in Geneva, where there would be an increased risk that 'the League of Nations will seek to involve itself in the question of the Rhineland pact, which would be an insupportable burden to negotiations that are already difficult'.[100] Berthelot was also dismissive of the very idea of guaranteeing arbitration as an attempt to achieve security with 'words alone'. Reliable commitments, he argued, must rest on 'shared interests'. The British, he predicted, would never surrender their freedom to interpret their own interests and act accordingly.[101]

This judgement was borne out when the British insisted that only 'flagrant' violations of the demilitarised zone could trigger their guarantee and reserved the right to interpret the precise meaning of 'flagrant' themselves.[102] Massigli pointed out that this qualification undermined the automatic character of the accords. This, in turn, removed a crucial legacy of the Protocol from the content of the Rhineland pact. Massigli argued again that France's security might be better served by holding out for a more precise and legally binding commitment in some other form of pact. 'It would be prudent not to let the Protocol disappear altogether,' he advised. 'We must not let the British argue that security can be assured by arbitration alone (something they are unwilling to accept for themselves) and lead us directly to disarmament.'[103] Massigli was arguing in essence for the integrity of the formula 'arbitration–security–disarmament'. Fromageot, interestingly, accepted Massigli's general critique but pointed out that limited British participation in French projects was preferable to none at all.[104] This was an argument to which Briand would return repeatedly when defending the accords in parliament.

---

[99] MAE, *Série Z, GB*, vol. 76, 'Sécurité: réponse au questionnaire anglais' (Laroche), 26 May 1925; Laroche, *Quai d'Orsay*, 211–12.

[100] MAE, *Série Z, GB*, vol. 82, Berthelot to London, 28 Aug. 1925.

[101] MAE, *Série Z, GB*, vol. 74, Berthelot's marginal comments; 'Sanctions et pacte de garantie', undated Berthelot note to Briand; also cited in G. Suarez, *Briand: sa vie, son oeuvre, avec son journal et de nombreux documents inédits*, 6 vols. (Paris, 1938–52), vol. VI: *L'Artisan de la paix, 1923–1932* (Paris, 1952), 83–4.

[102] MAE, *Série Z, GB*, vol. 80, 'Note: conversation avec M. Hurst' (Fromageot via de Fleuriau), 23 Jul. 1925; J. Jacobson, *Locarno Diplomacy* (Princeton, 1972), 32–4.

[103] MAE, PA-AP 217, *Papiers Massigli*, vol. 7, Massigli 'Note', 27 Aug. 1925; MAE, *Série Z, GB*, vol. 82, 'Lettre de Massigli' (from Geneva), 10 Sept. 1925.

[104] MAE, *Série Z, GB*, vol. 82, 'Note de M. Massigli: observations de M. Fromageot', 27 Aug. 1925; see also Ulrich-Pier, *Massigli*, I, 151–3.

Critics of the Rhineland pact strategy from outside the foreign ministry were marginalised. The archives of the general staff and CSDN reveal that army chief General Philippe Pétain and his staff were kept apprised of negotiations but not consulted. Marshal Foch, as we have seen, tried to intervene in policy debates but was ignored.[105] High-ranking officers were instead treated to lectures on international relations by Quai officials. Laroche informed sceptical members of the high command that 'Britain can provide the political and diplomatic support necessary to engage Germany in a system of security capable of assuring the peace of Europe'. The present negotiations were a window of opportunity before the Reich recovered its strength. It was essential, Laroche argued, to reinforce those elements inside Germany favourable to democracy and peace. 'The role of diplomacy for our national defence is more important than ever.'[106] The foreign ministry now enjoyed unquestionable dominance over security policy making.

VI

The significant sacrifices France had made to secure a common front with Britain paid dividends during direct negotiations with Germany in the summer of 1925. Stresemann's efforts to exploit differences between the French and British positions were almost entirely unsuccessful. In London in early September, and then at Locarno the following October, German negotiators made repeated efforts to link a Rhineland system of mutual guarantee to an early evacuation of the region. These initiatives met with joint resistance from Britain and France. Stresemann arrived at the Locarno Conference without any of the German demands having been met.[107]

In one area only did the German foreign minister manage to exact concessions in the negotiations that followed: Germany insisted that a French guarantee of the arbitration treaties with Poland and Czechoslovakia constituted an unacceptable form of encirclement. Fromageot proposed that France could instead guarantee to act as a League agent in the event the Council found Germany guilty of aggression against either Poland or Czechoslovakia. This attempt to intertwine an eastern guarantee with League obligations was also opposed by the German delegation. Briand was forced to give way after France did not receive British support over this issue. There was therefore no French eastern guarantee in the text of the Rhineland pact. French negotiators did, however, obtain wording (in Article 2 of the core Treaty of Guarantee) that

---

[105] MAE, *Série Z, GB*, vol. 76, 'Note du sous-directeur d'Europe' (Charles Corbin), 27 May 1925; see also the records of Foch's personal staff in SHD-DAT, 4N 92–3 (which contain no correspondence with either Herriot or Briand for this period).

[106] SHD-DAT, 2N 9–4, 'Délibération de la 1ère Section de la Commission d'études le 3 septembre 1925'.

[107] See esp. Steiner, *Lights that Failed*, 394–7.

reaffirmed France's right to intervene in support of Poland and Czechoslovakia under the Covenant.[108]

In the end the Locarno Accords comprised seven treaties. The most important was the five-power 'Treaty of Mutual Guarantee between the United Kingdom, Belgium, France, Germany and Italy'. This treaty guaranteed Germany's frontiers with France and Belgium as well as the permanent demilitarised status of the Rhineland. All three Rhineland powers agreed to submit 'any question with regard to which the parties are in conflict' to 'judicial decision'. They also pledged to comply with this decision. This provision for compulsory arbitration was backed up by interlocking commitments for mutual assistance to be triggered by a League Council declaration of aggression. As in the Protocol, a refusal to submit to arbitration was defined as aggression. The Treaty of Mutual Guarantee was supplemented by separate arbitration conventions between Germany and Belgium, Germany and France, Germany and Poland and Germany and Czechoslovakia. Two final accords between France and Poland and France and Czechoslovakia reaffirmed France's right under the League Covenant to assist its eastern allies in the event of unprovoked aggression. In this case the Rhineland Guarantee Pact would not be evoked against France.[109]

Another important result of the Locarno Conference was general agreement that Germany would join the League and assume the rights and obligations under the Covenant. Stresemann secured assurances of a permanent seat on the Council and a special dispensation to allow the Reich to renounce its obligations under Article 16 of the Covenant in the event of collective action against the Soviet Union. A number of other outstanding issues were agreed upon but not inserted into the treaty: the date of 10 December 1926 was set for the evacuation of Cologne; the Allies pledged to accelerate the withdrawal of the IMCC and that the League inspection regime that would replace it would not have a permanent presence inside Germany. Briand also assured Stresemann that détente engendered by Locarno would create circumstances conducive to the settlement of outstanding problems between France and Germany. This was an implicit commitment to negotiate over terms of the Rhineland occupation. Locarno opened the way for a long series of Franco-German negotiations over issues ranging from a commercial accord to industrial cooperation and a possible revision of the Dawes Plan.[110]

---

[108] MAE, SDN, vol. 754, 'Réunion du 8 octobre 1925 au palais de justice de Locarno' and 'Réunion du 15 octobre 1925'; Série Z, GB, vol. 86, 'Note au sujet du pacte rhénan', 2 Nov. 1925; 'Lettre collective: Accords de Locarno', Laroche (for Briand), 4 Nov. 1925; 'Rapport' on the Locarno Accords prepared by Paul-Boncour, 23 Feb. 1926; AN, C/14763, *CAEAN*, XIIIème Législature, Briand *audition*, 19 Dec. 1925.

[109] Reproduced in Johnson (ed.), *Locarno Revisited*, 214–18.

[110] Steiner, *Lights that Failed*, 396–7; Jacobson, *Locarno Diplomacy*, 26–41; Pitts, *German Problem*, 90–102.

VII

As a substitute for the Geneva Protocol, however, the Locarno treaties left much to be desired. The operation of the mutual assistance treaties, like action under Articles 10 and 16 of the Covenant, remained dependent on a unanimous vote of the League Council. This, when combined with the British determination to reserve the right to interpret the precise meaning of 'flagrant violation' for themselves, meant that France did not secure a guarantee of 'automatic assistance' embedded in the Protocol. Most importantly, however, the Locarno Accords provided implicit endorsement of the principle that European security was divisible. Germany was not obliged to recognise and guarantee its frontiers with Poland and Czechoslovakia. Nor were there any third-party guarantors of the eastern arbitration conventions. The operation of France's alliance with Poland, finally, had been made subordinate to League Council approval.

The Locarno Accords thus had far-reaching ramifications for the role of eastern Europe in French policy. But their impact on Franco-Czechoslovak relations was less harmful than on relations with Poland. Czechoslovakia was from the outset amenable to French initiatives to construct a multilateral security system that included Germany. The Czechoslovak foreign minister Beneš was a committed internationalist whose priorities were to secure a central position for Czechoslovakia, both in a regional security system in east–central Europe (organised around the Little Entente) and in the wider structures of the League. He was a prominent figure in the League Council and had been a driving force in drafting the Protocol. He therefore accepted the logic of French efforts to secure a British commitment on the continent – even if that commitment must, in the first instance, be limited to western Europe. He also approved of the strategy of bringing the Rhineland treaty as much as possible under the League umbrella, and of German entry into the League. Meeting with Herriot in March, Beneš indicated that he was 'not hostile to a five-power western pact' because 'anything that reinforces the security of France would be advantageous [for Czechoslovakia]'. He added, however, that 'any new pact must be based on existing treaties'. By this he meant the Treaty of Versailles and in particular the League Covenant. An eastern pact along these lines, Herriot and Beneš agreed, could even serve as 'a tactical means' to preserve 'the essence of the Protocol'.[111]

Berthelot made sure that his old friend Beneš was apprised of France's negotiating position as it evolved in the spring and summer of 1925. On 31 May the Czechoslovak foreign minister assured Berthelot that he considered the Rhineland arrangements 'the maximum that is obtainable' and 'a great

---

[111] MAE, *Série Z, GB*, vol. 74, 'Conversation avec M. Beneš', 16 Mar. 1925; see also M. Ádám, *The Versailles System and Central Europe* (London, 2004), 263–76; P. Wandycz, *The Twilight of French Eastern Alliances* (Princeton, 1988), 11–16.

success'. He observed to Seydoux that the time was not ripe for establishing such a guarantee system in eastern Europe, but predicted that such a system would in time follow on from the Rhineland pact. Poland, he added, would probably need to make some territorial concessions first.[112] These judgements shaped the Czechoslovak response to Locarno. Although concerned with the distinction between western and eastern security implied in the accords, Beneš would prove an enthusiastic supporter of all subsequent French efforts to extend the Locarno system eastwards.[113]

The Poles took a very different view. Elite and public opinion in Poland was alarmed at the first rumour of a western pact including France, Britain and Belgium. General Sikorski, the influential minister of war, warned that such an arrangement would 'incite Germany to act offensively against Poland'.[114] Laroche assured the Poles that all negotiations would 'conform as much as possible to the spirit of the Geneva Protocol'.[115] The decision to accept the British insistence on an east–west distinction therefore compromised France's credibility in Warsaw. Polish foreign minister Skrzyński all but accused France of betrayal. He warned that a pact limited to western Europe would 'deal a crippling blow to the League of Nations'.[116]

Skrzyński's protest exacerbated the antipathy of both Briand and Berthelot for Poland. Neither had supported the alliance in 1921 and neither would seek to solidify it in the years to come. Berthelot observed acidly that 'the Czechoslovaks, who also need security, understand that [a western pact] tied to arbitration treaties in the east is the maximum that can be obtained ... the Poles seem incapable of recognising their true interests in this affair'.[117] Official French responses, however, stressed the impossibility of obtaining a guarantee for the eastern frontiers. Polish representatives were assured that extending the guarantee system eastward was a central priority for French policy. Privately, however, Briand observed that an adjustment of the Polish–German frontier was both inevitable and desirable. He shared the view of most Quai d'Orsay officials that subordinating France's commitment to Poland to a prior declaration of unprovoked aggression by the League Council would reduce the risk of being embroiled in a future conflict caused by Polish adventurism.[118]

---

[112] MAE, *Série Z, GB*, vol. 76, 'Lettre de M. Beneš [to Berthelot]', 31 May 1925 and 'Visite de M. Beneš à M. Seydoux', 2 Jun. 1925.
[113] Ádám, *Versailles System*, 272–87; A. Marès, 'Locarno et la Tchécoslovaquie: le rôle d'Edvard Bénès' in J. Bariéty (ed.), *Aristide Briand, la Société des nations et l'Europe, 1919–1932* (Paris, 2007), 130–47; Wandycz, *Twilight*, 73–104, 163–91, 336–70.
[114] Quoted in Wandycz, *Twilight*, 13.
[115] SHD-DAT, 7N 3006-2, 'La Pologne et l'éventualité d'un pacte anglo-franco-belge', Herriot (Laroche) to Nollet, 10 Dec. 1924.
[116] MAE, *Série Z, GB*, vol. 76, Panafieu (Warsaw) to Paris, 4 Jun. 1925.
[117] Ibid., Berthelot's marginal comments.
[118] MAE, *Série Z, GB*, vol. 76, Briand (Berthelot) to Warsaw, 5 Jun. 1925; TNA-PRO, FO 408 (Foreign Office Confidential Print), no. 34, Chamberlain to Tyrell, 8 Jun. 1925.

Poland's leaders understood the implications of what they described as a 'second-class guarantee'. They proved much less enthusiastic about subsequent French attempts to construct a Locarno-inspired system in eastern Europe. Indeed, it was in the aftermath of Locarno that Polish policy began to move away from a position of strategic dependence on France.[119] This process was only reinforced by ongoing efforts by the French foreign ministry to revise the terms of the 1921 alliance. There was general agreement within the Quai d'Orsay that the traditional aspects of this alliance must be dismantled to make it compatible with what Briand called 'the new orientation of our foreign policy'.[120] The consistent aim of these initiatives was to limit France's obligations to assist Poland to those cases covered by Articles 10 to 16 of the Covenant. In the end, the alliance and military convention were never formally revised or renounced. But the atmosphere of ambiguity left by Locarno meant that they were not considered reliable pillars of national security policy on either side. The full consequences of the deterioration in Franco-Polish relations would not become apparent until the Czechoslovak Crisis of 1938.

VIII

Foreign ministry officials were so determined to revise the Franco-Polish alliance because it was incompatible with the multilateralist 'practical logic' that had emerged within France's political and diplomatic policy elite over the course of 1924–5. This logic, which would shape the policy responses of this elite for the next decade, was an interesting admixture of the internationalist and traditional currents that coexisted within the policy elite. Many of its central features emerge clearly in a fascinating memorandum on the Locarno Accords drafted by Massigli on 9 November 1925. In this document Massigli stressed a distinction that he saw between the traditional practices at the heart of French security policy after 1918 and the new approach that had evolved in 1924–5:

The basis of the 1919 system was the memory of the wartime alliance. In 1925 it seems that security resides in the organisation of the European continent for the pacific settlement of disagreements under the aegis of the League of Nations and with guarantees that accords will be respected. On one side relations of force; on the other the notion of harmony within a European society, of solidarity between nations rather than opposing power balances.[121]

---

[119] P. Wandycz, 'La Pologne face à la politique locarnienne de Briand', *RHD*, 2, 3, 4 (1981), 237–63; M. Zmierczak, 'La Pologne et Locarno' in Bariéty (ed.), *Briand*, 117–29; Steiner, *Lights that Failed*, 403–6.

[120] SHD-DAT, 7N 3006-2, Briand to Painlevé, 10 Nov. 1927; 'État actuel des question franco-polonaises', 13 Oct. 1927; 'Convention militaire franco-polonaise', 12 Nov. 1927; Soutou, 'Alliance franco-polonaise', 328–48.

[121] MAE, PA-AP 217, *Papiers Massigli*, vol. 7, 'Au Sujet des accords de Locarno', 9 Nov. 1925.

Summarising the course of events leading up to Locarno, Massigli observed that the collapse of the British and American guarantees strengthened those voices inside France that favoured 'a national solution to France's security problem'. Thereafter, however, pursuit of a 'national solution' had created 'international complications' that, in turn, pushed French policy in a more multilateral direction. Massigli cited efforts to internationalise the reparations problem, Briand's effort at Cannes and discussions in Geneva that led to the adoption of Resolution XIV and the Draft TMA as examples of this trend. The result was the Geneva Protocol, with its emphasis on compulsory arbitration as a means to identify aggression and trigger mutual assistance. Britain's refusal to accept the Protocol, combined with the German offer of a Rhineland guarantee pact, had forced the Herriot government to adapt its strategy. 'It became necessary to bring the German proposal, as much as possible, into the Geneva system.'[122] The result was Locarno.

Massigli submitted that 'to appreciate the importance of the Locarno Accords' it was necessary to 'take into account two essential factors'. First, the Great Powers had signed accords promising to accept compulsory arbitration to settle their political differences. 'For the first time,' he observed, 'in accordance with the theoretical example provided by the Geneva Protocol, sovereign states have undertaken not to make war under any circumstances.' This, he admitted, had 'hardly abolished war' but it had 'placed new and substantial obstacles in the way of such an eventuality'. Second, the League of Nations now played an important role in structuring relations between states. And the League had been strengthened, Massigli judged, 'not only by Germany's entry, but also by the fact that all of the [Locarno] Accords are dominated by the spirit of the Covenant and the Protocol'.[123]

There were at the same time clear limits to this move towards a more internationalist security policy. Massigli observed that 'because the benefits of a policy of détente are uncertain and will only be felt in the long term' it was essential for France 'to retain our rights under the treaty'. France had 'retained the right to stay in the Rhineland until it is clear that Germany has adapted to this new spirit'. The demilitarised status of the Left Bank, meanwhile, remained a vital element in France's security system for the foreseeable future. This status was now guaranteed explicitly by Britain. Britain's security commitment to France, Massigli added in conclusion, provided 'the element of force necessary to ensure the effective functioning of our system of security'.[124] There was, in other words, a need for caution and realism, a need to combine innovation with traditional practices. It was Massigli, after all, who famously observed that 'The "esprit de Locarno", "der Locarnogeist" and the "spirit of Locarno" are three different things'.[125] He was optimistic

---

[122] Ibid. [123] Ibid. [124] Ibid. [125] Quoted in Ulrich-Pier, *Massigli*, I, 156.

nonetheless that Locarno constituted a decisive step towards a more stable and peaceable Europe. This had been achieved not least because Germany was now part of the continental security system. 'Confidence has been placed in Germany and its willingness to adapt to the realities of the new European politics.' This was a significant innovation from the security policy under the Bloc national.

A core feature in the practical logic that had evolved under the Cartel was the interdependence of the rule of law and collective force that was expressed in the triptych 'arbitration–security–disarmament'. Security was understood as a process rather than an endpoint. Hope was placed in Germany's eventual socialisation as a responsible member of the international community. The enmeshing and constraining power of the League of Nations, finally, was envisaged as a potential source of security. But this approach was only viable if the process of German socialisation bore genuine results and if the League proved to be effective in enforcing the rule of international law. If these conditions did not prevail, France would need to count on Britain to fulfil its commitments under the Covenant and under Locarno. Belief in the importance of the British strategic commitment remained a key constituent element of the policy culture that emerged in 1924–5.

The influence of this new practical logic is nowhere more evident than in the defence of Locarno by Briand and Paul-Boncour in late 1925 and early 1926. Both argued forcefully that the Locarno treaties had laid the foundations for a forward-looking security strategy based on international cooperation under the rule of law. They contrasted this strategy with the fundamentally traditional conception advocated by critics of the accords to argue that Locarno reflected the changed international norms of the post-war period. Traditional Great Power alliances, both argued, were out of step with the new international political context and impossible to achieve in any case. Briand, in particular, argued for a forward-looking conception that envisaged the extension of the Locarno security regime into eastern Europe as a prelude to a wider political and economic federation of European states.

The signature of the Locarno Accords was greeted with enormous enthusiasm in the French public sphere. Internationalists trumpeted Locarno as a victory for their cause and a vital first step in the construction of an international system of peace through law. The failure to implement the Protocol had been a major setback for the internationalist cause. This led many leading juridical internationalists to embrace the concept of regional security accords as building-blocks towards a wider European security regime. Théodore Ruyssen observed that 'for the moment it appears impossible to place the peace of Europe under the guarantee of a universal pact'. He therefore recommended a less ambitious strategy of regional arrangements that could eventually be linked together in a system similar to the Protocol. Cassin took up this argument in the summer of 1925, arguing that regional accords under the auspices of the Covenant were the best means to preserve the 'directing principles' of the Protocol.[126] Locarno was interpreted as a welcome first step in this process.

Cassin praised the accords for outlining clear procedures for the juridical settlement of political disputes. Célestin Bouglé emphasised the importance of even limited British commitment to a juridical security system. The admission of Germany into the League was also welcomed as an additional source of security given the obligations that state would assume under the Covenant.[127] Alphonse Aulard judged that the 'spirit of Locarno' had laid the foundations for a 'United States of Europe' that would bring peace and prosperity to the continent. Joseph Barthélemy characterised the accords as 'the first links in a network of guarantees that will bind together all [European] states and maintain them in peace'.[128] Briand's celebrated speech welcoming the Reich into the League in Geneva on 10 September 1926 received a universally rapturous reception among French internationalists. The foreign minister had by this time become a major world figure in whom great hope was invested as a guide to a new and more peaceful epoch in European history.[129]

Support for Locarno was not restricted to internationalists on the centre and left of the political spectrum. A growing number of industrialists and business elites had come to advocate cooperation with Germany as a means to alleviate France's ongoing economic difficulties. In late 1925 France was faced with an acute budget deficit, a plummeting currency and very uneven economic growth. Over the course of that year the government had to borrow 36 billion francs from the Bank of France to avoid bankruptcy. The franc, meanwhile, lost well over half its value and by mid-1926 was trading at 226 to the pound sterling. The result was runaway inflation and a 70 per cent rise in the national wholesale index.[130] These developments hit the middle classes hardest. Public attention shifted away from international affairs to focus on France's economic difficulties. The only sectors that experienced growth were those industries able to take advantage of France's weak currency to export their manufactures. Iron and steel concerns, for example, increased their output substantially. But this increase only underlined their dependence on German coking coal. In the mid-1920s the metallurgical industry was united for the first time in calling for cooperative arrangements with German coal and steel. Prominent politicians

---

[126] T. Ruyssen, 'L'Échec au Protocole', *CDH*, 27, 4 (1925), 175–6; Guieu, *Rameau et glaive*, 144–5; J.-M. Guieu, 'Les Congrès universels de la paix et la question de l'unité européenne, 1921–1939' in M. Petricioli and D. Cherubini (eds.), *For Peace in Europe: Institutions and Civil Society Between the World Wars* (Berne, 2007), 387–406.

[127] Bouglé quoted in Guieu, *Rameau et glaive*, 146; J.-M. Guieu, 'Les Juristes français, la Société des nations et l'Europe' and N. Ingram, 'Les Pacifistes et Aristide Briand', both in Bariéty (ed.), *Briand*, 185–99 and 200–13, respectively.

[128] Aulard and Barthélemy, both cited in Guieu, *Rameau et glaive*, 147.

[129] M. Vaïsse, 'Oublié, Briand? La Mémoire du "pèlerin de la paix" en France' in Bariéty (ed.), *Briand*, 448–55.

[130] H. C. Johnson, *Gold, France and the Great Depression, 1919–1932* (New Haven, 1997), 76–89, 120–6.

with close connections to French heavy industry such as André François-Poncet and Pierre-Étienne Flandin called for an 'economic Locarno' to complement the security accords signed in October 1925.[131] Business and industrial elites were therefore part of a large cross-section of political opinion in favour of the greater Franco-German cooperation that was implied in the Locarno arrangements.

Yet there was also significant opposition to Locarno. Prominent advocates of the traditional conception of security advanced powerful criticisms of the accords in both the press and parliament. The most relentless press critic was Pertinax, who mounted a sustained attack on Locarno in *L'Écho de Paris*. He denounced the treaties as a 'palace of illusions', stressing that they added nothing of substance to French security in the west but undermined its network of alliances in the east. 'What means are envisaged to compel Germany to accept an arbitral sentence? None! Neither staff accords nor joint military plans.' The chief outcome of Locarno, Pertinax submitted, was to place Britain and Italy in a position to act as arbiters over France's right to respond to a German remilitarisation of the Rhineland. The implications for France's interests in eastern Europe were even worse. Pertinax concluded by lamenting the fact that France had surrendered its status as a victorious power in relation to Germany and warned of the consequences should the Reich return to aggression:

This is how we are repaid for our policy of engagement. A treaty of 'equality' that does not distinguish between victors and vanquished ... This system will function so long as Germany is a pacific power of good faith, but no safeguards are put in place for the case where Germany seeks once again to overthrow the map of Europe. We thus find ourselves before a great palace of illusions ... The greatest sadness is that all of this can only give encouragement to a bellicose Germany.[132]

Pertinax returned to the charge the following January and February with a series of articles characterised by Quai d'Orsay officials as 'the most comprehensive effort at systematically hostile criticism'.[133] He excoriated the process whereby the implementation of all mutual assistance was dependent on a unanimous decision of the League Council. And he poured ridicule on Paul-Boncour's assurance that the Great Powers had given the League's collective security machinery the automatic character that it lacked under the Covenant. 'Such an act of faith is more worthy of an apostle than a politician.'[134]

---

[131] J. Bariéty, 'France and the Politics of Steel: From the Treaty of Versailles to the International Steel Entente, 1919–1926' in R. Boyce (ed.), *French Foreign and Defence Policy, 1918–1939: The Decline and Fall of a Great Power* (London, 1998), 43–8; J.-N. Jeanneney, *François de Wendel en république: l'argent et le pouvoir 1914–1940* (Paris, 1976), 326–9; Wandycz, *Twilight*, 23–4.

[132] Pertinax, 'Après Locarno: le Palais des Illusions', *L'Écho de Paris*, 18 Oct. 1925.

[133] Quote from Wandycz, *Twilight*, 26.

[134] Pertinax, 'Locarno: le rapport de M. Paul-Boncour', *L'Écho de Paris*, 26 Feb. 1926; see also 'Les Accords de Locarno: aucun des orateurs n'a traité le sujet' and 'Les Accords de Locarno devant la chambre', *L'Écho de Paris*, 27 Feb. 1926.

The substance, though not the tone, of Pertinax's criticisms was taken up by the centre-right deputy and former army colonel Jean Fabry in a joint session of the chamber army and foreign affairs commissions on 19 December 1925. Fabry had been involved in negotiations related to the TMA in 1923. He was therefore familiar with the complexities surrounding all international discussion of security and disarmament. He began by praising the Locarno treaties for 'erecting a welcome juridical armature against war'. This was just a prelude, however, to a lengthy and trenchant critique of Briand's Locarno policy. At the heart of this critique was the failure to secure a guarantee of automatic and preplanned mutual assistance from Great Britain. Like Pertinax, Fabry argued that the need for a unanimous vote on the League Council meant that the Rhineland pact was in reality no more effective a guarantee than the Covenant. The Council was too slow and unreliable. 'As a juridical system,' he remarked, 'the Locarno arrangements have much to recommend them ... But can we base our security on the certainty that the rule of law will prevent aggression and end war?' What was needed, Fabry asserted, were 'military conventions providing details of the timescales as well as the number and type of units to be provided for this assistance'.[135] This was of course a systematic rearticulation of familiar criticisms of all projects for a multilateral security system made by the military establishment since 1923. The only true source of security in this highly traditional vision was a full-blown military alliance with Great Britain.

Fabry's criticisms were endorsed by nationalist deputy Louis Marin, who pressed for a more traditional security strategy policy based on alliances and the balance of power:

One day or another a pact will be forged that will reunite all of the victors of the war on the European continent, France, Belgium, Italy, Poland, Czechoslovakia, Yugoslavia, Romania ... The bloc of these continental victors constitutes a population three times as great and a force infinitely more powerful than that of Germany, even from the military point of view – despite that country's economic organisation, despite the widely recognised warlike qualities of that race.[136]

At the heart of this and similar condemnations of Locarno was a highly pessimistic understanding of international politics that was combined with an even more pessimistic interpretation of the German national character. Such pessimism was fundamentally incompatible with a policy based on interlocking mutual assistance pacts and the rule of law. Still less could it admit the possibility that Germany's aggressive tendencies might be curbed by enmeshing it in a multilateral system of political and legal commitments. 'They say that at Locarno you showed the true face of France,' Fabry remarked to Briand

---

[135] AN, C/14763, *CAEAN*, XIIIème Législature, joint session, army and foreign affairs commissions, 19 Dec. 1925.
[136] *JO*, Chambre, *Débats*, 1926, 1 Mar. 1926; also quoted in Hughes, *Maginot Line*, 182.

during the chamber debate. 'In reality it is the true face of Germany that worries me.'[137]

Briand's defence of his policy was an interesting mixture of pragmatism and idealism. He asserted repeatedly that Locarno was the best deal on offer for France. He argued that the treaties must be evaluated against the guarantees France enjoyed before they were signed. Responding to Marin's plea for a policy based on military alliances he pointed out that:

> It takes more than one party to make an alliance. At the time when the question of negotiations arose, I guarantee you that you would not have found a single one of the nations of which you speak ready to sign a pact the kind of which you are dreaming.[138]

Briand pointed out that the Treaty of Mutual Guarantee had secured at last the British guarantee to defend not only French soil but the demilitarised status of the Rhineland. The absence of this guarantee, he reminded members of the army and foreign affairs commissions, had been 'the great missing element of the Treaty of Versailles' and 'the central preoccupation of M. Clemenceau during the peace conference'. The Rhineland pact was 'an application of an article of the peace treaty that had remained unapplied'.[139] Briand reminded his critics that the abortive guarantee treaties had not included military conventions. The crucial factor, he insisted (repeating Clemenceau's arguments almost word for word, interestingly), was that Britain had signed a treaty and given its word. It was 'impossible to exaggerate the importance of Britain's commitment', he submitted. Locarno had 'given stability to the political situation on the continent and opened the way for a new era for Europe'.[140] All of this had been obtained, Briand emphasised, without sacrificing any of France's treaty rights. He defied his opponents to name a single clause of the Versailles Treaty that had been compromised by Locarno.[141]

The French foreign minister combined this emphasis on the strategic significance of the British guarantee with arguments of a very different kind. He asserted repeatedly that the accords were 'a new system' created in response to the changed character of international relations since the First World War.[142] And he deployed the language of *solidarité* to make this argument:

> A spirit of mutual assistance has replaced the old system of offensive and defensive alliances. It is a spirit of mutual assurance against all threats of war. It is the thesis of nations uniting to oppose aggressors from wherever they appear and making preparations in common to ensure that the threat of war is met swiftly with the threat of

---

[137] *JO*, Chambre, *Débats*, 1926, 26 Feb. 1926.
[138] *JO*, Chambre, *Débats*, 1926, 1 Mar. 1926.
[139] AN, C/14763, *CAEAN*, XIIIème Législature, joint session, 19 Dec. 1925 and Briand *audition*, 23 Feb. 1926.
[140] AN, C/14763, *CAEAN*, XIIIème Législature, joint session, 19 Dec. 1925.
[141] AN, C/14763, *CAEAN*, XIIIème Législature, Briand *audition*, 23 Feb. 1926.
[142] AN, C/14763, *CAEAN*, XIIIème Législature, joint session, 19 Dec. 1925 and Briand *audition*, 23 Feb. 1926; *JO*, Chambre, *Débats*, 1926, 1 Mar. 1926.

collective force ... This is the spirit in which the [Locarno] accords have been conceived.[143]

Briand described this approach as 'a practical application of the Covenant of the League'. But he could not resist taking credit for the concepts underpinning Locarno by linking them to his failed initiative in 1921–2. He claimed that 'the idea for a new type of system' first came to him in 1921 when

> I sensed that unless one considered the problem from a European point of view, it would be difficult to arrive at a workable solution ... I made clear to Great Britain that [my project] was not a matter of alliances standing in opposition to one another, but a pact of guarantee based on the spirit of mutual aid ... and that, once conditions for security were established, I saw no inconveniences – and indeed I saw important advantages – in integrating Germany into the pact.

Briand described his policy at the Cannes Conference as 'the origin of the Protocol', which was, in turn, the 'necessary antecedent' to Locarno. He made no mention of the negotiations regarding the TMA. Nor did he give credit to the intellectual contributions of Ruyssen, Bourgeois and other juridical internationalists in laying the conceptual foundations for a security policy based on arbitration and mutual obligation.[144] These were of course significant omissions to any narrative of the evolution of Locarno. But Briand was justified in underlining the importance of Cannes in the genesis of Locarno.

The foreign minister also emphasised the importance of German participation in the regime established at Locarno. He argued that this aspect of the 'new system' imbued it with greater legitimacy than the Versailles Treaty. 'A postwar treaty is a treaty imposed by victory to which the defeated party must submit ... the great weakness of such treaties is that they are always and necessarily understood as forced conventions.' Germany's commitment to Locarno, conversely, was 'not a signature imposed by victory, but a signature negotiated, deliberated and given voluntarily'. Briand argued that this was 'a very serious moral advantage'.[145] Germany now had a stake in a system that placed legal, political and moral restraints on its behaviour. Briand expressed his belief that the vast majority of Germans ultimately desired to live in prosperity in a stable Europe.[146] This strategy of enmeshing the Reich in a system that would have a socialising effect on its behaviour had been mooted at various moments since 1919. But it had never before been avowed publicly as an objective of French security policy.

Discussing French security policy after Locarno, Briand pledged to resurrect the long-standing internationalist objective of an international armed force to

---

[143] AN, C/14763, *CAEAN*, XIIIème Législature, Briand *audition*, 23 Feb. 1926.
[144] AN, C/14763, *CAEAN*, XIIIème Législature, joint session, 19 Dec. 1925.   [145] Ibid.
[146] AN, C/14764, *CAEAN*, XIIIème Législature, Briand *audition*, 19 Jan. 1927; C/14763, *CAEAN*, XIIIème Législature, Briand *audition*, 23 Feb. 1926; see also A. Barros, 'Briand, l'Allemagne et le "pari" de Locarno' in Bariéty (ed.), *Briand*, 160–72.

impose the rule of law. 'What is needed', he advised the army and foreign affairs committees of the chamber, 'is an association of forces to constitute a secular arm in the service of peace.' He explained that, in such an association, 'each nation will give what it can to constitute an international force that will be placed at the service of any country that is threatened ... We will need to do a sort of inventory where each country will be called to put some agreed portion of its forces at the disposition of the League of Nations, which will use these forces to prevent aggression.'[147] Briand was describing in effect the programme developed by the CISDN in 1918 and then put forward by Bourgeois at the peace conference in 1919.

Internationalist doctrine was present in almost every aspect of French security policy at this juncture. Explaining the details of the Locarno treaties, Briand underlined their innovative use of arbitration, not only as a means to define aggression and trigger mutual assistance, but also as a 'screen' to force states to stop and reflect before embarking on a war. 'The fact that compulsory arbitration is a unifying aspect of all the accords that were agreed upon at Locarno means that European powers are now prevented by law from using force as a first measure to resolve political disputes.'[148] 'Europe', he declared, deploying Massigli's argument, 'has for the first time been provided with a juridical means to settle conflicts and avoid war. This is a development without precedent in our history.'[149] Briand endorsed the hopes of the most optimistic juridical internationalists when he foretold that compulsory arbitration would in future constitute a central organising principle of international relations. 'When I reflect on the deeper forces that have changed international politics since the war,' he observed in December 1925, 'I am convinced that compulsory arbitration accords will become more important than ever in governing relations between states.'[150] The dream of peace through law would become a reality.

As a first step, Briand predicted, the system established at Locarno would be applied across the entire European continent:

I am in negotiations for a compulsory arbitration treaty with Spain. I anticipate other such treaties with other states with the end result that all of Europe will soon be included in a true network of accords aimed at resolving disputes through juridical processes, to the exclusion of any thought of recourse to force. There you have my conception of international politics, at least in Europe.[151]

The ultimate aim was 'the organisation of Europe on the core principles of the grand Protocol and along the lines of regional accords that complement one another in a global system'.[152] The juridical internationalist doctrine at the

---

[147] AN, C/14763, *CAEAN*, XIIIème Législature, joint session, 19 Dec. 1925. [148] Ibid.
[149] Ibid. [150] Ibid.; see also *JO*, Chambre, *Débats*, 1926, 1 Mar. 1926.
[151] AN, C/14763, *CAEAN*, XIIIème Législature, joint session, 19 Dec. 1925.
[152] AN, C/14763, *CAEAN*, XIIIème Législature, Briand *audition*, 23 Feb. 1926.

heart of the Protocol provided the conceptual framework for the Briandist conception of European peace.

The overriding theme in Briand's defence of Locarno, however, was that Locarno constituted 'a beginning' and 'a germ' that would grow and be extended across Europe:

> For me, Locarno is a germ ... the Treaty will render its best effects when it is enlarged by other accords ... Our preoccupation was to obtain peaceful solutions by arbitration and security through a vast system of mutual assurance, so that no nation can become the isolated victim of aggression on the part of another nation. We succeeded in achieving this aim for a small region. We hope to extend this system to other regions.[153]

The region where the extension of Locarno would most complement France's security aims was evidently eastern Europe. Responding to concerns that France's eastern allies were left more vulnerable than ever by Locarno, Briand assured parliament that a central aim of French policy in the immediate future would be 'the construction of a system of accords conforming to the model of Locarno ... [that will] ... be applied to Czechoslovakia, Poland, Germany and Russia'.[154] Briand proved true to his word. The holy grail of an 'eastern Locarno' would be the touchstone of French policy east of the Rhine throughout his long tenure as foreign minister and well into the 1930s.

This vision of an integrated European security regime lay at the heart of the final dimension of Briand's political vision: the notion of a federation of European states. This idea would evolve eventually into the 1930 'Briand Plan'. 'The larger aim of our policy', Briand advised the foreign affairs commission, 'must be to substitute, little by little, a narrow and selfishly nationalist spirit with a European spirit in which I believe France will find its best conditions of security.'[155] The first step down this road was a comprehensive economic accord with Germany. 'Economic accords constitute the best solder for peace between peoples, and such accords are manifestly in our interest ... but they are not sufficient in themselves to ensure our security for the future.'[156] Increased economic cooperation would instead constitute a preliminary phase in a process of economic and political federation. Briand underlined the importance of a new 'spirit' that had changed the character of European international politics:

> If one views the treaty only in its terms, one misses the larger picture ... If one considers the conventions signed as ends in themselves, one is mistaken and they lose the greater part of their interest. If one considers them as a beginning, however, one then has all kinds of reasons to be hopeful. The security pact of Locarno signifies the beginning of a new Europe founded on a spirit of solidarity between various

---

[153] Ibid. [154] AN, C/14763, *CAEAN*, XIIIème Législature, joint session, 19 Dec. 1925.
[155] AN, C/14763, *CAEAN*, XIIIème Législature, Briand *audition*, 23 Feb. 1926.
[156] AN, C/14763, *CAEAN*, XIIIème Législature, joint session, 19 Dec. 1925.

European states and the need for collaborative organisation to form a union that will permit them, to the greatest extent possible, to put an end to the danger of war and organise the continent economically.

Locarno, for Briand, provided foundations for a much more ambitious project. 'For me,' he explained, 'all of this must finally result in some kind of federal union of European states.' He admitted that this idea might seem 'unrealistic and even shocking to some'. But he assured deputies that 'we are moving down this road'.[157]

Paul-Boncour's contribution to the Locarno debate was of a different character. He made no reference to a new international spirit or European federation. He instead emphasised that the Locarno treaties were the latest stage in the inevitable evolution of an international legal regime that offered the best prospects of security for France. To make this argument, he asserted that 'Locarno cannot be understood independently of a continuous political effort to establish the authority of the rule of law and the League of Nations'.[158] The accords were 'not an end, but a "beginning" or, more exactly, a step'. Locarno was also 'the logical continuation of the project launched by the Geneva Protocol'.[159] Paul-Boncour argued that this process was driven by the onward march of international law as a force in international politics. The institution of compulsory arbitration as a means to settle both juridical and political disputes between nations was the decisive step in this process. 'The idea of arbitration', he declared, 'is the only idea that can bring nations together.'[160] In his *rapport* on the Locarno treaties for the chamber's foreign affairs commission, he further argued that using arbitration to designate aggressor states constituted a more powerful guarantee of assistance than traditional military alliances. This was because arbitration replaced the traditional pursuit of state interest, which was always subject to change, with 'a precise, automatic and permanent legal process'. As a result, 'once the aggressor has been thus automatically designated, the League Council will decree the application of sanctions in a simple act of procedure'.[161] This belief in the constraining potential of international law and the effective functioning of the League Council underpinned Paul-Boncour's recommendation that the accords be ratified.

Paul-Boncour acknowledged that the failure to extend the Locarno system eastward was 'the undeniable weak point' of the treaties. It meant that the accords constituted 'only a partial success for the principles of the Protocol'. He submitted, however, that, if an eastern equivalent to Locarno could be put in place, it would actually provide a much better guarantee for Poland than the

---

[157] Ibid.
[158] AN, C/14763, *CAEAN*, XIIIème Législature, 'Délibérations: accords de Locarno (suite et fin)', 23 Feb. 1926.
[159] MAE, *Série Z, GB*, vol. 88, 'Rapport', 23 Feb. 1926.
[160] AN, C/14763, *CAEAN*, XIIIème Législature, 'Délibérations', 23 Feb. 1926.
[161] MAE, *Série Z, GB*, vol. 88, 'Rapport', 23 Feb. 1926.

Franco-Polish alliance. The subordination of France's present commitment to Poland to the process of using arbitration to identify aggression, Paul-Boncour argued, would provide the Poles with 'absolute certainty' not only of automatic French assistance, but also of the immediate assistance of all those states adhering to the guarantee treaty. Such an outcome, he asserted, would 'constitute a formidable guarantee for Poland and for France'.[162]

The influence of internationalist doctrine on French foreign and security policy at this stage is striking. Nearly all of the key arguments deployed by Briand and Paul-Boncour in defence of Locarno rested ultimately on the power of international law, the effectiveness of the League procedures and the beneficial effects of a new international spirit to provide security for France. These kinds of arguments were never going to convince committed advocates of traditional security practices, however. Within the chamber's foreign affairs commission, for example, Paul-Boncour's *rapport* on Locarno was criticised as 'excessively legalistic' and 'full of evasions'. Édouard Soulier and Alfred Margaine both considered that the Locarno Accords would render France's alliance with Poland defunct and undermine its prestige and influence in eastern Europe. No number of arbitration treaties, Soulier warned, would prevent Germany from revising its frontier with Poland by force once it regained its military strength. 'The Locarno treaties', he concluded, 'have established the conditions for German hegemony.'[163] Franklin-Bouillon, the president of the commission and a long-time ally of Briand, observed that the chamber had no choice but to ratify the accord. But he did not believe that they would provide security. 'There is not one German in a million who is inspired by the "spirit of Locarno",' Franklin-Bouillon judged. 'It would be folly not to vote for the accords, but it would be even worse folly to believe in them.'[164]

In opposition to this 'tragic vision' of Locarno were the enthusiastic endorsements of centre-left internationalists such as Albert Milhaud, Pierre Renaudel and Charles Chaumet. All praised the accords for their pursuit of collective security under the League of Nations. Paul-Boncour's intervention in this debate illustrates the extent to which traditional and multilateral conceptions of security were understood in opposition to one another in early 1926:

It is necessary to decide between two conceptions. If one believes that old-style alliances are still possible and necessary, one is justified in opposing the Locarno Accords, because Locarno marks the start of a new era and a new approach.[165]

This was doubtless a rhetorical strategy to paint opposition to the accords as outdated devotion to a bygone era of traditional practices. But it also reflected a widely held conviction that the international political context had changed and that French policy must adapt to this change.

---

[162] AN, C/14763, *CAEAN*, XIIIème Législature, 'Délibérations', 23 Feb. 1926.   [163] Ibid.   [164] Ibid.   [165] Ibid.

The same argument was deployed with greater force by Briand. 'Our system', he explained, 'is based on the principle that international disputes must be settled by recourse to juridical methods.' He then invoked the experience of the Great War to argue for a new approach. 'Evidently,' he added, 'these are new ideas that are easy to dismiss with sarcasm ... but it is worth asking whether, had such a system been in place in 1914, war would have broken out? My answer would be no!'[166] The only alternative to Locarno, Briand asserted, was 'the organisation of international relations as they were practised in 1914, alliance systems based on the principle of mutual suspicion that led inevitably to arms races creating an extremely unstable and perilous atmosphere'. Locarno was 'a new system that takes the place of older practices ... [that have] ... produced a long succession of wars at great cost to the peoples of Europe'.[167] There was, in other words, no choice between the hopeful politics of Locarno and the traditional practices of the pre-war era of rivalry and arms races.

Two aspects of these debates are of particular interest. The first is the extent to which the arguments advanced by Briand and Paul-Boncour were based on the internationalist conception of peace and security. The importance both attributed to arbitration as an organising principle for international politics was a long-standing internationalist theme. The same is true of Briand's explanation of the principle of interlocking mutual assistance as a practical implementation of the solidarist principle of the mutualisation of risk. The second aspect is the optimism underpinning Briand's vision of future international politics based on cooperation and the rule of law. Germany, he predicted, would adapt its behaviour and accept a gradual and limited process of treaty revision on terms suitable to France. Britain, meanwhile, would come to embrace the principle that European security was indivisible and agree to participate in some form of east European mutual assistance system. Franco-German collaboration, finally, would drive forward a process of European economic and political organisation. In essence, Briand's position rested ultimately on the same basic assumption held by Bourgeois and other juridical internationalists: major powers would ultimately see the logic in surrendering a measure of their sovereignty and tempering pursuit of their individual interests in order to create a system of collective security under the rule of law. Briand's optimism on this score in 1925–6 would prove no better placed than that of Bourgeois in 1919.

It is fair at this stage to question the true extent of Briand's commitment to internationalism and his belief in the arguments he used to defend Locarno. At the same time that he was publicly lauding the opening of a 'new era in European politics', for example, he was privately mooting the rather traditional idea of inducing Poland to agree to the revision of its western frontier with

---

[166] AN, C/14763, *CAEAN*, XIIIème Législature, joint session, 19 Dec. 1925.
[167] AN, C/14763, *CAEAN*, XIIIème Législature, Briand *audition*, 23 Feb. 1926.

Germany by offering territorial compensations to its east at the expense of Lithuania.[168] Briand's political career to that point had been defined above all by a genius for sensing the ebb and flow of public and parliamentary opinion and adjusting his position accordingly. Yet, even if his arguments were not based on deeply held political convictions, the fact that he chose to defend his policy in these terms is no less important. It constitutes powerful evidence of the strength of internationalist ideas within both parliament and the public sphere. This point is further borne out by the results of the chamber and senate ratification votes. The chamber vote in favour of ratification was 413 to 71 (and the votes against included those of communist deputies who opposed Locarno en masse as an anti-Soviet conspiracy). The senate vote was even more decisive: 272 senators approved the accords against only 6 who opposed ratification. Briand's Locarno policy enjoyed overwhelming public and parliamentary support.[169]

IX

The vast majority of professional diplomats did not share the optimistic vision of a European future based on ever greater cooperation under the rule of law. Most did understand, however, that a multilateral system of binding political and legal commitments was the only viable means to enmesh and constrain Germany. It is doubtful that many at the foreign ministry believed that membership of such a system would socialise the Reich and transform it into a peaceful and responsible member of the international community. There were clear limits to the influence of such internationalist doctrines within the ministry.

The emergence of multilateralism as a practical logic within the foreign ministry is best understood as an adaptation of the traditional practices of Quai d'Orsay officials to the political conditions of the post-war era. The principle of the balance of power was too deeply ingrained in the predispositions of professional diplomats to disappear entirely. The policy conceptions of Philippe Berthelot are a case in point. Although Berthelot continued as secretary general for the rest of Briand's long tenure as foreign minister, his disdain for the League of Nations endured. He was always inclined to dismiss the League as 'an eloquent and respectable mess that offends my taste for reality, hard work and a job well done'.[170] Berthelot's scepticism regarding Briand's increasingly ambitious schemes to outlaw war or promote a European federation would ultimately lead to tensions with his long-time ally. By the end of his career Berthelot's influence with Briand was eclipsed almost entirely by that of his one-time protégé Alexis Léger. It was Léger who drafted the celebrated

---

[168] Soutou, 'Alliance franco-polonaise', 310–27.
[169] Bonnefous, *Cartel des gauches*, 120–2 and 136–7.
[170] MAE, PA-AP 72, *Papiers de Fleuriau*, vol. 3, Berthelot to de Fleuriau, 17 Nov. 1927.

memorandum calling for a European federation. Berthelot, for so long the great animating force at the Quai d'Orsay, was reduced to the role of spectator in the formulation of Briand's grand policy initiatives.[171]

The views of most foreign ministry officials in 1925 tended to fall along a continuum, with the more traditional instincts of Berthelot on one end and support for a League-based security policy on the other. In terms of their policy prescriptions, Berthelot and de Fleuriau moved some way along this continuum over the course of the 1920s but never came close to embracing the internationalist principle of peace through law. Others, such as Laroche, moved further, but saw the League primarily as a vehicle for obtaining security guarantees (mainly from Britain) that were impossible to secure using traditional balance-of-power practices. Others, such as Seydoux, Gout, Clauzel, Massigli and Léger, were willing to take the League seriously as a source of security for France. Not all, however, were willing to follow Briand down the road of European federalism. As a belief system, therefore, the internationalist conception of security made only limited inroads within the Quai d'Orsay. It never came close to displacing the traditional approach altogether.

Traditional predispositions were instead adapted to complement the changed international norms of the 1920s. The conviction that France required a strategic commitment from Britain to counterbalance German power remained central to policy calculations. The practical logic that emerged in 1924–5 was a marriage of the traditional balance-of-power reflexes of professional diplomats, on the one hand, and the muscular internationalist orientations of key French political leaders, on the other. It underpinned French pursuit of security through the construction of regional systems of mutual assistance based on the model of Locarno that Jean-Baptise Duroselle labelled 'pactomania'.[172] The Treaty of Mutual Guarantee served as a blueprint for a series of French initiatives in east–central Europe and the Mediterranean whose ultimate objective was the creation of a Europe-wide security regime. Projects for an 'Eastern Locarno', a 'Mediterranean Locarno', an 'Eastern Pact' or a 'Danubian Pact' sponsored by France over the next decade were all aimed at enmeshing Britain, Germany and, if possible, even the Soviet Union in a network of legal and political constraints that would ensure that any revision of the European status quo would be limited and peaceful rather than unilateral and violent.[173]

France's security policy had far-reaching implications for the structure of its armed forces and the specifics of its military strategy. Far-reaching reforms

---

[171] R. Meltz, 'Alexis Léger: de Philippe Berthelot à Aristide Briand' in Bariéty (ed.), *Briand*, 416–35; Barré, *Berthelot*, 397–408.

[172] J.-B. Duroselle, 'The Spirit of Locarno: illusions of pactomania', *Foreign Affairs*, 50 (1972), 752–64.

[173] G.-H. Soutou, 'La France et la problématique de la sécurité collective à partir de Locarno: dialectique juridique et impasse géostratégique' in G. Clemens (ed.), *Nation und Europa: Festschrift für Peter Krüger* (Stuttgart, 2001), 245–62.

introduced in 1927–8 resulted in a profound restructuring of the French army that rendered it incapable of any large-scale offensive action without full mobilisation. The corresponding evolution of French military strategy towards a fundamentally defensive conception resting on the inviolability of national territory was given material expression in the massive barrier of steel and concrete erected along the Franco-German border after 1928.[174] Unilateral military action to compel German compliance with the Versailles Treaty was a distant memory as construction began on the Maginot Line. Political and legal restraints to state behaviour replaced the overt threat of military force in a foreign and security policy that would result five years later in Briand's proposal for a European federation.

Paul-Boncour exaggerated when he characterised the Locarno Accords as 'the direct result of the movement set in train by the Protocol of 1924'.[175] The political and legal guarantees provided by the Rhineland Pact were far more circumscribed and less precise than those in the Protocol. They were limited to the Franco-German and German-Belgian frontiers and, by their very nature, precluded the regional defensive pacts envisaged under the Protocol. But the fact that France sacrificed key aspects of the 'doctrine of the Protocol' should not obscure the importance of juridical internationalist concepts in the design of the Locarno Accords. The interlocking compulsory arbitration agreements at the heart of the accords were an expression of the 'peace through law' approach to security. Never before had great powers pledged to abide by international arbitration over questions vital to their security. The contributions of a specifically French variant of internationalism to the conceptual framework of Locarno have been overlooked almost entirely in a historiography that has long represented the accords as having been imposed on France by Britain.

This reading of the origins and character of the Locarno Treaties has significant implications for the historiography of international relations in the 1920s. It is often argued that, because Germany was not forced to guarantee the inviolability of its eastern frontiers, Locarno marked the end of the Versailles order in Europe.[176] The problem with this argument is that it ignores the flexibility built into the peace treaty. All of the major peacemakers in Paris had anticipated that future territorial adjustments were likely, if not inevitable. The purpose of Article 19 of the Covenant, it should be remembered, was to provide for peaceful revision of the peace settlement. The Franco-Polish military alliance, which was intended to protect Poland's frontier with

---

[174] Vaïsse and Doise, *Outil militaire*, 324–62; Hughes, *Maginot Line*, 187–229; M. Alexander, 'In Defence of the Maginot Line: Security Policy, Domestic Politics and the Economic Depression in France' in Boyce (ed.), *French Foreign Policy*, 164–94.
[175] Paul-Boncour, *Entre-deux-guerres*, II, 162.
[176] See, among others, Wandycz, *Twilight*, 19–37; Cohrs, *Unfinished Peace*, 259–79.

Germany, was not an ineluctable consequence of the Treaty of Versailles. On the contrary, even Clemenceau admitted the possibility of future territorial revision. In his defence of the treaty before parliament, he stated explicitly that some territorial revision was to be expected.[177] The virtue of the Covenant, he argued, was that it made it more likely that revision would be peaceful and under terms acceptable to France. The Versailles Treaty was flexible enough to accommodate both the Ruhr and Locarno.

Another common misperception is that, because it was negotiated outside the specific structures of the League, Locarno constituted a revival of the nineteenth-century European concert of Great Powers.[178] This interpretation ignores the central role of arbitration as a trigger for the interlocking mutual assistance pacts at the heart of the accords. Nor does it take into account the role of the League of Nations in providing the wider legal structures that conditioned the operation of the treaties. There was no similar role for international law or international institutions in the operation of the European Concert even in its heyday between 1815 and 1848.[179] Finally, representing Locarno as a reversion to nineteenth-century practices ignores the crucial continuities between the Draft Treaty of Mutual Guarantee, the Geneva Protocol and the Locarno Accords. Locarno was very much a product of the post-war international environment.

---

[177] *JO*, Chambre, *Débats*, 1919, 25 Sept. 1919.
[178] Wandycz, *Twilight*, 19–20; G.-H. Soutou, 'Was there a European order in the twentieth century? From the Concert of Europe to the end of the Cold War', *CEH*, 9, 3 (2000), 332–5; P. Cohrs, 'The Quest for a New Concert of Europe' in Johnson (ed.), *Locarno Revisited*, 33–58.
[179] K. Hamilton and R. Langhorne, *The Practice of Diplomacy: Its Evolution, Theory and Administration*, 2nd edn (New York, 2011), 91–139; P. W. Schroeder, *The Transformation of European Politics 1763–1848* (Oxford, 1994), 583–801.

Conclusion

France's bitter war of survival from 1914 to 1918 shaped every aspect of its foreign and security policy. The conflict created the political conditions necessary for internationalist ideas about peace and security to become much more influential. Although internationalist impulses existed within the political and policy elite over this entire period, it was the experience of the Great War that presented internationalists with the opportunity to bring alternative conceptions of peace and security into the policy mainstream. French security professionals were forced either to adapt to changes in the internal and external environments or face marginalisation. This process took time. At no point was the internationalist vision of security ever dominant. But by the middle of the post-war decade the traditional conception no longer enjoyed the status of a practical logic. A new approach had evolved that combined traditional with internationalist approaches, the balance-of-power reflexes of French security professionals with the muscular internationalist doctrines of Cartel political leaders. The result was a multilateral security policy based on mutual assistance and the rule of international law that, at the same time, attributed decisive importance to British power. Reconsidering the course of French policy within an analytical framework of contending conceptions of security provides a new perspective on the international politics of this crucial period. The history of the period looks very different when the influence of internationalist ideas is taken seriously.

An analysis spanning the period before, during and after the Great War draws out interesting continuities that have been missed in the existing literature. Among the most important are the links between the legalist character of French internationalist thinking before 1914, the juridically inspired programme for a 'society of nations' put forward by Bourgeois at the peace conference in 1919 and French attempts to bolster the collective security provisions of the League Covenant in 1924–5. Also interesting and important is the role attributed to compulsory arbitration by juridical internationalists at the turn of the century and its pivotal status in French planning for both the Protocol and Locarno. One scholar of inter-war Europe has observed recently that a tendency to underestimate or ignore the vitality of internationalism is a distinctive feature of the international history of this period.[1] This is certainly true in the case of France. Also neglected, but equally important, is the persistent inclination to engage with democratic elements inside Germany throughout this period. Such engagement was of course a fundamental tenet of socialist internationalism and was advocated consistently by every SFIO spokesperson on foreign affairs. But it was also an important feature of the long-term policy conceptions of Clémentel, Aubert and Clemenceau in 1919 and of key figures such as Seydoux, Loucheur and Herriot in the 1920s. This current in thinking about long-term security would gain its fullest expression in Briand's project for a federal Europe.

There are also important continuities in various conceptions of economic security. Before the outbreak of war, French and German heavy industries seemed on the road to ever greater integration. At the heart of their relationship was France's shortage of coking coal and the German market for French-produced iron ore. Support for reviving this relationship after the war survived the ambiguities of French economic security planning during the conflict. The economic programme adopted by the Clemenceau government in 1919 aimed above all at the construction of a transatlantic regime of economic cooperation that would be strong enough to underpin Europe's economic recovery while at the same time enmeshing and restraining Germany. The assumptions underpinning this strategy endured even after hopes for American cooperation evaporated. The need for Franco-German commercial and industrial cooperation was at the centre of various plans to settle the reparations issue developed by Seydoux, Monnet and Loucheur in the early 1920s. The temporary resolution of this issue brought about by the Dawes Plan also hinged on international cooperation and was interpreted, on the French side at least, as a prelude to more extensive economic arrangements between France and Germany. This strategy came to partial fruition with the negotiation of the International Steel Entente in September 1926. It was given more comprehensive expression with the formation of the European Coal and Steel Community in 1951. The vision of a European economic community mooted by Seydoux in the 1920s anticipated in important ways that of Robert Schumann in 1950.

A longer chronological span at the same time highlights a number of interesting discontinuities. Among the most striking is Briand's evolution from a committed practitioner (and passionate defender) of power politics in 1916–17 to Europe's foremost prophet of multilateral cooperation under the League of Nations. Briand's political transformation probably tells us more about the underlying trends at work in the domestic and international political contexts than it does about the development of his personal belief system. His convictions evolved in response to deeper transformations in attitudes towards peace and security both in France and abroad.

---

[1] D. Lacqua, 'Preface' to D. Lacqua (ed.), *Internationalism Reconfigured: Transnational Ideas and Movements between the World Wars* (London, 2011), xii.

Another discontinuity is the sharp decline of military influence over this period. In 1919 France's senior military leadership enjoyed tremendous symbolic power in the realm of national security. Although Foch was outmanoeuvred by Clemenceau, his opposition to the Versailles settlement provoked a political crisis in France. Five years later, when the entire military establishment lined up to oppose the Geneva Protocol, their opposition was muted in the public sphere and easily brushed aside by Herriot and Briand. A necessary cause for the progressive marginalisation of the high command was the changed political context of the post-war era. Military prescriptions for security were profoundly out of step not only with international norms of the 1920s but also with the evolution of attitudes towards war and peace inside France.

Integrating the history of French policy making with the historical literature on internationalism provides other insights. French juridical internationalists were part of a much wider network of civil society activism not only through their involvement in the transatlantic peace movement but also by their membership in the emerging profession of international law. The similarities between the highly juridical visions of the Association de la paix par le droit in France and the League to Enforce Peace in the USA are striking. They are fascinating not least as an example of the way political ideas moved across linguistic and oceanic divides in the late nineteenth and early twentieth centuries. At the same time the episode of the peace conference illuminates the important differences between the French conception of international organisation, with its emphasis on automatic sanctions and a robust machinery of enforcement, and the more abstract ideas of Smuts, Cecil and Wilson. Lloyd George's private secretary Philip Kerr was right when he observed 'when we talk of peace we mean a moral situation ... [but] ... when the French talk about peace they mean a juridical situation ... Peace for them means the Treaty of Versailles as the political structure of Europe with irresistible force behind it.'[2] The use of force was a vital element in juridical internationalist doctrine. Pascal's maxim concerning the interdependence of force and justice was – and remains – central to all French thinking about political order. It has been invoked by politicians and political theorists of all ideological positions over the past two centuries. It has also been central to the interpretation advanced in this book, not least because it provided the necessary common ground for the marriage of traditional and internationalist visions that underpinned Cartel security policy in 1924–5.

It is strange that this dimension of French policy remains absent from the historiography of the League of Nations. Even the most recent work on the origins of the League, for example, fails to acknowledge that French proposals rested on a substantial and coherent body of theorising on the nature of

---

[2] National Archives of Scotland, GD40/17, *Papers of Philip Kerr, 11th Marquess of Lothian*, vol. 241, Kerr to Lord Houghton, 24 May 1928.

international peace and security.[3] Here, as in so many other cases, the untenable divorce between the history of internationalism and that of policy making has allowed basic misconceptions to endure and remain central to prevailing wisdom. The same is true of recent work done on the remarkable growth of civil society support for the League of Nations in France in the mid-1920s. This research sets the internationalism of the Cartel des gauches in its proper context. The Cartel's emphasis on a powerful League based on a robust regime of international law and with the power to impose military sanctions was an expression of French internationalist thinking stretching back into the nineteenth century. This vision of international security endured as a central principle of policy-making into the 1930s. It underpinned the 'constructive plan' for an international force put forward by Paul-Boncour at the World Disarmament Conference in November 1932. It was also at the heart of the demand for inspection and verification central to every French proposal for arms limitations through to the late 1930s. These and other connections between pre-1914 thinking and post-1918 policy have been missed almost entirely in the existing literature.

A different set of insights has been derived by integrating the cultural history of the First World War with that of security policy making. Official representations of the war as a struggle to restore the rule of law complemented the juridical internationalist campaign for 'peace through law' in fascinating ways. Just as important was the discourse of democracy versus autocracy that was deployed with increasing vigour after the collapse of Russia and the entry of the USA into the conflict. The unintended consequences of casting the meaning of the war in these terms came home to roost during the parliamentary crisis over war aims in June 1917. It was in the aftermath of the dramatic closed-session debates that the Ribot government followed through on its commitment to establishing a League of Nations by appointing the CISDN under the leadership of Bourgeois.

At the centre of wartime debates over France's security was a fascinating paradox. For some, the unprecedented sacrifices made to secure victory in 1918 illustrated the need for total security and thus the permanent transformation of the balance of power in France's favour. For others, however, these same sacrifices provided the most powerful argument conceivable for eradicating the balance of power as a source of security. The dynamic tension between these opposing conceptions of security has been the focus of this book. The year 1917 was the crucible within which popular attitudes towards peace and security began to be reshaped in the French public sphere. Traditional power politics were increasingly discredited as a basis for international security while support for alternatives based on international cooperation began to gain traction.

---

[3] See, for example, M. Mazower, *Governing the World: The History of an Idea* (London, 2012), 116–36.

These tectonic shifts in the structural environment had profound consequences for security policy. A persistent trope in memoir accounts of this period is a sense that the First World War had created a new and very different world that was 'big with new ideas'.[4] France would need to adapt to its new environment if it wished to retain its influence in international relations. Responses to this challenge were conditioned by the cultural backgrounds and practices of policy agents. Of the three major security policy constituencies, politicians and diplomats proved better equipped in a cultural sense to adapt to the rules and norms of post-1918 international politics. Negotiating skill is a fundamental requirement for both politicians and diplomats. Both constituencies tend to lose influence during wartime. The core function of the soldier, conversely, is to apply military force in pursuit of policy aims. It followed, then, that cultural predispositions of French military elites were less suited (and less easily adaptable) to policy making in a European context where military violence was increasingly ruled out as a legitimate tool of foreign policy.[5] Bourdieu's theory of cultural action has provided a helpful framework for better understanding these dynamics.

The concept of a 'practical logic' is also useful for identifying and understanding the role of traditions and beliefs in shaping policy responses. For most of this period, the traditional approach to security constituted a practical logic for both political leaders and security professionals. The existence of internationalist-inspired counter-currents did not threaten the dominant status of traditional practices. The advent of Clemenceau, and his decision to concentrate all important planning and decision making with himself and his close circle of advisers, posed a much greater threat to the traditional practical logic than did internationalist calls for a new approach to international politics. Clemenceau did not openly challenge the legitimacy of traditional practices. On the contrary, he proclaimed his commitment to traditional security concerns before parliament. Yet under his leadership, French security policy pursued an ideological vision based on a transatlantic community of democratic power into which a reformed Germany could eventually be integrated. The peace settlement that resulted was an ambiguous and open-ended arrangement that was far from a classic expression of traditional power politics. This change in course was in part a product of the structural limitations placed on French policy choices by the other peacemakers. But it also reflected Clemenceau's political convictions and those of his inner circle.

Although the end of Clemenceau's tenure marked a return to more traditional practices, the episode anticipated in interesting ways the confrontation

---

[4] Albert Thomas quoted in P. Clavin, 'Conceptualising Internationalism between the World Wars' in Lacqua (ed.), *Internationalism Reconfigured*, 6.

[5] This argument is developed in greater detail in P. Jackson, 'Pierre Bourdieu, the "cultural turn" and the practice of international history', *Review of International Studies*, 34, 1 (2008), 176–80.

between traditionalist and internationalist conceptions under the Cartel. The process that saw the traditional conception lose its status as a practical logic to be displaced by something new provides an interesting case study in the cultural sources of adaptation and innovation (and indeed the failure to adapt and innovate) within a policy-making elite.

Generational differences were also important in shaping diverse responses to the new structural environment within the policy establishment. It was no coincidence that divisions within the foreign ministry over fundamental questions of policy tended to fall along generational lines. There was a genuine appetite for new thinking and a new approach among the younger generation of diplomats. Jacques Seydoux acknowledged the existence of a pronounced generation gap when he observed that the war had 'made all things anew'. The older generation, he lamented, did not understand that 'the war of 1914 was not that of 1870 to the tenth degree. A new Europe has emerged, a new world, and it is this new world that they fail to understand.'[6] References to a generational cleavage are predictably absent from the official internal correspondence of Quai d'Orsay officials. But they are manifest in their personal recollections and in the fiction of younger writer-diplomats. They are central to Jean Giraudoux's *Bella* and also to Paul Morand's *Ouvert la nuit*.

It was no coincidence that the majority of officials belonging to this younger generation were protégés of Philippe Berthelot. For Berthelot the need to adapt to new conditions was an immutable law of policy making. 'There are a thousand imperatives that leave only a narrow way open for human agency and its execution,' he once reflected, 'and at every moment politics replies with a new reality that we must accept and to which we must adapt.'[7] This adaptability was by no means shorn of principle. If Berthelot accepted the need to adjust to the realities of the mid-1920s, seeking to embed a British commitment in a multilateral system, he refused to follow Briand in his initiatives for a bilateral arrangement with Germany or in his project for European federalism. The result was growing tension within the Briand–Berthelot partnership that led ultimately to the breakdown that provided Alexis Léger, one of Berthelot's protégés, with the opportunity to displace his mentor as Briand's chief confidant.[8]

Much of the evidence presented in the latter chapters underlines the remarkable flexibility of the European order as it was devised in 1919. The Treaty of Versailles provided a political and legal framework that could accommodate Franco-German economic cooperation as envisaged most notably by Seydoux, Loucheur and Briand (among others). But this same framework allowed for punishment and coercion. It could even

---

[6] Quoted in S. Jeannesson, 'L'Europe de Jacques Seydoux', *RH*, 299 (1998), 129.
[7] Quoted in J. L. Barré, *Philippe Berthelot: l'éminence grise, 1866–1934* (Paris, 1998), 350–1.
[8] R. Meltz, 'Alexis Léger: de Philippe Berthelot à Aristide Briand' in J. Bariéty (ed.), *Aristide Briand, la Société des nations et l'Europe, 1919–1932* (Paris, 2007), 431–4.

accommodate efforts to break up Germany under Poincaré in 1923. The extraordinary flexibility of the Versailles system has rarely been fully recognised, even in recent studies that seek to rehabilitate the efforts of the peacemakers in 1919. Clemenceau was right when he advised his parliamentary colleagues that 'this complex treaty will be worth only what you are worth; it will be what you make of it'.

Several of the findings of this study speak to core debates within international relations theory. The standard account of the evolution of twentieth-century thinking about the nature of international politics needs to be rewritten to take account of French theorising about peace and security. Léon Bourgeois fashioned the domestic political doctrine of *solidarité* into a reasonably coherent theory of international relations. What is more, he attempted to apply his ideas. His *solidarité*-inspired theory, with its focus on the mutual obligations of nation-states under the rule of international law, formed the conceptual core of the CISDN programme for a 'society of nations' rejected by British and Americans in 1919. The failure of the French conception of the League also has theoretical significance. Bourgeois' call for a binding regime of international law and an international armed force assumed a willingness on the part of all states to sacrifice a significant measure of their sovereignty in return for greater international security. This idea proved anathema to British and American delegates (as it was to most French policy elites). The French programme ran up against the same barriers as so many other propositions for collective action ever since: the stubborn refusal of the Great Powers to surrender their sovereignty for the benefit of collective enterprises. The same problem hampers contemporary efforts to control the international arms trade or to agree and enforce emissions standards that will protect the environment.

The book's evidence and arguments are also relevant to debates over the role of power and ideas among international relations theorists. In many ways, the foregoing analysis illuminates problems with realist international theory. It is hard to comprehend the massive influence of new normative standards based on international cooperation and collective security after 1918 from a purely realist perspective. One of the chief contributions of this book, moreover, is to illustrate the way that cultural dispositions conditioned French responses to the problems of peace and security. Structural realists get around these difficulties by pointing out that theirs is 'not a theory of foreign policy'. The explanatory power of structural realism, they argue, operates at the systemic level. The dynamics of anarchy place systemic pressures on states to pursue self-interested policies that inevitably undermine all prospects for collective security.[9]

At first glance the realist point of view seems persuasive – particularly when one reads the history of the post-1918 period through the lens of the 1930s and the Second World War. Yet it cannot account for the fact that many of the

---

[9] K. N. Waltz, 'International politics is not foreign policy', *Security Studies*, 6, 1 (1996), 54–7.

'systemic pressures' on French statesmen during this period ran in precisely the opposite direction. France's political and policy elites came under intense international pressure to renounce power politics and embrace new norms based on international cooperation under the auspices of the League of Nations. Nor can this pressure be understood in purely realist terms. Wilsonian rhetoric, for example, was not eyewash to disguise a traditional strategy to expand American power. Whatever his personal faults and political contradictions, Wilson was sincere in his desire to transform international relations. The result was that the system placed contradictory pressures on French policy. Some came from the threat posed by German demographic and industrial superiority. Others emanated from powerful inter-subjective expectations that the international system must be reformed to prevent another catastrophe on the scale of 1914–18. Both types of pressure were 'real'. Neither could be ignored.

This is not to say that a constructivist perspective offers a better understanding either of French policy or international politics during this period. German power existed independently of the cultural context of French policy making. The Reich posed a *potential* threat to France's existence that no amount of new thinking could remove entirely. Structures of power exercise a permanent and profound agency in international politics that policy makers ignore at their peril. The constructivist focus on culture and subjectivity tends to underplay this crucial fact. The influence of new international norms both during and after the conflict provides a good illustration of the way power and ideas are intertwined in the international realm. The pervasive influence of postwar norms, interestingly, derived in no small part from the fact that their most prominent advocate was also the president of the world's most powerful state. Wilson used his position to press for a thorough reorganisation of world politics. His message was hugely influential not least because it was backed up by economic and military power so formidable that it alarmed even America's allies.

In sum, realism and constructivism both offer valuable perspectives that can enrich the historical analysis of international politics. Both approaches force the historian to keep the wider picture in mind. Yet neither seems able, on its own at least, to capture the complex dynamics at work in the international system during and after the Great War. The historian, happily, does not need to choose between realist and constructivist approaches. Yet it is interesting and worthwhile to keep in mind the larger issues at stake in a theoretical debate that is unlikely ever to be resolved.

In the end, Foch was right. The great problem with the security strategy that evolved under the Cartel in the mid-1920s was that its success depended on the willingness of other European states to abide by the rule of international law. Jean-Baptiste Duroselle long ago dismissed this commitment to legalism and multilateralism in French foreign policy under Briand as 'illusions of pactomania'. Anthony Adamthwaite agreed that France's 'obsessive search for security through treaties' was 'a snare and a delusion'. More recently Robert Boyce has described the Locarno Accords as 'the emasculation of international security'.[10] There is considerable merit to these criticisms. Attempts to devise legal solutions to intractable political problems were naïve and probably always doomed to failure. Yet it may also be worth remembering that such an approach had never before been tried. The international convulsions of the next decade, the great depression, the collapse of transatlantic cooperation and the rise of Nazism, were unknowable to policy makers in 1925. The truth is that the most damaging policy failures, leading to disaster in 1940, were not the adaptations of the mid-1920s but instead the inability of French leaders to adjust to the political transformations of the early 1930s. They were not alone in this regard.

It should be acknowledged, finally, that the strategy of enmeshing and constraining Germany that failed so miserably during the 1930s was dusted off and applied with much greater success after 1944 (albeit with American support and towards a devastated and divided Germany). As I write the final lines of this book, France and Germany are preparing to celebrate the fiftieth anniversary of the 1963 Élysée Treaty of Friendship. This accord has underpinned one of the closest, most profitable and most durable partnerships in the long and troubled history of European politics. The success of this partnership suggests that the optimistic vision of the internationalist movement was not as misguided as the history of the period 1914–45 suggests. The tragedy is that it took another world war and the destruction of European society to realise this vision.

---

[10] J.-B. Duroselle, 'The Spirit of Locarno: illusions of pactomania', *Foreign Affairs*, 50 (1972); A. Adamthwaite, *Grandeur and Misery: France's Bid for Power in Europe, 1914–1940* (London, 1995), 229; R. Boyce, *The Great Interwar Crisis and the Collapse of Globalization* (London, 2009), 77–141.

Select bibliography

ARCHIVAL SOURCES
FRANCE
ARCHIVES NATIONALES (AN)

Archives privées
94 AP: *Archives Albert Thomas*
313 AP: *Archives Paul Painlevé*
324 AP: *Archives André Tardieu*
414 AP: *Fonds du maréchal Ferdinand Foch*
470 AP: *Archives Alexandre Millerand*
Ministère de l'intérieure
Série F7
Ministère du commerce
Série F12

ARCHIVES DU SÉNAT (AS)

Commission des affaires étrangères du Sénat (CAES)
Vol. 1891 / 69S 264: 1917
Vol. 1893 / 69S 266: 1919

BIBLIOTHÈQUE DE DOCUMENTATION INTERNATIONALE
ET CONTEMPORAINE (BDIF)

Archives Louis-Lucien Klotz

BIBLIOTHÈQUE NATIONALE DE FRANCE (BNF)

Nouvelle acquisitions françaises (NAF)
Papiers Poincaré / 16033: Notes journalières, 1 janvier à 30 mars 1919.

INSTITUT DE FRANCE

MS 4396: *Correspondance Stephen Pichon*
MS 5391: *Souvenirs du Général Edmond Buat*

MINISTÈRE DES AFFAIRES ÉTRANGÈRES (MAE)
Papiers d'agents (PA-AP)
PA-AP 008: *Papiers Camille Barrère*
PA-AP 12: *Papiers Maurice Horric de Beaucaire*
PA-AP 010: *Papiers Philippe Berthelot*
PA-AP 353: *Papiers Robert de Billy*
PA-AP 029: *Papiers Léon Bourgeois*
PA-AP 335: *Papiers Aristide Briand*
PA-AP 43: *Papiers Jules Cambon*
PA-AP 42: *Papiers Paul Cambon*
PA-AP 198: *Papiers Georges Clemenceau*
PA-AP 211: *Papiers Théophile Delcassé*
PA-AP 240: *Papiers Jean Doulcet*
PA-AP 72: *Papiers Aimé Joseph de Fleuriau*
PA-AP 77: *Papiers Charles de Freycinet*
PA-AP 196: *Papiers Jean Gout*
PA-AP 089: *Papiers Édouard Herriot*
PA-AP 93: *Papiers Jean Jules Jusserand*
PA-AP 113: *Papiers Pierre de Margerie*
PA-AP 217: *Papiers René Massigli*
PA-AP 118: *Papiers Alexandre Millerand*
PA-AP 133: *Papiers Maurice Paléologue*
PA-AP 141: *Papiers Stephen Pichon*
PA-AP 261: *Papiers Jacques Seydoux*
PA-AP 166: *Papiers André Tardieu*
Dossiers de personnel (Deuxième série nominative)
Vol. 157: Philippe Berthelot
Vol. 177: Robert Jules Daniel de Billy
Vol. 648: Henri Fromageot
Vol. 1185: Emmanuel Peretti de la Rocca
Vol. 118: Auguste Félix Charles de Beaupoil de Saint-Aulaire
Vol. 1426: Charles Louis Auguste Jacques Seydoux
Vol. 808: Joseph Maximilien Jarousse de Sillac
Relations commerciales
Série A (Administration)
Série B 81–82
Série B 84
Série A (Paix)
Série Guerre (1914–1918)
Série Y (Internationale)
Série Z (Europe 1918–1940)
Allemagne
Grande Bretagne

Rive gauche du Rhin
Pologne
Sarre
URSS
Société des nations (SDN)
Commission interministérielle d'études pour la Société des nations (CISDN)
Service français de la Société des nations (SFSDN)
Arbitrage, sécurité, désarmament
Service juridique
Fonds Fromageot

SERVICE HISTORIQUE DE LA DÉFENSE (SHD)

Département de l'armée de terre (SHD-DAT)

Série 1871–1919
3N: Comité de guerre
5N: Cabinet du ministre
6N: *Fonds Clemenceau*
Série 1918–1940
1N: Conseil supérieur de la guerre
2N: Conseil supérieur de la défense nationale
4N: États-majors particuliers
5N: Cabinet du ministre
7N: État-major général
Dossiers et états de service
Dossier Personnel du général Edouard Réquin
Fonds Privés [DITEEX]
Papiers du maréchal Ferdinand Foch

GREAT BRITAIN

BRITISH LIBRARY

Department of Manuscripts
MSS 51131: *Lord Cecil of Chelwood Papers*: 'Lord Cecil's Diary of the British Delegation: formation of the League of Nations, 1919'
India Office Select Materials
MSS Eur: F112: *Papers of Marquess Curzon* (George Nathaniel Curzon)

CAMBRIDGE UNIVERSITY LIBRARY: DEPARTMENT OF MANUSCRIPTS

GB 012 MS.Hardinge: Sir Charles Hardinge Papers
Add 1.26–1.29: Diary

CHURCHILL COLLEGE ARCHIVES, CAMBRIDGE

PHPP: *Sir Eric Phipps Papers*

NATIONAL ARCHIVES OF SCOTLAND

GD40/17: Papers of Philip Kerr, 11th Marquess of Lothian

THE NATIONAL ARCHIVES – PUBLIC RECORDS OFFICE (TNA-PRO)

CAB: Cabinet Papers
FO 608: British Delegation to the Peace Conference: Correspondence and Papers
FO 371: Foreign Office General Correspondence
30/69: James Ramsay MacDonald: Official and Literary Papers

UNITED STATES OF AMERICA

STERLING LIBRARY, YALE UNIVERSITY

MS 466: *Papers of (Colonel) Edward Mandell House*, Series II (Diary)

OFFICIAL PUBLICATIONS

FRANCE

Ministère des affaires étrangères, *Pacte de sécurité*, vol. I: *Neuf pièces relatives à la proposition faite le 9 février 1925 par le Gouvernement allemand et à la résponse du Gouvernement français (9 février 1925–16 juin 1925)*. Paris, Imprimerie des Journaux Officiels, 1925.

Pacte de sécurité, vol. II: *Documents signés ou paraphés à Locarno le 16 octobre 1925, précédés de six pièces relatives aux négociations préliminaires (20 juillet 1925–16 octobre 1925)*. Paris, Imprimerie des Journaux Officiels, 1925.

Annuaire diplomatique et consulaire de la République Française. Paris, Berge-Levrault, 1917 et seq.

Documents diplomatiques: l'alliance franco-russe. Paris, Imprimerie Nationale, 1918.

Documents diplomatiques français: série 1920–1932. Paris, Imprimerie Nationale, 1999–.

Travaux du Comité d'études. vol. I: *L'Alsace-Lorraine et la frontière du nord-est*. Paris, Imprimerie Nationale, 1919.

GREAT BRITAIN

HMSO, Cmd. 671, Miscellaneous No. 7, 2–7. London, 1920.

Cmd. 2105, *Reports of the Expert Committees appointed by the Reparation Commission*. London, 1924.

Secretary of State for Foreign Affairs, Cmd. 2169, *Papers Respecting Negotiations for an Anglo-French Pact*. London, 1924.

UNITED STATES

Papers Relating to the Foreign Relations of the United States: Paris Peace Conference, 1919, 13 vols. Washington, 1942–7.

DIARIES AND MEMOIRS

Aubert, Louis, Martin, Ivan, Missoffe, Michel, Piétri, François, Pose, Alfred and Puaux, Gabriel. *André Tardieu*. Paris, Plon, 1957.
Beau de Loménie, Emmanuel. *Le Débat de ratification du traité de Versailles à la chambre des députés et dans la presse en 1919*. Paris, Denoël, 1945.
Beaufre, André. *Mémoires: 1920–1940–1945*. Paris, Presses de la Cité, 1965.
Beneš, Edvard. *Souvenirs de guerre et de révolution (1914–1918): la lutte pour l'indépendance des peuples*, 2 vols. Paris, Ernst Leroux, 1929.
Benoist, Charles. *Souvenirs de Charles Benoist, 1902–1933*, vol. III: *Vie parlementaire, vie diplomatique*. Paris, Plon, 1934.
Bonsal, Stephen. *Unfinished Business*. New York, Doubleday, 1944.
Cecil, Robert. *A Great Experiment: An Autobiography*. Oxford, Oxford University Press, 1941.
Chambrun, Charles de. *L'Esprit de la diplomatie*. Paris, Corrêa, 1945.
Claudel, Paul. *Accompagnements*. Paris, Gallimard, 1949.
Clémentel, Étienne. *La France et la politique économique interalliée*. Paris, PUF, 1931.
Commynes, Philippe de. *Mémoires*, ed. Joël Blanchard, 2 vols. Paris, Agora, 2004.
Debeney, Marie-Eugène. *La Guerre et les hommes: réflexions d'après-guerre*. Paris, Plon, 1937.
Edmonds, James. *The Occupation of the Rhineland, 1918–1929*. London, HMSO, 1987.
Foch, Ferdinand. *Mémoires pour servir l'histoire de la guerre de 1914–1918*, 2 vols. Paris, L'Officine, 2007.
Freycinet, Charles de. *Souvenirs*, vol. II: *1878–1893*. Paris, C. Delagrave, 1913.
Herriot, Édouard. *Jadis*, 2 vols., vol. II: *D'une guerre à l'autre*. Paris, Flammarion, 1952.
House, Edward Mandell. *The Intimate Papers of Colonel House*, ed. Charles Seymour, 4 vols. New York, Houghton Mifflin, 1926.
Joffre, Joseph-Jacques Césaire, *Mémoires du Maréchal Joffre, 1910–1917*, vol. II. Paris, Plon, 1932.
Jouvenel, Bertrand de. *Après la défaite*. Paris, Plon, 1941.
Jouvenel, Robert de. *La République des camarades*. Paris, Grasset, 1914.
Lansing, Robert. *The Peace Negotiations: A Personal Narrative*. Ebook, 2003.
Laroche, Jules. *Au Quai d'Orsay avec Briand et Poincaré (1913–1926)*. Paris, Hachette, 1957.
Lenin, V. I. *Lenin: Collected Works*, trans. J. Katzer. Moscow, International Publishers, 1965.
Lloyd George, David. *War Memoirs of David Lloyd George*, 2 vols. London, Odhams, 1938.
Loucheur, Louis. *La Reconstruction de l'Europe et le problème des réparations*. Paris, Imprimerie Commerciale, 1922.
   Carnets secrets, 1908–1932, ed. Jacques de Launay. Paris, Brepols, 1962.
Madariaga, Salvadore de. *Disarmament*. Oxford, Oxford University Press, 1929.
Milhaud, Edgard. *Du Droit de la force à la force du droit*. Geneva, Atar, 1915.
Monnet, Jean. *Mémoires*. Paris, Fayard, 1976.
Mordacq, Jean. *Le Ministère Clemenceau: journal d'un témoin*, 3 vols. Paris, Plon, 1931–2.
Paléologue, Maurice. *La Russie des tsars pendant la Grande Guerre*. Paris, Plon-Nourrit et cie., 1921; republished as *La Crépuscule des tsars: journal (1914–1917)*. Paris, Mercure de France, 2007.

Paul-Boncour, Joseph. *Entre-deux-guerres: souvenirs de la IIIème République*, 3 vols., vol. II: *Les Lendemains de la victoire, 1919–1934*. Paris, Plon, 1946.
Pichot-Duclos, René Agisse. *Réflexions sur ma vie militaire: au GQG de Joffre*. Grenoble, Arthaud, 1948.
Pinot, Robert. *Le Comité des forges au service de la nation, août 1914–novembre 1918*. Paris, Colin, 1919.
Poincaré, Raymond. *Au Service de la France: neuf années de souvenirs*, 11 vols. Paris, Plon, 1926–74.
Recouly, Raymond. *Le Mémorial de Foch: mes entretiens avec le maréchal*. Paris, Éditions de France, 1929.
Ribot, Alexandre. *Lettres à un ami: souvenirs de ma vie politique*. Paris, Éditions Bossard, 1924.
  Journal d'Alexandre Ribot et correspondances inédits. Paris, Plon, 1936.
Saint-Aulaire, Comte de. *Confession d'un vieux diplomat*. Paris, Flammarion, 1953.
  Je suis diplomate. Paris, Éditions de Conquistador, 1954.
Serrigny, Bernard. *Trente ans avec Pétain*. Paris, Plon, 1959.
Seydoux, Jacques. *De Versailles au Plan Young: réparations, dettes interalliées et reconstruction européenne*. Paris, Arnavon et de Felcourt, 1932.
Stresemann, Gustav. *Vermächtnis: der Nachlass*, 3 vols. Berlin, Ullstein, 1932.
Tardieu, André. *La Paix*. Paris, Payot, 1921.
  Avec Foch. Paris, Flammarion, 1939.
Tirard, Paul. *La France sur le Rhin: douze années d'occupation rhénane*. Paris, Plon, 1930.

NEWSPAPERS, PERIODICALS AND POLITICAL REVIEWS

Action française
L'Avenir
Bulletin de l'Association française pour la Société des nations
Bulletin officiel de la Ligue des droits de l'homme
Bulletin du Parti républicain radical et radical-socialiste
Cahiers de droits de l'homme
Daily Mail
La Dépêche
L'Écho de Paris
L'Éclair
L'Europe nouvelle
Le Matin
L'Oeuvre
La Paix par le droit
Le Populaire
Le Progrès civique
Revue de deux mondes
Revue de métaphysique et de morale
Le Temps

OTHER PUBLISHED PRIMARY SOURCES

Anonymous. *Ceux qui nous mènent*. Paris, Plon, 1922.
Bainville, Jacques. *L'Allemagne*, 2 vols. Paris, Plon, 1939.

Select bibliography 529

Les Conséquences politiques de la paix. Paris, Godefroy, 1996.
Baker, Ray Stannard (ed.). *Woodrow Wilson and World Settlement*, 3 vols. London, Heinemann, 1923.
Barrès, Maurice. *La Grande pitié des Églises de France*. Paris, Émile-Paul Frères, 1914.
La Politique rhénane: discours parlementaires. Paris, Bloud et Gay, 1922.
Les Grands problèmes du Rhin. Paris, Plon, 1930.
Basch, Victor. *La Guerre de 1914 et le droit*. Paris, Ligue des droits de l'homme et du citoyen, 1915.
Benoist, Charles. *Les Nouvelles frontières d'Allemagne et la nouvelle care d'Europe*. Paris, Plon, 1920.
Blum, Léon. *L'Oeuvre de Léon Blum, 1924–1928*. Paris, Albin Michel, 1972.
Bouglé, Célestin. *Le Solidarisme*. Paris, Giard et Brière, 1907.
Bourgeois, Léon. *Solidarité*. Paris, Armand Colin, 1896.
Essai d'une philosophie de la solidarité. Paris, F. Alcan, 1907.
Pour la Société des nations. Paris, E. Fasquelle, 1910.
Le Pacte de 1919 et la Société des nations. Paris, Bibliothèque Charpentier, 1919.
Le Traité de paix de Versailles. Paris, F. Alcan, 1919.
Boyden, R. W. 'The Dawes Report', *Foreign Affairs* (June 1924), 583–97.
Buisson, Ferdinand, Thomas, Albert and Prudhommeaux, Jules. *Appel en vue de la fondation d'une Association française pour la Société des nations*. Paris, Les Droits de l'Homme, 1918.
Burnett, Philip Mason (ed.). *Reparation at the Paris Peace Conference from the Standpoint of the American Delegation*, 2 vols. New York, Columbia University Press, 1940.
Cambon, Jules. *Le Diplomate*. Paris, Hachette, 1926.
Cambon, Paul. *Correspondance, 1870–1924*, vol. III: *(1912–1924) Les Guerres balkaniques: La Grande Guerre. L'Organisation de la Paix*. Paris, Bernard Grasset, 1946.
Clemenceau, Georges. *Grandeurs et misères d'une victoire*. Paris, Plon, 1930.
Crafts, Wilbur Fisk. *A Primer of Internationalism: With Special Reference to University Debates*. Washington, D.C., International Reform Bureau, 1908.
Debeney, Marie Eugène. *Sur la Sécurité militaire de la France*. Paris, Payot, 1930.
Decharme, Paul (ed.). *VIIème Congrès nationale des sociétés françaises de la paix: compte-rendu du congrès (4, 5, 6 et 7 juin 1911)*. Clermont-Ferrand, 1911.
Dupuis, Charles. *Le Principe d'équilibre et le concert européen de la paix de Westphalie à l'acte d'Algésiras*. Paris, Perrin, 1909.
Durkheim, Emile. *De la Division du travail social*. Paris, F. Alcan, 1893.
Eitchal, Eugene d'. 'Solidarité social et solidarisme', *Revue politique et parlementaire* (July 1903), 96–116.
Glasgow, George. *MacDonald as Diplomatist: The Foreign Policy of the First Labour Government in Britain*. London, J. Cape, 1924.
Hanotaux, Gabriel. *Histoire du Cardinal Richelieu*, 2 vols. Paris, Plon, 1888.
Hauser, Henri. *L'Allemagne économique, l'industrie allemande considérée comme facteur de guerre*. Paris, Colin, 1915.
Les Méthodes allemandes d'expansion économique. Paris, Colin, 1915.
Keynes, John Maynard. *The Economic Consequences of the Peace*. London, Sterling, 1919.
Kriegel, Annie. *Le Congrès de Tours (1920): naissance du Parti communiste français*. Paris, Julliard, 1975.

Lapradelle, A. Geouffre de (ed.). *La Paix de Versailles*, 12 vols. Paris, Documentation Internationale, 1929–36.
Link, A. S. et al. (eds.). *The Papers of Woodrow Wilson*, 69 vols. Princeton, Princeton University Press, 1966–94.
Loménie, E. Beau de. *Le Débat de ratification du Traité de Versailles à la chambre des députés et dans la press en 1919*. Paris, Éditions Denoël, 1919.
Mangin, Général Charles. *Des Hommes et des faits: Hoche, Marceau, Napoléon, Gallieni*. Paris, 1923.
'Lettres de la Rhénanie'. *Revue de Paris* (April 1936), 481–526.
Mantoux, Paul (ed.), *Les Deliberations du Conseil des quatre (24 mars–28 juin 1919)*, 2 vols. Paris, Éditions du CNRS, 1955.
Montesquieu, Charles de. *De l'Esprit des lois*. Paris, Quadrige, 1999.
Morand, Paul. *Journal d'un attaché d'ambassade, 1916–1917*. Paris, Gallimard, 1963.
Nollet, Charles Marie Édouard. *Une Expérience de désarmement: cinq ans de contrôle militaire en Allemagne*. Paris, Gallimard, 1932.
Pascal, Blaise. *Pensées*, ed. P. Sellier. Paris, Mercure de France, 1976.
Péguy, Charles. *Charles Péguy: oeuvres en prose complètes, 1909–1914*. Paris, Bibliothèque de la Pléiade, 1992.
Pillet, Antoine. *De l'idée d'une Société des nations*. Paris, Rivière et cie, 1919.
Renault, Louis. *Introduction à l'étude du droit international*. Paris, L. Larose, 1879.
Renault, Louis (ed.). *Les Deux conférences de la paix de 1899 et 1907: recueil dex textes arrêtés par ces conférences et de différents documents complémentaires*. Paris, A. Rousseau, 1908.
Robespierre, Maximilien. *Oeuvres complètes*, vol. X. Paris, E. Leroux, 1967.
Rosenne, Susan (ed.). *The Hague Peace Conferences of 1899 and 1907 and International Arbitration: Reports and Documents*. The Hague, T. M. C. Asser, 2001.
Ruyssen, Théodore. *La Philosophie de la paix*. Paris, Rivière et cie, 1904.
Les Sources doctrinales de l'internationalisme, 3 vols. Paris, PUF, 1954–61.
Scott, James Brown (ed.). *The Hague Conventions and Declarations of 1899 and 1907: Accompanied by Tables of Signatures, Ratifications and Adhesions of the Various Powers and Texts of Reservations*, 2nd edn. New York, Oxford University Press, 1915.
Official Statements of War Aims and Peace Proposals, December 1916–November 1918. Washington, Carnegie Endowment for Peace, 1921.
Sharp, Walter R. *The Government of the French Republic*. New York, Van Nostrand, 1938.
Sorel, Albert. *L'Europe et la révolution française*, 8 vols., vol. I: *De l'Origine des traditions nationales dans la politique extérieure avant la Révolution française*. Paris, Plon, 1882.
L'Europe et la révolution française, 8 vols., vol. III: *La Guerre aux rois, 1792–1793*. Paris, Plon, 1885.
Lectures historiques. Paris, Plon, 1913.
Sorel, Albert and Funck-Brentano, Théophile. *Précis du Droit des gens*. Paris, Plon, 1887.
Stieve, Friedrich (ed.). *Isvolski and the World War: Based on the Documents Recently Published by the German Foreign Office*. Freeport, Books for Libraries Press, 1978 [repr. of 1926 edn].
Tardieu, André. *Notes sur les États-Unis*. Paris, Calmann-Lévy, 1908.
Valeur, Robert. *L'Enseignement du droit en France et aux États-Unis*. Paris, M. Giard, 1928.

Index

Aachen, Holy Alliance (1818) 385
Académie française 213
Aciéries réunies de Burbach, Eich et Dudelange 71
Action française 89, 124
Action française 221, 303
activism 445, 446, 516
  peace 6, 62, 64
Adamthwaite, Anthony 319, 432, 521
Africa, colonies in 209, 215, 244, 275
Agadir Crisis (1911) 76
aggression
  defining 458, 459, 460, 466, 473, 494, 498
  unprovoked German 484, 493, 502
alliance diplomacy 3, 5, 45, 78, 84, 85, 122, 130
alliances 11, 48, 502
  military 2, 59, 503, 509
Allied and Associated Powers 96, 100, 165, 182, 183, 184
  agreement on armistice conditions 195
  economic bloc 116, 185
  as Most Favoured Nations 261
  occupation of German port towns 363
  war aims 83, 151
Allied conference, Paris (1923) 403
Allied Economic Conference 175
Allied Supreme Council 214, 335
Allied Wheat Executive 175
Alsace-Lorraine 53, 105, 111, 113, 122, 130, 218, 249, 259
  northern frontier (1814) 288, 293, 295
  policy on 136, 143, 144, 145, 146, 150, 153, 158, 174, 192, 195
  return of 221, 279
  surrendered to Germany (1871) 164, 167
ambassadors 33, 335, 471
anarchists 22, 88
anarchy 11, 56, 64, 70, 520
anciens combattants see war veterans

Anglo-American guarantees 276, 279, 290–7, 298, 302, 305, 306, 308, 310, 313, 314, 392
  loss of 333, 498
Anglo-Franco-Belgian security pact proposed 474
annexations 95–6, 97, 104, 122, 129, 130, 313, 402
Anschluss 217, 239, 242
anti-communism 14
anti-militarism 321, 429, 443, 444
appeasement, and détente 479
arbitrage–sécurité–désarmament 2, 429, 431–68, 492, 499
arbitration 3, 6, 34, 62–5, 187, 229, 268, 272, 373, 388, 460, 466, 484, 489, 507, 509
  compulsory 1, 6, 14, 62, 74, 78, 127, 264, 270, 388, 429, 430, 457–63, 465, 470, 494, 498, 505, 514
  and general security and disarmament treaty 460, 461, 462, 507, 512
  as a means to define aggression 459, 460, 461, 473, 494, 498, 507
  and mutual obligation 504, 513
  permanent court of 179, 187, 455
  and sanctions 455, 456
arbitration treaties
  between Germany and Czechoslovakia 484, 486, 489, 490, 493
  between Germany and Poland 484, 486, 489, 490, 493
  in the nineteenth century 34, 39
aristocracy 20, 25, 28, 37
armaments policy, parliamentary control over 41–5, 92
Armenia 98, 245
armistice (11 November 1918) 190–5, 197, 210, 215
arms
  inspection regime for demilitarisation of Rhineland 476
  international trade in 520

531

arms reductions 63, 167, 186, 373–8, 383–90, 392, 418, 440, 451, 463
  criticisms of 424
  see also disarmament
army
  British troops in France 100
  Czech 416
  German 24, 96, 282
  international 186, 270, 271, 446, 520
  Polish 366, 367, 416
  Russian 140, 141
  Soviet Red Army 332, 365, 415
  US 189, 306
army (French) 36–41, 42, 75, 143
  casualties (1917) 143
  colonial soldiers 243, 246
  conscription 89
  crisis of morale 138–46, 165
  defensive role 442
  elite officer corps 39
  general staff 38–9, 44, 95, 104, 106–7, 125, 135, 157–9, 163, 236–8, 242, 259–60, 367, 424, 439, 463–4, 478, 493
  mutinies (1917) 133, 143, 145
  reform (1927–8) 472, 511
  republicanism of 23
  size 23, 376, 383, 442, 472
  and society 59
  symbolic power 442, 472
  'Time of Compromise' 472
Artaud, Denise 428
Asia, colonies in 209
Asquith, Herbert 101
Association de la paix par le droit 1, 64, 127, 516
Association française de la Société des nations (AFSDN) 222–3, 262, 372, 406, 419, 445
  membership 446
Atlantic 96
Atlantic Economic Union, proposed 250
Atlanticism 201, 232, 285, 286, 305, 313
Aubert, Louis 211, 229, 240, 284, 285, 374, 419, 515
  on Anglo-American guarantees 305
  memorandum on Atlantic alliance (1919) 286
  memorandum on Rhine frontier and the League of Nations 286, 289
  note on strategic importance of the Rhine 292
Augagneur, Victor 152, 432
Aulard, Alphonse 123, 370, 371, 390, 500
Auriol, Vincent 21, 405, 446
Australia 246
Austria 194, 217, 242, 342, 487
  Republic created 217
Austria-Hungary 50, 93, 96, 97, 98, 101, 130, 148, 159, 160, 190,
  call for dismantling of 105, 138, 161
  Functioning of the Dual Monarchy 139
Austro-Prussian war 53
Avenol, Joseph 345, 349, 350
aviation 416
avocats 20, 21, 64

Bainville, Jacques 58, 123, 221, 304
balance of power 2, 4, 5, 48–52, 78, 84, 263, 502
  American influence on 190
  and Anglo-American guarantees 305, 306
  economic 111, 249, 252, 253, 261
  European against Germany 5, 56, 169–71, 197, 275, 277, 366, 370, 391
  and frontier on the Rhine 303, 313
  the future 108, 122, 130
  and League of Nations 286
  overturning the European 132, 151–6, 287, 517
  the primacy of 85–132, 231, 275, 510
  and self-determination 286, 297
  structural shifts in the 11
  subjective meaning 12, 51
  transforming in France's favour 203, 322, 517
  see also équilibre européen
Baldwin, Stanley 411, 412, 468, 473, 475, 485
Balfour, Arthur 138, 143, 166, 225, 227, 290, 293
Balfour Note 394
Balkans, the 51, 96, 238
Balkan War, Second 97
Baltic states 96, 97, 139, 242
Bank of France 87, 219, 500
Banque industrielle de Chine 386
Bardoux, Jacques 300
Bargeton, Paul 465, 471
Bariéty, Jacques 362, 428, 432, 441, 454
Barrère, Camille 28, 108, 228, 298, 440, 465, 470
Barrès, Maurice 32, 68, 77, 87, 106, 123, 124, 221, 304, 318, 411
Barthélemy, Joseph 74, 419, 500
Barthélemy-Saint-Hilaire, Jules 28
Barthou, Louis 21, 86, 206, 302, 342, 358, 367, 383, 389, 402, 414, 419
Basch, Victor 74, 127
Basdevant, Jules 186, 271
Bavaria 51, 160, 341, 342, 416
Beaufre, André 40
Beauquier, Charles 74
Becker, Annette 324
Becker, Jean-Jacques 89, 144, 220
Belgium 51, 52, 93, 94, 95–104, 108, 148, 494
  claims on Luxembourg 213, 277
  coal and steel industry 7

Index

and the Dawes Plan 436
and France's Ruhr policy 402
German arbitration convention 494
'intimate cooperation' with France 105, 158
investment in France 71
liberation of 101, 130, 167
military alliance with 355
as Most Favoured Nation 250, 253
reconstruction 261
security pact with 474, 482, 486
trusteeship of mandates 246
western 104
see also Franco-Belgian agreement
Bell, P. M. H. 2
Beneš, Edvard 171, 214, 365, 417, 462, 489, 495
Benoist, Charles 124, 155, 229, 302, 303, 358
Bentham, Jeremy 61
Bergery, Gaston 450, 451, 475
Bergmann, Carl 331
Bergson, Henri 182, 211
Berstein, Serge 65, 90, 428, 431, 447
Berthelot, André 386
Berthelot, Marcellin 31
Berthelot, Philippe 31–6, 92, 107, 109, 114, 117, 241, 253, 342, 347, 471, 481, 491, 519
   on American involvement in the First World War 168
   on arms reductions 376
   and Beneš 495
   and Briand 359, 369, 425
   and British eastern policy 490, 519
   cordon sanitaire against Bolshevism 237
   energy policy 259, 260
   on Entente 342, 359, 465
   in exile 426, 490
   on federalism in Germany 283
   foreign policy 107, 108, 109, 110, 135, 137, 138, 166, 171, 193, 227, 235, 236, 238, 240, 341, 366, 368, 369
   on the League 266, 267, 273, 370, 373, 419, 510
   memorandum on Ottoman Empire 244–6
   on peace conference 210, 224, 225–9
   on Poland 366, 368, 496
   resignation 386
   Rhineland policy 278, 279, 280, 297, 298, 310, 313
   on the Russian Revolution 168
   on the Saar 285, 295
   on shared interests 492
Bethmann Hollweg, Theobald von 96, 139
Beugnot, Jacques Claude 280
Bismarck, Otto von 154, 277, 367
Black Sea Fleet, mutiny 328
Bliss, Tasker 460

bloc, use of term 325
Bloc national 323–30, 335, 358, 433, 447, 448
   arms reductions 422
   campaign strategy (1919) 329
   confrontational politics 390, 441
   foreign policy 319, 359, 405, 414
   ideological differences in 326
   relations with internationalists 419, 446
Blum, Léon 32, 75, 329, 390, 405, 413, 441, 444, 448, 450
Bohemia 172, 237, 238, 239, 240, 242
Bolshevik Revolution 79, 93–5, 141, 146, 162, 167, 236
Bolsheviks
   effect on French policy 149, 220, 222, 235, 238, 328, 329, 332, 414
   foreign policy 141, 147, 215
   as 'German agents' 168
   'Peace Decree' 141
Bordeaux, parliament and government exile in (1914) 81, 91
Bosphorus Sea 98
Bouchard, Carl 69
Boué de Lapeyrère, Admiral 44
Bouglé, Célestin 10, 74, 371, 500
Boulanger Affair 300
Boulanger, General Georges Ernest Jean-Marie 65
Boulangism 40
Bourbon-Parme, Sixte de 148, 169
Bourdieu, Pierre
   cultural action theory 518
   'practical logic' 9, 16, 60, 132, 162, 355, 514, 518
   sociology of 9, 12, 19, 207, 213
   'theory of practice' 16, 60
Bourgeois, Émile 125
Bourgeois, Léon 6, 10, 32, 34, 70, 74, 115, 128, 130, 134, 235, 268
   in the AFSDN 223, 372
   attitude compared with Clemenceau 272–5
   Commission (1918) 178–89
   on disarmament 68, 375, 378
   first president of League Assembly 374, 418
   for an international armed force 446
   government (1896) 65
   juridical conception of League of Nations 180, 262–75, 304, 447, 461, 468, 514
   juridical internationalism 65–7, 74, 127, 128, 462, 504, 505, 509, 520
   leader of CISDN 517, 520
   on the Left Bank of the Rhine 134
   and the proposed League of Nations 178–89, 210, 222, 286, 419, 457
   support for Poland 99
bourgeoisie 20, 26, 37, 62, 76
Boyce, Robert 5, 522

Brest-Litovsk Treaty (1918) 141, 171, 173, 194
Briand, Aristide 13, 21, 24, 32, 35, 65, 77, 91, 92, 112, 128, 129, 133, 134, 165, 166, 206, 318, 320
  and Berthelot 359, 369, 425
  career 358
  and Chamberlain 491
  commitment to internationalism 509
  compared with Poincaré 392–4, 405, 415
  economic security policy 378–83
  European security system 469, 499, 506, 509
  on federation of European states 499, 506, 515, 519
  on Foch 488, 516
  as foreign minister 92, 108, 119, 146, 147, 150–3, 161, 358–64, 429, 490–3
  on Franco-British cooperation 383–90, 452, 475, 491
  Franco-German economic cooperation 519
  and Geneva Protocol 468
  on German entry to the League 486
  government (1921) 259, 321
  on legal regime of the Covenant and Germany 484
  and Locarno Accords 494, 499, 502, 503–7
  meetings with Lloyd George (1921) 360, 362
  and Millerand 383, 389
  and multilateralism 357–90, 393, 461, 467, 515
  on peace 152, 203, 357
  on Poland 368, 415, 496, 497, 509
  premier (1915–17) 82, 92–3, 114, 115, 117, 128, 132, 335
  on reparations 351, 356, 378
  resignation (1917) 145
  resignation (1922) 389, 390
  Rhenish solution 397
  speech welcoming Germany to the League (1926) 500
  on Versailles 336, 357
Briand Plan (1930) 506
'Briandism' 4, 471
Briey–Longwy basin 95, 139
Britain
  attitude to eastern Europe 473
  bilateral treaty proposed 384, 387, 470
  Board of Trade 175
  Committee of Imperial Defence (CID) 43, 473
  and the Dawes Plan 436
  and disarmament 421–3
  Entente Cordiale (1904) 50, 164
  in Europe-wide security system 489
  fear of economic domination by 249
  financial crisis (1917) 102
  French economic dependence on 94, 95, 138, 255, 352
  and French Rhineland policy 290–7
  internationalism in 2, 6, 62, 68, 142
  and the League of Nations 264, 275, 520
  loans from USA 216, 255
  loans to France 219, 350
  opposed Seydoux Plan 354, 382, 387
  peace conference policy 203, 215, 225
  policy elites 3, 138
  post-war order attitudes 166, 334
  post-war policy 142, 200, 215, 317, 323, 333
  refusal to agree to financial controls on Germany 398
  refusal to guarantee German arbitration treaties 490
  refusal to ratify Geneva Protocol 429, 473–81, 498
  security policy (1924–5) 475
  strategic commitment (mid-1920s) 78
  strategic importance to France 100–1, 197, 227, 320, 361, 384, 471, 476, 491, 499, 503, 511, 514
  support for disarmament 374
  Treasury 142, 175
  trusteeship of mandates 246
  see also Anglo-American guarantees
British Empire 118, 167, 244, 250, 265
British Expeditionary Force (1914) 100
British League of Nations Union (LNU) 372
Brossolette, Pierre 445
Brugère, Raymond 409
Brussels Conference (1920) 354
Buat, General Edmond 281, 338, 367, 409, 439
budget (French)
  debates over 42
  post-war (1920) 328
  proposed for 1915 91
Buisson, Ferdinand 65, 74, 126, 222
Bulgaria 242
  entry into war 92, 97
Bülow, Bernhard von 205
Bureau des communications 34
Bureau d'études économiques 112–15, 116, 122, 174, 176, 251
Bureau international de la paix 372
bureaucracy 36, 41–6

cabinet 41, 43
  and alleged revolutionaries 89
  war 93
Cachin, Marcel 148, 149, 150, 151, 152
Caillaux, Joseph 145, 152, 162
Caix, Robert de 194, 244

Index

Cambon, Jules 28, 36, 107, 109, 110, 137, 138, 179, 184, 187
  on foreign policy 58, 109, 148, 166, 169, 241, 252, 298, 317
  on internationalist commitment to the rule of law 183
  peace delegate 206
Cambon, Paul 28, 36, 94, 95, 108, 109, 110, 136, 138, 190, 242, 266, 369, 386
  denounced Clemenceau 312
  instructions to Briand 133
  peace conference programme 224, 228
  on Prussia 281
  on Rhineland policy 278, 298
  on Wilson 224
Cambon Letter (1917) 138, 143, 146, 152, 391
Cameroon 246
Cannes Conference (1922) 358, 385, 386, 387, 388, 498, 504
Capetian dynasty 55
capitalism 200, 332
Caporetto, Battle of 189
Carnegie Foundation 64
Carnet B 89
Carr, E. H. 68
Cartel des gauches 1, 7, 10, 13, 418, 441
  distinguished from Bloc national 447
  election (May 1924) 427, 442, 444, 447
  finance policy 432
  Foch on 471
  foreign policy 431–68
  and internationalisation of security 427, 459, 469, 499, 514, 516, 517, 519, 521
  juridical internationalism 456, 468
  membership 448
  multilateral cooperation 458
  Ruhr policy 455, 456
  and Soviet Union 465
Cassin, René 445, 461, 488, 499
Catholicism 86, 89, 169, 284, 326, 341, 445
Cavallier, Camille 114
Cecil, Robert 185, 265, 268, 272, 293, 445, 516
  draft mutual assistance treaty (1923) 421–3
Cecil Plan 421–3
Cellier, Alexandre de 350, 351
censorship 79, 85, 87, 90, 122–4, 132, 144
  consignes 123
central Europe
  empires of 33
  inter-state war 324
  post-war policy 136, 166, 168–72
Central Powers 92, 94, 95, 102, 118, 119, 168–72, 214
  Bolshevik armistice with 141, 165

'Peace Note' (1916) 96
peace treaties with 216
chamber of deputies
  commissions 42, 302, 312
  resumes authority 325
  state of siege declared 87
Chamberlain, Austen 474, 475
  and Briand 491
  and German Rhineland proposal 482, 485
  and Herriot 481, 485
  refusal to commit to eastern Europe 490
  'The Necessity of the Early Consideration of the Question of French Security' 474
channel tunnel 291
Charle, Christophe 20
Chastenet, Jacques 317
Chaumet, Charles 508
Chemin des Dames, Battle of 93, 133, 143
Chicherin, Georgy 333
Church, separation of State and 23
Cilicia 245, 246
civil society
  and internationalism 74, 516
  and the League of Nations 222, 445, 517
  of peace activism 62, 64
  policy advice from associations 229
  and the security problem 122–30
  transnational 9
civil wars 324
civilians, German bombing of 94, 95
civilisation, crusade for, 9, 22, 67, 80, 94, 126, 151–6, 245, 285
Clark, Ian 63, 207
class struggle 22, 141, 441
Claudel, Paul 32, 35, 111, 511
Clemenceau, Georges 33, 42, 69, 155, 192, 235, 242, 258, 270, 327
  and armistice 189–96
  assassination attempt on 199
  Atlanticist orientation 201, 232, 286, 293, 308, 310, 314, 515
  attitude compared with Bourgeois 223, 272–5
  and Bolshevik Russia 236
  and British support 227, 476, 503
  career 163–6
  colonial policy 246
  constitutional crisis 298–305
  economic policy towards Germany 174, 175, 247–62, 348, 515
  eight-hour working day legislation 329
  Foch and 300, 310, 311, 516
  foreign policy 164, 172, 206, 364
  on German disarmament 282, 480
  and League of Nations 189, 223, 230, 235, 262, 267, 268

Clemenceau, Georges (cont.)
  meeting with Lloyd George (1918) 195, 227, 246, 291
  new international order 209, 232, 267, 306, 518
  as premier (1906–9) 164
  as premier (1917–20) 77, 146, 164, 206, 224
  relations with parliament 204, 325, 327
  on reparations 257
  retirement (1920) 164, 327
  Rhineland policy 276, 287, 291, 293, 294, 298–305, 310, 313, 314
  on Russian Revolution 148
  and the Saarland 295
  on self-determination 201, 241, 286, 293, 309, 310
  on Soviet regime 414
  style and image 198, 199, 206, 231, 309
  support for Poland 99, 239
  on territorial revision 513
  threat to resign 190
  two approaches to peace and security 314
  on Versailles Treaty 520
  war to the end 162
  wartime address 82
  and Wilsonianism 210, 227
Clémentel, Étienne 112, 115–16, 117, 165, 204, 248, 249–56
  economic plan 174, 176, 177, 185, 250, 275, 456
  as finance minister 450
  letter to Wilson (1917) 176–8, 190
  proposals for economic security 173, 175, 252, 254, 261, 454, 515
coal 7, 53, 70, 100, 111, 239, 258, 259, 260, 331, 337, 348, 349, 395, 404, 500, 515
Cobden, Richard 61
Cochin, Denys 92
Cocteau, Jean 32
Cohrs, Patrick 4, 319, 427, 454, 468
coke (metallurgical) 259, 349, 395, 401, 456, 500, 515
Cold War 285
Collette 32
Cologne 361, 452, 482
  evacuation scheduled 476, 477–81, 494
colonial issues 243–7, 275
Combes, Émile 92
Comintern (Communist International) 215, 329, 332, 413
Comité commercial franco-allemande 72
Comité de conciliation internationale 64
Comité de la rive gauche du Rhin 124, 221, 432
Comité de l'Afrique française 243
Comité des forges 72, 112–14, 229, 404

Comité des houillères 404
Comité d'études 44, 124, 156, 219–20, 229
Comité national d'études politiques et sociales 128, 180, 182
commemoration 324, 444
commerce ministry 112–15, 117, 132, 159, 348
  economic conditions of German peace 173, 175
  post-war cooperation rather than competition 248, 251
Commissariat of Foreign Affairs (Narkomindel) 215, 333
Commission des réformes administratives 33
Commission d'études 44
Commission d'études interministérielles pour la Société des nations (CISDN) 65, 178–89, 373, 457, 458, 465, 466, 475, 477, 493, 505
  first session (1917) 181, 408, 517
  meeting (1924) on Geneva 467, 472
  membership 179
  for a 'society of nations' 520
Commission du droit international 30
Commission on French Economic Expansion 112
Commission pour la rive gauche du Rhin 253
commissions
  expert in peace conference 230
  members 42
  role in war 91, 94
  standing 42
communications technology 31, 34, 60
communism 42, 215, 330, 332, 510
Communist International (Comintern) 215, 329, 332
Commynes, Philippe duc de 49
compensations 48, 158
Comptoir métallurgique de Longwy 72
Concert of Europe 265
Confédération générale du travail (CGT) 85, 128, 149, 304
  and Comintern 329, 330
  Comité confédéral 88
  Committee for the Resumption of International Relations 129
  membership 220, 329
  peace and self-determination 221
Confédération générale du travail unitaire (CGTU) 330
Confederation of the Rhine, Napoleonic 409
Conference of Ambassadors (1920) 335, 471
Conférence des avocats du barreau de Paris 21, 335
confrontational politics 391–426, 429, 441, 442, 465

Index

Bloc national 390
  Tardieu's 390
Congrès français de la Syrie 243
Congress of Vienna (1815) 225
conseil des ministres (cabinet) 41, 43
Conseil supérieure de guerre (CSG) 38, 338, 472
Conseil supérieure de la défense nationale (CSDN) 41–6, 338
  created (1906) 43
  and League of Nations 262, 268, 271
  membership 44
conseiller commercial et financier 34
conservatism
  in the French army 37, 38, 39
  nationalist 79, 90–1
Constantinople 98, 130, 141, 150, 245, 246
constitution 263
constructivist international theory 12, 521
consular service 31
Contrôle-général des territoires rhénans 283
contrôleur des dépenses engagées 42
Conty family 28
cooperation
  between state and private enterprise 205, 500
  democratic 286
  inter-state 5, 47, 115, 262
  international economic 70–4, 161, 163, 175, 177, 199, 200, 248, 250, 252, 351, 381, 419, 437, 506, 515
  international under rule of law 499, 517, 520, 521
  political dimensions of economic 178, 314, 320, 429
Corbin, Charles 465, 471
cordon sanitaire policy 414
Cosmos lodge 74
Coste, Émile 398, 402
Cot, Pierre 21, 69, 74, 446
Council of Four 228, 230, 241, 273, 298, 299, 301, 308
Council of Ten (Supreme Council) 230
Cours des comptes 43
Couyba, Maurice 303
credit, international 397, 398, 434, 447
Crewe, Lord Robert Offly 412
Crowe, Sir Eyre Alexander Barby Wichart 453
cultural action (Bourdieu) 518
cultural imperialism 244
culturalism 15
culture
  promotion of French 34
  role in explaining policy 11, 517
  role of predispositions 9, 16, 19, 518, 520
Cuno, Wilhelm 481
currency

French 413, 434, 500
French exchange crisis 433, 455
German 396, 399, 404, 407
Rhenish proposed 399, 407, 410
Curzon, Lord George Nathaniel 334, 387
customs unions 105, 116, 161, 253
Danzig and Poland 242
  with Left Bank 297
Czechoslovakia 170, 237, 238, 240, 241, 242, 275, 366, 369
  borders of 213, 214, 483, 484
  British refusal to commit to 473, 489
  Crisis (1938) 497
  effect of Locarno Accords 495–6
  foreign policy 365, 417
  French accords 494
  German arbitration treaty with 484, 486, 489, 490, 493, 494
  Germans living in 331
  as hub of east European order 368
  independence 171
  industry 369, 416
  military alliance with France proposed 417, 481
  relations with Poland 171, 194, 240, 365, 415, 418
  support for Geneva Protocol 462
Czechoslovak National Council 171

Daily Chronicle 344
Daily Mail 300, 387
Daladier, Édouard 431
Danton, Georges Jacques 303
Danubian confederation 368, 369
Danzig 242
Dardanelles Straits 97, 98, 130, 131, 141
  internationalisation of 245
  'Straits Agreement' (1915) 131
Darmstadt 337, 409
Daudet, Léon 353
Davis, Norman 291
Dawes, Charles 397, 434
Dawes Plan 431, 434, 435–7, 448, 451, 452, 454, 494, 515
  as German non-compliance 478, 480
Debeney, General Marie-Eugène 439, 458, 466, 467, 471, 472, 480
debt
  French 'floating' 433
  French war 173, 216, 219–20, 229, 248, 327
  German 350, 359, 435
  international mobilisation of German 378
  and reparations policy 255, 433
  Russian Tsarist 414, 447
Declaration of the Rights of Man 66, 80, 263

defence policy
  army and 472
  ideas in 59
  opposition to French 272
  organs 42
  parliamentary control over 19–24
Degoutte, General Joseph 340, 342, 362, 400, 401, 402, 409, 410
Degrand, Georges 239, 240
Delbos, Yvon 222, 431
Delcassé, Théophile 28, 29, 31, 82, 91, 92, 94, 95, 130, 131
  response to Wilson 109
democracy
  deliberative 21
  as a force for peace and security 281, 285, 313, 372
  and post-war order 150, 184, 199, 207, 210, 233, 307, 320
  the principle of 209
  and self-determination 208, 313
  as source of legitimacy 137
  versus autocracy 517
  war as a crusade for 83, 89, 103, 127, 148
Democratic Economic Union, proposed 250
democratisation 83, 102, 127, 161, 167, 170, 201, 314
demography 94, 95
Denis, Ernest 241
Département des affaires administratives et des unions internationales 34
deputies
  Chambre bleu horizon 327
  standing commissions 42
  in Third Estate 20
Deschanel, Paul 81, 134, 190, 327
d'Estournelles de Constant, Paul 64, 65, 74
détente 494, 498
  and appeasement 479
deterrence 416, 439
  and multilateralism 453, 467, 482
Deutsche–Französischer Wirtschaftsverein 72
Deutsche-Luxembourg 71
Deuxième bureau (French army general staff) 139, 160, 168, 169, 190, 339, 366
diplomacy 33, 57, 110, 167, 227, 229, 258
  'coercive' 360
  criticisms of traditional 370–8
  negotiation 518
  role in defence 493
  secret 370
  see also alliance diplomacy; summit diplomacy
diplomatic corps 25, 35, 43, 489
  entrance examination (*concours*) 25
  pessimism over Europe 510
  purge by Herriot 470

diplomatic history 54
Direction des affaires politiques et commerciales (DAPC) 34, 44, 171, 237, 238, 239, 241, 411, 460, 471
Direction du contentieux politique et commerciale 30
disarmament
  arbitrage–sécurité–désarmament formula 2, 429, 431–68, 492, 499
  clauses in Versailles Treaty 469
  Esher Plan for naval 420
  of Germany 264, 270, 282, 309, 320, 338, 343, 374, 375, 448, 449
  international 1, 68, 373–8, 415, 418–26
  moral disarmament of Germany 482
  opposition to future 441
  and security 421–4, 461
discourse
  civil society 122–30, 517
  popular and official 79, 86–91, 517
  strategies of 107
Dominique, Alfred 222
d'Ormesson family 28
Doulcet, Jean 111
Doumergue, Gaston 140, 146, 158, 244
  agreement with tsar (1917) 146, 153, 391
Draft Treaty of Mutual Assistance (1923) 423
Dreyfus Affair 23, 39, 59, 74, 164, 431
Driault, Edouard 123
Dubois, Louis 352, 378, 402
Dubost, Antonin 134, 301
Dumont, Charles 155
Dumont Resolution 155, 156
Durkheim, Émile, collective consciousness 66
Duroselle, Jean-Baptiste 90, 149, 511, 521
Dutasta, Paul 228

eastern Europe
  'Bolshevik danger' in 194
  British obligations to 462
  demographics 415
  'eastern barrier' to counterbalance Germany 170, 171, 313, 364–70, 414, 416, 417, 418
  effect of Locarno Accords on 495, 499, 506
  empires 33
  French right to intervene in 489
  frontier settlements 364, 484
  German aims in 96, 481
  guarantee system 496
  inter-state war 324
  and new multilateral security policy 439
  policy towards 14, 141, 148, 161, 166, 168–72, 221, 238, 322, 365, 413–18
  self-determination 240–3
  'successor states' 172, 237–43, 289, 331, 364, 369

Index

support for nationalities 170
territorial settlement 214, 235–43, 331
eastern front 94, 100, 141
Ebert, Friedrich 331
L'Echo de Paris 304, 354, 465, 501
École libre des sciences politiques 26, 29, 54, 57
École normale supérieure 75, 205
École polytechnique 37, 38, 59, 191
École spéciale militaire de Saint-Cyr 37, 38, 59
École supérieure de guerre 38, 59, 191
economic bloc
  Allied 116, 117, 118
  peacetime 119
economic community, European 515
Economic Conference (1916) 117, 119, 385
economic cooperation 7–8, 70–4, 132, 161, 229, 230, 275, 309, 320, 344, 349, 355, 437
economic coordination, inter-Allied 232, 249, 250
economic order, new international 163, 175, 176, 177, 248
economic policy
  planning approach 115, 117, 120
  Wilsonian 167
economic security 8, 13, 14, 73, 78, 84
  internationalist conception of 437, 515
  post-war planning 112–22, 132, 172–8, 247–62, 275, 320, 355
  programme (1918) 249–56
  Seydoux Plan 347, 351–6, 437
  under Briand 378–83
economics
  fixation with the primacy of 8
  in international relations 31, 219–20, 229
  liberal theories of interdependence 120
  in war 59
  western Europe 70–4
economy, structural dynamics of world 119
education
  Jesuit 191
  of policy elites 20, 26, 29, 54–60
electoral system
  alliances favoured 326
  new in 1919 326
elites
  cultural backgrounds of French 12, 15
  cultural predispositions 9, 12, 60
  peace policy 203
  see also diplomatic corps; military elites; policy elites; political elites
Élysée Treaty of Friendship (1963) 522
emissions standards 520

energy policy, post-war 248, 259, 260, 349, 404
enforcement 319, 336, 355, 376, 446, 469, 499, 516
  or engagement 323–56
Entente Cordiale (1904) 50
équilibre européen 49, 51
Erfüllungspolitik 331
Esher Plan (1922) 420
Essen 194, 404
Estates-General (1789) 20
ethnic conflicts 324
ethnicity 208
Europe
  in 1917–18 163
  balance of powers in 49
  'concert' 385
  economic community 515
  economic interdependence 437
  federation of states 499, 500, 506, 507, 510, 515
  juridical means to avoid war 505
  political future of 234, 519
  post-1945 projects for integration 178
  post-war international relations 317, 385, 505
  security of 138
  stabilisation by a multilateral security solution 385
  US financial assistance 333
  see also central Europe; eastern Europe; western Europe
L'Europe nouvelle 347, 406
European Coal and Steel Community (1951) 515
European Common Market 73
European Concert 513

Fabry, Jean 502
family dynasties 28
fascism 332
Faure, Paul 329
Fayolle, Marie Émile 212, 213, 281, 301, 310
federalism 320, 340, 341, 342, 400, 409, 410, 412
  European 499, 500, 506, 507, 510, 511, 515
Fédération française des associations pour la Société des nations (FFSDN) 372
Fédération nationale des anciens prisonniers de guerre 445
Fédération républicain 123
Fehrenbach, Constantin 350
Fénelon, François de Salignac de la Mothe 49
Ferry, Jules 28
Le Figaro 124, 470
finance commission 42, 92

finance ministry 42, 43, 350
  cuts to military spending 339
  Mouvement général des fonds 433
finances
  French post-war 327, 428, 432–4, 454
  German post-war 339, 435
  international committee of experts proposed 412
financial experts, committees of international (1924) 434, 447
First World War (1914–18)
  cultural history and security policy making 4, 9, 517
  effects 75, 77, 215, 514–22
  security policy during 6
Fisher, Sir Warren 43
Flanders 95, 139
Flandin, Pierre-Étienne 501
Fleuriau, Aimé de 471, 481, 482, 486, 491, 511
Foch, General (later Marshal) Ferdinand 40, 143, 148, 160, 191, 199, 201, 205, 227, 239, 342, 363
  annexation of the Saarland 279
  and Clemenceau 300, 310, 311, 516
  on Cologne evacuation 478
  critic of multilateralism 471, 521
  death (1929) 471
  deterrence strategy of eastern barrier 417
  draft memorandum on peace conditions 192
  Franco-Belgian military alliance 355
  geo-strategic conception 212–13
  on German character 281
  on German disarmament 282
  his stature 213
  on the League 266, 487
  marginalised from policy making 471, 493
  memoranda on the Rhine 278
  military conditions of armistice 195
  on military policy 339, 450
  note on neutralisation of the Rhine Left Bank (1919) 279
  on Poland 239, 366, 415
  policy towards Russia 237, 414
  on regional pacts 440
  on Rhine as natural barrier 279, 280, 299
  Rhineland policy 283, 287, 293, 298, 299–302, 337, 363, 409, 440, 487
  on Ruhr occupation 338, 361, 400, 402, 454
  studies of sanctions issue 361
  as supreme commander of Allied armies 189, 191–6
  on Versailles Treaty 312, 480, 516
Forcade, Olivier 60
force
  collective 6
  and guarantees 482, 498
  international 371, 520
  international law supported by collective 6, 68, 69, 78, 179, 265, 273, 446, 504, 520
  and justice 6, 68, 127, 181, 458, 461, 516
  military 45, 58, 59, 69, 185, 396
  over law 263
  role in international politics 474
foreign ministry (France) see Quai d'Orsay
foreign policy
  American 102, 104
  British 101, 104
  Cambon on 58
  Clemenceau's 164, 232
  evolution (1921) 357, 359
  of major powers 94, 95–104
  national traditions in 55
  opposition to (1922) 24
  organs 42
  parliamentary control over 19–24, 41–5
  predispositions shaping 24–36, 58, 59, 107–12
  radicalisation of French 394–404
  Russian 97–100, 103, 131
Fournier, Lieutenant Colonel Charles 416–17
'Fourteen Points' (Woodrow Wilson) 167, 175, 190–5, 209, 210, 217, 226
France
  anti-war sentiment in post-war 321, 429
  bilateral treaty with Britain proposed 384, 387, 470
  constitution (1875) 41
  culture de guerre 324
  and the Dawes Plan 436
  direct negotiations with Germany (1925) 493–4
  economic dependence 94, 95, 100, 102, 249, 259, 352, 434
  effective veto over *Anschluss* 243
  elections (1919) 323
  elections (1924) 407, 426, 446, 447
  empire 14, 244
  energy crisis (1920) 349
  financial crisis (1919–25) 327, 432–4, 454, 488, 490, 500
  German occupation 100
  German threat to 12, 82, 103, 119, 164, 173, 212, 219, 263, 348, 450, 521
  juridical internationalism 5, 6, 9, 14, 62, 63, 64, 65–7, 68, 74, 78
  League of Nations policy 262–75
  moral crisis in war effort (1917) 143, 144
  as Most Favoured Nation 250, 253
  national character 80, 334, 490
  national convention (1792–3) 52
  political crisis 151, 189, 516
  population levels 218
  relative decline in power post-war 317

Index

responses to German invasion 86
responsibility to preserve civilisation 81
strategic importance of Britain to 100–1, 197, 227, 320, 361, 384, 471, 476, 491, 499, 503, 511, 514
trusteeship of mandates 246
war losses 218, 324
see also Third French Republic
Franco-American affairs 166
Franco-Belgian agreement 393, 436, 451
Franco-Belgian Mission Interalliée de controle des usines et des mines (MICUM) 404
Franco-British Entente 33, 94, 95, 100, 101, 109, 117, 164, 189, 232, 246, 334, 336, 337, 342, 357, 359, 382, 383–90, 423, 438, 465
Franco-British pact (1922) 392–4, 422, 438–53, 459, 462, 473, 479, 480
rejected by British as it did not include Germany (1925) 474, 485–9
Franco-British summit, London (1921) 384
Franco-British–Belgian pact proposed 439, 475, 485–9
Franco-Czechoslovak 'Treaty of Alliance and Friendship' 417
Franco-German cooperation 7, 33, 70, 114, 235, 257, 275, 309, 311, 314, 320, 343, 522
economic 346, 347, 352, 355, 379, 399, 437, 454, 456, 506, 519
security 438, 469, 509, 519
Franco-Polish alliance 366–7, 415, 485, 497, 508, 512
Franco-Prussian War 201
Franco-Russian alliance (1895) 43, 50, 93, 94, 95, 97–100, 110, 145, 149
François I, alliance with Ottoman Empire 49
François-Albert, A. 449
François-Marsal, Frédéric 339, 350, 353
François-Poncet, André 501
Frankfurt 337, 409
Franklin-Bouillon, Henry 222, 238, 302, 447, 508
Franz Josef (emperor of Austria-Hungary) 148
Freemasonry 65, 74
French, as colonial language 245
French Communist Party *see* PCF
French Revolution 51, 53, 54, 107, 148
French security policy 1–2
ambiguity in 321
choice between force and economic integration 382
criticism of 312
during 1920s 319, 338–46

economic and financial preoccupations 428
internationalism 505
and the League of Nations 370–8, 446, 449
national solution 498
new European system 469
Poincaré's review 438
post-war dilemmas 323–56
post-war planning 85–132
revolution in 468
sources 15, 45–6
tension over British attitude to eastern Europe 473
Freycinet, Charles de 25, 29, 134
Fromageot, Henri 30, 179, 180, 184, 187, 336, 386, 422, 456, 460, 465, 466
on British support 489, 492
on Geneva Protocol 485
on German guarantee 483, 493
on international law 183, 264
and Laroche 476, 477, 478, 480

gages, rhetoric of 391, 397, 399, 407, 436
Gaiffier, Baron de 170
Galicia 97
Gallieni, Joseph 92
Gambetta, Léon 28, 54
Gamelin, Maurice 104
Gaul, myth of 52, 55
Gaulle, Charles de 54, 370
Geneva Protocol (1924) 14, 419, 422, 429, 431, 451, 458, 461, 462–8, 470, 482, 498, 513
aftermath 470–3, 481–5, 499, 504, 507
Britain declined to ratify (1925) 468, 475, 498
compulsory arbitration in 514
and guarantee treaties 491
opposition 429, 464, 516
'Optional Clause' 464
support for 488
Genoa Conference (1922) 394, 413, 414
Geoffray, Léon 111
Gérard, General Augustin 280, 301
Géraud, André ('Pertinax') 304, 310, 354, 465, 501
German, as language of education and administration 241
German Catholic confederation 169
German empire 215, 244
German West Africa 244
Germans, in Poland and Czechoslovakia 331
Germany
as aggressor 88, 94, 95–104, 281
arbitration treaties with Poland and Czechoslovakia 484, 486, 489, 490, 493
and Austria 217, 242, 243

542   Index

Germany (cont.)
  democratisation 127, 142, 154, 167, 170, 184, 188, 198, 209, 221, 233, 262, 263, 273, 281, 320, 332, 344, 371, 385, 405, 425, 515
  direct negotiations with (1925) 493–4
  dismemberment 340, 355, 391, 403, 410, 411, 520
  dual conceptions of 321, 372, 381, 405
  economic behaviour 117, 119, 121, 173, 381
  economic reconstruction 8, 348, 355
  effects of defeat 317
  elections (1919) 221
  enmeshing and constraining in a multilateral security system 5, 7, 78, 181, 235, 247, 249, 250, 261, 273, 275, 313, 321, 346, 358, 371, 384, 385, 389, 439, 463, 466, 468, 469, 473, 476, 499, 510–12, 515, 522
  financial controls on economy 378, 382
  financial settlement with 219, 248, 352
  Franco-Russian alliance against 50
  French strategic predominance over 2, 4, 51
  inclusion in new economic order 253, 318, 320
  inclusion in new security order 498, 509
  investment in France 71
  Kaiser's abdication 217
  membership of League mooted 263, 273, 275, 371, 386, 419, 448, 453, 461, 463, 483, 486, 494, 500
  military authority 96
  national character 80, 200, 281, 282, 283, 308, 502
  Nazi regime 469, 522
  need to come to terms with a reformed 311
  non-compliance with Versailles Treaty 330–2, 335, 376, 396, 476, 478
  offer of a Rhineland security pact (1925) 481–5
  outrage at territorial settlement 331
  participation in Locarno 504
  'passive resistance' 404, 407, 410, 424
  political culture 83
  population 94, 95, 287
  post-war limitation of power 115, 132, 142, 160, 184, 223, 248, 249, 260, 261
  pre-war commercial policy 116
  prevention of collusion with Russia 237, 241
  problem of power in Europe 5, 159, 170, 172, 198, 200
  reorganisation on federal basis 400, 409, 410, 412
  request for a ceasefire (October 1918) 192
  response to Ruhr occupation 402
  secret bilateral negotiations (1919) 257
  successes in 1914 93
  threat of rearmament 476, 487, 501, 508
  threat to France 12, 82, 94, 95, 103, 119, 164, 212, 219, 263, 348, 450, 521
  treating as an equal 440, 453, 463
  and Versailles Treaty 318, 327
  war indemnity to be imposed 105
  see also Reich; Weimar Republic
Gibson, Lora 474
Girardet, Raoul 28, 49
Giraudoux, Jean 32, 471, 519
Gout, Jean 179, 180, 182, 183, 186, 187, 271, 373, 420, 421, 422, 511
Grand Orient lodge 65, 74
Grand quartier général (GQG), 'Peace Conditions' (1916) 104–7
grands notables 20
Great Britain *see* Britain
Great War *see* First World War (1914–18)
Greece 97
Greffulhe, Comtesse Élisabeth, salon of 450
Grey–Cambon Letters (1914) 43
Grotius, Hugo 62, 186
Groupe parlementaire français de l'arbitrage international 64
Groupement universitaire français pour la Société des nations (GUSDN) 372, 419, 445
guarantees 340
  against aggression 439
  Anglo-American on the Rhine 276, 279, 333
  British military to France 382, 422, 478, 480, 492, 503
  on Cologne evacuation 479
  'contractual' 296
  demand for territorial from Germany 301
  'for execution' 451
  and force 482
  German 483
  international 451
  juridical rather than military 445
  legal and military 458
  material 193, 231
  'minimum' 376
  moral and material 231
  multilateral 383, 385
  mutual 273, 421–3, 494, 503, 511, 513
  need for 155, 191, 230, 238, 251, 267
  network of 500
  occupation as security 480
  'productive' 397, 398, 399, 403, 435
  on Rhineland pact 493
  supplementary 294, 297, 439, 459, 483
  see also gages rhetoric
La Guerre sociale 88

Index

Guesde, Jules 91, 92, 129
Guieu, Jean-Michel 126
Guillaumat, General Henri 478

'habitus' (Bourdieu) 16, 58, 162
Habsburgs 49, 52, 94, 96, 106, 139, 160, 161, 167, 169, 170, 172, 241, 242, 369
   collapse of 213, 224
   secret talks with 169
Hague Peace Conference (1899) 6, 35, 63, 65, 67, 127, 264
Hague Peace Conference (1907) 6, 35, 63, 65, 127, 264
Haguenin, François-Émile 257, 341, 343
Hankey, Sir Maurice 468
Hanotaux, Gabriel 50, 53, 99, 124, 179, 180, 184, 186, 224
   memoranda on 'grand peace' 277
   memorandum on new world order 210
   on the Rhine frontier 280, 410
Hanover 111
Harding, Warren 333
Hardinge, Baron Charles of Penhurst 363
Hauser, Henri 116, 120, 122, 173, 248–9, 260
   economic security programme (1918) 249–56
   reparations proposals 254
Hennessy, Jean 152, 370, 418
Henri IV 49
Herbette family 28
Herriot, Édouard 1, 6, 14, 21, 24, 124, 351, 390, 405–7, 413, 426, 428, 450, 478
   and Beneš 495
   and British accord 489
   cabinet 450
   career 431–2
   on Cologne evacuation 480, 482
   on disarmament 469
   on evacuation of the Ruhr 455
   fall of government (1925) 429, 490
   foreign policy 427, 429, 431, 432, 444, 447, 468, 473
   four 'barrages' (Cartel des gauches) 447
   on Geneva Protocol 475, 485, 486
   on German membership of the League 483, 487
   internationalist vision 431, 432, 441, 448, 515
   letter to Blum 448
   meeting with Chamberlain 481, 485
   meeting with MacDonald (1922) 451, 452, 465, 477
   multilateral security system 441–68
   peace motives 448
   purge of diplomats 470, 516
   on Rhineland proposals by Germany 482, 498

   support for League 427, 447, 476, 484
   and TMA 458
Herscher, Major Arnaud 159–60
Hervé, Gustave 76, 88
Hesse 341
High Seas Fleet (German) 215
Hindenburg, General Paul Ludwig von 96, 139, 488
historiography 2–5, 9, 23, 149, 157, 178, 197, 388, 427–9, 432, 468, 512, 516
Hoche, General Lazare 280
Hoesch, Leopold von 438
Hohenzollern Empire 106, 167, 184, 241
Holland 277
Holy Alliance (1818) 183, 385
L'Homme enchaîné 148, 165
Hoover, Herbert 252, 333
Horthy, Admiral Nicholas 368
House, Colonel Edward 103, 109, 267, 293, 295
Hughes, Charles 412
human rights 226
L'Humanité 88
Hungary 217, 242, 342, 365, 368
   Soviet Republic 217

idealism 2, 10, 197, 521
identities, and norms 12
ideology, of democratic peace 277, 289, 305, 307, 313
imperialism 33, 149, 209, 246, 372
   cultural 244
   new 51, 61–70
   'of the poor' 369
Independent Socialists 325
industry
   and Franco-German cooperation 500, 515
   French 7, 112, 132, 173, 219, 247, 260, 369, 399
   German 7, 94, 95, 287, 331, 352, 399
   interdependence in western Europe 70, 72, 380
   multilateral collaboration 456
   Russian 141
   see also metallurgical industry
inflation 396, 407, 433, 500
Information ouvrière et sociale 354
Inspection des finances 43
Institut de droit international 64
institutions
   international 3, 61, 78, 137, 178–89
   multilateral 33
   as social actors 16
inter-Allied conference (1917), on war aims 141, 170

inter-Allied conference (1919), of civil society associations for a league of nations 222, 223
Inter-Allied Control Commission in Germany 282, 450, 452, 476
Inter-Allied Maritime Transport Commission 252
Inter-Allied Military Control Commission (IMCC) 478, 480, 494
Inter-Allied Rhineland High Commission 340
inter-ministerial commission (1917) 65, 156, 178
inter-ministerial committee on the Rhine (1922) 363, 396, 399
inter-ministerial committee on the Ruhr (1923) 408
Inter-Parliamentary Union for Arbitration 63
interdependence
  commercial and cultural 61
  economic 70–4, 120
  and social solidarity 66
  theories of 61
interests
  'community of' 345
  moral and material 245
  national 56, 159
  national within an international institution 373
  power relationships determine 48, 49, 78
  of states 48–52, 56, 507
international council, proposed 179, 186, 187
International Court of Justice proposed 268, 270
International Labour Bureau 448
international law 5, 6, 34, 47, 156, 429, 516
  and arbitration 62, 78, 460
  codification and laws of war 63
  and collective force 6, 68, 69, 78, 265, 521
  compared with domestic law 57
  and 'contractual' guarantees 296
  defined (Renault) 57
  evolution of 57, 372
  League based on 179, 181, 269, 431, 499
  and Locarno Accords 507
  and multilateral cooperation 489, 514, 520
  'organised' 182
  peace through 182, 187, 320
  post-war rule of 150, 151, 209, 274
  and sanctions 262
  and sovereignty 271, 272, 273, 274
  teaching of 29
International Office for Public Hygiene 61
International Peace Bureau 74
international politics 10
  distribution of military and economic power 11
  establishment of a legal base for 187
  evolution of theory 68
  militarisation of European 45
  new spirit in European 506, 509
  pessimism in 502
  post-war attitudes 321
  role of war in 60
  sovereignty and anarchy problem 70, 264
  transformation of 33, 142, 196, 233, 304, 312, 449, 488
international relations
  changed character 503
  compulsory arbitration in 505
  'cultural turn' 15
  historiography 2–5
  norms in 207
  pessimistic view 47, 55, 59
  post-war 14, 190, 311, 317, 331, 335, 357
  and rights of individuals 263
  solidarité-inspired 263
  theory 10, 520
  Wilsonianism and 155, 216
  world opinion as arbiter in 216
international society, development of 63, 207
International Steel Entente (1926) 515
International Telegraphic Union 61
international theory
  constructivist 12, 521
  realist 10, 11, 12, 181, 275, 276, 314, 319, 520
International Tribunal at The Hague 182, 186, 448
International Union of Customs and Tariffs 61
International Union of League of Nations Associations 419
International Union for Weights and Measurements 61
internationalism 1, 2, 11, 162, 198, 203, 514–22
  comparison of French, British and American 69, 142
  the concept 2, 6
  economic 70–4
  French movement 370–8, 390, 419, 425, 428, 431, 445–7, 488, 500, 512, 514, 516
  juridical 1, 5, 6, 22, 30, 45, 63, 64, 65–7, 68, 74, 75, 78, 115, 127, 129, 133, 145, 163, 179, 182, 187, 222, 235, 271, 304, 372, 418, 441, 456, 499, 505, 509, 514, 516
  League-based 75, 103, 370–8
  liberal 68, 69, 75, 83, 142, 222
  and mutualisation 351
  or nationalism 321
  and patriotism 406, 443
  role of war in development of 84, 150–7, 319, 330

Index

socialist 75, 83, 85, 103, 129, 133
and technological change 61–70
intru 32, 33
investment, cross-border 71, 72, 73
iron ore 70, 71, 95, 112, 174, 248, 249, 258, 306, 380, 395, 404, 500, 515
iron and steel cartel proposal 261
Isaac, August 353
Italy 101, 106, 119, 135, 189, 226, 237, 242, 255, 257, 317, 494, 501
  border disputes 213
  Fascist Party 332
  nationalism and fascism 332
  unification 332

Japan 246, 257
Jarousse de Sillac, Joseph Maximilien 34, 180
Jaurès, Jean 74, 76, 88
  assassination 87
Jeanneney, Jean-Nöel 432
Jeannesson, Stanislas 410, 426
Joffre, Marshal Joseph 44, 91, 92, 94, 95, 104, 193
Joll, James 51, 207
Jordan, Nicole 428, 432
Jouhaux, Léon 87, 304, 330
Journal des Débats 124, 194
Jouvenel, Bertrand de 54, 445
Jouvenel, Henry de 74, 418, 422, 445, 461, 490
JP Morgan 434
July Crisis 73, 88
juriconsulte (legal counsellor) 30, 34, 179
jurisprudence, French 29
jusqu'au boutisme 115, 127, 145, 162
Jusserand, Jules 28, 110, 190, 341, 465, 470
justice
  and the rule of law 81, 86–91, 126, 132
  and use of force 6, 68, 181, 264, 314, 458, 461, 516

Kapp Putsch 337
Karl I (emperor of Austria-Hungary) 148
Kedward, Rod 76, 321
Keiger, John 77
Kerr, Philip Henry (Marquess of Lothian) 290, 291, 293, 516
Keynes, John Maynard 197, 350, 378
Klotz, Louis-Lucien 193, 194, 204, 206, 256, 266, 328
'Kreuznach Programme' (1917) 139
Krupp von Bohlen und Halbach, Gustav 71, 331
Kun, Béla 217

labour, movement across Europe 70
Lacroix, Victor de 411

Lancken, Baron Oskar von der 161
language
  colonial 245
  as guide to nationality 241
  promotion of French 34
Lansing, Robert 103
Larnaude, Ferdinand 235, 262, 268, 269, 270, 271, 274
Laroche, Jules 32, 210, 224, 259, 260, 342, 369, 388, 450, 465, 470
  on Allies in Russia 365
  Cologne policy 478
  defence of Geneva Protocol 465, 466, 486, 496
  and Franco-British security pact 386, 389, 473, 476, 478, 489, 491, 493
  on Franco-German relations 424, 483
  on League as providing guarantees 511
  memo on sanctions 360
  memo on security problem 438–40
  note on supplementary permanent guarantees to British 459
  Plan for deterrence and multilateralism 453
  on Poland 367–9, 485
  Rhineland policy 278, 283, 411, 477, 480, 485
  on TMA 457, 458
Lasteyrie, Charles de 397, 398, 402, 403, 411, 433
Laurent, Charles 348, 391, 410, 414
Laval, Pierre 21
Lavisse, Ernest 123, 124, 125, 156, 229
law
  as key to international peace 263
  role in French political history 20–2, 29, 64, 263
  see also international law; rule of law
'law of nations' 29, 86
Le Béguec, Gilles 20
Le Foyer, Lucien 74, 222
Le Rond, General Auguste 240, 279
Le Trocquer, Yves 401, 402
League Assembly 376
  Fifth (1924) 429, 458, 460, 477
  First 374
  Resolution XIV 422
League Council 65, 367, 462
  arms inspection 477
  commercial regime 261, 264, 308
  sanctions 459, 474, 507
League Covenant 216, 265, 268, 271, 274, 296, 355, 371, 373, 374, 389, 504, 514
  Article 10 457, 458, 484, 497
  Article 16 484, 494, 497
  Article 19 463, 512

League Covenant (cont.)
  French right to intervene in eastern Europe 493
  Hurst–Miller draft 268
  revisions 371
League of Nations 1, 13, 14, 65, 68, 70, 418, 469
  American view 175, 265, 333
  and balance of power 286, 289
  British view 264
  campaign to reform 446
  creation of 230
  Economic proposed 253
  and economic security 176, 249, 250, 253
  French policy towards 196, 220–4, 262–75, 370–8, 418–26, 429, 468, 520
  German membership 263, 273, 275, 371, 386, 388, 419, 448, 453, 461, 463, 483, 486, 494, 500
  historiography of 516
  idea mooted 75, 103, 134, 154, 156, 157, 203, 209, 320, 323
  planning for 163, 178–89
  popular support for 321, 429, 441, 443, 445–7, 517
  and a regional security system 387
  and reparations policy 254
  right of arms inspection 476, 494
  right to inspect German compliance 295
  role in multilateral strategy 486, 498, 513, 515
  as a source of security 477, 499, 511
  and sovereignty issue 188
  as transformer of international politics 304, 406, 431, 448, 521
  Wilson on 130, 142, 156, 216
League of Nations Commission 65, 235, 262, 268, 272, 295
League Secretariat, Disarmament Section 374
Lebanon 246, 247
Lebrun, Albert 219
Lefèvre, André 343, 376
left, in France 24, 79, 88–90, 128, 201, 221, 304, 330, 413, 444
  see also socialism
legal counsellors 30, 34, 179
legal experts, office of 30
legal profession 20–2
Léger, Alexis 32, 465, 471, 510, 511
legislature 21
Lenin, Vladimir 129, 332
Levant 244
Leygues, Georges 24, 238, 318, 342, 358, 376
liberalism 3, 68
  British 459
  economic 114, 121, 216
Liège 139

Ligue des droits de l'homme (LDH) 74, 127, 130, 431
Ligue des femmes contre la guerre 444
Ligue des mères et éducatrices pour la paix 445
Ligue des patriotes 87, 124
Ligue française 221
Lithuania 139, 510
'Little Entente' 369, 416, 495
Lloyd George, David 101, 138, 143, 225, 229, 257, 265, 290, 516
  and Anglo-American guarantee 333
  draft treaty of guarantee 389
  'European consortium' on Russia 414
  fall of 394
  and Foch 213, 300
  meeting with Clemenceau (1918) 195, 227, 246
  meetings with Briand (1921) 360, 362, 382, 387
  and Millerand 335, 336, 345
  peace strategy 215, 230, 337
  and Poincaré 392
  on the Polish settlement 242
  on reparations 363, 382
  Rhineland policy 276, 291, 293, 294, 295, 313
  and the Saarland 295
  speech on war aims (1918) 167
  style 215
  view of French post-war policy 334, 385, 388, 393, 394
  on the Wiesbaden Accords 381
loans, system of international 392, 397, 401, 403, 405, 411, 454
Locarno Accords (1925) 4, 7, 14, 78, 389, 428, 429, 468, 469, 513
  compulsory arbitration in 514
  criticisms of 495–7, 501, 502, 522
  different national attitudes to 498
  economic aspects 501
  effects on eastern Europe 495, 506, 507
  evolution 470, 482, 492, 493, 504
  importance of German participation 504
  juridical internationalist concepts in 512
  Massigli's memo 497–9
  as a process 469, 494, 499, 506
  ratification 510
  seven treaties 494
  support for 499, 500, 508, 510
London, Treaty of (1915) 101, 108, 213, 226
London Economic Conference (1924) 428, 431, 452, 453–7, 465
London Franco-British Summit (1921) 384
London Schedule of Payments (1921) 363, 378–82, 396, 411, 435
London settlement (1924) 4

Index

Longuet, Jean 89, 128, 151, 302
Loriot, Fernand 330
Lorraine, iron ore 51, 71, 260, 261, 396, 437
Loucheur, Louis 204, 256, 259, 261, 293, 349, 350, 461, 515
  career 205
  for financial controls on German economy 382, 515
  'Loucheur Plan' 363, 378, 379, 519
  and Rathenau 380, 381
Louis XIV 53, 108, 304
Louis XVI 50
Ludendorff, General Erich 96, 139
Luther, Hans 481
Luxembourg 71, 104, 105, 137, 139, 213, 253, 260, 261, 277, 310
  annexation of the Duchy of 101, 107, 109
Lyautey, General Louis-Hubert 92, 93

McAdoo, William 103
MacDonald, Ramsay 436, 451, 461
  Chequers summit with Herriot 452, 465, 477
  on international security 461
  London Conference (1924) 454
  Paris meeting (1924) 453
McDougall, Walter 427, 428
Madariaga, Salvador de 374, 375
Maginot, André 401, 402, 424
Maginot Line 512
Maison de la presse 34, 223
Malvy, Louis 89, 145
mandates 246
Mangin, General Charles 280, 301, 310, 409, 411, 458, 466
Manneville, Henri de 111
Margaine, Alfred 508
Margerie, Pierre de 28, 29, 107, 109, 110, 131, 169–71, 176, 179, 180, 410, 481
Marienwerder (region) 242
Marin, Louis 123, 502, 503
markets 113, 174, 352
  labour 220
Marne, Battle of the 81, 94, 95
Marx, Karl 89
Marx, Wilhelm 436
Masaryk, Tomas 171, 214
Mascuraud, Alfred 255
Masonic Congress of France 127
Massigli, René 258, 389, 450, 465, 478, 483, 511
  career 471
  on Franco-British cooperation 475
  on Geneva Protocol 486, 492
  juridical internationalism 505
  on Locarno Accords 497–9
  on Rhineland occupation 480, 485

Le Matin 124, 300, 419
Matter, Paul 179, 180, 271
Maurras, Charles 89, 124, 303
Max of Baden, Prince 190
Mayéras, Barthélémy 302
Mediterranean 95, 98, 511
Méline, Jules 123, 301
Mesopotamia 215, 245
metallurgy industry 112–15, 260, 401, 500
Mezes, 293
Michaelis, Georg 139
Middle East 244, 245, 247, 275
Milhaud, Albert 508
Milhaud, Edgard 75, 127
militarism
  French 80, 376, 378, 383, 384, 393
  Prussian 82, 94, 210, 281
  suspicion of 76, 443
military
  cuts to spending 339
  French presence in eastern Europe 364
  see also army
military academies 37, 54, 59
military conflict 5, 43
  post-1918 324–30
military conventions, and regional security pacts 438–53, 463, 502
military elites 19, 36–41
  core practices and beliefs 34, 58, 518
  Herriot and Briand and 471
  marginalisation 471, 493, 516
  opposition to Geneva Protocol 516
  on peacemaking 212
  post-war 45, 143
  and Rhineland policy 299–302, 409
  and Ruhr occupation 338–41
  security policy 104–7, 439, 440
  social and religious backgrounds 37, 38
  view of the League 266
military parades 76
military planning
  joint 48
  mobilisation plans 45, 89
  parliamentary control over 41–5
military service 23, 91, 339, 343, 442, 448, 472
Miliukov, Pavel 141
Mill, John Stuart 61
Millerand, Alexandre 13, 21, 24, 77, 91, 92, 165, 320, 425
  Allied solidarity 337
  and Briand 383, 389
  career 335–8
  and disarmament 420
  enforcement policy 336, 342, 345, 476
  on federalism 342

Millerand, Alexandre (cont.)
  on Franco-German economic cooperation 344, 349, 355, 519
  on Hungary 368
  and the League 419
  on Poland 366, 367
  as president (1921–4) 42, 318, 327, 358
  'realisation' policy 327, 331, 334, 345
  on reparations 349, 350, 354, 378
  resignation (1924) 449
  Ruhr policy 338–41, 401, 402
  on Russia 414
  speech at Évreux (1923) 449
  on Trianon Treaty 369
Millet, Philippe 406
mines, seizure of Prussian 398
ministers, French government 20, 43, 93
Mistler, Jean 32
Mitteleuropa 96, 116, 118, 122, 169, 248, 249, 364
Mittelhauser, General Eugène 416, 417
Moltke, Helmuth Johann Ludwig von 154
monarchy, French 50, 53
Monnet, Jean 178, 252, 291, 515
Montenegro 96, 101, 102
Montesquieu, Charles-Louis de Secondat 50, 52
Monzie, Anatole de 21
Morand, Paul 32, 33, 133, 142, 519
Mordacq, General Jean Jules Henri 195, 204
Morel, Jean 112
Morgan, J. P. 397
Morocco 472
Mosul 245, 246
Moutet, Marius 21, 148, 149
multilateralism 388, 389, 393, 420, 421, 438
  based on inter-Allied cooperation 364, 369, 383, 384, 385, 386
  Briandist 357–90, 465, 467, 519
  criticisms of 424, 466
  and deterrence 453, 467, 482
  and European stability 385
  in foreign ministry 510
  in French policy 498
  Herriot and the Radical Party 441–57
  and international law 489, 514
  League of Nations role in 486
  as restraint on German revisionism 466, 470
  to embed British military commitment 473, 519
Mun, Albert de 39, 87
munitions industry 92, 144, 205
Mussolini, Benito 332
mutual assistance
  against states guilty of aggression 459
  bilateral 438–53
  and binding arbitration 460, 469, 498, 509, 513
  European 473–81, 511
  multilateral 458, 514
  the principle of 429, 430, 438, 451
  see also solidarité; Treaty of Mutual Assistance (TMA)
mutual assistance pacts 78, 119, 366, 421, 422, 423, 429
  defensive 460
  Draft Treaty (1923) 423
  operation dependent on League Council vote 495, 502
  regional 388, 421, 458
  western Europe 486
mutual commercial preference 118
Mutual Guarantee, Treaty of (1925) 494, 503, 511, 513
mutuality 188, 273, 351, 509, 520

Napoleon Bonaparte 280, 304
Napoléon III 53
Napoleonic Wars 51, 53, 62, 385
Narkomindel (Commissariat of Foreign Affairs) 215, 333
National Convention (1792) 123
national security
  coordination of policy 43
  issues 23
  the principle of 43
national unity *see* Union sacrée
nationalism 73, 76, 86, 174, 372
  anti-German economic 174
  conservative 23
  eastern Europe 171
  French 233, 324, 325
  or internationalism 321
  and Italian fascism 332
  and national identity 208, 241
  'normative' 76
Nationalist Republicans 325
'natural frontiers', ideology of 49, 52–4, 55, 105, 106, 123–6, 132, 212, 280, 303
navy
  American 306
  British 100, 306
  French 36, 43, 237, 328, 383, 415
  German 101, 215, 282
Nazism 469, 522
Near East 93
negotiation 518
Neilson, Keith 3
New Zealand 246
Nice 52
Nicholas II, Tsar 108, 131, 146
  abdication 140
Niessel, General Henri 339

Index

Nivelle, General Robert Georges, offensives 143, 145
Nobel Peace Prize 64, 65
Nollet, General Marie Édouard 450, 451, 454, 472
Norman, Montagu 454
Normandy, exile of Belgian government in 101
norms 137, 200, 207–13, 233, 389, 427, 513, 520
  changed post-1918 45, 207–13, 233, 389, 393, 489, 518, 521
  defining 207, 208
  and identities 12
  internalisation of 207
  legitimacy of 175, 211
  new international 203, 499, 520, 521
  positivist 62
  regulative, constitutive or both 207
  on self-determination 283–6, 307
  'transformative' 209
North Atlantic Alliance (1947) 305
North Atlantic security community 277, 285, 290, 294, 305, 308, 311, 314
Noske, Gustav 331

Odessa 237
L'Oeuvre 124, 370, 449
Ogier, Émile 352
oil 238, 243, 245, 369
ordres du jour 154
Orlando, Vittorio Emanuele 230
Ottoman Empire 49, 97, 98, 130, 167, 244–6, 334
  Arab territories 244, 245
  collapse 224
  ethnic conflict 324
  settlement 246
  see also Turkey

pacifism 69, 85, 150, 429, 443
  anti-war sentiment in post-war France 321, 429
  British 371
  'integral' 68
  and internationalism 443
  'Jacobin' 69
  mocked 446
  revolutionary 129, 130, 138
  see also peace activism
'Pact of London' (1916) 97
Painlevé, Paul 74, 159, 160, 162, 169, 406, 429, 445, 450
  on army reform 472
  as premier 82, 145, 161, 490
La Paix par le droit 64, 128
Palatinate 131, 194, 301, 434

Paléologue, Maurice 29, 108, 131, 147, 148, 172, 228, 342
  foreign policy 341, 368, 369
  Paléologue–Pokrovsky letters (1917) 147, 152
Palestine 215, 245, 246
Paris
  siege of 163
  strikes (1917) 144
  war effort support 89
Paris Bar 20, 21
Paris Commune 39, 87, 163, 201
Paris Peace Conference (1919) 7, 10, 65, 203–6, 314, 324, 350, 505, 514, 516
  and Anglo-American guarantees 291
  eastern settlement 217, 235–43
  economic settlement 248–9
  planning for 210, 225–9
  plenary session (1919) 166, 273
  relations in 213–18, 224
  reparations debate 256
Parliament (French)
  authority rolled back 165
  control over foreign and defence policy 19–24, 39, 41–5
  crisis over war aims (1917) 141, 517
  debates 42, 83, 488
  debates on national security (1921–2) 390
  elections (1924) 42
  internationalist ideas in 510
  opposition 91
  post-war 325
  Rhineland policy 300, 301, 302
  and the Ruhr occupation (1923) 405–7
  secret sessions 149, 151–6, 162, 204
  support for Foch 301
  support for Locarno Accords 510
  twelfth legislature (1920–4) 325
  and the Union sacrée 91
  and Versailles Treaty 342
  war aims bloc (1915) 124, 300
Parmentier, Jean 433
Parti coloniale 243
Pascal, Blaise 68, 264, 371, 458, 461, 474, 516
Passy, Frédéric 63, 64, 65, 68
patriotism 22, 85, 126, 324, 325, 405–7
  anti- 76, 472
  and internationalism 406, 443
patronage 28
Paul-Boncour, Joseph 21, 457, 458, 461, 462, 466, 499, 501
  on enforcement 446
  on Locarno 467, 507–8, 512
PCF (French Communist Party) 330, 413, 510
peace 1, 59, 181, 462

550   Index

peace (cont.)
  democratic 103, 104, 154, 277, 285
  and Europe-wide security 485, 505
  French and British conflicting strategies of 334
  and international law 57, 78, 263, 509
  just 151
  moral or juridical 516
  political contexts for 203–34
  'Rhenish' 197
  and security (1918–19) 197, 235–75
  and social transformation expectations 220
  support for a compromise 133, 144, 161, 162
  through arbitration 62–5
  through international law 182, 187, 320
  transnational movements 9, 516
peace activism 6, 62, 64
  see also pacifism
peace conditions
  Foch's draft memorandum (1918) 192
  and self-determination 208
'Peace Conditions' (GQG)(1916) 104–7
peace programme (1919) 51, 197–201, 277, 305–15
peace settlement (1871) 163
'peace through law' 6, 62, 64, 74–8, 80, 126, 320, 373, 499, 505, 511, 512, 517
'peace treaty commission' 112–15, 302, 305
Péguy, Charles 81, 90
Pellé, General Maurice 239, 370
Peretti de la Rocca, Emmanuel 244, 367, 369, 379, 383, 393, 411, 415, 422, 450, 451, 453, 465, 470, 478
  against inclusion of Germany 441
  on deterrence and multilateralism 453
  on Rhineland policy 438
Permanent Advisory Commission on Military, Naval and Air Questions (PAC) 374, 375, 376
Permanent Court of International Justice (1919) 455, 464
Permanent International Court of Arbitration (1899) 63, 67, 187, 264, 460
'Pertinax' (André Géraud) 304, 310, 354, 465, 501
Pétain, General Philippe 40, 143, 190, 281, 284, 338, 339, 367, 408, 439, 467, 471, 472, 493
  'Army Directive No. 1' 144
Petit, Captain René 185, 186
Petrograd Soviet of workers' and soldiers' deputies 140
  'Army Order No. 1' 140
  'Petrograd Formula' 141, 148, 149
Pfister, Christian 125

Phipps, Eric 450
Pichon, Stephen 33, 35, 99, 165, 166, 170, 171, 172, 193, 194, 195, 204, 206, 228, 232, 251, 293
Pila, Fernand 116, 120–2, 174, 176, 179, 180, 185, 251, 253
  on national and collective economic measures 175
Pillet, Antoine 150
Piłsudski, Jozef 214, 365, 367
Pinot, Robert 112–15
Piou, Jacques 303
Pleven, René 445
Poincaré, Raymond 7, 13, 21, 29, 33, 87, 92, 124, 128, 145, 165, 199, 273, 308, 318, 320, 341, 358, 359, 368, 421, 428
  on the armistice 104, 190
  on 'casino politics' 336
  compared with Briand 392–4, 405
  confrontational style 424, 429, 431, 441, 444, 448, 465
  and the Dawes Plan 434, 436
  on disarmament 420, 421, 424
  end of government (1924) 24
  as foreign minister (1922) 391, 415, 424
  on Franco-British pact (1922) 393, 469
  on Franco-Russian alliance 50, 94, 95, 148
  on German disintegration 411, 520
  lack of fiscal policy 433, 434
  letters with Beneš 417
  and Lloyd George 392
  message to Parliament (August 1914) 86
  note to Ribot (1917) 157
  on Poland 415
  policy towards League of Nations 418–26, 446, 447
  as president (1912–19) 42, 77, 92, 123, 131, 164, 206, 223, 258, 300, 327
  on proposed German pact 487
  on reparations 350, 351, 354, 395–404, 412
  resigned (1919) 350
  on Rhineland policy 287, 298, 301, 313, 322, 408, 410, 411, 476, 481
  Ruhr occupation (1922/1923) 402, 404, 423, 426, 434, 444, 455, 465
  security policy review 438
  speech at Verdun (1920) 323
  and the Union sacrée 405
  war aims 82, 109, 126, 134
Pokrovsky, Nikolai, letters with Paléologue (1917) 147, 152
Poland 50, 96, 97, 98, 106, 111, 130, 237, 241, 369
  alliance with France 366–7, 415, 481, 507
  borders of 213, 214, 483, 484, 496, 508
  British refusal to commit to 473
  Corridor 415

Index

and Czechoslovakia 365
  effect of Locarno Accords 496–7
  First Partition (1772) 239
  French accords 494
  German arbitration treaty with 484, 486, 489, 490, 493, 494
  Germans living in 194, 331
  policy on 136, 139, 141, 146, 147, 151, 160, 169–71, 275, 366–8, 369, 370, 381
  population 416
  possibility of German–Bolshevik action against 376
  reconstituting 167, 169–71, 239–40, 241, 242, 260
  relations with Czechoslovakia 240, 415, 418
  and Soviet Union 324
  support for Geneva Protocol 462
  as vanguard of the west 170, 172
policy, role of culture in explaining 11
policy elites 19–46, 54–60, 86, 147, 162, 169, 233, 260, 277, 318, 320, 355, 358, 382, 422
  British 3
  French 2, 19–24, 25, 45, 54–60, 78, 87, 94, 95–104, 205
  German 217
  mixture of traditional and internationalist currents 497–510
  social networks 19–24
policy making
  civil associations and 229
  and cultural history 54–60, 517
  and economic planning 247–62
  foreign and security 41–6
  hybrid 78
  identities and norms as sources of 12
  and internationalism 517
  norms and 208
  for post-war settlement 190–5
  practical logic in 9, 16, 60, 132, 162, 355, 514, 518
  pre-1914 sources 8
  role of ideas in 15, 58
  social dynamics of 19–46
  structural constraints on 15, 200
Polish National Committee 214
political elites 19–24, 137
  internationalism among 157–62, 222, 330, 372
  revolutionary unrest and 328
political science, education 26
Pomerania 367
Pompidou, Georges 446
Pont-à-Mousson 114
Posen 97, 242
positive law tradition 29
positivism 29, 62, 64, 164

Posnania 287
post-war order 81, 84, 94, 95, 127, 150, 203
  British vision 215
  democracy in 199, 307
  economic security planning 172–8
  French draft memoranda on 277–83
  peace planning 203–6
  Wilsonianism 142, 216
power
  pursuit of 5, 48–52
  relational 48–52
  role in shaping ideas 12, 135, 520
  see also balance of power
power politics 197, 203, 277, 319, 392, 413–18, 424, 517, 521
'practical logic' (Bourdieu) 9, 16, 60, 132, 162, 355, 514, 518
  new in French policy 470, 489, 497–510, 511
'practice theory' (Bourdieu) 9, 16
Prague, French military mission 239
president of the Republic 41
press 33, 34, 113, 114, 124
  British 391
  on Cartel compared with Bloc national 449
  censorship 123
  European 482
  and multilateral security system 387
  nationalist 303
  opposition to Locarno 501
  on peace and security 223
  and reparations debt reduction 350
  support for Foch 301
profit, pursuit of 70–4
Progrès civique 449
Prost, Antoine 443
protectorates 246
Protestantism 169
Protocol for the Pacific Settlement of International Disputes *see* Geneva Protocol
Proudhon, Pierre Joseph 66
Proust, Marcel 32
Prudhommeaux, Jules 222, 488
Prussia 39, 53, 105, 108, 123–6, 130, 147, 161, 167, 253
  corridor through east 240, 242
  eastern 97
  militarism 82, 94, 210, 281
  and the Rhine 303
  and the Saar basin 278
public opinion 33, 34, 85, 123, 363
  British on military alliance 385, 394
  German on defeat 330
  on League of Nations 517
  on peace 203, 223
  power in international relations 216
  on reparations 195, 221, 255, 257, 351

552   Index

public opinion (cont.)
    on the Rhineland 283, 302
    support for League 429
    and treaty enforcement 321

Quai d'Orsay (ministry of foreign affairs)
        19–36, 42, 45, 46, 85, 92, 128, 166, 168,
        258, 355, 359, 438, 449
    and arbitration 460
    budget 42
    and commission interministérielle 179
    and continental security system 418
    and the eastern settlement 235, 238, 426
    elitism 25, 28
    Entente lobby 364
    and European balance of power 277
    generational differences 519
    and Geneva Protocol 464
    on Germany's Rhineland proposal 482
    ideological divide 367–9, 440
    and the League 419
    legal department 336
    and Locarno Accords 510–12
    peace planning 224–30
    on Poland 367–9
    policy recommendations 107–12, 342
    post-war planning 92, 116, 117, 132, 142,
        169–71, 223, 253, 320
    'Preliminary note on the reorganisation of
        Germany' (1917) 160
    purge by Herriot 470–3
    reforms 30–6
    republicanisation programme 25
    on Russia 148
    selection procedures 26, 27, 29–35, 57
    Sous-direction d'Afrique 244
    Turkish policy 334
Le Quotidien 370, 449

Radical Party Congress (1923) 445
Radical Socialist Party (French) 23, 24, 65,
        74, 75, 91, 124, 145, 222, 231, 301, 302,
        325, 447
    alliance with Socialists 442
    commitment to multilateralism 441–57
    in disarray post-war 325, 326
    Herriot in 432, 441–57
    internationalists 359, 445, 456
    juridical internationalism 441
    on military service 442
    patriotic 405–7
    reject confrontational politics 390
    revolution in security policy 431
    and the Ruhr occupation 406, 408
    and Russia 413
    support for League 441
    see also Cartel des gauches

railways 72, 73, 160
Rambouillet meeting (1922) 402
Rapallo Treaty (1922) 332, 394, 414
Rathenau, Walther 331, 343, 380, 381
raw materials
    access to 94, 95, 118, 149, 248,
        250, 251
    control of price 174–8, 248
    post-war sharing 173, 176, 190, 380
    Russian 168
realism 10, 11, 12, 181, 276, 314, 319, 520
    'objective laws' in 11
    structural or neo-classical 11, 520
realpolitik 198
regional defensive accords 421, 451, 512
regional security pacts 439, 441, 458,
        463, 499
Reibel, Charles 402
Reich
    refusal to accept defeat 330
    representations of the 283
Reichstag
    declaration (1915) 96
    federalism in 283
    increase in German army 24
    policy 139
religion 38, 40, 169
Renan, Ernst 241
Renaudel, Pierre 128, 129, 149, 151, 155,
        329, 508
Renault, Louis 30, 57, 65, 179, 180
Renouvin, Pierre 149
reparations 8, 119, 128, 153, 158, 247, 248,
        249, 263, 309
    as bargaining leverage 256, 257
    commercialising 350, 397, 403
    and community of interests policy 345
    Dawes Plan on 435–7, 449
    default 294, 296, 335, 362
    enforcement of 320, 327, 378
    final bill 363, 378, 395, 435
    and international loans 392, 397, 401, 403,
        405, 447
    internationalisation and mutualisation 351,
        498, 515
    in kind (Seydoux Plan) 347, 351–6
    London Schedule of Payments (1921) 363,
        378–82, 396, 411, 435
    moratorium request 382, 385, 388, 394,
        396, 403, 406
    policy 192, 193, 194, 215, 230, 254–7, 295,
        313, 360, 378
    public opinion on 195, 221, 222, 428
    and Ruhr occupation 391, 401, 455
    and the Saar coalfield 288
    and war debts 255, 328, 349, 392, 395–404,
        411, 433, 436

Reparations Commission 257, 350, 381, 397, 437, 452, 456
representative government 216
Républicains de gauche 448
'republican defence' movement 23, 75
Republican Socialists 406, 448
republicanism 23, 31, 83, 86, 432
république des avocats 64
république des camarades 22, 128
La République française 304
Réquin, Lieutenant Colonel Édouard 284, 419, 420, 421, 461, 464
  career 374
  disarmament and security policy 374, 377, 420
  on regional mutual assistance 421, 422, 423
revolution 324
  fear of 39, 79, 148, 159, 191, 198, 326, 328
revolutionary politics 22, 222, 330
Revue d'économie politique 347
Revue des deux mondes 124, 354
Revue générale de la droit international 64
Reynaud, Paul 21
'Rhenish peace' movement 123, 283–6, 298–305
Rheno-Westphalian state 391, 400, 402
Rhine, Left Bank 52, 105, 106, 109, 113, 123, 125, 129, 130, 132, 134, 136, 146, 152, 153, 160, 192
  customs barrier 341, 360, 362, 363, 379, 398, 407
  grouped with Ruhr as a single economic space 399
  as natural frontier 52, 56, 104, 105, 123, 212, 279, 280, 286, 299, 303
  as a strategic frontier 276, 277, 279, 280, 285, 286, 303, 340
Rhineland
  Anglo-American guarantees on 238, 239, 267, 272, 276, 430
  annexation of 107, 111
  as a buffer state 158, 167, 197, 221, 276, 284, 285, 287, 289, 297, 299–302, 322, 395, 397, 404, 411, 424
  character of Rhenish population 280, 284, 309
  coup attempts (1919) 301
  demilitarisation 278, 319, 388, 408, 476, 481, 486, 494, 498, 503
  evacuation 452
  German offer of security pact (1925) 481–5, 491, 493, 498, 502, 512
  gradualist solution 278, 283, 293, 295, 297, 400, 407
  independence call 221, 224, 233, 279, 313, 318, 320, 397
  liberation of industrial 94, 95, 109, 123
  myth of solidarity 53, 107
  policy discussions on 133, 134, 136, 141, 150, 166, 190, 198, 201, 287, 314, 396–404
  post-war occupation 128, 158, 181, 192, 195, 231, 257, 279, 287–90, 294, 297, 309, 320, 409, 455, 469
  right to reoccupy in event of German default on reparations 294, 296, 376, 498
  role in conditions of security 478
  separatism 284, 301, 309, 310, 340, 361, 386, 410, 411
  settlement 276–315
Rhineland Guarantee Pact 494
Rhineland High Commission 362, 478
Ribot, Alexandre 68, 91, 146, 161, 165, 166, 175, 184
  on CISDN 517
  on peace conditions 204
  premier (1917) 82, 145, 149, 150, 151, 153–7, 178, 206, 209
Richelieu, Armand-Jean du Plessis, Cardinal de 49, 50, 52, 303, 411
Riga, Treaty of (1920) 365
right, nationalist 24, 39, 76, 90–1, 124, 148, 221, 335
Robespierre, Maximilien de 68
Rohan, Henri de 49
Romania 97, 101, 102, 104, 105, 170, 171, 214, 237, 238, 239, 241, 242, 248, 275, 365, 366, 369, 415, 416
Roosevelt, Theodore 3
Roques, Pierre 92
Rousseau, Jean-Jacques 52
Roussellier, Nicolas 327, 358, 444
Royal Navy 100
Ruhr 71, 105, 111, 132, 194, 348
  British policy on 382
  ending occupation 438, 448, 451, 452, 454, 455, 478
  French control (1923) 4, 404–13, 444
  German troops in 337
  and Left Bank as a single economic space 399
  occupation 7, 194, 221, 321, 337, 338–41, 360, 362, 382, 391, 396, 400, 404–7, 434, 435, 436, 442
  occupation of port towns 379
rule of law 3, 5, 6, 9, 78, 127, 162, 167, 179
  and armed force 68, 181, 489, 499
  and disarmament 461
  and French war aims 81–2
  and Locarno Accords 507
  and social solidarity 66, 443
  society of nations based on 182, 207, 210, 448
  see also international law

554   Index

Russia
  alliance with 24, 43, 50, 93, 94, 95, 97–100, 106, 110, 145, 149
  Bolshevik regime 165, 214, 235
  civil war 324
  cordon sanitaire strategy 414
  debt to France 99
  fall of Tsarist regime 79, 93, 133, 137, 138, 148, 160, 168, 170, 190, 210, 213, 517
  foreign policy 97–100, 103, 131, 333
  France and Britain 'Pact of London' (1916) 97
  French delegation (1917) 148
  Imperial 275
  investment in Tsarist 73
  offensive against Germany (1914) 93
  policy towards 14, 164, 242
  post-war 170, 317, 318, 333, 413
  Provisional Government 93, 140–1, 148
  reintegration into European economy 382
  relations with Germany 96, 119, 130, 168, 248
  role in shaping French post-war security planning 97–100, 134, 140–1, 370
  withdrawal from war 133, 140, 189
  see also Soviet Russia
Russian Revolution 83, 93–5, 133, 140, 146, 158, 162, 168, 169, 214, 215, 220
Russo-German alliance, Rapallo (1922) 332, 394, 415
Ruyssen, Théodore 1, 6, 10, 64, 128, 371, 372, 390, 462, 499, 504

Saarland 53, 104, 105, 106, 111, 113, 132, 136, 146, 158, 287, 408
  annexation proposed 279, 285, 288, 289, 293
  coalfield 190, 231, 259, 260, 288, 295, 306
  granted to Prussia (1815) 278, 280
  occupation 260
  plebiscite to decide political status 295
Sagniac, Philippe 125
Saint-Aulaire, Comte Charles de Beaupoil de 26, 27, 28, 58, 386, 393, 394, 440, 451, 465
  forced to retire 470
Saint-Cyr academy 37, 38
Saint-Maixent academy 37
San Remo 337
sanctions
  arbitration and 455, 456, 462
  British opposition to Geneva 474
  credible threat of 360, 452
  economic 176, 180, 185, 250, 251, 341, 379
  enforcement and 320, 336, 516
  and international law 262, 264, 274, 308, 455

  international organisation with 152, 179, 184, 187, 230, 270
  military 69, 70, 78, 185, 187, 188, 361, 438, 440, 464
Sangnier, Marc 445
Sargent, Sir Harold Orme 450
Sarraut, Albert 80
Saumur academy 37
Savoy 52
Sazonov, Sergei 131
  'Thirteen Points' 97
Scelle, Georges 10, 222, 371, 372, 390, 419, 446
Schacht, Hjalmar 437
Schleswig-Holstein 194, 287
Schlieffen plan 88
Schneider 369
Schroeder, Paul 49, 51
Schuker, Stephen 319, 351, 428, 432, 454, 468
Schumann, Robert 515
seas, freedom of the 167, 229
Second World War (1939–45) 53
Secrétariat général de la défense nationale (SGDN) 44, 408, 423, 451
  on arms inspection 476
  on Cologne evacuation 479
  on Geneva Protocol 464, 466, 472
  proposed Franco-British security pact 473
  on TMA 458
Section d'études 20
Section française de l'Internationale ouvriere (SFIO) 22, 74, 75, 79, 85, 91, 128, 129, 130, 145, 146, 147, 149, 151, 152, 155, 156, 158, 335, 372, 413, 441, 448, 457
  in 1919 325, 327
  and Comintern 329, 330
  foreign policy 446
  internationalist agenda 390, 441, 515
  on military service 442
  opposition to Ruhr occupation 405, 444
  opposition to the war 145, 149, 165
  on peace conditions 304, 330
  peace and self-determination 221, 302
  policy on Russia 413
  post-war deputies 326
  radical wing 329
  and Radicals 432, 445, 448
  on reparations 222, 327
  on sanctions 184
  surveillance on 328
  Tours schism 359
  see also Cartel des gauches; Independent Socialists; PCF (French Communist Party); Republican Socialists
Section juridique (foreign ministry) 30

Index

security 1, 15, 47–78
  Anglo-American conceptions of 427
  arbitration–security–disarmament formula 431–68
  based on treaty enforcement 293, 317
  collective under League of Nations 365, 371, 389, 418–26, 446, 449, 462, 489, 520
  and disarmament 421–4, 461
  Entente-based strategy 337, 342
  Europe-wide 485, 489
  imperial and domestic 14
  internationalisation and the Cartel des gauches 427, 469
  internationalist concept 6, 47, 78, 79, 82, 84, 85, 320, 351
  multilateral approach 180, 457–63, 514
  multilateral and traditional approaches 484, 489, 517
  mutual approach to 273
  and peace (1918–19) 197, 235–75
  post-war planning 163–96
  as a process 499
  programme for post-war 85–132, 235–75
  traditional concept 4, 5, 47, 48–52, 60, 72, 77, 78, 79, 82, 84, 85, 133, 146–57, 162, 277–83, 289, 312, 323, 364, 391, 518
  transition 429
  and war debts 436
  see also economic security; French security policy; national security
Seignobos, Charles 156
self-determination
  and balance of power 286, 297
  Clemenceau's belief in 201, 210, 310
  and democracy 208, 313
  in eastern Europe 170, 171, 240–3
  national 52, 98, 102, 107, 127, 141, 150, 152, 161, 221, 223, 229, 233
  norms 283–6, 307
  the principle of 198, 199, 208, 210, 214, 223, 226, 278, 412
  in the Rhineland 277, 283–6, 293, 306, 313, 408
  Wilson on 290
Sembat, Marcel 21, 82, 91, 92, 99, 128, 129, 134, 304, 329
senate commissions 42, 303
Serbia 96, 97, 101, 102, 106
Serman, William 37
Serrigny, General Bernard 408, 441, 458, 464, 471, 473, 476
  on Cologne evacuation 479
Service de documentation pour le Congres de la paix 284
Service de la guerre économique 346

Service de presse et d'information 34
Service des écoles et des oeuvres françaises à l'étranger 34
Service du personnel et de la comptabilité 42
Service français de la Société des nations (SFSDN) 180, 373, 374, 419, 422
Sèvres, Treaty of 246, 324, 334, 384
Seydoux, Charles Louis Auguste Jacques 28, 58, 253, 259, 317, 318, 344–8, 363, 450, 465, 496, 511
  on British relations with France 361, 384
  career 346, 470
  on customs sanction 379
  on the Dawes Plan 437
  on European economic community 515
  for financial controls on German economy 382
  on Franco-German relations 425, 483, 519
  on generation gap 519
  on German entry to League 13, 201, 487
  on German relations with Britain 482
  multilateral vision 344, 364, 385, 386, 389, 401, 438, 515
  Relations commerciales 373
  and Ruhr policy 396, 398, 401, 407, 408, 411, 413, 425, 454, 455
Seydoux Plan 347, 351–6, 378, 379, 380, 437, 456, 515
Shotwell, James 460
Sikorski, Władysław 415, 496
Silesia 105, 160
  southern 98
  Upper 239, 242, 260, 331, 354, 367, 369, 381, 384
Simon, Henry 244
Skoda Works 369
Skrzyński, Aleksander 462, 496
Slovakia 171
Smuts, Jan Christiaan 208, 265, 516
Snowden, Philip 454
social capital 28
social debt (Bourgeois) 65–8
social order, French post-war 328
socialism 22, 42, 74, 82, 86, 90, 103, 130, 141, 142, 200
  internationalist 515
  moderate 329
  revolutionary Russian 140
Socialist Party *see* Section française de l'Internationale ouvriere
Société de géographie 243
'society of nations' 6, 34, 65, 67, 127, 132, 151, 152, 154, 156, 178–89, 210, 221, 222, 229, 253, 262, 432, 514, 520
solidarisme 65–8, 70, 262, 263, 273, 509
solidarité 188, 406, 445, 462, 489, 497, 503, 506, 520

Somme, battles of the 93, 104, 133, 192
Sorel, Albert 53–7, 58, 123
Soulier, Édouard 508
Sous-direction de droit public 30
Sous-direction des relations commerciales 347
South Africa 246
South Slav kingdom 214
Soutou, Georges-Henri 73, 116, 117, 119, 120, 121, 149, 157, 174, 211, 221, 261, 313, 364, 427
sovereignty 69, 70, 130, 271
  and arms limitation 374, 520
  German 382
  and individual rights 264
  and international law 185, 188, 271, 272, 273, 274
  state 372, 498
Soviet Russia
  Cartel's recognition of 465
  collective action against 494
  Communist regime 332
  membership of League mooted 388
  'New Economic Policy' 332
  and Poland 324, 365
  problems for French policy 332, 447
  White Russians and the Red Army 332
Spa Conference 336, 338, 339, 349, 351, 352, 360
Stalin, Joseph 53
standing commissions 42
State, separation of Church and 23
states
  arbitration in relations between 62
  changing standards of behaviour 12, 203, 207, 275
  democratic who recognised the reign of law 262
  duties of civilised 67, 273
  evolution of modern 36
  interests 48–52, 56
  'intermediary' as strategic buffers 50
  Most Favoured Nation status 174
  mutual obligations 182, 188, 273, 371
  neutral 110, 152, 153, 174, 285
  neutral 'buffer' 152, 153, 285
  with representative institutions 184
  shared interests in international law 57, 61, 274
  'successor' 172, 237–43, 289, 331, 364, 369
  'super' 186, 188, 376
Statut naval (1924) 383
Steeg, Théodore 329
steel industry 7, 70, 71, 95, 112, 174, 248, 249, 261, 306, 380, 395, 404, 437, 456, 500
Stefánik, Milan 171
Steiner, Zara 19, 468

Stevenson, David 149, 157, 207, 288
Stinnes, Hugo 71, 331
Stockholm meeting of socialist parties 134, 141, 149
Stresemann, Gustav 343, 410, 436, 456, 491, 493, 494
strikes
  calls for general 88
  French (1908) 164
  French (1917) 133, 138, 144, 145
  French (1918) 144
  French (1919) 220
  French (1920) 329
  French (1923) 404
  international general 76
  Russian 140
structuralism 11, 520
students, support for League by French 372, 419, 445
submarine warfare, German 96, 102
Sudetenland 172, 239, 240
summit diplomacy 33, 36, 336
Supreme War Council at Versailles 193
Sûreté nationale 25
surveillance, international 271
Sykes–Picot Agreement (1916) 244, 245
symbolic capital (Bourdieu) 40, 41, 213
symbolic power 442, 516
symbolism, of mourning and commemoration 325
Syria 243, 246, 247, 334, 472

Talleyrand, Charles Maurice de 30
Tangier 384
Tannenberg, Battle of 94
Tannery, Jean 399, 401
Tardieu, André 99, 104, 166, 242, 250, 255, 262, 267, 272, 273, 354, 374
  Atlanticism 251, 285, 286, 305, 306, 314
  career 205
  changed views 429
  Clemenceau's chief adviser 198, 199, 204, 206, 210, 229–30
  confrontational 390
  eastern policy 240
  and enforcement 343, 350
  on Franco-German military balance 306–8
  high commissioner to the USA 190, 206, 211, 227
  memo on the Rhine frontier 287–90, 313
  memo on the Saarland 287–8, 295
  proposed peace conference plan 229
  on reparations 257
  on the Rhine 276, 279, 283, 284, 286, 290, 291, 292, 293, 297
  on self-determination 293

Index

six conditions for accepting Anglo-American guarantee 294, 296
tariffs 72, 119, 174, 175
taxation 433
  double décime 433
teachers, pacifism 443
technology, communications 31, 34, 60
Le Télégramme du nord 304
Temporary Mixed Commission (TMC) 376, 377, 420, 423, 498
Le Temps 87, 201, 205, 354, 387
territory
  adjustments after Locarno 512
  mandates 246
  as a source of power 48, 49, 149, 151–6
  threat of occupation 321
Teschen 240, 365
Theunis, Georges 402
Thiers, Adolphe 28
Third Estate, deputies 20
Third French Republic 335
  clientélisme 28
  constitution (1875) 21, 41
  legalist political culture 6
  policy making in the 19–46
  religious politics 40
Third International *see* Comintern
Thomas, Albert 75, 82, 93, 99, 129, 134, 148, 156, 184, 205, 222, 232
Three Year Military Service Law (1912–14) 23, 91
Thyssen, Fritz 71, 72, 258, 331
Tirard, Paul 283, 310, 340, 341, 342, 402
  on Cologne evacuation 479
  on Franco-British military alliance 479
  notes on sanctions 362
  Rhineland policy 379, 400, 407, 408, 411, 478
Togoland 246
Toulouse-Lautrec, Henri de 32
Trachtenberg, Marc 116, 256, 343, 350, 354, 397, 428
trade
  British 216, 334
  free 167, 175
  French pre-war surplus with Britain 100, 363
  with Germany 174
  international 31, 61, 72
  protectionism 174
  US with the Entente 102
trade unions 22, 72, 75, 87, 88, 128, 129
  revolutionary element 330
  surveillance on 328
transatlantic economic community 204, 216, 247–61, 275, 515
transatlantic security community 277, 286, 313, 516, 522

treaties
  arbitration 62, 63, 64
  international 29, 62, 82
  Poincaré on 411
  ratification of 42
  secret Entente 141
  Treaty of Mutual Assistance (TMA) 451, 457–62, 463, 502, 504
  Draft (1923) 423
  rejected by British 457–62
Trianon, Treaty of (1920) 369
troisième bureau memorandum 158
Trotsky, Léon 129
Turkey
  crisis in 394
  French peace with nationalists 384
  Ottoman 97, 98, 245, 246, 334

U-boat squadrons 215
Ukraine 141, 170
Union des industries métallurgiques et minières de France 348
Union fédérale (UF) 443, 445
  'Message to the French People' (1922) 443
Union féminine pour la Société des nations 445
Union nationale des combattants (UNC) 443, 445
Union nationale des mutilés et réformés 443, 445
Union sacrée 22, 79, 83, 86, 132, 323, 326, 405, 442
  destruction of 133, 141, 145, 165
United Kingdom *see* Britain
United Nations, Security Council 188
United States
  as an 'Associated Power' (1917) 141
  at London Conference (1924) 453, 454
  Congress fails to ratify Versailles Treaty (1920) 333
  constitution 272
  and the Dawes Plan 436
  entry into the war 83, 93, 96, 133, 137, 138, 141, 162, 169, 189, 210, 517
  French economic dependence on 95, 138
  growing power 172, 318
  hostility to Allied trading bloc 119
  internationalism in 3, 6, 62, 64, 68, 190
  League to Enforce Peace 516
  Lend-Lease programme (1940–1) 102
  loans 99, 216, 219, 255, 333, 350, 394
  neutrality 102–3, 109
  and new economic order 248, 250, 251
  peace conference policy 203
  post-war attitude to Germany 167, 261
  post-war policy 3, 200, 317
  Rhineland policy 279

558　Index

United States (cont.)
  Russian order for armaments from 99
  strategic importance of 161, 197, 206, 227, 229, 281
  view of League of Nations 209, 265, 267, 275
  as a world power 33
  see also Anglo-American guarantees
Universal Peace Congresses 62, 63
Universal Postal Union 61

Vaillant, Edouard 87, 88, 129
Vaillant-Couturier, Paul 330
Vaïsse, Maurice 69, 319
Valmy, Battle of (1792) 148
Vatican, diplomatic relations with 448
Verdun, Battle of (1916) 92, 93, 104, 120, 133, 139
  commemoration 325
Verdun, Douaumont ossuary 325
Vergennes, Charles Gravier Comte de 50
Versailles military academy 37
Versailles, Treaty of (1919) 8, 24, 198, 199, 230, 261, 273, 335, 350
  American refusal to ratify 333
  commercial regime 454
  disarmament clauses 469, 476, 478
  enforcement of 317
  'execution of the' 318, 319, 321, 323, 342, 480
  flexibility of 309, 312, 469, 512, 519
  Foch on 312, 516
  on general arms limitation 374
  German non-compliance 330–2, 335, 376, 396, 476, 478
  government defence of 305, 476
  military restrictions on Germany 282
  ratification 302
  on the Rhineland 297, 320, 476
  right of arms inspection 476
  territorial settlement 320
La Victoire 88, 124
Viviani, René 21, 81, 82, 87, 92, 302, 457
  as premier 90, 92, 98, 123, 128
  resignation 92
  in TMC 377
Voltaire (François-Marie Arouet) 49

Waldeck-Rousseau, Pierre 205, 335, 457
war
  costs of 200, 218, 219–20, 229
  as a crusade for democracy 83, 89, 103, 127, 148, 210
  and economics 59
  Foch on 212–13
  juridical means to avoid 505, 510
  jusqu'au bout 115, 127, 145, 162

  laws of 63
  movement to eradicate 61, 78
  opposition to 22
  and the politics of national security 79, 132
  representations of 9, 79–84, 94, 126, 148, 151–6, 162, 324
  role in international politics 60
war aims
  Allies' 83, 151
  French 9, 81–2, 86–91, 124, 210
  German 95–6, 139
  inter-Allied conference (1917) 141, 517
  and peace conditions 138
  proclamations (1914) 81
  Russian 97, 103
war aims bloc (1915) 124, 300
war debts 8, 173, 333, 394
  and reparations 395–404, 411, 433, 436
  and Ruhr occupation 455
  and security 436
war ministers 92, 169
war ministry (1897) 44, 85, 393
war pensions 220, 256
war veterans 327, 442, 445
Washington Conference on security and disarmament in the Pacific (1921) 377, 384
Washington Naval Disarmament Conference (1921) 333, 420
Watt, Donald Cameron (D. C.) 19
Weimar Republic 217, 221, 331, 337, 352, 391
  Cartel's strategy 463
  policy of destroying currency 396, 407
Weiss, André 179, 180, 181, 187
  study of sanctions 185
Wendel, François de 112, 128
West European Economic Union, proposal 248–9
western Europe
  economy 70–4
  foreign nationals' rights of incorporation 71
  mutual assistance pact 486
  security in 14, 85–132, 418
  security pact 470, 486
western front 93, 138, 143, 158, 189
Westphalia 114, 195, 259
  peace of 304
Weygand, Maxime 415
Wiesbaden Accords (1921) 380
Wilde, Oscar 32
Wilson, General (later Field Marshal) Sir Henry 266
Wilson, Woodrow 6, 84, 108, 130, 182, 250
  armistice negotiations 190

Clémentel's letter to (1917) 176–8, 190, 204
on colonial subjects 244
commitment to League of Nations 130, 156, 216, 220–4, 230, 265, 269, 270, 521
Covenant for the League draft 265, 269
'Five Principles' 209
foreign policy 102, 104, 137, 142, 220
'Four Principles' (1918) 167
idealism 197, 521
international order conception 166–8, 200, 208, 216, 516
opposition to economic plan 175, 252
'Peace Note' (1916) 110, 132
'Peace Without Victory' speech 103, 142
on reparations 257
and the Rhineland 276, 291, 294, 313
and the Saarland 295
on self-determination 290, 309
as symbol of new approach to international relations 155, 203, 264, 272, 273, 521
see also 'Fourteen Points'
'Wilsonianism' 3, 102, 110, 142, 151, 154, 161, 210, 211, 313, 370, 521

Wirth, Joseph 379, 382, 383
women
  no right to vote 442
  in the workforce 220
women's movement, and peace activism 443, 445
workers' movement, French 328, 329
workers' revolution, international 332
world court 62, 70
world order
  'domestic analogy' 68, 70
  juridical internationalist vision for 187
  Wilson's call for a new 102, 104, 109, 166–8, 209, 521
Wurm, Clemens 428

Young Plan (1929) 435
Yugoslavia 172, 213, 214, 237, 241, 242, 257, 275, 365, 369, 416

Zeppelin airships 94, 95
Zimmerwald peace conference (1915) 129
Zinoviev, Grigory 332
Zola, Émile 164